CW01431978

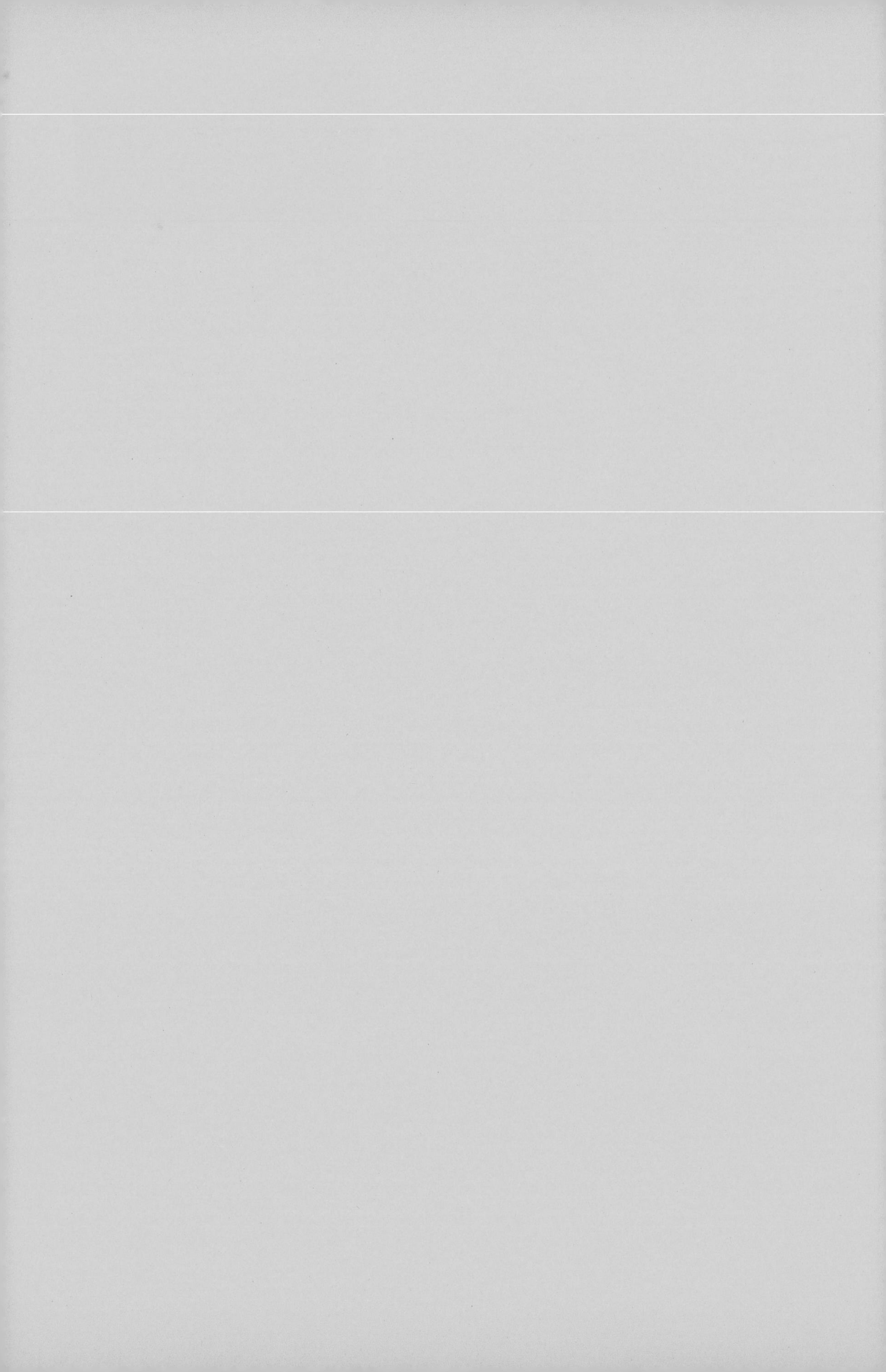

Early Peoples of Britain and Ireland

Early Peoples of Britain and Ireland

An Encyclopedia

Volume I: A–G

Edited by Christopher A. Snyder

Greenwood World Publishing
Oxford / Westport Connecticut
2008

First published by Greenwood World Publishing 2008

1 2 3 4 5 6 7 8 9 10

Greenwood World Publishing
Wilkinson House
Jordan Hill
Oxford OX2 8EJ
An imprint of Greenwood Publishing Group, Inc
www.greenwood.com

British Library Cataloguing-in-Publication Data: a catalogue record for this book is available from the British Library

Library of Congress Cataloging-in-Publication Data

Early peoples of Britain and Ireland : an encyclopaedia / [edited by] Christopher A. Snyder.
p. cm.
Includes bibliographical references and index.
ISBN 978-1-84645-009-9 (set: alk. paper); ISBN 978-1-84645-028-0 (Vol. 1: alk. paper); ISBN 978-1-84645-029-7 (Vol. 2 alk. paper)
1. Great Britain — History — To 1066 — Encyclopaedias. 2. Great Britain — History — Norman period, 1066–1154 — Encyclopaedias. 3. Ireland — History — To 1172 — Encyclopaedias. 4. Prehistoric peoples — Great Britain — Encyclopaedias. 5. Prehistoric peoples — Ireland — Encyclopaedias. 6. Ethnology — Great Britain — Encyclopaedias. 7. Ethnology — Ireland — Encyclopaedias. I. Snyder, Christopher A. (Christopher Allen), 1966–

DA135.E27 2008
941.0103—dc22 2008-005427

ISBN 978-1-84645-009-9 (set)
ISBN 978-1-84645-028-0 (Vol. 1)
ISBN 978-1-84645-029-7 (Vol. 2)

Designed by Fraser Muggeridge studio
Typeset by TexTech International
Printed and bound by South China Printing Company

This encyclopedia is dedicated to the Rabbi, the Magister and the Teacher.

Contents

Acknowledgements

I would like to thank the members of my Advisory Board—Richard Abels, Ben Hudson, Lloyd Laing, Tom O'Loughlin and Aidan O'Sullivan—outstanding scholars all; Thomas Burns, Philip Freeman and Andrew McDonald for reading various entries; Katharine Torrey for her tremendous help with editing and formatting text; editorial assistants Martha Rogers, Liz Kalk and Sarah James; programmer Pipop Nuangpookka; the librarians at Marymount University; Simon Mason at Greenwood World Publishing for his patience and encouragement; and Renée, Carys, Ceili and Hart at Glynnehaven for their love and understanding. Lastly, I would like to acknowledge the love and support of my first history teacher, Donald Snyder, and my first editor, Betty Snyder (*in memoria tui*).

Board of Advisors

Richard Abels
United States Naval Academy

Benjamin Hudson
Pennsylvania State University

Lloyd Laing
University of Nottingham

Thomas O'Loughlin
University of Wales-Lampeter

Aidan O'Sullivan
University College, Dublin

Alphabetical List of Entries

Guide to Related Topics

Figures

Adminius
Adomnán
Áed
Aedán mac Gabráin
Ælfric of Eynsham
Ælle
Æthelbald
Æthelberht
Æthelflaed
Æthelfrith
Æthelred the Unready
Æthelstan
Agricola
Aidan, Saint
Alain II
Alain III
Alban, Saint
Alchfrith
Aldfrith
Aldhelm
Alexander I
Alfred the Great
Ambrosius Aurelianus
Aneirin
Anselm
Arthur
Asser
Augustine of Canterbury, Saint
Aulus Plautius
Bede
Benedict Biscop
Bertha
Boudica
Bran the Blessed
Brendan, Saint
Brian Boru
Brigid, Saint
Bruce Family
Brude mac Maelchon
Brutus
Cædmon
Caesar, Julius
Caratacus
Carausius
Cartimandua
Cassivellaunus
Castus, Lucius Artorius
Ceolfrith
Cerdic
Cernunnos
Chad
Ciarán of Clonmacnois
Claudius
Cnut
Coel Hen
Cogidubnus
Columba, Saint
Columbanus, Saint
Constantine I the Great
Constantine III
Constantius I
Cú Chulainn
Cummian
Cunobelinus
Cunomorus
Cuthbert, Saint
Cynewulf
David I
David, Saint
Dicuil
Donald III Bán
Duncan I
Duncan II
Dunstan, Saint
Edgar, King of England
Edgar Atheling
Eddius Stephanus
Edmund, Saint
Edward the Confessor
Egbert I of Kent
Egbert II of Kent
Egbert of Wessex
Eleanor of Aquitaine
Elfoddw
Emma of Normandy
Éoganacht
Eric Bloodaxe
Fursa, Saint
Geoffrey, Count of Anjou
Geoffrey of Monmouth
Geraint
Germanus of Auxerre, Saint
Gildas
Godfrey Haraldsson
Godwin
Gruffudd ap Cynan
Gruffudd ap Llywellyn
Gruffudd ap Rhys
Guthram
Hadrian
Harold I 'Harefoot'
Harold Godwinsson (Harold II)
Harthacnut
Hengest and Horsa
Henry I
Henry II
Henry of Huntingdon
Hilda
Hywel Dda
Ida of Bernicia
Illtud, Saint
Ine of Wessex
Ivar the Boneless
John of Salisbury
John Scottus Eriugena
Kenneth I MacAlpin
Kentigern, Saint
Kevin, Saint
Lug
Macbeth
Maelgwn Gwynedd
Magnus Barefoot
Magnus Haraldsson
Magnus Maximus (Macsen Wledig)
Malcolm Canmore
Marcher Lords
Marianus Scotus
Matilda
Merfyn Frych
Merlin
Montgomery Family
Muirchú
Nennius
Ninian, Saint
O'Connor, Kings of Connacht
Óengus
Offa
Olaf Cuarán
Olaf Tryggvason
Olaf the White
Orkney Jarls
Oswald of Northumbria
Oswiu of Northumbria
Owain ap Urien
Palladius
Patrick, Saint
Paulinus of York
Pelagius
Penda
Prasutagus
Rædwald of East Anglia
Ranulf II of Chester
Rhodri ap Merfyn (Rhodri Mawr)
Rhydderch
Rhys ap Tewdwr
Richard Fitz Gilbert de Clare 'Strongbow'
Robert, Duke of Normandy
Samson, Saint
Ségéne
Silures
Somerled
Stephen of Blois
Suetonius Paulinus
Tacitus
Taliesin
Theodore
Theodosius
Tristan
Urien Reghed
Vortigern
Wilfrid
William I the Conqueror
William II Rufus
William of Malmesbury
William Marshal, Earl of Pembroke
Wulfstan II, Bishop of Worcester and Saint

Monuments, Works, Treasures and Burials

Aberlemno Stones
Alfred Jewel

Places and Events

Peoples and Ages

Themes

Introduction

Celts, Romans, Anglo-Saxons, Scots, Picts and Vikings are evocative terms, perhaps now more than ever. Variously neglected, romanticised and misunderstood, the early peoples of Britain and Ireland now dominate popular histories, films and the Internet. They attract thousands of visitors each year to museums and 'living history' exhibitions; they inspire artists, craftspeople, musicians and dancers. Television programmes celebrate their histories and follow archaeologists as they search for clues about their material cultures. Scholars, most bemused and befuddled by all of this attention, continue to produce specialised studies and struggle to explain the historical realities to enthusiastic students and lay audiences.

While such explanation is no easy task, it is the aim of this work. Scholarly encyclopedias must be both scholarly and encyclopedic; that is, they must give a sense of current scholarly consensus (or debate) and be broad, inclusive and accessible. The authors of the essays and entries in this encyclopedia are scholars from the United States, Canada, the United Kingdom, Ireland and Continental Europe. Most work in colleges, universities and museums, and they are specialists in archaeology, art history, history, classical and European languages and literature. They have all been asked to cover complex topics, some with centuries of accumulated literature, and present them to the reader in a brief narrative with accessible, jargon-free prose. A dozen thematic essays and over 500 shorter entries are arranged in alphabetical order. The first sentence of each entry is usually a concise definition of the term. Following this, there will be a more detailed narrative, usually chronological. At the conclusion of each essay and entry is a brief bibliography containing a list of sources used by the author and suggestions for further reading.

The parameters of this encyclopedia require some explanation. Geographically, the scope is Britain, Ireland and their associated islands. Cornwall and the Isle of Man have their own entries, but England, Scotland, Wales and Ireland are not treated separately, for such entries would be entirely too long and unwieldy. There has been a conscious attempt by the authors to extend balanced coverage to each of these geographic areas, but in some areas – Cornwall, Ireland and the Scottish Highlands and Islands – there are periods for which few written sources are available. Having said this, we have perhaps differed from the traditional Anglocentric approach by including many topics from the 'Celtic fringe' (especially archaeological and art historical) that would not have appeared in other reference works.

Chronologically, the encyclopedia ranges from the Stone Age to AD 1154, the year the Plantagenet dynasty came to rule Britain (and eventually Ireland) with the accession of Henry II. The early periods – Palaeolithic, Mesolithic, Neolithic, Bronze Age, Iron Age and Roman – have their own entries, while the medieval period is covered in entries pertaining to various groups of people, such as Britons, Scots, Picts, Angles, Saxons, Vikings and Normans. Since, apart from coin legends and inscriptions, no written records appear in Britain before the Roman period (and in Ireland before the early Middle Ages), the prehistoric periods are covered herein by archaeological and anthropological methods. From the Roman period on, history surpasses archaeology in terms of entries included. If the twelfth century does not here have the coverage it deserves, this is because it does get covered in other medieval or nationalistic reference works.

It is, of course, impossible to cover every topic in a reference book, especially one as broad in scope as this work. If you do not find a particular person, place or topic in the entry list, please consult the index and you will probably find that what you are looking for is covered in one or more entries under a different title. You will also find following the entries other useful aids: A 'Timeline' covering the most important peoples and events in Britain and Ireland for the period covered by the encyclopedia; 'Royal Genealogies' illustrating the pedigrees of the major Brittonic, English, Anglo-Norman, Scottish and Irish dynasties covered by the encyclopedia; and several large maps (scattered throughout) to help locate places mentioned in the essays and entries.

Lastly, a word or two needs to be said about the conventions used in this encyclopedia. British spellings (e.g. 'colour' rather than 'color') and European-style dates (e.g. '10 November 1134' rather than 'November 10,

1134') have been employed throughout. The dating system used herein is the traditional *Anno Domini* (AD, 'in the year of the Lord') system made popular in England by the historian Bede. Whereas BC ('before Christ') and AD are, in our own times, often being replaced by BP ('before the present', used by some archaeologists and anthropologists) and BCE/CE ('before the common era/of the common era'), most readers will follow the Julian/Gregorian calendar and will therefore be more familiar with this convention.

Prehistory

Britain and Ireland were connected to each other and to Continental Europe until the end of the **Palaeolithic** ('Old Stone Age'), about 10,000 BC. There was sporadic hominid occupation dating back to the Cromerian Interglacial period, about 500,000 years ago, when evidence of stone tools and animal butchery first appear. Burial rituals first occur in the Middle Palaeolithic, about 300,000 years ago, and may be associated with **Neanderthals** in Britain living in caves and rock shelters. Modern humans (*Homo sapiens*) first appear in Britain in the Upper Palaeolithic and with them appeared the specialised and composite tools and mobilary art. Ireland, however, does not show substantial evidence of human occupation until the **Mesolithic** ('Middle Stone Age'), which begins with the end of the last Ice Age. Warmer climates in the British Isles resulted in the gradual transformation of the tundra into deciduous woodlands – which hosted deer, elk and wild pigs – divided by lakes, rivers and freshwater lagoons teeming with wildfowl and freshwater fish. Mesolithic hunter-gatherers followed a seasonal pattern of settlement and subsistence, following the herds and schools of fish with an occasional base camp for more prolonged periods of residence. At Mount Sandel in County Antrim, there is evidence of circular huts with hearths and storage pits, while Aveline's Hole, a cave in the Mendips, may have been used as a cemetery.

The **Neolithic** ('New Stone Age') begins around 4000 BC in Britain and Ireland and is marked by the introduction of pottery, polished stone axes and, most importantly, settled agriculture. These early farming communities raised animals (cattle, pigs, sheep and goats) and grew cereals (particularly wheats and barleys), supplementing their farming with gathered and hunted food. Houses proliferated, and large tombs (long barrows and round barrows) appear in Ireland and the Orkneys. Various types of causewayed enclosures also appear in the Early Neolithic, including ones with circular areas surrounded by banked ditches, but it is unclear whether they were settlements, cattle enclosures or ritual sites. The Late Neolithic is characterised by an abundance of circular enclosures known as **henge** monuments. These include timber circles, stone circles and a variety of stone tombs; **Stonehenge** and **Avebury** are perhaps the most notable examples, but Wiltshire in particular and the Scottish Highlands and Islands are dotted with henges, standing stones and barrows. The emergence of henge monuments and prestige burials has indicated to scholars wider changes in settlement practice and the rise of a socio-political elite. It is assumed that such rulers would have been needed to command the labour forces needed to construct the larger henges and hilltop enclosures of the Late Neolithic.

Elites also required more sophisticated weapons and adornment, and so began to turn to **metalworking** during the Early **Bronze Age**. Copper smelting was first introduced into Ireland, from the Continent, around 2500 BC. Copper was mined in Ireland and North Wales to produce copper axes from open stone moulds. This has traditionally been associated with the **Beaker people**, called this because of the beaker-shaped pottery they produced (possibly to consume alcohol), who may have brought the art of copper smelting from Iberia (though not, as was once thought, through large-scale invasion). The Beaker people of Britain and Ireland also produced decorated gold 'sun disks' and necklets called lunulae from their crescent-moon shape. Around 2000 BC, British smiths learned to alloy copper and tin to produce bronze tools and weapons, which held a much harder edge than pure copper. **Cornwall** became the main supplier of tin for much of Europe, and in the Roman period, tin was known as the Brettanic metal. Bronze Age warriors came to prefer the dagger to the axe, and in the Middle Bronze Age, these daggers evolved into elongated 'rapiers' and spearheads. Stone houses, palisaded enclosures, round barrows, cairns and the reuse of Neolithic monuments are characteristic of the Middle Bronze Age, as are richly furnished burials in southern England associated with a warrior aristocracy known as the **Wessex culture**. However, around 2000 BC, there was a general shift in Britain from inhumation to cremation.

The Late Bronze Age saw the appearance of the first leaf-shaped swords (c.1300 BC) and wheeled-vehicles in Britain, which indicate more extensive contact with the Continent. Sizeable cremation cemeteries in Britain are comparable with the **Urnfield culture** of Continental Europe, once assumed to be the immediate predecessor of the **Celts**. The weapon and shield types produced in Britain at the end of the Bronze Age have been associated with the **Hallstatt** culture of central Europe, who were almost certainly Celtic-speaking. However, the theory that large groups of invaders (Beaker people, Urnfield culture and Celts) were responsible for cultural and linguistic changes in the British Isles began to fall out of favour with archaeologists in the 1960s, and archaeologists now prefer to see such changes as the result of trade, kinship, political alliances and the occasional movement of smaller groups from the Continent.

The Iron Age

It is a matter of some debate as to when the Iron Age began in Britain and Ireland. As early as 1000 BC, there is evidence of iron smiths working in Britain, but we do not know what they were producing. Iron was more readily available than copper or tin, and iron production was cheaper and more efficient. The earliest iron tools and weapons – a sword and a sickle – date to the Hallstatt C period and come from Llyn Fawr in South Wales. Iron daggers appear in the Early **La Tène** period (fifth century BC), which, like Hallstatt, is defined by typology and motifs originating in central Europe. Iron weapons, chariot fittings and other items appear in the fourth-century high-status burials of Yorkshire, the so-called **Arras culture**, but overall iron objects are scarce in Britain until the first century BC.

Iron Age warfare in Britain is defined by distinctive La Tène swords, the use of horse and chariot and the proliferation of **hillforts**. The successors of the hilltop enclosure of the Late Bronze Age, Iron Age hillforts became larger and contained more varied activities within (examples include **Danebury**, Hod Hill, **Maiden Castle** and **South Cadbury**). Some also developed multiple ramparts and increasingly elaborate entranceways, often with accompanying 'guard chambers'. The areas with the most extensive hillfort building and refortification are Wales and the south-west of Britain. By the Late Iron Age, social differentiation increases, with individual houses being enclosed and the appearance of gold **torcs**, **brooches** and **coins** (eventually bearing the names of tribal rulers who call themselves 'king'). Formal temple sites first appear, and, in Ireland, ceremonial centres such as **Tara** and the **Navan Fort**. In the Late Pre-Roman Iron Age, a new settlement type also emerges – the *oppidum* – which was a larger, usually low-lying area enclosed by ramparts. The ***oppida*** were truly proto-towns and served as tribal centres (examples can be found in or near **St Albans**, **Colchester**, Winchester and **Silchester**).

By the first century AD, we have not only increasing archaeological evidence of trade with Gaul and the Mediterranean (e.g. amphoras which carried wine) but also the first extensive written descriptions of Britain and Ireland in the classical sources. The names *Britanni*, *Britannia* and *Hibernia* now become the standard Roman terms for describing **Britons**, Britain and Ireland, though the inhabitants of Britain and Ireland seem to have self-identified in tribal terms. From coinage and texts, we see the emerging dominance in lowland Britain of two large tribes or tribal confederacies: the ***Brigantes*** in the north and the ***Catuvellauni*** in the south-east. The *Catuvellauni* and their neighbour the ***Trinovantes*** are part of the archaeologically defined '**Aylesford**-Swarling culture', whose elites displayed their high status through imported Mediterranean goods found in their graves. **Cassivellaunus**, presumably the ruler of the *Catuvellauni* and the first Briton to be named in a written history, led the resistance against **Julius Caesar**'s British expeditions in 55 and 54 BC. Caesar, looking to extend his fame and sphere of influence (and to prevent the Britons from aiding the Gauls), brought a small force to Britain and experienced some military success before taking oaths and hostages and returning to Gaul. In his famous memoirs of this period, the *Commentaries on the Gallic Wars*, Caesar provides lengthy descriptions of the geography of Britain and the culture of the Britons, including references to chariot-fighting and **Druids**.

The Roman Period

No Roman legions followed up on Caesar's British expeditions until AD 43. Again, from archaeology and written sources, we see increasing trade contacts between Britain and the Roman world, and it is possible that some British rulers may have become formal clients of Rome. The dominant figure of this period is **Cunobelinus**, Shakespeare's 'Cymbeline', who expanded the influence of the *Catuvellauni*. His sons Togodumnus and **Caratacus** led the British resistance against the Roman invasion force of AD 43, commanded by **Aulus Plautius** in the name of the Emperor **Claudius**. Plautius and the future emperor Vespasian had tremendous success against the *Catuvellauni* and their allies, capturing hillforts and eventually the tribal capital of Camulodunum (Colchester). Claudius arrived to witness the final moments of the Roman conquest of Britain, and Colchester was remade into a veterans colony and the first capital of the new province.

Recently scholars have debated both the process and the success of Romanisation in Britain. Some have pointed out the large number of client-kings and consumers of Roman goods in Britain during the first century AD, suggesting that many Britons were content to see the Romans seize control of lowland Britain from the *Catuvellauni*. Others have emphasised the ferocity of native resistance in the first decades after the Claudian conquest, particularly the revolts of Caratacus and **Boudica**, wife of the king of the ***Iceni***. Our most important witness for these years is the Roman historian **Tacitus**, who chronicled these revolts as well as writing a biography of his father-in-law **Agricola**, the Roman military governor who completed the conquest of Wales and northern Britain culminating in his famous victory over the **Caledonians** (a tribal confederation in Scotland) at Mons Graupius in AD 84. Agricola was said to have even contemplated a Roman conquest of Ireland. Tacitus, not always a fan of Roman colonialism, states that the strategies of Romanisation in the provinces include building Roman-style towns and buildings and encouraging native consumption of Roman goods and the adoption of Latin and Roman clothing. There is evidence, in the old tribal capitals at least, that this process was both quick and successful, while much of Scotland, Wales and the north and south-west of Britain remained virtually untouched by Roman culture.

The famous **Roman roads** linked the new Roman towns in Britain and provided a quick and easy route for military and trade. Villas were built in the south and began to transform the British economy, and the towns began to compete with one another by building ever grander masonry baths, basilicas and theatres. The most magnificent construction, however, was that of **Hadrian's Wall** in the north beginning in the year 120. The Wall stretched from one side of the island to the other and was used as a means of controlling the movement of peoples and goods between the southern provinces and the unconquered north (which contained some client tribes). A great source of information about military and civilian life in the Roman north are the **Vindolanda** writing tablets which were discovered (in an amazingly preserved state) in 1973. Rome maintained a significant military presence in Britain up to the end of Roman control of the island in AD 410. The province of Britannia, which was later reorganised into two provinces and then four (within 'the diocese of the Britains'), flourished in the second and third centuries but never became as wealthy as its eastern counterparts. Sea piracy and more organised raids from Ireland, Scotland and northern Europe increased in the third and fourth centuries, and Britain also established a reputation as a launching pad for imperial usurpations. Even the presence of emperors such as Septimius Severus, **Constantius I** and **Constantine the Great** on military campaigns in Britain could not dispel the belief that Britain was a remote and barbaric island.

The Early Middle Ages

Details about the end of Roman Britain are sketchy, leaving much up to interpretation. Some have argued that the Roman towns in Britain remained small in comparison with other parts of the Roman empire, and that true urban life was dead by the beginning of the fifth century, along with a coin-based economy. The few written sources emphasise the role played by barbarian raiders and invaders, resulting in a quick and cataclysmic end to Roman rule. Archaeologists have pointed out that there is little material evidence for such a cataclysmic attack, and indeed many scholars point out the continuities – the survival of some towns, Christianity and Latin literacy – from Roman to medieval Britain.

The British provinces are seldom mentioned in the chronicles of the Late Empire, with the exception being the discussion of a series of 'tyrants' – **Magnus Maximus** in 383 and Marcus, Gratian and **Constantine III** in 406/407 – who were raised to the purple by their British troops. Both Maximus and Constantine III took troops from Britain to fight in Gaul, as perhaps did the general Stilicho around 402. A concerted attack by **Saxons**, **Scoti** (from Ireland) and **Picts** (from Scotland) in 367 led to the death and capture of several important Roman officials in Britain, and barbarian raiding increased again in the first decade of the fifth century. The western Roman emperor Honorius then informed the British towns that they were to see to their own defences (though this so-called Rescript of Honorius has been questioned by some scholars) and there is no evidence that Roman troops, officials and coinage ever returned to Britain after 411. The now-independent Britons turned to a variety of kings and local magnates (together termed *tyranni*) for organisation and defence, ultimately following the advice of a *tyrannus superbus* (who some sources call **Vortigern**) to hire a group of Saxon mercenaries to fight against the **Scots** and the Picts. They came at first in small numbers (three ships) and were successful, but after demanding more lands and supplies, they rebelled against the Britons and pillaged several towns. The remnant Britons fled to 'high, fortified places' (possibly refortified hillforts) or to 'lands across the seas' (probably Brittany and Galicia) or stayed to face their enemy under the leadership of one **Ambrosius Aurelianus**. He led the Britons to some victories over the Saxons, and then, around the year 485, the Britons won a decisive victory at the Battle of **Badon Hill**, which halted Saxon expansion for a generation or more. Later sources attributed the victory at Badon to a warrior or king named **Arthur**.

This is the version of events given by a British cleric named **Gildas**, writing in the early sixth century. His writings, and those of **St. Patrick**, are the only contemporary insular sources for Britain and Ireland until the late sixth century. The fifth and sixth centuries have been variously ignored or treated as a transition period between Roman and Anglo-Saxon; it has been labelled sub-Roman, post-Roman, early Christian or simply the Dark Ages. I have proposed the label of **Brittonic Age**. In any case, a lack of written records and the difficulty in dating and interpreting archaeological evidence has led to many questions and a wide variety of theories. What happened to the population of Roman Britain, estimated at nearly four million in the fourth century? Did plague, famine or genocide kill large numbers of Britons? Could a small number of highly militarised mercenaries have replaced British political authority and led to the creation of Anglo-Saxon England or must it have been a large invasion force? Or perhaps the Britons were not killed in large numbers but survived in what became 'England' by eventually adopting the language of their conquerors?

No less controversial are the most famous figures associated with this period: Patrick, Arthur and **Merlin**. Though we have Patrick's own writings (including a spiritual autobiography, the *Confessions*), they describe contemporary Ireland (where he lived as a slave and later returned as a missionary) more than Britain and contain no dates. There is no contemporary evidence at all for a historical Arthur, for he does not appear in written histories until the ninth and tenth centuries. He and Merlin (in the earlier form 'Myrddin') appear in the Britons' vernacular poetry (i.e. in Welsh poetry), but the earliest stories do not even make them contemporaries. Similarly the great **Old English** epic ***Beowulf*** seems to refer to this period in history but was written down centuries later and in a very different context.

What we can say for sure is that the fifth and sixth centuries were when the separate nations of England, Scotland and Wales first began to emerge, and written evidence finally exists for some of the happenings in Ireland. These lands all participated in what has been termed the Age of Saints, and indeed, it is the monastic saints and scribes who dominate and sometimes write the surviving texts. The missionary efforts of Patrick and his successors brought both Christianity and Latin to Ireland, and Irish hagiography celebrates the achievements of Irish-born saints such as **Brigid**, **Brendan** and **Columba**. The latter is given credit for bringing Christianity to the Scottish Hebrides and Highlands, following the missionary work of **St. Ninian** in the Scottish Lowlands. From Columba's monastic school at **Iona**, monks such as **Aidan** and Colman brought Christianity to the English of **Northumbria**, where it met a Roman mission led by **Augustine of Canterbury** and **Paulinus of York**. The two traditions varied in the dating of Easter and liturgical matters, leading to a politically tinged clash at the **Synod of Whitby** described by the first English historian, **Bede**. Much has been made of the so-called **Celtic Christianity** since the 1980s, with its seemingly egalitarian and ecologically aware mysticism, but scholars have tended to dismiss this concept as misleading neo-Romanticism and wishful thinking.

Bede also describes the process of Anglo-Saxon state formation, as does the much later ***Anglo-Saxon Chronicles***. From these written sources as well as distribution patterns of Germanic pottery and jewellery, we can glimpse a rough political outline of early medieval England. Following the rebellion of Saxon mercenaries in the mid-fifth century, charismatic warlords began expanding their territorial bases from the northeast and the south-east until small kingdoms emerged a century later, most notably **Wessex**, **Kent**, **East Anglia**, **Bernicia** and **Deira**. These last two, perhaps Anglian takeovers of British polities, merged to form **Northumbria** in the sixth century, by which time the Anglian kingdom of **Mercia** along the Welsh border was also coming into prominence. A handful of rulers from these early Anglo-Saxon kingdoms became *bretwaldas*, 'Britain rulers', by asserting hegemony over their neighbours. The rulers of Northumbria enjoyed perhaps the greatest initial success, expanding into northern Wales and southern Scotland at the expense of British, Scottish and Pictish kingdoms.

The political arrangements of Wales and Scotland in the early Middle Ages are a little less clear. The expansion of Wessex and Northumbria seems to have isolated British communities in Cornwall, Wales and northern Britain, resulting in the gradual disappearance of British kingdoms such as **Dumnonia**, Craven, **Elmet**, **Rheged**, **Gododdin** and **Strathclyde**. Wales, segmented from the very beginning, witnessed the struggle between powerful **Gwynedd** and **Powys** and the isolation of smaller kingdoms such as **Dyfed**, **Ceredigion**, **Brycheiniog** and Gwent. Internal dynastic rivalries and the expansion of Mercia and Wessex prevented the emergence of a united Wales, which instead remained culturally conservative. Competition in Scotland pitted the Britons of Strathclyde and Gododdin (who held the districts around Glasgow and Edinburgh, respectively) against Northumbria, the southern Picts and the emerging Scottish state of **Dalriada** in Argyll. Dalriada had been settled by an Irish aristocracy from Antrim beginning in the late fifth century, and the area was quickly becoming **Gaelic** in language and culture. Ultimately **Kenneth MacAlpin** was able to unite the thrones of Dalriada and Pictland to create the kingdom of Alba, later termed Scotland. The mysterious Picts, though they converted to Christianity and remained potent militarily, lost their language and much of their culture in this merger.

Early medieval Ireland is known to us from Irish hagiography, monastic annals and the first vernacular texts written in Old Irish using the Latin alphabet (an earlier alphabet, Ogam, survives mainly in stone inscriptions). As monastic communities grew and proliferated on the island, Ireland remained divided politically and suffered from the dynastic rivalries of its dozens of clans or royal families. Of these, the most powerful was the **Uí Néill** ('descendants of Niall'), a tribal confederation which split into northern and southern branches who contended for the title 'king of Tara', which had become nearly synonymous with 'king of Ireland' in the seventh century. The northern Uí Néill was dominated by Cenél Conaill and Cenél nÉogain, while the southern Uí Néill was dominated by Clan Cholmáin, kings of Mide (**Meath**), and Síl nÁedo Sláine, kings of Brega. Around the year 730, Cenél nÉogain and Clann Cholmáin ousted their rivals from their claim to the overkingship and, henceforth, settled into an uneasy alternation in the kingship of Tara, supported by marriage alliances. Ecclesiastical rivalries were also characteristic of northern Ireland in this period, and the so-called **Ulster Cycle** (written down in the eighth and ninth centuries) celebrates the exploits of the **Ulster** hero **Cú Chulainn** against Queen Medb of Connacht.

The Viking Age

Ireland, the Isle of Man, the Scottish Isles and much of northern Britain were transformed dramatically by Viking raids in the ninth and tenth centuries. Seasonal raiding from Denmark, Sweden and Norway, which was mostly small scale and targeting portable wealth, was aided by new ship-building technology in the eighth century. The first Viking raid in the British Isles, according to the *Anglo-Saxon Chronicle*, was in 789. By the end of the eighth century, the **Vikings** attacked churches on the Isle of Skye, Iona and **Lindisfarne**. The early raids concentrated on the northern part of the Frankish realms, northern Britain and north-western Ireland. By the middle of the ninth century, the Vikings had begun building fortresses and other permanent camps in Britain and Ireland, using these strongholds to concentrate their attacks on specific regions throughout the year, and Viking fleets increased in size as well. One such Viking force was the 'Great Army' that, after 865, toppled the Anglo-Saxon kingdoms of Mercia and Northumbria.

In Ireland, the Vikings (most from Norway) turned from sporadic raiding to establishing permanent fortified naval bases (*longphorts*) along the east and south coasts at places such as **Cork**, **Dublin**, **Limerick**, **Waterford** and **Wexford**, which became Ireland's first true towns. Many smaller Irish kingdoms were destroyed by the Vikings, and the powerful families that survived were thus able to consolidate their position and dominate their regions. The greatest of these survivors, the powerful Uí Néill confederation, had some success in destroying Viking settlements which enabled them to claim supremacy in Ireland. Danish raids on Ireland in the middle of the ninth century resulted in their takeover of Dublin, which became a base for **Olaf the White** and his ally Ivar to raid Meath, **Munster**, the Isle of Man and Scotland. On Man, there is a high density of Viking graves and Scandinavian place names, and though no records survive detailing events, Scandinavian culture on Man can also be seen in the distinct Manx stone crosses and the still-active Court of Tynwald, a legislative assembly descended from the Norse Thing (*þing*). In the tenth century, the Norse on Man converted to Christianity, and in 1079, the Gaelic–Norse mercenary Godred Crovan conquered Man and founded a dynasty of **Manx 'sea kings'** that controlled Man and many of the Scottish islands until 1265.

Viking attacks on the Picts of northern Scotland opened the way for **Kenneth MacAlpin** to unite the Scots and the Picts, while the Norse remained a dominant presence in Shetland, Orkney and the Hebrides for centuries.

The Viking threat in England also made the career of another political unifier, **Alfred the Great**. After conquering Northumbria, the Vikings came to dominate northern England from their base at Jorvik (York). Though the Great Army had split into three parts, they pushed southwards and decisively defeated Mercia and East Anglia and seriously threatened the then most powerful Anglo-Saxon kingdom, Wessex. An unlikely heir to the throne of Wessex, Alfred managed to flee and survive until his force was strong enough to face the Vikings at the **Battle of Eddington** in Wiltshire in 878. His victory at Eddington over **Guthram**'s Danes, and subsequent land and naval victories over Vikings in the east, led to an Alfredian religious and cultural revival and a Wessex-led consolidation of the Anglo-Saxon kingdoms to become 'England'. This feat was accomplished in the tenth century by Alfred's grandson, **Æthelstan**, but only after Alfred had halted Viking expansion by building an English navy, fortifying towns (**burgs**) and sponsoring the conversion of Danish princes to Christianity. Henceforth, the Danes were restricted to lands in the north-east which became to be known as the **Danelaw**, where Scandinavian customary law was the norm and Scandinavian influence was evident in the local dialect.

The Anglo-Norman Period

The Northmen continued to have an impact on the politics of Anglo-Saxon England throughout the tenth and eleventh centuries. **Cnut**, who held power in both Denmark and Norway, seized control of England in 1016, as did his sons **Harold Harefoot** and **Harthacnut**. But it was the **Normans**, descendants of the Danish warlord Rollo who had settled in north-west France, who were to have the greatest impact on the history of the British Isles. **Edward the Confessor** succeeded his half-brother Harthacnut in 1042 and ruled with the support of the most powerful English earls. However, Edward began favouring his Norman advisors and, in 1151, named his cousin **William**, duke of Normandy, as his heir. This led to a mercurial relationship with **Godwin**, earl of Wessex, and his sons. There is no greater debate in English history than what *really* happened in 1066 when Edward died childless and the throne went to **Harold Godwinsson**. According to Norman sources, Harold had sworn an oath to support William's succession, and the latter prepared an invasion force to settle the dispute.

The Norman victory at the **Battle of Hastings** and the thorough Norman takeover of Anglo-Saxon political and ecclesiastical control are issues that have long interested historians. William's commission of ***Domesday Book*** benefited more than just royal tax collection: it is an invaluable source for local and regional history. The reign of William and his sons, **William II** and **Henry I**, require English historians to have an understanding of French medieval politics, for England was just one – and not always the most important – possession of these French-speaking dukes of Normandy. This changed only slightly with the civil war between **Stephen** and **Matilda** and the succession of Matilda's son, Henry **Plantagenet**, in 1154. **Henry II** constructed the so-called Angevin Empire by inheriting and marrying into vast continental holdings, but he also sought to extend his insular power through wars in Ireland, Scotland and Wales. The traditional explanation is that feudalism and monastic reform was brought into these Celtic-speaking lands by the Normans. Ireland, which witnessed great political strife following the death of the hegemon **Brian Boru** at **Clontarf** in 1014, was claimed by Henry as an English possession following his invasion of 1171. The island was later given to his youngest son, John, who was the first king of England since Harold II to speak fluent English.

There are several good reasons to end an encyclopedia such as this with the accession of Henry II. Henry worked and fought hard to re-establish central royal power over baronial authority. The enormous size of his empire prompted the expansion of local administration, causing government in England to become exceedingly more complex and bureaucratic. These and Henry's interest in legal matters led to the beginnings of English common law. In the next century, Magna Carta would be promulgated, expressing the limits of royal authority and the rights of other political groups, and the English Parliament would emerge from the Great Council of the Plantagenet kings. In Ireland, royal administration and English colonists would spread from the area around Dublin known as the Pale, while the princes of Wales and Scotland would give up their power (albeit in Scotland's case temporarily) to Henry's great-grandson, the conqueror and reformer Edward I. The Old English language was undergoing transformations, under the influence of Norman French, to becoming the English of Chaucer and Shakespeare. The early peoples of Britain and Ireland were truly becoming the modern peoples of Britain and Ireland.

In conclusion, I would point out a few general trends in the recent scholarship of early Britain and Ireland. The traditional invasion explanation of cultural change, derived mainly from written sources, has given way since the 1960s to archaeologists espousing a 'post-processual' view in which cultures adopt new languages, technologies, dress, etc. through trade contacts and alliances rather than conquest. Though still dominant in the discussion of prehistory, Iron Age and Roman Britain, the post-processual view has recently been challenged by historians and archaeologists studying the early Middle Ages, who have revived the notion of large-scale population displacement in, for example, the Anglo-Saxon migrations to Britain. Many have turned to emerging scientific measurements – particularly genetic (chromosomal) studies and stable isotope analysis – to answer questions about the percentages of Celtic, Anglo-Saxon and Scandinavian types in medieval and modern populations. A general distrust of written sources has also led to a re-evaluation of the Vikings as beneficent Scandinavian traders and explorers who liked to exaggerate tales of blood-thirsty heroes in their saga literature. Historians have turned less to poetry and hagiography and more to legal texts, charters and other seemingly more objective written sources, and the dominance of social history has led to the greater investigation of gender, marriage and kinship among the early peoples of Britain and Ireland. Finally, both archaeologists and historians have recognised the need for interdisciplinarity and awareness of what is happening in other parts of Europe (contextualising change in Britain and Ireland) or even drawing inspiration from anthropology, and conducting comparative studies of ancient and medieval cultures with modern and non-western societies.

We are living in an era of many answers, or at least many theories, rather than certitudes. For some students, this may be frustrating, for others inviting and challenging. My hope is that this work will reveal many paths for beginning the investigation of these compelling peoples and periods.

A

Aberlemno Stones

Several carved stones in and near Aberlemno in Angus, Scotland, are associated with the **Picts** of the early Middle Ages. Three stones stand by the roadside at Aberlemno, two of which are carved with Pictish symbols. Another Pictish stone stands at the west of Aberlemno church within the burial ground. In 1962, a fifth Pictish symbol stone was ploughed up on Flemington Farm, Aberlemno, about 98 feet (30 metres) east of the church. The fifth stone is now in the McManus Galleries, Dundee. In the nineteenth century, Jervise (1854–1857, 192) reported that a circle of stones or a cairn approximately 7 feet (2 metres) across was located to the south of one of the roadside stones and local people informed him of cists in the field.

Two of the roadside stones, both sandstone pillars, are regarded as Class I monuments, because they are incised on one face with Pictish symbols (on Pictish stone classification, *see* **Hilton of Cadboll**). They have (from top to bottom) symbols consisting of a serpent, a double disc and Z-rod and a mirror and comb. Both the serpent and the double disc and Z-rod symbols are deeply incised. The Flemington Farm stone has a horseshoe-shaped symbol above the so-called elephant or Pictish beast symbol. This combination of symbols also occurs in Pictish stones found elsewhere: Bruceton (Perthshire), Clatt (Aberdeenshire) and Congash (Highland).

The slab standing within Aberlemno churchyard is a Class II monument. One face bears a Latin cross, which stands proud off the background. Its arms are connected by a ring forming a quadrilobate shape rather than a true circle. This shape has the effect of enclosing a circle at each of the quadrants where the cross arms meet, a feature also characteristic of the Eassie (Angus) cross-slab. The background of the Aberlemno slab is carved in relief with interlaced and coiled beasts.

The other face is framed by a pair of fierce-toothed serpents, whose heads meet at the apex of the slab. Immediately beneath are two symbols side by side: a two-legged rectangle and Z-rod and a triple-circular disc symbol. Underneath is a battle scene, which has received much comment. Alcock (2003, 149) used the pictorial evidence of mounted warriors and foot soldiers in his discussion of the Pictish army. Cruickshank (2000) suggested that the scene is a narrative one, commemorating the Battle of Dunnichen (or **Nechtansmere**) in which the Picts defeated the **Angles** in AD 685. The dating of this stone is problematic. According to Cruickshank (2000, 86), the face with the battle scene was carved first, shortly after the events at Dunnichen, and the cross face later in the 720s. Laing (2001) examined the sword types and other iconographic features related to metalwork. Concluding that these features are not characteristic of the seventh or eighth century, Laing (2001, 250) proposed a ninth-century date for both faces, attributing correspondences that other authors have seen on the cross face with eighth-century insular manuscripts to a revival of earlier styles.

There is more consensus about the dating of the second Aberlemno cross-slab which is by the roadside. Most authors assign a later date to it (ninth century). It is large, measuring 9.25 feet (2.82 metres) high, and carved on four sides. This is also a Class II monument, whose design features a Latin cross on one face. Much of the carving is in high relief. Circular bosses appear within a ring, which connects the cross arms, whose ends are ornamented by rectangular mounts resembling settings for stones. A ringed boss is at the centre of the head. The cross appears to have been inspired by a metal-encased altar cross set with precious gems, few of which have survived. One rare example of such an altar cross dated to the eighth or ninth century is the Tully Lough Cross, Ireland. In common with Pictish conventions, the Aberlemno cross is that of the resurrected Christ, and it does not display the crucifixion. It is unusual because the shaft is flanked by two angels, whose heads are bowed as if in mourning.

The other face displays a large crescent and V-rod and double disc and Z-rod symbols. Immediately below them, a panel contains a hunting scene in which hounds attack two hinds and a fawn. There are two trumpeters in the upper right-hand corner of the panel, a feature which also occurs on the Hilton of Cadboll cross-slab. At Aberlemno, they are depicted on one plane, one following the other. Two further panels at the bottom of the slab contain a centaur and a scene with a frontal standing figure rending the jaw of a lion. A sheep and a harp accompany the man, indicating that this figure represents the biblical David.

Further Reading

Alcock, Leslie. 2003. *Kings and Warriors, Craftsmen and Priests in Northern Britain AD 550–850*. Society of Antiquaries of Scotland, Monograph Series.

Cruickshank, Graeme D. R. 2000. 'The Battle of Dunnichen and the Aberlemno Battle-Scene'. Pp. 69–87 in *Alba: Celtic Scotland in the Medieval Era*. Edited by E. J. Cowan and R. Andrew McDonald. Tuckwell Press.

Jervise, Andrew. 1854–1857. 'Notices Descriptive of the Localities of Certain Sculptured Stone Monuments in Forfarshire'. *Proceedings of the Society of Antiquaries of Scotland* 2: 187–199, http://ads.ahds.ac.uk/catalogue/adsdata/PSAS_2002/pdf/vol_002/2_187_201.pdf (cited 27 February 2008).

Laing, Lloyd. 2001. 'The Date of the Aberlemno Churchyard Stone'. Pp. 241–251 in *Pattern and Purpose in Insular Art*. Edited by Mark Redknap, Nancy Edwards, Susan Youngs, Alan Lane and Jeremy Knight. Oxbow Books.

RCAHMS. 1999. *Pictish Symbol Stones: An Illustrated Gazetteer*. Royal Commission on the Ancient and Historical Monuments of Scotland.

Penelope Dransart

Adminius (dep. AD 39)

Adminius, or 'Amminus' or 'Amminius' as he was styled on some of his coins, was a native British prince who lived in the early first century AD. The son of **Cunobelinus** of the ***Catuvellauni/Trinovantes*** tribe, who installed him as ruler in eastern **Kent** over the ***Cantiaci*** tribe, he is perhaps best known for his exile and flight to Rome in search for imperial intervention. As far as the rest of his family is concerned, his brother Epaticcus was given reign over portions of the Atrebatic kingdom, but little is known of Adminius's early life, other than that the distribution of his coins places him in the first half of the first century AD in the Kent region, and it is not until Suetonius that the firm date AD 39 is provided for a specific event in his life: his deposition.

Why exactly he was exiled is not certain, but it was possibly the result of a revolt amongst his tribe or the result of one led by two of his other supposed brothers, Togodumnus and **Caratacus**, against the pro-Roman faction of their father. Regardless of the precise motives, he fled to the emperor at the time, Gaius (Caligula), and appealed to him with the promise of submission. This created a perfect opportunity for Roman intervention, and though the prepared invasion force in AD 40 was subsequently abandoned, it revived Roman interest in the possibility of British occupation. Why exactly the initially planned campaign was cancelled is not known, but it seems that the refusal to return Adminius to Britain afterwards contributed to rising anti-Roman sentiment, followed by the successful Claudian invasion in AD 43. To a certain degree then, he was partially responsible for bringing about the destruction of the indigenous kingdoms. As with his beginnings, little is known of what became of him, although an inscription at **Chichester** naming 'Lucullus, son of Amminus' has been argued by Miles Russell as making Adminius the father of Sallustius Lucullus, a Roman-British governor in the late first century.

See also Roman Army; Roman Britain.

Further Reading

Birley, Anthony. 1980. *The People of Roman Britain*. University of California Press.

Branigan, Keith. 1985. *The Catuvellauni*. Alan Sutton.

Cunliffe, B. W. 2005. *Iron Age Communities of Britain* (4th edn.). RKP.

Russell, M. 2006. 'Roman Britain's Lost Governor'. *Current Archaeology* 204: 630–635.

Todd, Malcolm. 1999. *Roman Britain* (3rd edn.). Blackwell.

Anne Sassin

Adomnán (c. AD 628–704)

Adomnán (c. AD 628–704), monk and scholar, from the same Donegal family as Colum Cille, became **Iona**'s ninth abbot in 679. During his abbacy, he brought new renown to Iona not simply because of his scholarship but through his, now less well-known, diplomatic and legal work. His interest in mitigating the effects of war took him to **Northumbria** (he visited there at least twice, as a guest at the monastery of Wearmouth–**Jarrow**, when **Bede** was an oblate, and he presented a copy of his *De locis sanctis* to King **Aldfrith** who had earlier stayed with Adomnan on Iona) on behalf of Irish captives. Moreover, he was the central figure at the Synod of Birr (697), which produced the *Lex innocentium* (and later known as the *Cáin Adomnáin* after him) for the protection of women, children and other non-combatants. He is credited in a series of canonical manuscripts as the author of a short collection of *Canones* (church law), and there is no reason to doubt his authorship. He is the most recent named authority in some recensions of the *Collectio canonum hibernensis*: he possibly had a role in its creation as it has many links with Iona, which required a large well-organised library such as the one we see Adomnán use elsewhere, and there are some unusual items of information common to the *Collectio* and the *De locis sanctis*. Adomnán also took part, according to Bede, in the Easter-date controversy.

Adomnán is best remembered today for his *Vita of Colum Cille* which – despite hagiographical commonplaces, it claims to record his miracles, prophesies and visions (a scheme he took from Gregory the Great) – is a major source for the history of Iona and insular monasticism. Its account of royal anointing influenced the development of kingship in Europe, however, it is little more than a fine specimen of the Latin genre of the period. His other book, *De locis sanctis*, deals with places mentioned in the Scriptures. Posing as information received from a bishop, a Gaul named Arculf, who had travelled in the East, in addition to what Adomnán knew from books, it is a complex manual for solving exegetical problems using geographical knowledge. Much of the work may, in fact, have been derived from information available in Iona's relatively well-stocked library. The contradiction-laden figure of 'Arculf' is best understood as the rhetorical device of prosopopoeia; his presence offering narrative unity to the snippets of information. Among the many attempts to reconcile conflicting geographical statements found in the Scriptures (Adomnán was particularly inspired by the hope that Augustine had placed in using geographical knowledge who desire that someone should write a work on this), his is one of the most competent and original in method, and on one occasion, he deliberately sought to improve on Augustine's method. The book was immediately recognised as a key resource as the number of copies circulated Europe-wide testify, while Bede recognised its potential as a textbook and wrote a summary (also called *De locis sanctis*) intended for students not yet ready for Adomnán's book – and Bede's was only the first of a series of classroom abbreviations. His European medieval reputation – one of the few Irish writers who were labelled 'illustrious' – as a scholar rested on this work, and through *De locis sanctis*, he is the only Irish writer who can be said to have played a role in the growth of the medieval propositional approach to Scripture. It was one of the first early Irish works in print.

Adomnán's fame in medieval Ireland seems related principally to his being the author of one of 'four laws (*cána*) of Ireland' and as a saintly abbot, for he is specially noted in the martyrologies and is the subject of a *vita* in Irish. However, his reputation as a scholar must also have continued (a Bede-inspired abbreviation of the *De locis* survives under his name in Irish), for he was made the worthy seer of a vision/tour of heaven and hell, the *Fís Adomnáin*: the most elaborate specimen of the genre extant in Irish.

See also Celtic Christianity.

Further Reading

Herbert, Máire. 1988. *Iona, Kells, and Derry: The History and Hagiography of the Monastic Familia of Columba*. Oxford University Press.

Lapidge, Michael, and Richard Sharpe. 1985. *A Bibliography of Celtic-Latin Literature 400–1200*. Royal Irish Academy.

O'Loughlin, Thomas. 2007. *Adomnán and the Holy Places: The Perceptions of an Insular Monk on the Locations of the Biblical Drama*. T. & T. Clark.

Thomas O'Loughlin

Adventus Saxonum

The Latin term *adventus Saxonum*, 'the coming of the **Saxons**', although not appearing in precisely this form in any early medieval source, has become the scholarly shorthand for the events or processes that initiated the settlement of Germanic-speaking peoples in eastern Britain in the fifth century. The most influential account, from which the phrase is derived, is that of **Bede** who, writing in 731, opens Book I, chapter 15 of his *Historia Ecclesiastica*:

> In the year of Our Lord 449 Marcian, forty-sixth from Augustus, became emperor with Valentinian and ruled for seven years. At that time the *gens* of the **Angles** and the Saxons (*Saxonum*), invited by **Vortigern**, came (*advenitur*) to Britain in three warships and by his command were granted a place of settlement in the eastern part of the island, ostensibly to fight on behalf of the fatherland, but their real intention was to conquer it.

Bede's account is largely, although not entirely, based on that found in *De Excidio Brittaniae* written 200 years earlier by the Briton **Gildas** and also bears a close, though ill defined, relationship to the account of the same events found in the ninth-century

Cambro-Latin ***Historia Brittonum***. All three accounts, as they come down to us, seem already to have combined oral tradition with documentary sources.

Bede is the only one of the three authorities who gives a precise date, although this seems to have been calculated from the account of Gildas who places the invitation to the Saxons after the rejection of an appeal by the **Britons** to the Roman general Aëtius for military aid against their insular enemies, the **Picts** and the Irish. Gildas cites the address from the appeal, 'to Aëtius, thrice consul', thus dating the appeal, if his report is genuine, to the period between Aëtius's third consulship, in 446–447, and his murder, in 454. Bede seems to have presumed that the appeal was sent in the year of Aëtius's third consulship and to have allowed for a brief interval, perhaps on grounds of common sense, before charting the coming of the Saxons in 449.

Bede's narrative remained, with minor modifications, the basis for all accounts until modern times and is not entirely without influence even today. Recently, however, this treatment of the *adventus Saxonum* has come under attack from three directions. First, whatever may be made of the account by Gildas, which contains far fewer details than that of Bede or the *Historia Brittonum*, the eighth- and ninth-century versions of the story are now recognised as national origin legends constructed within an established genre. Certain elements of the story, such as the invaders arriving in three ships, have been recognised as international folklore motifs, and the names of the Saxon leaders supplied by Bede and the *Historia Brittonum*, **Hengest and Horsa** ('stallion/gelding' and 'horse'), are not otherwise attested as personal names nor do they fit into the widely spread Germanic practice of using dithematic names combining two complimentary elements (as in Theodoric, 'people + sovereignty', or Ælfwald, 'elf + rule'). The monothematic names given the leaders of the *adventus Saxonum* look more like mythological or totemic labels.

Secondly, archaeological and, to some extent, linguistic studies suggest that the Germanic-speaking peoples in Britain did not share a single common origin but settled following a number of discrete events. Archaeological evidence has also been claimed to demonstrate that the settlement preceded the dates given by Bede, but there are problems of circularity here since the *adventus Saxonum* has traditionally provided something of a Rosetta Stone which has enabled the relative chronologies of brooch and pottery typologies to be tied into absolute dating systems. There are also questions to be raised as to how specifically dated events relate to broader processes of cultural change visible in the archaeological record.

Thirdly, a more fatal blow is dealt to Bede's dating of the *adventus Saxonum* by the contemporary *Gallic Chronicle of 452*, probably composed in southern Gaul by Faustus, abbot of Lerins, himself a Briton, or someone in his circle. This chronicle records, under the year 441–442: 'The provinces of Britain, having up to this time suffered various defeats and calamities, were reduced to Saxon rule.' Since this entry relates to an event only a decade before the compilation of the chronicle, it is likely that this date is fairly accurate and it receives some confirmation from the *Chronicle of 511*, which appears to record the same event under the year 440–441. The *Chronicle of 452* also has an earlier entry recording a devastation of the island by the Saxons in 408–409. This earlier entry is more distant from the time of compilation but would seem to relate to the barbarian attack on Britain in 409 recorded in the sixth-century history of Count Zosimus (who lifted most of this part of his work from a now-lost early fifth-century history by Olympiodorus of Thebes). If we accept the witness of the Gallic chronicles, then a major military success was gained by the Saxons up to half a dozen years before the third consulship of Aëtius, and it might be possible to imagine that some part of the island had been occupied since 409.

Various attempts have been made by modern scholars to square Gildas's account of the appeal to Aëtius with that of the Gallic chronicles. Some have suggested that the phrase 'thrice consul' was not in the document Gildas appears to have been citing but that he added it as a rhetorical flourish somewhat anachronistically, the original document relating to an earlier period. Others have suggested that Gildas's account relates only to the northern frontier of Roman Britain and was never intended to relate the first Saxon settlement in the island as a whole.

The appeal to Aëtius is perhaps best taken at face value. In the late 440s, this Roman general appears to have won a victory over the Franks at Vicus Helena, a place not far from Arras, and to have restored imperial hegemony over the hinterland of the channel ports. The text of the appeal, as quoted by Gildas, refers only to the conflict between the Britons and unnamed barbarians, and the simplest solution to the conundrum is to accept that the appeal is genuine but that Gildas misplaced it in his sequence when he presented it as preceding an appeal for Saxon help rather than as an appeal for help against the Saxons who had overwhelmed the British provinces at the beginning of the decade. Once this chronological marker has been removed, we are left with an account of the Saxons apparently gaining a definitive upper hand c. 441 but with no clue as to the date of their arrival.

An alternative dating scheme is preserved in the *Historia Brittonum*, written in Wales c. 820. Like the Gallic chronicles, the account in chapter 66 of the *Historia* uses consular dating rather than years from the incarnation of Christ. It reads:

> Vortigern, however, held power in Britain in the consulship of Theodosius and Valentinian, and in the fourth year of his reign the Saxons came to Britain, in the consulship of Felix and Taurus.

Theodosius and Valentinian shared the consulship in 425 and Felix and Taurus in 428. This alternative dating has attracted some support from scholars over the years, but it is not clear that it is truly independent of the dating provided by Bede. Bede reckoned the end of Roman rule in Britain to the year 409, forty years before his date for the *adventus Saxonum*. The *Historia Brittonum*, in chapter 31, also makes the period between the ending of Roman rule and the coming of the Saxons forty years, but, in contrast to Bede, it reckons **Magnus Maximus** to be the last Roman emperor to rule over Britain. Maximus was slain in 388, so the fortieth year after this was 428, the consulship of Felix and Taurus.

In conclusion, we shall probably never know the precise date for the arrival of Saxon forces in Britain nor the extent to which something approaching history can be drawn from the story of the invitation offered them by Vortigern. Nonetheless, we can be confident that these matters will continue to excite speculation for many years to come.

Further Reading

Brooks, Nicholas. 2000. 'The English Origin Myth'. Pp. 79–90 in *Anglo-Saxon Myths: State and Church, 400–1066*. Edited by Nicholas Brooks. The Hambledon Press.

Howe, Nicholas. 2001. *Migration and Mythmaking in Anglo-Saxon England*. University of Notre Dame Press.

Jones, Michael E. 1996. *The End of Roman Britain*. Cornell University Press.

Morris, John (ed. and tr.). 1980. *Nennius: British History and the Welsh Annals*. The Phillimore Press.

Sowerby, R. 2007. 'Hengest and Horsa: The Manipulation of History and Myth from the *Adventus Saxonum* to *Historia Brittonum*'. *Nottingham Medieval Studies* 51: 1–19.

Alex Woolf

Áed (d. AD 700)

Áed Dub, bishop of Slébte in County Carlow, was a key figure in mid-seventh-century Irish ecclesiastical matters who, amongst other aspirations as conforming to the Roman church, is notable for having the *Life of Saint Patrick* dedicated to him. Brother of Faélán mac Colmáin, king of the north **Leinster** Uí Dúnlainge dynasty, it is most probable that Áed may have already been one of the *Romani* – those in favour of union with Rome – when he inspired his disciple **Muirchú** moccu Machtháni of North Leinster to write his life of the saint, as Slébte in the southern half of Ireland had already conformed to the controversial Roman calculation of Easter by the 630s. This life of **Patrick**, which was contained within the ***Book of Armagh***, may have been the means by which Áed and Muirchú attempted to win over the north and Armagh to the Roman viewpoint, as it certainly contained the correct keeping of Easter figures.

Another document preserved in the same manuscript describes the process of Áed negotiating with Bishop Ségéne of Armagh and establishing the overlordship of the latter, making it one of the only known instances of formal overlord acknowledgement in such a context. From this, it has been suggested that Armagh and Áed may have been in sympathies with each other, as much of Muirchú's material seems to have been supplied by the authorities of Armagh, and as Áed certainly joined the *paruchia Patricii* while Ségéne was still bishop and would not have probably been so attached if the two churches differed on such an important issue as Easter, Armagh most probably conformed as well before 688. Most of the other events in Áed's life rely on documentation in the annals, and he was known to have recognised the Primacy of Armagh in 680 and along with Muirchú attending **Adomnán**'s Synod of 697. Yet by the time of this latter event, he seems to have been succeeded by Conchad, who died in 692 and incidentally had accepted the successor of Ségéne, Flann Febla, continuing the tradition of the overlordship of Armagh. According to the ***Annals of Ulster***, Áed died in AD 700, and it seems that this was after several quiet years of retirement which had been spent at Armagh.

See also Celtic Christianity.

Further Reading

Farmer, D. H. (ed.). 2003. *The Oxford Dictionary of Saints*. Oxford University Press.
Hughes, Kathleen. 1966. *The Church in Early Irish Society*. Methuen.
Ó Cróinín, Dáibhí. 1995. *Early Medieval Ireland, 400–1200*. Longman.
———. 2003. *Early Irish History and Chronology*. Four Courts Press.

Anne Sassin

Aedán mac Gabráin (r. AD 574–c. AD 606)

In both medieval legend and modern historiography, Aedán mac Gabráin fulfils the role of an archetypical early Scottish king. In modern literature, he is perhaps best known as a contemporary and sometime co-worker of St. **Columba**. In medieval Irish literature, his main function was perhaps as both the apical figure of the Scottish royal house and the representative of Gaelic north Britain in the constructed heroic age of the later-sixth and early-seventh centuries. In this latter role, he also attained a somewhat sinister reputation, whether as the tempter of Columba, as in Manus Ó Domhnaill's *Life of Saint Columba*, or as the intimate of Satan and betrayer of his kinsmen, as in *The Saga of Cano Son of Gartnait*.

In reality, Aedán seems to have been a particularly active king, reigning from 574 until c. 606, in western Scotland and north-east Ireland. If we discount the later saga material, most of our information about Aedán is derived either from the Irish chronicles or from Adomnán's *Vita Columbae*, supplemented by some genealogical material. Aedán was the ancestor of many later kings of **Dál Riata**, but this kingdom, as we know it, may have been largely the product of his long and eventful reign. Aedán's reign is presumed to have begun with the death of Conall mac Comgaill, who precedes him in the later king lists, in 574. The first of his own activities to be noted in the chronicles are an expedition to Orkney in 580 or 581 and a victory won in *Manu* in 582. *Manu* here probably indicates the British kingdom of Manaw lying to the east of Stirling rather than the **Isle of Man**. The year 590 saw a victory at the unidentified site of Leithreid, while in 596, the killing of two of Aedán's sons, Bran and Domangart, is noticed. The *Vita Columbae* identifies Domangart's killers as the **Saxons**. The final battle attributed to Aedán, a defeat inflicted upon him by the Saxons, is dated to 600. Since this battle is almost certainly the same conflict as that noted by Bede as having occurred in 603, it is possible that all the above dates may be two or three years too early. The geographical range of Aedán's battles, from Orkney to the modern Anglo-Scottish border area, is unparalleled by any later king of Dál Riata, and later Irish material makes it clear that he was active across much of the north of Ireland as well although here the record is more of diplomatic contacts with both the **Uí Néill** ruler Aed mac Ainmirech (d. 597) and the **Ulster** over-king Báetán mac Cairrell (d. 581). It is possible that his hegemony in Antrim supplied the resources which supported his British campaigns.

Aedán is said to have had many sons, a number of whom had British rather than **Gaelic** names. Unusually for a Gaelic ruler, he found a place in Welsh tradition in which he seems to have also been regarded as a sinister character. Adomnán's protestation that he was not Columba's first choice for the kingship, on Conall's death, may suggest that his negative reputation was already in place by the 690s.

See also Scots.

Further Reading

Bannerman, John. 1974. *Studies in the History of Dalriada*. Scottish Academic Press.
Sharpe, Richard (tr.). 1995. *Adomnán of Iona: Life of St Columba*. Penguin.

Alex Woolf

Ælfric of Eynsham (b. c. AD 953–955)

Ælfric of Eynsham, also known as Ælfric the Homilist, was one of the most prolific authors of **Old English** texts. The majority of what remains of Old English comes from his pen, and interestingly enough, two of the four surviving manuscripts of Old English poetry come from those associated in some way with Ælfric. He was a very well-educated and learned man, drawing on many sources, writing in an elegant and sometimes poetic style suitable for preaching and, most importantly, remembering his words. Nothing is known of his origins or familial background. Because it was so late in his career that he rose to abbot, and that he did not rise to bishop, it has been supposed that he was not of noble origins. His dialect seems to place him firmly in the south of England. His birth is believed to have occurred c. 953–955.

It is not until 987 and the transfer to Cern Abbas from Winchester that anything definitive may be said about Ælfric, and what may be said is mostly in regard to his literary output. His earliest known works are the *Sermones Catholici*, the Catholic Homilies, consisting of two series of forty homilies each proceeding through the church year on the Gospels, some saints lives and some doctrinal themes. He tells us in the preface that he was concerned for the ignorance of basic Christian doctrine by both monk and lay person and that he prepared these homilies for both readers and preachers. These were widely circulated. Throughout his career, Ælfric continued to revise the collection and added to it some forty additional homilies and organised and reorganised these homilies into different collections. A third collection of homilies soon followed consisting in the main lives and passions of the saints. Ælfric produced a Latin grammar, written in English, for his students at Cerne Abbas and also a colloquy on the trades to assist his students mastering Latin. He is also responsible for a series of translations of portions of the *Old Testament* and summaries of other *Old Testament* books into English, and these were taken and later collected into a single work to form an illustrated Hexateuch; the material that Ælfric had not translated was provided by another translator. He also wrote pastoral letters, was a considered authority on canon law and church practices and may have even advised King **Æthelred**.

Between 1002 and 1005, Ælfric became abbot of a refounded monastery at Eynsham where he continued the work he had begun at Cern Abbas. His death year is not known, but cannot be later than 1012, and is probably a good deal earlier. Ælfric was certainly the most prominent product of the Benedictine reform, and as a scholar, he was cognizant and drew on a wide range of patristic and early medieval authors. He worked closely with both clergy and noble laity in educating monks and lay people in the ideals of the Reform movement. His few works in Latin reveal a competent Latinist who preferred a simpler style in contrast to most of his contemporaries who wrote what has come to be called the 'hermeneutic style' which was flowery and favoured obscure words. The vast majority of his work is in Old English, and his style became a model for late Old English and a standard against which Old English prose is often measured.

See also Literature.

Further Reading

Clemoes, Peter. 1966. 'Ælfric'. Pp. 176–209 in *Continuations and Beginnings: Studies in Old English Literature*. Edited by E. Stanley. Nelson Publishing.

———. 1980. *The Chronology of Ælfric's Works*. Old English Newsletter Subsidia 5 repr. CEMERS.

Hurt, James. 1972. *Ælfric*. Twayne.

Reinsma, Luke. 1987. *Ælfric: An Annotated Bibliography*. Garland.

Larry Swain

Ælle

Ælle was a name borne by two Anglo-Saxon kings of the pre-Christian period and one in the ninth century. The best known of these was the father of Eadwine of **Deira** (617–632), who was apparently king of Deira at some earlier period. The ***Anglo-Saxon Chronicle*** claims that this Ælle became king of the Northumbrians in 560, following Ida, and was succeeded in 588 by Æthelric. This is at odds with the Bernician regal list preserved from the late eighth century in which Ida is succeeded by a number of his sons in turn, including Æthelric, and which has no place for Ælle. Probably, the chronicle account reflects a late attempt to synthesise Northumbrian history prior to the union of Deira and **Bernicia**. No king list survives for Deira, but a pedigree of Eadwine makes him the son of Ælle, the son of Yffe, the son of Uuscfrea. It is possible that Ælle continued to rule over Deira until its conquest by Æthelfrith of Bernicia in 604; perhaps it was his brother Ælfric, the father of Eadwine's successor Osric (632–633), who ruled at some point in this latter period. Ælle's daughter Acha married the Bernician conqueror Æthelfrith and bore him a son, Oswald.

The other pre-Christian Ælle was a king of the South Saxons whose *floruit* was placed by the *Anglo-Saxon Chronicle* in the gap between the career of Hengest and the beginnings of West Saxon history (c. 477–491). He is otherwise known only from **Bede**'s famous list of seven kings who held *imperium* south of the Humber. He is the first in this sequence, and since each of the others has a *floruit* overlapping his neighbours in the list, probably Ælle's career overlapped with that of his successor Ceawlin of the Gewisse that seems to have begun c. 581. Thus, Ælle of Sussex was probably a contemporary of his Deiran namesake, and traditions concerning them may have become confused.

The third king named Ælle was another Northumbrian whose descent is unknown. He contested the kingship with Osberht (c. 848–867). It was during their civil war that the Great Army came to **Northumbria**. In the face of Viking aggression, Ælle and Osberht set their differences on one side and joined forces. It was to no avail, however, and the two were slain. In later legend, English and Scandinavian, much of the blame for the Viking conquest of Northumbria was laid at Ælle's door.

See also Kings and Kingship.

Further Reading

Kirby, David P. 1992. *The Earliest English Kings*. Routledge.

Yorke, Barbara. 1990. *Kings and Kingdoms of Early Anglo-Saxon England*. Seaby.

Alex Woolf

Æthelbald

There were two rulers named Æthelbald, one a king of the Mercians in the early eighth century and the other a king of the West Saxons in the middle of the ninth century. Æthelbald, king of the Mercians, holds the distinction of ruling for forty-one years from AD 716 to 757, the longest reign credibly recorded in Anglo-Saxon history. He established overlordship of southern England through military conquest and even claimed the title *rex Brittaniae*, 'King of Britain'. The other King Æthelbald ruled over the West Saxons from 855 to 860. Æthelbald of **Wessex** came to power when his father Æthelwulf undertook a pilgrimage to Rome in 855, leaving Æthelbald the suzerainty of Wessex. Æthelbald is most famous for having rebelled against his father, attempting to impede his return from pilgrimage in 856.

Æthelbald of Mercia's reign expanded Mercian power. In 716, he came to rule through the help of Guthlac, a respected hermit and eventual Anglo-Saxon saint. The two had associated in the fens when Æthelbald, who was from a rival royal bloodline, was exiled by Ceolred, king of Mercia. Guthlac prophesied Æthelbald's ascendancy, which occurred after the death of Ceolred in 716. King Æthelbald expanded his power both through military victory and through negotiation. He absorbed several sub-kingdoms into the Mercian domain, such as the Magonsaetes, the Hwiccians and the Middle Anglians. Against more powerful rivals, Æthelbald also found success. He waged war on the West Saxons expanding the Mercian border southwards. Kentish charters reveal Æthelbald extending power by patronising Kentish churches. Additionally, he controlled **London** and its tolls. He attacked the Welsh and the Northumbrians, perhaps in an alliance with the **Picts**. In 757, these successes came to an end when a bodyguard murdered him.

Æthelbald of Mercia also strengthened ties with the Christian Church. He convened the Council of Clofesho in 746/747. Boniface, the famous Anglo-Saxon missionary, may have prompted this gathering. In 745/746, Boniface sent Æthelbald a scathing letter, rebuking him for seizing church property, abusing monks and nuns and neglecting the needs of the church. At the Council of Clofesho, bishops gained greater supervision over monasteries to ensure their proper conduct. At Gumley in 749, Æthelbald conceded royal privileges to the church, including exemptions from financial obligations.

The latter Æthelbald became king of the West Saxons in 855. Æthelbald of Wessex was the oldest of four brothers, **Æthelberht**, **Æthelred** and **Alfred**. When Æthelwulf abdicated his kingship in 855 to travel to Rome as a pilgrim, he established a will, some of which can be reconstructed from Asser's *Life of Alfred*. Æthelbald, as the eldest, inherited western Wessex and the kingship, while the eastern part of Wessex passed to Æthelberht. In 856, Æthelwulf returned, perhaps unexpectedly. With the assistance of other nobles, Æthelbald attempted to bar his father's entrance. The two negotiated a compromise, whereby Æthelbald retained control of western Wessex and Æthelwulf took control of eastern Wessex. After the death of Æthelwulf, Æthelbald fell into a scandal by marrying Judith, Æthelwulf's widow. Æthelbald died in 860.

See also Kings and Kingship.

Further Reading
Campbell, James, Eric John and Patrick Wormald. 1982. *The Anglo-Saxons*. Edited by James Campbell. Cornell University Press.
Kirby, D. P. 1968. *The Making of Early England*. Schocken Books.
Yorke, Barbara. 1995. *Wessex in the Early Middle Ages*. Leicester University Press.
———. 1997. *Kings and Kingdoms of Early Anglo-Saxon England*. Routledge.

James Williams

Æthelberht

There were several kings with the name of Æthelberht in the early medieval period, two kings of **Kent**, a king of East Anglia and a king of **Wessex**. Æthelberht I of Kent was regarded as the most powerful ruler in England in the second half of the sixth century and is best known as the first of the Anglo-Saxon kings to convert to Christianity. Æthelberht II ruled Kent, perhaps as a co-ruler with his brother Eadbert, around the middle of the eighth century, as Kentish power waned. Little is known about Æthelberht of East Anglia except that he died around 794. Æthelberht of Wessex ruled the West Saxons for six years beginning in 860, reuniting the sub-kingdoms within Wessex.

Historians have struggled reconciling with conflicting source information about the life and chronology of Æthelberht I of Kent. The two main sources, **Bede**'s *Historia Ecclesiastica Gentis Anglorum* and Gregory of Tours's *Historia Francorum*, differ substantially in motive and perspective. It is believed that Æthelberht was born c. 560. Twenty years later, he married the Frankish princess **Bertha**, the daughter of Charibert. Despite the normal prestige associated with a marriage to a continental royal family, Æthelberht's marriage to Bertha probably garnered him little clout because of the proliferation of Merovingian kings at the time. Æthelberht's political career is unclear, but sometime after the fall of Caewlin of Wessex in 592 he became overlord of the southern British kingdoms. In 597, he received the papal mission of St. Augustine and converted to Christianity, because of either the influence of his Christian wife Bertha or a desire to escape conversion at the hands of the Franks, an act which may have signified political subordination. Æthelberht I died sometime between 616 and 618.

Documentary evidence for Æthelberht II also creates problems for historians, obscuring the later Kentish kings. Wihtred of Kent died in 725 leaving three sons, Æthelberht, Eadbert and Alric. Æthelberht as the oldest may have assumed the title of king, but it seems that he ruled jointly with his brother Eadbert until Eadbert's death in 748. From 748 until 762, Æthelberht II ruled alone. Kent under Æthelberht II had trouble competing against its rivals, ceding control of London and the ability to appoint archbishops of Canterbury to **Æthelbald** of the Mercians.

Æthelberht, king of East Anglia, died at the hands of **Offa** of Mercia in 794. Little is known about his rule due to the dearth of written sources from East Anglia.

Æthelberht of Wessex was the second son of King **Æthelwulf** of the West Saxons. When Æthelwulf abdicated his kingship in 855 to go on a pilgrimage to Rome, Æthelberht as the second son received the eastern half of Wessex, while his older brother Æthelbald received the title 'King of the West Saxons' and the western half. Upon the death of Æthelbald in 860, Æthelberht reunited the two halves, the last time the kingdom of Wessex would be separated.

See also Kings and Kingship.

Further Reading
Brooks, Nicholas. 1989. 'The Creation and Early Structure of the Kingdom of Kent'. Pp. 55–74 in *The Origins of Anglo-Saxon Kingdoms*. Edited by Steven Bassett. Leicester University Press.
Campbell, James, Eric John and Patrick Wormald. 1982. *The Anglo-Saxons*. Edited by James Campbell. Cornell University Press.
Kirby, D. P. 1968. *The Making of Early England*. Schocken Books.
Yorke, Barbara. 1997. *Kings and Kingdoms of Early Anglo-Saxon England*. Routledge.

James Williams

Æthelflæd (d.918)

Æthelflæd (d. 918), ruler of the Mercians, was the daughter and first-born child of Alfred – king of the West Saxons and later of the English – and his wife Ealhswith, daughter of Æthelred, ealdorman of the 'Gaini'. By c. 893, she married the Mercian ealdorman **Æthelred**, who had come to rule over the part of **Mercia** left to native rule after the kingdom's dismemberment by the **Vikings** and had submitted to Alfred's overlordship. After Æthelred fell ill, leadership of the Mercians is accorded by the sources to Alfred's son Edward the Elder or to Æthelflæd, and after his death in 911, Æthelflæd is described by the 'Mercian Register' as *Myrcna hlæfdige*, 'Lady of the Mercians'. Succeeding to the West Saxon kingdom, Edward the Elder took over jurisdiction of formerly Mercian **London** and Oxford.

Æthelflæd shared in her brother's enterprise to reconquer the **Danelaw**. As its precursor, she was instrumental in extending into **Mercia** a system of fortified settlements or ***burhs***. **Worcester** (887–899) and **Chester** (907) had been fortified, and the unlocated 'Bremesburh' had been built. Thereafter, paralleling Edward's programme, she had *burhs* constructed at Bridgnorth and 'Scergeat' (912), Tamworth and Stafford (913), Warwick and Eddisbury (914) and Runcorn, Chirbury and perhaps 'Weardburh' (915). Around this time too, she built the defences of **Gloucester** and Hereford.

This activity provided the basis for the successes of 917. In that year, three separate Viking forces attacked English territory but were rolled back, and before the end of the year, all the Scandinavian armies of East Anglia had submitted to Edward. In the meantime, Æthelflæd sent an army that captured Derby and its region, the first of the Viking 'Five Boroughs' of the east Midlands to fall. In the following year, a co-ordinated campaign to capture the four remaining Viking strongholds took Edward to Stamford, while Æthelflæd entered Leicester without opposition. There may be a kernel of truth behind the reports of the late Irish source, the *Three Fragments*, that she co-ordinated military action with the **Picts** and the **Scots** and led a combined army against the Viking Ragnall at the second battle of Corbridge. In 918, according to the 'Mercian Register', the men of **York** offered her their submission, which laid the foundation for Edward's pacification of the north in 920.

Æthelflæd did not share this final triumph, dying on 12 June 918. She was buried in St Peter's Abbey, Gloucester. Edward initially allowed her daughter Ælfwynn to hold a nominal rulership over the Mercians, but after six months she was taken off to **Wessex** and the *Anglo-Saxon Chronicle* reports that all the people of Mercia submitted to Edward.

See also Kings and Kingship.

Further Reading

Wrainwright, F. T. 1975. *Scandinavian England*. Phillimore.

Marios Costambeys

Æthelfrith (r. c. AD 592–616)

Æthelfrith, who ruled **Bernicia** from c. AD 592 until his death in 616, was the son of Aethelric and the grandson of Ida, legendary founder of the ruling dynasty of **Northumbria**. He was the last great pagan warlord, and it is as a warrior that **Bede** presents him in his *Historia Ecclesiastica*. As well as ruling the northern part of what would eventually become Northumbria, following his marriage in 604 to Acha, daughter of **Ælle** and princess of **Deira**, he then added the southern part of the kingdom. He was thus the first king of a united realm of Northumbria and the earliest ruler of Bernicia, and according to Stenton, 'the continuous history of Northumbria, and indeed of England' begins with his reign.

Bede compared Æthelfrith with the Old Testament king Saul, describing him as 'a most worthy king and ambitious of glory', and he 'ravaged the Britons more than all the great men of the English'. In 603, **Aedán mac Gabráin**, king of **Dál Riata** in modern Argyll, challenged Æthelfrith's expansion and raised a large army against him. Bede describes how Aedán's 'immense and mighty army' was beaten by Æthelfrith's inferior force and was put to fight at Degsastan. Although Æthelfrith's brother, Theodbald, was killed with most of the men he commanded, the victory was so great that 'no king of the **Scots** durst come into Britain to make war on the English to this day'.

The circumstances of Æthelfrith's annexing Deira in 604 are unclear; it may have taken place through conquest or by more peaceable means. His union with Acha might have already taken place, or he might have married her to consolidate his new position. The ***Historia Brittonum*** gives Æthelfrith's queen as Bebba, to whom he gave the coastal fortress of Din Guaire, renamed 'Bebbanburgh' (**Bamburgh**) in her honour. However, his son, Oswald, was born to Acha in 604.

Æthelfrith's expansion policy continued; later in his reign, his campaign reached as far as **Chester** where he defeated the army and killed the local king. In this same battle, he attacked and killed a large company of monks from the monastery of **Bangor**, who had assembled to pray for the success of the defending British Army. According to Bede, Æthelfrith thought the monks are legitimate prey as, although unarmed, they were involved in the battle by aiding his enemies by their prayers. This victory may have had strategic significance in that it separated the British in the north from those in Wales; on the other hand, the importance may have been dynastic in that Edwin, exiled son of Ælle and a threat to Æthelfrith while still at large, had taken refuge in Mercia.

Edwin moved on to seek sanctuary under the powerful protection of **Rædwald** in East Anglia, but Æthelfrith repeatedly sent threats and bribes to Rædwald to force him to kill Edwin or surrender. Rædwald would ultimately have given in to these threats, but his wife dissuaded him on the grounds that to do so was unworthy of his honour. Rædwald raised an army and marched north against Æthelfrith, who, according to Bede, was unprepared for battle. The two armies met on the banks of the river Idle, where Æthelfrith was killed and his army defeated. Edwin assumed the kingship of both Bernicia and Deira, while Æthelfrith's sons went into exile in the west of Scotland. After Edwin's death in battle in 632 at Hatfield, Æthelfrith's sons regained the throne, and his dynasty ruled Northumbria until well into the eighth century.

See also Kings and Kingship.

Further Reading

Colgrave, B., and R. A. B. Mynors (eds. and tr.). 1969. *Bede: Historia Ecclesiastica Gentis Anglorum.* Claredon Press.

Stenton, Frank. 1971. *Anglo-Saxon England.* Clarendon Press.

Patricia Rumsey

Æthelred the Unready (r.979–1013 and 1014–1016)

The rule of Æthelred the Unready (r. 979–1013 and 1014–1016), son of King Edgar and Queen Ælfthryth and younger half-brother of Edward the Martyr, was destined to be viewed by history as a failure from the start. A month after witnessing Edward's murder, probably by Ealdorman Ælfhere, in 978, Æthelred was elected king among constant rumours that his household had murdered Edward to place the young prince on the throne. It is this cloud of suspicion, combined with Æthelred's violent temper and his lack of military success which won him the epithet 'Unræd', meaning not 'unready', but rather 'unadvised' or 'ill-advised' in opposition to his name, 'Æthelred', meaning 'noble counsel'. This witticism of Anglo-Saxon semantics was possibly added to his title not in his lifetime, but rather in the eleventh or twelfth century, after history had already judged his long rule a failure. The primary source for Æthelred's failed political career comes to us from the *Abingdon Chronicle*, a text written after the loss of the country to Danish invaders, which gives a decidedly negative view of the events leading up to King **Cnut**'s reign. Given his inauspicious ascension to the throne and disastrous negotiations with the **Vikings** and being an unfavourable historian, it is little wonder that Æthelred has been painted so poorly.

A mere two years into Æthelred's reign, the Danish resumed their raids after a twenty-five-year break. Initially, Æthelred was able to withstand the Danish forces, despite their new organisation under the direct leadership of Danish kings and increasing numbers. However, the Danes were able to retreat to Normandy to restock and rest. Unable to muster a sufficient defence against the refreshed Danes, Æthelred accepted the suggestion of his advisors to buy peace from the Danes – an action that was deplored in the ***Anglo-Saxon Chronicle*** as particularly foolhardy (and one that was destined to be repeated in 994, 1002, 1007 and 1012). The taxes required to raise these sums crippled the treasury and the countryside and only convinced the Danes that there was further wealth to be gained on the island and the attacks increased. In 991, Æthelred, under the advisement of Archbishop Sigeric, negotiated a treaty with Normandy to halt the aid given to the Danes, in exchange for Æthelred's marriage to Emma, daughter of Richard, duke of Normandy.

Although the English forces were insufficient to stop the Viking invasions, it is in 991 that a small band of **Essex** warriors held a causeway against the larger Danish force led by **Olaf Tryggvason** near Maldon. Although the English eventually lost the field, and their lives, the heroism of Earl Brythnoth and those who died in defence of their land have been immortalised in the celebrated Anglo-Saxon verse, '**the Battle of Maldon**'.

The turn of the millennium brought little relief from the Viking attacks. On 13 November 1002, Æthelred ordered the slaughter of all Danes in England as a result of a rumoured plot to take the throne. While few regions of his realm were likely to carry out the sentence as many of the towns were predominantly Danish, there was a substantial massacre of Danish settlers in many towns, such as Oxford. Far from being invading interlopers, however, some of the Danes slaughtered had familial ties in England that extended back for generations. It is traditionally believed that the Danish princess, Gunnhild, sister of King Svein Forkbeard of Denmark, had been held in England as a hostage to secure peace at this time and was numbered among the dead. Svein's retaliation, perhaps fuelled by the murder of his sister, began in 1003 and continued with few interruptions until England fell to his rule. In the summer of 1013, Æthelred, recognising the perilous state of his country, sent his wife, Emma, and their two sons to Normandy. Shortly thereafter, Æthelred followed his family and took up residence in Normandy in exile. Upon Svein's death, loyalties in England were divided between the Danish heir, Cnut (know as 'the Great' in Scandinavian histories), and the restoration of Æthelred. Although Æthelred was nominally returned to England as its king, it was his son Edmund who was actually fighting for the throne, while his father remained in London, awaiting death. Fighting resumed between the now-divided kingdom and ended only with the death of Æthelred on 23 April 1016 and his son and heir Edmund Ironside on 30 November 1016. Upon Edmund's death, Cnut reunified the English territories, married Æthelred's widow and ruled over England and Denmark. It was not until Cnut's death in 1035 that England was again unified under an English king of Æthelred's bloodline, **Edward the Confessor,** and, through his marriage to Emma, under William the Conqueror.

Although it is Æthelred's shortcomings that receive the most historical commentary, his thirty-eight-year reign also saw a proliferation of literature as well as economic improvements. It is between 993 and 1006 that Byrhtferth, **Ælfric** and Wulfstan of Winchester wrote. The four great manuscript collections that contain virtually all the Anglo-Saxon verse known today (the *Junius Manuscript*, the ***Exeter Book***, the *Nowell Codex* and the *Vercelli Book*) are all argued to have come from, or close to, this period of Benedictine reform and flourishing. Æthelred was also instrumental in funding building projects, such as the great tower for New Minster from 979 to 988.

Also under Æthelred's rule, **London** established itself as the most influential city in England. Able to withstand the Viking attacks without royal aid, London won for itself the right to participate in the election of kings, a unique standing that held well into the later Middle Ages.

See also Kings and Kingship.

Further Reading

Hunter Blair, Peter. 2003. *An Introduction to Anglo-Saxon England*. Cambridge University Press.

John, Eric. 1991. 'The End of Anglo-Saxon England'. Pp.214–239 in *The Anglo-Saxons*. Edited by James Campbell. Penguin Books.

Lapidge, Michael, et al. (eds.). 1999. *The Blackwell Encyclopedia of Anglo-Saxon England*. Blackwell Publishing.

Stenton, F. M. 1971. *Anglo-Saxon England*. Clarendon Press.

Williams, Ann. 2003. *Æthelred the Unready: The Ill-Counselled King*. Hambledon Press.

Britt Rothauser

Æthelstan (r. AD 925–941)

Æthelstan was the king of **Wessex** from AD 925 until his death in 941 and, through a series of alliances and shows of military strength, was the first ruler of this line to have a realistic claim on the title 'king of all the English' (or, more correctly, the '**Anglo-Saxons**'), and for the last twelve years of his life, he also held overlordship over a region approaching the geography of modern Britain. While contemporary records say little about Æthelstan, later medieval traditions took a great deal of interest in him as a heroic warrior king, and thus almost all historical traditions concerning his reign contain fabulous and often fanciful accretions (see, in particular, **William of Malmesbury**'s account of Æthelstan in his *Gesta Regum Anglorum*).

Æthelstan was the eldest son of King Edward the Elder and thus the grandson of **Alfred the Great**. If we believe the twelfth-century record of William of Malmesbury, then he was thought to have been the illegitimate son of a concubine with only a questionable claim to the throne; certainly, he faced opposition for the throne and suffered a rebellion from within the royal family (lead by his brother Eadwine). He was fostered in the Mercian court of Edward the Elder's sister, **Æthelflæd**, and perhaps ruled that region as an under-king after her death in 918. On 17 July 924, his father died, and in 925, Æthelstan succeeded to the kingdom of **Wessex**, unifying it with that of **Mercia** and the regions of the **Danelaw**, which had been reconquered by the West Saxons and the Mercians in the previous decades.

As a ruler, he appears to have been an active and vigorous administrator and began wide-ranging reforms of the Anglo-Saxon coinage. However, he is best remembered for his military successes and his steady consolidation of power over the regions which bordered Wessex and Mercia. From the very beginning of his reign, he began to extend his reach beyond the borders of Wessex and Mercia, and immediately after his coronation, he entered into some form of alliance with King Sihtric of **York**. Sihtric married Æthelstan's sister on 30 January 926, presumably to cement their agreement. Unfortunately, Sihtric died before the summer of 927 and was replaced by his more quarrelsome heir Olaf. This Olaf appears to have received military support from his Hiberno-Norse uncle, Guthfrith of Dublin, and in 927, they caused enough trouble to warrant Æthelstan leading an army against them. This campaign was successful, and on 12 July 927, Æthelstan received the public submission of a number of kings of Scotland and **Strathclyde** and the English lord of **Bamburgh**. Soon after a number of Welsh kings submitted to him at Hereford, a tenth-century Welsh poem, the '**Armes Prydein Vawr**', records that Æthelstan exacted an annual tribute from them. He appears then to have turned his attention to the **Britons** of **Cornwall** and, by 931, had sufficient overlordship there to establish a see at St Germans.

This form of political body, held together only through the bonds of nominal overlordship and the fear of military retribution, was far from stable. In 934, in response to some part of Scotland going into revolt, Æthelstan led an army north and harried as far as Fordun in Kincardineshire, while his fleet ravaged the coastline up to Caithness. However, this only temporarily quelled rebellion, and in 937, Olaf Guthfrithsson of **Dublin** (the son of the Guthfrith whom Æthelstan had expelled in 927), Constantine, king of the **Scots**, and a number of their allies combined their forces in a joint revolt against his authority. They met Æthelstan's forces in battle at **Brunanburh** (which, despite a great deal of debate, has so far escaped conclusive identification) and were victorious, and the battle is the subject of a triumphant poem in Old English (which bears the name of the battle-site in modern editions).

Æthelstan's alliance building can also be detected on the Continent. He married his sister, Eadgyth, to Otto of the Saxons (who subsequently became Emperor Otto I) and married another sister, Eadhild, to Hugh, duke of the Franks. Such alliances were clearly not just empty agreements, and he appears to have supported military interventions in Brittany and perhaps France. Additionally, late-Scandinavian historical traditions remember Æthelstan as the foster father of Hákon, son of Haraldr Hárfagri (d. c. 933), king of a large region of medieval Norway, and it seems probable that there is a significant kernel of truth in these accounts.

Æthelstan was a devoted supporter of the English Church, and much evidence survives of his donation of manuscripts (mainly liturgical) and saints' relics to various communities. Moreover, he appears to have used some of his European contacts to bolster the English Church and continue his grandfather's campaign of ecclesiastical refoundation.

Some pieces of contemporary evidence indicate that Æthelstan was conscious of the new political body he had created in Britain and that he may have begun to assume a limited form of imperial status. As David Dumville has observed, Æthelstan's charters 'exhibit a Latinity of Aldhelmian bombast and royal styles which bespeak imperial pretension' (1992, 149), and similar traces can be found in his coinage reforms. These reforms aimed to establish a strictly controlled system across most of England, which issued coins bearing the inscription *rex totius Brittaniae* ('king of all Britain') alongside the first English depiction of the ruler with a crowned head.

Æthelstan died on 27 October 941, leaving no apparent heirs, and was succeeded by his brother, Edmund. There are no historical records which allow us to identify any wives or concubines, and much can be speculated here and little proved. While we can be reasonably certain that Æthelstan was unmarried, we cannot state that he did not have concubines and a number of illegitimate heirs who have been ignored by the historical record, and an unwillingness to marry may have its origins in religious beliefs or dynastic motivations.

See also Kings and Kingship.

Further Reading

Dumville, D. N. 1992. *Wessex and England from Alfred to Edgar*. Boydell.

Stafford, Pauline. 1989. *Unification and Conquest: A Political and Social History of England in the Tenth and Eleventh Centuries*. Edward Arnold.
Wood, M. 1983. 'The Making of King Æthelstan's Empire: An English Charlemagne?' Pp.250–272 in *Ideal and Reality in Frankish and Anglo-Saxon Society: Studies Presented to J. M. Wallace-Hadrill*. Edited by P. Wormald with D. Bullough and R. Collins. Oxford University Press.

Timothy Bolton

Æthelwulf

See Æthelbald; Æthelberht; Alfred.

Agricola (AD 40–93)

Julius Agricola is the best known of the governors of Britain by virtue of the biography written by his son-in-law, the Roman historian, **Tacitus**. He is also exceptional for other reasons, not least the length of his governorship (AD 77–84) and the fact that he is the only senator known to have held all three military commands in the same province. Agricola is the first governor to be attested epigraphically in Britain, both on a stone inscription (probably from the forum-basilica) at ***Verulamium*** (Frere 1983, 69–72) and on three inscribed lead pipes at **Chester** (Collingwood and Wright 1995, vol. II, RIB 2434.1–2434.3).

Agricola was born in AD 40 at *Forum Iulii* (modern-day Fréjus) as the son of a senator who was executed soon after by Caligula. Brought up by his mother, he studied at Marseilles before entering the army. His first recorded post was *tribunus laticlavius* (second in command of a legion), wherein he saw service in Britain under **Suetonius Paulinus** at the time of the Boudiccan revolt (AD 60–61). After his return to Rome, he married Domitia Decidiana, with whom he had at least two sons (who died in infancy) and one daughter (who later married Tacitus). Successive offices followed as quaestor in Asia (AD 63–64), tribune of the plebs at Rome (AD 66) and praetor (AD 68). So far his career had been unexceptional. Then during the civil war of AD 69, following the death of his mother at the hands of supporters of Otho, he joined the party of the future Emperor Vespasian and successfully raised troops for his cause in Italy. Thence, he was sent to Britain as a *legatus legionis*, taking charge of Legio XX and seeing service under Petilius Cerialis. Upon returning to Rome by AD 73, he was made a patrician, ahead of taking up the governorship of Aquitania in south-west France (AD 73–76). The consulship followed (AD 76 or 77?), well before the normal minimum age of forty-two, after which he was assigned once again to Britain, this time as the provincial governor (*legatus Augusti pro-praetore*).

The precise chronology of Agricola's governorship has been a matter of considerable debate, with much depending upon the presumed date of his final victory at Mons Graupius. The earlier of the two possibilities – AD 77–84 and AD 78–85 – is followed here, though the alternative is equally plausible. In the first season (AD 77), late in the campaigning season, Agricola is recorded as completing the conquest of north-west Wales, by defeating the ***Ordovices*** and invading Anglesey. In the second season (AD 78), he is said to have been equally active, though Tacitus's account is remarkably short on geographical detail; it is usually assumed that Agricola was operating in northern England and southern Scotland. Over the winter, he instituted measures to promote 'Romanisation', by encouraging the natives to build temples, fora and houses. In the third season (AD 79), Agricola moved against new peoples and advanced as far as the river Tay, after which there was even time to establish forts. On the expectation that he would be replaced in AD 80 (the fourth season), Agricola focused his attention on consolidation. The Forth–Clyde isthmus is said to have been secured by garrisons, with a suggestion that this might be a convenient provincial 'terminus' or boundary.

The fifth season (AD 81) has been the subject of much debate; it started with a sea crossing, followed by operations against new peoples and ended with the whole of the coast facing Ireland being lined with troops. While some have seen this as an advance on the north of the Clyde, most have located the operations in south-west Scotland, north of the Solway. In the sixth season (AD 82), Agricola advanced beyond the Forth–Clyde, by moving the army north-eastwards along Strathmore with the fleet in support, but it proved impossible to engage the enemy in open battle. In the seventh, and final, season (AD 83), further land and sea operations culminated in the Battle of Mons Graupius, whose precise location remains unknown, despite the claims for Bennachie in Aberdeenshire. At the end of the season, the fleet circumnavigated the island.

Agricola is likely to have left Britain early in the following year (AD 84), whence he returned to Rome to be awarded the *triumphalia ornamenta*. No further commands followed, principally (according to Tacitus) because of jealousy on the part of the Emperor Domitian. Agricola chose not to stand for the proconsulate in Asia or Africa (probably in AD 90), perhaps because of ill health or veiled threats at the time of the ballot. He died in AD 93, at the age of fifty-three.

See also Roman Army; Roman Britain.

Further Reading

Birley, A. R. 1981. *The Fasti of Roman Britain* (pp. 73–81). Oxford University Press.
Collingwood, R. G., and R. P. Wright. 1995. *The Roman Inscriptions of Britain*, vol. II. Alan Sutton.
Dobson, Brian. 1981. 'Agricola's Life and Career'. Pp. 1–13 in *Agricola's Campaigns in Scotland*. Edited by J. Kenworthy. Scottish Archaeological Forum 12.
Frere, S. S. 1983. *Verulamium Excavations*, vol. II. Society of Antiquaries of London, Research Report No. 41.
Hanson, W. S. 1987. *Agricola and the Conquest of the North*. Edinburgh University Press.
Ogilvie, R. M., and I. A. Richmond (eds.). 1967. *Cornelii Taciti de Vita Agricolae*. Oxford University Press.

Barry C. Burnham

Aidan, Saint (d.651)

Aidan, founder and bishop of **Lindisfarne** (634–651), was chosen in 634 to convert the Northumbrians to Christianity. He was a principal in the wave of peregrination that earned for Ireland the designation 'Isle of the Saints'. Peregrination, derived from *peregrini*, is a form of exile taken as an act of penance or piety by monks of the Celtic church. A result of peregrination was the dissemination of Celtic monasteries into northern Britain, throughout the Rhineland and into central Europe. As part of this movement, Aidan initiated the expansion of Celtic monasticism southwards from Scotland to **Northumbria**.

Scholars place Aidan in Ireland at the monastery of Iniscathy (Scattery Island) under St. Senan and later at the monastery of Clogher as bishop (Grattan-Flood 1907). Most of what is known of Aidan is derived from **Bede**'s *Ecclesiastical History of the English* (c. 731). Bede's information starts with Aidan's departure from **Iona** to England. In 563, **St. Columba** founded a monastery on Iona, off the western coast of Scotland. When Aidan arrived c. 630, Iona was under the guidance of Abbot Segene (d. 652) who cultivated relations with Ireland and Northumbria.

Seventh-century Britain was a composite of kingdoms – Northumbrian, Mercian, Saxon and Angle – over which a sovereign, the *bretwalda*, occasionally ruled. The sub-kingdoms of Northumbria, **Bernicia** and **Deira** were administratively independent and clashed repeatedly over the sovereignty of Northumbria. At the beginning of the seventh century, rule passed from **Æthelfrith** of Bernicia (593–616) to Edwin of Deira (616–632). Æthelfrith's sons went into exile. Oswald (634–642) and Oswiu (642–670) went to Iona; Eanfrith (d. 633) lived among the Pictish nobility. At Iona, Oswald and Oswiu converted to Christianity. Aidan's residence at Iona coincides with the end of their exile.

In 633, Oswald returned from exile and established himself as *bretwalda*. In medieval Europe, abbots and bishops were involved in the machinations of sovereignty. The advances made by earlier Roman missionaries, i.e. Augustine (d. 569) to Paulinus (c. 610), were in decline. Oswald looked to Iona for missionaries. Segene assigned Corman. When Corman proved incompatible with the English, Segene chose Aidan. The introduction of **Celtic Christianity** to Northumbria under Aidan went hand in hand with Bernician dominance of the bretwaldship.

Oswald granted Aidan the island upon which he founded Lindisfarne. Under Oswald's auspices, Aidan, as bishop of Lindisfarne, administered the Northumbrian diocese and appointed an abbot to head the monastery. Aidan and his disciples modelled their foundations on Celtic monasteries. The combination of monastery and bishopric was characteristic of Irish foundations (Stancliffe 1989, 104). So too were double monasteries and adjacent communities of monks and nuns. Monastic compounds included *scriptoria* where monks and nuns worked to transcribe manuscripts. The rule imposed on the monasteries emphasised asceticism, private confession, scholarship, labour and prayer.

Lindisfarne under Aidan produced leading figures of the seventh century. St. Chad (d. 672), among the first of Aidan's students, was bishop of the Mercians. Hild (d. 680), a member of the Deirian royal house, was appointed abbess of Hartlepool by Aidan and later founded a double monastery at Whitby;

the Synod of Whitby was set in 664. The synod was ostensibly to prohibit Celtic peculiarities of practice.

In 642, Penda of Mercia defeated Oswald and Northumbria was divided. Oswine (644–651) ruled Deira and Oswiu (642–670), Oswald's brother, ruled Bernicia. In 651, Oswiu had Oswine murdered. According to Bede, the treachery broke Aidan's heart and he died twelve days later. An indication of the power Iona held in Northumbria is the appointment of Finan (651–661) to the see of Lindisfarne. Finan was chosen by Iona, not by Oswiu. In 654, Oswiu installed his son Alchfrith over Deira. Alchfrith used Deirian separatism and Roman Christianity as leverage against his father. Oswiu convened Whitby in response to this threat. At Whitby, **Wilfrid**, who departed Lindisfarne the year after Aidan's death, led the Roman side of the debate while Colman, third bishop of Lindisfarne, represented the tradition of Aidan and Iona. To protect his position, Oswiu decided for Roman Christianity.

After Whitby, Aidan represented a heretical position as well as the ties that bound the daughter houses of Lindisfarne to Iona (Stancliffe 1989, 22). **Whitby**, on another level, marked the beginning of the separation of the Northumbrian churches from Iona. Colman resigned and Oswiu granted his last request that Eata, another of Aidan's students, be appointed bishop of Lindisfarne.

Although Aidan's relics were venerated, the cult of Cuthbert, bishop of Lindisfarne (685–687), overshadowed Aidan's. After Whitby, some of Aidan's relics were carried by Colman to Ireland, and in the late eighth century, when Lindisfarne was evacuated to escape the Vikings, the monks dismantled the chapel Aidan built, gathered the relics of Oswald, Aidan and Cuthbert and transported the lot to safety; today, the relics that remain are housed at **Durham** Cathedral.

Further Reading

Abels, Richard. 1983. 'The Council of Whitby: A Study in Early Anglo-Saxon Politics'. *The Journal of British Studies* 23.1: 1–25.

Charles-Edwards, T. M. 2000. *Early Christian Ireland.* Cambridge University Press.

Grattan-Flood, W. H. 1907. *The Catholic Encyclopedia,* vol. 1. Robert Appleton Company.

Stancliffe, Clare. 1989. 'Cuthbert and the Polarity Between Pastor and Solitary'. Pp. 21–42 in *St. Cuthbert, His Cult and His Community to AD 1200.* Edited by Gerald Bonner, David Rollason and Clare Stancliffe. The Boydell Press.

Susan Schulze

Alain II (d.952)

Alain Barbetorte was a tenth-century Breton ruler who spent time at the court of the English king **Æthelstan**. Grandson of Alain I 'le grand', ruler of Brittany, Alain Barbetorte was sent abroad with many other Bretons, as well as ecclesiastical treasures, during the Viking raids of the early tenth century which temporarily obliterated central rule in the kingdom of Brittany. The presence of many of these Bretons at Æthelstan's court was probably responsible for a significant increase in continental cultural and ecclesiastical influences in tenth-century Britain, in particular in the south-west, a region which had strong historical, linguistic and cultural ties with Brittany. On his return, Alain II was unsuccessful in founding a new ducal dynasty to rule over Brittany, but his relative success in regaining Breton territory set the stage for the advent of future dukes (rather than princes or, as Alain I had styled himself, *rex*) of Brittany.

Sometime after 913, in the face of devastating Viking raids, in particular on Cornouaille (in the south-west of Brittany), and the resulting political fragmentation exacerbated by the death of Alain I in 907, Alain I's son-in-law, Mathuedoi, went to England along with his infant son, Alain II, who came to be called Barbetorte, 'twisted-beard'. Our only narrative source for this portentous episode is the later-medieval *Chronique de Nantes*, an unreliable source, which relates that Mathuedoi, *comes de Poher* (apparently some part of Cornouaille), along with his son Alain II (by an unnamed daughter of Alain I) and a large number of Breton rulers (*comites, vicecomites ac mathiberni*), fled to Æthelstan's court, where Alain II was baptised with Æthelstan as godfather (Merlet 1896, 80–83). After a series of devastating raids, by 919 at least, Viking control of Brittany was complete. In 931, as Scandinavians in Brittany gathered for a concerted attack on the Franks, the Bretons rebelled and made gains in several battles. The rebellion was soon crushed by the Viking leader, Incon, with the help of William Longsword who, according to Hugh of Fleury (as quoted by Guillotel 1979, 64, n. 9), negotiated a treaty with one of the two most powerful Breton leaders, Judicael Berengar; the other, Alain II, was forced to flee. This would seem to have been an unsuccessful attempt on the part of Alain Barbetorte to return to Brittany. According to the Frankish annalist Flodoard, in 936 the Bretons regained their territories with the help of Æthelstan. Dudo of St Quentin relates a suspiciously partisan elaboration of this episode, saying that Æthelstan interceded successfully with William Longsword on behalf of Louis IV and Alain II. We have only one charter of Alain II's to illuminate this obscurity: a charter of Landévennec seems to support the thrust of Dudo's account by implying that Alain II only returned to Brittany once peace had been established, with the help of Jean, abbot of Landévennec.

In Brittany, Alain II's attempts to restore a central rule had mixed results. His conquests south of the Loire were only partially maintained, and he died in 952 after a relatively short reign. The rule of Brittany passed to the family of Judicael Berengar of Rennes, the other of the two powerful Breton leaders mentioned by Hughes of Fleury in connection with the Breton rebellion against the Vikings in 931, but Alain's rule had helped consolidate the duchy to which they succeeded.

Further Reading

Guillotel, H. 1979. 'Le premier siècle du pouvoir ducal breton (936–1040)'. Pp. 63–68 in *103e Congrès des sociétés savantes*, Nancy-Metz, 1978. Section philologique et historique jusqu'à 1610. Principautés et études d'histoire lorraine. Paris.

Merlet, R. (ed.). 1896. *La chronique de Nantes*. Alphonse Picard et fils.

Price, Neil S. 1989. *The Vikings in Brittany*, vol. 22. Saga Book: The Viking Society for Northern Research.

Smith, Julia M. H. 1992. *Province and Empire: Brittany and the Carolingians*. Cambridge University Press.

Karen Jankulak

Alain III (d. 1146)

Count Alain III (d. 1146) was one of many Bretons established in England after the Norman Conquest. Alain is of interest not only because he exemplified a particular faction's support of King Stephen in the war against **Matilda** but also on account of the fact that it was through his marriage to the Breton ducal heiress Berthe that the significant 'Honour of Richmond' came into the possession of the Breton ducal family, providing a vast source of revenues to the duke and paving the way for the duchy's brief integration into **Henry II**'s Angevin empire.

Alain's grandfather Eudo of Penthièvre, so called by modern historians to distinguish his descendants from those of his brother the Breton duke Alain III (with whom Alain count of Richmond should not be confused), left several sons, including two Alains: Alain Rufus ('the red', also known as 'Alain *comes*', d. 1089) and Alain Niger ('the black', d. 1093). While Eudo was active in Brittany during a turbulent period of minorities and revolts, several of his sons established themselves in Britain. A large part of Alain Rufus's wealth was granted to him after a revolt in the north of England in 1070, including crucial estates seized from Earl Edwin, in Yorkshire. These estates formed the nucleus of what would become known as the 'Honour of Richmond'. Alain Rufus, having built the great stone castle at Richmond, was succeeded as lord of Richmond by his brother Alain Niger and then by their brother Stephen (d. c. 1135?). During Stephen's lifetime, a lasting rivalry grew up between two of his sons, Geoffrey II Boterel of Lamballe, who seized his father's Breton possessions, and his elder brother, Alain, often called Alain III (following on his uncles Alain I and II as lords of Richmond) as well as sometimes 'Niger' (like his uncle). Alain III, who is at issue here, had been sent to England by 1123 to look after his father's estates there (Clay 1935, 89, n. 7). Sometime before his father's death, Alain gained hereditary title to the Honour of Richmond and began to style himself 'earl' (*comes*) of Richmond. During this period, he was also recalled to Brittany to marry Berthe, the daughter of the Breton duke Conan III. The marriage between Berthe and Alain, which Keats-Rohan reasonably characterises as an attempt to reconcile the Breton ducal family with their cadet Penthièvre branch, was brief and apparently unhappy (1992, 70). Alain died before his father-in-law, thus losing the chance to succeed to the duchy, and Berthe quickly married Eudo of Porhoet.

Alain's name occurs in several accounts of King Stephen's reign, chiefly John of Hexam's *Historia*, William of Malmesbury's *Historia Novella,* Henry of Huntingdon's *Historia Anglorum* and the anonymous *Gesta Stephani.* The support of Bretons with English interests followed particular factions determined by both Breton and English politics. While his brother Geoffrey, Alain's rival in Brittany as well, is mentioned among Matilda's supporters, Alain was loyal, if self-interestedly so, to King Stephen: in 1140, he captured a castle at the somewhat obscure 'Galclint', built another one at 'Hoton' and ravaged Ripon and property of the archbishop of York. He was granted the earldom of Cornwall by Stephen but lost it on his capture by the earl of Chester, having withdrawn his forces from Stephen's army either before or during the battle of Lincoln in February 1141. The *Gesta Stephani* describes him as 'a man of boundless ferocity and craft' (*uir ... immensae truculentiae et doli*) (Potter 1976, 116–117), noting with somewhat surprising approbation that he was relentless, although unsuccessful, in avenging the capture of Stephen who had been shamefully abandoned (the *Gesta Stephani* does not name Alain in this connection, but others do) at Lincoln in the first place. He is described in a Breton obituary as 'when a youth, very cruel (*crudelissimus*) and a marauder (*praedo*)', but 'as a man, the father of his country (*pater patriae*) and a vigilant friend of the Church (*ecclesiae uigilantissimus amator*)' (Morice 1742, 5). Having gone to Brittany in 1145, he died there on 15 September 1146. His son with Berthe, Conan IV, went on to become duke of Brittany, but only after he wrested power from his stepfather who had presided over his minority. The union between Berthe and Alain ensured that revenues from the Honour of Richmond were henceforth vested in the Breton duchy, and they as such were not only an important source of revenue but also a significant weapon in the hands of Henry II, who was in a position to withhold them, or enforce his authority over his vassal, as earl of Richmond. The culmination of this situation was the marriage between duke Conan IV's daughter Constance and Henry II's son Geoffrey, which ultimately led to the integration, albeit temporary, of the Breton duchy into the Angevin empire.

See also Normans.

Further Reading

Clay, C. T. (ed.). 1935. *Early Yorkshire Charters, Volume IV: The Honour of Richmond Part I.* Yorkshire Archaeological Society.

Keats-Rohan, K. S. B. 1992. 'The Bretons and Normans of England 1066–1154: The Family, the Fief and the Feudal Monarchy'. *Nottingham Medieval Studies* 36: 42–78.

Morice, P.-H. (ed.). 1742. *Mémoires pour servir de preuves á l'histoire ecclésiastique et civile de Bretagne. Tome I.* Osmont.

Potter, K. R. (ed. and tr.). 1976. *Gesta Stephani.* Clarendon Press.

Karen Jankulak

Alban, Saint

Alban, after whom the town of St Albans (***Verulamium***) – just north of **London** – is named, was remembered during the Middle Ages as 'the protomartyr of Britain' (Bede's *Martyrology*, 22 June, but curiously this entry is found in only one Irish martyrology: Gorman's). First mentioned in Constantius's *Vita Germani*, the standard account of Alban is based on a passage in **Gildas**'s *De Excidio Britianniae* 10–11. This was followed by **Bede** in his *Historia Ecclesiastica Gentis Anglorum* (1,7) who cited extensively the anonymous, but no longer extant, *Passio Albani*.

Combining our two sources, we get this composite *vita* (a brief biography). During the persecution of Dioceltian 302–305 (both Gildas [9,1] and Bede are explicit on this point, but some scholars have argued that the events occurred during Decian's persecution in c. 250 or even earlier), the pagan Roman soldier Alban, stationed in *Verulamium* (known to Bede as Uerlamacaestir), encountered a Christian on the point of arrest. This man was being arrested because he would not worship the imperial gods – Gildas uses the word *confessor*, a detail which Bede interpreted as implying that the man was a cleric. Alban hid him and was converted, swapped clothes with him and thus took his place for the arresting party (this is what Gildas says; Bede offers motives and explanatory detail and generally makes the tale more pious). Between arrest and execution, Gildas has Alban as a great wonder-worker somewhat like Moses at the Nile (Exodus 14); Bede, by contrast, offers a classic of the *passio* genre, questions and retorts between judge and accused which bring out the sanctity of Alban. At the execution, both Gildas and Bede have similar miracle tales about the man due to behead Alban being suddenly converted; and both note that Alban's burial place became a place of cult. Gildas presents Alban's death as causing a revival of faith among the British exactly in accordance with his theology of divine justice, while Bede simply remarks that his tomb is a place of healing miracles.

See also Celtic Christianity; Roman Britain.

Further Reading

Colgrave, Bertram (tr.). 1969. *Bede's Ecclesiastical History of the English People.* Oxford Medieval Texts.

Winterbottom, Michael (ed. and tr.). 1978. *Gildas: The Ruin of Britain and Other Documents.* Phillimore.

Thomas O'Loughlin

Albion

Albion is the most ancient name for Britain, first cited in the sixth century BC. It would later come to refer to the kingdom of Scotland after its formation in the ninth century and reappear as a poetic name for Britain used by writers like William Blake.

The *Massiliote Periplus*, a manuscript which only survives in fragments but is quoted in the fourth century AD *Ora Maritima* by Rufus Festus Avienus, provides an account of a sea voyage c. 600 BC from *Massilia* (Marseilles) along the Atlantic seaboard, in which the Oestrymnians traded with the inhabitants of two large islands, *Iernē* and Albion. These earliest references to Ireland and Britain are the Greek forms of the names which survived among the Irish (as *Eire* and *Albu*) into the second millennium AD, but it is not quite known whether they should be argued as **Celtic** in origin or an adaptation from an older language (i.e. Proto Indo-European). Though the two names certainly seem to have become generally known amongst the Greek geographers by the third century BC, the next most ancient source on Britain, Pytheas of Massilia (c.325–323 BC), referred to them as the *Pretanic* islands, rather than their older names. While this may suggest an arrival by this time of a group of immigrants (*Pretanni* or **Britons**) who had not been there in the sixth century, this cannot of course be substantiated.

By the time of Pliny the Elder (AD 23–79), Albion was in use again. In his *Natural History*, he made it very clear that the whole island of Britain was being referred to: 'It was itself named Albion, while all the islands about which we shall soon briefly speak were called the *Britanniae*' (iv.xvi.102), though his additional note of the *Albione* tribe in Spain created later confusion. Only a century later, Ptolemy (AD 90–168) cited it as *Alouion* in his *Geography*, and to the Romans, the name had its derivative in *albus* (Latin for 'white'), possibly in connection to the cliffs of **Dover**, though others seeking Celtic origins have drawn attention to the Welsh *elfydd*, meaning 'world' or 'land', which was derived from the stem *albio*. The origins of Albion have been widely debated, and up until the twelfth century, a derivative form continued to be used in Gaelic tradition, with the Kingdom of *Alba* created after the unification of **Dál Riata** and Pictland in AD 843 under **Kenneth I MacAlpin**, though some Irish writers maintained its use to refer to Britain as a whole.

Further Reading

Cunliffe, Barry. 2003. *The Extraordinary Voyage of Pytheas the Greek*. Penguin.
Jackson, K. H. 1953. *Language and History in Early Britain*. Edinburgh University Press.
Murphy, Trevor Morgan. 2004. *Pliny the Elder's Natural History: The Empire in the Encyclopedia*. Oxford University Press.
Powell, T. G. E. 1980. *The Celts*. Thames & Hudson.
Rivet, A. L. F., and Colin Smith. 1981. *The Place-Names of Roman Britain*. Book Club Associates.

Anne Sassin

Alchfrith (r. c. AD 655–c. AD 664)

Alchfrith, sub-king of Anglian **Deira** from c. AD 655 to 664, is a shadowy figure in **Bede**'s *Historia Ecclesiastica*. Although Bede is silent on the subject, evidence from elsewhere (the ***Historia Brittonum*** and the *Liber Vitae Lindisfarnensis*) seems to indicate that before his marriage to Eanfled, **Oswiu** had married a British princess and that Alchfrith was the son of that marriage.

Alchfrith first appears in Bede's writings as his father's ally on the battlefield; he fought at Oswiu's side at the Battle of the Winwaed, where Oswiu and Alchfrith and their 'very small army' were victorious against **Penda** of **Mercia**. Alchfrith is presented as an ally of Penda's son, Peada, when the latter sought the hand of Alchfrith's sister, Alchfled, in marriage. Peada was told this would not be possible unless he embraced the Christian faith, which, at Alchfrith's encouragement, he declared ready to do. Alchfrith, according to Bede, was already married to Penda's daughter and so was already brother-in-law to Peada.

He next appears at the so-called **Synod of Whitby** as a protegé of **Wilfrid**, by whom he had been instructed in the Christian faith and from whom he had received a high regard for all things Roman. Alchfrith was also the sub-king of **Deira**, and recent commentators have suggested that his espousal of the Roman cause was partly to challenge his father Oswiu's authority. Possibly Alchfrith was using the council to try to increase his own influence in Northumbria at the expense of that of his father; if this was the case, he was disappointed by Oswiu's own change of loyalty. After the Synod, Alchfrith is not mentioned specifically again in any source.

See also Angles; Celtic Christianity.

Further Reading
Barnwell, P. S., L. A. S. Butler and C. J. Dunn. 2003. 'The Confusion of Conversion: *Streanaeshalch*, Strensall and Whitby'. Pp. 311–326 in *The Cross Goes North*. Edited by Martin Carver. York Medieval Press.
Colgrave, B., and R. A. B. Mynors (eds. and tr.). 1969. *Bede: Historia Ecclesiastica Gentis Anglorum*. Claredon Press.
Mayr-Harting, Henry. 1972. *The Coming of Christianity to Anglo-Saxon England*. Batsford.
Webb, J. F. (tr.). 1965, repr. 1998. 'Eddius Stephanus: The Life of Wilfrid'. Pp. 105–184 in *The Age of Bede*. Edited by D. H. Farmer. Penguin.

Patricia Rumsey

Aldfrith (d.705)

Aldfrith reigned over the powerful English kingdom of **Northumbria** during the second half of the seventh century AD. He was the son of **Oswiu of Northumbria** and, reputedly, an Irish princess who is named in the *Félire Óengusso* (the *Martyrology* of Óengus the Culdee) as Fína, daughter of Colmán Rimid, a northern **Uí Néill** overlord from the clan of the Cenél nÉogan. Thus, Aldfrith was of the royal blood of both Northumbria and Ireland; he appears in Irish sources as Flann Fína mac Ossu.

His early life is shrouded in mystery and the year of his birth is unclear. The earliest suggested date is early in the 630s; the latest is c. 650. Oswiu's relationship with Aldfrith's mother was not considered to be a legitimate marriage (**Bede** describes Aldfrith as 'said to be' the son of Oswiu and as an 'illegitimate brother' to Ecgfrith). Presumably, Aldfrith was conceived when his father Oswiu was exiled in Ireland or **Dál Riata**. According to Irish law, his mother would have been responsible for his upbringing. At some stage, Aldfrith returned to England and formed a close friendship with **Aldhelm** of Malmesbury, with whom he studied and was confirmed. Letters from Aldhelm to Aldfrith survive. His accession to the throne of Northumbria seems to have been unexpected, occasioned by his half-brother Ecgfrith's death at the **Battle of Nechtansmere** in 685 without a male heir.

Bede several times describes Aldfrith as a man of great learning, well versed in the Scriptures, and says he spent time in Ireland or 'in the regions of the Irish' for the sake of his love of learning. **Adomnán** presented him with a copy of *De locis sanctis*, and Aldfrith had this work copied and distributed. Aldhelm exhorted Aldfrith not to neglect his study of scripture, even amongst his many secular responsibilities. All these instances reveal Aldfrith as an unusually scholarly man; at his death in 704, the *Annals of Ulster* gave him the title of *sapiens*. He has been described as 'an early example of the Anglo-Saxon philosopher king'.

His reign is of importance because it coincides with the beginning of the 'Golden Age' of Northumbria; the ***Lindisfarne Gospels*** were begun in Aldfrith's time; these were the years of **Bede**'s scholarly activity and the beginning of Anglo-Saxon missionary activity in Europe. However, there were difficult issues also. Early in Aldfrith's reign, he allowed **Wilfrid** to return from exile, and from then on, as described by Wilfrid's biographer **Eddius**, his relationship with Wilfrid was stormy until finally Aldfrith banished Wilfrid, who went into exile in **Mercia**. Wilfrid was eventually excommunicated, and he travelled to Rome to plead his cause with Pope John VI and returned with papal letters for Aldfrith asking for Wilfrid to be reinstated. Aldfrith ignored the letters and Wilfrid remained out of favour.

Aldfrith married Cuthberg, sister of Ine, king of **Wessex**; according to the ***Anglo-Saxon Chronicle***, they eventually separated and Cuthberg founded the abbey at Wimbourne Mister where she became abbess. It is not clear whether she was the mother of Aldfrith's sons, Osred and Osric. Aldfrith died in December 705, having been ill for sometime previously.

See also Literature.

Further Reading
Colgrave, B., and R. A. B. Mynors (eds. and tr.). 1969. *Bede: Historia Ecclesiastica Gentis Anglorum*. Claredon Press.
Ireland, Colin. 1994. 'Aldfrith of Northumbria and the Learning of a Sapiens'. Pp. 63–77 in *A Celtic Florilegium: Studies in Memory of Brendan O Hehir*. Celtic Studies Publications II.
Webb, J. F. (tr.). 1965, repr. 1998. 'Eddius Stephanus: The Life of Wilfrid'. Pp. 105–184 in *The Age of Bede*. Edited by D. H. Farmer. Penguin.

Patricia Rumsey

Aldhelm (b. c.640)

Aldhelm was the abbot of Malmesbury and, after 705, bishop of Sherborne. Little is known of Aldhelm's early life. It is supposed that he was born c. 640 and that he was of noble family and had royal connections in **Wessex**. It is known that at c. 670, he was a student at the school of Canterbury founded by Archbishop Theodore and Abbot Hadrian. **William of Malmesbury** has preserved a section of a letter from Aldhelm to Hadrian. He lists the subjects he was studying there as law, metre and poetry, mathematics and astrology. His breadth and depth of learning and familiarity with classical and patristic literature is impressive, and his writings display his learning. He left the school to become abbot of Malmesbury at an unknown date but early charters place this as c. 680, though William of Malmesbury gives the date as 675.

As abbot of Malmesbury, Aldhelm built several churches and increased the endowment of the foundation. He travelled to Rome and throughout southern England working to place the church of Wessex on firm ground religiously and financially. The bishopric of Sherborne was created in 706, and Aldhelm was a natural choice for the see. He held the office until his death in 709/710. In **Anglo-Saxon** calendars, he is celebrated on 25 May, and interestingly enough two post-conquest authors wrote *vita* of Aldhelm.

Aldhelm's literary output is better known than the details of his life, but even so, his works are too seldom studied. This is in part because Aldhelm's ornate Latin is often very difficult since Aldhelm favours obscure words often borrowed from Greek, alliteration, rhyme and complex grammatical constructions. A dozen letters from Aldhelm survive including letters to his students to convince them of the superiority of English over Irish education. He also wrote to King **Geraint** of Dumnonia explaining the Roman method of Easter calculation, a subject he also undertook in a letter to the bishop of Wessex. He also wrote to Irish scholars and sent a treatise on metrics to the king of **Northumbria**. He wrote *Carmen ecclesiasticum*, poems for church and altar dedications. He is best known for his work *Aneigmata*, 100 riddles written in Latin demonstrating metrics, and is also well known for his *opus geminatum* titled *De Virginitate*, the prose version was dedicated to nuns at Barking. Less well known but no less important is his work *De Metris* on metrics and *De pedum regulis* on scansion of Latin poetry. Another short poem describes a journey from Cornwall to Devon.

All these works are written in Latin. According to later traditions, Aldhelm also composed songs and poems in **Old English**, some of which were yet known to Alfred and later to William of Malmesbury. Regrettably, none has survived.

Aldhelm's writings were certainly influential. His student Æthilwald imitated him as did also near contemporaries Tatwine, Eusebius, Felix and Bonfiace. **Bede** quotes him too. A generation later, Alcuin of York also owes a debt to Aldhelm's works. His Latin style influenced the Benedictine reform in the tenth century and the 'hermeneutic style' of Latin then current.

See also Literature.

Further Reading

Lapidge, Michael, and Michael Herren. 1979. *Aldhelm: The Prose Works*. Cambridge University Press.

Lapidge, Michael, and J. L. Rosier. 1985. *Aldhelm: The Poetic Works*. Cambridge University Press.

Orchard, Andy. 1994. *The Poetic Art of Aldhelm*. CSASE 8. Cambridge University Press.

Winterbottom, Michael. 1977. 'Aldhelm's Prose Style and Its Origins'. *Anglo-Saxon England* 6: 39–76.

Larry Swain

Alexander I (r. 1107–1124)

Alexander I, king of **Scots** (1107–1124), was known for his piety and vigour of rule. His reign was instrumental in the development of the Scottish kingdom as he continued the assimilation of foreign influences begun by Malcolm III and continued with Edgar.

Little is known of Alexander's early years. In all probability, he left Scotland for the English court in the uncertain political environment that followed the death of his parents, Malcolm III and St. Margaret in 1093. Historians believe that he returned upon the succession of his brother Edgar in 1097. Alexander succeeded to the kingship when Edgar died childless in 1107. Tension with his brother David over the Scottish lands left to him in Edgar's will marred the early years of Alexander's rule, and the relationship between the two brothers remains enigmatic.

Unsurprisingly, given Alexander's sojourn at the English court, relations with England were close and reasonably cordial during his reign. This amiability was secured through his marriage to Sibylla, an illegitimate daughter of **Henry I** (England), and equally through Henry's marriage to Alexander's sister Matilda. Sources describe the marriage between Alexander and Sibylla as both loveless and childless. Alexander was also instrumental in achieving a peaceful resolution to Welsh campaigns led by Henry in 1114. However, closer to home, he skirmished with the descendants of Lulach around the Moray firth.

During his seventeen years of rule in Scotland, Alexander demonstrated his piety by continuing the reform of the Scottish church begun by his mother. Evidence from papal letters suggests that to improve the respectability of the Scottish people, Alexander introduced the four seasons of fasting, more frequent communion and confessions to priests rather than to lay people. He also encouraged a reformed liturgy and clerical morality and discouraged simony and vagrancy.

Alexander's larger church reforms focused on the strategic placement of bishoprics and monasteries as strongholds in the provinces and frontiers of Scotland. These developments reflected the continental centralisation evident in Benedictine and Augustinian reforms. This is most notable in the foundation of the Augustinian priory at **Scone** in 1114. Alexander also appears to have entertained the hope of securing metropolitan and archiepiscopal status for **St Andrews**. This appears to be an attempt to maintain a distinctly Scottish influence over the church. This met with little success as the bishopric remained vacant and under dispute for much of Alexander's rule.

Alexander also incorporated foreign influences through a castle-building campaign, most notably Stirling Castle. He also integrated Norman ideals of court by granting land in return for military support. This garnered him support from the **Gaelic** nobles, which he later bequeathed to his brother David. In some ways, Alexander's attempts at reform to both the ecclesiastical and the secular landscapes of Scotland lay the foundation for his successor's future accomplishments.

When Alexander died in 1124, he left no legitimate heir and was succeeded by his brother **David I**. Speculation, however, remains that Alexander may have had an illegitimate son, Malcolm, who challenged the rule of David I in the 1120s and 1130s. Alexander is described by Ailred of Rievaulx as 'a man of great heart, applying himself in all things beyond his strength' (Anderson 1908, 155), an apt epithet for a pious king whose ventures appear to have met with limited success.

See also Kings and Kingship.

Further Reading

Anderson, A. O. (ed. and tr.). 1908. *Scottish Annals from English Chroniclers AD 500 to 1286*. Paul Watkins.

———. 1922. *Early Sources of Scottish History AD 500 to 1286*. Paul Watkins.

Barrow, G. W. S. 1981. *Kingship and Unity: Scotland 1000–1306*. University of Toronto Press.

Duncan, A. A. M. 1975. *Scotland: The Making of a Kingdom*. Oliver and Boyd.

———. 2002. *The Kingship of the Scots 842–1292*. Edinburgh University Press.

Trudy Tattersall

Alfred the Great (848/849–899; r.871–899)

Alfred (848/849–899; r. 871–899) is the most celebrated king of the Anglo-Saxon era and the only English king to be called 'the Great'. Alfred's accomplishments included preserving his kingdom of **Wessex** from Viking conquest, inaugurating a literary and educational programme that promoted Old English as a literary and administrative language and laying the institutional foundations of what was to become the kingdom of England. He began his reign as king of the West Saxons, ruling England south of the Thames and parts of southern Essex. When he died in 899, he was also 'King of the **Anglo-Saxons**', a title which perhaps exaggerated his actual power – he ruled only Wessex and western **Mercia** – but which accurately reflects the new status of kingship in England.

Alfred was the fifth son of King **Æthelwulf** of Wessex. He succeeded his brother **Æthelred** as king in 871 in the midst of a Viking invasion of Wessex. In the preceding winter, a Viking army under the command of Danish chieftains Halfdan and Bagsecg had suddenly crossed the Thames and seized the strategically important royal estate at Reading. From this point, they had easy access to the major lines of communications, **Roman roads**, trackways and rivers, in the middle of the Thames valley. King Æthelred and his brother Alfred raised forces to meet the threat. The year was marked by a series of battles, skirmishes and raids. The West Saxons managed to win a major victory at Ashdown on the Berkshire Downs but were unable to capitalise on it. Upon his brother's sudden death on 15 April, Alfred ascended the throne and immediately confronted the Vikings at Wilton but was defeated, which led him to purchase peace from the Vikings. The peace lasted for five years. After an abortive attack in 876, the Danish sea-king Guthram struck again during the Christmas season of 877. Alfred, who had been celebrating Christmas at the royal estate of Chippenham in Wiltshire, was taken completely by surprise and barely managed to escape capture. To save himself and his family, he took refuge in the marshes of Somerset. There Alfred built a fortress on the isle of Athelney, which he used as a base for raiding. The decisive Battle of Edington in the spring of 878 saved the throne for Alfred, and the Treaty of Wedmore with Guthram provided Alfred with some breathing space. The terms of the treaty included Guthram's conversion to Christianity and the recognition of a territorial border between Wessex and the **Danelaw**, a border that ran through the old kingdom of Mercia. Alfred's insistence that Guthram and his chief men convert is significant. He stood sponsor for Guthram at his baptism and, hence, became his spiritual father. Guthram adopted the 'Christian' name 'Æthelstan', which had been the name of Alfred's deceased older brother. Carolingian rulers such as Louis the Pious and Charles the Bald also demanded conversion to Christianity as an essential precondition for peace and recognition of territorial authority. By standing sponsor for Guthram at his baptism, Alfred was recognising the Danish king's legitimacy as ruler of East Anglia. He was welcoming him into the company of 'civilised' rulers. How seriously Guthram took the conversion is unknown. We do know that he issued coins as king of East Anglia under his baptismal name Æthelstan. If Guthram truly converted, it was because Edington had persuaded him of the great power and majesty of the Christian God, the Lord of Battles and, of his agent on earth, King Alfred.

The near disaster of the winter of 878 left its mark on Alfred even more than the victory in the spring and shaped his subsequent policies. It was one thing to win a battle; quite another to secure a lasting peace and to ensure the common weal. The latter called for hard work and resolution and the course Alfred chose for himself and his people was not easy. Over the last two decades of his reign, Alfred undertook a radical reorganisation of the military institutions of his kingdom, strengthened the West Saxon economy through a policy of monetary reform and urban planning and strove to win divine favour by resurrecting the literary glories of earlier generations of Anglo-Saxons. Alfred pursued these ambitious programmes to fulfil, as he saw it, his responsibility as king. This justified the heavy demands he made upon his subjects' labour and finances. It even excused the expropriation of strategically located Church lands. The royal army (the *fyrd*) had been an ad hoc levy of local landowners and their followers, quite unsuitable to oppose a highly mobile enemy. Alfred ordered his soldiers to be mounted and reorganised the *fyrd* into a standing army consisting of two contingents, which served two-month rotations in the field. Simultaneously, he ringed Wessex with some thirty garrisoned fortified towns (called ***burhs***), situating them along the coasts, on navigable rivers and on Roman roads. He created military districts for each of these *burhs*, placing the responsibility for garrisoning the towns and maintaining their defences upon local landowners. Alfred's thirty boroughs were distributed widely throughout the West Saxon kingdom in such a manner that no part of the kingdom was more than 20 miles (32 kilometres), a day's march, from a fortified centre. They were also sited near fortified royal villas, to permit the king better control over his strongholds. Alfred seems to have had 'highways' (*hereweges* – 'army roads') linking the burhs to one another.

Alfred's borough system was revolutionary in its strategic conception and extraordinarily expensive in its execution. The cost of building the boroughs was great in itself, but this paled before the cost of upkeep of these fortresses and the maintaining of their standing garrisons, which together amounted to 27,071 troops. (We know this because a remarkable early tenth-century document known as the 'Burghal Hidage' provides a formula for determining how many men are needed to garrison a town on the basis of one man for every 5.5 yards [5 metres] of wall.) Alfred, lacking the institutions of bureaucratic coercion, was forced to persuade and cajole the magnates of his realm to fulfil his vision. It is a testament to his greatness that they did. Thirteen years later when the Vikings returned in force, they found the kingdom defended by a standing, mobile field army and a network of garrisoned fortresses that commanded its navigable rivers and Roman roads. Characteristically, all Alfred's innovations were firmly rooted in traditional West Saxon practice, drawing as they did upon the three so-called common burdens of bridge work, fortress repair and service on the king's campaigns that all holders of bookland and royal loanland owed the Crown. Where Alfred revealed his genius was in designing the field force and *burhs* (as these fortified sites were called) to be parts of a coherent military system. Neither Alfred's reformed *fyrd* nor his *burhs* alone would have afforded a sufficient defence against the Vikings; together, however, they robbed the Vikings of their major strategic advantages: surprise and mobility. Alfred, in effect, had created what modern strategists call a defence in depth system and one that worked. Alfred's boroughs were not grand affairs like the massive stone of late-Roman shore forts that still dot the southern coast of England (e.g. Pevensey and Richborough 'Castle'). Rather, the borough defences consisted mainly of massive earthworks, large earthen walls surrounded by wide ditches. The earthen walls probably were surmounted with wooden palisades, which, by the tenth century, were giving way to stone walls. (The Alfredian defences are well preserved at Wareham, a town on the southern coast of England.)

Alfred also tried his hand at naval design. In 896, he ordered the construction of a small fleet, perhaps a dozen or so longships, which, at sixty oars, were twice the size of Viking warships. The Anglo-Saxon Chronicler flattered his royal patron by boasting that Alfred's ships were not only larger, but swifter, steadier and rode higher in the water than either Danish or Frisian ships. Alfred had sea power in mind: if he could intercept raiding fleets before they landed, he could spare his kingdom from ravaging. In conception, Alfred's ships may have been superior, but in practice they left a bit to be desired. His ships proved to be too large to manoeuvre well in the close waters of estuaries and rivers, the only places in which a 'naval' battle could occur. The warships of the time were not designed to be ship killers but troop carriers. A naval battle entailed a ship coming alongside an enemy vessel, at which point the crew would lash the two ships together and board the enemy. The result was a land battle at sea.

The failure of a Viking 'Great Army' to take Paris in 886 and other difficulties led them to cross back to England in 892. A force of 250 ships sailed across the channel carrying horses with them and landed in south-east Kent. A second (probably independent) Viking fleet of eighty ships followed and sailed into the Thames estuary and made camp in northern Kent. Opportunistic Vikings settled in East Anglia, and Northumbria broke the peace to raid Wessex once more. For the next four years, Alfred waged war on several fronts against invaders. Alfred's defensive measures were not yet complete, and the Vikings even captured one ill-defended, half-built borough. But Alfred had created a strong enough defensive system to harry the Vikings and negate their threat. In 896, the Viking army dispersed and returned to Francia.

In the 880s, at the same time that he was 'cajoling and threatening' his nobles to build and man the burhs, Alfred, perhaps inspired by the example of Charlemagne a century before, undertook an equally ambitious effort to revive learning. It entailed the recruitment of clerical scholars from Mercia, Wales and abroad to enhance the tenor of the court and episcopacy; the establishment of a court school to educate his own children and those of his nobles; an attempt to require literacy in those who held offices of authority; a series of translations into the vernacular of Latin works the king deemed 'most necessary for all men to know'; the compilation of a chronicle, known today as the ***Anglo-Saxon Chronicle***, detailing the rise of Alfred's kingdom and house; and the issuance of a law code that presented the West Saxons as a new people of Israel and their king as a just and divinely inspired law-giver. This enterprise was to Alfred's mind as essential for the defence of his realm as the building of the *burhs*. As Alfred observed in the preface to his translation of Pope Gregory the Great's *Pastoral Care*, kings who fail to obey their divine duty to promote learning can expect earthly punishments to befall their people. The pursuit of wisdom, he assured his readers, was the surest path to power: 'Study Wisdom, then, and, when you have learned it, condemn it not, for I tell you that by its means you may without fail attain to power, yea, even though not desiring it' (Alfred, Boethius's *Consolation of Philosophy*). Alfred undertook translations of Pope Gregory the Great's *Pastoral Care*, Boethius's *Consolation of Philosophy*, Augustine's *Soliloquies* and the first fifty psalms. Neither the **Old English** *Orosius* nor the *Anglo-Saxon Chronicle*, formerly attributed to Alfred, is now thought to be his work, but the two, along with the Old English translation of **Bede**'s *Ecclesiastical History*, may well have been part of a court-directed programme of translation. The portrayal of the West Saxon resistance to the Vikings by Alfred's biographer **Asser** and the authors of the *Anglo-Saxon Chronicle* as a Christian holy war was more than mere rhetoric or propaganda. It reflected Alfred's own belief in a doctrine of divine rewards and punishments rooted in a vision of a hierarchical Christian world-order in which God is the Lord to whom kings owe obedience and through whom they derive their authority over their followers. He believed, as did other kings in ninth-century England and Francia, that God had entrusted him with the spiritual as well as physical welfare of his people. If the Christian faith fell into ruin in his kingdom, if the clergy were too ignorant to understand the Latin words they butchered in their offices and liturgies and if the ancient monasteries and collegiate churches lay deserted out of indifference, he was answerable before God, as Josiah had been. Alfred's ultimate responsibility was the pastoral care of his people.

Alfred's military reforms saved his kingdom from Scandinavian conquest, while the Alfredian Renaissance not only revived learning but helped create a strong, theocratic conception of kingship that helped Alfred and his successors rule more effectively. Alfred's burghal system provided the West Saxon monarchy with islands of royal power throughout southern England. The boroughs, which were to serve as sites of royal mints and as trading centres as well as fortresses, gave Alfred and his successors more wealth and a greater amount of coercive power than that their predecessors have enjoyed. In short, the response to the Viking invasions in England was *not* the destruction of central authority, as it was in Francia, but the consolidation and growth of kingly power. England did not become decentralised as did France. Instead, the king managed to control his nobility and to exact from their lands taxes and military service. Both the taxes and the military service were based on the value of the land. The result was a monarchy that was able to exploit systematically the wealth of its realm. Alfred's son, Edward the Elder, and his grandsons used their wealth and military resources to conquer the areas of Viking settlement ('the Danelaw') north of the Thames. By the reign of Edgar 'the Peaceable' (959–975), the kings of Wessex had fully become kings of England and lords of Britain.

See also Alfred Jewel; Coinage and Trade; Kings and Kingship; Literature; Wessex.

Further Reading

Abels, Richard P. 1998. *Alfred the Great: War, Culture and Kingship in Anglo-Saxon England.* Longman.

Frantzen, Allen J. 1986. *King Alfred.* Twayne.

Keynes, Simon D., and Michael Lapidge (eds.). 1984. *Alfred the Great: Asser's Life of King Alfred and Other Contemporary Sources.* Penguin.

Nelson, Janet L. 1999. *Rulers and Ruling Families in Early Medieval Europe: Alfred, Charles the Bald, and Others (Variorum Collected Studies Series, Cs 657).* Ashgate.

Pratt, David. 2007. *The Political Thought of King Alfred the Great.* Cambridge University Press.

Reuter, Timothy (ed.). 2003. *Alfred the Great: Papers from the Eleventh-Centenary Conferences.* Ashgate.

Smyth, Alfred P. 1996. *King Alfred the Great.* Oxford University Press.

Wormald, Patrick. 2004. *Oxford Dictionary of National Biography*, s.v. 'Alfred (848/9–899)'. Oxford University Press.

Richard Abels

Alfred Jewel

This gold and enamel ornament consists of a composite unit comprising a cloisonné enamelled plaque displaying a figure holding sceptres beneath a polished rock-crystal plate, with a back plate decorated with a plant motif and with an inscription in goldwork round the side which reads AELFRED MEC HEHT GEWYRCAN, 'Alfred ordered me to be made'. The jewel fits into a gold filigree and granular mount in the shape of an animal head with a socket. It was found in 1693 near Athelney in Somerset.

1. The Alfred Jewel, ninth century AD (gold, rock crystal and enamel).

There has been considerable debate about the meaning and function of the object, though most seem to think that the 'Alfred' is King Alfred of **Wessex** (871–899) and that it was intended as the top of a reading pointer or *aestel.* Alfred ordered reading pointers to be sent out to all the dioceses in Wessex, along with copies of his translation of Gregory's *Regula Pastoralis.* We are also told that each *aestel* was worth fifty mancuses, which was a very valuable amount. This interpretation would fit the fact that the socket was at the bottom (and thus the jewel was not a pendant) and that the socket would fit a fairly slender rod, perhaps of ivory, inappropriate for a sceptre or similar object.

The figure depicted has been variously interpreted as King Alfred, Alexander the Great, Christ or, most probably, a personification of Sight or Holy Wisdom. The latter two would be appropriate for a reading pointer, but the former interpretation is supported by the depiction of Sight in a similar style on the late-Saxon Fuller Brooch, which displays the five senses.

It is likely to be a composite, the enamel panel and its rock crystal being cut down from a larger item. The recent discovery of a number of enamelled pieces from late-Saxon England would allow for this being native, though the rock crystal is probably imported, but the back plate may well be of Carolingian inspiration. It is closely related to the Minster Lovell jewel from Oxfordshire (which may have been from the foot of just such a pointer) and two recent finds.

See also Art and Architecture.

Further Reading

Bakka, E. 1966. 'The Alfred Jewel and Sight'. *Antiquaries Journal* 46: 277–282.

Hinton, D. A. 1974. *A Catalogue of the Anglo-Saxon Ornamental Metalwork 700–1100 in the Department of Antiquities, Ashmolean Museum* (pp.29–48). Oxford.

Webster, L., and J. Backhouse. 1991. *The Making of England* (pp.282–283). British Museum.

Lloyd Laing

Ambrosius Aurelianus

A British general who fought successfully against the Saxon rebellion in the fifth century AD, Ambrosius Aurelianus is a historical figure who later finds his way into Arthurian legend. He first appears in **Gildas**'s *De Excidio Britanniae* ('Concerning the Ruin of Britain'), written around the year 500. After describing how the Saxon mercenaries turned on their British employers, destroying their towns and butchering them in the mountains, Gildas states that the surviving **Britons** rallied around a new leader:

> Wretched people fled to them from all directions.... Their leader (*duce*) was Ambrosius Aurelianus, a gentleman (*viro modesto*) who, perhaps alone of the Romans, had survived the shock of this storm; certainly his parents, who had worn the purple, were slain in it. His descendants in our day have become greatly inferior to their grandfather's excellence. Under him our peoples regained their strength, and challenged the victors to battle. The Lord assented, and the battle went their way. (Winterbottom 1978, 28)

That is all we hear about Ambrosius in Gildas's narrative, which is adopted without elaboration by **Bede**. Ambrosius next appears in the ninth-century ***Historia Brittonum***, in three distinct episodes. First, he is the prophetic boy who confronts the British tyrant **Vortigern** at **Dinas Emrys**, which translates as 'The Fortress of Ambrosius'. Next is the brief mention of strife between Ambrosius and a Vitolinus at Guolop (possibly Wallop near Amesbury). Lastly is an Ambrosius Aurelianus who resembles Gildas's champion, though here he is the opponent of both Vortigern and his Saxon allies and becomes 'king among all the kings of the British nation'. **Geoffrey of Monmouth** in his *History of the Kings of Britain* (c.1136) calls the prophetic boy Merlin and makes 'Aurelius Ambrosius' the brother of Uther Pendragon, and thus King **Arthur**'s uncle.

Not much can be said about the historical Ambrosius beyond the information provided by the near-contemporary Gildas. *Aurelius* is a common late-Roman family name, but *Ambrosius* may suggest a connection to St. Ambrose. It is similarly conjecture to state, as many have done, that Ambrosius (rather than Arthur) was the leader of the Britons at Badon Hill, that Ambrosius *is* the historical Arthur or that there were two or more men named Ambrosius behind these events.

See also Roman Army; Roman Britain.

Further Reading

Hunter-Mann, Kurt. 2001. 'The Last of the Romans: The Life and Times of Ambrosius Aurelianus'. *The Heroic Age* 4, <http://www.heroicage.org/issues/4/Hunter-Mann.html> (cited 27 February 2008).

Lapidge, Michael, and David Dumville (eds.). 1984. *Gildas: New Approaches*. Boydell.

Morris, John (ed. and tr.). 1980. *Nennius: British History and the Welsh Annals*. Phillimore.

Snyder, Christopher A. 1998. *An Age of Tyrants: Britain and the Britons, AD 400–600*. Penn State Press.

———. 2003. *The Britons*. The Peoples of Europe Series. Blackwell.

Winterbottom, Michael (ed. and tr.). 1978. *Gildas: The Ruin of Britain and Other Works*. Phillimore.

Christopher A. Snyder

Angevins

See Plantagenets.

Angles

The Angles were one of the three major groups of Germanic incomers who according to **Bede** (*HE*, 1, XV) settled in Britain in the fifth century AD. Bede tells us that they came from Anglia ('which it is said from that time to remain desert to this day'), a land between the **Jutes** and the **Saxons**. This is modern Schleswig, in North Germany, where there is still a district called Angeln. Bede further explains that from the Angles were descended in his own time the East Angles, the Middle Angles, the Mercians and the Angles north of the Humber River; these represent the kingdoms of East Anglia, Middle Anglia, **Mercia** and **Northumbria** (which came to encompass the Anglian sub-kingdoms of **Deira** and **Bernicia**).

Bede's account of the settlements was an oversimplified one, as the homelands of the settlers were more diverse than what he implies; there is evidence of settlement from Norway, for example, and also from Sweden. It is, however, the case that there are close similarities between the pottery in Anglia and that of North Germany and some direct evidence for settlers in the form of the travels of potter's stamps. The burial ritual of cremation, found in North Germany, is also

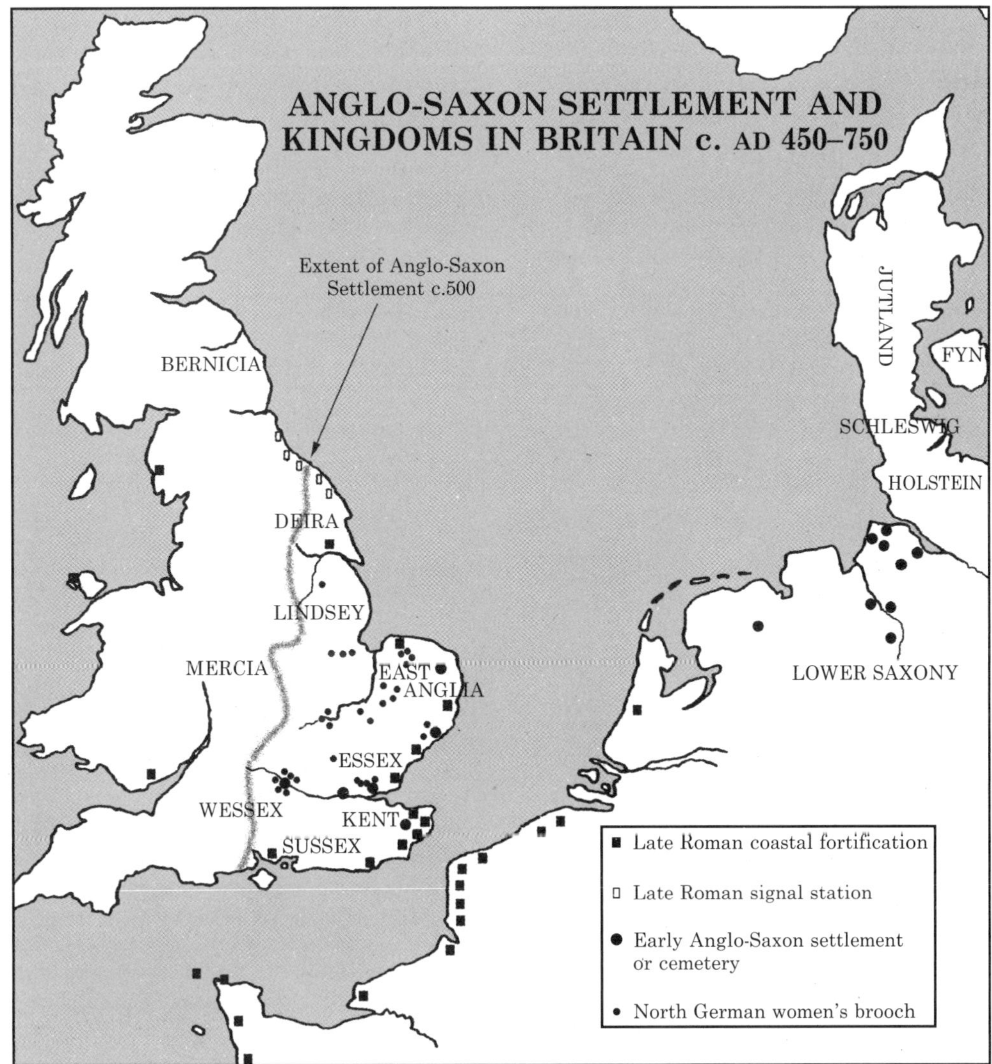

1. The Anglo-Saxon Kingdoms.

the predominant rite in north of the Thames, with inhumation being more fashionable in south of it, in keeping with Bede's Saxons, though neither practice is found exclusively in defined geographical areas. There is also some evidence to support Bede's assertion about desertion in the homelands. Between the Elbe and Weser rivers are to be found cemeteries of the fourth to fifth century AD with artefact assemblages very similar to those in eastern England. These seem to come to an end on the Continent around the end of the fifth century.

Bede also claims that seven early Anglo-Saxon kings claimed 'rule over all the southern kingdoms'; the ***Anglo-Saxon Chronicle*** coined the term *Bretwalda*, or 'Britain ruler', for these kings and added to Bede's list. Among these Britain rulers (the concept is now disputed by scholars) are the Anglian kings **Rædwald of East Anglia** and Edwin, **Oswald** and **Oswiu of Northumbria**; **Æthelbald** of Mercia exercised similar authority. Broadly speaking, Northumbrian rulers dominated English politics throughout the seventh century (though our information is perhaps skewed by our Northumbrian informant, Bede), and Mercian rulers held this position throughout the eighth century. The two Anglian kingdoms suffered from Viking raids and settlements beginning in the late eighth century, which led to their supplanting by the West Saxons under **Alfred the Great** in the ninth.

See also Art and Architecture; Literature.

Further Reading

Bassett, Steven (ed.). 1989. *The Origins of the Anglo-Saxon Kingdoms*. Leicester University Press.

Higham, N. J. 1992. *Rome, Britain and the Anglo-Saxons*. Seaby.

James, Edward. 2001. *Britain in the First Millennium*. Oxford University Press.

Welch, Martin G. 1992. *Discovering Anglo-Saxon England*. Pennsylvania State University Press.

Wormald, Patrick. 1983. 'Bede, the *Bretwaldas* and the Origins of the *gens Anglorum*'. Pp. 99–129 in *Ideal and Reality in Frankish and Anglo-Saxon Society*. Edited by Patrick Wormald et al. Oxford.

Yorke, Barbara. 1990. *Kings and Kingdoms of Early Anglo-Saxon England*. Routledge.

Lloyd Laing

Anglo-Saxon Chronicle

The *Anglo-Saxon Chronicle* is the most important documentary source for Anglo-Saxon history. It was written in **Old English** by many hands, in several places, over more than 200 years, and purports to cover the period from 60 BC to AD 1154, although for the first few centuries it is entirely derivative, and only one version of it goes all the way to 1154. It survives in six main manuscripts, conventionally labelled A through F. The differences between them give many clues as to how the work was compiled and passed on, but complete agreement has not been reached.

It is generally accepted that the *Chronicle* began as an initiative of the last decade of the reign of King **Alfred the Great** (849–899), during a lull in campaigns against the **Vikings**. The manuscript A is written in the same handwriting up the end of the entry for AD 891, after which the same scribe has written 892 in Roman numerals as preparation for the next entry, which is, however, in a different hand, as if the *Chronicle* was now being written up at the end of each year, like a diary. All versions of the *Chronicle* retain the form of an 'annal', that is events are recorded year by year, though there are occasional exceptions, as when the entry for 755 records a deposition and killing in that year but goes on to complete the story with an attempt at revenge made twenty-nine years later. The annalistic form suggests that the major source for events before the lifetime of the first chronicler was a set of 'Easter Tables'. Calculation of the proper date of Easter necessitated writing down a string of facts for each year, usually organised in columns, and it was a natural continuation to note in the margin the major event or events of that particular year – usually, the deaths and successions of kings and archbishops, major battles and disasters.

The first chronicler also had available to him written sources such as **Bede**'s *Ecclesiastical History of the English People*, and royal genealogies and bishop lists, as well as some forms of oral tradition. In later years, when 'Chronicles' were being continued in different places, material was incorporated from further sources. The compiler of the manuscript C had access to information about **Mercia** in the early tenth century, while the manuscript D is especially well informed about northern and Scottish affairs. The manuscript E is a copy made in 1121 at Peterborough, and in the process of making the copy, the scribe seized the opportunity to add detailed accounts of local events, such as the 1070 sacking of the monastery by 'Hereward and his gang'. This 'chronicle' was continued up to the year 1154, in a language which deviated increasingly from standard Old English.

The *Anglo-Saxon Chronicle* as a whole has been much admired by modern scholars. Its tone is hard-headed and practical. The chroniclers avoid moralistic explanations for events, record failure as well as success, and do not regularly indulge in flattery. In A 897, the summary of damage done by the Vikings before they were forced to give up is even-handed and judicious; the similar summary in E 1011, while angrier, shows an attempt to analyse as well as record. Nevertheless, the chroniclers did have individual biases, from which modern scholars have derived further insights. The chronicler of the 890s is strongly pro-Alfred, and can be detected minimising failures of policy, and whose withholding facts he was probably aware. The manuscripts C, D and E agree on major events during the last years of the Anglo-Saxon kingdom up to 1066 but take different political positions as to the repeated clashes between King **Edward** and members of the house of **Godwin**. Especially problematic is the long account, presumably compiled by the first chronicler, of the conquest of **Wessex** by King **Cerdic** and his descendants. As we have it, this is a heroic tale of continuous expansion from a precarious beachhead in the year 495, but the story is not supported by archaeology. Like the praise-poems inserted in ABCD 937 and 942, on '**The Battle of Brunanburh**' and 'The Capture of the Five Boroughs', respectively, this shows most clearly what the chroniclers wanted to believe. Nevertheless, the *Chronicle* as a whole is the most impressive vernacular history written anywhere in Europe for many centuries. It was heavily used by contemporary and later historians writing in Latin, who sometimes seem to have had access to versions now lost.

See also Literature; Wessex.

Further Reading

Bately, Janet. 1991. *The Anglo-Saxon Chronicle: Texts and Textual Relationships*. University of Reading.

Keynes, Simon, and Michael Lapidge (tr.). 1983. *Alfred the Great: Asser's Life of King Alfred and Other Contemporary Sources*. Penguin.

Swanton, Michael (ed. and tr.). 2000. *The Anglo-Saxon Chronicles* (rev. edn.). Phoenix.

Tom Shippey

Anglo-Saxon Language

See Old English.

Anglo-Saxons

See Angles; Saxons; Jutes.

Angus mac Fergus, King of the Picts

See Óengus.

Aneirin

An early **Welsh-language** poet, to whom '**Y Gododdin**' is generally attributed. It is also assumed that his *floruit* belongs to sometime between the mid-sixth and the early seventh century, although no contemporary historical records mention his name. The earliest reference to Aneirin (or Neirin) appears in the ***Historia Brittonum*** where he is named alongside four other *Cynfeirdd* poets, Talhaearn Tad Awen (Talhaearn 'Father of the Muse'), Taliesin, Blwchfardd and Cian.

The 'Gododdin' is a poem celebrating the disastrous attack by 300 British horsemen upon the **Angles** of **Deira** and **Bernicia** (in modern-day Northumberland and Yorkshire) at ***Catraeth*** (Catterick). Before sallying forth to certain death at the hands of overwhelming numbers of Angles, the small warband had been at the court of Mynyddog Mwynfawr in the region of Din Eidyn (Edinburgh) where, in return for the year-long largesse and patronage of Mynyddog, they had entered into a *de facto* contract to fight to the death in an attempt to recover the strategically important town of Catterick from their encroaching enemies.

Although composed of a series of elegies, the 'Gododdin' cannot be said to be simply a lament since its tone so often celebrates the unflinching heroism of the warband and their unstinting loyalty to Mynyddog Mwynfawr. To paraphrase *Book of Aneirin*, they had acted honourably and their fame (through the medium of verse) would be cherished in perpetuity. Neither can the 'Gododdin' be said to be an epic, since it contains not a single narrative but a series of vignettes or stanzas dedicated to individual warriors. Despite its form, however, no other poem in Welsh literature embodies more fully the heroic ideals of the period. Its style is vigorous and memorable, often containing sharply contrasting statements which are reinforced by hyperbole (and sometimes by meiosis). Its language is varied and complex, and metaphor occurs more frequently than simile. Syntax, metre, rhythm and imagery are all employed to praise and memorialise the heroes of the 'Gododdin' whose martial capacity for ferocity and bravery is accorded due attention. An emphasis is also placed, however, upon their liberality, munificence, geniality and kindness in peace and in female company. Emphasised in many of the stanzas and underscoring much of the imagery are the bonds made during the year-long carousal at Edinburgh between Mynyddog Mwynfawr and his warriors: they were bonds which could not be broken, and in the slaughter at Catterick, the heroes of the 'Gododdin', it is declaimed, repaid their overlord's mead with their own lives.

The style of 'Gododdin', however, may not have been unique: 'Moliant Cadwallon' ('Praise of Cadwallon') and an elegy to Cynddylan ap Cyndrwyn have a style, pattern and vocabulary resembling those of the 'Gododdin' and suggest an early British literary heritage common to the Old North and Wales. Some allusions to Christianity do exist in parts of the 'Gododdin', but the earliest text, belonging orthographically to the ninth century, contain none: Aneirin was, arguably, a pre-Christian heroic poet. The 'Gododdin' proved an inspiration for medieval vaticinatory poets and continues to have an impact upon modern Welsh readers (with the aid of critical apparatus). The only source for the 'Gododdin' is a medieval manuscript known as the *Book of Aneirin*, which belongs to the thirteenth century. The manuscript contains more than 1,000 lines of verse attributed in two texts to the 'Gododdin', one of which belongs orthographically to the thirteenth century and the other to the ninth. The earlier orthography contains Old Welsh but is a subject of some debate as is the history of the transmission of 'Gododdin' from oral to written record. It is conceivable that the early heroic poetry of northern Britain, including the 'Gododdin', was preserved in Strathclyde and was later transferred to North Wales.

According to a Welsh triad, Aneirin was killed by an axe-blow from Eidyn. Another triad notes that he was assassinated by Heiddyn mab Enygan. Whether or not these triads contain mutually contradictory evidence, however, remains inconclusive.

See also Literature.

Further Reading

Jackson, K. H. 1969. *The Gododdin: The Oldest Scottish Poem*. Edinburgh University Press.

Jarman, A. O. H. 1990. *Aneirin: Y Gododdin: Britain's Oldest Heroic Poem*. Gomer Press.

———. 1992. 'Aneirin'. Pp. 68–80 in *A Guide to Welsh Literature*, vol. 1. Edited by A. O. H. Jarman and Gwilym Rees Hughes. University of Wales Press.

Koch, John. 1997. *The Gododdin of Aneirin: Text and Context from Dark-Age North Britain*. University of Wales Press.

Lewis, Ceri W. 1992. 'The Historical Background of Early Welsh Verse'. Pp. 11–50 in *A Guide to Welsh Literature*, vol. 1. Edited by A. O. H. Jarman and Gwilym Rees Hughes. University of Wales Press.

Roberts, Brynley F. (ed.). 1988. *Early Welsh Poetry, Studies in the Book of Aneirin*. National Library of Wales.

Williams, Ifor. 1972. *The Beginnings of Welsh Poetry*. University of Wales Press.

Owen Thomas

Annales Cambriae

Annales Cambriae is the name given by modern scholars to a family of Latin chronicles from medieval Wales. Three versions of the chronicle survive: manuscripts A, B and C. A covers the period from AD 445 to 954, while B and C cover the period from AD 682 to 1288. The exemplars for B and C probably originally began in 444, but in the surviving manuscripts the text survives only as a continuation of **Geoffrey of Monmouth**'s *Historia Regum Britanniae*, and thus the earlier material, dealing with a period Geoffrey covered in much greater detail, was omitted. Text A, which survives interpolated into the earliest recension of ***Historia Brittonum*** in the famous Harley Manuscript 3859, written c. 1100, seems to represent a genuine mid-tenth-century recension of the chronicle. Its annalistic framework continues beyond the last entry until the annal for 977 suggestion that it reached its present state, give or take a few minor scribal errors and emendations, between 954 and 977. The later material, found only in texts B and C, has not attracted as much attention as text A; Welsh scholars preferring to approach this tradition through the later thirteenth-century vernacular translations of *Annales Cambriae* known variously as *Brut y Tywysogyon* or *Brenhinoedd y Saeson*. A good modern edition and translation of the Latin text after 954 is still awaited.

More scholarly and popular attention has been paid to text A, and a considerable amount concerning its construction has been discerned.

At its core lies a chronicle kept at or near **St David's** from c. 800. This contains many references to the kings and bishops of **Dyfed** and occasional notices of events elsewhere in Wales. In c. 950, this chronicle was augmented by a considerable amount of material drawn from an Irish chronicle sharing a common source with the *Annals of Tigernach* and *Chronicum Scottorum*. In addition to these two major sources, additional material relating to early British history, not found in the Irish chronicles, was added. Much though not all of this early British material is concerned with the Old North, the Brittonic kingdoms of northern England and southern Scotland. The origin of this early British material has been the main focus of debate concerning *Annales Cambriae*. It is too meagre and discontinuous in nature to represent a single additional chronicle source, and it is not clear whether it originated as annalistic entries or whether all or some of the details derive from literary and hagiographical material which was inserted into the annalistic framework provided by the Irish chronicle as part of a self-conscious historical endeavour in the tenth century. This problem has excited much attention because amongst this material lie the earliest absolute dates attributed to King **Arthur** as well as to other figures known otherwise only from unspecific literary texts. Thus, much hangs on the reliability of this material.

See also Literature; Welsh People.

Further Reading

Dumville, David N. 2002. *Annales Cambriae, AD 682–954: Texts A–C in Parallel.* Department of Anglo-Saxon, Norse and Celtic, University of Cambridge.

Hughes, Kathleen. 1980. *Celtic Britain in the Early Middle Ages.* Boydell.

Alex Woolf

Annals of Ulster

See Irish Annals.

Annals of Wales

See Annales Cambriae.

Anselm (c. 1033–1109)

Anselm of Bec was an influential theologian and ecclesiastical leader in both Normandy and England in the later eleventh century. Abbot of the Norman monastery of Bec from 1078, he succeeded his friend and mentor, Lanfranc, as archbishop of **Canterbury** in 1093. According to tradition, Anselm only grudgingly accepted appointment to England's primatial see, perhaps anticipating that he would enjoy very few peaceful years in that position. Anselm's insistence that kings of England obey the church's laws and uphold its traditions at a time when the relationship between secular and ecclesiastical authority was coming under increasing scrutiny by the papacy led to two major periods of exile for the archbishop and many uncomfortable moments for Anglo-Norman kings and bishops alike. Anselm spent only the last two years of his life to concentrate fully on his pastoral duties, but he managed to write, throughout these years, some of the most influential works of theology of the eleventh century. Some 500 archbishop's letters are also extant. Anselm was the subject of a contemporary biography by his friend and colleague at Canterbury, Eadmer, and he figures prominently in Eadmer's chronicle of eleventh-century Canterbury, the *Historia Novorum*.

Anselm was born c. 1033 to a noble family in Aosta, on the border of Burgundy and Lombardy. Fleeing an overbearing father, he gave up his patrimony in his early twenties, making his way to the prominent Norman abbey of Bec. Although a relatively new foundation, the abbey was already famous due to its intellectually gifted prior and schoolmaster, Lanfranc of Pavia. Although Eadmer portrays Anselm as initially uncertain in his choice, once he took his vows in 1060 Anselm rose rapidly in the ranks of this prestigious community, replacing Lanfranc as prior and schoolmaster in 1063 and the abbey's founder, Herluin, as abbot in 1078. For the fifteen years that Anselm was abbot of Bec, he continued to increase its fortunes and extend its influence through the establishment of dependencies on the Continent and in England. Anselm's later skirmishes with secular authority were foreshadowed by his steadfast repudiation of the claim of Robert, count of Meulan, to overlordship over the abbey in the early 1080s.

Anselm was in England in 1093, perhaps seeing to the abbey's English interests, when King **William II** finally decided to fill the vacancy at Canterbury left by Lanfranc's death in 1089. Anselm was the obvious choice, but he was apparently initially unwilling to accept the appointment. Invoking the humility *topos* required of pious churchmen, Anselm sought to evade the appointment until, according to Eadmer, he came to accept it as God's will. Anselm was enthroned at Canterbury on 25 September 1093 and consecrated by Thomas, archbishop of **York**, on 4 December 1093. One of Anselm's first goals was to restore the see's patrimony, which had been ruthlessly exploited by the king during the four-year vacancy. He was also intent on reasserting Canterbury's primacy over York and reforming English clerical practices through the convocation of regular synods. Owing to technicalities, restoring the see's lands took longer than anticipated, as did settling the primary issue. Anselm was never, however, to receive permission from William Rufus to convoke primatial synods, much to his regret. Indeed, Anselm's relationship with William Rufus was difficult at best, even from the beginning. Anselm's insistence that he receive the pallium from Pope Urban when Rufus had not yet decided which rival pope to support only deepened the rift between them. Anselm was exiled to the Continent in 1097 while the pope worked to reconcile the two sides. The archbishop's exile only ended when Rufus was killed in a hunting accident in August 1100. Anselm was immediately recalled by the new king, **Henry I**, and when he arrived back in England in late September 1100, he had every reason to believe that his relationship with Henry would be a much more cordial one.

Unfortunately for king and prelate, the Gregorian papacy had recently banned lay investiture, and when Henry refused to give up the royal rights of investiture and receiving homage, Anselm was forced to choose between his loyalty to the king and his obedience to the pope. Quite apart from the principle involved, Anselm was on record as having participated in the papal council that had approved the measure. The English Investiture Controversy was drawn out over the period 1100–1107, during which time Anselm spent another three years in exile awaiting its resolution. A compromise was finally reached in 1105, whereby Henry gave up the right to invest bishops but maintained the right to receive homage. Anselm finally returned to England and spent the last two years of his pontificate working once again to ensure Canterbury's primacy over York and enforcing laws against clerical marriage and simony. He died on 21 April 1109 and was entombed at Canterbury beside Lanfranc.

Anselm's legacy at Canterbury was to safeguard its most important prerogatives for future archbishops, but his influence in the intellectual world was far greater. His phrase, *fides quaerens intellectum* ('faith seeking understanding'), became the motto of scholastic theologians seeking to reconcile faith with reason. Anselm wrote widely on topics from the Trinity to original sin, but his methodology proved most influential. Among his most important works was *Cur Deus Homo*, a rational argument for why God had to become human to save humankind, which he completed in exile in 1099.

Further Reading

Davies, Brian, and Gillian Evans (tr.). 1998. *Anselm of Canterbury: The Major Works*. Oxford University Press.

Southern, Sir Richard. 1990. *St Anselm: A Portrait in a Landscape*. Cambridge University Press.

Vaughn, Sally N. 1987. *Anselm of Bec and Robert of Meulan: The Innocence of the Dove and the Wisdom of the Serpent*. University of California Press.

Mary Frances Giandrea

Antonine Wall

The Antonine Wall, the short-lived successor to **Hadrian's Wall**, formed Rome's northern frontier under the Emperor Antoninus Pius (r. AD 138–161). Visible remains extend for 37 miles (60 kilometres) across the Forth–Clyde isthmus, from Old Kilpatrick in the west to Bridgeness in the east. The decision to re-advance to the Forth–Clyde came early in the new reign, with the resulting campaigns being entrusted to the Governor Q. Lollius Urbicus (AD 139–142). Both the war and the decision to build a wall of turf are briefly mentioned in a fourth-century life of Antoninus Pius (*Scriptores Historiae Augustae* [*SHA*], *Ant. Pius* 5.4). Various reasons have been advanced to account for these events, which resulted in the abandonment of Hadrian's Wall, the most cogent of which is the emperor's need to gain military prestige; this is reinforced by the fact that, following the campaigns, Antoninus took the title of *Imperator* in AD 142, the only time he did so during his reign.

Recent research has shown that the Antonine Wall, like its predecessor, had a complex structural history. Several features have been identified. The first is a linear barrier of turf or earth with clay/turf cheeks, erected on a stone base, around 15 feet (5 metres) wide and 10 feet (3 metres) high, with dressed stone kerbs, incorporating culverts from the outset. The second is a ditch, lying more than 20 feet (6 metres) north of the wall; though its dimensions varied, it averaged about 40 feet (12 metres) wide and 13 feet (4 metres) deep in the central sector. There are also seventeen forts of varying sizes, some clearly primary features, while others were later additions; their close spacing, at intervals of about 2.25 miles (4 kilometres), contrasts with Hadrian's Wall. Additionally, there are several fortlets, typically about 70 by 60 feet (21 by 18 metres), not unlike the milecastles of Hadrian's Wall, all of them either contemporary with or earlier than the wall; some are known to underlie later forts. Several enigmatic and irregularly spaced 'expansions' and small ditched enclosures have also been identified, though their function remains uncertain. Lastly, a military road was laid behind the wall.

From the relative relationship of these different features, it is clear that the Antonine Wall underwent changes in design during its construction, much like its predecessor. Two broad blueprints have been recognised: (1) an original plan comprising the rampart and ditch, six large forts at intervals of about 7–8 miles (11–13 kilometres), a series of fortlets at intervals of a mile and the 'expansions' and small ditched enclosures; (2) a secondary plan involving the suppression of the fortlets and the addition of a further eleven smaller forts at much closer intervals. Later in the process, annexes were also added to several forts. The fact that two primary forts were built in stone has suggested that there may even have been an early plan to build a stone wall which was rapidly abandoned.

Epigraphic evidence makes it clear that work began under Lollius Urbicus in AD 142, prior to his departure from the province, no doubt with the expectation that it would be completed by his unnamed successor. Precisely how long this took remains a matter of speculation, however, with at least one recent commentator suggesting that it may not have been achieved before the mid-150s, perhaps because of interruptions caused by problems in Mauretania (between AD 145 and 150) and by fighting on the northern frontier (in the early 150s). All three legions participated in the construction of the frontier, while several auxiliary units are attested working on the forts. The work of the legions is commemorated by twenty inscriptions, known as 'distance slabs', which demonstrate that the wall was divided into very precise lengths (e.g. Collingwood and Wright 1995, RIB 2139, RIB 2173, RIB 2186); these inscriptions suggest the existence of a detailed specification for the actual building operations.

The date at which the Antonine Wall was abandoned has been much debated, and it is only recently that a new consensus has begun to emerge. This argues that the epigraphic evidence for rebuilding on the curtain of Hadrian's Wall in AD 158 (Collingwood and Wright 1995, RIB 1389) is *prima facie* proof of a decision to abandon the Antonine Wall and to re-commission its more southerly counterpart. The pottery evidence, however, suggests that the more northerly line was not fully relinquished before c. AD 163, while epigraphy demonstrates that rebuilding operations on Hadrian's Wall continued into the early 160s under the Governor Calpurnius Agricola. The simplest interpretation of this material would see a protracted process of withdrawal over a period of more than five years. This view is not without its detractors, but it has the considerable merit of fitting current evidence.

See also Roman Army; Roman Britain; Roman Roads.

Further Reading

Bailey, G. B. 2003. *The Antonine Wall: Rome's Northern Frontier*. Falkirk.

Breeze, D. J. 2006. *The Antonine Wall*. John Donald.

Collingwood, R. G., and R. P. Wright. 1995. *The Roman Inscriptions of Britain. Volume 1: The Inscriptions on Stone*. Alan Sutton.

Hanson, W. S., and G. S. Maxwell. 1983. *Rome's North-West Frontier, the Antonine Wall*. Edinburgh University Press.

Barry C. Burnham

Ardagh Chalice

While digging for potatoes in 1868 near the village of Ardagh, County Limerick, Ireland, a young man came across a hoard of early Irish metalwork, which may well have been hidden during a period of Viking raiding in the area. The most important item in the hoard was the highly ornate two-handed chalice we now refer to as the 'Ardagh Chalice', which on the basis of its decorative style has been dated to roughly 710–735. The decoration of the chalice displays remarkable artistic inspiration and technical skill by the metalworkers. Its filigree ornament resembles in miniature some of the interlace illuminations found in contemporary manuscripts. It was intended for use as the

2. The Ardagh Chalice, Celtic, early eighth century (silver with silver gilding, enamel, brass and bronze).

single cup, which, when filled with wine (it has a capacity of 3 pints [1.5 litres]: enough for about sixty communicants), is one of the focal symbols in the central Christian ritual of the Eucharist ('the Mass'). Cups such as this are extraordinarily rare from the Latin west because with changes in the ritual these large cups gradually became redundant and were recycled as scrap. Those that have survived have usually been items that were preserved as relics of specific saints or, like this one, were hidden, forgotten and then recovered by accident.

However, for more than a century after its discovery, this cup was viewed solely in terms of its virtuosity as metalwork as some doubted if such chalices were ever actually used. These doubts were removed with the 1980 discovery of a similar, if later, cup at Derrynaflan together with that other essential piece of Eucharistic metalwork: a paten. This ensemble (two cups, one paten and the wine strainer) when placed within the framework of what we know of the pre-Carolingian liturgy in the west and when the metalwork is used to give shape to descriptions found in documents such as the Stowe Missal allow us to see that these were functioning liturgical vessels in a rite where there was one cup used for all present at the Eucharist. There are two handles to facilitate the handing to and fro of the cup between the deacon and the recipient at the liturgy, while the lip of the cup was there to enable the recipient to drink from it without spillage. The significance of this cup as understood can be established not only from sources such as law codes, which prescribe a penance for those who scratch such a cup with their teeth, but also from a distinctive feature of the Ardagh Chalice: it has the names of twelve apostles inscribed around the cup indicating that the recipient is being brought into the circle of the apostles around the Eucharistic table.

See also Celtic Christianity; Metalworking.

Further Reading

O'Loughlin, Thomas. 2003. 'The Praxis and Explanations of Eucharistic Fraction in the Ninth Century: The Insular Evidence'. *Archiv für Liturgiewissenschaft* 45: 1–20.

———. Forthcoming. 'The List of Saints on the Bowl of the Ardagh Chalice'. *Journal of Celtic Studies* 5.

Ryan, Michael. 2000. *Early Irish Communion Vessels.* Country House/National Museum of Ireland.

Rynne, Etienne. 1987. 'The Date of the Ardagh Chalice'. Pp. 85–89 in *Ireland and Insular Art: AD 500–1200.* Edited by Michael Ryan. Royal Irish Academy.

Thomas O'Loughlin

Ardwall Isle

Ardwall Isle is an uninhabited tidal island that lies off the coast of Kirkcudbright, in south-west Scotland. Extensively excavated in 1964–1965, it produced a long sequence of structural phases. The first phase involved the establishment of a Christian cemetery, which was followed by the construction of a putative timber oratory or chapel demarcated by a series of post-holes. At this stage, it is possible that an oval enclosing bank was constructed round the cemetery. This was in turn succeeded by a stone-built chapel that partly overlaid the supposed timber oratory and was on a slightly different axis from it and from the burials apparently oriented on it. Two rows of inhumations were, however, oriented on the stone structure. At a later date when the chapel was roofless, there were further burials in the body of the church.

The original excavator believed that a hollow associated with the earliest burials had been a special grave, the bones from which had been translated first to an above-ground slab-shrine and then to a relic cavity in the stone-built altar of the stone chapel. While the relic cavity (which still contained bones) was clearly used as such, the supposed corner-post shrine, reconstructed on the basis of unaligned post-holes, remains very speculative, as does the 'special grave'. The oratory, being represented by four post-holes belonging to two sides, is also open to other interpretations.

A series of inscribed stones were found on the site, of which the most significant was one inscribed with the name Cudgar, which is Germanic rather than Celtic, and a series of fragments of crosses which are most closely matched in **Northumbria**, particularly **Whitby**. Other inscribed stones have their counterparts in the Celtic-speaking world. The chronology and affinities of the site are problematic; no finds demonstrate a use before the eighth century AD. At some point, the churchyard and church were abandoned, and a medieval hall house (c.1250–1350) was built on the site. This was in turn replaced by a late-eighteenth-century tavern.

See also Art and Architecture.

Further Reading

Thomas, A. C. 1967. 'An Early Christian Cemetery and Chapel on Ardwall Isle, Kirkcudbright'. *Medieval Archaeology* XI: 127–188.

Lloyd Laing

Armagh

Armagh is an archdiocese of Ireland, traditionally founded by **St. Patrick** around AD 445, when a **rath** was given to the saint by the local king. It was the principal monastery of Ireland and had a famous school. Nothing remains of the original monastery, but aerial photographs reveal its concentric planning in the layout of the streets of the modern town, and a seventeenth-century map provides a bird's-eye view of the town, which shows the later medieval buildings in the inner enclosure. Rescue excavation has, however, revealed a substantial ditch (21 feet [6.4 metres] wide and up to 10 feet [3 metres] deep) datable to the fifth through ninth century, which probably encircled the hilltop perhaps enclosing an area 164 feet (50 metres) in diameter. The ditch had two periods of fill, the first dated by radiocarbon dating to between the late-second and mid-sixth century AD, the second lying somewhere between the fifth and eighth centuries when material was tipped in from the outer bank, along with metalworking debris which included interlace-ornamented clay moulds. Excavations elsewhere have produced evidence for an early cemetery. A fragmentary cross of the late-ninth or tenth century is preserved in the Anglican cathedral.

The ***Book of Armagh*** (Trinity College Dublin, Ms 52) is a manuscript that most unusually can be both dated precisely and assigned to a specific scriptorium. It was made by Ferdomnagh for Torbach, abbot of Armagh, in 807, aided by another, anonymous, scribe. Measuring 0.6 feet × 0.5 feet (195 millimetres × 145 millimetres), it consists of 217 folios now rebound in two volumes. It contains a complete text of the New Testament, canon tables, prefaces and explanations of Hebrew names. In addition, it contains a version of the *Confession* of St. Patrick, two seventh-century lives of the saint and Sulpicius Severus's *Life of St. Martin*.

It is noteworthy for its limited use of colour, though there are considerable similarities in the decoration to some in the ***Book of Kells***. It was guarded by a Hereditary Keeper in the medieval period but later passed into other hands and was bought late in the seventeenth century by the chancellor of Dublin University for Trinity College library. Associated with it is a leather budget or book satchel which dates from the fifteenth century AD, but which was originally made for a larger object. This is elaborately decorated with moulded ornament in cuir bouilli technique, the ornament comprising roundels with interlace and animals, the roundels intertwining where they conjoin, as on the so-called Harp of **Brian Boru**.

See also Celtic Christianity; Literature.

Further Reading

Alexander, J. J. A. 1978. *A Survey of Manuscripts Illuminated in the British Isles. Volume 6: Insular Manuscripts 6th to 9th Century*. Harvey Miller.

Gaskell-Brown, C., and A. E. T. Harper. 1984. 'Excavation at Cathedral Hill, Armagh, 1968'. *Ulster Journal of Archaeology* 47: 109–161.

Waterer, J. W. 1968. 'Irish book satchels or budgets'. *Medieval Archaeology*. 12:70–82.

Lloyd Laing

'Armes Prydein Vawr'

'The Great Prophecy of Britain', a poem of 199 lines predicting an ambitious alliance of the Celtic world which collectively would drive the encroaching English invaders out of Britain. The alliance, under the leadership of Cynan and Cadwaladr, would consist of Norsemen from **Dublin**; **Gaels** from Ireland, Anglesey and Pictland; and British warriors from **Cornwall**, Brittany, the Old North and Wales. In a combined effort, the poem envisages, they would rout **Æthelstan**'s forces to Winchester, the centre of **Wessex**.

The style of 'Armes Prydein Vawr' combines exhortation and exultation with the conventions of vaticination in a series of nine *awdlau* (a poem of a single main-rhyme), with many lines using a metre known as *Cyhydedd Naw Ban* (lines of nine syllables) and embellished with internal rhyme and alliteration. The author remains anonymous, but on the basis of the poem's political content, historical context and allusions to saints such as Dewi (**David**) and Garmon, he was arguably a South Wales monk opposed to **Hywel Dda**'s rapprochement with Æthelstan. Sir Ifor Williams has suggested that the poem was composed during the period of Æthelstan's aggressive policy of expansion (927–937) and before the attempt of the Norse of Dublin and the kings of Scotland and Strathclyde to form a pan-Celtic alliance ended in calamity at **Brunanburh** in 937. Furthermore, the poem's many allusions to taxes may suggest a link with the heavy tributes exacted by Æthelstan from the Welsh at the council of Hereford between 927 and 930.

Despite its propaganda against Æthelstan, 'Armes Prydein Vawr' also reveals anti-Hywel Dda sentiments in tenth-century Wales by emphasising a pride in ancient British tradition and a belief that the sovereignty of Britain belonged to the British, and not to the Saxons, and would by the grace of a *mab darogan* ('son of prophecy') be delivered back into their possession. It has also been posited that the poem demonstrates an embryonic sense of national Welsh identity. At the very least, it can be said that the poem's antagonism towards Wessex is conspicuous. 'Armes Prydein Vawr' is to be found among the prophetic poetry of the thirteenth-century *Book of Taliesin*. Its preservation in such a prestigious manuscript gives some indication of the high regard in which the poem was held in Wales by later generations.

See also Literature; Welsh People.

Further Reading

Dumville, David. 1983. 'Brittany and *Armes Prydein Vawr*'. *Etudes Celtiques* 20: 145–159.

Jarman, A. O. H. 1992. 'The Later Cynfeirdd'. Pp. 98–122 in *A Guide to Welsh Literature*, vol. 1. Edited by A. O. H. Jarman and Gwilym Rees Hughes. University of Wales Press.

Lewis, Ceri W. 1992. 'The Historical Background of Early Welsh Verse'. Pp. 11–50 in *A Guide to Welsh Literature*, vol. 1. Edited by A. O. H. Jarman and Gwilym Rees Hughes. University of Wales Press.

Williams, Ifor (ed.). 1972. *Armes Prydein: The Prophecy of Britain from the Book of Taliesin*. Dublin Institute of Advanced Studies.

Owen Thomas

Arras Culture

Located near Market Weighton, and named for the town of Arras, this group of distinctive, **Iron Age** burial sites on the Yorkshire Wolds was first excavated in the early nineteenth century. As in adjacent areas of central and western France, in Britain we have little evidence for burials during the Iron Age, in contrast to northern France and western Germany. One exception in Britain is on the Yorkshire Wolds and adjacent areas of the Vale of Pickering, the Tabular Hills and the Vale of **York**, where large numbers of distinctive burials are found, the earliest dating to the fifth century BC, the latest to the beginning of the first. The group is named after the village of Arras near Market Weighton where burials were excavated in early nineteenth century. Characteristically, the burials consist of a crouched inhumation, buried either on the ground surface (in the earlier graves) or in a pit, and this is then covered by a chalk and earthen mound, apparently originally shaped like a pyramid. Around this was dug a square ditch; in most cases, the mound has disappeared, and most sites are only known from the distinctive square enclosures visible on aerial photographs.

Most graves contain no or few grave goods, perhaps a **brooch**, a simple pot or pig bones from a joint of meat or simply half the pig's head. A small group are accompanied by two-wheeled chariots, which, though they were used in war, seem to be mainly for daily transport; they are found with both men and women. The carts may be dismantled or buried whole and are distinguished by the bronze fittings of the harness (bits and strap junctions), the yoke (terret rings) and wheel fittings (linch pins) and by the iron tyres of the wheels. Weapons are rare but can include swords as in two burials at Wetwang Slack and spears, shields and bone points at Grimthorpe or chain mail at Kirkburn. Weapons become more common in the later burials when there is also a shift to extended inhumation.

The most distinctive features of the Late **Bronze Age** to Roman period are the linear dykes forming blocks of lands, divided by ditched trackways. The burials occur singly, in small groups or as large cemeteries of up to 500 burials (Danes' Graves, Wetwang) that can by aligned along the tracks or the dykes. Settlement is scattered throughout the enclosed areas, with small roundhouses, accompanied by occasional grain storage pits, laid out along internal pathways (Wetwang). Though parts of the Wolds are best suited to pastoralism, agriculture was also important, and at Kilham and Burton Agnes, there are large numbers of storage pits, suggesting some sort of centralised communal storage. Iron smelting was important in Vale of York.

Comparisons have been made with continental burials in Champagne and western Germany. The burials of chariots, the square enclosures and the **La Tène** material culture: all this has been interpreted as evidence of an invading group. But the burial rite also differs from the continent (relative importance of pottery and weapons, crouched as against extended inhumation), and the material culture shares more with other groups in Britain than with the continent. There were certainly contacts with the continent (e.g. the importation of coral), but no more than are found in other British groups.

Further Reading

Stead, I. M. 1979. *The Arras Culture*. Yorkshire Philosophical Society.

———. 1992. *Iron Age Cemeteries in East Yorkshire*. English Heritage, Archaeological Report No. 22.

John Collis

Art and Architecture

Prehistoric

Art in Britain may be said to have begun in Britain in the Upper **Palaeolithic** Period, at a time when magnificent cave paintings were being executed in France and Spain. The only site in Britain to have produced any examples of this art is Cresswell Crags, Derbyshire, where a series of engravings on the cave walls in Church Hole date from around 13,000 years ago and include a bird, a series of superimposed animals and a stag, as well as a painting of a horse's head.

The next stage in the development of prehistoric art in Britain and Ireland was in the Neolithic Period, when abstract ornament is to be found on pottery of a type known as Grooved Ware and as carvings on stones. Although there are some designs on portable objects, such as the Folkton Drums from Yorkshire, the majority appear on stones connected with chambered tombs, and the style is accordingly termed from the type of tomb they most often decorate, Passage Grave Art. These designs are predominantly abstract patterns of spirals and zigzags, though there are some examples of stylised human faces. Some of the finest examples are to be seen in Irish passage graves on the Boyne, notably those at **Newgrange**, **Knowth** and Dowth. The style is also apparent in Britain, for example in North Wales at Barclodiad y Gawres and Dyffryn Ardudwy. This art was also on occasion carved on exposed rock faces in northern Britain, a tradition which continued through to the Bronze Age. The designs change somewhat with time and presumably also in terms of their significance – typical of the later rock carvings are 'cup and ring' marks. There are few examples of purely representational art from Neolithic Britain and Ireland, but a wooden figure from Dagenham, Essex, has been dated to this period.

Abstract art is manifest on the *lunulae* (gold collars) made by the **Beaker people** in Britain, which have patterns which seem to mirror some of those on their pottery beakers. Linear and curvilinear ornament was used on goldwork of the earlier Bronze Age, for example on the finds from Bush Barrow, Wilts, and on the gold 'pectoral' from Mold, Clwyd.

Iron Age

The Iron Age is characterised by its use of the so-called Celtic art, a term which is rather loosely applied to a tradition which displays a considerable degree of abstraction, with curvilinear patterns employing spirals, trumpets, peltas (crescentic shapes seen to resemble a type of Greek shield) and concave-sided triangles among other motifs. Celtic art developed first on the Continent, drawing upon native traditions of abstract ornament and new ideas from the Mediterranean world and further East. It was classified for the Continent into a number of styles by Paul Jacobsthal. This art coincided with the **La Tène** phase of the European Iron Age and spanned the period from the fifth century BC until **Julius Caesar**'s conquest of Gaul in the mid-first century BC. Recent writers on insular Celtic art have favoured a similar system for Britain. A numerical scheme for the earlier stages, roughly following Jacobsthal, has been adopted by Dr Ian Stead, who has recognised Styles I–V. In point of fact, the use of style labels is misleading for Celtic art, since one object may display more than one style and their usage overlaps chronologically.

Styles I and II are the counterparts of the terms called by Jacobsthal 'Early' and 'Waldalgesheim' and seem to have been inspired by some early imports. Examples include the Standlake scabbard plates and the Wandsworth scabbard chape. Style III followed

Jacobsthal's 'Plastic' and 'Sword' styles but has few direct counterparts in England.

Some scholars have not accepted, however, that any insular art was produced until the influence of what was termed on the Continent the Hungarian Sword style. One of the manifestations of Jacobsthal's 'Sword' style led to the distinctively insular Style IV. Typical of this style is asymmetrical engraved foliage ornament, often found in scabbards, though a relief-modelled version is also encountered. Good examples are the Wandsworth boss, the Torrs horns and the Witham shield. Style V is without Continental parallel but is derived from Style III. The patterns are more symmetrical, with basketry filling. One manifestation is seen on relief work, such as the famous series of **torcs** from **Snettisham**, Norfolk. Another manifestation is engraved and seen to best effect on mirror backs, such as that from Desborough, Northants.

A number of later developments take the story of Celtic art in Britain past the Roman conquest, when manifestations include the Casket style (used in the decoration of die-stamped plates for caskets and other objects) and the Brigantian and Caledonian schools, which flourished into the second century AD and employed high relief work with slender-stemmed trumpet patterns.

Romano-British Art

Art in **Roman Britain** comprises imports from other parts of the empire, items in purely Classical style, perhaps created by immigrant craftsmen, and native products which represent purely British manifestations of an art of Mediterranean origin. A great deal of art survives from Roman Britain, in a diversity of media: sculpture, metalwork, pottery and glass, wall paintings and floor mosaics.

Floor mosaic was an art of Mediterranean origin but was first employed in Roman Britain in the late first century. There are two main periods when it was particularly fashionable, in the second century and then again in the fourth, when most of the surviving mosaics were laid down. Mosaics are found in both towns and villas in the countryside. The great majority are made up of abstract patterns, but pictorial mosaics are also found. The largest assemblage is at **Fishbourne** in Sussex, where the techniques used include the rare *opus vermiculatum* (using very tiny tesserae or cubes for the inlays) and *opus sectile*, which used stone cut to different shapes. Mosaics which may have employed flowers made up from shaped pieces of stone are known from Piddington, Northants. Different mosaic schools of the fourth century have been recognised, including a Corinian (based on **Cirencester**, Glos) and a Durnovarian (based on **Dorchester**, Dorset). Among the most notable of the pictorial mosaics are some with Christian subject matter, from Hinton St Mary and **Frampton**, Dorset.

Wall painting was used in town houses, villas, forts and mausolea. Most of the designs are abstract and linear, but a number of more sophisticated schemes are apparent, such as the Christian subject matter of the wall paintings at **Lullingstone**, **Kent**, or the figural scenes from Southwell, Nottinghamshire and Sparsholt, Hants.

Most of the metalwork was probably imported and includes the hoards of silver plate from **Mildenhall**, Suffolk, **Traprain Law**, East Lothian and **Water Newton**, Cambridgeshire, all of the fourth century: the last two containing items of Christian significance. The story of the hoards of silver plate is carried into the fifth century with the **Hoxne** find, which like Water Newton also contained items of gold. Isolated items reflecting the wealth of Britain in the fourth century include the Corbridge lanx, a large silver dish. Not all metalwork was imported, however, and probably British in manufacture are a series of items of enamelled bronze, ranging from different types of **brooches**, model 'stools', belt buckles and bronze bowls. Two of these are distinguished by depicting **Hadrian's Wall** with a name for the forts, one early find, the Rudge Cup, another recently discovered in Derbyshire.

Anglo-Saxon Art: Pagan

The art of pagan Anglo-Saxon England is almost entirely confined to ornamental metalwork and the decoration of pottery; no sculpture survives from this period with the exception of a three-dimensional pottery lid from Spong Hill, Norfolk, depicting a seated human figure in fairly naturalistic form and a couple of carved whetstones from **Sutton Hoo**, Suffolk, and Hough-on-the-Hill, Lincs.

The arrival of the Anglo-Saxons in what became England was marked by new ornamental traditions. Germanic art had developed in northern Europe, particularly Scandinavia, out of late-Roman provincial styles. Some of the same models were available in late Roman Britain, displayed in particular on a series of buckles and strap attachments in what may be termed the Vermand style, named after a Frankish cemetery on which they were well represented. These items were decorated with chip-carving (a technique imitating woodworking) of animal patterns including dolphins and sea horses. The Quoit Brooch style was a British development of the Vermand style which evolved in the early fifth century, in which the most characteristic features are crouching, semi-naturalistic animals with hatched fur and double outlines, often looking back. These are arranged in processions or bands, as on the Sarre parcel-gilt Quoit brooch from Kent. The origins of the Quoit Brooch style have been vigorously debated (similar types of ornament are found on the Continent), but it is now widely believed to have been developed by fifth-century Romano-**Britons** in the south-east, from whom Quoit Brooch-style objects were traded to the neighbouring Anglo-Saxons.

Soon after the development of the Quoit Brooch style, new, purely Germanic, art styles are apparent in pagan England. The two main styles are Styles I and II, which were first defined by Bernhard Salin in his classic *Altgermanische Thierornamentik* (1904).

Style I originated in Scandinavia out of the earlier Nydam style (named after the finds from a fourth-century boat deposit). It made its appearance on the Continent around AD 475 and is found in England before the end of the fifth century. The main characteristics of Style I are the use of chip-carved patterns employing disjointed animals and human and animal masks which are employed in all-over decoration. The style was probably introduced separately from Denmark (Jutland) to Kent and from Norway to East Anglia. It is first seen in England on square-headed brooches found in Kent but was used to ornament a wide range of personal items: brooches, buckles, pins, sleeve-fasteners and mounts. It seems to have lasted through most of the sixth century.

Style II seems to have evolved soon after the middle of the sixth century, and it is characterised by the use of a snake-like creature or creatures with interlacing bodies, sometimes termed lacertines. Simple interlace without zoomorphic features is sometimes found, especially at the start of the use of Style II in England, but most Style II creations are zoomorphic, with snake-like heads. The origins of this style have been very vigorously debated; Salin believed it to have been a purely Scandinavian development out of Style I, but other later scholars have suggested input from the Late Antique world and have also suggested that it evolved separately in different areas in north-west Europe. In England, some non-zoomorphic interlace appears soon after the mid-sixth century, for example on a sword pommel from Coombe, Kent, and on a number of square-headed brooches most notably from Lincolnshire. Current opinion sees the development of Style II as an English evolution, probably under Continental influence. In East Anglia, this probably stemmed from Sweden and, elsewhere in Kent, from Frankish as well as Scandinavian contacts.

Styles I and II flourished alongside one another in the late sixth century, until Style II became dominant in the seventh. It is very apparent in the treasures from the **Sutton Hoo** ship burial in Suffolk.

The Crundale style is the third animal style to be found in pagan Anglo-Saxon England. It seems to have evolved out of Style II in the early seventh century, possibly out of an East Scandinavian version of the style, and is characterised by a compact dragonesque animal with long jaws that may bite itself or another similar creature. It takes its name from a sword pommel from Crundale Down, Kent, and is well represented in the Sutton Hoo find and on the back of a disc brooch from Faversham in Kent. It survives into Christian art, appearing in a variety of guises not just in England – it occurs for example in the ***Book of Durrow***.

Apart from these animal styles, pagan Anglo-Saxon art saw other achievements particularly in the field of abstract ornamental metalworking. From the middle of the sixth century, new metalworking techniques appeared in England, notably the use of filigree (gold-twined wire), granulation (beads of gold) and cloisonné work (the insetting of inlays in cells on a metal ground). These techniques have their origin in the East Mediterranean workshops of the Byzantine Empire but were widely taken up by the barbarian incomers in north-west Europe; cloisonné work appears in the grave of the Merovingian king Childeric at Tournai in the late fifth century, and the technique is encountered in Visigothic contexts in Italy as early as c. 450. The immediate inspiration for the Anglo-Saxon work was probably Frankish. Cloisonné work does not appear in England until around 550, when it was first employed in the decoration of Kentish disc brooches. The most ornate of these were the gold composite brooches produced in the early seventh century, which employed cloisonné settings of garnet, glass and shell, the most famous examples of which were the Kingston, the Amherst (Sarre II) and Dover brooches. The same techniques, however, were used in a variety of other objects, such as buckles, and can be seen at their finest in the Sutton Hoo treasure.

Pottery is a less accomplished art but serves to show the kind of ornamental techniques employed on a lower social level by the Anglo-Saxons. Different decorative schemes were employed on pagan Anglo-Saxon cremation urns, employing stamps to build up often quite sophisticated designs. Although the stamps were mostly geometric, more elaborate stamps were also used, depicting different animals, swastikas, etc. Some of the later cremation urns, for example those by the so-called Illington-Lackford potter, are noteworthy products of a folk art.

Anglo-Saxon Art: Christian

With the advent of Christianity in the late sixth century, the repertoire of Anglo-Saxon art is extended to manuscripts, stone sculpture, ivories and some evidence for embroideries. The arrival of **St. Augustine** in Kent in AD 597 did not result in an immediate change of direction in Anglo-Saxon art. St. Augustine, however, arrived bearing books and other items from the Christian Mediterranean, which introduced Anglo-Saxon England to the traditions of the Late Antique world. One book brought by him, *St. Augustine's Gospels*, still survives (in Corpus Christi College, Cambridge, Ms 286) and, although only a minor Italian work of the sixth century, was to prove very influential in the development of Anglo-Saxon manuscript art.

Manuscript ornamentation was probably the most notable innovation of conversion period art. During the period from the late seventh century, two distinct traditions of manuscript art flourished in England: one in the south, centred on St Augustine's foundation at **Canterbury**, and one in the north, in the kingdom of **Northumbria**. The earliest surviving decorated manuscripts are those that emanated from Northumbria, though it is usual to speak of *insular* manuscripts since provenance is often disputed and only some are certainly Northumbrian. Indeed, the two earliest manuscripts surviving are probably produced in the Irish foundation at **Iona**, off the west coast of Scotland. Undoubtedly, the earliest English manuscript is the **Durham** Cathedral A II 10, of which only twelve pages now survive, of which only two are decorated. Produced perhaps shortly before the middle of the seventh century, the ornament is very limited, one page having a design of stacked, interlace-decorated D-shapes with what are known as pelta patterns, the other with an ornate initial letter for the opening of the *Gospels of St. John*. It was produced probably at **Lindisfarne**, which became the home of a scriptorium producing the finest surviving Northumbrian manuscripts.

The most famous of these is the ***Lindisfarne Gospels***, written and decorated by the monk Eadfrith probably around 698, perhaps for the enshrinement of **St. Cuthbert** in that year. Arguably the finest achievement of Anglo-Saxon art is that it has fifteen elaborately decorated pages as well as embellishments to the text. Typical of Lindisfarne are long-legged and long-beaked birds and animals, juxtaposed with traditional 'Celtic' (i.e. Romano-British) motifs such as spirals, trumpets and three-legged patterns known as triskeles. The book is also decorated with full-page evangelist portraits, 'carpet pages' (pages of all-over ornament) and canon tables (for the concordance of events chronicled in the Gospels).

Also noteworthy is a group of Northumbrian manuscripts which comprise the *Durham Gospels* (Durham Cathedral A II 17), *Echternach Gospels* (made for the monastery at Echternach in Luxembourg) and the Corpus Christi College, Cambridge, Ms 197 (which was similar to the Echternach Gospels). All seem to have been produced by the same scribe, now dubbed the 'Durham–Echternach Calligrapher'. Besides these, a manuscript which more closely follows classical tradition also survives: the *Codex Amiatinus*, produced at Monkwearmouth or **Jarrow** for Abbot **Ceolfrith** before 716. This was one of three similar books, of which this was intended as a gift for the pope.

In the south (or Southumbria as it is sometimes termed, meaning 'area south of the Humber'), a separate tradition flourished in the eighth century. Canterbury was a major centre for manuscript production, but there were others, such as the Mercian centres at **Worcester**, **Hereford** and Lichfield.

Of the Southumbrian works, the *Stockholm Codex Aureus* was partly inspired by *St. Augustine's Gospels* and was made in Canterbury as was the Canterbury or **Vespasian Psalter**, decorated around 725. These books had more classical-looking figures than those employed in the north and drew inspiration from Oriental, Italian, Frankish and native sources for their embellishment.

A mainly Mercian group of manuscripts is that named the 'Tiberius' group, made around the beginning of the ninth century. These display distinctive, yapping animals. The 'Tiberius Bede' is one of them, the *Book of Cerne* another.

Manuscript art was disrupted by the Viking raids and settlements, but in the mid-tenth to mid-eleventh century there was a remarkable revival of manuscript art, which went hand in hand with the development of art in other media. The incentive behind this was the monastic reform movement which had originated on the Continent and was taken up in England at Winchester under **St. Dunstan** and St. Æthelwold. The movement began in the 930s and had royal support. Artistically, the movement was enriched by inspiration from the Carolingian Renaissance, with its return to Antique artistic taste. This late-Saxon movement is usually referred to as the 'Winchester school', though it was not confined to Winchester, and manifested itself in other media including stone and ivory carving and wall painting. The style is first apparent in embroideries produced by southern English needlewomen as a gift for the shrine of St Cuthbert at Chester-le-Street, County Durham, and was probably presented to the shrine in 934. In manuscript art, however, it is first displayed in a copy of **Bede**'s *Life of Cuthbert* now in Cambridge, perhaps also made for the shrine of the saint and presented in the same year. This has a picture showing the king (**Æthelstan**) presenting a copy of the book to the saint, set in a frame employing the Carolingian motif of acanthus foliage, ultimately of classical inspiration. Rather lighter in style is a sketch in St. Dunstan's own notebook, now of the Bodleian library in Oxford (Ms Auct.f. 4. 32), showing the saint kneeling at the foot of Christ. The penmanship is superb and heralds a long tradition of English drawing which lasted into the later Middle Ages and beyond.

The finest Winchester manuscript is probably the Benedictional of St. Aethelwold, decorated soon after 971 by a scribe called Godeman and intended perhaps to mark the translation of the relics of St. Swithun in Winchester. It is richly coloured, with abundant use of gold and silver, and relates to various feasts. It is without parallel on the Continent. Related to it are the Benedictional of Archbishop Robert and the Grimbald Gospels, written and illuminated by a scribe called Aedui Bassan.

Later, 'Winchester school' manuscripts continue two traditions of decoration, lightly coloured drawings following the tradition started by St. Dunstan's drawing of Christ and more richly coloured and painterly works, following the trend manifested in the Benedictional of St. Aethelwold. Of the former, both the Ramsey Psalter (Harley Manuscript 2904) and the Harley Psalter (Harley Manuscript 603) stand out.

Not surprisingly, little painting other than in manuscripts survives (though a number of stone sculptures still retain traces of the paint that once adorned them), but fragmentary Winchester school paintings survive from Winchester cathedral and from Nether Wallop, Hants.

With the possible exception of a limited amount of decoration found in a couple of early Kentish churches, Anglo-Saxon sculpture first developed in Northumbria in the late seventh century. This work was essentially architectural and is to be found at Hexham, Monwearmouth and Jarrow. The inspiration seems to have been from Frankish Gaul and perhaps Italy, and the ornament was mostly inanimate, with the exception of some animals from Hexham where they seem to have been employed in friezes. Around AD 700, other types of sculpture can be discerned in Northumbria, of which most notable are some grave markers (such as the Herebericht stone at Monkwearmouth and some other simple monuments from **York**, Hartlepool and Lindisfarne).

Around 725–750, Northumbrian sculptors began erecting elaborately ornamented free-standing crosses, the first of their kind in Europe. Outstanding are the **Ruthwell Cross** (in Dumfriesshire, now in Scotland) and the **Bewcastle Cross** (in **Cumbria**), though other notable monuments include Acca's Cross at Hexham. Once established, crosses continued to be erected in Northumbria through the early medieval period. Slightly later, the custom of erecting stone crosses spread to **Mercia**, where again the custom continued throughout the early Middle Ages. One of the earliest Mercian crosses is a fragmentary example from Repton, Derbyshire, with a mailed rider on the front and a human-headed serpent on the side, swallowing the heads of two humans. The same tradition does not seem to have caught on to the same extent in the south – there are a few isolated monuments, such as the Winchester-influenced Reculver Cross from Kent or crosses from Winchester and Gloucester, which date from the tenth century. Of exceptional merit is the cross-shaft from Codford St. Peter in Wiltshire.

Eighth- and ninth-century crosses were erected under the patronage of major monasteries, to which were sometimes attached workshops. In the tenth century, secular patronage became increasingly important in the Anglo-Scandinavian areas, and the aristocracy of the Viking Age was enthusiastic about endowing local churches. Northumbrian crosses of this period far outnumber those of the pre-Viking Age and display a hybrid Anglo-Scandinavian art.

In Mercia, the earlier tradition of architectural sculpture continued with the carving of friezes in churches, most notably at Breedon on the Hill in Leicestershire where the growing influence of Carolingian art is apparent; the Breedon sculptures date mostly from the ninth century and influences upon them may include designs based on Syrian textiles acquired by King **Offa**. Also distinctive is a stone shrine tomb (a solid block replica of a house-shaped shrine) known as the Headda Stone, now in Peterborough cathedral and dated to the later ninth century. Other such block shrines from Mercia include examples from Bakewell and Wirksworth in Derbyshire.

In **Wessex**, the Winchester school tradition seen in manuscripts is also apparent in sculpture. A flying angel in the style can be seen at Bradford-on-Avon, Wilts, and the same motif occurs at Winterborne Steepleton, Dorset. Other sculptures in the Winchester style include a fine rood at Romsey Abbey, Hants.

Conversion to Christianity had little immediate effect on metalworking traditions, but techniques used in the creation of gold and garnet jewellery in the pagan period were additionally turned to the production of specifically Christian objects, such as the Ixworth Cross from Suffolk, St. Cuthbert's Pectoral Cross from his grave in County Durham and the Westgate, Canterbury pendant from Kent. Gold (previously derived from melted-down Merovingian coins), however, became increasingly much rarer, and few items of goldwork survive from the later part of the Christian period, the most notable dating from the ninth century and comprising a plaque from Brandon, Norfolk and the **Alfred** and Minster Lovell Jewels, the two probably from aestals or reading pointers, the former made on the orders of Alfred the Great.

The Crundale style of animal continued to be used in the Christian period, but in Mercia a new type of animal with long legs and yapping mouth similar to those seen in manuscripts are to be found, the best example being on a linked pin set from the river Witham in Lincolnshire. Similar creatures can be seen on a brooch from Flixborough, South Humberside.

Some outstanding pieces of ecclesiastical metalwork survive from the late eighth and ninth centuries, several from the Continent where they were spared the Viking raids. Several of these show strong Carolingian features and may have been made abroad by craftsmen trained in English workshops. They include the Tassilo Chalice, with gilt chip-carving and a depiction of Christ, from Kresmünster, Austria, dated to 777–778, the cover of the Lindau Gospels and the Rupertus Cross from Bischofhofen in Austria.

A new type of small, contorted creature developed on metalwork of the ninth century. The style of this metalwork is distinctive and known as Trewhiddle after a find made in **Cornwall** coin dated to c. 868 which included both ecclesiastical and apparently secular objects. The Trewhiddle style is found on occasion on gold and frequently on copper alloy, but it is best represented on silverwork where the ground was inlaid with niello, a silver sulphide paste which contrasted black against the silver ground. The use of silver and niello at an earlier (late-eighth-century) stage is well exemplified by the Fetter Lane sword pommel from London. The developed Trewhiddle style is found on a series of strap ends, many of them copper alloy but originally probably silvered or tinned. In a related style is a series of swords with silver mounts.

The earlier tradition of circular brooch production continued in later **Saxon** England and is well exemplified by a hoard of brooches from Pentney, Norfolk, which date from the early ninth century and display relatives of the animals found on the Witham pins, and the magnificent Fuller Brooch, executed in silver and decorated with personifications of the five senses which dates from the latter part of the same century.

A number of important ivory carvings survive from Anglo-Saxon England, among the earliest of which is the **Franks Casket**, a whalebone box with sophisticated iconography taken from both pagan and Christian sources. This dates from the earlier eighth century. The Brunswick Casket is a late-eighth-century reliquary box produced probably in East Anglia, which displays in ivory features of Mercian art. Late-Saxon ivories include a noteworthy group in the Winchester tradition.

Organic materials do not survive well, but surviving examples include St. Cuthbert's wooden coffin, decorated with Christ and figures of saints, and a boxwood reliquary casket, now in the Cleveland Museum of Art, Ohio. Leatherwork is well exemplified by the cover of the Stonyhurst Gospels, originally buried with St. Cuthbert. Mention has already been made of the embroideries produced for St. Cuthbert's shrine, and other manifestations of the art of Anglo-Saxon needlewomen include these, and a few other works such as the Maaseik embroideries, now in Belgium and dating from the eighth century, serve as a reminder of how much must now be lost.

Anglo-Saxon Architecture: Secular

The architecture of the pagan Anglo-Saxons was in timber, and nothing of it survives above ground. A variety of timber-framed buildings were constructed, ranging from sunken-floor huts (***grubenhäuser***) to more substantial rectilinear halls, well exemplified by excavated examples from Chalton (Hants), Catholme, Staffs, Cowdery's Down, Hants and West Stow (Suffolk).

Secular architecture in the Christian period remained mostly of timber construction. Sunken-floor huts were still constructed until the end of the period, but they were comparatively rare, the majority of buildings being of larger rectilinear plan, with post-hole or post in beam-slot construction predominating. Few secular buildings survive in the archaeological record from the Middle Saxon period (i.e. c. AD 600–800), though some are known from Maxey, Northamptonshire, and from North Elmham, Norfolk. In Northumbria, however, there is an important royal complex at **Yeavering**, in use during the late sixth and early seventh century. The structures at Yeavering began with an enclosure conjectured as a cattle compound, of uncertain date, outside which were a series of halls which were progressively enlarged, the largest being 82 feet × 39 feet (25 metres × 12 metres) with huge timbers set in foundation trenches 7 feet (2 metres) deep. The site also possessed a 'grandstand', shaped like the segment of a circle, with tiers of seats and a small stage. This is so far unique in England. Other royal halls are mostly known from aerial photography, but one later complex has been excavated at Cheddar, Somerset, which was known to have been used by a succession of kings in the tenth century. The first constructional phase, dated to the ninth century, comprised a two-storey hall in an enclosure with subsidiary buildings. In the time of Æthelstan in the 930s, the original storm-water ditch was extended and an eastern façade of fence and ditch was constructed with a gateway and free-standing pole. A new hall was built, with further subsidiary buildings and a stone-built royal chapel. There was further rebuilding in the tenth to eleventh century.

Stone was rarely employed in Anglo-Saxon secular architecture, but at Northampton a large eighth-century timber hall was replaced in the ninth by a stone one, which seems to reflect Carolingian influence and royal patronage. First seen as a palace, it is now interpreted as more probably associated with a monastic complex. A series of huge cement mixers were located adjacent to it. Other evidence of late-Saxon stone building in a secular context comes from Sulgrave (Northamptonshire).

A timber horizontal watermill of the ninth century has been excavated at Tamworth, Staffs, perhaps connected with a Mercian palace complex there. Urban buildings are generally similar to those in the countryside, a good series having been excavated at Thetford, Norfolk, but a distinctive group is characteristic of York, where at Coppergate a series of Anglo-Scandinavian structures were excavated with wattle-filled or plank-built walls. These were up to 13 feet (4 metres) wide and over 26 feet (8 metres) long. Viking-period longhouses with stone footings are known from Ribblehead, North Yorkshire, Simy Folds (County Durham) and Bryant's Gill (**Cumbria**).

Anglo-Saxon Architecture: Ecclesiastical

Ecclesiastical architecture in England begins with the arrival of St. Augustine in 597. He initiated a programme of building, possibly assisted by Gaulish masons. The first group of churches to be built had a nave and chancel with a stilted apse, the latter separated from the nave by a chancel arch. Flanking nave and chancel were side chapels known as *porticus* which were sacristies and, in the case of those flanking the nave, were used for burials as burial was prohibited in the body of the church. Roman building materials were reused in the earliest churches, where available. Classic examples are St Peter and Paul's, St Pancras's and St Mary's, all within the confines of St Augustine's Abbey in Canterbury, the earliest structure underlying Canterbury cathedral, Reculver and Minster (also Kent) and Bradwell-on-Sea, Essex. The formative influence behind these churches was essentially Mediterranean. An early outlier of the Kentish group does not have a stilted apse and was built by Kenwahl at Winchester around 648.

With the spread of the Kentish mission to Northumbria, where Christianity was already established as an offshoot of Iona, churches were built that differed from the Kentish group and seem more directly influenced by Gaul. These were buildings with long, tall naves and small, rectangular-ended chancels; some had *porticus*. The classic examples are those founded by **Benedict Biscop** at Monwearmouth and Jarrow (County Durham) and **Wilfrid** at Hexham and Ripon, where crypts were constructed. An undocumented but good example of the early Northumbrian type of church is at Escomb, County Durham, which displays the reuse of building materials from Hadrian's Wall and which gives its name to a type of construction using quoins placed alternately upright and flat in openings – 'long and short work'.

The period from c. 750 to c. 950 has caused some debate among architectural historians, as for a long time it was believed that little building was carried out during the period of the Viking raids. It is now, however, apparent that some buildings attributed to other periods may belong to this horizon, such as the aisled basilican building at Brixworth, Northamptonshire (once believed to be seventh century but now re-attributed to the later eighth), St Mary's, Wareham, Dorset (dated to c. 800), and excavated churches at **Cirencester** and Canterbury cathedral, where the earlier church was rebuilt around 810. Basilican plans were probably the result of Carolingian influence.

Late-Saxon churches often display architectural features such as pilaster strips (raised bands of stone) which are now seen to have begun earlier, probably in the ninth century. In ninth-century Mercia, a number of important churches were built or underwent major rebuilding, such as the complex multi-period site at Deerhurst, Glos, part of the present church at Repton, Derbys (where the crypt probably started out as a mausoleum), and St Oswald's in Gloucester.

The Winchester monastic reform of the tenth century saw renewed building activity, though few structures that belong to this phase survive to any extent above ground. Of the churches known to have been built or partly rebuilt at this time mention may be made of the Old Minster, Winchester, Romsey Abbey and the Lincolnshire church of Barton-upon-Humber.

The period from the late tenth to the twelfth century was one of active church building, the traditions lasting past the Norman Conquest to survive alongside the new Romanesque. Many parish churches were built in stone for the first time. A feature of this period was the construction of sophisticated churches with Westworks on the Continental model: this seems to have been the case with the excavated churches of the Old Minster, Winchester, and Canterbury cathedral. The same feature may be noted at Sherborne, Dorset.

Celtic Art

Celtic art of the early Christian period began as a continuation of that of Roman Britain. During the fifth and sixth centuries, most of the evidence for it comprises brooches and pins, displaying a limited range of ornamental devices already present in later Roman Britain and a series of bronze hanging bowls ornamented with escutcheons, frequently enamelled, of which the most noteworthy designs are those involving triskeles (three-legged designs) made up of confronted trumpets.

The impact of Christianity resulted in the appearance of manuscripts, the earliest surviving examples of which were probably produced by Irish monks in the Italian monastery of Bobbio; the ornament on these is very restricted, as is that in the earliest surviving Irish manuscript, the Cathach of **St. Columba**, produced probably in Iona in the early seventh century. The only ornament in this is decorative initials, but by the time the ***Book of Durrow*** was produced, probably also on Iona, the range of ornament was extended to pages with evangelist symbols and carpet pages. Durrow is closely related to the far more sumptuous ***Book of Kells***, which though started on Iona may have been finished at **Kells** in Ireland after monks from Iona fled there following Viking raids. Produced probably in the late eighth century for the enshrinement of St. Columba, it was very influential on later art. Between Durrow and Kells, a number of small books were produced for personal devotion, known as 'pocket gospels'. These include the *Book of Dimma* and the *Book of Mulling*. After Kells, there were relatively few manuscripts of major note, the ***Book of Armagh*** showing some features in common with Kells, and the *Book of MacRegol* (early ninth century), the *Book of MacDurnan* (c. 900) and the Cotton Psalter (early tenth century) being the most notable. Little manuscript art survives from Scotland or Wales, but the Psalter of Rhygyfach (or Ricemarch) was illuminated by a Welsh scribe at Llanbadarn Fawr around 1079, and the ***Book of Deer*** may well have been produced by a not very artistic Pict in the tenth century. In the twelfth century, there was something of a late *floruit* of manuscript art, revitalised by Viking and English art, of which the Corpus Missal and Cormac's Psalter are noteworthy examples.

From the early seventh century, Celtic ornamental metalwork became very much more elaborate, much of it now produced under the patronage of the Church. Although there is a certain amount of Pictish metalwork, ranging from that represented in some early silver hoards and the fine **Monymusk reliquary** through to a series of superb silver brooches produced around AD 800 and represented along with other items in the **St Ninian's Isle**, Shetland hoard, most of this metalwork is Irish. There is growing evidence for some metalwork in Wales, but none of it is particularly fine. Irish metalwork reached an apogee in the eighth century, to which time some of the pieces in a series of hoards can be ascribed. The finest is perhaps the Ardagh hoard, which contained the **Ardagh Chalice**, one of the finest pieces of metalwork to survive from early medieval Europe, followed by the **Derrynaflan** and Donore hoards, the first of which takes the story of metalworking into the later ninth century. Eighth- to ninth-century Irish metalwork was influenced by techniques and ornament derived from Anglo-Saxon England as well as from a native past. Other major pieces of metalwork from this 'golden age' include the Moylough Belt shrine, the Rinnigan Crucifixion Plaque and the recently discovered Tully Lough Cross. Metalworking was disrupted by the Viking raids in the ninth century, and work tended to be coarser, but a number of crosiers in particular can be used to trace development of styles. These include the Crozier of Cú Dúilig, also known as the Kells or British Museum Crozier, which like many pieces of Celtic ecclesiastical metalwork in multi-period, its final form dating from the late tenth century. In the eleventh and twelfth centuries, there was a resurgence in ornamental **metalworking**, stimulated by Viking art, in particular by the Ringerike and Urnes styles. The first centre responsible for the production of this metalwork was Kells, followed soon after by **Clonmacnois** and possibly Roscommon. Major pieces of metalwork from this phase include the **Shrine of St Patrick's Bell**, the **Lismore Crosier**, the Shrine of St Lachtin's Arm and the Cross of Cong.

Sculpture in the Celtic lands begins with the series of enigmatic symbol stones, with incised designs carved by the **Picts**. These seem to be pre-Christian in origin and perhaps owe something to Roman traditions of carving. The earliest seem to date from the sixth if not the fifth century. With the advent of Christianity, various inscribed stones are found. An important group is the recumbent cross-slabs, of which 800–900 have been recorded, with a rich collection from **Clonmacnois**. None, however, is probably earlier than the eighth century. In Scotland, a similar series of crosses may start with a group from Iona, one of which has been argued to belong to the late seventh century. Free-standing cross-slabs are found in both Ireland and Scotland. A few, with false relief work such as that at Reask, County Kerry, may date from seventh or even late sixth century, but most are later. The fine series of free-standing High Crosses of Ireland date from the early ninth century onwards, starting with a group of limited figural ornament from County Offaly, including the crosses at Ahenny, then continuing in the later ninth and tenth centuries with a series of complex figural iconographical schemes, of which the crosses at Kells, Clonmacnois and **Monasterboice** are the most important. Slightly earlier, High Crosses had appeared on Iona at the end of the eighth century, with St Orans and St John's Crosses and with an outlier at Kilnave on Islay. Outside **Dalriada**, the free-standing cross was not popular, and instead Pictish sculptors favoured relief-decorated cross-slabs, some still bearing Pictish symbols. These slabs are all, or almost all, of the ninth and tenth centuries and thus represent a parallel development to the High Cross in Ireland. In Wales, there is a certain amount of sculpture from the ninth century but little displays of figural work. Viking influence led to the production of a notable series of sculptures in the **Isle of Man** and south-west Scotland.

Celtic Architecture

No secular architecture survives above ground in Celtic areas, and our knowledge of houses is confined to plans recovered in excavation. **Brittonic Age** (fifth to sixth century) buildings tend to be small rectangular or sub-rectangular structures of stone or (more often) timber, though the large timber complex at **Wroxeter** shows that classical architectural forms could survive in Romanised areas of Britain. The earliest ecclesiastical architecture is similarly only known from archaeology and mostly comprises small timber-built oratories or chapels, usually in the proportions of 3:2, with a door in one of the short sides. A classic example is at Church Island, County Kerry (where it was replaced by a stone chapel). Stone structures are first mentioned in documentary sources in Ireland in the early eighth century, the first recorded being that at Duleek documented in 724. Thereafter, references are more frequent, becoming common in the eleventh and twelfth centuries. Scientific dating has assigned a corbelled stone oratory at Illaunloughan to a date between 640 and 790, which seems to have had a stone and two turf predecessors, while at Croagh Patrick a large stone oratory existed, probably corbelled, in the seventh century. Early surviving stone chapels are unicameral and small, with stone roofs, and display such features as cyclopean masonry, inwardly inclined door jambs and projecting antae at the front, probably to support large barge boards. Corbelling is a feature of stone roofs, the most famous example being at **Gallarus Oratory** in County Kerry. A good, early example of a surviving church is St Columba's House at Kells, which probably dates from the early ninth century. This has a steep stone roof with a relieving arch. St Kevin's Kitchen at **Glendalough** started out as a simple building, but a chancel and sacristy with stone roofs were added and a round tower was added to the west gable.

Stone beehive corbelled structures exist in Ireland in both secular and ecclesiastical contexts. Known as clochans, the earliest may date from the eighth century, but most are later, some probably of relatively modern date. The classic examples can be seen in the monastery of **Skellig Michael**, off the coast of Kerry. Also distinctive of Ireland are round towers, which are isolated structures in monastic complexes, with a single door above ground level and timber floors originally reached by ladders. They are first documented in the tenth century, but most date from later, mainly the twelfth century. There are outliers at St Patrick's Isle, Peel, Isle of Man, and at Abernethy and Brechin in Scotland.

3. An early Christian monastic outpost on the Skellig Michael Island, Waterville, Ireland.

Outside Ireland, there is very little evidence for ecclesiastical stone building before the twelfth century, though a Pictish stone church has been identified in the crypt of the later church at **Portmahomack** dating from the eighth century. Other stone church remains found belong to the tenth century and later.

See also Literature.

Further Reading

Backhouse, J., et al. 1984. *The Golden Age of Anglo-Saxon Art.* British Museum Press.

Fernie, E. 1983. *The Architecture of the Anglo-Saxons.* Batsford.

Henig, M. 1995. *The Art of Roman Britain.* Batsford.

Jope, E. M. 2000. *Early Celtic Art in the British Isles.* Clarendon Press.

Laing, Jennifer. 1997. *Art and Society in Roman Britain.* Alan Sutton.

Laing, Lloyd. 2006. *The Archaeology of Celtic Britain and Ireland, c. AD 400–1200.* Cambridge University Press.

Laing, Lloyd, and Jennifer Laing. 1992. *Art of the Celts.* Thames & Hudson.

———. 1995. *Celtic Britain and Ireland, Art and Society.* Herbert Press.

———. 1996. *Early English Art and Architecture.* Alan Sutton.

Megaw, Ruth, and Vincent Megaw. 1989. *Celtic Art, from Its Beginnings to the Book of Kells.* Thames & Hudson.

Powell, T. G. E. 1966. *Prehistoric Art.* Thames & Hudson.

Sandars, N. K. 1965. *Prehistoric Art in Europe.* Penguin.

Stead, I. M. 1996. *Celtic Art.* British Museum Press.

Taylor, H. M., and J. Taylor. 1965–1968. *Anglo-Saxon Architecture*, 3 vols. Cambridge University Press.
Toynbee, J. M. C. 1964. *Art in Britain Under the Romans*. Clarendon Press.
Webster, L., and J. Backhouse. 1991. *The Making of England: Anglo-Saxon Art and Culture, AD 600–900*. British Museum Press.
Wilson, D. M. 1984. *Anglo-Saxon Art*. Thames & Hudson.

Lloyd Laing

Arthur

Arthur was the legendary king of the **Britons**, founder of the Round Table, husband of Guinevere and disciple of **Merlin**. He is depicted as a mighty British warrior in medieval Welsh literature and as the ideal Christian monarch in medieval French romances of Chrétien de Troyes and in Thomas Malory's English epic *Morte D' Arthur*. Books, films and Internet sites continue to speculate about his origins and deeds. But was there a real, historical person behind the literary figure?

A historical Arthur remains a possibility, but good evidence is lacking. The name Arthur may be British in origin (*arth* is the modern Welsh word for bear) or it may be a vernacular version of the Latin name Artorius. The first written accounts of Arthur's deeds – the sparse ***Annales Cambriae*** ('Welsh Annals') and the fabulous ***Historia Brittonum*** ('History of the Britons') – were produced in the ninth and tenth centuries AD, some 300 years after the date given for Arthur's death (537 in the *Annales Cambriae*). A casual reference to Arthur in the Welsh bardic poem '**Y Gododdin**' may be older (the poem was probably composed c. 600), but it did not appear in written form until the thirteenth century. There is simply no primary source evidence for Arthur's existence. **Gildas**, a fellow Briton writing in the early sixth century, does not mention Arthur, nor does **Bede**, writing his famous history two centuries later but using Gildas and other primary sources. Without contemporary records, historians have not been able to make a very strong case for Arthur.

In 1191, monks at **Glastonbury** Abbey excavated their ancient cemetery and uncovered a remarkable grave. Inside a hollowed-out log coffin were the bones of a large man and a woman whose golden hair was still intact. A lead cross near the grave bore the Latin inscription: *Hic iacet sepultus inclitus rex Arturius in insula Avalonia* ('Here lies buried the famous King Arthur in the Isle of **Avalon**'). Had this excavation been without controversy, there would not be much of a mystery about Arthur and Avalon. But the Glastonbury monks knew what they were looking for – a bard had allegedly 'tipped off' their patron, King **Henry II** – and finding Arthur's bones was expected to bring in revenues from pilgrims to help pay for rebuilding at the Abbey. The book that had made Arthur famous throughout Europe – **Geoffrey of Monmouth**'s *History of the Kings of Britain* (written in 1136) – was by then being roundly criticised by contemporary scholars. Moreover, modern scholars have concluded that the letter forms on the inscribed cross (now lost, along with the bones) are too late to belong to the era in which Arthur allegedly lived, and many now accuse the monks of having pulled off a brilliant hoax.

Devious or not, the Glastonbury monks were the first to look for material evidence for clues to Arthur's existence. The search for Camelot fascinated early antiquarians, who recorded Arthurian associations with sites like **South Cadbury** in Somerset. But with the development of modern archaeology in the twentieth century, new and compelling evidence concerning what came to be called 'the Age of Arthur' (the fifth and sixth centuries) began to emerge. The first discovery was at **Tintagel**, **Cornwall**, the site of Arthur's birth in Geoffrey's *History*. Excavations revealed, beneath the later Norman castle, the remains of several small buildings of stone and slate associated with thousands of pottery sherds. Though the structures were unremarkable, the pottery was evidence of a fifth- to sixth-century trade in luxury goods between Britain and the Mediterranean. Moreover, excavation in 1998 uncovered a slate bearing the inscription PATER/COLI AVI FICIT/ARTOGNOV ('Artognou, father of a descendant of Coll, has had [this] made'). Although this is not evidence for a historical Arthur (ARTOGNOV represents the Welsh name Arthnou), it *is* evidence for Latin literacy in a secular context at Tintagel in the fifth or sixth century. Subsequent excavations at South Cadbury, Glastonbury Tor, and numerous **hillforts** in western and northern Britain yielded more imported pottery and evidence of military and industrial use.

Despite this flurry of archaeological activity, however, nothing has been found which is explicitly identified with a historical

4. King Arthur and his Court, on vellum, fourteenth century.

Arthur. Still, a veritable industry of Arthur books has taken off in Britain and America. These detective-like tales posit candidates for *the* Arthur which include the second-century Roman general **Lucius Artorius Castus**; the Breton warlord Riothamus; an obscure Welsh king of **Gwynedd**; and one Artuir, son of the Scottish king **Aedán mac Gabráin**. While these theories rest on later medieval written evidence, some scholars have suggested that Arthur's roots lay in prehistoric ritual, classical mythology or medieval folklore. Still other scholars are entirely sceptical, seeing Arthur as non-historical and more than a bit distracting to serious study of the history of early medieval Britain.

This quest to possess a piece of Arthur is nothing new. Richard the Lionheart gave to a crusading companion a sword alleged to be Excalibur, while Henry VIII showed Emperor Charles V the *real* Round Table hanging in Winchester Castle (though it bore a painted likeness of Henry himself). Both English and Welsh princes used Merlin's prophecies about Arthur to support their own political aims, and latter-day bards such as Spenser and Tennyson wrote new tales about Arthur to magnify the glories of reigning monarchs. It seems destined that the once and future king is to be dug up and debated over by each new generation.

See also Literature.

Further Reading

Alcock, Leslie. 1971. *Arthur's Britain*. Penguin.

Dumville, David. 1977. 'Sub-Roman Britain: History and Legend'. *History* 62: 173–192.

Green, Thomas. 'The Historicity and Historicisation of Arthur', http://www.arthuriana.co.uk/historicity/arthur.htm (cited 1 January 2006).

Higham, N. J. 2003. *King Arthur: Myth-Making and History*. Routledge.

Lacy, Norris J., Geoffrey Ashe and Deborah N. Mancoff. 1997. *The Arthurian Handbook*. Garland.

Snyder, Christopher A. 2000. *The World of King Arthur*. Thames & Hudson.

———. 2006. 'Arthurian Origins'. Pp.1–18 in *A History of Arthurian Scholarship*. Edited by Norris J. Lacy. Boydell & Brewer.

White, Richard (ed.). 1999. *King Arthur in Legend and History*. Routledge.

Christopher A. Snyder

Arthurian Legend

See Arthur.

Asser (d.908/909)

Asser was a Welsh monk, bishop of Sherborne and author of the *Vita Ælfredi Regis* ('Life of King Alfred'). Much of what we know about

Asser comes from autobiographical asides in the *Vita*. He tells us that he was 'raised, educated, tonsured and, eventually, ordained' at **St David**'s, a monastery in **Dyfed** in the farthest reaches of south-western Wales. A kinsman of a bishop of St David's, Asser may have been that monastery's bishop in 885 when King **Alfred** first summoned him to his court. With the approval of his fellow monks, Asser agreed to serve in Alfred's household for six months out of each year. Over the next few years, King Alfred bestowed upon Asser two monasteries in Somerset, Banwell and Congresbury, and, sometime later, a far larger monastery in Exeter with its various dependencies in Cornwall and Devonshire. Sometime between 892 and 900, Asser succeeded Bishop Wulfsige in the see of Sherborne. He survived into the reign of Alfred's son, Edward the Elder, and died in 908 or 909.

Asser was among the court scholars who helped Alfred translate Gregory the Great's *Pastoral Care* into English and (less certainly) Boethius's *Consolation of Philosophy*. He wrote the *Vita* in 893 at a time of crisis when Alfred was fighting off a second Viking invasion of his kingdom. Much of the historical information in the *Vita* derives from the ***Anglo-Saxon Chronicle***, which had been 'published' only a few months before Asser began writing. Indeed, the first half of the work consists mainly of a Latin translation of the *Anglo-Saxon Chronicle*'s account of the years 851–887. Asser added to this a personal account of the king's efforts to revive learning, restore religion and administer his realm justly, while fighting to preserve it from 'pagan' invaders.

The authenticity of Asser's *Vita* has been challenged, most recently by Alfred Smyth, but the consensus among historians is that it is an authentic and invaluable source for the reign of King Alfred. It is also a problematic text that must be used critically. There is no extent medieval manuscript of the *Vita*. An early eleventh-century copy, at least twice removed from the original, survived until 1731, when it was destroyed in the fire that ravaged the priceless Anglo-Saxon collection of Sir Robert Cotton. All modern editions of the *Vita* are reconstructions based on early modern transcripts of the lost Cotton MS Otho A.xii, checked against excerpts of the work incorporated into Byrhtferth of Ramsey's historical miscellany (c.1000) and two chronicles compiled in the second quarter of the twelfth century, John of Worcester's *Chronicle from Chronicles* and the so-called *Annals of St. Neots*.

The *Vita*'s loose organisation, repetitions, inconsistent use of verb tenses and lack of conclusion suggest a work in progress rather than a polished text. But the greatest stumbling block to the historian is the nature of the work itself. Asser's *Life of King Alfred* is not a biography in the modern sense. Asser did not strive for historical accuracy and objectivity. Underlying Asser's image of Alfred are received models: Biblical exemplars of virtuous kingship, Solomon and David in particular; Carolingian mirrors for princes; and, most importantly, the teachings and personal example of Pope Gregory the Great. Asser explicitly shaped his presentation of the king's life, actions and character along the lines of Einhard's *Life of Charlemagne*, just as Einhard modelled his biography on Suetonius's Augustus.

The *Vita* was intended as a celebration of Alfred's greatness for the edification of its multiple audiences: the monks of St David's, the royal court, the king's sons and, first and foremost, Alfred himself, to whom the work was dedicated. Asser's Alfred is presented as a model of ninth-century Christian king: a lover of wisdom, truthful, patient, munificent in gift-giving, just, a defender of the poor and weak, incomparably affable, intimate with his friends, faithful to his God and a victorious warrior in a holy war.

See also Literature; Wessex.

Further Reading

Abels, Richard. 1998. *Alfred the Great: War, Kingship and Culture in Anglo-Saxon England*. Longman.

Campbell, James. 1986. 'Asser's Life of Alfred'. Pp.115–135 in *The Inheritance of Historiography 350–900*. Edited by Christopher Holdsworth and T. P. Whiteman. Exeter University Press.

Galbraith, V. H. 1964. 'Who Wrote Asser's Life of Alfred?' Pp.88–126 in *An Introduction to the Study of History*. Edited by V. H. Galbraith. C. A. Watts.

Keynes, Simon. 1996. 'On the Authenticity of Asser's *Life of King Alfred*'. *Journal of Ecclesiastical History* 47: 529–551.

Keynes, Simon, and Michael Lapidge. 1983. *Alfred the Great: Asser's Life of King Alfred and Other Contemporary Sources*. Penguin.

Smyth, Alfred P. 2002. *The Medieval Life of King Alfred the Great: A Translation and Commentary on the Text Attributed to Asser*. Palgrave.

———. 1995. *Alfred the Great*. Oxford University Press.

Stevenson, W. H. (ed.). 1904. *Asser's Life of King Alfred*. Oxford University Press.

Whitelock, Dorothy. 1968. *The Genuine Asser*. Stenton Lecture 1967. University of Reading.

Richard Abels

Atrebates

The *Atrebates* were a Belgic client kingdom of **Roman Britain** who had **Iron Age** origins, and their original territory seems to have consisted of the modern counties of Surrey, West Sussex, Hampshire and parts of Wiltshire, though the borders would fluctuate. Their ceramic traditions (e.g. saucepan pots) have suggested that there was some kind of cultural unity in place in the Atrebatic territory going back to the second or third century BC, from which three zones developed: an eastern group of the Sussex coastal plains and Downs, a southern group of the rest of Sussex and Hampshire and a northern group which was centred on the Salisbury Plain and the edge of the Thames valley, implying possible political fragmentation thereafter.

Whether or not the British kingdom was the result of a population movement by their Gaulish counterparts has been debated, though there may have been some intrusive Belgic element with Commius's arrival in c. 30 BC to join his Atrebatic people already established in Britain. Inscribed coinage and references by Roman sources can provide broad outlines of their politics, which due to commercial and cultural contacts with the continent appear to have developed into a strong socio-political unit. Such coin portraits include Commius's sons Tincommius, king of the south British *Atrebates* c. 25 BC to AD 5, Verica, and Eppillus, who represent well the British rulers' aspirations of cultural equality with Rome. The distribution of Commius's coins suggest that, at its greatest extent, his kingdom stretched from Beachy Head to the Salisbury Avon and from the Berkshire Downs to the Channel coast, though during Verica's reign (c. 25 BC) the **Silchester** region was lost to the ***Catuvellauni***, and after the Roman invasion, the kingdom was split into the *civitas Regnensium*, *civitas Atrebatum* and *civitas Belgarum*, with capitals at **Chichester**, Silchester and Winchester, respectively, resulting in a greatly shrunken realm. Its overall central weakness, as well as possible wealth, can be gauged by the numerous coin hoards minted by local leaders that have been found within the territory, probably a reward for its crucial buffer position against the hostile south-west ***Durotriges*** and ***Dobunni*** tribes. Why exactly the artificial *civitas* creation was imposed on the old tribal structure is uncertain, though it may have been to isolate those *Atrebates* who had shown opposition.

A difference in settlement type after the imperial invasion can be detected, and while there was continuous occupation of **hillforts** (e.g. **Danebury**) especially in East Sussex, they were abandoned overall and replaced by ***oppida*** in West Sussex and Hampshire, implying anti- and pro-Roman factions, respectively. The northern part of the kingdom, which had realigned with the *Catuvellauni* while the eastern became associated with the Kentish tribes, had its nucleus at Silchester (*Calleva Atrebatum)*, becoming the capital of the Atrebatic *civitas*. Industries included numerous potteries around the settlement at Farnham, where later Roman villas were also plentiful. Burial rites in Atrebatic territory were varied, with inhumations clustered in the south (e.g. Owslebury) and cremation in the north (e.g. Marlborough), as well as **Romano-Celtic temples** and rural shrines all over. The *civitas* continued until the end of the Roman period and the coming of the **Saxons** in the fifth and sixth centuries.

See also Coinage and Trade.

Further Reading

Bean, S. C. 2000. *The Coinage of the Atrebates and Regni*. Oxford University School of Archaeology.
Cunliffe, Barry. 1973. *The Regni*. Duckworth.
———. 2005. *Iron Age Communities of Britain* (4th edn.). RKP.

Anne Sassin

Attacotti

The *Attacotti* were a tribal group that raided **Roman Britain** and beyond in the late fourth century AD. Classical authors state that the *Attacotti* (also *Atticoti*, *Atacotti* and *Atecotti* in various manuscripts) were warlike people of questionable morals who harassed the north-west Roman frontier for decades, but also served as auxiliaries in the **Roman army**. Almost certainly Celtic in origin, probably they were Irish.

The *Attacotti* first appear in the writings of the Roman historian Ammianus Marcellinus as allies of the barbarian **Saxons**, **Picts** and

Scoti (Irish) in their raids on Britain in the 360s AD (*History* 26.4.5, 27.8.5). The Christian scholar Jerome claims that he met a group of *Attacotti* cannibals face-to-face in northern Gaul (*Against Jovinian* 2.7). Jerome also asserts that they shared their wives in common (*Epistle* 69.415). A final source on the *Attacotti* is potentially the most interesting. The *Notitia Dignitatum*, a record of Roman troops serving throughout the empire written c. AD 395, lists the *Attacotti* as auxiliary troops in Gaul, Italy and Illyria (*East* 9.8; *West* 5.48, 51, 70, 197, 200, 218, 7.24, 74, 78).

Although our information on the *Attacotti* is sparse, we can make an intelligent guess regarding their homeland. Linguistically, the elements of the name *Attacotti* have clear cognates with other Celtic tribes, ruling out a Germanic origin. Jerome, moreover, identifies them as a British people, meaning in classical terms that they originated from the British Isles, including Ireland and Scotland. Finally, in both Ammianus and Jerome, they are always paired with the Scoti from Ireland. If indeed the *Attacotti* were Irish, as is reasonable to assume, the *Notitia Dignitatum* provides a remarkable record of Irish auxiliaries serving in the Roman legions as far away as Italy and the Balkans in the late fourth century AD.

Further Reading

Freeman, Philip. 2002. 'Who Were the Atecotti?' Pp.111–114 in *Identifying the 'Celtic': CSANA Yearbook 2*. Edited by Joseph Falaky Nagy. Four Courts Press.

Philip Freeman

Augustine of Canterbury, Saint

St. Augustine of Canterbury is sometimes called the 'apostle of the English' since he is responsible for the first English converts to the Christian faith. He is sometimes styled 'Augustine the Lesser' to distinguish him from Augustine of Hippo. He was the first archbishop of **Canterbury**.

Nothing is known of Augustine's life prior to Pope Gregory I choosing him to inaugurate the Roman mission to the English. At the time of his mission, Augustine was the prior of the monastery of St. Andrew in Rome, located on the Coelian Hill. In 595 or 596, Augustine set out from Rome with forty monks. Mid-journey, Augustine returned to Rome to beg Gregory not to send them on so dangerous a journey only to be sent back to England. They arrived in **Kent** in 597 where they were received by King **Æthelbert**. Æthelbert's wife, a Frankish princess named Bertha, was already a Christian and undoubtedly through her intervention Augustine was given a hearing by the king, on the Isle of Thanet. Augustine was granted land in Canterbury, the former church of St. Martin, and given permission to preach in Kent. They made headway baptising 10,000 in the first months of the mission. In the same year, Augustine returned to Gaul from Arles to be consecrated the archbishop of the English church by Ætherius. In 601, an additional group of missionaries arrived who brought with them books and '... *universa quae ad cultum erant ac ministerium ecclesiae necessaria*' (all things which were necessary for the worship and ministry of the church).

Gregory's plan had been to have two Episcopal sees on the island of Britain at the traditional Roman centres, **London** and **York**. Augustine's see, however, remained in Canterbury and was not moved by his successors. But by 604, Augustine had consecrated two of the missionaries who had come with him to Episcopal office, Justus who was consecrated to the see of Rochester and Mellitus who went to London. Augustine also established Christchurch in Canterbury and established the monastery of St. Peter and St. Paul outside the city, which later became known as St. Augustine's.

Augustine did not bring Christianity to the island, though he certainly seems to have brought it to the Anglo-Saxons, since there is no record that either the Franks or the British made efforts to christianise them. Augustine did meet with the bishops of the British Christian church, but he had certain conditions that the British refused to accede to. Among those conditions was acceptance of Augustine as their archbishop, to practice Easter and baptism according to the Roman rite and to preach to the English. All conditions were refused and Augustine rebuffed, creating a rift between the British and English churches, at least as reported by **Bede**.

It is unknown in what year Augustine died, but the date of his death is May 26, and he died sometime between 604 when he consecrated Justus and Mellitus and 609. When he died, the essential structure for the English church had been established and could grow and the fledgling organisation was supplied with books, church furniture, vestments as well a number of men dedicated to establishing a firm foothold for the Roman rite.

Literarily, Augustine left nothing to posterity. In Book I of his *Ecclesiastical History*, Bede records a number of letters from Pope Gregory, known as the *Libellus Responsionum*, but none from Augustine himself. One letter from Gregory purports to be answers to questions that Augustine had sent to Gregory regarding the governance of the English church, but all that remains of Augustine's letters are the questions themselves. There is a possibility that two anonymous sermons in a Mainz manuscript may be Augustine's as well.

One book that Augustine brought with him from Italy does survive although probably not copied or written by him. The so-called *St. Augustine's Gospels*, Corpus Christi College, Cambridge, Ms 286, is a gospel book of the Italian type written in the sixth century and was certainly in England in the seventh century when it received corrections in an insular hand. There is little reason to doubt the traditional attribution of the book as coming with Augustine to England. It is assumed that Augustine and his monks established a school since the purpose of the mission was to as quickly as possible provide native leadership of the church and as such they would need training. But the evidence of writing and its impact dates from early in the mission with the Laws of Æthelbert, which although surviving in a twelfth century copy is the earliest example of written **Old English**.

See also Celtic Christianity; Literature.

Further Reading

Attenborough, F. L. 1922. *The Laws of the Earliest English Kings*. Cambridge University Press.

Brooks, Nicholas. 1984. *The Early History of the Church of Canterbury: Christ Church from 597–1066*. Leicester University Press.

Meens, R. 1994. 'A Background to Augustine's Mission to Anglo-Saxon England'. *Anglo-Saxon England* 23: 5–17.

Meyvaert, Paul. 1986. 'Le libellus responsium à Augustin de Cantorbèry: une oeuvre authentique de saint Grégoire le Grand'. Pp. XX in *Grégoire le Grand*. Edited by J. Fontaine.

Wood, Ian. 1994. 'The Mission of Augustine of Canterbury to the English'. *Speculum* 69: 1–17.

Larry Swain

Aulus Plautius

Aulus Plautius was governor of **Roman Britain**, AD 43–46, and responsible for the military direction of the Roman advance following the Emperor **Claudius**'s landing in AD 43. Little is known about him before this time, though his campaigns in Britain are documented in Cassius Dio's *History of Rome* (bk.LX, ch.xix) and in Suetonius's account of *Claudius* (Chap. xvii, *Lives of the Caesars*). He is mentioned in **Tacitus**'s *Agricola* as the first consular governor of Britain (14.1).

Commanding Legio IX, Plautius advanced northwards through the tribal lands of the ***Catuvellauni*** and ***Corieltauvi***, establishing small fortresses at Water Newton (Cambridgeshire) and Newton on Trent (Derbyshire) on the Corieltauvian borders. Meanwhile, Legio XIV annexed the territory of the ***Dobunni*** in the Cotswolds – a fort was founded at Mancetter, Warwicks. Legio II Augusta moved into the south-west under the leadership of the future Emperor Vespasian conquering the lands of the ***Belgae*** in Hampshire and Wiltshire and the ***Durotriges*** of Somerset and Dorset.

The *Regnenses* of Sussex had already become a client kingdom under their leader **Cogidubnus**, and Roman supply bases for the fleet were established at **Chichester**, Hamworthy (Poole, Dorset) and Topsham (Devon). Legio XX remained in **Colchester**, where it replaced the pioneer roads with permanent metalled roadways and posting stations of which Watling Street was of prime importance.

By the end of Aulus Plautius's governorship, the area south of a line drawn roughly between the estuaries of the Trent and the Severn was in Roman hands. On his return to Rome, he was given an *Ovatio* (triumphal parade).

See also Roman Army; Roman Roads.

Further Reading

Manley, J. 2002. *AD 43: The Roman Invasion of Britain*. Tempus.

Todd, Malcolm. 1999. *Roman Britain* (3rd edn.). Blackwell.

Webster, Graham. 1981. *The Roman Invasion of Britain*. Batsford.

Jennifer Laing

Avalon

A mysterious place to which **Arthur** is taken after his last battle, gravely wounded, but alive. Medieval authors picture it as an island. There he is healed, perhaps rejuvenated, and continues living indefinitely. The theme is related to various folk tales of his survival, which were current among the Bretons, Cornish and Welsh, but the image of the immortal king in an insular Elysium is literary rather than popular.

Avalon is akin to enchanted islands in the Irish *immrama* or sea-fantasies, such as the *Voyage of Bran*. Its name is of Celtic origin and probably means *apple-place* or *apple-orchard* (from Old Welsh *aballon*, 'apple'). One early Welsh form of the name is *Avallach*. Here an ambiguity is sometimes detected, because *Avallach* occurs in Welsh genealogical legend as the name of a person, so that *Ynys Avallach* might mean 'Avallach's Island'. However, an equivalent Irish word *ablach* does mean 'rich in apples' and is an epithet of a mythical island belonging to the sea-god Manannán mac Lir. Hence, there is every reason to think that *Ynys Avallach* has a similar meaning. The Avalonian apples may be magical or supernatural fruit, but a theory that made out the island to be an abode of departed spirits is now discounted; the whole point of Arthur's presence is that he is alive.

Geoffrey of Monmouth, in his Latin *History of the Kings of Britain* (c.1138), informs his readers that Arthur's wonderful sword was forged in the *Insula Avallonis* long before he was there. He says later that after the final battle, in **Cornwall**, the king was 'carried off to the Isle of Avalon so that his wounds might be attended to'. Geoffrey goes no further at this point, and does not commit himself to a belief in Arthur's survival, but he leaves the door open for it, doubtless aware that some of his readers may cherish that belief and would resent its dismissal.

In a subsequent work, the *Vita Merlini* (*Life of Merlin*), he does go further. He introduces the bard **Taliesin** as visiting the aged **Merlin** and talking of 'the island of apples which men call the Fortunate Isle', where nature is marvellously bounteous and the inhabitants live to be a hundred or more. It is ruled by the wise enchantress Morgen, who presides over a sisterhood. Taliesin tells Merlin that he was one of the party that conveyed Arthur to it over the water. He describes how Morgen examined the king's most serious wound and undertook to heal him if he remained there. Back in Britain, Taliesin suggests to Merlin that Arthur may have recovered by now and might even return to lead his people again, but Merlin knows by prophetic insight that this cannot happen soon.

Though Geoffrey gives Avalon enduring status as the terminus of Arthur's career, he is vague as to its whereabouts. Romancers who adopt it move it in various directions with no pretence of veracity. In 1191, however, **Glastonbury** Abbey in Somerset gave it a place on the map, if in a comparatively mundane sense. Some at least of the Welsh bards had accepted that Arthur was dead but were still reticent about his grave. Reputedly, one of them revealed the secret to the English king **Henry II**: Arthur was buried in Glastonbury's monastic graveyard between two memorial pillars. The abbot ordered an excavation, which uncovered a rough coffin containing the bones of a tall man with a damaged skull and also, allegedly, the remains of a woman who might be Guinevere. Modern examination of the site has shown that the monks dug where they said and unearthed an early burial. The question was whether the person buried was, or could have been, Arthur. In corroboration, they produced a lead cross said to have been taken from the grave, with a Latin inscription, *Hic iacet sepultus inclitus rex Arturius in insula Avalonia* ('Here lies buried the famous King Arthur in the Isle of Avalon').

Until the onset of academic scepticism (which has perhaps been too dogmatic in asserting a total fabrication), the Abbey's claim was widely accepted and taken to prove that the real Avalon, Arthur's final destination, was simply Glastonbury – or, to be more precise, the hill-cluster cradling the town. It was there long before the town was and, in the early Christian era, was almost surrounded by water. This quasi-island may have been a pagan sanctuary of some kind. While clues offered by archaeology do not go very far, the attachment of the spellbinding name to the place may have had a certain aptitude. Gerald of Wales, who was much interested in the exhumation, tries to rationalise Geoffrey's resident enchantress by explaining her as the ruler of this part of the country in Arthur's time, who tried to cure him.

The name 'Avalon' survived, with the location which the monks had given it, and became lastingly familiar as an alternative to Glastonbury. Somerset, after all, is apple-growing country. It is not clear why 'Avallach' became 'Avalon' in the twelfth century when it was not a true Latinisation. Rachel Bromwich observes: 'It is difficult to avoid the conclusion that the form has been influenced by the name *Avallon* which is that of a town in Burgundy' (1978, 267). This Burgundian name has the same 'apple' derivation. The connection is not due to proximity. It seems to be an etymological loose end.

See also Kings and Kingship; Literature.

Further Reading

Ashe, Geoffrey (ed.). 1968. *The Quest for Arthur's Britain*. Pall Mall.

Ashe, Geoffrey. 2003. *The Discovery of King Arthur* (rev. edn.). Stroud.

Bromwich, Rachel. 1978. *Trioedd Ynys Prydein: The Welsh Triads, with Translation and Notes* (2nd edn.). University of Wales Press.

Geoffrey of Monmouth. 1966. *The History of the Kings of Britain*. Translated by Lewis Thorpe. Penguin.

———. 1990. 'Vita Merlini'. Translated by John Jay Parry. Pp. 71–98 in *The Romance of Merlin*. Edited by Peter Goodrich. Garland.

Gerald of Wales. 1978. *The Journey Through Wales and the Description of Wales*. Translated by Lewis Thorpe. Penguin.

Geoffrey Ashe

Avebury

Avebury, Wiltshire, is one of the most important prehistoric ritual complexes in England. Within a short distance of the modern village are located Avebury **henge** and stone circles; the Kennet Avenue (a processional way leading to the Sanctuary on Overton Hill); Silbury Hill (the largest human-made mound in Europe); the **Neolithic** causewayed enclosure on **Windmill Hill**; the **West** and East **Kennett** Neolithic long **barrows**; and a large number of **Bronze Age** round barrows.

5. Avebury contains one of the best examples of Neolithic monuments in Europe, which dates from about 5,000 years ago.

The most impressive remains are those of the Avebury stone circles. Recent reappraisal of the dating of Avebury suggests that the first phase of construction took place around 3200 BC when two, possibly three, 'coves' were erected, inspired by the central chambers of some megalithic tombs. Adjacent to one of these grew up a small settlement. Around 2800 BC, the *South Circle* of stones was erected, focused on the 'cove'; of this original circle of thirty-two stones five survive. To the NNW of this, a second circle, the *Central Circle* (or just possibly a horseshoe-shaped setting), was constructed, originally possibly of thirty stones (four survive). The *North Circle* (of which the only surviving evidence were three stone holes) was erected probably somewhat later and then demolished.

The main phase can be dated to around 2600 BC when an approximately circular ditch with flat bottom was dug, broken by four entrances (three known to be ancient and the fourth assumed to be), the quarried material being banked up outside the ditch with a berm. This bank originally had a revetment of chalk blocks on the inside. It has been calculated that bank and ditch took 1,560,000 man hours to construct. Within the ditch is the *Main Circle* of what were originally about 100 sarsen stones, the largest flanking the entrances. These are of two shapes, tall monoliths and lozenges buried at one corner. This enclosed the two smaller circles and occupation area.

The two lines of standing stones (the Kennet Avenue) were constructed perhaps around 2400 BC, being erected in a piecemeal fashion. The Sanctuary, to which the Kennet Avenue leads, had at least two structural phases, the first of which has been dated to around 3600 BC, which was subsequently replaced by two concentric circles of stones (now no longer visible) probably around 2600 BC. Against a stone of the inner circle, a young girl was buried around 2000 BC. Avebury as a ritual centre seems to have been abandoned in the Early Bronze Age. Nearby Silbury Hill was probably built around 2700 BC, the original small circular mound being heightened by a series of chalk cones.

Further Reading

Burl, A. 1979. *Prehistoric Avebury*. Yale University Press.

———. 2000. *The Stone Circles of Britain, Ireland and Brittany*. Yale University Press.

Malone, C. 1989. *Avebury*. Batsford/English Heritage.

Jennifer Laing

Aylesford

The **Iron Age** cemetery at Aylesford, Kent, was excavated in 1886 by Sir Arthur Evans, the future discoverer of the Minoan civilisation of Crete and the palace of Knossos.

The publication was a major development in archaeological thought, for the discussion introduced the concept of prehistoric invaders of Britain, an idea taken up by Lord Abercromby in his work on **Bronze Age** pottery a few years later. Evans argued that the pottery and associated metalwork were distinctive of a group of people in south-east England, and through a study of the imports he argued that the cemetery post-dated 150 BC and probably represented the graves of immigrants from Belgic Gaul documented by **Julius Caesar**. Subsequent work at Swarling in the same county by J. P. Bushe-Fox firmly established the concept of an immigrant 'Belgic' culture in southern Britain, which became known variously as 'Belgic,' 'Swarling-Aylesford' or '**Iron Age** C'.

The cemetery was distinguished by its use of elegant wheel-made pottery, the most distinctive type of which was the pedestal urn, and by its use of cremation. The rich finds came from three graves, those from grave Y being closely matched by finds on the continent dating between 50 and 30 BC. These consisted of a bronze jug and pan, manufactured in Italy, and an imported brooch. The burial, accompanied by pots, was interred in a bronze-plated wooden bucket. Grave X contained a burial in an iron-bound bucket, and grave Z a tankard and pots. The graves at Aylesford seem to have been arranged in a circular setting and may represent a few rich burials with a series of satellites, a phenomenon noted elsewhere.

The concept of a 'Belgic' immigration has been questioned in recent years, and certainly the Aylesford cemetery is too late to be associated with Caesar's immigrants. The appearance in Britain of imported coins in the late second century BC certainly points to close links with Belgic Gaul at this time; they were soon copied in Britain. Even if there was no large-scale invasion, influence from Belgic Gaul was very much apparent in the Late Iron Age in south-east England.

Further Reading

Birchall, A. 1965. 'The Aylesford-Swarling Culture: The Problem of the Belgae Reconsidered'. *Proceedings of the Prehistoric Society* 31: 241–367.

Cunliffe, B. W. 2005. *Iron Age Communities in Britain*. RKP.

Evans, A. J. 1890. 'On a Late Celtic Urnfield at Aylesford, Kent'. *Archaeologia* 52: 315–388.

Hawkes, C., and G. C. Dunning. 1930. 'The Belgae of Gaul and Britain'. *Archaeological Journal* 12: 411–430.

Lloyd Laing

B

Badon Hill, Battle of (c. AD 500)

The Battle of Badon Hill was a key battle fought c. AD 500 between the **Britons** and the **Saxons** during the English settlement and conquest of lowland Britain. Writing some time in the first half of the sixth century, the British cleric **Gildas** describes an important victory of the Britons over the Saxons at *obsessio Badonici montis*, literally 'the siege of the Badonic Mount'. He claims that the battle was fought during the year of his own birth and that forty-four years had passed since then (though here his Latin is a bit obscure). **Bede** adopted Gildas's account of the battle and added that it took place about forty-four years after the Saxons arrived in Britain (which he dates as AD 449), whereas the ***Anglo-Saxon Chronicle*** is silent on Badon. The ***Annales Cambriae*** give the date AD 518 for *bellum Badonis* ('battle of Badon'). (A second battle is recorded for AD 667.) Both the *Annales* and the ***Historia Brittonum*** attribute the British victory to **Arthur**.

Modern scholarship on Badon has focused on the date and the location of the battle as well as on the identity of the general who led the Britons to victory. Not surprisingly, the latter goal has often come in the context of investigating a historical King Arthur. Celticist Kenneth Jackson argued that the primitive Welsh name *Badon* would have become *Badon-byrig* (or Badbury) in **Old English**, assuming that it was a **hillfort** that was besieged. There are several Badburys that fit this description, including Badbury Rings (Dorset), Badbury Hill (Berkshire) and Liddington Castle (Wiltshire), which was once known as Badbury Camp.

In the twelfth century, **Geoffrey of Monmouth** had speculated that the battle was fought at the city of **Bath**. There have been many modern proponents of this Bath theory, including the archaeologist Leslie Alcock. Alcock accepted the evidence of the *Annales Cambriae* and the *Historia Brittonum* as confirming the identity of Arthur as leader at Badon and dated the battle c. AD 490, in accordance with Bede's statement that the battle occurred forty-four years after the coming of the Saxons. However, Alcock rejected the Badbury hypothesis on linguistic grounds, arguing that the British name *Badon* was pronounced with a soft *th* rather than a hard *d*, thereby making Bath a more apt location. The battle, he wrote, would not have been fought in the Roman town (*Aquae Sulis*) itself but rather on an adjacent hilltop or at a nearby pre-Roman Iron Age hillfort, although this location seemed less likely for Alcock.

Recently, Nicholas Higham went against conventional wisdom by arguing that Badon was fought early on in the British-Saxon wars (c. AD 440) and that it was the Saxons, not the Britons, who were the victors. It remains to be seen whether Higham's provocative thesis will spark new investigations of the location and character of the battle of Mount Badon.

See also Warfare and Weapons.

Further Reading

Alcock, Leslie. 1971. *Arthur's Britain: History and Archaeology, AD 367–634*. Penguin.

Burkitt, T. and Burkitt, A. 1990. 'The Frontier Zone and the Siege of Mount Badon: A Review of the Evidence for Their Location'. *Proceedings of the Somerset Archaeological and Natural History Society* 134: 81–93.

Higham, N. J. 1994. *The English Conquest: Gildas and Britain in the Fifth Century*. Manchester University Press.

Hirst, Susan and Philip Rahtz. 1996. 'Liddington Castle and the Battle of Badon: Excavations and Research 1976'. *The Archaeological Journal* 153: 1–59.

Jackson, K. H. 1958. 'The Site of Mount Badon'. *Journal of Celtic Studies* 2.2: 152–155.

Christopher A. Snyder

Ballinderry

Ballinderry is known for two ***crannogs*** (artificial islands) located on the same *lough* (lake), which, though adjacent, lie on either side of a county boundary. Both were subject to excavation by the Harvard expedition before the Second World War, under the leadership of Hugh O'Neill Hencken of the Peabody Museum, Harvard.

Ballinderry 1 in county Westmeath, built in a swampy area of shallow water in tenth century AD, is the later of the two. On the artificial island, which was constructed with a palisade of piles round the perimeter and a second partial palisade of planks within it, a large house was constructed, with a horseshoe plan, 56 feet (17 metres) across, which was replaced in the eleventh century by another and replaced again by a third after AD 1200. The waterlogged deposits produced a rich array of finds, most notably organic, which included a gaming board decorated with a type of ring-chain (developed by the Norse sculptor Gaut in the **Isle of Man**) and wooden bowls. Other finds included a copper-alloy hanging lamp. The house has recently been the subject of reassessment, and it is now believed to be a **Viking** settlement, constructed during the time of Norse occupation in **Dublin**. In the centre of the building was a raft, on which the main roof support was situated as well as a hearth. There was activity on the site, continuing down to the nineteenth century.

Ballinderry 2 in county Offaly began as a **Bronze Age** lakeside settlement, with wicker huts and a larger building. Ballinderry 2 was swamped because of a rise in the level of the lough. Around the end of the sixth century AD, a crannog was built on the site, which was occupied until the mid-eighth century. As with Ballinderry 1, the site produced an important array of finds, including woodwork, an assortment of shoes and a fine penannular brooch with enamel and millefiori inlay.

Further Reading

Hencken, H. O'Neill. 1936. 'Ballinderry 1 Crannog'. *Proceedings of the Royal Irish Academy* 43C: 103–226.

Hencken, H O'Neill. 1942. 'Ballinderry 2 Crannog'. *Proceedings of the Royal Irish Academy* 47C: 1–75.

Johnson, R. 1999. 'Ballinderry Crannog no. 1: A Reinterpretation'. *Proceedings of the Royal Irish Academy* 99C: 23–71.

O'Sullivan, Aidan. 1998. *The Archaeology of Lake Settlement in Ireland*. Royal Irish Academy.

Lloyd Laing

Bamburgh

Located in **Northumbria**, Bamburgh has been regarded as one of the most important **Anglo-Saxon** centres in Britain. It is best known for its **Norman** castle, which underwent a major restoration in the nineteenth century and is still undergoing excavations. The history of the site has origins dating back to before the **Iron Age**. Evidence for such early occupation has come from pottery found in trial excavations, but despite its precarious position on the Roman frontier, it was not until the eighth century that the site was first recorded. Bamburgh appears as 'Dinguoaroy' in **Bede**'s ***Historia Ecclesiastica***, with a foundation date of AD 547 under its conquering king Ida. In the mid-sixth century, Northumbria became the frontline of Anglian expansion, with

Bamburgh serving as the principal stronghold, and it may have been around this time that the site was named after the sixth-century Bernician queen Bebbe, wife of Ida's grandson **Æthelfrith**, becoming 'Bebbanburgh' in the sources.

It is apparent that the site had associations with royalty, as every one of Bede's references, whether they were *civitas* or *urbs*, had the added adjective *regia*. Some of this royal standing may have had to do with the dismembered hand and arm of St. Oswald, which were preserved in a silver casket in the church at Bamburgh. Bede was also the source for much of Bamburgh's early history, including its defence by Theoderic against a coalition of British kings and its burning in the seventh century by **Penda of Mercia**. Although its original Anglian fortifications were destroyed by the **Vikings** in the late tenth century, the castle was rebuilt after the Norman conquest and even unsuccessfully besieged by **William II**.

Although the site's 5-acre (2-hectare) area was large enough for both a town and a timber-palisaded stronghold in the mid-sixth century, the Norman castle occupied the whole of the rock, leaving room for only a small village to be able to grow around the castle walls. The excavations of Brian Hope-Taylor in the 1960s and 1970s focused on the north end and west ward of the castle, and in addition to the numerous Anglian finds (e.g. coins), animal bones and carbonised cereals, a gold plaque known as the Bamburgh Beast was found, which may have been originally inset on a book cover or reliquary. The plaque bears an engraved motif of a beast biting its own forepaw. In 1998, the Bamburgh Research Project was able to relocate a cist burial ground from the post-Roman era. A geophysical survey work of the castle conducted by Durham University revealed definite evidence of fortification prior to the Roman conquest.

Further Reading

Alcock, Leslie. 2003. *Kings and Warriors, Craftsmen and Priests in Northern Britain AD 550–850*. Society of Antiquaries of Scotland.

'Archaeology', Bamburgh Castle, http://www.bamburghcastle.com/archaeology.html (cited 17 March 2008).

'History of Bamburgh', Bamburgh Research Project, http://www.bamburghresearchproject.co.uk/history.html (cited 17 March 2008).

Webster, L. and J. Backhouse (eds.). 1991. *The Making of England, Anglo-Saxon Art and Culture AD 600–900*. British Museum Press.

Anne Sassin

Bangor (Gwynedd)

Bangor, a city in **Gwynedd**, North Wales, and one of the oldest bishoprics in Britain, dates back to the early sixth century AD when its first cathedral was established. It continued to remain fundamental to the Welsh Church throughout the Middle Ages. Largely contained by Bangor Mountain to the south and the Rivers Adda and Cegin to the east and west, Bangor began as a very small monastic community and hamlet, with St. Deiniol (d.584), the first Bishop of Bangor and a saint supposedly consecrated by **St. David**, founding the see and building a monastery c. 525 at the site of the present cathedral. The land itself was said to have been granted to St. Deiniol by **Maelgwn**, king of Gwynedd, and it was a site which saw more than one sacking by **Viking** marauders, including the one of 1073 which may have done damage to the cathedral. Some of the archaeology of Bangor includes a coin hoard from c. 930 of thirteen coins, mostly **Northumbrian** and Danish including a few oriental ones, attesting to the high level of commercial activity which the monastery saw due to its coastal proximity.

The cathedral itself has little of its original Romanesque fabric remaining other than short sections of the south transept and a blocked window and pilaster buttress in the south presbytery wall. Excavation was able to reveal the typical cruciform plan about 131 feet (40 metres) in length, a comparatively small cathedral for the time. Possibly incorporating slabs with insular-type plaitwork from the earlier tenth century structure into the screen, the earliest part of the present cathedral was built around the first quarter of the twelfth century under the patronage of **Gruffudd ap Cynan**, who was buried by the high altar, as were his sons Owain Gwynedd and Cadwaladr, and it underwent massive destruction under King John's troops in 1211, necessitating extensive reconstruction in the following centuries.

Though it is believed that **Elfoddw**, who was the Archbishop of Gwynedd, was also Bangor's bishop in the early ninth century, most of the better-known bishops of Bangor were the ones after the Norman invasion, being the period which was best evidenced. These included Hervé le Breton, bishop from 1092 to 1109 who was elected in an attempt to enforce Norman authority onto North Wales, and David the Scot (1120–1139), who was responsible for the rebuilding of the cathedral and was appointed after a lull in the bishopric due to the contention between Gruffudd and **Henry II** over its assignment. Other noted bishops of Bangor include Alban (1195–1197) and Robert of Shrewsbury (1197–1212) at the end of the century; the latter was forcibly removed by John's forces. It was the introduction of monumental architecture to Gwynedd under the earlier bishops that was the true sign of the changing religious reforms under Norman rule, while at the same time attesting to the Hiberno-Norse background of the patrons of North Wales, such as Gruffydd.

See also Welsh People.

Further Reading

Clarke, M. L. 1969. *Bangor Cathedral.* University of Wales Press.

Davies, W. 1982. *Wales in the Early Middle Ages.* Leicester University Press.

Dodd, A. H. (ed.). 1969. *History of Bangor Diocese.* University of Wales Press.

Thurlby, M. 2006. *Romanesque Architecture and Sculpture in Wales.* Logaston Press.

Anne Sassin

Bards

In the English language, the word *bard* (Greek βαρδ, Irish *bard*, Welsh *bardd*) encompasses a wide variety of poets, writers, singers, musicians and storytellers inhabiting ancient and medieval Europe. In the Celtic-speaking lands, especially Ireland and Wales, the bard was held in high esteem and often performed the additional functions of historian, genealogist and seer.

Greek and Roman writers vividly described the functions of bards among the ancient **Celts**. Strabo (c. 64 BC–AD 21) writes: 'There are three classes of men held in special honour: the Bards, the Vates, and the **Druids**. The Bards are singers and poets' (*Geography* 4. 4. 4). According to Diodorus Siculus (c. 60–30 BC), 'They have also lyric poets whom they call Bards. They sing to the accompaniment of instruments resembling lyres, sometimes a eulogy and sometimes a satire' (5. 31. 2). Caesar claimed that the druids could commit vast amounts of poetry to memory. The bard is thus related to the druid in antiquity, but that relationship is not clear. Since the druids were wiped out by the Romans in nearly all of their conquered territories, the bard may have survived into the Middle Ages taking over some of their functions, but in a Christian context. **Gildas** complains about the sycophantic poets who hang about the courts of British tyrants like Maglocunus (**Maelgwn Gwynedd**), and says that even the British clergy enjoyed hearing their 'foolish stories'. The vast number of bards, jugglers and entertainers at the courts of early medieval Europe go mostly unnoticed by historians because they formed a vernacular oral culture that did not take written form until the tenth and eleventh centuries (see Richter 1994).

The British bard (*crota Britanna*, in Middle Welsh *crwth*), with his ever-present harp, retained his privileged position in medieval Wales. Welsh law texts refer to two classes of bard: the *pencerdd*, 'chief of song' and the *bard teylu*, 'poet of the war-band'. Welsh tradition long celebrated the earliest poets, the *cynfeirdd*, a group that included **Aneirin**, **Taliesin** and **Myrddin**. In addition to their surviving poems, we have elegiac poetry, vatic (prophetic) poetry (e.g. '**Armes Prydein Vawr**'), the Welsh Triads and the four branches of the ***Mabonogi*** and their associated **Arthurian** poems. In 1176, the Lord Rhys celebrated the first *eisteddfod* in Cardigan by awarding prizes for *cerdd dafod* ('the craft of the tongue') and *cerdd dant* ('the craft of the string'). Welsh bards are said to literally inhale their inspiration from a muselike spirit called the *awen*.

In early medieval Ireland, the ***filid*** were the most learned poets and experts in tradition, forming one of the subclasses of the *áes dana* ('people of skill or knowledge'). There were also seven different subclasses of *filid*, significantly the same number of subclasses of the clergy (Charles-Edwards 2000, 128). They were called upon to praise their patrons, princely or otherwise, but could also employ satire. In the eleventh and twelfth centuries a Bardic Oder emerged from the *filid*, with its own schools and schoolmaster (the *ollam*).

See also Irish Language; Welsh Language; Welsh People.

Further Reading

Charles-Edwards, Thomas. 2000. *Early Christian Ireland.* Cambridge University Press.

Green, Miranda J. 1997. *The World of the Druids.* Thames & Hudson.

Koch, John T. (ed.). 1995. *The Celtic Heroic Age: Literary Sources for Ancient Celtic Europe and Early Ireland and Wales.* Celtic Studies Publications.

Moisl, Hermann. 1980–1982. 'A Sixth-Century Reference to the British *bardd*'. *Bulletin of the Board of Celtic Studies* 29: 269–273.

Richter, Michael. 1994. *The Formation of the Medieval West: Studies in the Oral Culture of the Barbarians.* St. Martin's.

Williams, J. E. Caerwyn. 1984. 'Gildas, Maelgwn, and the Bards'. Pp.19–37 in *Welsh Society and Nationhood: Historical Essays Presented to Glanmor Williams*. Edited by R. R. Davies et al. University of Wales Press.

Christopher A. Snyder

Barrows

A barrow is any mound covering a burial or group of burials. In Britain they range in date from the **Neolithic** to the Early Medieval periods. The earliest type of barrow found in Britain and Ireland is termed the *Long Barrow* or *Long Cairn* (barrows being of earth, cairns of stone), of which several thousands survive. They started to be constructed around 2,800 BC and comprised rectangular or trapezoidal mounds, often higher at one end than the other, and sometimes as much as 329 feet (100 metres) in length. They are associated with the expansion of farming in the period down to c. 2,500 BC. They were considerable undertakings, involving up to an estimated 7,000 to 16,000 man-hours to construct. They were collective tombs, i.e. they contained up to fifty burials, interments being added over long periods of time – up to 500 years. These were mostly inhumations, and in some cases the bodies may have been exposed to decompose before burial. A few barrows in northeast England contain massed cremations, and one or two mounds are devoid of burials entirely.

The diversity in long barrows and long cairns is considerable. In the West (western and northern Scotland, North and South Wales, the Cotswolds) and in northeast England, barrows are found to contain megalithic structures (i.e. built with huge stones), sometimes with a long mound encapsulating two or more such stone chambers. The variety in plan and overall shape of these mounds is very variable, with two basic traditions of Passage Graves (long passages leading to a terminal chamber) and Gallery Graves (a passage with lateral chambers for burials) being discernible. These burial mounds usually have some kind of forecourt, usually at the wider, higher end, and were re-opened at intervals to add burials. Sometimes, the stones of which the chambers and passages were composed have carvings on them (megalithic art). Classic megalithic-chambered tombs include Maes Howe, Unstan and Midhowe in Orkney, Knowth, Dowth and **Newgrange** in Ireland, Bryn Celli Ddhu and Dyffryn Ardudwy in north Wales, Wayland's Smithy in Oxfordshire and West Kennet in Wiltshire.

In **Wessex**, the east of England, and in some areas in eastern Scotland, stone interior structures are replaced by timber. These mounds may or may not have some kind of façade, and many seem to have had several phases of use before the final act of piling up a barrow. During the period from c. 2500 BC, round barrows became fashionable in some areas, and round barrow burial, now usually with a single interment, became the norm from the start of the Beaker period. These barrows are often found in barrow cemeteries, smaller barrows being clustered round a pre-existing long barrow or an early **Beaker** grave. In some cases, the construction of barrows over a cemetery of flat graves was carried out as a final stage in the use of the cemetery. Many different types of round barrows are known: bowl barrows, bell barrows, disc barrows, saucer barrows and pond barrows. There is also a diversity of associated burial rituals, such as the use of cremation or log coffin burial.

Barrows are sometimes found in the **Iron Age**. The most significant group are the **Arras** graves on Eastern Yorkshire, which were demarcated by rectangular enclosures and contained a burial with an associated cart or 'chariot'. These have been seen as the result of limited settlement from the Marne. Later Iron Age barrows include a small group of 'princely' burials immediately pre-dating the Roman conquest, such as the tumulus at Lexden, Colchester and Essex. Barrow burial is not common in **Roman Britain**, but there are some notable barrow groups such as that at Bartlow Hills, Essex, or another group outside **Canterbury**, **Kent**. These belong to the earlier part of the Roman period.

Prehistoric barrows were sometimes used as a focus for early medieval cemeteries, and sometimes medieval burials were inserted into the side of the mounds. In pagan Anglo-Saxon England, barrow burial is a feature of the 'Final Phase,' as it is termed, which in general dates from the seventh century. Barrow burial was used for high-status interments, and classic examples from Anglo-Saxon England include **Sutton Hoo**, Suffolk, Taplow, Bucks and Swallowcliffe Down, Wilts. A notable group is found in the Peak district of Derbyshire, where prehistoric round barrows were used for Anglo-Saxon interments.

Recent archaeological research is also showing that in the Iron Age/Early Christian tradition in Ireland, inhumation burials were often placed under circular, earthen mounds, possibly being the boundary burial mounds termed 'ferta' in the early Irish texts. The **Vikings** also employed barrow burial. Some of the finest examples are from the **Isle of Man** (Balladoole, Ballateare, Knock y Doonee, Cronk Moar), but they also are found in the North of England. A small Danish barrow cemetery is known at Ingleby, Derbyshire. A number of square-enclosure barrow burials are also known in northeast Scotland, among the **Picts**.

Further Reading

Ashbee, P. 1960. *The Bronze Age Round Barrow in Britain*. Phoenix.

———. 1970. *The Earthen Long Barrow in England*. Dent.

Daniel, G. 1950. *The Prehistoric Chamber Tombs of England and Wales*. Cambridge University Press.

Grinsell, L. V. 1953. *The Ancient Burial Mounds of England* (2nd edn.). Methuen.

Lucy, S. 2000. *The Anglo-Saxon Way of Death*. Sutton Publishing.

Stead, I. 1979. *The Arras Culture*. Yorkshire Philosophical Society.

Lloyd Laing

Bath

Bath is a Roman thermal and religious complex, focused around several hot springs that rise to the surface north of the river Avon. These springs account for its Roman name, variously recorded as *Aquae Sulis* in the Antonine Itinerary (Route XIV) and as Υδατα Θερμα (*Aquae Calidae*) in Ptolemy's *Geography*. The Bath complex is significant both for the richness of its monumental architecture and for the wealth of its sculptural and epigraphic collections.

Little trace of any **Iron Age** use of the springs has survived the extensive Roman operations. The central focus was the King's Bath spring, where engineers constructed a polygonal reservoir to control the daily output of over one million litres. This reservoir lay in the southeast corner of a paved and colonnaded precinct, which housed the Temple of Sulis Minerva towards its western end, with an axially aligned altar in front. Enough survives to reconstruct a tetrastyle Corinthian façade, surmounted by the well-known Gorgon pediment. To the south, the reservoir connected with a large suite of baths, comprising a spacious entrance hall flanked by a series of rooms to the south and west and a sequence of thermal baths to the east. Stylistic assessment of the architecture and the associated pottery indicates a surprisingly early date, c. AD 65–75, for these monumental developments in marked contrast with many other Romano-British urban sites.

Both temple and baths underwent significant changes during the second and early third centuries. The former was doubled in size by the addition of a raised ambulatory around the original podium, with a monumental façade across the east, incorporating a flight of steps flanked by two small rooms. The baths had new or extended suites of rooms added at the eastern and western ends, while the original timber roofing was replaced by vaulting. Contemporary with the bath, the reservoir was enclosed within a vaulted chamber. When the reservoir began to collapse later in the century, a raised portico was added along its northern side, providing a foundation for several buttresses, the central one of which took the form of a monumental doorway surmounted by a pediment incorporating the head of the sun god. Parallel changes in the northern part of the temple precinct may have mirrored this, if this was the original location of the Façade of the Four Seasons; this too had a pediment incorporating the head of the moon goddess.

The area occupied by the three springs and their related facilities was surrounded by defences enclosing around 24.71 acres (10 hectares). An initial earthwork phase of the later second century has been identified, followed later by the insertion of a stone wall. Whether this was part of a wider pattern of 'urban' defence, or simply a marker for the religious precinct, remains uncertain. The provision of defences seems to have been accompanied by an increase in the number of buildings within the intramural area, most apparently of some size and pretension. Outside the walls, ribbon developments extended along the frontages of various roads, most of which were focused on an assumed river crossing some distance to the north of the later walled area. Beyond these extramural areas lay several large cemeteries, with a mixture of cremations and inhumations spanning the whole of the Roman period.

Bath has produced a wealth of epigraphic evidence (Collingwood and Wright, 1995), which clearly attests the cosmopolitan nature of the population. Several soldiers certainly came to Bath, while citizens are recorded from as far away as modern Chartres and Metz. There is also reference to a priest of Sulis, a *haruspex* (soothsayer/seer/prophet) and an eye specialist represented by his oculist's stamp. The religious importance of the site is further emphasised by the finds from the reservoir, which included a large number of coins, numerous metal vessels, some 130 lead curses and a range of other ritual objects; the curses, in particular, represent the most significant archive yet published for Romano – Celtic religion.

From c. AD 350 onwards the character of the temple precinct began to change; the evidence suggested that the associated monuments were being progressively dismantled as their function lapsed. Activity continued, however, in the form of an accumulation of rubbish and soil interspersed by various phases of cobbling and repaving, which must have extended well into the fifth century if not beyond. Subsequent activity involved deliberate demolition. The fate of the baths remains less clear, though their demise may well have been hastened by the problem of periodic flooding. The final stage would have seen the collapse of the vaulting to leave 'The Ruin', so vividly described in an eighth century poem.

See also Roman Britain.

Further Reading

Collingwood, R. G., and R. P. Wright. 1995. *The Roman Inscriptions of Britain. Volume 1: The Inscriptions on Stone.* Alan Sutton.

Cunliffe, B. W. 2000. *Roman Bath Rediscovered.* Tempus.

Cunliffe, B. W., and Davenport, P. 1985. *The Temple of Sulis Minerva at Bath. Volume 1. The Site.* Oxford University Committee for Archaeology, Monograph No. 7.

Cunliffe, B. W. (ed.). 1988. *The Temple of Sulis Minerva at Bath. Volume 2. The Finds from the Sacred Spring.* Oxford University Committee for Archaeology, Monograph No. 16.

Cunliffe, B. W., and Fulford, M. G. 1982. *Corpus signorum Imperii Romani. Great Britain. Volume 1. Fasc. 2, Bath and the Rest of Wessex.* Oxford University Press.

Barry C. Burnham

Battersea Shield

The Battersea shield is one of the masterpieces of **La Tène** Celtic ornamental metalwork from the British Isles. Found in the River Thames, it measures 77.5 cm (0.775 metres) long, roughly

6. Battersea Bronze Shield, c. second to first century BC.

oblong, with a slightly waisted profile. It was not, however, suitable for use in battle and comprises copper alloy plates for a wooden or leather base. The decoration comprises three roundels with central bosses, these containing enamelled swastika patterns. Behind the central boss is an openwork mount which may have served as a handgrip, decorated with dot-filled curved triangles. When the shield was taken apart for technical examination in 1980, it was determined that the enamel is of identical composition to that employed on the early La Tène Basse Yutz flagons from France. The modelling is symmetrical and in high relief, and though at first sight apparently abstract, it in fact contains animal and human masks. Open-mouthed duck heads are made from the outer spirals of the smaller roundels. The shape and general design is similar to that of the Witham Shield, from the river Witham in Lincolnshire, which also seems to have been a votive offering, as may have been the mounts for another shield from Wandsworth, also from the Thames in London.

There has been considerable debate about the date of the shield. Apart from the enamel, the symmetry of the design and the use of masks have led some authorities to believe it belongs to the earliest phase of **Iron Age** art in Britain, with parallels in the 'Early Style' of Continental La Tène art. In this interpretation, it should be dated to the third century BC, or earlier. Other authorities have argued that its symmetry is due to the influence of Roman art, which has also been seen as the inspiration for some of the decorative elements. According to this view, it dates from around the first century AD.

See also Ceramics and Glass; Warfare and Weapons.

Further Reading

Fox, C. 1958. *Pattern and Purpose, Early Celtic Art in Britain*. National Museum of Wales.
Jope, E M. 2000. *Early Celtic Art in the British Isles*. Clarendon Press.
Megaw, J. V. S. 1968. *The Elusive Image: Art of the European Iron Age*. Adams & Dart.
Megaw, R., and Vincent Megaw. 1989. *Celtic Art: From Its Beginnings to the Book of Kells*. Thames & Hudson.
Stead, I. M. 1985. *The Battersea Shield*. British Museum.

Lloyd Laing

Battle Abbey

William I the Conqueror built Battle Abbey, a Benedictine monastery in East Sussex, in the wake of the Norman Conquest of England. According to house tradition, the foundation was intended to atone for the blood spilled by the **Normans** in the course of the **Battle of Hastings** in October, 1066. Construction of what would become the king's victory church began shortly after William's consolidation of power in England in the 1070s. The high altar, which was installed in 1076, supposedly stood on the spot where King **Harold** fell during the battle. The abbey was completed in the 1080s but it was not consecrated until 1094, during the reign of William's son, **William II Rufus**.

William chose a Norman model in St Etienne, Caen, for his new abbey, but the abbey's combination of an eastern apse and an ambulatory with radiating chapels was distinctive even by Norman standards. It was a relatively small church compared to other churches built in England by the Normans, measuring about 225 feet (68.58 metres) in length. William imported monks from Marmoutier-on-Loire to staff his abbey, which contributed to its continental character. The Marmoutier connection perhaps also accounted for the abbey's dedication to St. Martin. Battle Abbey was further distinguished by its impressive endowment in **Domesday Book**, which included lands in at least six other counties besides Sussex. Although the abbey suffered predation of its lands during the period of the anarchy, as many churches did, later abbots maintained close ties with royal courts, thus ensuring its return to prosperity. The community benefited greatly from the appointment of Walter de Lucy, whose brother, Richard de Lucy, was chief justiciar under **Henry II**. Diplomatic and narrative evidence reveals how Walter utilised his considerable legal acumen, as well as his court connections, to restore the abbey's patrimony. Abbots of Battle Abbey also enjoyed considerable autonomy from the bishops of **Chichester**, a privilege that they zealously guarded. The efforts of the community to safeguard the abbey's lands and privileges are documented in the two-part house chronicle composed in the twelfth century. Battle Abbey remained a wealthy and influential abbey from its inception until its dissolution in 1538.

Further Reading

Fernie, Eric. 2000. *The Architecture of Norman England*. Oxford University Press.
Searle, Eleanor (ed.). 1980. *Battle Chronicle: The Chronicle of Battle Abbey*. Oxford University Press.
Searle, Eleanor. 1974. *Lordship and Community: Battle Abbey and Its Banlieu, 1066–1538*. Pontifical Institute of Medieval Studies.

Mary Frances Giandrea

'The Battle of Maldon'

'The Battle of Maldon' is an **Old English** poem purporting to describe events of 991 in which Byrhtnoth, the Earl of **Essex**, was defeated at Maldon on the Panta (Blackwater) river by **Viking** raiders. The poem focuses on the issues of warrior ethics and loss in battle. Consequently it holds interest as an occasional poem, as a statement of heroic codes, and as a display of martial rhetoric; contemporary readings of the poem tend to explore historiography, linguistics and identity politics.

What is known about the event at Maldon in 991 has been derived from 'The Battle of Maldon' and two short accounts of the battle and its circumstances in two recensions of the ***Anglo-Saxon Chronicle***. One of the *Chronicle* texts for the year 991 reads in translation: 'Here Ipswich was raided. Very soon after that, ealdorman Byrhtnoth was killed at Maldon. And on that year it was decided to pay tax to Danes for the great terror that they made by the seacoast; that first [payment] was 10,000 pounds. Archbishop Sigerīc decided first on the matter'.

The existing version of the poem begins at some point after its original opening which has not survived. Byrhtnoth, whose fame and status appear to have been established prior to the composition of the poem, prepares his men to confront a Scandinavian raiding party that has landed on an island in the Panta—now the Blackwater—river. A messenger from the Viking party offers Byrhtnoth ransom in place of being raided. In a dramatic gesture of refusal, Byrhtnoth raises his shield and shakes his spear, sending back his message that there will be no such capitulation. Because of the river, neither army could approach the other until the tide ebbed; Byrhtnoth's men led by **Wulfstan**, Ceola's son, then hold the causeway, thwarting the Vikings' access to the land. The Vikings ask leave of Byrhtnoth to advance their troops, and 'on account of his pride', the earl invites his enemies to a foothold across the causeway. The battle ensues full-scale, with terrible consequences on both sides and the poem describes Byrhtnoth's urging both his trained knights and supporting conscripts until he himself is wounded. He continues to fight until an arrow strikes him and Byrhtnoth goes down. The hero thanks God for his life, asks for safe passage to heaven and dies. Numerous men flee the battle. Some, however, vow to continue the fight, recalling boasts they had made, but they cannot avail. The words of one old retainer, Byrhtwold, are frequently recalled from this part of the poem:

> The spirit must be the firmer, the heart the bolder,
> courage must be the greater as our strength diminishes.

He dies fighting and falls by the slain Byrhtnoth, his lord. The poem breaks off in mid-sentence.

The source of the text of 'The Battle of Maldon' is, presumably, British Library Cotton MS Otho A.xii, but this manuscript was destroyed in the fire in Ashburnham House in **London** in 1731. Until the 1930s, the only known text of the poem was its first edition by Thomas Hearne in the second volume of his *Johannis Confratris et Monachi Glastoniensis Chronica sive Historia de Rebus Glastoniensis* (Oxford, 1726). Although John of Glastonbury's history does not provide a logical context for 'The Battle of Maldon', Hearne noted in a preface that 'certain noble Anglo-Saxon fragments should be appended to the end of the work, just as Richard Graves ... caused them to be transcribed from the Cotton Codex by a learned man John Elphinston.... Neil Ker found a transcript in Oxford, Bodleian Library MS. Rawlinson B.203, fols. 7r-12v, which answered to the one Hearne edited and described, and this has therefore been known as the Elphinston transcript. Subsequent study has determined that the transcript was in fact the work of David Casley, who succeeded Elphinston as deputy keeper of the Cotton library. It is on this transcript that all recent editions of 'The Battle of Maldon' depend, although there do not appear to be significant discrepancies between the transcript and Hearne's *editio princeps*.

See also Literature.

Further Reading

Gordon, E. V. (ed.). 1976 (reprint). *The Battle of Maldon*. Manchester University Press.

Scragg, Donald (ed.). 1991. *The Battle of Maldon, AD 991*. Basil Blackwell for the Manchester Centre for Anglo-Saxon Studies.

Patrick W. Conner

Bayeux Tapestry

The Bayeux Tapestry is a unique object that provides a visual and textual account of the **Norman Conquest** of Anglo-Saxon England. Despite its name, the work is an embroidered cloth of white linen on which coloured wool threads are stitched. It is presently 230 feet (70.104 metres) long by 20 inches (0.508 metres) high, made of eight joined strips, although the end has been lost. The precise details of its production are not known, but the Tapestry was almost certainly made in England, very shortly after the Conquest in 1066, and was likely commissioned by **William I the Conqueror**'s half-brother, Odo, Bishop of Bayeux, who appears prominently in it. The ideological position of the Tapestry has been debated, but it seems to argue for the justness of the Norman cause.

The Tapestry is the only visual account of the Conquest close in date to the actual events and so it is often utilised as if it were a photojournalistic record of the battle and is not assessed with the critical approaches used for the textual sources. It is dealt with as if it were an impartial means of reproduction. This illusion is fostered by the work itself which aims to conceal beneath its brief inscriptions and straightforward images any rhetorical position.

7. Detail of parley between Harold II and William I from the Bayeux Tapestry, eleventh century.

In brief, the story told by the Tapestry is as follows: The aging **King Edward** has no heir, so there is an unclear line of succession. **Harold Godwinsson**, his English brother-in-law, and William, Duke of Normandy and a distant cousin to Edward, will both eventually lay claim to the throne. Harold gets lost on a hunting expedition and winds up in Normandy, captured by Count Guy. William ransoms him, and in one of the most interesting moments in the tapestry, Harold swears an oath of allegiance to William. William is shown seated, holding his sword, while Harold swears on a pair of relics. Textual accounts describe one relic so the second, which appears behind him, has been interpreted as representing a prior oath to Edward. Harold returns to England, Edward dies and Harold declares himself king. William builds a fleet and sails to England. This begins the most intense portion of the Tapestry, the Battle of **Hastings**, which is characterised by the relentless charge of the Normans. The horrors of war are depicted clearly, with women and children forced to flee burning homes and dismembered corpses lying in the lower margin. The battle images are justly famous, showing Normans on horseback, charging in powerfully from the left. They are met by the stalwart shield wall of the Anglo-Saxons. The Normans push through and eventually kill Harold. The Anglo-Saxons flee and the Tapestry breaks off, so no image survives of William as king, though it seems reasonable to conjecture that one was there.

The Tapestry's account seems designed to show that William was justified in his conquest, but it tells the story, via the Anglo-Saxon artists responsible for its physical production, in English terms. The unadorned prose of the text gives the appearance of a factual account, but also participates in constructing the program justifying William's claims to the throne.

Colours are used throughout for impact and contrast, not for naturalism, so we find blue horses and horses with legs of four different colours. Almost the entire work is bordered at its top and bottom. These bands contain heraldic beasts, human figures and scenes from fables. Some of these have been noted as having some of the most explicit imagery of naked bodies from Anglo-Saxon England, including visibly aroused men chasing women. Many of the marginal elements have been connected through metaphor and symbolism with the main narrative. The margins are also tied directly to the main narrative; particularly at moments of great dynamism, the central scenes spill over into the margins. We find, for example, beside the coronation of Harold, figures pointing into the upper margin at Halley's Comet, which was visible in 1066 and seen as a bad omen. Likewise, in the great battle scenes, archers and corpses appear in the lower register.

The Tapestry is now housed in its own museum, the Centre Guillaume le Conquérant, in the city of Bayeux, Normandy.

See also Art and Architecture.

Further Reading

Bouet, Pierre, Brian Levy and François Neveux (eds.). 2004. *The Bayeux Tapestry: Embroidering the Facts of History. The Proceedings of the Cerisy Colloquium* (1999). Presses Universitaires de Caen.

Brown, Shirley Ann. 1988. *The Bayeux Tapestry: History and Bibliography*. Boydell Press.

Lewis, Suzanne. 1999. *The Rhetoric of Power in the Bayeux Tapestry*. Cambridge University Press.

Foys, Martin Kennedy. 2003. *The Bayeux Tapestry*. Scholarly Digital Editions.

Wilson, David. 1985. *The Bayeux Tapestry*. Thames & Hudson.

Asa Mittman

Beaker People

The term 'Beaker People' is used in reference to an assemblage of archaeological material found in Britain in the Late **Neolithic**/Early **Bronze Age**, the significance of which has been under debate over the past century. The definitive artefacts are pottery vessels called Beakers which first appeared around 2,700 BC and were still in use a millennium later. From the start, Beakers seem to have been status objects, probably associated with the consumption of alcohol. The distinctively shaped and decorated pots are usually found with other artefacts including barbed and tangled arrowheads, archers' wrist guards and flat copper daggers. Initially, archaeologists thought that the appearance of Beaker pottery implied the presence of invaders from the continent, but this is no longer felt tenable. The idea of Beaker invasions was first advanced in 1912, by Lord Abercromby in his *Bronze Age Pottery*. By the 1960s it was being suggested that there had been seven Beaker invasions of Britain, introducing different lifestyles to the north and south of the country. The Beaker People, or Beaker culture, was also seen to be associated with the rite of single-grave burial and with the introduction of horse riding. It was considered that the occurrence of two distinctive types of skull that were found in graves of the period furthered the arguments for invasions of Beaker People. The invaders were seen to be those who were brachycephalic (wide skulled) as opposed to the native population, which were dolichocephalic (narrow skulled).

More recent research has shown greater variation in early prehistoric skull shapes than hitherto believed, so the differences between the burials in early Neolithic chambered tombs and Beaker graves are now explained as gradual indigenous changes rather than invasion. Current thinking, while not dismissing the idea of some settlers in Britain from the Continent, generally rejects the idea of 'invasions' by Beaker People. Beaker pottery certainly originated on the Continent rather then being developed in Britain. The vessels vary considerably in shape and were usually decorated with cord impressions. The earliest (which probably originated on the lower Rhine or in the Low Countries and are found in Britain along the south and east coasts and along the east coast of Scotland) were decorated with all-over cord impressions (AOC or Bell Beakers). Later Beakers have necks, long-necked and short-necked forms representing regional variations. Eventually, Beakers deteriorated in quality, for example the crudely decorated (barbed wire beakers). Occasionally they had handles.

Around the same time, the people who used Beakers seem to have introduced both copper working and gold working to Britain. Gold 'sun discs' have been found, as well as crescent shaped gold collars (lunulae) which are often decorated with similar designs to those found on Beakers. Early copper daggers and pins as well as flat axes were later augmented by bronze work, the skills for which probably originated in Saxo-Thuringia. The people associated with Beakers were certainly active traders. Early copper knives from **Wessex** have been shown to have been made from central European copper, while one Wiltshire knife was made of metal from Ireland. Axes and lava were imported, and some lunulae reached the other side of the Channel.

See also Ceramics and Glass; Metalworking.

Further Reading

Clarke, D. 1970. *Beaker Pottery of Great Britain and Ireland*. Cambridge University Press.

Clarke, D. V., T. G. Cowie and A. Foxton (eds.). 1985. *Symbols of Power at the Time of Stonehenge*. HMSO.

Harrison, R. J. 1980. *The Beaker Folk: Copper Age Archaeology in Western Europe*. Thames & Hudson.

Pearson, M. Parker. 2005. *Bronze Age Britain* (2nd rev. edn.). Batsford.

Jennifer Laing

Bede (c.673–735)

Bede, known as 'the Venerable', was born in England, became a monk in **Jarrow** and has left behind the largest corpus of theological writings in Latin by any insular writer in the first millennium by far. He is, without doubt, the foremost Anglo-Saxon theologian; but because he wrote on the history of his people as Christians (he entitled this the *Historia Ecclesiastica Gentis Anglorum*), he is more often used as a source for insular history than as a theologian. Bede was born somewhere in the north of England (exactly where we do not know), and when aged seven he was given by his parents to the monastery of Wearmouth (**Monkwearmouth**), under **Abbot Benedict Biscop** (ob. 690). Soon afterwards, he was transferred to a daughter house of Wearmouth, Jarrow, which was not far along the river Tyne and lived under Abbot Coelfrid (ob. 716). Apart from a couple of short trips to gather information, he remained there for the rest of his life. Ordained as a priest c. 703, the life of his community, the liturgy and his work (teaching and writing) seem to have been his only concerns.

In 731, Bede drew up a list of his works. Although incomplete, the thirty works mentioned can be divided thus: twenty-one pieces of biblical exegesis, four pieces of hagiography (into this category he would have placed his historical writings), one work on science (and we could add others on chronology), two works on grammar, a book of letters and a book of liturgical material (and we could add many homilies). The range is expressive of the concerns of theology at his time and of the monastic curriculum in particular. It is in his commentaries on the Christian scriptures that we see him at his best. They are largely derivative from the great Latin fathers: Augustine, Ambrose, Jerome and Gregory; but while Bede was anxious to display his dependence (to show how unoriginal he was he developed the use of marginal codes to identify sources: e.g. *HI* indicates that he is drawing on *HIeronymous* [Jerome]) he did not act as a simple excerptor. His aim was to smooth over differences and omissions to provide a seamless exegesis that seems to show all four (and others) speaking 'with one voice'. It was this ability that made his work so popular. Bede is, therefore, the ideal of the pre-Carolingian schoolmaster, and because of that reputation he has long been regarded as the last of the 'Latin Fathers'. Through his writings Bede also further refined the notion of western monasticism as that became identified with 'Benedictinism'.

Today Bede is less known as a theologian but more as a historian as exemplified by his *Historia Ecclesiastica Gentis Anglorum* ('The History of the English Nation as a Church' ['as a church' is the best way to render the adjective *ecclesiastica* which qualifies *historia*]). However, his aim was theological: to show that his own 'nation' was an elect one, a people that figure in God's providence. It is to be noted that he was not writing the history of 'the English church' or the history of 'the English people', but of one of the *gentes* of the Earth (his notion of a *gens*, a nation, is based on Paul's *Letter to the Romans* [e.g. in Ch. 9]), and his aim was to show that they are now part of the group of peoples who make up the church. This is a view of history that is foreign to us but was fundamental to Bede's role models: Eusebius, Orosius and Gregory of Tours. To this end he had to show that the pagan ancestors could be brought within the sphere of God's saving plans, given the gospel and then grow into a church, with all that involved. Although in most matters Bede followed Augustine closely, on the issue of the conversion of the Anglo-Saxons he developed Augustine's notion of the 'Egyptian God' beyond recognition to produce a theory of God's working outside the Church as well as a theory of inculturation whereby missionaries could build upon pagan customs and practices by redirecting them towards their true end. This theory was an important element in the armoury of Anglo-Saxon missionaries.

Bede can be seen as typical of early Anglo-Saxon learning. He lived in **Northumbria** (a geographical term which was defined by his work) whose Christianity was a legacy of Irish missionaries from **Iona** and many of the books in his library came by way of Iona. Yet, he was also conscious of the larger world of Latin Christianity which he felt was represented by the work of **Augustine** of **Canterbury** coming from the very centre of the Latin West: Rome. His writings show familiarity with scholarship in both directions, but he was insistent that if there was any disparity between these traditions then the whole should determine the part, and not vice versa. Hence, within his *Historia* he created out of a pragmatic decision by a prince at Streanaeshalch (now often identified **Whitby** – but this is not certain) on a minor point of practice an image of a council as momentous as Nicaea in 325, whereby the Anglo-Saxons pledge their loyalty to Rome.

However, nothing in the culture of the Anglo-Saxons was either as clear-cut or as organised as Bede presents it to us.

Bede's larger legacy is complex; he fixed the message of the Fathers for much of the Middle Ages, popularised the use of AD dating in historical writing, became the expert on *computus* (Easter dating) and, at a local level, canonised a particular picture of early Christianity in the British Isles.

See also Celtic Christianity; Literature.

Further Reading

Bede. *Ecclesiastical History of the English People.* Trans. Bertram Colgrave (1969), edited with Introduction and Notes by Judith McClure and Roger Collins (1994). Oxford University Press.

Bonner, Gerard (ed.). 1976. *Famulus Christi: Essays in Commemoration of the Thirteenth Centenary of the Birth of the Venerable Bede.* Society for the Promotion of Christian Knowledge.

Dekkers, Eligius, and Aemilius Gaar. 1995. *Clavis Patrum Latinorum.* Brepols. Items: 1343–1384; 1565–1567; 2032; 2273; 2318–2323b; and 2333.

Jones, Charles W. 1969. 'Some Introductory Remarks on Bede's Commentary on Genesis'. *Sacris Erudiri* 19: 115–198.

Ward, Benedicta. 1990. *The Venerable Bede.* Geoffrey Chapman.

Thomas O'Loughlin

Belgae

The *Belgae* occur as a group of tribes who lived in Gallia Belgica (an area between the Seine, Marne and Rhine, now roughly corresponding to Belgium) who were defeated by **Julius Caesar** in 57 BC. The latter suggested that there were close ties between Britain and Belgic Gaul and referred to one Divitiacus as a king who ruled in both areas c. 80–60 BC, shortly before Caesar's own expeditions to Britain. The fact that coins originating in Belgic Gaul were imported to Britain from the second century BC led to archaeologists developing a theory of complex invasions and settlements of Belgic people in south-east England down to the time of Caesar, similarities in pottery, burial rites and other cultural attributes being taken as evidence for invasions. Although it is not doubted that the culture complex often termed by archaeologists as '**Swarling-Aylesford**' shows close ties between Britain and the Continent. It is now less widely accepted that invasions should account for it and more subtle processes of cultural transmission are now evoked as explanation.

After the conquest, the Romans seem to have defined a Belgic tribal canton with its *civitas* capital at Winchester (*Venta Belgarum*), which was formerly of the Atrebatic territory. Ptolemy also attributed **Bath** (*Aquae Sulis*) to the region, with Portsmouth being another known town of importance. Although it has been disputed whether it was entirely a Roman creation, current opinion favours the view that the only reason for the Roman appellation was a pre-existing native one. Under the Romans, the pottery industry seems to have flourished, with a large number of villas appearing by the end of the Roman period, though the time of the **Saxon** invasions in the fifth century affected the *civitas* similarly to others in **Roman Britain**. A tradition of Belgic royal genealogy may have survived in Wales throughout their occupation, being treasured later, especially in medieval times, and it is possible that a branch of *Belgae* also settled in Ireland, though this is based largely on mythological references to the *Fir Bolg*.

See also Ceramics and Glass.

Further Reading

Birchall, A. 1965. 'The Aylesford-Swarling Culture: The Problem of the Belgae Reconsidered'. *Proceedings of the Prehistoric Society* 31: 241–367.

Cunliffe, B. W. 2005. *Iron Age Communities of Britain* (4th edn.). RKP.

Hawkes, C., and G. C. Dunning. 1930. 'The Belgae of Gaul and Britain'. *Archaeological Journal* 12: 411–430.

Todd, Malcolm. 1999. *Roman Britain* (3rd edn.). Blackwell.

Anne Sassin

Beltaine

In Irish mythology, Beltaine is the beginning of the Summer season which started on the first of May. Beltaine (Modern Irish *Bhealtaine*) derives from the Old-Irish word *Bel-tene*, 'bright fire'. The name is also linked to *Belenus*, or *Bel*, the 'bright' or 'shining' Celtic god of light and patron of the Beltaine celebration.

The Celtic year was divided into two main parts, beginning with Beltaine, which marked the light and bright season, and followed by **Samhain**, the first of November, which heralded the end of summer and the coming of the dark winter days. On Beltaine, the cattle were driven out of their confined and secured winter stables to graze on the summer pastures and meadows. It was a feast of abundance and fertility. Even now, wreaths are hung on doors, and trees are decorated with ribbons, flowers and garlands, resulting in maypole dancing. These were expressions of gaiety, light and life. The decorating of the May Tree was also a festivity on the Continent, especially in Germany, Switzerland and the Slavic countries.

Great bonfires lit up on *Oidhche Bhealtaine* ('the Eve of Beltaine'), and cattle from the surrounding villages would be gathered on the hill of Uisneach (present day County **Meath**). The herd would be driven through two big bonfires to ensure an abundant fertility of the herd and to make sure that the people had a good harvest at the end of the season. It was part of a ritual cleansing ceremony.

The Continental Celtic year was not only divided into the main festivals of Beltaine and Samhain, two more existed: Imbolc and Lughnasadh. *Imbolc*, the first of February, was also a fertility season, even though little is known about the festivities surrounding it. Later, Imbolc was Christianised as **St Brigid**'s Day, after the fifth-/sixth-century saint, Brigid of **Kildare**. *Lughnasadh*, the first of August, was celebrated in honour of the sun god **Lugh** and it was a harvest festival. It was a time when the clans and tribes came together and games were held. 1 August is still a National Holiday in Switzerland (Helvetia), which could well be the original place of this Celtic tradition as the ancient Helvetians worshipped Lugh.

Like the festival of Samhain, the dark opposite of Beltaine, on 33 October, Beltaine was a time when the gates of the Otherworld were believed to be open and supernatural beings were able to wander around. Human beings could also enter the other, immortal world, but they never knew what price they would have to pay for that extraordinary trip.

The ***Tuatha Dé Danann***, the Otherworldy tribe who invaded prehistoric Ireland, are believed to have arrived in Ireland on Beltaine.

See also Irish Language.

Further Reading

Danaher, Kevin. 1972. *The Year in Ireland*. Mercier Press.

Koch, John (ed.). 1995. *The Celtic Heroic Age: Literary Sources for Ancient Celtic Europe, Early Ireland and Wales*. Celtic Studies Publications.

O'Rahilly, Thomas R. 1971. *Early Irish History and Mythology*. Dublin Institute for Advanced Studies.

Nicki Bullinga

Benedict Biscop

Benedict Biscop, inveterate traveller and innovator, laid the foundations for English scholarship in **Northumbria** that would culminate in the works of **Bede**. Biscop was born c. 628 in Northumbria and was of a noble family close to the king. His given name was Biscop Baducing. When he was twenty-five and a minister to King **Oswiu** and a layman, Biscop decided to travel to Rome to view the Christian relics and the resting places of the apostles. In **Kent**, he met and then travelled with the young **St. Wilfrid**, who was also on his way to Rome. Wilfrid stopped for sometime at Lyons in Gaul, Biscop continued onto Rome and returned to Northumbria. Twelve years later he made another pilgrimage to Rome, and while there he went to the monastery at Lérins, an island off the coast of France in the Mediterranean, and took monastic vows, took the name Benedict and studied for two years. His return to Rome coincided with the journey of his countryman Wigheard, the archbishop elect of **Canterbury** who was in Rome to receive the pallium. Wigheard died of plague and Pope Vitalian then appointed the Byzantine monk **Theodore of Tarsus** to the post and deputed Biscop to accompany him to Canterbury and temporarily take the position of abbot of St Augustine's until Hadrian could come and take over. Biscop and Theodore departed Rome 27 May 668 and arrived almost a year later; Hadrian arrived in 670. Biscop went again to Rome in 671, this time with the express purpose of purchasing books and other materials to furnish a monastic foundation. He then returned to Northumbria and received land from King Ecgfrith at the mouth of the Wear River and founded in 673 or 674 the monastery of **Monkwearmouth**.

Biscop went to Gaul and brought back masons, glaziers and other workmen and erected a church in the Roman style; the building was completed in about a year. Upon completion, both Biscop and his prior, Ceolfrith, went to Rome again and returned with additional books, pictures and images to decorate the church and also brought with them John, then presenter of St Peter's in Rome, to teach their monks the proper method of chanting. Monkwearmouth was extremely successful and by c. 681 Ecgfrith had given Biscop additional land to endow a second monastery, **Jarrow**, some 12 miles (19.31 kilometres) from the first foundation. When completed, Biscop appointed **Ceolfrith** abbot of Jarrow, and the latter remained there with some twenty monks, including a young Bede. In 685, Biscop made his fifth and final trip to Rome and, as was by now his custom, returned with books and other materials to enrich his foundations in every way. Shortly after his return, he developed a 'paralysis', as Bede calls it, which became worse over the course of three years, until he died in 689.

It is largely through the efforts of Biscop that Monkwearmouth-Jarrow became the important and vital centres they did at the centre of the Northumbrian Renaissance. From this foundation, within a few years of Biscop's death, Ceolfrith would have produced three great pandects of the Bible according to the Vulgate. Of these three, the one that survives, known as *Codex Amiatinus,* is the earliest witness to the Vulgate text. From this foundation would come the important author Bede. It is difficult to assess the full impact of Biscop's life, but his zeal and his foundation directly influenced and affected the rest of the medieval period.

See also Celtic Christianity; Monasticism.

Further Reading

Bede. 1965. *Lives of the Abbots of Wearmouth and Jarrow*. Trans. J. F. Webb. Penguin.

Robson, H. L. 1974–1976. 'Benedict Bishop of Wearmouth'. *Antiquities of Sunderland* 26: 34–46.

Wormald, Patrick. 1976. 'Bede and Benedict Biscop'. Pp.141–169 in *Famulus Christi: Essays in Commemoration of the Thirteenth Centenary of the Birth of the Venerable Bede*. Edited by Gerald Bonner. SPCK.

Larry Swain

Beowulf

Literary historians have claimed since the early nineteenth century that *Beowulf* is the oldest, best Germanic epic to have survived to our period. The action of the poem is centred on the three exploits of a *Geatish* (a Scandinavian ethnic group located in Jutland) hero named Beowulf, for whom there are potential comparisons in Norse and **Anglo-Saxon** writings but who is not directly traceable in any surviving text. In the first of the three exploits, Beowulf and his followers voyage to Denmark and the court of King Hrothgar whose meadhall Heorot is being regularly ravaged by a cannibalistic, man-like monster named Grendel. Beowulf vanquishes this troll in hand-to-hand combat, tearing off his arm in the battle. In the second exploit, Grendel's mother comes to Heorot seeking vengeance for her slain son, and murders Æscere, Hrothgar's favorite, in retribution for her son's death. Beowulf traces her to an underground lair and, with the help of an enchanted sword hanging on the cave wall, he slays her. At the centre of the third exploit is a fight with a dragon which has been ravaging the *Geatish* countryside which an aged Beowulf finally dispatches with the help of one remaining loyal retainer, Wiglaf, although the epic hero dies from a mortal wound sustained in the fight. All three events are properly framed with careful descriptions of courtly behaviour and oratory appropriate to the cultures portrayed here. The end of Grendel and subsequent death of his mother are celebrated by the Danes and Geats, and the fight with the dragon leads to Beowulf's funeral and the close of the epic.

Numerous digressions into early Germanic legends, many of which are found in other Scandinavian, Anglo-Saxon and continental Germanic traditions, are woven into the narrative. While it is true that there are no other complete poems extant similar in theme, style and structure to *Beowulf*, it would also seem to be likely that this epic poem reflects an important literary tradition. Although the poem is written in **Old English**, the language of the Anglo-Saxons, a passing reference to King **Offa** of **Mercia** (d.796), who was well-known throughout Europe in the early Middle Ages, constitutes the only English reference in the poem. A reference to King Hygelac's raid on Frisia recorded by Frankish scribes in the early sixth century, wherein a military force led by Theudebert, son of the king of the Franks, killed the *Geatish* King, provides the earliest event mentioned in the poem which can be historically documented outside of it. Unlike Attila or the eponymous heroes of Norse saga, there is no historical personage to be associated with Beowulf; in spite of the name 'Beow' appearing in the legendary portions of some surviving West Saxon genealogies.

In his famous lecture, *Beowulf: The Monsters and the Critics*, first published in 1936, J. R. R. Tolkien demonstrated how the poem had been seen for too long as a document to be mined by historians for information about institutions and culture in the so-called Dark Ages; he hoped he could persuade his auditors to understand the poem as a work of literary art, using the conventions and language appropriate to its time and place.

He had to dispel the notion that Grendel, Grendel's mother and the dragon were primitive or unrefined images incapable of expressing sophisticated conflict. 'A dragon is no idle fancy', he wrote most memorably. 'Whatever may be his origins, in fact or invention, the dragon in legend is a potent creation of men's imagination, richer in significance than his barrow is in gold.' If there has been one single moment in the poem's critical history when readings of it began to change, this may have been that moment.

For several decades after Tolkien's intervention, however, one debate that he might have quelled continued and continues today, although on different terms. Historians might be willing to abandon *Beowulf* as a source of cultural data, but a large number of people wanted a pre-conversion, if not outright pagan, touchstone for reasons that sometimes seemed to touch identity politics or other ideological concerns. In fact, the poem is ambiguous. As Roy Liuzza has observed, '*Beowulf* is a secular Christian poem about pagans which avoids the easy alternatives of automatic condemnation or enthusiastic anachronism'. Its complexities as a work of literature are perhaps unmatched before we get to Chaucer. Liuzza further adds:

> recent work recognised that *Beowulf*, like the culture of the Anglo-Saxons themselves, reflects a variety of interdependent and competing influences and attitudes, even a certain tension inherent in the combination of biblical, patristic, secular Latin, and popular Germanic material.

Most recently, the poem has developed a place in popular culture that is unusual for any poetic work, let alone one written at least 1,000 years ago in a language that has had no native speakers for at least 700 years. Since 1999, it has been the subject of at least four feature-length commercial films, an opera and a best-selling translation by Nobel prize-winning poet, Seamus Heaney, whence it landed on the *New York Times* bestseller list. Actor Benjamin Bagby has memorised a large portion of the poem in Old English and has performed it regularly to sold-out crowds in Europe and America. In February 2007, he gave four such performances in the eastern United States and returned in April of the same year for yet another engagement in New York City. All of this suggests an incredible market for material derived from this poem, whose only parallel may be the popularity of the Arthurian legend throughout the twentieth century.

Contemporary critics of the poem now look to *Beowulf* for subject matter demonstrating their positions in a variety of post-modern analyses, such as those embracing gender theory, semiotics, post-colonial readings and psychoanalytical approaches, to name a few. While these approaches are regularly used with many medieval texts, *Beowulf* has been particularly productive of important new readings, possibly because of the high tension the poem maintains among the binaries of youth and age, violence and order, the human and the monstrous, and the governed and those that govern. Furthermore, new discoveries in archaeology as well as new techniques in pan-Germanic and Anglo-Saxon anthropology and medieval historiography have all found appropriate applications with this text. It is one of incredible richness.

The unique manuscript containing *Beowulf* now belongs to the British Library, where it is known by the shelf mark, Cotton MS Vitellius A.15, which identifies it as having belonged to Robert Cotton (d.1631). Cotton must have acquired the book directly or indirectly from Laurence Nowell (d.1571) because Nowell's name is inscribed on the first leaf of the second part of what is now a two-part codex, having been first bound together in the seventeenth century. The first of these dates is from the twelfth century and contains four works of prose. The second volume contains the Old English poems *Beowulf* and *Judith*, accompanied by three prose works: a life of St. Christopher, a description of the fantastic beings which inhabit distant lands called *Marvels of the East* and a translation of *A Letter of Alexander to Aristotle*. The Nowell codex is usually dated around AD 1000; the date of the composition of *Beowulf* is possibly earlier than the single manuscript in which it survives, which we often know to be true in the case of the textual history of a number of Greek and Latin classical texts. The date of composition of the poem ranges from the seventh century to the eleventh, a problem for the student of the poem that is not likely to be resolved soon, because the methodologies for dating ancient poetry depend for their acceptance on debatable assumptions in other areas of scholarship, such as linguistics and archaeology.

Modern editions of *Beowulf* begin with John Mitchell Kemble's publication of his edition of the poem in 1833. The best known edition and the edition most often cited by scholars today is the third edition of Friedrich Klaeber's *Beowulf and the Fight at Finnsburg* (Boston: D. C. Heath & Co., 1950). A fourth edition of Klaeber's *Beowulf and the Fight at Finnsburg*, under the editorship of R. D. Fulk, Robert E. Bjork and John D. Niles, appeared in 2008. A digital edition of the manuscript, *The Electronic Beowulf*, has also been prepared by Kevin S. Kiernan with Ionut Emil Iacob for the British Library Publications in 2004.

See also Literature.

Further Reading

Bjork, Robert E., and John D. Niles (eds.). 1998. *A Beowulf Handbook*. University of Nebraska Press.

Fulk, Robert D. (ed.). 1991. *Interpretations of Beowulf: A Critical Anthology*. Indiana University Press.

Joy, Eileen A., and Mary K. Ramsey (eds.). 2006. *The Postmodern Beowulf: A Critical Casebook*. West Virginia University Press.

Luizza, Roy M. 1999. *Beowulf: A New Verse Translation*. Broadview.

Orchard, Andy. 2005. *A Critical Companion to Beowulf*. D. S. Brewer.

Patrick W. Conner

Bernicia

The most northerly of the **Anglo-Saxon** kingdoms was the province of the Bernicians. Its boundary with its southern English neighbour, **Deira**, seems to have lain at the river Tees and it expanded, at the expense of Brittonic-speaking kingdoms towards the west and north. By the time of **Bede,** in the early eighth century, it comprised three dioceses which probably reflected either secular divisions of the kingdom or the ghosts of earlier kingdoms. Along the north seacoast, the diocese of Hexham ran from the river Tees to the river Aln and the diocese of Lindisfarne from the Aln to as far as the Avon in modern West Lothian. To the West the third Bernician diocese lay at **Whithorn** in modern Galloway. Its boundaries with Hexham and **Lindisfarne** are unknown.

Most of our information concerning early Bernicia is derived from Bede's *Historia Ecclesiastica* and from ***Historia Brittonum*** supplemented by king-lists and hagiography. The first king of the Bernicians was said to have been Oesa (sometimes Eosa), but it is not until the days of his grandson **Ida**, the apical figure of the later dynasty, that a narrative begins to emerge. Ida's reign seems to have run from about 541 to 552 and he is credited with having added the fortress of **Bamburgh** (originally *Bebbanburh* – named from his wife Bebba) to the kingdom. This tradition probably represents a record of the expansion of the kingdom north of the Aln into the territory of the **Brittonic Gododdin** tribe. Bamburgh overlooks the island of Lindisfarne where, according to *Historia Brittonum*, the British king **Urien** briefly besieged Ida's son Theodoric (568–575). Regional hegemony passed to Bernicia during the reign of Ida's grandson and Theodoric's nephew **Æthelfrith** (589–616) who Bede claimed 'ravaged the **Britons** more extensively than any other English ruler ... for no other ruler or king had subjected more land to the English nation or settled it, having first either exterminated or conquered the natives' (*Historia Ecclesiastica* 1. 34). In addition to British territories, Æthelfrith also conquered Deira to the south. Following Æthelfrith's death in battle, Bernicia was briefly conquered by a resurgent Deira, but from 634, his sons welcomed Christian missionaries into the kingdom and restored its regional hegemony. From 679, Deira and Bernicia were ruled by a single king of the Bernician royal house and this kingdom came to be known as **Northumbria**.

Although the Bernicians spoke **Old English** and were regarded as English by themselves and their neighbours, their archaeological imprint is not distinctively Anglo-Saxon and in their use of fortified citadels such as Bamburgh, the **Mote of Mark** and Dunbar, they resembled their British neighbours. Whether this impression reflects a more mixed population or perhaps the fact that they were largely settled outside the old Roman frontier is unclear. Even after the union of Deira and Bernicia this most northerly of English provinces retained its distinctive character and identity. In later centuries, this identity was most obviously focused upon the veneration of St. **Cuthbert**.

Further Reading

Colgrave, Bertram, and R. A. B. Mynors (eds. and tr.). 1969. *Bede's Ecclesiastical History of the English People*. Oxford University Press.

Kirby, David P. 1992. *The Earliest English Kings*. Routledge.

Yorke, Barbara. 1991. *Kings and Kingdoms of Early Anglo-Saxon England*. Seaby.

Alex Woolf

Bertha (c.565–c.601)

Bertha (c. 565–c. 601) was a Merovingian princess, wife of **Æthelbert** of **Kent** (560–616) and mother of Eadbald of Kent (616–640). She was the daughter of the Frankish king Charibert of Paris (r. 561–567) and his wife Ingoberga (d. 589). At some point after Bertha's birth, Charibert repudiated Ingoberga, who moved to the area of Tours, where she maintained a close relationship with Gregory of Tours (c. 539–594). Bertha married Æthelbert of Kent c. 580. When she arrived in Kent, she was accompanied by the Frankish bishop Liudhard. Bertha continued to practice her Christian faith in Kent, worshipping at a church dedicated to St. Martin of Tours just outside **Canterbury**. **Augustine** and the other Christian missionaries sent to England by Pope Gregory I (590–604) also used this church before Æthelbert converted to Christianity some time in 601. After Bertha's death, she was buried in a chapel dedicated to St. Martin of Tours within the church of Saints Peter and Paul in Canterbury. Æthelbert was buried beside her.

Bertha's marriage to Æthelbert is virtually unique in the history of Anglo-Saxon England, as it is the only confirmed marriage between an Anglo-Saxon king and a Merovingian princess. The marriage has been highlighted as an example of political contact between England and Gaul in the late sixth century. In addition to any political dimension, the marriage was also important to the conversion of the English. Although Bertha did not personally convince her husband to convert to Christianity before Augustine's mission of 597, she was a strong Christian presence within Kent. After Augustine's arrival, she provided assistance for the mission, and she was praised by Pope Gregory I for her efforts.

See also Celtic Christianity.

Further Reading

Colgrave, Bertram, and R. A. B. Mynors (eds. and tr.). 1992. *Bede's Ecclesiastical History of the English People*. Clarendon Press.

Thorpe, Lewis (tr.). 1974. *Gregory of Tours: The History of the Franks*. Penguin.

Wood, Ian. 1994. *The Merovingian Kingdoms: 450–751*. Longman.

Yorke, Barbara. 2006. *The Conversion of Britain: Religion, Politics and Society in Britain, c. 600–800*. Pearson.

Deanna Forsman

Bewcastle Cross

Along with the **Ruthwell Cross**, the tapering shaft, 14.44 feet (4.4 metres) high, that now stands in the churchyard at Bewcastle, **Cumbria**, is one of the major early works of Anglo-Saxon sculpture. Although always assumed to be a cross, no head is ever known to have existed, and it may simply have been a shaft. The churchyard in which it stands lies within a Roman fort, one of the subsidiaries to **Hadrian's Wall** and is a reminder that forts were often given by Anglo-Saxon kings to clerics for their churches, though there is no evidence for an early ecclesiastical foundation on the site.

The ornament on the Bewcastle Cross displays John the Baptist, Christ in Majesty, and a falconer, probably St. John the Evangelist, with vine-scroll, interlace and chequered patterns on the sides. Additionally, it carries a sundial and six panels with runic inscriptions, the reading of which has caused some dispute. The style is close to that at Ruthwell, and it is of approximately the same date (perhaps slightly later), in the second quarter of the eighth century.

See also Art and Architecture.

Further Reading

Bailey, R. N., and R. J. Cramp (eds.). 1988. *Corpus of Anglo-Saxon Sculpture. Volume 2. Cumberland, Westmorland and Lancashire North of the Sands*. Oxford, 19–22; 61–72.

Lloyd Laing

Birdoswald

Birdoswald (*Banna*) is a fort along the western portion of **Hadrian's Wall** built to guard the Irthing bridge crossing. Covering nearly 4.94 acres (2 hectares) in area, the outline of this fort along with the foundations of some of its gates and buildings can still be seen today. Excavations lead by Tony Wilmott in the late 1980s revealed the reuse of Roman military buildings as domestic structures in the **Brittonic Age**. Two stone Roman granaries were, in their finals stages, renovated and turned into long timber halls. A stone hearth in the south granary led to the interpretation of the buildings as 'feasting halls', as commonly described in early medieval poetry (e.g. the 'mead hall' of ***Beowulf***). Also in the immediate post-Roman years timber buildings were constructed against the renovated gateway. The post-Roman occupation of Birdoswald lasted until about 520 and has been attributed to a remnant of local Roman soldiers who set up their own independent power base, or perhaps one that was part of a new defence system along the Wall.

Birdoswald also has tenuous connections to both St. **Patrick** and King **Arthur**. Charles Thomas has argued that Patrick was born at a small estate near the fort, *Banna* then being Patrick's *Bannavem Taburniae* (Thomas 1981). Since it was once thought that Birdoswald was named *Camboglanna*, some have argued that the fort was the sight of Arthur's last battle (***Camlan***) or even Camelot itself. The most recent excavator has rejected both of these claims.

See also Roman Army; Roman Britain.

Further Reading

Dark, K. R. 1992. 'A Sub-Roman Re-Defense of Hadrian's Wall?' *Britannia* 23: 111–120.
Selkirk, Andrew, and Tony Wilmott. 1989. 'Birdoswald: Dark-Age Halls in a Roman Fort'. *Current Archaeology* 116: 288–291.
Thomas, Charles. 1981. *Christianity in Roman Britain to AD 500.* University of California Press.
Wilmott, Tony, et al. 1997. *Birdoswald: Excavations of a Roman Fort on Hadrian's Wall and Its Successor Settlements, 1987–92.* English Heritage.

Christopher A. Snyder

Bog Bodies

Bog Bodies is a term used to describe ancient human remains, typically those that are perfectly preserved, that have been recovered from bogs and mires. Bog bodies can consist of entire corpses, or portions of them (heads, legs, torsos), frequently with their skin, hair, fingernails, internal organs and even facial features intact. Bog bodies can date from the **Neolithic** to the post-medieval period, but there is a distinct and large group scientifically dated to the **Bronze Age** and **Iron Age** that has attracted a range of archaeological interpretations. Bog bodies are a widespread phenomenon across northern and western Europe with hundreds found in Germany and Denmark in particular, while the Netherlands, Britain and Ireland have also produced numerous examples. Bog bodies have been recovered in bogs since the eighteenth century at least, when local people cutting turf uncovered startlingly well-preserved bodies in the peat (which being anaerobic and cold, inhibits the actions of organisms that typically rot organic materials such as wood, leather and skin, while acidic chemical compounds in the peat can also lead to a literal tanning of the skin). Most early discoveries were either hurriedly reburied on site or buried in coffins in graveyards, so that their qualities of preservation were quickly lost. These early discoveries were typically interpreted at the time as being the result of accidental deaths of people crossing bogs or as suicide or murder victims. The latter explanation was popular because bodies often seemed to be strangely mutilated, or merely consisted of body parts or were deliberately buried with hides and other objects.

Bog bodies continue to be found in modern times, although the large-scale mechanised extraction of peat has meant the discoveries are now often damaged. Modern influential research and publications have included those by the Danish archaeologist P. V. Glob in the 1960s and an increasing number of modern projects such as that by Ian Stead, Don Brothwell and colleagues on **Lindow Man**, an Iron Age bog body found in 1984 in Cheshire, England. Bog bodies have been subject to a variety of scientific and forensic analytical techniques. It is possible to X-ray bodies; investigate the person's age and social status (many show evidence for a lifestyle free of physical work, meaning that they may have been wealthy or from the upper social classes); reconstruct their diet and health in the period preceding their death and record the precise details of traumatic injury they suffered. The seemingly miraculous survival of bog bodies often evokes an emotional response in us today, as we can gaze into the face, or at fingerprints or intact hands of an individual person who has been dead for thousands of years.

Archaeologists have recognised that many Bronze Age and Iron Age bog bodies were the result of formal or deliberate ritual depositions of human remains in wetland contexts for a range of symbolic and ideological reasons, and that later prehistoric bog bodies in particular relate in some way to the contemporary deposition of bronze, gold and iron metalwork hoards and objects in waterlogged places in Europe. The writings of Classical authors have often been used to claim that Iron Age bog bodies were **druids**, outlaws, traitors or executed homosexuals, but it has been recognised in more recent times that these accounts, loaded with ideological agendas in the portrayal of northern peoples, are not necessarily accurate or truthful. Nevertheless, many bog bodies exhibit evidence of brutal treatment prior to death, being stabbed, decapitated, strangled or beaten often all at once.

One of the most famous bog bodies is Tollund Man, found in 1950 in Tollund Mose in Jutland, Denmark. This body of a male aged thirty to forty years was found in a small bog, at a depth of 8.20 feet (2.5 metres). The body, which was naked except for a leather cap and belt, lay on its right side, with its legs drawn up and arms bent. Around his neck was a noose of leather that had probably been used to garrotte or hang him. His last meal lay in his stomach and consisted of a gruel of porridge of barley, linseed and willow herb seeds (including the up to thirty different types of wild seeds) and he may have been buried (like many bog bodies) in the winter or early spring. Some mutilations may also be ritualistic. An Irish Iron Age bog body found in 2003 at Old Croghan, County Offaly, consisted only of a torso (the head and lower body had been removed) and the man had his nipples cut through with a blade. The Iron Age Clonycavan Man, County **Meath** (dated to c. 400–200 BC), found in 2003, consisted only of a head and torso and had probably been murdered through blows to the head with an axe. Interestingly, his hair had been gelled with a substance made of plant oil and resin (presumably only available to the upper social classes) that had to be imported from France or Spain. Some, but certainly not all, European Iron Age bog bodies seem to have been formally pinned into bog pools using hazel and other wooden stakes. Recently it has been suggested that Iron Age bodies in Ireland were often formally deposited in those bog lands that lay on significant territorial boundaries and that both the treatment of these individuals and the location of their remains relates in some way to the performance of power and **kingship** in early Ireland.

See also Barrows; Iron Age; Bronze Age; Kings and Kingship; Urnfield Culture.

Further Reading

Aldhouse Green, M. 2002. *Dying for the Gods: Human Sacrifice in Iron Age and Roman Europe.* Tempus/Stroud.

Brothwell, D. 1987. *The Bog Man and the Archaeology of People.* British Museum Publications.

Glob, P. V. 1969. *The Bog People: Iron-Age Man Preserved.* Faber.

Kelly, E. P. 2006. 'Secrets of the Bog Bodies: The Enigma of the Iron Age Explained'. *Archaeology Ireland* 75: 26–30.

Stead, I. M., J. B. Bourke and D. Brothwell. 1986. *Lindow Man: The Body in the Bog.* British Museum Publications.

Turner, R. C., and R. G. Scaife (eds.). 1995. *Bog Bodies: New Discoveries and Perspectives.* British Museum Publications.

Van der Sanden, W. 1996. *Through Nature to Eternity: The Bog People of Northwest Europe.* Museum Batavian Lion International.

Aidan O'Sullivan

Book of Armagh

The *Book of Armagh* is a manuscript (Trinity College Dublin, 52) of 222 folios which was produced in **Armagh** in Ireland around 807 at the instigation of Abbot Torbach (d. 808) by the scribe Ferdomnach (d. 846) and assistant scribes. While it is primarily a copy of the New Testament, it contains important documents relating to St. **Patrick**. Its contents, almost entirely in Latin, show why it is so important to modern scholarship, as well as showing that it was intended as a prestige book – it was well written with several illuminations – that could demonstrate the dignity and historical claims on Armagh at the time of its production when Armagh was claiming primacy over all the churches in Ireland and when the central argument in that claim was that it was the see of Patrick. In such an environment, a large gospel book also containing virtually every document in the early cult of Patrick could act as a 'charter' for those claims.

The manuscript contains these texts: (1) the entire New Testament (the Vulgate version); (2) an exegetical drawing of the New Jerusalem offering an interpretation of The Apocalypse of St. John 21–22; (3) materials elaborating the Eusebian apparatus used in Gospel studies; (4) Sulpicius Severus's *Vita Martini* (this text was paradigmatic for Latin hagiography); (5) Patrick's *Confessio*; (6) **Muirchú**'s *Vita Patricii*; (7) Tirechan's *Collectanea*; (8) the *Liber angeli* (a book claiming to be a heavenly revelation of the future status of Armagh); (9) six other fragments relating to Patrick's cult (see Lapidge and Sharpe 1985, n. 354–359) including the *Dicta Patricii* (three sayings attributed to Patrick and which may be genuine); (10) two liturgical fragments (see Lapidge and Sharpe 1985, n. 538–539); and finally (11) a note of a gift made to Armagh in 1002 by King **Brian Bóru** (see Lapidge and Sharpe 1985, n. 616).

The presence of the technical exegetical apparatus (items 2 and 3 in the list) shows that it was copied from a functional text intended for use by a scholar and to this was added the Patrician material. But why a single book had so wide a range of material — as seen in this agglomeration of texts – remains obscure. However, its dignity as a vehicle of the basic texts of Armagh increased with time, and it became a relic whose rightful possessor was the *comarba Padráig* (i.e. the bishop of Armagh) – as witness its use as a suitable place to record Armagh's links with Brian Bóru. The book remained with the hereditary stewards of Armagh until the seventeenth century, then after various owners it passed to Trinity College in the mid-nineteenth century.

See also Art and Architecture; Celtic Christianity; Literature.

Further Reading

Bieler, Ludwig. 1979. *The Patrician Texts in the Book of Armagh*. Dublin Institute for Advanced Studies.

Gwynn, John, 1913. *Liber Ardmachanus: The Book of Armagh*, edited with introduction and appendices. Royal Irish Academy.

O'Loughlin, Thomas. 2000. 'The Plan of the New Jerusalem in the Book of Armagh'. *Cambrian Medieval Celtic Studies* 39: 23–38.

Sharpe, Richard. 1983. 'Palaeographical Considerations in the Study of the Patrician Documents in the Book of Armagh'. *Scriptorium* 36: 3–28.

Thomas O'Loughlin

Book of Deer

The *Book of Deer* is a gospel book of likely early tenth or possibly ninth century production from the church of Deer in Aberdeenshire, and it is best known for having the earliest known instance of Gaelic written in Scotland, though it also contains Latin and an Old Irish colophon. The Latin text consists of the Gospels of all four Evangelists, though only that of John is complete, as well as the Office for the Visitation of the Sick and Apostles Creed. Despite having been produced in Scotland, the script itself is an Irish miniscule. The peculiar nature of portions of the Vulgate and tradition in keeping with Irish pocket gospels at 54 by 107 millimetres (0.054 by 0.107 metres) has led to a theory that it was executed from memory by a scribe who did not have a copy of the Gospels in front of him to copy. On the other hand, the Gaelic portion of the book is confined to the margins and is the work of at least five different hands, which includes an acknowledgement of the monastery's foundation under St. **Columba** and a deed by **David I**.

The eighty-six folio manuscript is illuminated, although the full-page Evangelist portraits have been viewed as little more than caricatures and of inferior quality and other decoration consists of borders of fret interlace surrounding the text, decorated initial letters and sketches of both animals and men with some elements possibly recalling the Pictish stone at nearby Elgin. The *Book of Deer* is currently housed in Cambridge University Library, having arrived there in 1715 from the library of Bishop Moore of Norwich. Though the history of when it left Scotland is uncertain, it has been put forward that it left during the Wars of Independence in the thirteenth and fourteenth century.

See also Art and Architecture; Celtic Christianity; Literature.

Further Reading

Geddes, J. 1998. 'The Art of the Book of Deer'. *Proceedings of the Society of Antiquaries of Scotland* 128: 537–550.

Laing, Lloyd. 2006. *The Archaeology of Celtic Britain and Ireland, c.* AD *400–1200*. Cambridge University Press.

Laing, Lloyd, and Jennifer Laing. 1995. *Celtic Britain and Ireland: Art and Society*. Herbert Press.

Anne Sassin

Book of Durrow

The *Book of Durrow* (so named as it was placed in a metal shrine in 916 in Durrow, a monastery of the Columban family) is an elaborate copy of the four gospels. It consists of 248 folios (page size: around 245 by 145 millimetres), was written in Irish majuscule and contains eleven full-page pictures. It also contains a remarkable pure and accurate text of the Vulgate, presents the gospels in the familiar Vulgate sequence of Matthew, Mark, Luke and John and presents the reader with an elaborate scholarly apparatus. Therefore, unlike gospel books that were intended mainly for the eye as beautiful artefacts – artistic monuments to the 'word of God' as a book, such as the ***Book of Kells*** – this is a book whose marginal additions render it more suitable for use in formal exegetical work by a scholar.

There is no agreement as to when or where it was produced. While some art historians note Northumbrian influences in the decoration, most scholars dealing with the codex see it as an Irish production. Many scholars are prepared to link it in some way with **Iona** (where in the period there were good connections with **Northumbria**) or a monastery with some connection to Iona (it does, after all, first enter the historical record in such a monastery). Dates for its production – all based on comparisons of the style of writing and decoration in this codex with other gospel books – vary from between 650 to the early years of the eighth century, but a good 'working date' (on which there is widespread agreement) would be the last decades of the seventh century. Since the late seventeenth century, it has been housed in Trinity College, Dublin (MS 57 [A. 4. 5]).

Given the unique place of the gospels in Christian memory, it is not surprising that these gospel books were produced with great splendour, commitment of resources and effort. However, what distinguishes this codex is that its apparatus indicates that it belonged to a distinct category of gospel manuscripts whose origins lie in the second century. Some manuscripts – often containing the whole New Testament (e.g. the ***Book of Armagh***) – were produced with the intention of having the whole canon, or part of it (e.g. the gospels in the case of 'pocket gospel books') available in one place. Others, such as the ***Book of Durrow***, were produced so as to show that the four-fold gospel was also one gospel and that the four evangelists spoke with a single consistent voice. This aim was achieved by providing a specific codex for the gospels and adding the Eusebian apparatus (canons at the beginning and then marginal numbers throughout) which was designed to harmonise the gospels without merging them into a single narrative and other introductory materials that serve to guide the reader through the gospels as whole documents. *The Book of Durrow* is a model of this process for not only does it have the canons but these have also been put into grids for easy reference. Moreover, the marginal numbers have been expanded to a degree never envisaged by Eusebius, which allows their use with an accuracy and speed unavailable in the majority of such codices, each section beginning is marked, and this ease of use is further facilitated by running heads with the names of the evangelists.

The presence of some of this apparatus is quite common in a gospel book, but having all of it points to a deliberate choice to provide a codex for study purposes. Producing this 'added value' was a very considerable work of scholarship in itself. The presence of the apparatus precludes the possibility that this book was produced for use in the liturgy – an assumption commonly found in references to it. The question which should be asked is, why was the reconciliation of the four gospels a major scholarly concern in the insular world in the seventh century? Only one place shows this concern: Iona in the time of **Adomnán** – a period and location that fits with all our other evidence. We know that Adomnán was interested in this problem and had the necessary skill to develop the apparatus to the form we find in the *Book of Durrow*.

See also Art and Architecture; Celtic Christianity; Literature.

Further Reading

Henderson, George. 1987. *From Durrow to Kells: The Insular Gospel Books 650–800.* Thames & Hudson.

Meehan, Bernard. 1996. *The Book of Durrow: A Medieval Masterpiece at Trinity College Dublin.* Roberts Rinehart/Town House Dublin.

O'Loughlin, Thomas. 1999. 'The Eusebian Apparatus in some Vulgate Gospel Books'. *Peritia* 13: 1–92.

Thomas O'Loughlin

Book of Kells

The *Book of Kells*, housed in Trinity College Library, Dublin, is one of the most significant of the surviving manuscripts of early medieval Europe. It comprises a text of the four Gospels in Latin, written on vellum (calf skin) on 340 folios (i.e. 680 pages), only two of which are without colour embellishment. About 30 folios are now missing; these include some of the preliminaries and the end of the *Gospel of St. John*. The pages are large 33 by 24 centimetres (0. 33 by 0. 24 metres), and the text is written in insular majuscule script. It takes its name from the monastery at **Kells**, County **Meath**, where it was in the eleventh century and from where it was stolen in 1006, to be found buried in the ground 'twenty nights and two months' later, stripped of the gold on its binding. It still bears some of the scars of its burial. After passing through several hands, it was given by one Henry Jones, Vice-Chancellor of the University of Dublin, to the college probably prior to 1681.

8. Irish manuscript illumination from *Book of Kells*, eighth century. Page bearing ornate initial of the *Gospel of St. Mark*, Trinity College, Dublin.

It was subsequently bound and rebound and the pages trimmed. The last rebinding was done in 1953, when it was bound in the four volumes in which it is now kept.

The decoration in the *Book of Kells* comprises six main elements: (1) canon tables, to enable specific events in the life of Christ recorded in the Gospels to be collated; (2) evangelist symbols; (3) portraits of Christ and the evangelists; (4) full-page illustrations of the Temptation of Christ (the 'Temple Page'), the Virgin and Child and the Betrayal; (5) prefatory cruciform 'carpet' pages before each gospel; (6) decorative text pages, most notably the *Christi autem* or 'Chi-Rho' page. There are additional decorative details throughout the book.

Debate has surrounded when and where it was made. The fact that it was in Kells at the beginning of the eleventh century does not mean it was necessarily made there. Kells was a monastic foundation that was established in 807 by Columban monks from **Iona** who fled the **Viking** raids. For it to have been entirely written and decorated at Kells, it would have been made after the beginning of the ninth century; it is difficult to believe that such a sumptuous book was one of the first things done by the refugee monks. Most scholars now believe it to have been a product of Iona, executed before the Viking attacks, though some favour the view that it was taken unfinished to Kells, perhaps after a Viking raid in AD 878, for further embellishment. There are strong arguments to support the view it was made on Iona, not least because of its close textual relationship to the ***Book of Durrow***, which could not possibly have been made at Kells but which could have been brought to Ireland along with the *Book of Kells* by the fleeing monks. There is also a context for its production at Iona, namely the enshrinement of the relics of St. **Columba** sometime between AD 752 and 767, under the patronage of Oengus mac Fergus, a Pictish king who ruled **Dalriada** and had wide contacts with the **Anglo-Saxon** world. It was never made for daily use, only for special occasions, and this explanation for its creation is paralleled by the creation of the ***Lindisfarne Gospels***, another great early medieval manuscript, for the enshrinement of St. **Cuthbert**. Many details in the *Book of Kells* can be paralleled on Pictish sculpture, and the link makes more sense if it were made by the neighbours of the **Picts**, the Dalriadic **Scots**, rather than across the water in Ireland.

Different hands are apparent in the decoration. Françoise Henry distinguished a number of separate artists: the 'Goldsmith' who produced metalwork effects (most notably in the Chi-Rho page), the cruciform page known as the 'page of eight circles' and the initial page of each gospel (except Luke); the 'Illustrator' who did the full-page pictures, the *Tunc crucifixerant* page' and the symbols at the start of the *Gospel of St. John*; and the 'portrait Painter' who did the portraits of evangelists and Christ and the initial page for Luke. A fourth painter did the *Nativitas Christi* page and one of the Canon pages. He may also have been responsible for much of the naturalistic animal ornament in the book, which is very Pictish in style – he may have been a Pict.

The decoration is extremely varied, with traditional 'Celtic' elements deployed alongside others of Mediterranean inspiration. In keeping with other manuscripts of the time, some of the ornament was produced geometrically, employing compasses and ruled lines. The colours (which did not include gold) were mostly minerals, dissolved in water with egg albumen as a binder. These minerals included orpiment (for yellow – a piece was found on the nearby Dalriadic site of **Dunadd**), red and white lead, verdigris (green), ultramarine (blue) and lapis lazuli, the last possibly imported from Afghanistan. Some shades of blue, pink and purple were obtained from folium, other shades of blue from woad and kermes (for red).

The iconography of Kells is extremely sophisticated and continues to intrigue art historians with the complexity of its symbolism, which required a very wide learning on the part of the artists.

See also Art and Architecture; Celtic Christianity; Literature.

Further Reading

Farr, C. 1997. *The Book of Kells*. The British Library.
Henderson, G. 1987. *From Durrow to Kells*. Thames & Hudson.
Henry, F. 1974. *The Book of Kells*. Thames & Hudson.
Meehan, B. 1994. *The Book of Kells*. Thames & Hudson.
O'Mahony, F. (ed.). 1994. *The Book of Kells*. Trinity College Library.

Lloyd Laing

Boudica (?–c. AD 61)

Boudica was the wife of **Prasutagus**, mother of his two daughters and queen of the ***Iceni***, a British tribe which occupied roughly the area of modern Norfolk in East Anglia.

In his will, Prasutagus left the Emperor Nero joint-heir with his own daughters in an attempt to safeguard his kingdom and family. After his death in AD 60, the provincial procurator, Decianus Catus, and the officials of the Roman governor ignored the terms of this will and treated the *Iceni* as if they had been forcibly conquered and subjugated. The Romans plundered, evicted and looted the British tribespeople mercilessly; when the queen objected, she was flogged and her daughters raped. Anti-Roman feeling, which had smouldered since the earlier revolt in AD 47, burst into flame and the humiliated Boudica launched a full-scale revolt against Rome, calling neighbouring British tribes to join the *Iceni* in their rebellion.

The ***Trinovantes***, neighbours of the *Iceni* to the south in present day Essex, had their own grievances. Discharged veterans from the Roman army had settled in the colony at **Colchester** (*Camulodunum*, the provincial capital) and drove these native British from their own homes and lands, treating them as slaves and captives. The *Iceni* and the *Trinovantes* both smarted under pressure from Roman moneylenders to supply funds for Roman projects, such as the Imperial cult based in Camulodunum. The two tribes joined forces under Boudica and attacked Camulodunum, which stood open and undefended. The rebels fired dwellings and shops, and a small band of soldiers who barricaded themselves inside the hated temple of Claudius were overcome within two days. Boudica swept on towards London.

An attempt was made to halt the rebels by Q. Petillius Cerialis, the legate of the Ninth legion, and a small force under his command, but these were cut to pieces by the British, and the terrified procurator, Decianus Catus, fled to Gaul.

The Roman governor of Britain, Suetonius Paullinus, was in North Wales, mounting an attack against Anglesey. When news reached him of the uprising he set out at speed with the cavalry for **London**, leaving the infantry to follow. However, on reaching London he found there were no other troops there and his own force was insufficient to defend the town. The only alternative was to withdraw and 'sacrifice the one town to save the general situation' (**Tacitus**, *Annals*, 14. 33). So London was abandoned to its fate and the British vented their hatred of Rome on its citizens. They burned, slaughtered and crucified, 'took no prisoners, sold no captives as slaves and went in for none of the usual trading of war' (Tacitus, *Annals*, 14. 33).

Their next target was ***Verulamium*** (modern **St Albans**) where the scene was mercilessly repeated. Archaeology has revealed the burned debris of what is presumed to be the destruction wrought by Boudica and her army. Tacitus gives the official reckoning as 70,000 Romans and allies slain between the three sites. Suetonius Paullinus by this time had regrouped and had added other forces till the total numbered around 10,000 men. He chose a site protected by woods and hills to the sides and rear and drew up his troops for battle somewhere in the Midlands (near Mancetter?). Here he engaged with Boudica's vast and unwieldy warrior horde. The superior discipline and weaponry of the Romans more than compensated for their fewer numbers; the Britons were overcome by a javelin attack and a legionary charge which fragmented their army and drove them back against their own wagons, which they had drawn up for the women and children to watch the battle. These wagons now proved a death trap for the warriors, who could not escape and were slaughtered by the Romans. Tacitus claimed 80,000 British dead for the loss of 400 Romans. Boudica was not slain on the battle field, but died soon after, by poison at her own hand according to Tacitus, though Dio Cassius said she died of illness.

Boudica's rebellion calls into question the whole issue of the place of women in early British and Irish society, especially in warfare. Although the *Cáin Adamnáin*, an **Old Irish** law tract which was aimed specifically at protecting 'innocents' (women, children and clerics) particularly in battle, dates from the late seventh century it describes what was seen as a woman's duty:

> The work which the finest of women used to do was to proceed to battle and battlefield, division and encampment, killing and slaughter. On one side she carried her provision-bag, on the other side her infant. Her wooden pole upon her back, thirty feet in length. On one end of it [there was] an iron hook, which she would thrust into the opposite battalion at the hair of the other woman. Her husband behind her, a fence-stake in his hand, flogging her on to battle. For at that time it was a woman's head or two breasts which were taken as trophies. (Ní Dhonnchadha 1995, 66)

However, the picture presented here is that of women forced to fight and Ní Dhonnchadha comments: '[t]his does not suggest that women willingly engaged in warfare and, in fact, the evidence for women opting for the warrior life in medieval Ireland is insubstantial (Ní Dhonnchadha 1995, 66).

Tacitus, in the speech he puts on the lips of Boudica at the beginning of her uprising, presents her as saying: 'We British are used to women commanders in war' (Tacitus, *Annals*: 14.35). However, Boudica and her contemporary, **Cartimandua** of the northern tribe of the ***Brigantes***, are the only women leaders known in British society. Their exploits prove that British tribeswomen could show enormous courage, leadership qualities and some political skill when the need arose, but it is possible that they only assumed these positions of authority because of the extraordinary circumstances of that time. As Prasutagus' widow, Boudica was the focus of the humiliation, outrage and affront to the *Iceni's* honour that suffered at the hands of the Romans. In more normal and settled times when there was no brutal foreign power tyrannising the tribe would a woman have been acknowledged as a ruler? If there had been a son to inherit the leadership would she have been accepted as the successor of Prasutagus? We do not know. What is sure is that her revolt very nearly drove the Romans out of Britain in AD 61.

See also Britons; Roman Army; Roman Britain.

Further Reading

Frere, Sheppard. 1978. *Britannia: A History of Roman Britain.* Routledge and Kegan Paul.

Koch, John T., and John Carey. 1997. *The Celtic Heroic Age: Literary Sources for Ancient Celtic Europe and Early Ireland and Wales.* Celtic Studies Publications.

Ní Dhonnchadha, Máirín. 1995. 'The *Lex Innocentium*: Adomnán's Law for Women, Clerics and Youths, 697 AD'. Pp. 58–69 in *Chattel, Servant or Citizen, Women's Status in Church, State and Society.* Edited by Mary O'Dowd and Sabine Wichert. The Institute of Irish Studies, Queen's University of Belfast.

Ní Dhonnchadha, Máirín. 2001. 'Birr and the Law of the Innocents'. Pp. 13–32 in *Adomnán at Birr, AD 697.* Edited by Thomas O'Loughlin. Four Courts Press.

Salway, Peter. 1981. *Roman Britain.* Clarendon Press.

Patricia Rumsey

Boudiccan Revolt

See Boudica.

Bran the Blessed

Bran the Blessed (Medieval Welsh, *Bendigeidfran*; Modern Welsh, *Brân ap Llyr Llediaith*) is a British and Welsh mythological figure, whose name *Bran* means 'raven' (a bird often associated with battle in Celtic and Germanic mythology) in both Welsh and Irish. He features prominently in Medieval Welsh **Literature**, particularly in the tale *Branwen Uerch Lyr* ('Branwen daughter of Llyr') from the collection of stories known as the ***Mabinogi***, where the fullest description of Bran is given.

In *Branwen*, Bran is portrayed as a giant so large that he is unable to fit inside a normal house, and he possesses a magic cauldron which can resurrect warriors slain in battle. He is also the brother of Branwen, who is married to the Irish king Matholwch. In this story, Matholwch mistreats Bran's sister, and Bran and his followers travel to Ireland in order to punish Matholwch. Although Matholwch attempted to calm Bran by building him a house that could hold his enormous size, hostilities resume when Bran's half-brother Efnisien mutilates Matholwch's horses. Bran and his warriors were victorious;

however, Bran was mortally wounded and only six others survived. Bran then had his remaining followers decapitate him and bring his head back to Britain, where it was kept as a talisman; it was later buried at a hill in **London** called Gwynfryn as instructed by Bran. Gwynfryn has been located at both the Tower of London and St Paul's Cathedral. Bran's head was believed to bring prosperity and protect Britain from invasion, a circumstance declared in no. 37 of *Trioedd Ynys Prydein* ('Triads of the Island of Britain'). Interestingly, there is an Arthurian connection to Bran's head in this same Triad, where Arthur exhumes it out of an arrogant belief in his own power as a sufficient deterrent to invaders.

Bran has been presented as the grandson of Beli Mawr, a Welsh 'ancestor deity' from whom many prominent Welsh ruling families derived their origin. He has been named as the son of Llyr Lledyeith. It has been suggested that Llyr (which means 'sea' in Welsh and is cognate with the Irish *ler*) derives from Irish mythology; however, this is uncertain. Bran has also been called the brother of Manawydan and father of Caradawc. Interestingly, Manawydan is a Welsh deity who may be identical with the Irish sea-god Mannanan mac Lír. Because of this possibility, it has also been speculated that Bran the Blessed himself is the same individual as the Irish hero Bran, who is the subject of the eighth or ninth century Irish tale *Immram Brain* ('Voyage of Bran'). In this tale, Bran even encounters Mannanan mac Lír, a fact which could justify the identification of the two figures, particularly since much of the action in *Branwen Uerch Lyr* takes place in Ireland. Nevertheless, the equation of the Irish Bran with Bran the Blessed cannot be proven definitively, especially since Bran is the son of Febal in *Immram Brain*.

See also Welsh People.

Further Reading

Bartrum, Peter C. 1993. *A Welsh Classical Dictionary*. The National Library of Wales.

Bromwich, Rachel. 2006. *Trioedd Ynys Prydein* (3rd edn.). University of Wales Press.

Chadwick, Nora. 1986. *The Celts* (13th printing). Pelican Books.

Ford, Patrick K. (ed. and tr.). 1977. *The Mabinogi*. University of California Press.

Ross, Anne. 1992. *Pagan Celtic Britain* (rev. edn.). Constable.

Joseph Calise

Brehon Laws

The Brehon Laws were the law tracts governing the daily life and politics in early medieval Ireland which were compiled in the seventh and eighth centuries and have been regarded as probably the oldest surviving laws in Europe in their inspiration, as they were in theory unaffected by Roman law. The word 'Brehon' itself is an Anglicised version of *Brithem* or *Breitheamh,* meaning 'judge', but they are more properly known as the *Fénechas* ('the law of the *Féine*' or 'land tillers'), as they served more as legal advisors to the rulers who actually passed judgment, though they are still officially statements of customary practices rather than the king's laws.

The Brehon Laws are assumed to be reflective of ancient pre-Christian traditions and customs, probably prior to the **Iron Age** though their precise origins may never be known, and despite being relatively reliable, they are also an expression of the ideals to which society was supposed to tend. At times, the Laws were also in conflict with canon (ecclesiastical) law, providing a different insight into the eighth-century Irish church than do the *Irish Annals*. As civil laws, they were concerned with compensation payment rather than punishment itself for crimes committed. Contracts dealing with issues such as inheritance and property took into account the social hierarchies that were in place, often defining degrees of status within individual classes. Thus they were not so much a legal system, but rather a number of treatises devoted to special subjects. There are indications that some were originally composed in poetry, suggesting that their intended means of transmission was to be passed down orally, probably by professional jurists in secular law schools.

The early legal poem 'Críth Gablach' provides insight into farming practices at the time, describing a strict hierarchy of farmers, each with their individual possessions listed, which they were required to own in order to maintain their status. Thus a *boaíre* was required to own a barn and pens for his animals, of which there was a specific number for each, in addition to a house and outhouse of precise dimensions, while an *ocaíre* (a smaller grade of farmer) had fewer animals to possess. The Laws describe what the ideal relationship between a man and woman should be with such issues as, the terms of a marriage contract, the duties of the marriage and to a child, fosterage laws, adultery, abduction, abortion and divorce. With regards to marriage and sexual matters, it is obvious that the laws were rather liberal towards women, who had more independence and rights to property than in any other European society of the time, even being able to divorce their husbands on the grounds of impotence or violence which left a mark. Though property was divisible equally, with each party being allowed to leave with what they put in, women were considered biased in the matter of testimony and they were rarely allowed to serve as witnesses.

Matters of hospitality were thoroughly covered in detail, as were the laws of the ***túath*** and its inheritance by kings, the matter of clientship and the process by which one could move up or down the social ladder. The system of what served as legal tender, whether cattle, a *cumal* (female slave) or a *sét* (honour price), was discussed in detail, with the value of a *sét* established as one third that of a *cumal,* half of a milch cow or two ounces of silver. Distraints were discussed, especially in relation to the maintenance of cattle and other livestock as were contracts and the conditions under which they were not valid (e.g. in drunkenness, ignorance or fear). The classes which made up the social structure were all recognised, as were their duties and privileges, and they included the *Ri* (rulers), *Nemedh* (nobles), *Aíre* (rent-paying freemen), *Céile* (free tenants), and the non-free *Bothach, Sencleithe* and *Fuidir*. Clearly, the Brehon Laws covered all aspects of life and were a true force throughout the land up until the thirteenth century, at which point Anglo-Norman control made the Irish subject to English law. Though there was some revival in the thirteenth century following intermarriage and the adoption of certain aspects of Irish culture by the Norman overlords, the Statutes of Kilkenny outlawed the Laws in 1367, with the Tudor conquest in the seventeenth century destroying all remnants.

See also Irish Language.

Further Reading

Hughes, Kathleen. 1972. *Early Christian Ireland: Introduction to the Sources*. Sources of History Limited.

Kelly, Fergus. 1988. *A Guide to Early Irish Law*. Dublin Institute for Advanced Studies.

Power, Patrick C. 1976. *Sex and Marriage in Ancient Ireland*. Mercier Press.

Ó Cróinín, Dáibhí. 1995. *Early Medieval Ireland 400–1200*. Longman.

Anne Sassin

Brendan, Saint

St. Brendan of **Clonfert** was the **Munster**-born founder and abbot of the monastery of Clonfert in County Galway. Apart from having a considerable cult in Ireland, Scotland and Brittany he is best known as the hero of the immensely popular Latin tale, *Navigatio Sancti Brendani Abbatis* ('The Voyage of St Brendan the Abbot'). His feast day is on 16 May.

St. Brendan was probably born in the early sixth century. In the earliest references to the saint his ancestry is consistently described as *moccu Altai* (for example, **Adomnán**, *Vita Columbae* I.26 and III.17), i.e. amongst the Altraige, a people based around Tralee. His father was named Findlug and his mother Cara. Early Irish tradition places him in the second generation of monastic founders in Ireland, along with figures such as **St. Columba** of **Iona**, **Ciarán of Clonmacnois** and St. Ruadán of Lorrha, as well as his namesake Brendan of Birr, with whom he is sometimes confused in medieval tradition. A number of versions survive of an early *Life of St. Brendan* (*Vita Sancti Brendani*), but these are all corrupted in some way and it is difficult to reconstruct the original *Life*. The extant *Life* presents the young Brendan as a pupil of St Erc in his native region who travels north to found monasteries at Inis-dá-Dromma (Coney Island, County Clare), Eanach nDúin (Annaghdown) and Inis Moccu Cuinn (Inchiquin) on Lough Corrib. The ***Irish Annals*** give the date of the foundation of Clonfert as AD 558 and record the date of Brendan's death as AD 575. His death probably occured at Clonfert though his Latin *Life* places it at Annaghdown, whence his body was returned to Clonfert. This is probably a legend arising from rival claims over the saint's relics. The monastery of Clonfert came under the control of the **Éoganacht** of Loch Léin in the seventh century, when Cuimmíne Fota was bishop, which may account for the unique ascription of Éoganacht Locha Léin ancestry to St. Brendan at the opening of the *Navigatio*.

Brendan's cult spread early via Britain to Brittany, where the ninth-century *Life of St. Malo* (*Vita Sancti Machutis*) presents Brendan as a companion of St. Malo. The *Vita Sancti* Brendani also indicates that Brendan was the patron of monasteries in Brittany, at Alet and Cézambre. A cluster of dedications to the saint are still to be found around St. Malo and in Finistére, though there the cult of Brendan is conflated with that of a different saint, Brévelaire (Branwaladar). Though Brendan is recorded in Adomnán's *Life of Columba* (*Vita Sancti Columbae*) as visiting Scotland, most of the existing Scottish dedications to him appear to be foundations of the later Middle Ages, when a lost Latin *Life* of the saint, possibly of Anglo-French origin, was circulated.

St. Brendan, however, achieved greatest fame for a fictional voyage. The *Navigatio*, written around 800 and one of the most remarkable and original works in medieval literature, describes a marvellous sea voyage undertaken by the saint. The tale presents Brendan as the ideal abbot, by analogy with Moses, who leads his followers through the 'desert' to the brink of the Promised Land. It is both monastic journey in the wilderness (***peregrinatio***) and an adventure tale ultimately inspired by native genres. Though the *Navigatio* evocatively depicts life at sea and is set amongst islands (such as the Faroes and Iceland) that were known to the Irish in the 700s, this is an allegorical, not an actual, journey fraught with apocalyptic motifs, albeit subtly presented. The monks encounter phenomena on the ocean such as giant beasts and a column of crystal that owe their inspiration to real encounters, at least in part, with whales and icebergs in the eighth century but claims that St. Brendan or his later counterparts sailed as far west as Canada are not likely to be correct. The *Navigatio*, in making St. Brendan the only Irish monk to lead his community to the Promised Land, shows the reputation he enjoyed throughout the Middle Ages as one of the founding-figures of Irish monasticism. He remains an iconic figure in the church of the Irish 'diaspora'.

See also Celtic Christianity; Monasticism.

Further Reading

Barron, W. R., and G. S. Burgess (eds.). 2001. *The Voyage of St Brendan: Themes and Variations*. Exeter.

Burgess, G. S., and C. Strijbosch. 2000. *The Legend of St Brendan: A Critical Bibliography*. Dublin.

Jonathan M. Wooding (ed.). 2000. *The Otherworld Voyage in Early Irish Literature*. Dublin.

Jonathan Wooding

Brian Boru (c.941–1014)

Brian Boru (Bórumha, 'Cow Tribute') was a renowned Irish king whose career was memorialised in the *Cogad Gáedel re Gallaib*. He ruled as king of Dal Cais and Thomond (AD 976–1014), king of **Munster** (978–1014), high king (*ard rí*) of Ireland (1002–1014) and the emperor of the Irish (1005–1014).

Born c. 941, the son of Cennétig mac Lorcan, Brian came to power after his brother Mathgamain was murdered in 976. Brian inaugurated his reign by raiding Scattery Island and killing the **Viking** leader Ivar of **Limerick**. He then proceeded to pillage the town. In 978, at the Battle of Belach Lechta, he defeated Máel Muad, his primary rival for the kingship of Munster and the chief instigator in the murder of Brian's brother Mathgamain. After this battle, Brian was recognised as the king of Munster. The following years saw Brian in a back and forth struggle with the High King of Ireland Máel Sechnaill, king of **Tara**. During this time, Brian put several fleets on the Shannon River as well as raids in Osraige and **Leinster**. In 985, responding to a revolt by the subordinate kingdom of the ***Déisi*** in the southeast, he attacked and defeated the *Déisi*. He fortified several locations within Munster and conducted a circuit of the South, collecting the hostages of Emly, Lismore and **Cork**. Brian ensured the support of the southern churches by installing his brother Marcán as abbot of Killaloe, Terryglass and Emly effectively securing his position in the South. In 997, Brian and Máel Sechnaill reached an agreement to divide Ireland in half, with the High King giving Brian the hostages of **Dublin** and Leinster and Brian collecting and turning over the hostages of Connacht to Máel Sechnaill.

In 999, Brian defeated the combined forces of the men of Leinster and Dublin in the Battle of Glen Máma after which he plundered Dublin and then expelled Sitric, the Viking king of the town. Sitric was unable to find support for his resistance and returned to Dublin, submitting to Brian's overlordship. In 1001, hostilities between Brian and Máel Sechnaill flared and the king of Tara joined with the king of Connacht in building a causeway at Athlone to deny Brian access up the Shannon River. This attempt failed and Máel Sechnaill submitted to Brian in 1002.

Brian travelled to **Armagh** in 1005 and gave an offering of 20 ounces (567 grams) of gold, acknowledging Armagh as the primary church of Ireland. On this occasion Brian's scribe Máel Suthain celebrated him as the Emperor of the Irish. Two years later, Brian took advantage of conflict among the northern kingdoms. Continued fighting between the Cenél Eóghain and the **Ulaid** left the Ulaid weakened. Brian conducted a host to the north and took the hostages of Ulaid in 1007, and in three subsequent northern expeditions – in 1008, 1011, and again in 1011 – reduced the Northern **Uí Néill**. Brian brought the king of Cenél Conaill to Kincora to symbolise his victory and the submission of the entirety of Ireland to his rule. Irish unity lasted barely a year.

In 1012, the Cenél Conaill in the North, and the men of Leinster in the South, revolted against Brian's authority. Dublin joined the revolt. After a failed siege of Dublin in late 1013, Brian returned to the Viking town in 1014. Brian, supported primarily by the men of Munster and southern Connacht, faced the combined forces of Leinster, Dublin and their allies led by Earl Sigurd of Orkney. Prior to the battle, Máel Sechanill and the men of **Meath** left the field. On Good Friday, 23 April 1014, the two forces fought the **Battle of Clontarf** outside the town of Dublin. Fighting lasted the entire day and casualties on both sides were high. Brian, his son Murchad, and his grandson Tadc died along with Máel Mórda of Leinster and Sigurd, Earl of the Orkneys. Brian's body was taken to Armagh for burial and his son Donnchad led the forces of Munster back to Kincora.

Brian Boru's death ushered in a period of Irish history called the 'kings with opposition'. Brian's incredible military success exacerbated the weakened state of the families that traditionally filled the High Kingship. After his death, provincial kings considered themselves legitimate claimants, heightening the internecine warfare that disrupted any trend towards centralised authority.

See also Gaels; Kings and Kingship.

Further Reading

Ryan, John. 1938. 'The Battle of Clontarf'. *The Journal of the Royal Society of Antiquaries of Ireland* 68: 1–50.

———. 1967. 'Brian Boruma, King of Ireland'. Pp.230–241 in *North Munster Studies*. Edited by Etienne Rynne. Thomond Archaeological Society.

David Beougher

Brigantes

The *Brigantes* were a powerful tribe, or tribal grouping, in northern Britain during the Late **Iron Age** and Roman period. Their territory, largely based on both the writings of Ptolemy and dedications to the goddess Brigantia, seems to have stretched from coast to coast between the Tyne and Humber Rivers and from north of **Hadrian's Wall** to include possibly the Peak District of Derbyshire, making them the largest British tribe of those mentioned by **Tacitus**. The name itself seems to have been derived from a Celtic root, possibly meaning something to the effect of 'The High Ones' or 'Hill Dwellers'. It seems that many smaller tribes of **Britons** once existed in this area, and were combined to form a confederation. These may have included the ***Carvetii*** and *Parisi* who later became separate *civitates*. Presumably this confederacy was under a very powerful leader, probably an immediate ancestor of **Cartimandua**, though it does seem that classical writers may have used the 'Brigante' term rather generically to encompass all the tribes of northern Britain.

Although it is assumed that the Iron Age populace was descended from the **Bronze Age** one, Iron Age groups are often difficult to distinguish due to a dearth of finds, and one of the trademark settlement types of the period, the hillfort, is not common in the Brigantian region. It is arguable that this may point to more stability, i.e. the lack of hillforts indicating the lack of large-scale warfare. Records for most of the first century AD are rare, though it is known that the south-western region of Brigantia rebelled against Cartimandua's decision to ally with Rome and interfered with Ostorius Scapula's North Wales expedition. Despite the location of Cartimandua's base being uncertain, Stanwick has been seen as a potential spot for the palace for her consort Venutius, who took the kingdom away from her sometime after 69. This possibly opened up the territory to conquest and fighting. By Agricola's time, the whole of the Brigantian area was garrisoned and appears to have been pacified by the end of the first century, with a thinning out of the garrisons east of the Pennines for the establishment of Hadrian's Wall. This in turn lead to more towns and Romanised farms, including Catterick, Corbridge and Aldborough, the last viewed as the *civitas* centre (*Isurium Brigantum*) based on an entry in the Antonine Itinerary. There was also the colonial settlement at York, which by the later Roman period was a wealthy establishment, and many smaller settlements within the *civitas*, with a fair number existing alongside auxiliary forts and even continuing after their evacuation, such as Adel. In the late second century, there seems to have been unrest amongst the *Brigantes*, and it is perhaps at this time that the creation of the Civitas

Carvetiorum took place, though there is no evidence that the third or first half of the fourth century was anything but peaceful within the territory.

While the pre-Roman rural pattern seems to have been rather dispersed, it seems that the arrival of the army did not initially make much impact on native settlement and agriculture patterns, and even when villas and rural shrines were introduced they were of much lower density than those in the south. However, the army did come to stimulate the marketplace with prominent industries of the period including metalworking (both iron and decorative, e.g. the Aesica brooch), tiling and pottery and it is not an unreasonable assumption that the excess of livestock in the *civitas* may have been used for trade, as the main basis of the economy seems to have been pastoral. There is nothing to suggest that the tribe possessed currency, as previously attributed coins have since been assigned as Corieltauvian though luxury items do suggest that trade took place. While the later fourth century does not show substantial evidence for destruction in Brigantia or the immediate abandonment of sites, the defences at Aldborough seem to have been updated, and by the fifth century there is no longer evidence for administration continuing in the *civitas*. A return to an older Iron Age tradition may therefore have taken place in the late Roman period, at least until the northern part of the Brigantian territory fell under the British kingdom of Rheged and subsequent Anglian invaders.

See also Roman Britain.

Further Reading

Branigan, Keith (ed.). 1980. *Rome and the Brigantes: The Impact of Rome on Northern England.* Department of Prehistory and Archaeology, University of Sheffield.

Hartley, B. R., and R. L. Fitts. 1988. *The Brigantes.* Alan Sutton.

Cunliffe, B. W. 2005. *Iron Age Communities of Britain* (4th edn.). RKP.

Snyder, Christopher A. 2003. *The Britons.* Peoples of Europe Series. Blackwell.

Todd, Malcolm. 1999. *Roman Britain* (3rd edn.). Blackwell.

Anne Sassin

Brigid, Saint (c. AD 450–525)

Brigid (c. AD 450–525), a patron saint of Ireland along with **Patrick** and **Columba**, was founder, abbess and bishop of the double monastery at *Cill – Dara* (i.e. 'church of the oak'), now **Kildare**. The fundamental connection between St. Brigid and the *pagan goddess* Brigid (or Brig), a deity of three manifestations from the central pantheon of Celtic Ireland, is substantiated in parallels between the two; e.g. the celebration of St. Brigid's feast day on 1 February and *Imbolc* also 1 February. *Imbolc* was a pre-Christian ritual associated with the goddess Brigid intended to mark winter's end and the beginning of spring. A question for scholars is the degree to which the Brigitine material represents an appropriation and reconfiguration of the goddess's legends to suit the world-view of a recently Christianised Ireland (c. 400). Some argue that St. Brigid did not exist, that she is a Christianised pagan deity; others argue that she did exist, but that the memory of her was conflated with that of the goddess.

According to the hagiographical tradition, Brigid was born c. 451 to Dubhthach, a chieftain and Brocca, a slave. Brigid's tribal descent is traced through Dubhthach to the Fotharta of north **Leinster**. In her youth, Brigid was fostered to a **Druid**. She was returned to her family and when she reached marriageable age refused matrimony, plucking out her own eye to deter one suitor, choosing a life of religion instead. St. Macaille administered her vows. Around 470, Brigid settled on the *Magh Life* (i.e. the Liffey Plain), where she founded the double monastery of *Cill – Dara*. Either St. Mel or Bishop Ibor conferred abbatial and, by mistake, episcopal authority upon Brigid. She appointed Bishop Conleth to administer the sacraments and to oversee the monks of the Kildare community. The abbey became a centre of learning as well as an important *scriptorium*. The *Book of Kildare*, according to Giraldus Cambrensis (d. 1223) a magnificent example of the illuminators' arts, was lost after the sixteenth century. The memory of Brigid was such that parity between the abbesses of Kildare and the bishops of Ireland continued until the Synod of **Kells** in 1152.

A remarkable number of medieval copies of Brigid's *Lives* exist indicating the importance of St. Brigid's cult during the Middle Ages. The known *Lives* are the *Vita Prima* attributed to Ultan and *Vita Sancti Brigidae* by Cogitosus, composed in the late seventh century; a *Life* attributed to Coelan of Inis-celtra (d. 750) written in the eighth century; the *Ní car Brigit* (i.e. Broccán's Hymn) and *Bethu Brigte* (also termed 'Second Irish *Life*' and 'Old Irish *Life*') as yet to be dated; the *Vita Metrica* dated to the ninth century; a *Life* attributed to Animosus (Colgan's *Vita IV*) dated to the tenth century; and the *Life* by Laurence of Durham (d.1154) and the First Irish *Life* dated to the twelfth century.

Scholars have determined that, over time, redactors, copyists and compilers influenced the contents of the *Lives*, embedding original compositions in an aggregate of the *Lives*' evolution. So, Brigid became the 'Mary of the Gael' due to a tale in which she served as Christ's wet nurse that was incorporated into her legends. It is also a characteristic of hagiography that contemporary political and economic relationships of the monasteries are reflected in the material. The production of the early Brigitine *Lives* was in part a reaction to the rivalry for primacy between the churches of Armagh (which associated itself with St. Patrick) and Kildare from the seventh to the tenth centuries, while Brigid's connections with the Fotharta and, as a detail introduced in later *Lives*, with the Ui Dunlainge is an indication of the dynastic relations the Kildare community maintained over time.

Brigid died 1 February 525 and was interred in the Cathedral of Kildare. During the **Viking** raids of the ninth century, her relics were re-interred at Downpatrick where, in 1185, the remains, minus Brigid's skull, were translated to the Cathedral. Brigid's skull was carried to Portugal.

See also Celtic Christianity; Monasticism.

Further Reading

Bhreathach, Edel. 2001. 'Abbesses, Minor Dynasties and Kings in *clericatu*: Perspectives of Ireland, 750–850'. Pp.113–125 in *Mercia: An Anglo-Saxon Kingdom in Europe*. Edited by Michelle P. Brown and Carol A. Farr. Leicester University Press.

Connolly, Sean. 1987. 'Cogitosus's *Life of St. Brigit*: Content and Value'. *Journal of the Royal Society of Antiquaries of Ireland* 117: 5–27.

McCone, Kim. 1984. 'An Introduction to the Early Irish Saints' Lives'. *The Maynooth Review* 11: 26–59.

Ó hAodha, Donncha. 1974. 'The Early Lives of Saint Brigit'. *The Journal of County Kildare Archaeological Society* 15: 397–405.

Sharpe, Richard. 1991. *Medieval Irish Saints' Lives: An Introduction to Vitae Sanctorum Hiberniae*. Clarendon Press.

Susan Schulze

Britons

Britons was the name given to the early inhabitants of the island of Britain, used by the Cornish and the **Welsh** in the early Middle Ages and (officially) of all inhabitants of the United Kingdom after the 1707 Act of Union. While the first Greek explorers apparently used ***Albion*** and *Albiones* for the island and its inhabitants, the words Ρρεττανια and Ρρεττανοι (later Βρεττανια and Βρεττανοι) soon replaced the earlier terms and became *Britannia* and *Britanni* in Latin. It has been suggested that Ρρεττανοι was a Gallo-Brittonic word introduced to Britain during the P-Celtic linguistic innovations of the sixth century BC (Cunliffe 154–156). In any case, it is very similar to both *Priteni*, the Britons' term for the **Picts**, and to *Prydein*, the Welsh word for Britain. Isidore of Seville, the early medieval etymologist, wrote that *Britto* (an alternate form for *Britanni*) derived from *brutus*, 'unwieldy or dull', and in the ninth-century ***Historia Brittonum*** a Trojan refugee named **Brutus** is made the founder of the race of Britons.

Whether or not the Britons used the term for themselves, or for a particular British tribe, **Julius Caesar** and other Roman authors consistently used it as a blanket term for all of the peoples of Britain (until Roman expansion took them to Scotland, whose inhabitants they called **Caledonians** and later **Picts**). Caesar's description of the culture and customs of the Britons in the late pre-Roman Iron Age has now been complemented by archaeological and numismatic evidence. This shows that the Britons had developed coinage and proto-towns called *oppida* under the hegemonic kings of the southeast. The powerful kingdoms of the ***Catuvellauni***, the ***Trinovantes***, the ***Iceni***, and the ***Brigantes*** would continue to cause Rome trouble after the Claudian conquest of Britain in AD 43, even though client relationships were established with several pro-Roman native rulers.

The level of Romanisation varied greatly in the province of Britain, and a syncretism with native British styles can be seen in art, architecture and religion. Despite significant numbers of British troops in the Roman army, there is little evidence of native Britons rising to prominence in the politics and culture of the empire. A notable exception is the heresiarch **Pelagius**, born in Britain in the later fourth century but achieving prominence elsewhere. The terms *Britannus* and *Britto* appear in Latin inscriptions throughout the empire, but in the twilight years of the fifth century AD there was a particular burst of 'British pride' especially from expatriates living in Gaul and Spain. By this point there were new settlements of Britons in Galicia, in northwest Spain and in the Armorican peninsula in western France which was renamed *Bretagne* (Brittany) or 'Lesser Britain' in their honour. This immigration, perhaps led by bishops and later including monastic saints, began before the Anglo-Saxon takeover of Britain but was no doubt accelerated by it.

Declaring their independence from Rome in 410 (or, some would say, having been abandoned by the emperor), the Britons remained the majority population and held political control over most of Britain throughout the fifth and sixth centuries. This **Brittonic Age** is chronicled by native clergymen **Patrick** and **Gildas**, who emphasise political fragmentation under the rule of native *tyranni* and their corrupt partners, the bishops. **Vortigern** (infamous for inviting the first Saxons to Britain) and other tyrants inhabited shrinking Roman towns, crumbling Roman forts and refortified native hillforts in an attempt to assert local control over agriculture and industry. Many of these tyrants lived in grand style, importing such luxuries as olive oil and fine wine from a revived trade with the eastern Mediterranean (see '**Tintagel Ware**'). Ultimately, however, they gave ground to Germanic mercenaries who rebelled by seizing large portions of the eastern (**Kent**, East Anglia) and north-eastern (**Northumbria**) parts of the island and established warrior kingships.

This period also gave rise to the Age of the Saints in the Celtic churches (Gildas, **Illtud**, **David**, **Kentigern** and Samson are only a few examples of influential British clergy), the growth of monasticism (and a British innovation – monastic **penitentials**) and the legends of **Arthur** and **Merlin**. In his first literary appearance (in the *Historia Brittonum*), Arthur is depicted as leading the kings of the Britons to victory in twelve battles against the treacherous Saxons, in the year 518 according to the tenth-century ***Annales Cambriae***. Though these sources are too late to be taken as historical evidence for the sixth century, they do point to a consistent trend in Welsh literature to mark the declining fortunes of the Britons by looking back to a time when they possessed the Sovereignty of the Island.

Several victories by expansionist Anglo-Saxon kings (especially those of **Wessex** and Northumbria) in the late sixth and early seventh centuries seem to have driven permanent wedges between Britons living in the southwest (**Devon** and **Cornwall**), the west (**Wales**) and the north (**Cumbria** and **Strathclyde**). Though ecclesiastical and linguistic ties between these areas (as well as to Brittany) will continue until the **Norman Conquest**, the Britons' political power was quickly evaporating and even the conservative Welsh came to give up the term *Britanni* for ***Cymry***. While some Britons chose to ally with the **Vikings** against Anglo-Saxon kings, the process of unifying Britain south of **Hadrian's Wall** under one *English* king began with **Alfred** and **Æthelstan** and was aided by the introduction of Norman **feudalism**.

While we can trace the history of the Britons in their diaspora, the fate of the Britons within Anglo-Saxon England is less clear. The conventional picture, derived from Gildas and other written sources, is that an increasing number of Saxons (hundreds of thousands) were able to eventually overwhelm the native Britons due to their military superiority (or to the alleged cowardice of the Britons). Archaeologists, unable to detect physical evidence of large-scale invasion and massacre, began to challenge this picture beginning in the 1980s. An alternate model was then proposed: a smaller number (tens of thousands) of highly militarised Saxons were able to impose their rule and culture on the indigenous population, which remained numerically superior. Anglo-Saxon cemeteries have been scanned – bones measured, military gear counted – to try to distinguish between Germanic newcomers and native Britons. Early genetic studies, and detailed analyses of oxygen isotopes found in human teeth from Romano-British and early Anglo-Saxon cemeteries, showed little evidence of Germanic intrusion in Britain before the Viking Age (Budd et al.). However, recent studies of the Y-chromosome variation have indicated a great similarity between haplotypes in Central England and Friesland on the one hand and a dissimilarity between Central England and North Wales on the other. Rather than massive numbers of Germanic invaders, it has been suggested that early Anglo-Saxons created an 'apartheid-like' society with legal and economic disincentives for intermarriage with the native *Wealas* (Thomas, Stumpf and Härke).

Regardless of which of these theories prevails, it is clear that Anglo-Saxon, Viking and Norman invaders did not wipe out the Britons' laws, language and myths. The British or Brittonic tongue, which had survived four centuries of Roman occupation, splintered into Welsh, Cornish, Cumbric and Breton in the early Middle Ages. Pre-Christian British mythology survives in the medieval Welsh wonder tales known as the ***Mabonogi*** as well as the legends of Arthur and Merlin, **Tristan** and Isolde and the Holy Grail. While the fight to preserve the Welsh and Cornish languages continues with varying success, the fascination with the Arthurian legends and 'Celtic' music and spirituality is bringing the ancient Britons to greater attention than, perhaps, they ever enjoyed.

See also Brythonic Language; Celts; Cornwall; Kings and Kingship; Roman Britain.

Further Reading

Budd, Paul, et al. 2004. 'Investigating Population Movement by Stable Isotope Analysis: A Report from Britain'. *Antiquity* 78.299: 127–141.

Cunliffe, Barry. 1997. *The Ancient Celts*. Oxford University Press.

Higham, N. J. 2003. *King Arthur: Myth-Making and History*. Routledge.

Snyder, Christopher A. 1998. *An Age of Tyrants: Britain and the Britons, AD 400–600*. Pennsylvania State University Press.

———. 2003. *The Britons*. The Peoples of Europe Series. Blackwell.

Thomas, Mark G., Michael P. H. Stumpf and Heinrich Härke. 2006. 'Evidence for an Apartheid-Like Social Structure in Early Anglo-Saxon England. *Proceedings of the Royal Society B* (published online May 19): 1–7.

Christopher A. Snyder

Brittonic

See Brythonic Language.

Brittonic Age

The Brittonic Age is the name given to the period between the withdrawal of the Romans from Britain (c. AD 410) and the arrival of St. **Augustine** at **Canterbury** (597). Other labels have been used to describe this period, including Dark Age Britain, the Early Christian period, the Age of **Arthur** and Sub-**Roman Britain**. All of these have serious flaws. 'The Dark Ages', although used as a description of various things medieval since at least Petrarch and still used in common parlance, has been rejected by modern historians of the early Middle Ages for it's obvious derisive and somewhat misleading connotations. 'Early Christian' is more accurate but perhaps too broad, for it would include much of the Roman period and has no obvious terminus. 'The Age of Arthur', 'The Arthurian Period' and 'Arthur's Britain' all rest on the assumption (now questioned by scholars) that there was a historical Arthur. Historical or not, Arthur still remains the biggest draw for most people to the period.

'Sub-Roman Britain' became the preferred term for specialists around the 1970s. It was a popular term used by archaeologists to describe pottery, buildings and other objects datable to the last years of the Roman Empire in the West. It often assumes, however, both a deterioration from Roman standards and a continuing connection to the empire or things Roman. 'Post-Roman' is also occasionally used by archaeologists, but like the other terms used, it also lacks an obvious ending point.

In 1998, Christopher Snyder suggested 'The Brittonic Age' as an alternative to these labels. It describes Britain more accurately, Snyder argued, for most of the fifth and sixth centuries. Few would now question that **Britons** or Brittonic/Brythonic speakers remained the majority population in Britain south of the Forth-Clyde line throughout the Roman period and well into the early Middle Ages. All of the written texts from the island in this period and nearly all of the epigraphic evidence come from Britons, most notably **Patrick** and **Gildas**. Lastly, Britons likely remained in political control of the majority of towns and provinces in Britain until the last couple of decades of the sixth century. One hundred and seventy five years is too long to be treated as a transitional period, so we should not merely consider these years a transition from Roman to **Anglo-Saxon** rule. The Brittonic Age is not only more accurate; it gives the Britons (and their descendants, the Cornish and the **Welsh**) their due. This is more in keeping with recent historiographic trends, which have called for the replacement in books and curricula of 'English History' with a history of the *peoples* of the British Isles.

See also Cornwall.

Further Reading

Alcock, Leslie. 1971. *Arthur's Britain*. Penguin.

Dark, K. R. 1993. *Civitas to Kingdom: British Political Continuity, 300–800*. Leicester University Press.

Davies, R. R. 1994. 'The Peoples of Britain and Ireland, 1100–1400, Identities'. *Transactions of the Royal Historical Society* 6th series, 4: 1–20.

Dumville, David. 1977. 'Sub-Roman Britain: History and Legend'. *History* 62: 173–192.

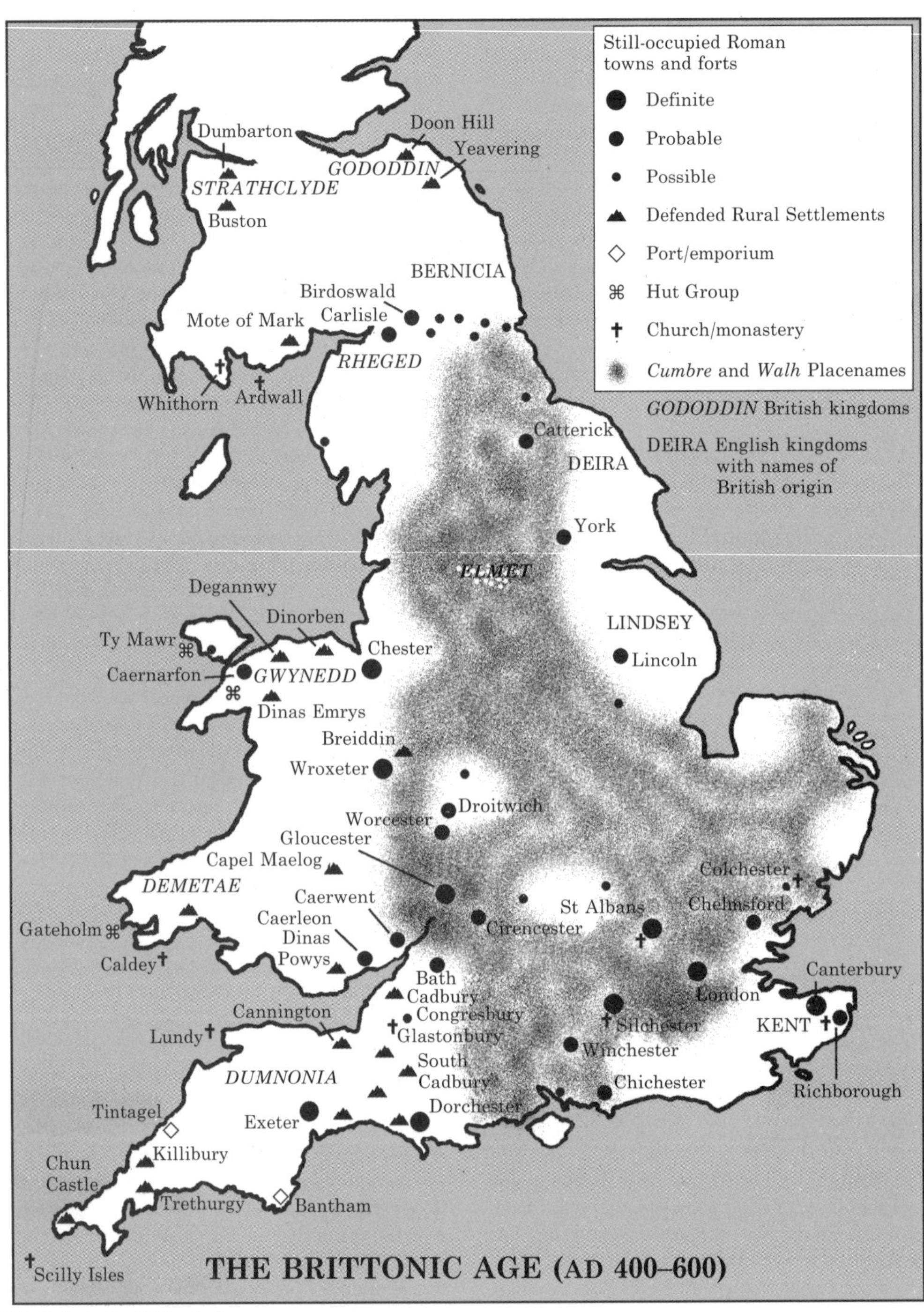

2. Britain in the Brittonic Age.

Snyder, Christopher A. 1998. *An Age of Tyrants: Britain and the Britons, AD 400–600*. Pennsylvania State University Press.

———. 2003. *The Britons*. The Peoples of Europe Series. Blackwell.

Thomas, Charles. 1981. *Christianity in Roman Britain to AD 500*. Batsford.

Christopher A. Snyder

Brochs

The term *broch* is applied to a type of developed round house found in Atlantic Scotland in the **Iron Age**. Typically, they are circular towers with a double dry stone wall tied together with slabs. These slabs created intra-mural galleries, linked by stairs, and had openings which gave

9. A round house of the Iron Age, c. 200 BC–AD 100, at Dun Carloway Broch, Lewis, Scotland.

access to upper timber floors that have now vanished. Scarcements still visible on some sites provided the supports for timber floors. They have a single entrance, sometimes furnished with guard chambers, and lack windows. They average between 26.24 feet (8 metres) and 39.37 feet (12 metres) in diameter. The highest surviving example is in Mousa, Shetland, which stands 43.64 feet (13.3 metres) high and there are often rows of voids in the interior walls, which have never been adequately explained. It has been suggested that the broch towers was so constructed to facilitate insulation, the intra-mural galleries keeping out the extremes of weather. Only at Mousa is it possible to reach the top of the tower by way of the intra-mural stairs, and the use of the galleries for storage was probably a subsidiary function – only some galleries seem to have been so used while others are too narrow for adult access. A group of brochs have solid bases and it has been suggested that the ground floor was only used for storage and for stock, the living occurring on the upper floors.

Brochs seem to have evolved from earlier stone-built roundhouses. The starting point seems to have been houses constructed in Orkney around the end of the seventh century BC, when stone-built houses with very thick walls first appeared. These however lacked most of the architectural features of brochs, which started to make their appearance around 400 BC in 'complex roundhouses'. The stages of development are attested at Howe, Orkney, where a thick-walled roundhouse was demolished before 200 BC and replaced first with a building that had many of the features of brochs, namely intra-mural staircases leading to upper timber floors and an entrance passage flanked by guard chambers. This in turn was followed by a true broch, built between 200 BC and AD 100, which was the centre of a village of smaller huts. Such broch villages are widespread in Orkney and the north mainland of Caithness, but absent from Shetland and the Western Isles, where wheelhouses were developed. By the end of the second century AD, brochs ceased to be built, but their sites continued to be a focus for occupation until the **Viking** Age.

The best known brochs include the substantial towers at Glenelg, Invernesshire, Dun Carloway on Lewis and the more truncated towers at **Clickhimin**, Shetland and the Broch of Gurness and Midhowe in Orkney.

See also Art and Architecture.

Further Reading

Armit, I. (ed.). 1990. *Before the Brochs*. Edinburgh University Press.

Armit, I. 1997. *Celtic Scotland*. Batsford.

Harding, D. W. 2004. *The Iron Age in North Britain: Celts and Romans, Natives and Invaders*. Edinburgh University Press.

Henderson, J. 2007. *The Atlantic Iron Age*. Edinburgh University Press.

Lloyd Laing

The Bronze Age

Traditionally, the Bronze Age in Britain and its social changes were seen to be determinate on technological innovation (i.e. the use of bronze), as was the view in the classic 1930 study *The Bronze Age* by V. G. Childe. However, it has now been seen that many facets of that society (e.g. the construction of monuments and certain subsistence practices) existed both before and after bronze was adopted. As Britain at this time was behind many other parts of Europe in the use of metal, no proper Copper Age has been indicated, and both the earliest bronze and copper tools seem to belong to the same date range, with copper metallurgy appearing to originate in Ireland. The earliest date for metal tools that can be firmly established, in this instance by dendrochronology, is 2268–2251 BC, when timbers were felled by a metal axe at Corlea, County Longford. Furthermore, a hoard of such axes found at Castletown Roche in County Cork may pre-date the introduction of **Beaker** pottery, which along with single grave burial is an association often made in Britain with the arrival of metallurgy, exemplifying one more prior conception that may have been refuted in recent years.

The Bronze Age in Britain can be placed into a tripartite division: the Early Bronze Age (2600–1600 BC), the Middle (1600–1200 BC) and the Late (1200–700 BC). A two-part scheme has occasionally been undertaken as well, with an Earlier (2600–1400 BC) and Later (1400–600 BC) Bronze Age. There are various chronologies that have been put forward for the first half of the Bronze Age, some based on industrial stages (e.g. Burgess 1980) and others on the assemblage of metal artefacts themselves (e.g. Needham 1988). Burgess' broad period division can be summarised as follows: the Mount Pleasant phase (2700–2000 BC), in which flat axes, Beaker pottery and the practice of inhumation were used; the Overton phase (2000–1700 BC), in which flanged axes, flat-tanged daggers, various vessels (e.g. collared urns) and elaborate grave goods were used; the Bedd Branwen phase (1700–1400 BC) which saw the regionalisation of pottery and continued cremation, though not with golden grave goods; and the Knighton Heath phase (1400–1250 BC).

Pottery analysis and typology have often governed Bronze Age studies, ever since Lord Abercromby's work on urns in the early twentieth century, and despite subsequent work on assemblages as Beaker pots and food vessels, a finely honed ceramic chronology for the Earlier Bronze Age is not easily established, with much overlap apparent: Beaker pottery (2700–1700 BC), food vessels (2200–1800 BC), collared urns (2000–1700 BC) and bi-conical urns (1800–1400 BC) and with the Beakers standing out in the overall crude tradition as finely made ceramics, perhaps to be viewed at rather than used although they are certainly not limited to funerary or ceremonial contexts. Flint knapping from the Early Bronze Age has often been viewed as similar to that of the Late **Neolithic**, yet the careful working of certain daggers and arrowheads suggests a division between everyday blades and specialist manufacture for prestigious items, a tradition of stone working that also saw the quarrying and dressing of large stones (e.g. Stonehenge). Such standing stone monuments and circles have been the subject of study for centuries, and though most are thought to belong to the Early Bronze Age, few have been dated with any relative certainty, with exceptions such as Machrie Moor on the Isle of Arran and the Rollright Stones of Oxfordshire and **Stonehenge**, leaving their function as memorials, calendars etc. still open to debate. Though personal adornment was also well known in the Late Neolithic, it becomes especially prominent in the subsequent period, including jet necklaces, amber beads, dress pins and amazingly a gold cape from Mold in Clwyd, possibly signifying an increased individualism or various status grades. The 'fancy goods' of this Earlier Bronze Age have been seen to mark a sharp distinction from everyday artefacts (e.g. pottery), possibly drawing a contrast between the private and domestic realms by this time, with other changes involving the move from the axe of the Neolithic to a preference for the dagger which by the Middle Bronze Age had evolved into rapiers and spearheads.

There are a few house remains from the period known from western Britain, mainly constructed of stone (e.g. Alt Chrysal, Rosinish and Stanydale) and in small and dispersed groups and there is a prominent alteration detected in the architecture by the end of the Earlier Bronze Age to a more substantial scale, often involving palisaded enclosures and ditches (e.g. South Lodge). Round barrows (e.g. Normanton Down, Wiltshire and Irthlingborough, Northamptonshire) and cairns from the Early and Middle Bronze Ages have seen investigation and excavation since antiquarian times, and though there is possible regionalisation and considerable variation in the funerary practices (e.g. skulls from the Thames suggesting water deposition), there does seem to be a noted change around 2000 BC from inhumation to cremation. Other patterns that can be inferred may include patrilineal descent, because females as primary burials were rarely followed by adult males, and earlier Neolithic monuments often seem to have been re-used, establishing large zones of sacred space (e.g. **Avebury**, Rudston and the Bend in the Boyne in Ireland), perhaps coinciding with a shift in emphasis of personal identity to territory rather than lineage.

The Later Bronze Age has much less evidence for human burial; with the tradition of barrow burial having died out, the lack of content associated with burials necessitated different chronological schemes, and archaeological focus has tended to shift to changes in agricultural practice and settlement organisation. Falling into the Later Bronze Age is the final stage of Burgess' division, the Knighton Heath phase (1400–1250 BC), the end of the burial sequence with predominantly pottery-cremations. Bronze metalwork typologies thereafter have been used to establish a chronology for the remainder of the period (Taunton 1400–1250 BC and Penard 1300–1100 BC, when the first leaf-shaped swords appear; Wilburton 1150–950 BC, Ewart

3. Prehistoric Britain and Ireland (Bronze Age).

Park 950–750 BC and Llyn Fawr 750–600 BC, the final of which overlaps with the beginning of the **Iron Age**), with a corresponding sequence for pottery of the Deverel-Rimbury type of southern Britain, though this last chronology has since seen some adjustments through radiocarbon calibration.

The Later Bronze Age varies considerably in the regional archaeological assemblage, with **Wessex** and the Thames Valley having undergone more extensive excavation, most likely due to the high concentration of sites (e.g. Aldermaston Wharf, Berkshire, and Runnymede Bridge, Surrey), as well as Fengate and Flag Fen near Peterborough in Cambridgeshire. The latter site is perhaps one of the best known for the whole Later Bronze Age period, where a massive wooden platform was assembled in the open water c.1000 BC, with many of the other sites of the period appearing to have been defensive (e.g. **Mucking**, Essex). Though there is slighter evidence for settlements of the early first millennium BC, they are by and large unenclosed clusters of round houses, with a few 'high-status' sites possibly presented (e.g. Potterne and East Chisenbury). However, by 1000 BC the beginnings of climatic deterioration saw the abandonment of many sites, a period by which mixed agriculture had become exploited more intensely than ever before, coinciding with a greater concern for feasting practices, use of wheeled vehicles and more elaborate weapons of warfare, which revealed through their style and techniques of production an increased contact with the Continent.

See also Ceramics and Glass.

Further Reading

Champion, Timothy. 1999. 'The Later Bronze Age'. Pp.95–112 in *The Archaeology of Britain*. Edited by J. Hunter and I. Ralston. Routledge Press.

Pearson, M. P. 1999. 'The Earlier Bronze Age'. Pp.77–94 in *The Archaeology of Britain*. Edited by J. Hunter and I. Ralston. Routledge Press.

Pearson, M. P. 1993. *Bronze Age Britain*. B. T. Batsford.

Raftery, Barry. 1994. *Pagan Celtic Britain*. Thames & Hudson.

Anne Sassin

Brooches

Brooches have a long history in Britain and were employed both as a means of fastening clothing and for ornamental purposes. In the **Bronze Age** however different types of pins were used as dress-fasteners and it is not until the Early **Iron Age** that brooches became fashionable. These were inspired by Mediterranean prototypes and are of the safety-pin or 'fibula' type with a bow, spring and catchplate. Some brooches used in the earlier Iron Age were imported and include Italic types of the 'leech' family with wide, curved plates and a few ornate examples of **La Tène** I brooches including some with coral inlays or Waldalgesheim style ornaments. The development of La Tène brooches follows an evolutionary sequence that can be traced in Britain, the foot being first turned up (La Tène I), then folded over to join the bow (La Tène II) and then finally made in one piece (La Tène III). The last type remained current in Britain in the early years after the Roman Conquest (they are known as Nauheim Derivative brooches). A few circular brooches appear also to have been made at the end of the Iron Age.

A great diversity of different types of brooches was in use in Roman Britain, the majority being of the bow-and-spring variety. The widest range of types belongs to the first and second centuries; by the fourth century only a few types were current. Romano-British brooches belong to three main categories: penannular, plate and bow. Penannular brooches originated in the pre-Roman Iron Age and comprised a hoop with a break through which a pin could pass which swiveled on the hoop. By turning the hoop, the cloth was caught. The earliest have simple rolled-over terminals, but by the second century the 'zoomorphic' type evolved, with cast terminals that look vaguely like an animal head facing the hoop. New types of these developed in the fourth century, which were developed in the post-Roman period.

Bow brooches have a head with some form of cross-bar incorporating the spring mechanism. They sometimes have spring pins and sometimes hinged pins, and both mechanisms were found on ordinary and sophisticated examples. A number of different types of bow brooches were introduced by the **Roman army**, such as the Langton Down brooches (named after a site in Sussex), which had flat, reeded bows; Aucissa brooches (so-called on account of the name 'Aucissa' which sometimes appears on the bow and is that of the Gaulish maker); and Hod Hill brooches (named after a site in Dorset) which seem to have originated round Trier and were popular until c. AD 70. These have square head-plates with projecting knobs. The most important however were Colchester brooches, which had been worn in the pre-Roman Iron Age but continued through the first century, when the earlier one-piece construction was replaced by a two-piece mechanism. From such brooches evolved dolphin brooches, current in the later first century, which as the name suggests were somewhat like a diving dolphin in profile, and the distinctively British trumpet brooches, which have ornate trumpet-shaped heads and often moulded bows. These continued being fashionable even in the second century. Various types of bow brooches continued through the second and into the third century, when a new type, the crossbow brooch, made its appearance. These brooches had long cross pieces on the head, at first with simply round knobs but later with elaborate terminals. The ornate versions were a feature of the fourth century and were the only type of bow brooch to be in use at that period.

Plate brooches were fashionable in the second century. They are essentially round or lozenge shaped, usually flat brooches, sometimes with projections and often enamelled. A special series have applied die-stamped plates, sometimes modelled on coins of the emperor Hadrian, or with a triskele (three-legged) pattern. Other plate brooches were shaped like a pelta (a shield seen in profile), a horse-and-rider, a hare, fish or other animals. More richly modelled are brooches shaped like birds. These were frequently enamelled. A specific type of plate brooch developed in the fourth century, which was disc-shaped and was often set with a glass or stone in the centre.

In the areas outside those settled by the Anglo-Saxons, penannular brooches and various types of pins were used as dress fasteners in the fifth to seventh centuries. Some types of zoomorphic brooch had arrived in Ireland probably before the end of the Roman period, and these were taken up and the designs developed. The main trend was towards enlarging the terminals, which were then decorated with '**Celtic**' designs, enamel and sometimes inlays of millefiori glass. The acquisition of new techniques of decoration, involving filigree, granular work and chip-carving from the Germanic world led to the production of such sumptuous works as the **Hunterston** and '**Tara**' **brooches**. This tradition continued into the ninth century, when such masterpieces as the Queen's Brooch and Westness Brooch were created. Brooches in the Celtic world were worn as marks of status and rank, and this led to their importance in both secular and ecclesiastical society.

In Anglo-Saxon England, the incomers introduced new brooch types, among the earliest being supporting-arm brooches (which looked a little like Roman crossbows) and equal-armed brooches, which were popular with the **Saxons**. An unusual type, the applied plate brooch was the successor of Roman versions of the same idea. A brooch of Romano-British derivation, the Quoit Brooch (basically a penannular attached to a broad flat hoop) found its way into Anglo-Saxon graves. The main brooch types of the pagan period comprised plate (possibly derived from Romano-British), quoit and various types of bow brooches of which the cruciform (originally with one, later with three projections from the plate head) and the square-headed were particularly noteworthy. Alongside grander versions were smaller everyday brooches, known confusingly as 'small long brooches'.

The bow brooch went out of fashion in the seventh century, and the dominant type of brooch was disc-shaped. The ornate gold-and-garnet disc brooches of the last phase of the pagan period were succeeded by more modest types, though few brooches were worn in the eighth century and it was not until the ninth that new versions became fashionable. They were sometimes executed with openwork (as in the Pentney hoard), sometimes as plates (as in the case of the Fuller Brooch). Alongside these were a number of enamelled brooches, disc brooches imitating coins, and cheaper bronze and pewter plate brooches with ornaments of **Viking** inspiration.

See also Art and Architecture; Metalworking.

Further Reading

Hattatt, R. 1982. *Ancient and Romano-British Brooches.* Dorset Publications.

———. 1985. *Iron Age and Roman Brooches.* Dorset Publications.

Hines, John. 1997. *A New Corpus of Anglo-Saxon Great Square-Headed Brooches.* Society of the Antiquities. Res. Rep. 51.

Jessup, R. 1950. *Anglo-Saxon Jewelry.* Faber & Faber.

Johnson, R. 2001. 'The Development of Irish Brooch Forms and Pins in the Viking Age, c. 850–1170'. *Peritia* 15: 321–362.

Laing, Lloyd. 2006. *The Archaeology of Celtic Britain and Ireland c.* AD *400–1200.* Cambridge University Press.

Lucy, S. 2000. *The Anglo-Saxon Way of Death.* Alan Sutton.

Whitfield, N. 2001. 'The "Tara" brooch: An Irish Emblem of Status in its European Context'. Pp. 211–247 in *From Ireland Coming: Irish Art from the Early Christian to the Late Gothic Period and Its European Context.* Edited by Colum Hourihane. Department of Art and Archeology, Princeton University.

———. 2004. 'More Thoughts on the Wearing of Brooches in Early Medieval Ireland'. Pp. 70–108 in *Index of Christian Art Occasional Papers VII.* Edited by Colum Hourihane. Four Courts Press.

Lloyd Laing

Bruce Family

The Bruce family, lords of Annandale, is principally associated with its most famous son, the Scottish king Robert Bruce (r.1306–1329), but the family had been among the foremost cross-border lords holding lands in both England and Scotland for around two centuries before King Robert.

The progenitor of the family was Robert I de Brus, who arrived in England as a follower of **King Henry I** (r.1100–1135) in about 1100. The name Bruce or Brus is derived from Brix in the Cotentin Peninsula of Normandy, and the family's **Norman** origins are clear though its history is obscure until c.1100. Robert I's support for Henry I was rewarded with extensive estates in Yorkshire between c.1103 and c.1110. Robert's close affiliation with Henry I brought him into contact with another of Henry's protégés, the future **David I** of Scotland (r.1124–1153). When, in the reign of his brother, **Alexander I** (r.1107–1124), David took control of lands in southern Scotland, Robert I de Brus accompanied him and became one of David's most influential companions. When David succeeded to the kingship in 1124, one of his first acts was to grant Robert the lordship of Annandale, with its castles at Annan and Lochmaben, in the critical southwest frontier of Scotland.

Robert I de Brus was a close companion of King David in Scotland but he continued to hold his English lands, illustrating the phenomenon of what is known as cross-border lordship. When King David invaded England in 1138 and the English and Scottish armies met at Cowton Moor near Northallerton, Robert was forced to choose between his two allegiances and ultimately took his place in the English army. But his younger son Robert II fought on the Scottish side and Robert I may have returned to favour with David I by 1139 or 1140. Robert I de Brus died in spring 1142 and was buried at the priory of Guisborough that he had founded in Yorkshire. His lands were divided between his two sons. Adam (d.1143), the eldest, received the English lands while Robert II (d. c.1194), the second son. received Annandale, and the fortunes of the two families began to diverge. The English branch lost prestige in the thirteenth century and died out in 1272, but the Scottish Bruces remained powerful and influential. In the 1290s, the Scottish Bruces began their pursuit of the Scottish kingship, which culminated in the coronation of King Robert I in 1306.

Annandale was adjacent to the **Gaelic**-speaking region of Galloway in southwest Scotland and the grant to Robert I de Brus was initially intended to guard this vital frontier zone. But the Bruces gradually associated with the Gaelic-speaking aristocracy of the region, and Robert Bruce VI (d.1304; the father of King Robert I) married the daughter of the last Gaelic earl of Carrick. Characterisations of the Bruce family as either 'Celtic' or 'Anglo-Norman' are therefore over-simplistic, and the family provides an excellent example of the processes of cultural assimilation and interaction among the British nobility as well as a classic example of cross-border landholding and trans-national lordship that characterises this period of medieval British history.

See also Kings and Kingship; Scots.

Further Reading

Barrow, G. W. S. 1981. *The Anglo-Norman Era in Scottish History*. Oxford University Press.

Barrow, G. W. S. 1988. *Robert Bruce & the Community of the Realm of Scotland* (3rd edn.). Edinburgh University Press.

Blakely, Ruth M. 2005. *The Brus Family in England and Scotland 1100–1295*. Boydell.

Duncan, A. A. M. 1994. 'The Bruces of Annandale, 1100–1304'. *Transactions of the Dumfriesshire and Galloway Natural History and Antiquarian Society* 69: 89–102.

R. Andrew McDonald

Brude mac Maelchon

Bridei, son of Meilocon, known to the Irish as Brude mac Maelchon, was a powerful Pictish king who is most famous for having been visited by Saint **Columba**. He began to rule in 554 or 556 and his death occurred in 584 or 586. Most of what we know about him is recorded in **Adomnán**'s *Vita Columbae*. Here we are told that he had a royal fortress near the mouth of the river Ness in the north of Scotland and that his foster father, Broichan, was a *magus* – possibly meaning a druid. Broichan is presented as an opponent of Columba. According to Adomnán, Columba encountered a tributary king from Orkney at Bridei's court. Though later hagiography claims that Columba successfully converted Bridei to Christianity, this is not clear from Adomnán's work, although the two men are presented as enjoying cordial relations. Nonetheless, recent archaeological excavations at **Portmahomack** in Easter Ross suggest that a monastery was founded there during Bridei's time.

Bridei's father's name, Meilocon, or, in Irish, Maelchú, is a form of the Brittonic name Maglocunos. There has been much speculation that he may in fact have been the son of the king of **Gwynedd** to whom **Gildas** addressed part of his *De Excidio Britanniae* and who is known in modern Welsh as **Maelgwn**. It is possible but far from proven. This theory is based on the belief that royal succession amongst the **Picts** passed through the female line and that a number of Pictish kings were the children of foreign princes.

It is not clear how extensive Bridei's power was amongst the various Pictish tribes. At least one other king reigned alongside him for a time, but he features in a late Pictish king list indicating that later kings of Pictland saw themselves as his heirs. According to **Bede**, it was Bridei who gave the island of **Iona** to Columba although the later Irish chronicles claim Conall mac Comgaill king of **Dál Riata** was the donor. This has led some to speculate that Bede's knowledge of these things came from a Pictish rather than a Gaelic source. By coincidence, during Adomnán's term of office as abbot of Iona (672–704) two kings called Bridei reigned over the **Picts** (Bridei son of Beli, 672–693, and Bridei son of Derile, 696–706) and it may be that Adomnán's account of the son of Meilocon was coloured by his own relations with these men.

See also Gaels; Kings and Kingship.

Further Reading

Sharpe, Richard (tr.). 1995. *Adomnán of Iona: Life of St Columba*. Penguin.

Anderson, Marjorie O. 1973. *Kings and Kingship in Early Scotland*. Scottish Academic Press.

Alex Woolf

Brunanburh, Battle of (AD 937)

The Battle of Brunanburh was fought in AD 937, where the English won against the combined forces of the **Scots** and the **Dublin** Norse. Little is known about the Battle of Brunanburh, and our primary source for the battle comes from a poem entered into the ***Anglo-Saxon Chronicle***. The English King, **Æthelstan** (r. 924–939) and his brother Eadmund declared war on the Scottish king, **Constantine**, in 934, harrying the Scots by land and sea. In 937, the Scottish king allied with Olaf, the Norse king of Dublin, realising that the English were too powerful to be defeated by the Scots alone. The climax came with the Battle of Brunanburh, where the English defeated the invaders with heavy causalities on both sides and according to the poem, five kings died along with seven of Olaf's earls. With victory at the Battle of Brunanburh, Æthelstan ended the invasions from the north and fully consolidated and secured the kingdom of England from threats from the north. It was not only important in the victory itself but it was also the first time that the Mercians fought as an integral part of the English army. The exact location of the battle is unknown, though it is thought to have occurred somewhere in the northwest of present day England. It is also likely that the invaders had penetrated far into the new kingdom of England before the English repelled them.

When Æthelstan came into power there already was an England, consisting mainly of Wessex, where he was crowned king, and western **Mercia**, where he was recognised as a king independent of **Wessex**. In 926, he arranged the marriage of his sister to the Norse king Sihtric, who held **York** and much of **Northumbria**, in an attempt to continue good relations and bring the north into his new kingdom. However, Sihtric died the following year, leaving his son Olaf as heir. Æthelstan then decided that he wanted to add Northumbria to England for good, so after a short campaign in the summer of AD 927 he defeated the Norse, driving them back to Ireland, and claimed Northumbria as his own. In the next four years he extended his supremacy to include much of western and northern Britain, securing tribute from the various kings and princes. When Guthfrith died in 934, Olaf became king of the Dublin Norse. It was with this hold in the north that the kings of Scotland, the kings of **Strathclyde** and the English lord of Bamburgh became Æthelstan's men as they were in his new domain. It is unclear what broke the six-year peace, but by 934, war broke out between the Scots and Strathclyde against the English. The Battle of Brunanburh was the climax to this war.

See also Warfare and Weapons.

Further Reading

Campbell, James. 1982. *The Anglo-Saxons*. Penguin Books.

Crossley-Holland, Kevin. 1982. *The Anglo-Saxon World: An Anthology*. Oxford University Press.

Stenton, F. M. 1943. *The Oxford History of England: Anglo-Saxon England*. Oxford University Press.

Gregory Hays

Brutus

Brutus is one of several legendary figures identified as the eponymous founder of Britain in medieval Welsh tradition. He was established as the definitive British founder by his appearance in this role in **Geoffrey of Monmouth**'s *Historia Regum Britanniae*.

In the ninth-century Cambro-Latin text ***Historia Brittonum*** the name is found, apparently interchangeably, as 'Britto' or 'Brutus'. The *Historia Brittonum* states that Britain takes its name from 'one Brutus, a Roman consul' (Morris 1980, 18, 59). Later, the *Historia* helpfully states that there are 'two alternative explanations' for Britain's origins: the first, ascribed to the 'Annals of the Romans', relates how Brutus, the grandson of the Trojan hero Aeneas, was prophesied as 'the child of death', who would 'kill his father and mother and become hateful to all men' (Morris 9, 60). Having accidentally killed his father, Brutus was driven away from Italy and eventually wandered to Gaul, where he founded Tours, before coming to Britain to be its founder and eponym. The source of the name of Brutus was the *Chronicon* of Eusebius, translated by St. Jerome, which also provided a chronological scheme within which most early medieval national histories positioned themselves. According to the *Chronicon*, Brutus, the Roman consul Decimus Junius Brutus Callaicus, conquered Spain in 142 BC. The *Historia Brittonum* appears to have added Britain to Brutus's conquests and inserted the tale into a Trojan context. Brutus's epithet 'hateful' may well derive from Isidore of Seville's *Etymologies,* which suggests that the British are so called because they are 'brutes' (Barney *et al.* 198).

The second explanation given in the *Historia Brittonum,* perhaps originally attached to a separate figure, Britto or Britus, eponym of the *Brittones,* traces Brutus's descent, via Aeneas, to Japheth, son of Noah (Morris 1980, 22, 63). This lineage connects Brutus to the founding ancestors of several other European barbarian kingdoms and was derived from an early medieval text examining the supposed genealogical relations between the various Roman and post-Roman barbarian ethnic groups, known as the Fränkische Völkertafel, or 'Frankish Table of Nations'. To this text's enumeration of Romans, **Britons** (*Brittones*), Franks and Alamans among the descendants of *Istio,* the *Historia Brittonum* added material of Irish provenance as well.

Geoffrey of Monmouth ignored the second explanation in the *Historia Brittonum* entirely, and expanded on the material given in the first (Thorpe, 54–74). He falsely claimed Homer as a source for part of his account and made the foundation of Britain follow on a prophecy from the goddess Diana that Brutus would found 'a second Troy' to which the entire world would be subject. According to Geoffrey, Brutus came to what was then called **Albion**, found it empty except for a few giants, founded the British race and built *Trinovantum* (from *Troia Nova,* according to Geoffrey), later London. The name Brutus passed via Norman French usage into the Welsh language as *brud, brut,* meaning 'chronicle' or 'history' with the additional sense of 'prophecy'. Despite this, Brutus the character appears surprisingly infrequently in medieval Welsh literature apart from translations of Geoffrey into Welsh (under the title *Brut y Brenhinedd*) and their derivatives in the genre of genealogy. There are hints of an entirely separate, probably pre-Geoffrey, story whereby the founder and eponym of Britain (*Prydein* in Welsh) was *Prydein fab Aed*; the medieval tract *Enweu Ynys Brydein* claims that Britain takes its name from him, although it also states that the Britons came from Troy, albeit with no mention of Brutus (Bromwich, 228–229). Nevertheless, the character Prydein, like Brutus, is only otherwise mentioned in *Brut y Brenhinedd*'s genealogical reckonings.

See also Literature.

Further Reading

Barney, Stephen A., et al. (tr.). 2006. *The Etymologies of Isidore of Seville.* Cambridge University Press.

Bromwich, Rachel (ed.). 1978. *Trioedd Ynys Prydein* (2nd edn.). University of Wales Press.

Goffart, Walter. 1983 'The Supposedly "Frankish" Table of Nations: An Edition and Study'. *Frühmittelalterliche Studien* 17: 98–130. Reprinted in Walter Goffart, *Rome's Fall and After* (London and Ronceverte, 1989), pp.133–65.

Jaski, Bart. 2003. 'We Are All Greeks in Our Origin: New Perspectives on the Irish Origin Legend'. *Cambrian Medieval Celtic Studies* 46: 1–53.

Morris, John (ed. and tr.). 1980. *Nennius: British History and the Welsh Annals.* Phillimore.

Thorpe, Lewis (tr.). 1966. *Geoffrey of Monmouth: The History of the Kings of Britain.* Penguin.

Karen Jankulak

Brycheiniog

Brycheiniog was a kingdom in the uplands of the Usk River in south central Wales which was purportedly founded by a quasi-mythic figure called Brychan, who had Irish connections. The kingdom persisted for several centuries before it was conquered by the Anglo-Norman baron, Bernard de Neufmarché in 1093. Thereafter it was known as Brecon or Brecknock and was held by Bernard's descendants until 1521.

According to Welsh genealogical tradition, Brychan's mother was Marchell, the daughter of King Tewdrig of Garthmadrum. She had gone to Ireland to marry Anlach, son of Coronac, and returned to Wales after Brychan was born. During the mid fifth century, Brychan eventually became ruler of Garthmadrum, which was renamed Brycheiniog after him. The genealogies report that Brychan had several dozen children, many of whom were saints. While the historical reality of Brychan may be suspect, there is archaeological evidence of Irish settlement in the Brecon region during the early medieval period, including a cluster of six ogam stones with inscriptions of Irish names. Further evidence for the Irish connection of this region and its ruling family comes from the distribution over the southern half of Ireland of churches dedicated to the names of many of the reported saintly children of Brychan. There is documentary evidence for existence of kings of Brycheiniog by the eighth century, including references in chronicles and charters, like the *Book of Llandaff*. The political court of these kings was probably a *crannog* (an artificial island) in **Llangorse** Lake (Welsh Llyn Syfaddan). Kings of this dynasty were associated in charters with Llandeilo'r fân, Llanfihangel Cwm Du and Llangorse – all places clustered near Brecon. The last known king of Brychan's line was Tewdwr ab Griffri, who sought alliance with King **Alfred the Great** to have protection against the depredations of Anarawd ap **Rhodri Mawr** of **Gwynedd** late in the ninth century. Tewdwr attended the English royal court and witnessed some charters as a *subregulus* – a sub-king dependent upon the English ruler. Tewdwr's last known grant dates from 925, and in Welsh genealogies his line peters out with his son. When Llywarch ap Hyfaidd, the king of **Dyfed**, died in 904, his sister's husband, Hywel ap Cadell ap Rhodri the king of Seisyllwg, took control of Dyfed. It seems likely that after the death of Tewdwr ab Griffri, Hywel ap Cadell also gained control over Brycheiniog, thus creating the kingdom of **Deheubarth**.

The **Vikings** attacked Brycheiniog and Gwent in 896. In 916, King Alfred's formidable daughter **Æthelflaed**, the 'Lady of the Mercians', led an attack on the region. Another attack by English forces occurred in 983. In 1093, Bernard de Neufmarché conquered Brycheiniog, erected a strong castle at Brecon and killed **Rhys ap Tewdwr**, the king of Deheubarth. However, Bernard also used marriage as part of his strategy to control the region, for he married Nest, a granddaughter of **Gruffudd ap Llywelyn**, who had controlled all of Wales until his death three decades earlier.

See also Kings and Kingship; Welsh People.

Further Reading

Davies, John. 1993. *A History of Wales*. Allen Lane/Penguin.

Davies, Wendy. 1982. *Wales in the Early Middle Ages*. Leicester University Press.

Maund, K. L. 1991. *Ireland, Wales, and England in the Eleventh Century*. Boydell Press.

Frederick Suppe

Brythonic Language

The term *Brythonic* refers to those languages native to Britain (although not restricted to use in Britain), which belong to the so-called P-Celtic branch of Indo-European languages. The P-Celtic language developed from the ancestral tongue of all the Celtic languages, which is called Common Celtic. Before the **Iron Age** this Common Celtic became differentiated into two branches:

1. Q-Celtic, which was initially spoken in Ireland and is represented in modern times by (a) Modern Irish (spoken mainly in western Ireland), which dates from c.1250 to present; (b) Scottish Gaelic (spoken mainly in the Highlands and Islands of Scotland), which dates from c.1400 to present; and (c) Manx (spoken on the Isle of Man), which dated from c.1600 to early twentieth century.

2. P-Celtic, which was spoken in Ancient Gaul and Britain and later developed into Brythonic. In modern times Brythonic is represented by three languages: (a) Modern Welsh, which dates from c.1500 to present. (b) Modern Cornish, which dated from c.1600 to c.1800. (c) Modern Breton, which dates from c.1600 to present.

During the Iron Age, P-Celtic transformed into two distinct types: 1. Gallic (spoken in Ancient

Gaul), represented by the now extinct Gaulish. 2. Brythonic (*or* Brittonic) (spoken throughout Britain). The Brythonic language evolved until c. 325 BC at which time it became the language known as British, a language characterised by an early phase (Early British, c. AD 43–450) and a late phase (Late British, c. 450–550). During the Early Medieval Period around AD 550, British gave way to five separate languages:

1. Pictish (spoken primarily in northern and eastern Scotland), which died out around 900 when it was replaced by the Q-Celtic Gaelic language used by the Scots of **Dál Riata**.

2. Cumbric (spoken in Cumbria and other parts of northern Britain), which died out by c. 100.

3. Primitive Welsh (spoken in Wales), which dates from c. 550 to c. 750.

4. Primitive Cornish (spoken in **Cornwall**), which dates from c. 550 to c. 850.

5. Primitive Breton (introduced to Brittany by **Britons** migrating to France), which dates c. 550–c. 850.

The three surviving remaining Brythonic languages further evolved into Old Welsh, which dates from c. 750 to c. 1150; Old Cornish, which dates from c. 850 to c. 1300; and Old Breton, which dates from c. 850 to c. 1000. It is during this period that the oldest manuscripts with Brythonic languages used in them were written. The earliest Old Welsh texts are the '*Surexit-memorandum*' (an Old Welsh and Latin text of a lawsuit) and the '*Ostenditur hic*' entry (containing Old Welsh names written above a Latin text discussing Gospels being given to the church of Llandaff). Both of these are from the *Book of St. Chad* and date from the late seventh and eighth centuries. The earliest Old Cornish text is the *Vocabularium Cornicum* ('Vocabulary of Cornish') or 'Old Cornish Vocabulary', which dates from c. 1000. The earliest Old Breton text is the *Venice Orosius*, a manuscript of Orosius' *Historia Adversus Paganus* which contains Old Breton glosses and dates from the middle of the ninth century. During the High Medieval Period these three languages became Middle Welsh; which dates from c. 1150 to c. 1500; Middle Cornish, which dates from c. 1300 to c. 1600; and Middle Breton, which dates from c. 1000 to c. 1600.

See also Celts; Literature; Welsh People.

Further Reading

Chadwick, Nora. 1986. *The Celts*. Pelican Books.
Jackson, Kenneth. 1994. *Language and History in Early Britain*. Four Courts Press.
Jackson, Kenneth. 1955. 'The Pictish Language'. Pp. 129–166 in *The Problem of the Picts*. Edited by F. T. Wainwright. Thomas Nelson.

Joseph Calise

Burgh Castle

Burgh Castle, a village in Norfolk near Great Yarmouth on the river Waveney, is a site with a long history of occupation from the remarkable preserved Roman fort of *Garrianonum* (or *Garrianum*) to the Norman motte-and-bailey castle. Garrianonum is one of the Roman **Saxon** Shore forts, part of a defensive network along eastern and southern Britain, with Caistor-on-Sea nearby to the northeast, which seems to have been built in the later third century AD. Evidence suggests that the garrison at Burgh Castle consisted of Greek Stablesian cavalry who had been stationed in Holland. Burgh Castle's comparatively well-preserved remains are especially apparent in the south wall, whose mortared masonry face is clearly evident, showing flints separated by courses of red Roman tiles, approximately 8.20 feet (2.5 metres) thick at the base and 14.76 feet (4.5 metres) high. Massive circular bastions stand at the corners and along certain sections of the walls, one of which shows evidence for an anchoring socket for a Roman ballista to hurl weapons at attackers, with gates in the middle of each standing wall, though the eastern is the only one of significance, at approximately 11.48 feet (3.5 metres) wide. The quadrilateral plan of the fort, with the east end about 49.21 feet (15 metres) shorter than the eroded west one, is approximately 5.93 acres (2.4 hectares) total, and it continued its occupation until the fourth century when its troops were withdrawn to face problems on the continent.

The existing church at Burgh Castle, likely Late **Saxon** in date and dedicated to Saints Peter and Paul, is one of the round-tower types, a distinctive ecclesiastical form which was especially prevalent in East Anglia due to the difficulty in obtaining neat corners with flint. Within the fort walls themselves, however, are the remains of an earlier, possibly seventh century, Anglo-Saxon

Christian community, which according to Bede was founded by **Fursa**, an Irish monk, the site having been given to him by the local king. Excavations by Charles Green in 1960–1961 found a cemetery of 144 burials. There were also post-Roman structural phases, associated with Middle and Late Saxon pottery. The interpretation of the remains however is open to some doubt.

In the **Norman** period, a motte-and-bailey earthwork was constructed at the former fort's southwest corner, only to be levelled by the eighteenth century, leaving fragments of the earthworks behind.

See also Roman Britain.

Further Reading

'Burgh Castle', Norfolk Archaeological Trust, http://www.norfarchtrust.org.uk/burgh/index.htm (cited 22 August 2007).

Johnson, S. 1983. *Burgh Castle: Excavations by Charles Green 1958–61*. Norfolk Archaeological Unit.

Wallis, H. 1998. 'Excavations at Church Loke, Burgh Castle, 1993–4'. *Norfolk Archaeology* 43: 62–78.

Anne Sassin

Burghal Hidage

The Burghal Hidage describes a system of defence designed to protect **Wessex** from Danish invasions in the early tenth century AD. It establishes several fortified areas, assigns specific amounts of land to each fortified area and indicates the number of men required to defend each fortified area from attack. According to the formula preserved in one manuscript version of the Burghal Hidage, the system provided each fortified area with enough land to support four men for each pole – or standard section – of wall surrounding the fortified area. Each of the fortified areas in Wessex was located within approximately 20 miles (32.19 kilometres) from neighbouring fortifications. The fortifications were of various types, including old Roman towns and forts, **Iron Age** fortifications and new sites built on a rectangular grid pattern. In addition to serving as places of refuge and defence, the fortified sites also served as centres of trade and commerce.

In its original manuscript forms, the Burghal Hidage has no official title. 'Burghal Hidage' was the name given to the document in 1897. The **Old English** word ***burh*** (thus 'Burghal') refers to a fortified location, while the term 'hide' (thus 'Hidage') refers to a unit of taxation in Anglo-Saxon England. Since the late nineteenth century, the 'Burghal Hidage' has been used as an important source for urban history, place-name studies and archaeology.

See also Vikings.

Further Reading

Campbell, James. 1991. *The Anglo-Saxons*. Penguin.

Hill, David, and Alexander R. Rumble (eds.). 1996. *The Defence of Wessex: The Burghal Hidage and Anglo-Saxon Fortifications*. Manchester University Press.

Deanna Forsman

Burhs

Burh is a term used in Anglo-Saxon England to describe fortified places, more specifically the fortified towns of the ninth and later centuries. The term appears in the ***Anglo-Saxon Chronicle*** to refer to prehistoric fortifications or sometimes to monasteries. The first reference to the building of fortifications occurs in **Mercia** in a royal privilege of AD 749. Under **Offa**, there is evidence for the building of defensive works, of which **Offa's Dyke** is the most notable, but also includes the earliest known fortified settlements. Classic examples are the sites of Hereford and Tamworth, where archaeological work has helped to elucidate the nature of the defences, and Winchcombe, where the defences are pre-tenth century but not provably as early as those on the other sites.

It was in **Wessex**, however, that the development of burhs took place. The earliest reference to fortifications there was in 846, and it is usually assumed that the first building of such defended towns was in the time of **Æthelwulf** (r. 839–858), though the real impetus behind their construction was due to the policies of **Alfred the Great**. Some of the burhs in Wessex were re-occupied Roman towns which utilised the Roman walls and gates, some were re-defended prehistoric sites, while some were no more than promontories cut off with a landward defence.

The burhs of Alfred and his son, Edward the Elder, are documented for us in the '**Burghal Hidage**', drawn up by Edward the Elder probably after 914 (but devised by Alfred in the 880s), which lists the burhs stating how many hides of land each contained, one hide having to provide one man for the maintenance of the defences. One pole of the rampart about 5.5 yards (5 metres) was defended by four men. Archaeology has confirmed that the length of the ramparts coincides with the length indicated in the 'Burghal Hidage'. The scheme, which echoed some Carolingian plans, was undoubtedly partly developed in response to the **Viking** threat. The document lists thirty burhs for Wessex. The defences were of earth-and-timber, and it was usual to leave an open area between the built-up part of the interior and the rampart, to facilitate the rapid manning of the defences. Streets were laid out on a grid-iron pattern (where the burhs were occupying Roman sites, the street plan did not coincide with the Roman, except insofar as it was dictated by the gates), and each burh had a mint. No area of Wessex was to be more than about 18.64 miles (30 kilometres) from a burh.

The scheme set out in the 'Burghal Hidage' was extended to Mercia by **Æthelflaed**, Alfred's daughter, in a similar document known as the *Mercian Register*.

See also Warfare and Weapons.

Further Reading

Clarke, H., and B. Ambrosiani (eds.). 1991. *Towns in the Viking Age*. Leicester University Press.

Hill, D., and A. R. Rumble. 1996. *The Defence of Wessex: The Burghal Hidage and Anglo-Saxon Fortifications*. Manchester University Press.

Hodges, Richard. 1989. *The Anglo-Saxon Achievement*. Duckworth.

Lloyd Laing

C

Cadbury Castle

Cadbury Castle is a substantial refurbished **Iron Age** hillfort situated on Cadbury Hill in South Cadbury, Somerset, and is most famously affiliated with King **Arthur** and his legendary **Camelot**. Though generally the site name *Cadbury* is considered to be a Saxo-Brythonic hybrid, meaning 'Battle-Fort', the name *Camelot* may be derived from the land (lot) by the river Cam. Camelot first appears as the court of Arthur in the poetry of Chrétien de Troyes (twelfth century), and its identification with South Cadbury is first recorded by the antiquarian John Leland in 1532. However, modern archaeological excavations, first conducted by Leslie Alcock from 1966 to 1970, have found nothing to substantiate this association, though still providing a wealth of information on the history and development of south-west Britain.

One of the few hillforts of the period to be located over 19 miles (30 kilometres) from the sea, this considerable multivallate structure had the advantage of a steep position in addition to agriculturally suitable land and a water supply within its defences, and it seems to have first been built around 500 BC, though there is some representation of Neolithic pottery and flints, as well as **Bronze Age** occupation. The Iron Age structure, consisting of large ramparts and elaborate timber defences, suggests refortification at more than one stage over the following centuries, with excavation revealing both round houses and rectangular six-post house foundations, what may have been the workshop of a blacksmith and a putative temple, which may have still been in some use as late as the fifth century AD. These *oppida*-like features attest to the prominence the site must have had, necessitating a Roman takeover, which evidence (e.g. ballista bolts) suggests was particularly violent, probably c. AD 50. A survey of the hinterland showed certain agricultural developments from the third to the fifth century, and by the mid-fifth century, it seemed that settlement had definitely shifted from Ilchester to Cadbury, following the withdrawal of Roman administration.

The period of the early medieval reoccupation of the site, associated with Arthur's reign, is the one which has seen the most investigation and interpretation. The site is thought to have been in use from c. 470 and its use lasted until the mid-sixth century. One of the more substantial revelations of the excavation is the 'Great Hall', an approximately 66 feet × 33 feet (20 metres × 10 metres) rectangular feature with bowed ends, whose outline was evidenced by post-holes and suggested a dividing partition, providing proportions of 1:2:1. Near the Great Hall is a small structure which has been interpreted as a kitchen. This period of occupation also saw the innermost Iron Age defences refortified, a series of four (or possibly five) sets of banks and ditches, with an outer facing of timber for the stone bank (about 16 feet [5 metres] wide) with tie beams running into the core. Cadbury also boasts of the only known and excavated early medieval gateway, a timber tower approximately 10 feet (3 metres) squared at the south-west entrance, consisting of four corner posts linked by beams, to which may have been added double-leaved gates in Roman fashion. A major road appears to have run through the gateway, with a late-sixth-century Anglo-Saxon buckle discovered beneath the upper surface, with other finds including a rare example of a long narrow-bladed saw, iron weapons including knives and axe-hammers and sherds of glass beakers and pottery from the East Mediterranean and North Africa, indicating extensive trading links.

Between 1009 and 1020, the hill was reoccupied under Æthelred II and briefly by **Cnut** for use as a temporary late-Saxon mint, some bearing the mint-mark CADABYR, with defences including a gate and an unfinished church constructed, which the presence of iron nails suggests, of timber, but in his conquest Cnut managed to revert the site back to its original agricultural function. The gap in centuries between this phase and the earlier sub-Roman occupation cannot be readily explained, other than the readily available defensive site of the eleventh century being made use of. Whether or not Arthur really had any affiliation with Cadbury, the refortification in the fifth century could credibly have been a response by the **Britons** to an Anglo-Saxon advance into the valley, and as the site itself would have allowed for a much smaller fort to have been built, the huge scale undertaken attests to the effort and the strong political power that would have been required; presumably under a king.

See also Warfare and Weapons.

Further Reading

Alcock, L. 1972. *'By South Cadbury Is that Camelot ...' The Excavation of Cadbury Castle 1966–1970.* Thames & Hudson.

———. 1982. 'Cadbury-Camelot: A Fifteen-Year Perspective'. *Proceedings of the British Academy* LXVIII: 355–388.

———. 1995. *Cadbury Castle, Somerset: The Early Medieval Archaeology.* University of Wales Press.

Barrett, J. C., P. W. M. Freeman and Ann Woodward. 2000. *Cadbury Castle Somerset: The Later Prehistoric and Early Historic Archaeology.* English Heritage.

Davey, J. E. 2005. *The Roman to Medieval Transition in the Region of South Cadbury Castle, Somerset.* Archaeopress.

Anne Sassin

Cædmon

According to **Bede** (d. 735) in his *Ecclesiastical History of the English People*, Cædmon was the first poet to compose poetry with Christian content in English. Although Bede says that Cædmon wrote numerous poems on biblical subject matter, scholars now agree that only nine lines survive of his *oeuvre*:

> Nu scylun hergan hefaenricaes uard,
> metudæs maecti, end his modgidanc,
> uerc uuldurfadur – sue he uundra gihuaes,
> eci dryctin, or astelidæ!
> He aerist scop aelda barnum
> heben til hrofe, haleg scepen;
> tha middungeard, moncynnæs uard,
> eci dryctin, æfter tiadæ
> firum foldu, frea allmectig.
> Now we ought to praise the Guardian of Heaven's Realm,
> The power of the Creator, and his grand design,
> The work of the Father of Glory – as he, the Eternal Lord,
> Established all wonders from the start!
> For the sons of men, the Holy Creator made first
> Heaven as a roof; then the Guardian of mankind,
> the Eternal Lord, the Lord Almighty, spun out Middle Earth,
> the place for people.

The poem is traceable in **Old English** in twenty-two manuscript witnesses, twenty-one of which are fully legible. This means that we possess twenty-one copies of this short text, which vary from one another more or less significantly, from which the *Hymn* has to be edited. Although the versions exist in both northern and western Saxon dialects, they appear to have generated as many as five 'recensions' or related groups of texts. (The Old English version given above is based on Daniel O'Donnell's edition of the poem reconstructed from all the manuscripts. The translation is added for the purpose of this article.)

The occasion for Cædmon's short poem is remarkable, as Bede makes clear in his retelling of the epiphanic moment when Cædmon, a hired hand on a monastic farm belonging to **Whitby**, discovers his gift. Lacking the confidence to join in recitation to the accompaniment of the harp, Cædmon had a habit of absenting himself when occasion might call him to perform. On one such evening, he adjourned to the barn where he was to sleep with the cattle for their safety. As he slept, an angel appeared to him and asked him to sing, that is to recite or chant, presumably in the manner of those whose company he had recently quit. Cædmon objected, saying that he could not sing, and the angel persisted. When the cowherd asked what he should sing about, the angel told him to sing about the Creation. The poem, given above in the form it appears in the oldest Latin manuscript of Bede's history and perhaps in a dialect fairly close to Cædmon himself, if he is not a creation of legend, surprised Cædmon and subsequently all who heard it, except the angel. He afterwards embraced monastic orders and used his gift to compose English poetry on Biblical themes until his death, which Bede records in detail to stress the sanctification Cædmon's gift of poetry provided. Many others tried subsequently to write such poetry in English, Bede declares, but none were as good as Cædmon.

Much has been learned during the last half century about the nature of poetic improvisation of the sort that Cædmon demonstrated, and there is nothing improbable in the event Bede describes, although his evaluation of Cædmon as the first and the best composer of English Christian poetry may be coloured by the northern parameters Bede brings to his narrative. Because there are so few names to be associated with the production of pre-conquest English poetry, early literary historians divided much of the poetic corpus into 'Cædmonian' or 'Cynewulfian' (**Cynewulf** q.v.) works. Scholars now agree that only the above 'Hymn', can be ascribed to Cædmon, and some scholars argue about how closely these lines come, or ever can come, to represent the text elicited by the angel from the hired man. Recently, contextualised studies of literary works have led to much historical investigation pertaining to Anglo-Saxon literary culture, and Cædmon's story and *Hymn* have offered ways to access the complex interconnections between vernacular and learned texts, matters of oral and textual performance and even issues about monastic and lay social organisation.

See also Literature.

Further Reading

Frantzen, Allen J., and John Hines (eds.). 2007. *Cædmon's Hymn and Material Culture in the World of Bede*. Medieval European Studies 10. West Virginia University Press.

O'Donnell, Daniel Paul. 2005. *Cædmon's Hymn: A Multi-media Study, Edition and Archive*. D. S. Brewer in association with SEENET and the Medieval Academy. [Digital edition on included CD.]

Patrick W. Conner

Caerleon

Caerleon (*Isca*) was a legionary fortress built by the Second Augustan Legion on the river Usk in South Wales. It was built in the AD 70s as one of three permanent legionary fortresses in Britain (the others being **Chester** and **York**) with the intention of controlling and subduing the Welsh tribe known as the ***Silures***. Caerleon acted as the principal base for the Second Augustan Legion for more than 200 years. The site continued to be occupied into the late Roman period, although it is generally thought to have been abandoned as a military base in the later part of the third century. Substantial remains, notably of the baths and amphitheatre, are still visible on the site.

The fort was begun around AD 70 and its earliest ramparts were in earth and timber, with internal buildings also constructed in timber. The defences were rebuilt in stone around AD 100; the timber buildings were also replaced by buildings on cobbled foundations in the late first century. The fort covered around 52 acres (21 hectares) and its interior was divided into 24 *insulae* of varying sizes, a number of which have been excavated to some degree (although the confidence with which the fort's plan is sometimes reconstructed belies the often rudimentary nature of some of the excavations).

The interior contained barrack blocks, arranged along the north-west and south-east sides of the fort and to the north of the *via principalis* (the main axial street that ran from south-west to north-east). Larger accommodation including hypocaust systems associated with the barracks to the west of the *principia* may well have been that of the centurions commanding the first cohort. In the angle formed by the *via principalis* and the *decumanus maximus* was a major bath complex built on a symmetrical plan and decorated with mosaic pavements. Finds from a drain at the baths include beads, hairpins and jewellery, suggesting that women were regular users of the baths, while milk-teeth finds show the presence of children. The discovery of a lead admission token suggests that the use of the baths was granted to members of the civilian community that lived outside the fort.

On the basis of very limited evidence, it has been suggested that a hospital complex existed to the east of the bath complex. The *principia* or headquarters building was placed at the centre, underlying the present parish church, and to its north lay the commanding officer's house. This was a palatial building, arranged around a central colonnaded area with curving ends, which probably surrounded a garden. Little excavation has been carried out in the southern quarter of the fort, although further barracks and possible granaries have been recently identified through recent geophysical survey.

A substantial amphitheatre was built to the south-west of the fort, close to the rampart. Construction seems to have begun around AD 80, immediately after the initial construction of the fort, although later modifications occurred in the second and third centuries. Two external bath complexes have also been identified, one adjacent to the amphitheatre and the other close to the medieval castle at the eastern corner of the fort.

See also Roman Britain; Warfare and Weapons; Welsh People.

Further Reading

Boon, George C. 1987. *The Legionary Fortress of Caerleon-Isca*. National Museum of Wales.

University of Cardiff. 'Caerleon Research Committee', http://www.cf.ac.uk/hisar/archaeology/crc.html (cited 4 September 2007).

Zienkiewicz, J. David. 1986. *The Legionary Fortress Baths at Caerleon*, 2 vols. National Museum of Wales.

William Bowden

Caernarfon

Caernarfon, in north-west Wales, was the site of a Roman fort (*Segontium*) and a medieval castle. The Romans, under Governor Gnaeus Julius **Agricola**, established a major fortress in the territory of the ***Deceangli*** around AD 77 after suppressing a rebellion of the neighbouring ***Ordovices*** and then capturing *Mona* (Anglesey). Segontium, overlooking the Menai Strait, was linked to several other forts in north-western Wales by a strategic road network, supported by the legionary bases at **Chester** and **Caerleon**. The fort was designed to accommodate a regiment of 1,000 auxiliary infantry, but by the fourth century, the garrisons were probably smaller. Throughout the Roman occupation, Segontium served as both the military and the administrative centre of north-western Wales. A small civilian settlement (*vicus*) grew up alongside the fort, which included the garrison's bathhouse and a *mithraeum* (temple of Mithras).

The fort underwent extensive internal modifications in the fourth century and appears to have been manned up to about 400. Sub-Roman activity is indicated by the new sentry box built in the south-east guardroom of the south-west gate. An early medieval church was founded just outside of Segontium, at Llanbelig, and Roman terms such as *civis* and *magistratus* appear on early Christian memorial stones found in the area. Segontium appears as *Caer aber Seint* in 'The Dream of Macsen Wledig', one of the medieval Welsh tales associated with the **Mabinogi**. A Norman motte-and-bailey castle was built to the west of Segontium by Hugh of Avranches around 1090. Edward I encompassed this work within his imposing castle of Caernarfon following his Welsh campaigns of 1282–1283. A year later, his son, the first English Prince of Wales and future King Edward II, was born here, and the current Prince of Wales, HRH Prince Charles, took his oath of investiture here in 1969.

See also Roman Britain; Romano-British Towns; Warfare and Weapons; Welsh People.

Further Reading

Casey, P. J., and J. L. Davies. 1977. *Segontium: Excavations at Caernarfon 1976, an Interim Report*. University of Durham Press.

Davies, J. L. 1988. 'Segontium, Caernarfon'. Pp.115–116 in *Early Medieval Settlements in Wales AD 400–1100*. Edited by Nancy Edwards and Alan Lane. University of Wales Press.

———. 1990. *Segontium Roman Fort*. Cadw.

Jones, M. L. 1984. *Society and Settlement in Wales and the Marches, 500 BC to AD 1100*, 2 vols. British Archaeological Reports No. 121.

Laing, Lloyd. 1977. 'Segontium and the Roman Occupation of Wales'. Pp. 57–60 in *Studies in Celtic Survival*. Edited by Lloyd Laing. British Archaeological Reports No. 37.

Christopher A. Snyder

Caerwent

Caerwent is the Roman town of *Venta Silurum* ('market place of the ***Silures***'), recorded in the Antonine Itinerary (Route XIV) and Ravenna Cosmography. The city is the presumed administrative centre of the tribal community (*civitas*) of the *Silures*, whose existence, together with a council (*ordo*) that could pass decrees, is recorded in a third-century inscription (Collingwood and Wright 1995, RIB 311). Almost two-thirds of the Caerwent site was explored between 1899 and 1913, though the resulting plan is essentially that of the late town.

The town lay on a slight rise in a broad open valley, about 2 miles (3 kilometres) from the river Severn. Its origins remain uncertain; there is no obvious **Iron Age** predecessor and little evidence for an early fort. Instead, it apparently began life in the late first century as a roadside settlement, with timber shops and workshops flanking an east–west road linking **Gloucester** and **Caerleon**. These shops were replaced by a series of stone strip-buildings, which form a characteristic feature of the late plan. Eventually, the town possessed a planned street layout, though this may not have been fully formalised before the construction of the defences in the late second century; the streets divided the defended area into twenty blocks (*insulae*), arranged in two rows of five to either side of the main road.

Such evidence links Caerwent with the better-known 'planned' towns of Britain, as do its public buildings and amenities. The central area is dominated by the forum-basilica, occupying a full *insula* north of the main road; built in the early second century, probably under **Hadrian**, it provides confirmation of the site's self-governing status. In the *insula* to the south, across the road, lay the bathhouse, also built in the second century. Other structures include a possible official inn (*mansio*), just inside the south gate, and several temples; the one east of the forum overlay earlier structures and was not built until c. AD 330. Other religious finds include two inscriptions recording the deities Mars Ocelus (Collingwood and Wright 1995, RIB 310) and Mars Lenus/Ocelus Vellaunus (Collingwood and Wright 1995, RIB 309).

Further evidence of the site's status is provided by the earthwork defences, probably constructed at the end of the second century, perhaps with contemporary stone gates; they enclosed about 44 acres (18 hectares). These were later reinforced by a stone wall, most probably in the late third century. Later still, c. AD 349–350, external towers were added along the north and south sides. The town's relative prosperity in the later third and fourth centuries is signified by the presence of wealthy town houses, several of them arranged around a courtyard in Mediterranean fashion; some town houses were clearly involved in agricultural activities.

Evidence indicates that activity continued to the end of the fourth century at least, perhaps reinforced by a military garrison. Little is known about the early medieval period, beyond the discovery of two cemeteries, one near the present church and the other outside the east gate. Radiocarbon dates taken from graves in the latter show that the people of Caerwent continued to be buried in this cemetery in the fifth and sixth centuries. There is also a tradition in the *Life of Tatheus* that the Irish saint was given the town site, where he founded a monastic settlement. Four stone buildings may have belonged to this monastery, and a penannular brooch and two spiral pins provide a glimpse of the early medieval occupants of Caerwent.

See also Roman Britain; Romano-British Towns; Warfare and Weapons.

Further Reading

Brewer, R. J. 1993. 'Venta Silurum: A Civitas Capital'. Pp. 56–65 in *Roman Towns: The Wheeler Inheritance*. Edited by S. Greep. Council for British Archaeology Research Report 93.

Collingwood, R. G., and R. P. Wright. 1995. *The Roman Inscriptions of Britain. Volume 1: The Inscriptions on Stone*. Alan Sutton.

Knight, J. K. 1996. 'Late Roman and Post-Roman Caerwent: Some Evidence From Metalwork'. *Archaeologia Cambrensis* 145: 34–66.

Knight, J. K., and Alan Lane. 1988. 'Caerwent'. Pp. 35–38 in *Early Medieval Settlements in Wales 400–1100*. Edited by Nancy Edwards and Alan Lane. University of Wales Press.

Manning, W. H. 2003. 'The Defences of Caerwent'. Pp. 168–183 in *The Archaeology of Roman Towns*. Edited by P. Wilson. Oxbow Books.

Wacher, J. S. 1995. *The Towns of Roman Britain* (2nd edn.). Batsford.

Barry C. Burnham

Caesar, Julius (b. 100 BC)

Gaius Julius Caesar, born in 100 BC, five times Roman consul (once sole), five times dictator (last in 44 BC, for life), a patrician of distinguished ancestry, the most famous Roman, invaded Britain in 55 and 54 BC, with no lasting result other than greater honour for himself. He studiously avoided kingship while courting honours accorded to Alexander the Great. Shortly before his assassination, he adopted Octavian, better known to posterity as Augustus, the first emperor. Caesar's calendar reforms are still with us.

Julius Caesar rose to ever-greater prominence by virtue of his early political acumen, assisted by a series of well-placed marriages, but primarily because of his rather unexpected abilities to lead men in battle. By 55 BC, he had eight legions, consisting of approximately 40,000 men, under his command, five of which accompanied him to Britain in 54 BC. The survival of his *Gallic War* and the *Civil Wars* has assured, since ancient times, that his views of Rome and its imperial destiny have occupied a central position in the evolution of Western political thought and military history. His accounts of the **Britons** and of Britain are our earliest extant eyewitness reports, but they must be considered within the contexts of his rhetorical training, his political aspirations and ancient ethnographic traditions. History and ethnography were two related but separate literary genres that Caesar and others frequently combined to strengthen their rhetorical arguments. There was nothing simple about Caesar, and there is nothing straightforward about his accounts of his campaigns. The campaigns in Britain occupy parts of two books (modern chapters) of the *Gallic War*. As with the Celts and the Germans in Gaul, Caesar provides a brief ethnographic treatise on the Britons (4.14–4.17) that is heavily dependent upon Greek ethnographies, particularly that of Posidonius, but with some traditions going back more than two centuries. In ancient ethnographies, the farther removed people were from civilisation geographically, the more primitive was their social and cultural development. Even after two brief campaigns, Caesar displays little new knowledge of either the peoples or the geography of Britain. As a part of the *Gallic War*, Caesar's narrative on his campaigns in Britain are extensions of his desire to justify his role in the northwards expansion of Roman power and influence into Gaul at a time when his own political success threatened the traditional structure of the Roman republic.

By the time he could spare troops from Gaul for an invasion of Britain, it was already late August 55 BC, and the sailing season for crossing the Channel was rapidly closing. He despatched Commius, a Celtic chief thought to have much influence with the locals in south-east Britain, since tradition had it that Belgic peoples from northern Gaul had recently settled in this area. Commius was transported on the single ship that Caesar sent to reconnoiter the coast. Unfortunately for Caesar, Commius's contacts were not in the area of the landing but farther west, and he was quickly taken captive. Even more foreboding was the haste at which the scouting was accomplished, entirely missing the harbour at **Richborough**, for example, and this proved nearly catastrophic for both of Caesar's campaigns. The inhabitants of southern Britain had already become familiar with Roman wares, even coinage, and in return had traded minerals, especially tin, to the Continent.

Consisting of two legions sailing in eighty transports of traditional Roman design, the first expedition amounted to a reconnaissance in force, but even so small a force might have succeeded in extending the Roman client system to the area had not Channel storms wreaked havoc with the Roman fleet drawn up on a gradual beach, a short distance north from the last of the cliffs of **Dover**, somewhere between Kingsdown and Deal. The Roman cavalry did not land until four days after the legions, thereby denying Caesar any chance to pursue the barbarians as they retreated in disarray, routed by a legionary charge at water's edge. Salvaging parts from disabled ships, Roman shipwrights were able to repair sufficient transport for a return to Gaul. The campaign was a failure in Britain, but a success in the Senate, which declared twenty-seven days of thanksgiving, an unparalleled honour. The Senate and the Roman people were delighted to learn that their sway had reached beyond the ocean and into worlds scarcely known. Nobody cared to note that Caesar had greatly overstepped his assigned territory, Gaul.

A year later, again after setting Gaul in order, Caesar returned to Britain with a very powerful force, 5 full legions and 2,000 cavalrymen transported by 800 ships, many especially designed for the mission. Once again, however, a good harbour was not found and the fleet disgorged its troops on the same beach as before. Caesar – ever true to form – hastened to move inland and forced the issue before organised defences could take shape, but this meant delaying hauling his ships above the tide line and building an encampment large enough to protect them and his supplies. Storms struck as before with similar results. Although the landing was unopposed, it was hardly a surprise as thousands of onlookers followed the passage of the fleet up the coast. The exact route of Caesar's march inland cannot be established, despite much effort and speculation. His force probably forded the Thames near the future site of **London**. The various British tribal groups that had long been skirmishing against one another came together under a single leader, **Cassivellaunus**, the earliest Briton known by name and a military leader of genuine ability. The ***Trinovantes*** were the first to break ranks and go over to Caesar in return for his support and protection. Parallels between Cassivellaunus and Vercingetorix, the great leader of the last Gallic uprising against Roman oppression, are clear; however, unlike the latter, Cassivellaunus agreed to favourable terms and lived to fight another day. Caesar declared victory and rushed back to Gaul to put down yet another rebellion. Before the decade was out, he had crossed the Rubicon and suffered the consequences; so too did Rome.

See also Roman Army; Roman Britain.

Further Reading

Frere, Sheppard. 1987. *Britannia: A History of Roman Britain* (3rd rev. edn.). Routledge.

Gelzer, Matthias. 1968. *Caesar: Politician and Statesman*. Translated from the sixth edition by Peter Needham. Harvard University Press.

Wistrand, Erik. 1979. *Caesar and Contemporary Society*. Vetenskaps- och Vitterhets-samhället.

Thomas S. Burns

Caistor-by-Norwich

Caistor-by-Norwich is the site of the Roman town of *Venta Icenorum*, which was the *civitas* capital of the ***Iceni***. The town lies in open fields on the valley of the river Tas, slightly to the south of modern Norwich. The name *Venta Icenorum* is preserved in the third-century AD document known as the Antonine Itinerary (Iter V AI 474 6; Iter IX AI 479 10), although Ptolemy (II 3.11) also refers to *Venta* in the second century AD. The site has produced only one illegible inscription, but its identification as *Venta Icenorum* has been widely accepted.

The origins of the Roman town may lie in the period immediately following the Boudiccan revolt. It is probable that the town was placed on the site of an earlier **Iron Age** settlement, although this continues to be a source of debate. A street grid was laid out perhaps in the late first century AD, and public buildings including a forum and basilica were erected during the second century AD. Two temples are known from the interior of the town, while a third temple complex has been identified beyond the town to the north-east. A large set of public baths was situated on the west of the site, and an amphitheatre is known to lie outside the town to the south-west. The wall circuit, which remains the site's most visible feature, was probably built in the third century and enclosed a much smaller area (around 32 acres [13 hectares]) than that which was covered by the original street plan. As well as being connected by road to **Colchester** and **London**, it is thought that Caistor could be accessed via the river Tas, which connected to a major inland estuary (the remnants of which now form the Norfolk Broads).

The fate of *Venta Icenorum* following the end of formal Roman rule in Britain in the fifth century is unclear, although the discovery of significant Anglo-Saxon cemeteries to the north, south-east and west of the town, together with concentrations of seventh- and eighth-century material to the west of the Tas, is certainly indicative of continued occupation of the area. It has been hypothesised that the site of *Venta Icenorum* continued to function as a centre of trade and exchange into the eighth century. The present church of St Edmund, which is situated in the south-east corner of the walled area, dates to the twelfth century and later, although its relationship to the Roman street grid suggests an earlier church on the site.

Archaeological interest in the site began in 1928, when a remarkable vertical air photograph was taken over Caistor. This image clearly showed the outlines of streets and buildings as a series of parch marks against the darker grass that covered the site. Donald Atkinson carried out excavations on the forum, the bath complex, the south gate, some pottery kilns and the two temples between 1929 and 1935. These excavations unfortunately remained largely unpublished during Atkinson's lifetime.

See also Britons; Roman Britain; Romano-British Towns.

Further Reading

Davies, John A. 2001. *Venta Icenorum. Caistor St Edmund Roman Town*. Norfolk Archaeological Trust.

Frere, Sheppard. 1971. 'The Forum and Baths at Caistor by Norwich'. *Britannia* 2: 1–26.

———. 2005. 'The South Gate and Defences of Venta Icenorum: Professor Atkinson's Excavations, 1930 and 1934'. *Britannia* 36: 311–327.

William Bowden

Caledonians

The Caledonians (*Caledonii*) were a tribal grouping located north of the Forth–Clyde line by Roman geographers. They are one of two major northern peoples, the northern neighbours of the Maeatae, a group not documented before AD 197–200 in Roman sources. The Caledonians first figure in Roman historiography when, according to **Tacitus**, the Roman general **Agricola** advanced in AD 82–89 into their territory. The Caledonians under the leadership of Calgacus met Agricola at *Mons Graupius*, whose location has been much debated (claims have been made for Aberdeenshire near the **Iron Age** fort of Bennachie, and also for Perthshire). Despite numbering over 30,000 men, the Caledonians suffered a resounding defeat. Agricola then established a series of marching camps at Strathmore and what were intended as permanent forts at Strathcathro and Inchtuthil in Perthshire. Inchtuthil was abandoned before completion in AD 86, as troubles on the Danube caused the withdrawal of Roman troops from Britain. From this point onwards, the Roman frontier was established between Clyde and Forth (the line that was demarcated later by the **Antonine Wall**), but the Caledonians continued to be a threat to the Romans. Around 180, according to Cassius Dio, tribespeople from north of the Antonine Wall crossed into what is now southern Scotland, doing considerable damage and cutting down a Roman general and his men. Order was restored, but Caledonii and Maeatae allied to threaten Roman Britain towards the end of the second century, to be bought off by the British governor. In 209, following further troubles from the Caledonians, Emperor Septimius Severus came to Britain with his sons and campaigned vigorously in the north, but following his death at York in 211, his son Caracalla left Britain to become emperor in Rome.

There is good reason to suppose that the Caledonians were one of the northern peoples who later became known as the **Picts**, and it is extremely unlikely that they only came into existence when they are first mentioned in Classical sources. In the later Roman period, sources refer to Dicalydones and Verturiones forming the Picts: the first must be the Caledonians in a new guise, the new name reflecting perhaps a bipartite division. Associated with the Caledonians is a school of art, stylistically related to that of the ***Brigantes*** of northern England, which favoured high-relief modelling and slender-stemmed trumpet patterns. This is displayed on a series of massive armlets and on the 'Deskford carnyx', a boar-headed war trumpet. The Caledonians also manufactured other distinctive artefacts, most notably knobbed terminals for the butts of their spearheads and massive terrets, which were rein-guides for chariots.

See also Roman Britain; Scots.

Further Reading

Breeze, David. 1981. *The Northern Frontiers of Roman Britain*. Batsford.

Harding, D. W. 2004. *The Iron Age in Northern Britain: Celts and Romans, Natives and Invaders*. Routledge.

Maxwell, G. 1987. 'Settlement in Southern Pictland: A New Overview'. Pp. 31–44 in *The Picts: A New Look at Old Problems*. Edited by A. Small. Aberdeen University.

———. 1989. *The Romans in Scotland*. Edinburgh University Press.

Strang, A. 1998. 'Recreating a Possible Flavian Map of Roman Britain with a Detailed Map for Scotland'. *Proceedings of the Society of Antiquaries of Scotland* 128: 425–440.

Lloyd Laing

Camelot

See Arthur; Cadbury Castle.

Camlan, Battle of

This is the site of **Arthur**'s last battle, where he was mortally wounded along with Mordred. Camlan was not named in the earlier battle-list of the ***Historia Brittonum*** and is first mentioned in the ***Annales Cambriae*** under the year AD 539: *Gueith Cam lann in qua Arthur et Medraut corruerunt* 'The battle of Camlan in which Arthur and Medraut fell' (Morris 1980, 45). Camlan can be translated as either *cam* + *lann*, 'crooked enclosure' or *cam* + *glan*, 'crooked bank', as in a riverbank. Although later sources make Mordred the enemy of Arthur, the entry in the *Annales Cambriae* merely states that both fell at the battle, not that they fought each other.

The first person to try and locate Camlan was **Geoffrey of Monmouth** in his *History of the Kings of Britain* (written c. 1136), who locates it on the river Camel in Cornwall, not far from **Tintagel** Castle. Geoffrey also creates a background to the battle by making Mordred, depicted here as the nephew of Arthur, steal the crown of Britain and Arthur's wife Guinevere. Mordred had gathered together a massive army made up of **Saxons**, **Picts** and **Scots**, forcing Arthur to return from Europe and face him. After several clashes in southern Britain, they ended up at the river Camblan in Cornwall where Mordred was killed and Arthur, mortally wounded, was carried off to the Isle of **Avalon**.

The medieval Welsh tale *Culhwch and Olwen* states that three people survived the battle, a theme that is also referred to in later antiquarian texts, where seven survivors are named. *The Dream of Rhonabwy* names Iddog the Embroiler as the person who caused the battle by kindling strife between Arthur and Medrod when he could have brought peace. In medieval Welsh poetry, Camlan became synonymous with a disastrous defeat and was used as a proverbial expression for a confused mob. The Welsh Triads describe the battle as one of 'The Three Futile Battles of the Island of Britain' (Bromwich 2006, 217). The exact location of Arthur's last battle has been the cause of much debate. The French romances of the thirteenth century locate it on Salisbury plain, as does Thomas Malory, and following Geoffrey of Monmouth, many have located it in Cornwall. On the basis of linguistic similarity, Crawford (1935, 289) identified the site with the Roman fort of Camboglanna on **Hadrian's Wall**. The place name Camlan survives in several instances in a small area of mid-Wales. Near the village of Dinas Mawddwy is an area still known as Camlan; a nearby mountain pass which anciently formed the border between **Gwynedd** and **Powys** also bears the name and a river called Afon Gamlan exists nearby just to the north of Dolgellau. The exact site of the battle, however, remains uncertain.

See also Literature; Roman Britain; Warfare and Weapons.

Further Reading

Bromwich, Rachel. 2006. *Trioedd Ynys Prydain* (3rd edn.). University of Wales Press.

Crawford, O. G. S. 1935. 'Arthur and His Battles'. *Antiquity* 9: 277–291.

Morris, John. 1980. *Nennius British History and the Welsh Annals*. Phillimore.

Padel, Oliver James. 1984. 'Geoffrey of Monmouth and Cornwall'. *Cambridge Medieval Celtic Studies* 8: 1–28.

Scott Lloyd

Calmulodunum

See Colchester.

Canterbury

Canterbury, in **Kent**, is a city with an ancient history which became, in the Middle Ages, the heart of the English Church. Once an important Roman town, Canterbury is the site of one of the oldest English cathedrals, the seat of the archbishop and the home to one of the wealthiest monastic foundations in England, renowned for its architecture and manuscript tradition.

10. Aerial view of Canterbury Cathedral and city walls, United Kingdom.

Not much is known about the origins of the town, but excavation and coin finds indicate that **Iron Age** Canterbury may have been a royal site which focused on a ford across the river Stour. Canterbury's Roman name, *Durovernum Cantiacorum*, indicates that it was an important centre of the ***Cantiaci*** tribe, from which the name Kent is derived. *Durovernum* seems to have begun as a planned civilian settlement, with impressive public baths, a large temple precinct and a rare stone-built theatre, whose seats could have accommodated some 7,000 people. Later, *Durvernum* was given walls and took on defensive measures, perhaps related to increasing piracy in the Channel. Despite the demolition of many of the town's public buildings, there are many signs of continuity in the fourth and fifth centuries. New timber structures were built over the baths complex, and other fifth-century structures were built over Roman roads. In the Marlowe area, timber structures were inserted into the shell of an earlier stone building, and the find of a Visigothic gold coin nearby, probably a copy of a Roman *tremissis*, indicates trade activity in c. 480. A wealthy Christian community in the town is represented by the find of a silver hoard outside the London Gate, dated c. 407–411, which included silver ingots, a gold ring and numerous silver spoons decorated with the *Chi-Rho* monogram.

The transfer of political control from Briton to Saxon in Kent is not recorded, but it is clear that at least some Christian **Britons** remained in the area and maintained their church. The Cathedral Priory of Christ Church was founded by St. **Augustine** in 598, beginning the eventual victory of Roman Christianity over **Celtic** forms. Augustine was sent to Britain by Pope Gregory I ('The Great') in 597, with forty missionaries. **Bede** provides an account of their successes in the *Ecclesiastical History*. He chose Canterbury because Æthelburga, wife of King **Æthelbert** of Kent, was a Christian. Augustine first worshipped with the queen at St Martin's Church, which dates to the Roman period and remains the oldest English church continuously in use. Augustine converted Æthelbert, who ruled much of southern England, and established a see at Canterbury. Christ Church was thereafter ruled by a series of influential bishops including Cuthebert, **Dunstan**, **Ælfric**, Lanfranc, **Anselm** and, perhaps most famously, Thomas à Becket, who was murdered in the Cathedral in December 1170. Canterbury's influence spread through its seventeen subordinate sees: **Bangor**, **Bath** and Wells, **Chichester**, Coventry and Lichfield, Ely, **Exeter**, Hereford, **Llandaff**, **Lincoln**, **London**, Norwich, Rochester (which was so closely tied to Christ Church that products of their scriptoria are often indistinguishable), St Asaph's, **St David's**, Salisbury, Winchester and **Worcester**. Throughout the Middle Ages, the nearby monastery of St. Peter and St. Paul, later known as St. Augustine's, was something of a rival.

The **Anglo-Saxon** structure is known primarily through Eadmer, biographer of Anselm, who primarily focuses on holy sites within it, such as shrines and relics. He describes the fire which destroyed the church in 1067. The current structure was begun under Lanfranc (d. 1089), the first Norman archbishop, appointed in 1070. He had been the prior of the prominent Norman abbey of Bec and then abbot of St Etienne at Caen and brought with him monks from both foundations. From his new post, Lanfranc sought to increase ecclesiastical discipline and to assert the primacy of Canterbury over **York**. He reorganised the monasteries, though he did meet with resistance at times, as St. Augustine's, Canterbury. Here, the Anglo-Saxon monks left the monastery to protest the Norman abbot appointed by Lanfranc. Lanfrac also left an architectural legacy. He oversaw the construction of new ecclesiastical buildings to replace those damaged by the fire in 1067. These were designed to impress the conquered English with their grandeur. The most significant element of the new cathedral was the nave which, in typical Norman style, was extremely long, so much so that the Gothic replacement for it 300 years later was no larger.

Lanfranc was succeeded by Anselm (d. 1109), also a former prior and later abbot of Bec. For his loyalty to the pope rather than to the king, he was exiled by **William Rufus** and again by his successor, **Henry I**. A bargain was made whereby the archbishop would pay homage – and lay fees – to the king, who in turn gave up the right of investiture of abbots and bishops. Anselm was a renowned scholar and, after death, was canonised. He also commissioned the massive crypt and choir, designed by the French master builder, William of Sens, thereby setting a new standard for Anglo-Norman architecture and inspiring a number of other structures (most notably Salisbury) with its striking black Purbeck marble columns. The nave and choir are capped with a large chapel dedicated to the Trinity and the Corona, built by William the Englishman in the late twelfth century to house the relics of Thomas à Becket.

In addition to its noteworthy architecture, Christ Church also possessed an impressive library, begun by Augustine and enlarged by his many successors, particularly Lanfranc and, during the tenth-century reform, by St. Dunstan. In this period, the cathedral was a major centre for manuscript production and illumination, including the great Harley Psalter, a copy of the Carolingian Utrecht Psalter. Christ Church came to great prominence following the martyrdom of Thomas à Becket at the order of **Henry II**, resulting from a series of bitter disputes between the two former friends. He was killed by four knights in the north-west transept, at a spot still revered. His shrine became a major pilgrimage site, as memorialised by Geoffrey Chaucer's *Canterbury Tales*.

See also Art and Architecture; Celtic Christianity; Romano-British Towns.

Further Reading
Kahn, Deborah. 1991. *Canterbury Cathedral and Its Romanesque Sculpture.* Harvey Miller.
Keates, Jonathan, and Angelo Hornak. 1980. *Canterbury Cathedral.* Philip Wilson.
Ottoway, Patrick. 1996. *Archaeology in British Towns.* Routledge.
Snyder, Christopher A. 1996. *Sub-Roman Britain (AD 400–600): A Gazetteer of Sites.* British Archaeological Reports British Series 247.
Woodman, Francis. 1981. *The Architectural History of Canterbury Cathedral.* Routledge and Kegan Paul.

Asa Mittman

Cantiaci

The *Cantiaci*, or *Cantii* as cited by Ptolemy, were an indigenous Celtic tribe living in the **Iron Age** and **Roman Britain**. The territory of these **Britons** seems to have been centred on modern **Kent**, stretching north to the East Anglian rivers, west to the Chiltern ridge and south to the High Weald of **Sussex**, the inhabitants of which may have been local groups of merely regional consequence, as only the rulers were described by **Julius Caesar**. Different ethnic groups in the first century BC are also indicated by pottery traditions, with commercial links with Rome and a money market utilising Gallo-Belgic coinage, leading to settlements along trade routes, including the **hillforts** at Bigbury and Oldbury, the *oppidum* at Quarry Road, loose and lesser settlements at Rochester and **Canterbury**. Numismatic evidence may indicate their involvement with other tribes and their dynastic upheavals after Caesar's departure; their involvement with non-Kentish rulers is also indicated on multiple series of coins, including Tasciovanus, his son **Cunobelinus** and his son Adminius, though the limit of sites indicative of wealth (i.e. the cemetery at **Aylesford**) may suggest that hostility to Rome affected the area's economic development. Unlike other Romano-British *civitates* which were able to retain their tribal names, the *Cantiaci* territorial district lacked a tribal identity and was composed of both **Belgic** and non-Belgic ethnic groupings, brought together by the Romans within the **Atrebates's** territory and composed of two *pagi* (administrative districts), one in east Kent centred around the capital of **Canterbury**, whose name derived from that of the tribe, and one in the west administered from Rochester, where settlement and industry seem to have been concentrated.

The system of roads in the territory seem to have developed independently from Iron Age tracks and included Watling Street and the road to Hastings, connecting Rochester and Canterbury to other regions, with the proximity of the latter to the Channel ports possibly explaining its choice as the tribal capital. Other Romano-British settlements along such routes included Springhead (*Vagniacae*), which has had at least seven religious structures revealed through excavation, Dartford and Crayford, though the evidence for other urban settlements is mostly inconclusive. The rural towns and farms of the Roman period seem to have developed from existing Belgic settlements and farmsteads and though most did not progress much beyond their Iron Age forms, a small number near Canterbury may suggest that farming was undertaken by the centre's citizens, with the more prosperous farms having an easterly distribution, including the villa estates of the later Roman period (e.g. **Lullingstone** and Faversham). Though several temples, shrines and rural cemeteries are known in the region, little can be said for certain about the Cantiaci's religion beyond conjecture, at least until fourth-century Christian establishments as at Lullingstone and Canterbury. The *civitas*' economy seems to have been a mixture of light industry and agriculture, with farming and animal husbandry well established before the invasion. With as many as nine pottery kilns and two tileries found at Canterbury, the level of manufacturing seems to have been intended to extend beyond the *civitas*, and other industrial activity seems to have involved the stone quarries, iron-working and salt-panning sites of the region. What happened to the *Cantiaci* in the late Roman period is only conjectural, though defensive measures taken such as strengthening the Saxon Shore forts suggest external threat and instability. Some houses at Canterbury clearly continued in use into the fifth century, after which Saxon settlement overtook the *civitas*, leaving the impression of the *Cantiaci* in place names only.

See also Celts.

Further Reading
Cunliffe, B. W. 2005. *Iron Age Communities of Britain* (4th edn.). RKP.
Detsicas, A. 1983. *The Cantiaci.* Alan Sutton.

Anne Sassin

Canute

See Cnut.

Caratacus

Caratacus was a British chieftain who headed the resistance to the Roman invasion of Britain in AD 43 and, subsequently, a sustained and serious rebellion. The son of the pro-Roman **Cunobelinus**, king of the ***Catuvellauni/Trinovantes*** (a tribal grouping located roughly in modern Essex and Hertfordshire), Caratacus and his brother Togodumnus inherited much land and power when their father died c. AD 40. Having gained his wealth probably as a result of his pro-Roman stance, Cunobelinus seems to have extended his territory into what is now Kent, taking it over from the ***Atrebates*** tribe (centred on Hampshire). Significantly, at this time, the coins issued by the ruler of the *Atrebates* were replaced with identical issues bearing the name CARA (presumably Caratacus).

Soon after this, *Catuvellaunian* territory was extended even further, into the tribal area of the ***Dobunni*** (centred in Gloucestershire). Cassius Dio relates that the 'Bodunni [*sic*] were subject to Catuvellaunian rulers' (bk. LX, ch. 6). This aggressively expansionist policy led to the Atrebatan king Verica fleeing to Rome seeking help against the *Catuvellauni*. This provided an excuse for the Roman invasion of 43, ordered by Emperor Claudius. The **Britons** suffered an early and overwhelming defeat at Roman hands in a battle, probably at the river Medway, in which Togodumnus was killed. Caratacus then abandoned his capital at Camulodunum (**Colchester**) and fled to south Wales, where, having united the local tribes, he started operating from the lands of the ***Silures*** to attack Roman-held areas in modern Gloucestershire.

Ostorius Scapula, governor of Britain from 47 to 52, drove Caratacus back across the Severn and moved his military base from Colchester to **Gloucester**, where he founded a legionary base. Caratacus migrated northwards into central Wales and the lands of the ***Ordovices***, but Scapula followed, making a new military base at **Wroxeter**, Shropshire. Caratacus was caught in a pincer movement by the two Roman forces and defeated around AD 50. He fled to the ***Brigantes*** in the north-east, whose queen, **Cartimandua**, was pro-Roman and promptly handed him over to Scapula. After being paraded in triumph through the streets of Rome, he was spared by Claudius and allowed to live with his family in Rome.

See also Celts; Roman Army; Roman Britain; Warfare and Weapons.

Further Reading

Snyder, Christopher A. 2003. *The Britons.* Peoples of Europe Series. Blackwell.

Todd, Malcolm. 1999. *Roman Britain* (3rd edn.). Blackwell.

Webster, Graham. 1981. *Rome Against Caratacus: Roman Campaigns in Western Britain, AD 48–58.* Batsford.

Jennifer Laing

Carausius (d. 293)

Marcus Aurelius Maus[aeus] Carausius is a securely attested historical figure, an usurping Roman emperor in Britain and northern Gaul at the time of co-emperors Diocletian and Maximian. **Geoffrey of Monmouth** presented him as a founding figure in his account of early British history.

According to late antique sources, Carausius was from the province of *Menapia* (made up of parts of northern France, Belgium and the Netherlands) and was a sailor or helmsman of humble origins. Around 286, he was raised to the command of a Roman fleet based at Boulogne on account of his successes in Maximian's campaign against *bagaudae* (peasants in revolt). His further achievements against pirates infesting the Gaulish coast are described as having been achieved at the expense of the areas he was supposed to be protecting, as he allowed the pirates to proceed with their raids, attacked them on the way home and did not pay the proceeds into the treasury as expected. When Maximian ordered his death, he seized his fleet, fled to Britain and set himself up as emperor.

Numismatic evidence suggests that Carausius's revolt had a significant Gaulish component in the early stages, and following the utter failure of a significant campaign against him in Britain in 289, Carausius recovered territory in Gaul as well. He seems to have enjoyed considerable support. A Latin panegyric of 297 (Mynors 1964, viii (v), 12) lists among his supporters a Roman legion, several auxiliary units, Gaulish merchants and barbarian allies; they were all engaged in skilled shipbuilding and seafaring, notes the panegyricist, in pointed contrast to their Roman foes. In Britain, Carausius conducted a functioning government; the coinage in particular shows a relatively stable, peaceful and sophisticated reign with traditional imperial trappings and claims for Caurasius's co-emperorship with Diocletian and Maximian. Ultimately, Carausius's forces were besieged at Boulogne by Constantius, who was then newly appointed by Caesar. Carausius was killed in somewhat obscure circumstances by his colleague Allectus, who then held Britain for three more years until his own death.

Carausius was mentioned in several early medieval histories, but it was Geoffrey of Monmouth who gave what was for a long time the definitive account in his *Historia Regum Britanniae*. Geoffrey's main innovations were to make Carausius British and to make him responsible for settling the **Picts** in Scotland, perhaps due to a perceived connection between Carausius's name and that of the river Carron in Stirlingshire on the borders of Pictland. As such Carausius became a significant figure in medieval and modern Scottish histories. A second Carausius has been proposed due to mid-fourth-century coins found in Britain bearing that name, but the matter is controversial. The name was also known in medieval Wales, appearing on an early medieval inscribed stone from Penmachno in north Wales (Macalister no. 393). Despite this, and despite the considerable interest medieval Welsh literature showed in Romano-British figures such as **Magnus Maximus**, Carausius did not impinge on Welsh historical tradition until translations of Geoffrey's *Historia* into Welsh (as *Brut y Brenhinedd*) related his story, under the name Carawn. By the fourteenth century, as suggested by the poetry of Lewis Glyn Cothi, the name of a village in mid-Wales, Caron (probably a river name), had become Tregaron (understood as *tre(f)-*, settlement, + personal name), and by the late eighteenth century, at least, St. Caron was misidentified as the founder of the church of Tregaron. By the nineteenth century, the biography of St. Caron of Tregaron depicted him as a British rebel against Roman power in Wales rather than the British plunderer/king, according to Geoffrey, or the leader of an at least effectively legitimate, if short-lived, Roman government, according to historical evidence.

See also Roman Army.

Further Reading

Casey, P. J. 1994. *Carausius and Allectus: The British Usurpers*. BT Batsford.

Jankulak, Karen. 2007. 'The Many-Layered Cult of St Caron of Tregaron'. *Studia Celtica* 41: 101–114.

Macalister, R. A. S. 1945–1949. *Corpus Inscriptionum Insularum Celticarum*, 2 vols. Stationary Office.

Mynors, R. A. B. (ed.). 1964. *XII Panegyrici Latini*. Clarendon Press.

Karen Jankulak

Carlisle

Carlisle, in north-western Britain, was the site of a Roman fort and town (*Luguvalium*), a British and Anglian royal centre and a medieval border castle. The Romans built a small fort here, in the territory of the ***Carvetii***, around AD 75. This fort was abandoned when Stanwix, the largest of the wall forts, was built, and the site eventually became a civilian settlement. Luguvalium was granted *civitas*-capital status rather late, perhaps by Caracalla (or even Postumus) in the third century. By the fourth century, Luguvalium had become part of the defensive system of **Hadrian's Wall**, possibly its headquarters, and some have argued that it became the capital of the newly formed Valentia province. A defensive wall was built around the city at this time, and there is some evidence of early Christians in the vicinity. Probably, Carlisle became the seat of a bishop, and Charles Thomas has argued that both **St. Ninnian** and **St. Patrick** would have been associated with the town (Thomas 1981).

Carlisle (*Caer Luel*, from the British name *Luguvalos*) is one of a handful of Roman towns where new construction (mostly in timber) continued in the fifth century after the Roman withdrawal. It seems that Carlisle remained an administrative centre of some political import among the **Britons**, perhaps as the seat of the kingdom of **Rheged**. Most remarkable of all is the story of **St. Cuthbert** visiting the town in the seventh century, greeted by a man described as *praepositus civitatis*, walking along the town walls and viewing a working fountain (implying that there was a still-functioning aqueduct). Then under the control of the **Angles** of **Northumbria**, the British church at Carlisle was granted to Cuthbert, probably a native Cumbrian. The area was still under Northumbrian control during the reign of Macbeth, but Malcolm III may have taken it over and held it as late as 1092, when

William II Rufus built a castle over the Roman fortifications. This structure was rebuilt in stone, probably by Henry I. English and Scottish kings continued to fight over this strategically important stronghold for centuries.

See also Romano-British Towns.

Further Reading

Barrell, A. D. M. 2000. *Medieval Scotland*. Cambridge University Press.

Dark, K. R. 1992. 'A Sub-Roman Re-Defense of Hadrian's Wall?' *Britannia* 23: 111–120.

Higham, Nicholas, and Barri Jones. 1985. *The Carvetii*. Sutton.

McCarthy, M. R. 1990. *A Roman, Anglian and Medieval Site at Blackfriars Street*. Cumberland and Westmorland Antiquarian and Archaeological Society.

Salway, Peter. 1993. *The Oxford Illustrated History of Roman Britain*. Oxford University Press.

Snyder, Christopher A. 1996. *Sub-Roman Britain (AD 400–600): A Gazetteer of Sites*. British Archaeological Reports No. 247.

Thomas, Charles. 1981. *Christianity in Roman Britain to AD 500*. Batsford.

Christopher A. Snyder

Carmarthen

Carmarthen is the site of the Roman town of *Moridunum* ('sea fort'), presumed administrative centre of the tribal community (*civitas*) of the ***Demetae*** in south-west Wales. Its name is recorded in the Antonine Itinerary (Route XII) and Ptolemy's *Geography*. It lay on a broad terrace on the north side of the river Tywi, close to the tidal limit and the lowest bridging point.

The first Roman presence took the form of a fort, founded in the mid-70s AD, on a site west of the later town; traces of a possible annexe have also been located. Like other forts in Wales, this fort was later reduced in size, before being abandoned altogether by AD 120, at the latest. If there was ever an associated civil settlement (*vicus*), it remains poorly known, though the discovery of a **Romano-Celtic temple** and a possible official inn (*mansio*) within the area of the later town clearly indicates some level of development in the later first and early second century; little of this early fabric was retained.

From the mid-second century onwards, things become clearer within the town, with the discovery of several discrete lengths of street, all clearly part of a more co-ordinated layout. Such elements of planning align Carmarthen with the better-known 'planned' towns of Britain, as does the presence of public buildings and amenities in the form of a theatre/amphitheatre east of the later defences and a bathhouse and possible *mansio* in the south part of the town; nothing is yet known, however, about the central area where we might have expected the forum-basilica, a key indicator of self-governing status. Further evidence of the site's status is provided by the construction of its earthwork defences, probably towards the end of the second century; these were later reinforced by the insertion of a stonewall, probably during the course of the third century. They enclose an area of 33 acres (13.2 hectares), making Carmarthen the smallest of the British *civitas* centres.

Excavation has also identified a range of other structures, the majority of which conform to the pattern of shops and workshops so typical of other provincial towns (even if they are somewhat small and unprepossessing by comparison), together with a small number of larger stone or part stone-built town houses belonging to the third and fourth centuries. In this respect, Carmarthen conforms to a late trend noted elsewhere, though none of the 'houses' comes up to the standard of the courtyard houses so typical of the later plan at **Caerwent**. Amongst the identifiable trades are those associated with metalworking and baking, both on a scale capable of serving more than local domestic needs.

Evidence indicates that activity continued down to the end of the fourth century at least, though how the town fared beyond this period remains difficult to assess with current evidence. There is a suggestion that the earliest centre for the cult of Teilo may have been in or adjacent to the Roman town, though there is nothing to substantiate this in the archaeological evidence.

See also Roman Britain; Romano-British Towns.

Further Reading

James, H. 2003. *Roman Carmarthen: Excavations 1978–1993*. Britannia Monograph Series No. 20. Society for the Promotion of Roman Studies.

Jones, G. D. B. 1970. 'Excavations in Carmarthen, 1969'. *Carmarthenshire Antiquary* 6: 4–14.

Little, J. H. 1971. 'The Carmarthen Amphitheatre'. *Carmarthenshire Antiquary* 7: 58–63.

Wacher, J. S. 1995. *The Towns of Roman Britain* (2nd edn.). Batsford.

Barry C. Burnham

Cartimandua

Cartimandua (whose name means 'sleek filly') was the scandalous queen of the ***Brigantes*** tribe in northern Britain in the first century AD. The *Brigantes*, a confederation of northern British tribes, came under the control of Cartimandua through reasons unknown. A diplomatic marriage with Venutius, ruler of a neighbouring tribe, and an early alliance with Rome helped Cartimandua consolidate power in northern Britain. In AD 51, she displayed her loyalty to Rome when she handed over **Caratacus**, the British chieftain who had come to the *Brigantes* to seek Cartimandua's aid in his rebellion. Rome rewarded her with imperial support when, after taking Venutius's armour-bearer Vellocatus as her lover, Venutius tried to depose his queen. However, Venutius was successful in his efforts in 69, and we hear no more about Cartimandua.

Tacitus states that Cartimandua exercised power over the *Brigantes* 'by virtue of her noble birth' but lost the support of some of the *Brigantes* due to 'wealth and the self-indulgence of success' (*Annals* 12.40 and *Histories* 3.45). Like her contemporary **Boudica**, Cartimandua was an intelligent and energetic ruler who fascinated the Romans and continues to fascinate us today.

See also Britons; Celts; Roman Britain.

Further Reading

Braund, David. 1996. *Ruling Roman Britain: Kings, Queens, Governors, and Emperors from Julius Caesar to Agricola*. Routledge.

Rankin, H. D. 1987. *Celts and the Classical World*. Croom Helm.

Snyder, Christopher A. 2003. *The Britons*. Peoples of Europe Series. Blackwell.

Christopher A. Snyder

Carvetii

The *Carvetii* were an indigenous Celtic tribe living in **Iron Age** and **Roman Britain**, whose territory broadly encompassed modern Cumbria and Lancashire, though habitable terrain was limited to the coastal plains and river valleys of the Solway basin. Overall, it was an area which has seen little archaeological research into the pre-Roman community, though a **Bronze Age** population is apparent through the pottery and metalwork concentrated in the central Eden Valley, and the best evidence for a late prehistoric tribal centre has been seen as the **hillfort** at Carrock Fell, with other important native settlements at Clifton Dyke, Dobcross Hill and Dalston, a pattern which saw continuity until the second century AD. It is quite difficult to determine who the *Carvetii* were, as Roman writers tended to automatically use the name ***Brigantes*** to cover the tribes of North Britain, and the tribe is only able to be identified from an inscription at Old Penrith and a milestone from Brougham referring to their *civitas* (*Carvetiorum*).

The size of Clifton Dyke has led to possible arguments for it being the *Carvetii caput*, though arguments have also been made for **Carlisle**, and Roman forts at sites like Brougham and Stanwick may suggest that the territory was the power base of Venutius, husband of **Cartimandua**. It was not until **Agricola** in the late 70s that permanent forts began to be established in the region, including the major settlement at Carlisle and several *vici*, many of which were exceptional in size (e.g. Old Carlisle and Old Penrith), and this frontier development culminated in the Stanegate Frontier and **Hadrian's Wall**. The tribal territory of the *Carvetii* suffered from a shortage of low-lying fertile soil, with the regional distributions suggesting that the majority of sites were circular enclosures south of the Solway, and though little excavation has been done on rural settlement, the overall pattern is one of scattered communities practicing mixed agriculture in lowlands, often associated with Roman trackways or forts. Pottery production was on a very localised basis, though by the mid-second century military sites were losing their markets and being replaced by imported ware, and there seems to have been the widespread use of quarrying and lead mining. Native religion outside of Roman control is apparent with gathering places for the god Maponus, with the area boasting some of the best early Christian evidence for the Irish Sea province (e.g. **Whithorn**, Kirkmadrine, **Ardwall Isle** and Hoddom), and many of the region's forts, especially along the Cumbrian coast, may have still been garrisoned against seaborne threat, undergoing heavy destruction during the 'barbarian conspiracy' of the 360s. However, from this period on, there is only uncertainty, as no Carvetian site has produced the imported wares known from other Dark Age sites, despite evidence of occupation continuing into the fifth century at Old Carlisle, and by the sixth century, the territory was succeeded by the early medieval kingdom of **Rheged**.

See also Britons; Celts.

Further Reading

Birley, Anthony. 1980. *The People of Roman Britain.* University of California Press.
Cunliffe, B. W. 2005. *Iron Age Communities of Britain* (4th edn.). RKP.
Higham, N. J., and Barri Jones. 1985. *The Carvetii.* Alan Sutton.
Todd, Malcolm. 1999. *Roman Britain* (3rd edn.). Blackwell.

Anne Sassin

Cashel

The Rock of Cashel in County Tipperary, Ireland, may have been a prehistoric royal centre, after the manner of **Tara** or **Navan**, and a Roman brooch has been found on the hill. The surviving remains are, however, all medieval. Traditionally, **St. Patrick** converted the local king and founded the bishopric at Cashel. It was the seat of the Éoghanachta kings of **Munster**, and **Brian Bóruma** was crowned king of Munster at this site in 977. The rock was given to the church in 1101 by Muircheartach O'Brien.

The earliest structure is Cormac's chapel, which was started in 1127 by Bishop Cormac MacCarthac. This is arguably the finest Romanesque church in Ireland. It has a nave and chancel (not on exactly the same alignment) with a very steeply pitched stone roof (at an angle of 65 degrees), which may have been a contribution from native Irish tradition. Towers flank the nave at the eastern end, which may, along with other features (such as the design of the south front), reflect influence from Germany. It contains a carved sarcophagus, decorated in the **Viking** Urnes style, which is of exceptional quality and is the only such representative of Urnes in Irish sculpture. Cormac's chapel seems to have been preceded by a timber church, traces of which were found in excavation.

Around the same time that Cormac's chapel was built, a round tower was erected. Dating from the time of Cormac's chapel or slightly earlier is a very weathered High Cross. The cathedral, now ruinous, dates from the thirteenth century.

Further Reading

Leask, H. G. 1955. *Irish Churches and Monastic Buildings, in the Early Period and the Romanesque.* Dundalk.

Lloyd Laing

Cassivellaunus

Cassivellaunus, king of the *Catuvellauni,* was one of the most powerful kings of the late pre-Roman **Iron Age** and the first Briton to be named in a written history. Using primarily hit-and-run tactics, he led a confederacy of tribes in resistance to **Julius Caesar**'s second expedition to Britain, in 54 BC. Upon landing in Kent, Caesar faced the first thrust from the **Britons**, which reached all the way to his legionary standard. After the Romans repelled these advances, Cassivellaunus dismissed the confederate infantry and retained only his own army – 4,000 charioteers – to harass Caesar's march towards the river Thames. At this point, a British prince of the *Trinovantes* named Mandubracius, whose father had allegedly been killed by Cassivellaunus, came to Caesar and offered the *Trinovantes*'s surrender in return for assistance against Cassivellaunus. Other tribes of the south started to go over to the Romans, and these defectors disclosed to Caesar the location of Cassivellaunus's stronghold. While Caesar besieged the Catuvellaunian king, his allies in Kent attacked Caesar's beach camp, but in the end Caesar was able to take the stronghold and receive Cassivellaunus's surrender. The Roman general took hostages, demanded annual tribute and instructed Cassivellaunus to leave the *Trinovantes* alone.

After Caesar's withdrawal from Britain, the ***Catuvellauni*** continued their expansion. It seems perhaps that they merged with the ***Trinovantes*** by about 15 BC, with Camulodunum (**Colchester**) as their new capital. This work was carried out by Tasciovanus (possibly the son or grandson of Cassivelluanus) and **Cunobelinus**, Shakespeare's *Cymbeline*. It is unlikely that Cassivellaunus continued to pay tribute to Rome nor that he kept his promise regarding the *Trinovantes*. Britain's first great hegemon, however, disappears from records after 54.

See also Roman Army.

Further Reading

Branigan, Keith. 1985. *The Catuvellauni.* Sutton.
Jiménez, Ramon L. 2001. *Caesar Against the Celts.* Castle Books.
Julius Caesar. 1999. *Commentaries on the Gallic War.* Translated by Carolyn Hammond. Oxford University Press.
Snyder, Christopher A. 2003. *The Britons.* Peoples of Europe Series. Blackwell.

Christopher A. Snyder

Castus, Lucius Artorius (b. c. 140)

Lucius Artorius Castus was a Roman military commander who served briefly in Britain in the middle of the second century AD. He stands out among hundreds of other Roman soldiers serving in Britain because his *nomen gentilicum* – Artorius – makes him the first recorded 'Arthur' in British history and, some have argued, the historical figure behind the legendary King **Arthur**.

The primary evidence for Lucius Artorius Castus comprises an extensive autobiographical résumé on three fragments from a sarcophagus found in modern Croatia. The Artorii were an equestrian family, possibly from Campania. Castus was born around 140 and entered military service, serving with several legions and rising to the rank of procurator. The fullest of the inscriptions gives a list of his tours of duty:

> Centurion of the III legion Gallica, also centurion of the VI legion Ferrata, also centurion of the II legion Adiutrix, also centurion of the V legion Macedonica, also *primus pilus* of the same [the V legion Macedonica], *praepositus* of the *classis Misenatium* (the fleet on the Bay of Naples), *praefectus* of the VI legion Victrix, *dux* of the legions of cohorts of cavalry from Britain against the Armoricans, *procurator centenarius* of the province of Liburnia. (Malcor 1999a)

We are given no more details about his activities in Britain. Sometime after his service as procurator in Liburnia (in Dalmatia), but before 200, Castus died and presumably was buried in Spalato in the sarcophagus he had commissioned.

Beginning with the linguist Kemp Malone in 1924, several scholars have argued that the exploits of Lucius Artorius Castus in Britain and in Armorica provided the basis for the military career ascribed to Arthur (Snyder 2006). Helmet Nickel and Scott Littleton pointed out that, at the time Castus was serving in Britain, a unit of the Sarmatian heavy cavalry was sent to northern Britain to help fight against the barbarians. Could these 'knights', fighting under a dragon banner and telling folktales about magic swords from their Caucasian homeland, have been assigned to a commander named 'Artorius' and helped him to achieve legendary victories? Linda Malcor has elaborated on this theory, adding details about the career of Castus and the role of Sarmatians in the Roman army (Littleton and Malcor 1994; Malcor 1999b), and Hollywood producer Jerry Bruckheimer was so drawn to it that he made it the basis for his film *King Arthur* (Touchstone Pictures 2005). It remains, however, like all other theories about an historical Arthur, an interesting conjecture.

See also Roman Army.

Further Reading

Littleton, C. Scott, and Linda A. Malcor. 1994. *From Scythia to Camelot*. Garland.

Malcor, Linda A. 1999a. 'Lucius Artorius Castus: Part 1: An Officer and an Equestrian'. *The Heroic Age* 1, http://www.heroicage.org/issues/1/halac.htm (cited 12 February 2008).

———. 1999b. 'Lucius Artorius Castus: Part 2: The Battles in Britain'. *The Heroic Age* 2, http://www.heroicage.org/issues/2/ha2lac.htm (cited 12 February 2008).

Snyder, Christopher A. 2006. 'Arthurian Origins'. Pp. 1–18 in *A History of Arthurian Scholarship*. Edited by Norris J. Lacy. D. S. Brewer.

Christopher A. Snyder

Catraeth, Battle of

The Battle of Catraeth was a sixth-century military engagement fought at an unidentified location. Catraeth has been identified with Catterick in North Yorkshire, England; however, this has yet to be established definitively. The exact date of the encounter is unknown but has usually been placed c. AD 600; however, c. 540, c. 570, 580–600 and 588–600 have also been suggested. The battle, which is not mentioned in medieval Welsh, English or Irish chronicles, is known primarily through poetic references, the most significant of which is 'Y Gododdin', attributed to the poet **Aneirin**. Although this work has its origins in a seventh-century original, it is only extant in one poorly preserved manuscript dating from the thirteenth century. According to 'Y Gododdin', 300 British warriors fought against a superior force of 54,000 or 100,000 Anglo-Saxons. The British warriors mounted an epic struggle but were defeated, and the entire host of **Britons** was killed but for the bard who survived to tell the tale. The poem primarily consists of elegies praising the heroism of the warriors who fell at Catraeth, but it also includes interpolated material concerning events unrelated to the Battle of Catraeth. The battle is also mentioned in other medieval poetic works, such as the works attributed to Taliesin and *Trioedd Ynys*

Prydein ('Triads of the Island of Britain'), but with much less detail.

Traditionally, the Battle of Catraeth has been seen as a conflict of Britons based at Edinburgh (then part of the British kingdom of Gododdin) with allies from other parts of Britain (including Pictland) fighting against **Anglo-Saxons** from **Deira** and **Bernicia**. The British warriors apparently attacked Catraeth, which earlier had been part of the British kingdom of **Rheged**, to recapture it from the Anglo-Saxons who had taken it after the death of the **Urien**, king of Rheged. However, the Anglo-Saxons, who greatly outnumbered the British force from Gododdin, were victorious. It has also been suggested that the Battle of Catraeth may have been part of a larger campaign which included the **Battle of Degsastan**, in which the **Scots** of **Dál Riata** under their king **Áedán mac Gabráin** (r. 574–608) were defeated by Bernicia under their king **Æthelfrith** (r. 593–605 in Bernicia; r. 605–617 over a united **Northumbria** consisting of Bernicia and Deira) in 603. This association of the Battle of Catraeth partly stems from the fact that Áedán mac Gabráin may be mentioned in 'Y Gododdin'. Some scholars have even equated the Battle of Catraeth with the Battle of Degsastan since Catraeth is not recorded in annals and chronicles, an omission which appears incongruous for a battle which drew such attention by poets. However, the reality of either of these possibilities is uncertain. There have also been challenges to the accepted view that the battle was a struggle of the Britons and the Anglo-Saxons; it was instead viewed as a struggle of territories and dynasties in which Bernicia fought on the same side as the warriors of Gododdin against the forces of Deira as part of Æthelfrith's efforts to conquer Deira (Koch 1993). Again, this view has been subject to much debate.

See also Literature; Warfare and Weapons.

Further Reading

Bartrum, Peter C. 1993. *A Welsh Classical Dictionary*. The National Library of Wales.

Jackson, Kenneth. 1969. *The Gododdin*. Edinburgh University Press.

Jarman, A. O. H. 1990. *Aneirin: Y Gododdin*. Gomer Press.

Koch, John T. 1993. *The Gododdin of Aneirin*. University of Wales Press.

Williams, Ifor. 1978. *Canu Aneirin*. University of Wales Press.

Joseph Calise

Catuvellauni

The *Catuvellauni* were an **Iron Age** tribe of south-east Britain who seemingly emerged in the aftermath of **Caesar**'s invasion of 54 BC. The name of the *Catuvellauni* does not appear in Caesar's account, although they are often assumed to be the tribe of Cassivellaunus, who led the British response to Caesar's attack. This is partly because the territory of Cassivellaunus is noted by Caesar as being divided from the maritime tribes by the Thames and lying about 70 miles (113 kilometres) from the sea (*Gallic Wars* v. 11). Caesar crossed the Thames at what he describes as its only fordable point, which led directly into Cassivellaunus's territory (*Gallic Wars* v. 18). The two statements suggest that Cassivellaunus's territory broadly corresponds to the later *civitas* of the *Catuvellauni*.

The *Catuvellauni* appear to emerge as an entity in the latter part of the first century BC, when a certain Tasciovanus emerged as the ruler of a substantial area covering Hertfordshire, south Bedfordshire, much of Buckinghamshire and the part of Oxfordshire west of the river Cherwell. The polity was centred on ***Verulamium***, from where most of Tasciovanus's coins were minted. Tasciovanus was succeeded by **Cunobelinus**, described by Suetonius as 'king of the Britons' (*Caligula* XLIV), who greatly enlarged the territory under his control, although the form of this rule and the means by which it was achieved are not clear. The expanded area included the territory of the ***Trinovantes***, as by AD 7 Cunobelinus was minting coins at **Camulodunum**, before starting to mint coins at *Verulamium* from around AD 10. It should be noted that no sources directly state that Cunobelinus was ruler of the *Catuvellauni*, and it has been conversely argued that he was leader of the *Trinovantes*. As with many of the Iron Age tribes of Britain, probably the value ascribed to fragmentary Roman sources by earlier scholars has conferred a degree of political unity and coherence on the *Catuvellauni* that may not have existed.

British opposition to **Claudius**'s invasion of AD 43 was led by **Caratacus** and Togodumnus, the two sons of Cunobelinus. Cassius Dio (ix, 20.1–20.2) tells us that the Bodunni, an otherwise unknown tribe who defected to the Romans, were tributaries of the *Catuvellauni*. This fact implies that the forces of Caratacus and Togodumnus were the *Catuvellauni* and constitutes the first direct literary evidence for the existence of the tribe as a social and political entity. They are listed as one of the *civitates* of Britain by Ptolemy (II. 2), who mentions the towns of *Salinae* (currently unidentified) and *Urolanium* (*Verulamium*).

Archaeologically, the *Catuvellauni* cannot be distinguished from the *Trinovantes* and, like the *Trinovantes*, are part of the broader '**Aylesford**-Swarling culture', partly characterised by the increasing adoption of products imported from Gaul and the Roman world, which are found in burials where they were apparently used as a means of status display. The region associated with the *Catuvellauni* also saw the development of major nucleated centres or ***oppida***. The earliest of these seem to have been at Wheathampstead, where massive earthworks defined an area of almost 99 acres (40 hectares). Wheathampstead was apparently supplanted around 15–10 BC by *Verulamium*, which was the political centre of the *Catuvellauni*, judging from the coin evidence, before Camulodunum became the pre-eminent settlement of the region. Other major settlement sites are known from Braughing and Baldock.

See also Britons; Celts; Roman Army; Roman Britain.

Further Reading

Branigan, Keith. 1987. *The Catuvellauni*. Duckworth.
Creighton, John. 2006. *Britannia: The Creation of a Roman Province*. Routledge.
Cunliffe, Barry. 2005. *Iron Age Communities in Britain*. Routledge.
Julius Caesar. 1999. *Commentaries on the Gallic War*. Translated by Carolyn Hammond. Oxford University Press.
Suetonius. 1998. *Lives of the Caesars*. Translated by J. C. Rolfe. Harvard University Press.

William Bowden

Céli Dé (Culdees)

The *Céli Dé* were a group of monastics first mentioned around AD 750 in Ireland. *Céli Dé* (anglicised to 'Culdees') is usually translated as 'servants' or 'companions' of God. The movement centred round the houses of Tallaght and Finglas, but spread to other parts of Ireland and then to Scotland and the north of England.

The first detailed study was by Reeves in 1864, followed by O'Dwyer in 1977, which until recently remained the standard study. Both these studies regarded the *Céli Dé* as a reform movement within early Irish monasticism. More recent work prefers to see them as considering themselves to be a 'religious élite' (Lambkin 1999, 142), as there seems to have been no desire on their part to return to a stricter regime after deterioration into a more lax observance. Hence, to call them a 'reform' movement is now seen as inaccurate. Writers such as Etchingham and Lambkin deny that there was such a deterioration in Irish monastic observance, claiming that strict and less strict observances had always existed side by side in Irish **monasticism** (Etchingham 1999, 463).

Various texts survive from the movement: *The Teaching of Maelruain*, *The Rule of the Céli Dé*, *The Martyrology of Tallaght*, *The Félire of Óengus* and the *Stowe Missal*. The first one is classed as a 'wisdom text', containing wise sayings of senior monks; the second one, although professing to be a monastic rule, is more accurately described as an anecdotal collection, with some legislation and prescriptive material added. These texts portray a monasticism with an overemphasis on minutiae of observance, particularly with regard to fasting, exercises of penance, confession and sabbath observance, and an approach to liturgical prayer which was innovative to the point of idiosyncrasy, putting the recital of the 'Three Fifties' (the complete psalter, which had to be recited daily in its entirety before the monks could eat) before the praying of the canonical hours and encumbering these hours with other paraliturgical prayers such as the 'Breast-plate of Devotion'.

Along with claims of strictness of observance, the *Céli Dé* have usually been understood as anchorites and solitary ascetics, but recent research has produced evidence from the *Rules* of the *Céli Dé* to show that they were monks who lived, ate, prayed and worshipped together in community.

This monastic movement seems to have begun in Munster under the influence of Ferdácrích of Darinis (d. 747), MacÓige of Lismore (d. 753) and Samthann of Clonbroney (d. 739). The greatest figure, however, was Máel Rúain of Tallaght (d. 792), who with his contemporaries, Dublittir of Finglas (d. 796), Máel Dithruib of Terryglass (d. 840) and Elair of Loch Cré (d. 807), did much to spread the movement and whose rather grim personality imposed itself on the character of the whole movement. The monasteries mentioned most often in connection with the *Céli Dé* are Tallaght, Finglas, Terryglass, Dairinis, Lismore, Clonbroney, Derrynaflan, Clonmacnois, Loch Cré (Monaincha, near Roscrea), **Iona**, Clonfert and Louth. Some of these were monasteries inhabited by *Céli Dé* monks alone, such as Tallaght; in some monasteries, these monks lived in a separate house at a short distance from the main monastery, as in Roscrea; in other houses, they lived together in the same monastic enclosure with other monks who did not share their particular vision of the monastic life, as in **Armagh**.

See also Celtic Christianity.

Further Reading

Etchingham, Colmán. 1999, repr. 2000. *Church Organisation in Ireland AD 650 to 1000*. Laigin Publications.

Gwynn, Edward J. (ed.). 1927. *The Teaching of Máel Rúain and The Rule of the Céli Dé*. Hermathena 44, Second Supplemental Volume. Hodges, Figgis & Co.

Lambkin, Brian. 1999. 'Blathmac and the Céili Dé: A Reappraisal'. *Celtica* 23: 132–154.

Rumsey, Patricia M. 2007. *Sacred Time in Early Christian Ireland: The Monks of the Navigatio and the Céli Dé in Dialogue to Explore the Theologies of Time and the Liturgy of the Hours in Pre-Viking Ireland*. Continuum.

Patricia Rumsey

Celtic

See Celts.

Celtic Christianity

Few notions in early medieval history provoke such strong reactions as that of 'Celtic Christianity' or the 'Celtic Church'. Indeed, not only are these vigorously contested terms, but reactions range from those who hold that these notions are bogus and without any significance for our understanding of the past, to staunch defenders of these ideas who believe, often passionately, that they refer to realities in the past about which we not only know a great deal, but which can be contrasted in detail with other 'Christianities' from both the past and indeed today. This essay is unlikely to convince anyone one way or the other, so its main task is to sketch how such a diversity of opinion has arisen and continues.

The Conceptual Difficulties

If we allow any validity to the term 'Celtic' – and few scholars would use it as widely as was done only a generation ago – then its primary referent is linguistic: a group of closely related Indo-European languages in western Europe with profound similarities in grammar and vocabulary. However, at no time in Late Antiquity or the Middle Ages did the users of these languages think of themselves as a having any unity. So while they had the Christian religion in common – and personnel may have moved between regions – that religion was also consciously shared with all other Christians in the Latin west and even beyond – and within these much broader areas there was also a movement of personnel. So clearly, if there was a 'Celtic Church' or a distinctively different Christianity, then none of its members knew of this.

However, 'Celtic' is also used in a much looser way, covering the fringes of north-western Europe or the western and north-western British Isles where it is used as a vaguely racial term, where their peoples are supposed to share characteristics of thought, temperament and behaviour (traits that can be as diverse as 'fiery' and 'disorganised' or 'spiritual rather than materialistic' and 'emotional rather than rational') which render them 'a people apart', who are either a threat or a resource for the others. The rhetoric of this approach can be either colonialist ('the Celtic temperament is not given to detailed organisation' = they cannot govern themselves) or romantic ('they are inherently attuned to the spiritual' = they are not like us moderns who have lost this virtue), but it is a rhetoric that is applied from the outside in the first instance, which is then sometimes adopted as an identity. If such stereotypes have a validity – other than their use as bonding factors in cultural and nationalist politics – then one would expect that there would be a specific religious temperament among these peoples and this would result in a distinctive Christianity. While we await the work of psychologists that might prove the existence of these distinctive shared traits, it is as well to concentrate our study on the evidence of the actual Christianity found among these diverse social and political groups and the actual church structures they lived within.

Another strand of confusion arises from two different ways of understanding what 'history' is. For the majority of modern academics, this study is an investigation of mentalities and

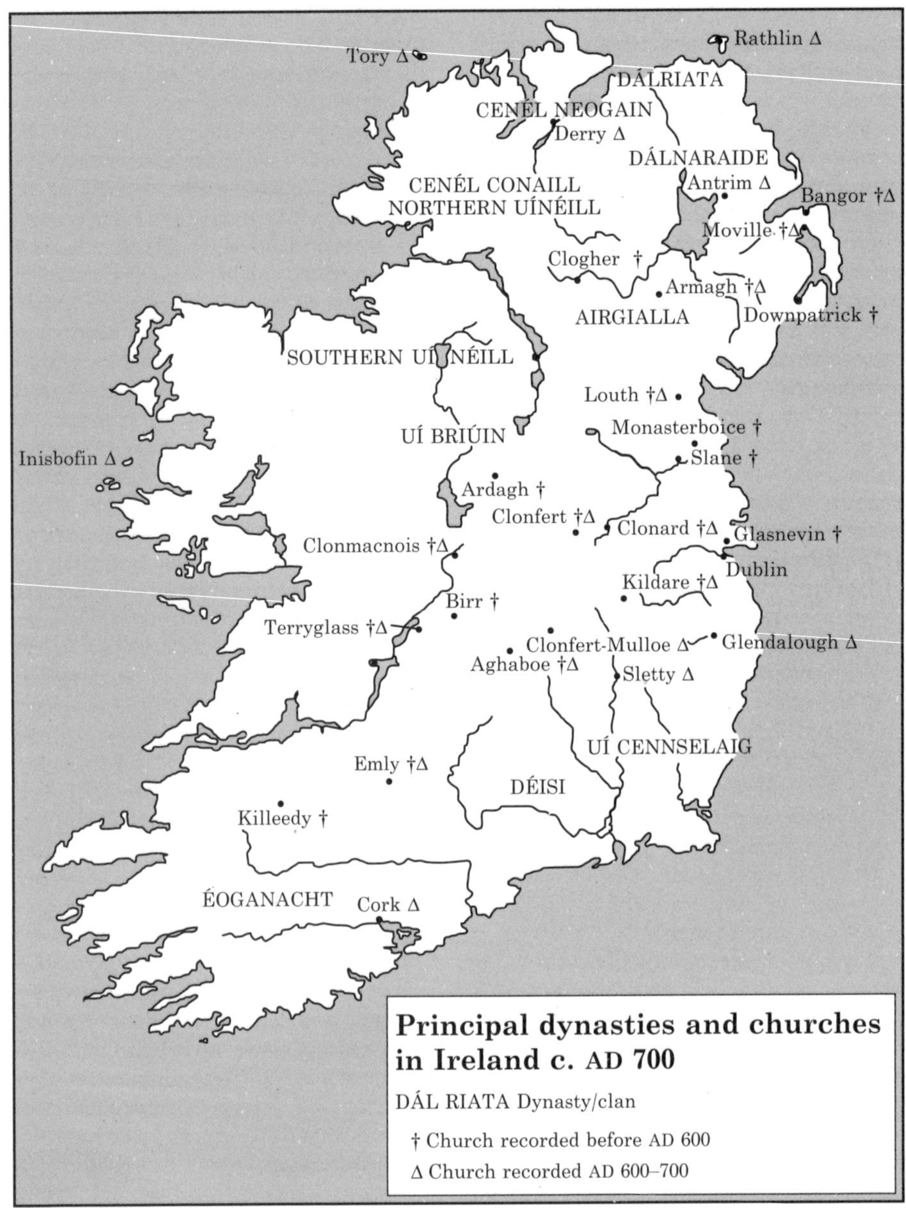

4. Ireland c. AD 700.

structures as they existed within a given period in the past. The starting point is that *the past is different*. Even though there must be a sequence between the people in the past and later times, or even today, there is a working assumption of continual change so that what exists later or today is inevitably different. History is not a key to an Aladdin's cave of beautiful artefacts, nor is it a return to a golden age of purity and splendour, but it is a genetic investigation of realities in the flux of time.

However, many groups of Christians think of history as not only the treasure trove of memories, but as that which provides credentials for what they are doing in the present. Hence, if there is change or a desire for change in the present, this change can be justified and shown to be true in so far as it can be presented as being a return to the past or the reform of a modern corruption in favour of a pristine time. The most common 'golden moment' that is invoked in these 'forward to the past' evolutions is the halcyon days of 'the Bible', 'the New Testament' or 'the Early Church' (the precise formulations of the myth depend on the flavour of Christianity involved). But for Anglophone Christians, one other moment in history has attractions: the pre-Norman church or the non-Anglo-Saxon period. Here is a time (1) with which they can feel a geographical continuity (and Christianity as a religion thinks of itself in geographical blocks); (2) that is distant enough to be the 'other' (and so not contaminated with their own perceived problems); (3) sufficiently obscure that it can be imagined in any number of forms (and so can provide prototypes for what they seek for the future); (4) that has left many beautiful artefacts (and, assuming that quality of art is linked to quality of faith – an assumption with its own history – it must have been religiously vibrant); and (5) that is apparently free of other associations such as with the continent or Rome (and so anything introduced as 'Celtic' does not provoke allergic reactions as being 'Romish', ritualist or superstitious). While secular historians may debunk this use of 'the Celtic past' as being little more than theatre, it is nothing other than the way the past is used by groups to further their identity, where that identity involves chronic continuity as one of its constituent parts – one need only recall how older universities reuse their pasts.

Another element that generated the debate about 'Celtic Christianity' flows from assumptions about the nature of the consistency of the set of ideas designated as 'Christian'. In many forms of modern Christianity, there has been a doctrinal desire to present 'Christianity' as an intellectually systematic and socially highly organised religion of well-defined creeds, acceptable behaviour and characteristic practices, all of which are presented as of great antiquity and consistency. In this presentation, uniformity with the present is stressed, and variation is suspect if not condemned as 'syncretistic' or as an 'impurity'. If one starts from these assumptions, then when someone looks at a particular period in the past that situation is either an 'alternative' Christianity (if one likes one's edited picture of the past) or a period of 'corruption' in need of reform (if one's edited picture is not to one's liking). This can be illustrated by recalling the fact that during the plague of 743, the relics of many Irish saints were brought in procession through the countryside to halt the plagues. How is this viewed by someone who assumes that 'genuine' Christianity has no place for relics or that religion can have any benefit except through divine-willed intervention which could not be coerced by a ritual? The procession could then be another illustration of the superstitious corruption of the medieval church which has adopted pagan notions of *arete/virtus* and inherent spiritual power either from its immediate environment or at some point in the past. If one admires what one sees, it is equally alien to many modern presentations of what Christians should believe, so it must be another form of Christianity and 'Celtic' is a convenient label. To one person, the relics equal superstition, and to the other, they point to a 'sense of connection between holy people and healing and earth'. Interestingly, neither explanation engages with the history of ideas and asks how the Christians in 743 imagined what they were doing. If, however, one does not start with such a definite unhistorical image of Christianity, one expects to find changes, differences and variations over time, locality and in relation to other factors shaping society. In such a view of the history of Christianity, one has a tapestry of beliefs and practices that are always changing and in looking backwards the historian is not isolating some pure moment but seeking a genetic understanding of each cultural situation.

Approaching the Concept Through Its History

Before looking at any of the early medieval Christian texts that are extant from regions which spoke a Celtic language, one awkward issue has to be addressed: Was there a form of Christianity in those places which was distinctive from the rest of the Latin world at that time? If one responds to this using the notion of the 'Celtic Church', one then fails to recognise the most obvious facts: the early medieval writers whose writings survive all sought that theological ideal that the truth of their witness to their religion was what was held always, everywhere, by everyone, and if they had suspected that there were in any way idiosyncratic, they would have been the first to adapt their ideas to that of the larger group. Equally, when we look at where their works have survived, we find that for the most part it is in continental manuscripts, which demonstrates to us that not only the scholars but their works were received and appreciated without any awareness of deviancy. The acid test is this: Did the Christians in the Celtic lands have a markedly different liturgy or system of law? Here, the briefest sampling of the evidence shows that the insular material is no more distinctive than materials from any other part of the Latin world of the time. For example, the *Stowe Missal* contains the Roman rite and its local additions would not amount to judging it a distinct rite. The best example for legal structures is the *Collectio canonum hibernensis*: it reflects the social situation in Ireland, but it was used throughout Europe and many of its *sententiae* can be followed from collection to collection until they are found in Gratian.

The counter-example of the Easter-dating controversy does not undermine this position. At issue was a very technical piece of mathematics that only bothered a small number of people for a limited time and would hardly have surfaced on the horizon of history save that it was a technical matter close to the heart of **Bede**. In any case, the disagreements were as much among theologians in one culture – e.g. the Irish clerics **Ségéne** and **Cummian** – as between 'the Celts' and 'the others'. We should remember two things. First, that Bede had his own religious and ethnic reasons for recalling the question in the way he did – it was part of his aim to create a Christian Anglo-Saxon identity as an elect people. Second, the matter of dating Easter could not be finally settled by anyone in the early Middle Ages, and therefore – just as a matter of mathematics – each side could pick holes in the calculation methods of the other side. The fundamental assumption was that the Creator had to work with perfect numbers – upon that assumption every calculation could be destroyed if the calculations were projected far enough into the future. The problem was only solved in 1582 by the Jesuit mathematicians working for Pope Gregory XIII. They tacitly abandoned the notion that the calculation would result in perfect whole numbers by eliminating eleven days from the calendar and then proposing a perpetual system of corrective balances. Hence, the whole debate that lies behind the so-called **Synod of Whitby** of 664 is better evidence of the endurance of monks from **Iona** in learned argument than for some distinctive version of Christianity.

If the 'Celtic Church' is a concept that disappears the more one scrutinises it, then why has it had so many supporters? This is not just a question about the history of recent scholarship, but one about the various groups who have sought to bring 'history' in on their side. The notion's origin lies within the aftermath of the Reformation: Could someone who rejected Rome (the 'old religion') in the present still appropriate the past as his or her own? If the past was *their past*, and their present involved the very conscious rejection of Rome, then the past had to be non-Roman as well. This desire to claim the past could be formalised in many ways, for example through changing the date of Rome's corruption until after the period one wished to claim or through holding that the bonds with Rome were recent and that in the earlier period there were no important links. Later, this was further formalised into 'the branch theory' of the church whereby the Church Universal was made up of many branches: Antioch, Constantinople, Roman and, *inter alia*, the Celtic branch. The effects of this were two-fold: first, it made the study of the early Irish church a battleground for sectarian warfare and generated as much heat as light in the process; second, it led to an inordinate interest in anything that could be considered 'exceptional'. The exceptional became the guarantee of ecclesial distinctiveness, and after many generations of noting what was exceptional, an impression was formed among the general public that the 'Celtic' and continental churches were as different as chalk and cheese. Each local difference was not simply an instance of that variety of Christian expression that occurred of every diocese in the medieval Latin church, but was a token of a difference as great as that between Latin Christianity and the Christians of Ethiopia or Armenia. For many today who seek to link their Christian faith more closely with their locality, and to enliven their spirituality and worship with a more expressive liturgy, but for whom anything that 'smacks of High Church or Romish practice' sparks an allergic reaction, this image of the 'Celtic Church' still has great attractiveness.

Another prop of the 'Celtic Church' came from nationalists in Ireland. If the present Ireland was to stand alone as a nation, then it must have the antiquity and dignity of a nationhood which had been conquered. To be just an island on the western fringe of Europe was of no avail – that merely was an argument that it should be a rural province ruled by a centre, which happened to be in London. For an island 'long a province, to be a nation once again' (the phrase is taken from Thomas Davis's ballad, 'A Nation once again', which was the *de facto* anthem of Irish nationalism in the nineteenth century), it was necessary to have a language, an ancient history and a pride in its individual and distinctive achievements. The notions of 'the island of saints and scholars', of the Irish language as an offshoot from the Indo-European stock just as ancient as Latin or Greek and of the ancient books as 'the work of angels' (the phrase came from their great enemy: Giraldus Cambrensis) were all ammunition for argument. The church in Ireland was distinctive not in its theology but in its purity, holiness and zeal. While for Anglicans seeking to reclaim a past notion of the 'Celtic Church' that church was essentially *non-Roman*, for the nationalist group it was essentially *distinctive*. Since this distinction was its antiquity, cultural brilliance and zeal, it was a distinctiveness that was very acceptable to Roman Catholics. The important thing for all concerned was that there was a great, world-envied Celtic culture long before there were any **Anglo-Saxons**, **Normans** or English. In a head-to-head comparison between the 'English Church' and the 'Celtic Church' – then for antiquity, purity and brilliance the Celts won! Such a gloriously distinctive church was another indication that here was an ancient free land that had a right to freedom once again. This may now seem a far-off battle, but it still flares up from time to time. Among scholars, it has a residual life in the energy devoted to refuting any suggestion that an insular manuscript with nice pictures (e.g. the ***Book of Kells***) was produced in a Northumbrian rather than an Irish centre. At a popular level, it can be found among many Catholics who wish to distance themselves from their church's formal positions – for such people, the 'Celtic Church' was not constitutionally distinct, but rather an eco-friendly, Augustine-free zone without formal theology or law.

The third group are those in France, Germany and, more recently, the United States, who see the 'Celtic World' as a romantic alternative to the corruption and decay that was found in the decadent Roman Empire and then as the noble bearers of civilisation to its barbarian successors. In imagery, this is the most powerfully coloured of the 'Celtic Church' myths: it reduces the 'fall of Rome', the 'barbarian invasions' and the 'conversion of Europe' down to a simple narrative of black and white. Finally, a 'saviour' appears in the form of a band of rugged Irish monks. The theme has all the stuff of drama, and it is not so long since (in a refined form) it could find academic supporters. This notion, it could be argued, could be found as early as Bede's presentation of the Irish missionaries in Britain as men of 'simple faith' and 'apostolic courage', but it drew its attraction for many on the continent from the nineteenth-century image of the Celts as a group of quaint mystics forgotten by time, whose spiritual energy was great, but whose practical skill meant that they would be crushed by their crude neighbours. This theme of a 'church out there' which could send missionaries to help an ailing continental church had a wide appeal, particularly in France, before the Second Vatican Council (1962–1965); it was favoured in Ireland as a proof of spiritual and intellectual prowess; and recently, it has been adopted in promoting a strong, positive cultural image abroad with benefits in terms of tourism and as historical credentials for closer European links. Today, this image is reserved for ceremonial rhetoric at symbolic events which draw together Scottish, Irish and, sometimes, Welsh politicians with their continental counterparts. However, as is the wont of strong narratives, it can still attract the crowds. As recently as 1995, an American author, Thomas Cahill, retold the whole myth – without a blush of embarrassment or a nod to scholarship – and had enormous sales!

A common factor linking all these uses of the notion of a 'Celtic Church' is their emphasis on the distinctness and separation of the Celtic fringe from a 'mainland'. 'Out there', things are different: as times move more slowly, ideas take fantastic forms and the learned activities are not those common to Franks, Italians and Germans, but of 'a race apart'. Essentially this is just a variant on the myth of rustic simplicity and the longing for a simple, worry-free life. However, this dream has had a pernicious effect on studies of these early churches because it has turned that study into a search for the peculiar, the unique and the bizarre: what is common between that culture and the rest of Christendom becomes invisible, and what seems jarring becomes the norm. At a learned level, it can be seen in the practice of continental librarians who, when faced with an otherwise unattributable and unusual text, use the label 'insular' as an escape hatch. Equally, in the rumbling debate about the extent of 'Irish exegesis', there seems to be an assumption among many scholars that either those products of the early Irish were wholly distinctive or they must be non-Irish! At a popular level, the willingness to believe any story, no matter how far-fetched, about the beliefs and practices of early insular monks. What we need is a model that allows for differences but does not measure difference by the exceptional.

Measuring Differences

When one looks at any period or region, one notices distinctive features, items of belief or practice or teaching that are different from other regions at the time or from Christianity at an earlier or later date. So how should such differences be described by the historian? A useful working hypothesis is that the theological and pastoral work of the early churches in the Celtic lands constituted a 'local theology' or a collection of local theologies. This concept of a 'local theology' requires some elaboration. First, it is a notion that most scholars who work in the history of theology take, often unwittingly, for granted. Among historians of Christianity in England in the eighteenth and nineteenth centuries, it is assumed that there was an 'Oxford' and a 'Cambridge' theology, that each had its *genius loci* and produced divines of differing temperaments and churchmanship. John Henry Newman (1801–1890), for instance, reflected on how his life might have developed differently if, on the day he was sent by his father to university, a chance encounter had not pointed his father towards Oxford rather than Cambridge. In these cases, it is largely the result of how people function in the group to which they physically belong and with whom they share a sense of belonging. This sort of difference can be seen today in the way that particular universities become 'schools of thought'. In the past, there were the 'Sorbonne theologians', the 'Tübingen School' and the 'Louvain approach' to Thomism; and still today, a gathering of like-minded scholars – while sharing the same belief system with scholars elsewhere – can give a particular place a prominence in advancing one aspect of theology so as to make it distinctive.

A concept of a 'local theology' does not entail that those who share its positions are close geographically or temporally. The Catholic religious orders provide many examples of how a group can have a distinctive view of theology but where distinctiveness is relative to a community of belief, rather than the symptoms of a sectarianism. Thus, 'Dominican' and 'Jesuit' theologies were, in the days before teaching clusters, two camps which inducted their own disciples into distinct ways of going about theology, pastoral work and prayer. The awareness of such differences was not confined to those who could follow the distinctions regarding the theologies of actual grace (the 'Thomists' versus the 'Molinists') in the textbooks of each order. The local parish priest knew that a mission from the Redemptorists or the Passionists was very different from one preached by Vincentians or Jesuits. The parishioners knew likewise that one's reception 'in the [confession] box' would vary with the confessor's stable. Yet, such differences lived within Catholicism, despite the post-Trent cult of uniformity, the existence of print and an ever more centralising canon law.

Second, wherever a group of Christians have cultural experiences in common and share specific pastoral difficulties, a local theology will develop. Again, we take such groupings for granted. The worker-priest movement in France was largely confined within France as it arose out of the circumstances of the Second World War there and its aftermath. Today, the Episcopal Church in the United States and the Church of England draw apart on issues relative to the place each holds in their different societies, but that is not the separatism desired by some of their African co-religionists. The attractiveness of some theological issues in the First World is in sharp contrast to the lack of interest in poorer countries. Liberation theology is a vital issue in Latin America, though it is often little more than a curiosity in Europe. In a similar way, the theology of early medieval Europe has to be seen not as a continental monolith with a distinctive Celtic rock lying off to one side but as a patchwork of local theologies which influence one another for good and ill.

The religious interests of Gregory the Great (made pope 590; d. 604) in Italy, with his love of the new Benedictine **monasticism** on the one hand and his dealings with Constantinople on the other, seem far removed from Visigothic Spain and the works of Isidore of Seville (made bishop c. 600; d. 630). In some ways, the works of Isidore are more reflective of the classical past than the Visigothic present. Both Spain and Italy seem distant from the dioceses and monasteries in Frankish lands that we meet in the course of **Columbanus**'s life (on continent from 590 to 615); and all seem different to the Ireland of **St. Columba**'s time (d. 597 on Iona) and the England upon which **St. Augustine of Canterbury** landed (arrived in **Kent** 597;

d. 604/605). Yet, all these people are linked one with another. Isidore used Gregory's works, Columbanus wrote to him, the monasticism of Columba and Columbanus was formed from the same Gaulish materials – mainly John Cassian – that produced the Frankish monasteries and which influenced the *Rule* Gregory championed, and within a few years, the works of Gregory were being read on Iona and those of Isidore were the basic textbooks on that island, while today people sometimes assert that they see an eastern influence in Iona's monasticism and fail to notice that the connection with the sands of Nitria is through the pages of Cassian. To say that all these expressions of Christianity were merely one, 'western', 'Latin Catholicism' blinds us to the rich diversity of texture, to split them up into 'churches' dismisses the abundant links and their own perception of their unity in Christ. Reality is more complex than either the 'clumpers' or the 'splitters' would have it. The notion of 'local theologies' is an attempt to hold links and differences in tension. As such, it is 'Celtic' or 'Irish' or 'Welsh' or 'Scottish' not because it can be brought into contrast with some other theology imagined as a highly consistent unity, but because its practitioners would have recognised their common links with a particular land, and that in many ways they shared cultural and linguistic experiences which set them apart from their fellow Christians elsewhere in the Latin West.

The Ongoing Life of the Concept

The concept of the 'Celtic Church' has all but disappeared from scholarly discourse, while that of a 'Celtic Christianity' never had much exposure among historians of religion and seemed but a publishers' catch phrase from the start. However, among popular writers and among a diverse range of Christian religious groups, the terms are so valuable – for both commercial and religious purposes – that there seems little likelihood that they will disappear from use. This is partly due to the very vacuity that scholarship eschews. The term conjures up a past that seems so distant that anything might have been the case 'back then', while at the same time the claims relate to a period of western European history that is so little studied in terms of its religious ideas – roughly between the time of Augustine (354–430) and Anselm (c. 1033–1109) – when one can attribute many things to western Christianity with some assurance that it will be difficult to refute one's claims. Moreover, 'Celtic Christianity' combines the attractiveness of the familiar (Christian religion) with an attractive set of images (manuscripts illuminated with knotwork, the ruggedness of Skellig Michael, rolling hills without urban sprawl) with an exotic element that seems to lure supporters in the same way as the myth of Shangri-la. This is a cultural myth to which scholarship has not yet devoted sufficient attention.

However, to those who begin to question the myth, there is no better starting point than the concluding paragraphs of **Adomnán**'s *Life of Columba* (bk. 3, epilogue 135b). Written in the quintessential 'Celtic' monastery on an Irish island belonging geographically to Britain, and now considered Scottish, standing out amid the Atlantic's storms, we are told of the holy fame of the founder. It is a fame that is truly great not because it is known in the locality, but through Gaul and Spain, and then across the Alps and down into Italy, and is even celebrated in the city of Rome itself. Moreover, this fame was expressed using phrases from the Evagrius's Latin translation of Athanasius's *Life of Antony of Egypt* – a link with the eastern deserts made through Latin books in the library rather than by far-wandering Orientals. Whether or not people in Rome in the late eighth century kept the feast of Columba is not the issue; rather, we should note that those monks on Iona saw themselves as part of a world-wide church that reached from Rome to their island at the ends of the earth.

Further Reading

Adomnán of Iona. 1995. *Life of St Columba*. Translated by Richard Sharpe. Penguin.

Davies, Wendy. 1992. 'The Myth of the Celtic Church'. Pp. 12–21 in *The Early Church in Wales and the West: Recent Work in Early Christian Archaeology, History and Place-Names*. Edited by Nancy Edwards and Alan Lane. Oxbow Monographs.

Etchingham, Colmán. 1999. *Church Organisation in Ireland: AD 650 to 1000*. Laigin Publications.

Hughes, Kathleen. 1981. 'The Celtic Church: Is This a Valid Concept?' *Cambridge Medieval Celtic Studies* 1: 1–20.

Meek, Donald E. 1996. 'Modern Celtic Christianity'. *Studia Imagologica: Amsterdam Studies on Cultural Identity* 8: 143–157.

———. 1997. 'Surveying the Saints: Reflections on Recent Writings on "Celtic Christianity" '. *Scottish Bulletin of Evangelical Theology* 15: 50–60.

O'Loughlin, Thomas. 1994. 'St Patrick and an Irish Theology'. *Doctrine and Life* 44: 153–159.

———. 1998. 'Medieval Church History: Beyond Apologetics, After Development: The Awkward Memories'. *The Way* 38: 65–76.

———. 2000a. *Celtic Theology: Humanity, World and God in Early Irish Writings*. Continuum.

———. 2000b. *Journeys on the Edges*. Orbis.
———. 2001. 'Theologians and Their Use of Historical Evidence: Some Common Pitfalls'. *The Month* 261: 30–35.
———. 2002a. ' "Celtic Spirituality", Ecumenism, and the Contemporary Religious Landscape'. *Irish Theological Quarterly* 67: 153–168.
———. 2002b. ' "A Celtic Theology": Some Awkward Questions and Observations'. Pp. 49–65 in *Identifying the 'Celtic'*. Edited by J. F. Nagy. Four Courts Press.
———. 2004. ' "Things New and Old": Contemporary Cultural Tensions and the Tradition of Liturgy in Ireland'. Pp. 140–159 in *City Limits: Mission Issues in Postmodern Times*. Edited by J. Egan and T. R. Whelan. Milltown Institute of Theology and Philosophy.
Sims-Williams, Patrick. 1981. 'Celtomania and Celtoscepticism'. *Cambrian Medieval Celtic Studies* 36: 1–35.

Thomas O'Loughlin

Celts

Celts and *Celtic* are currently popular terms used to describe many of the ancient inhabitants of northern Europe (including those in Britain and Ireland) and their distinctive culture or cultures. There are usually three components to this identification: historical, archaeological and linguistic. The term Κελτοι was first used by Greek writers such as Herodotus and Plato to describe a warlike peoples who lived along the Danube and beyond the Pillars of Hercules (Gibraltar). Diodorus Siculus (c. 60 BC) says that those in the east, from the present-day Czech Republic to southern Russia, are properly called *Galatae* (Galatians), while those around the Alps and the Pyrenees are Celts, though the Romans tend to group all the tribes together and call them *Galli* (Gauls). **Julius Caesar**, during his conquest of Gaul, described western and central France as *Galllia Celtica*. No ancient (or medieval) writer used the terms Celt or Celtic to describe the inhabitants of Britain and Ireland.

Archaeologists began to associate specific sites and artefacts with the Celts in the mid-nineteenth century. The two most important excavations were **Hallstatt** in Austria (1846–1863) and **La Tène** in Switzerland (1857–1917). The former uncovered about 1,000 graves, spanning the seventh and sixth centuries BC, richly furnished with weapons, bronze and ceramic vessels and jewellery. At the latter excavation, submerged in the north-west corner of lake Neuchâtel, were dozens of swords, spears, shields, bronze vessels and ornamental objects dating to the fifth century BC. By the end of the century, archaeologists had agreed upon a dating system for Celtic cultures by classifying object types and artistic styles with reference to these two sites. Hence came the labelling of the Hallstatt Culture, from the Late **Bronze Age** (c. 1200 BC) to the Early **Iron Age** (c. 450 BC), and the La Tène Culture, from c. 450 BC to c. 50 BC. The two were deemed to be Celtic, and La Tène art in particular, with its distinctive motifs and curvilinear designs, was thought of as 'Celtic art'. Hallstatt elements were identified in British artefacts, and La Tène styles were associated with both Britain and Ireland into the early Christian period.

Many believe the strongest identifier of Celtic is language. While medieval authors such as St. Jerome and Gerald of Wales noticed the similarities in the languages spoken in Gaul and Galatia (in Asia Minor) and Ireland and Wales, it was not until 1695 that the Oxford linguist Edward Lhuyd applied the term 'Celtic' to Gaulish (the language spoken in ancient Gaul), **Irish** and British (i.e. **Welsh**, Cornish and Breton). From then on, linguists considered a Celtic branch of the Indo-European language tree to have developed sometime after 4000 BC and spread throughout western and central Europe. From place-name evidence, it can be argued that by around 300 BC, Celtic was probably the most widespread language in Europe. This contrasts greatly with the state of the Celtic languages today, which have survived only in small pockets of the Atlantic fringe (e.g. Brittany, Wales, western Ireland, the Scottish Highlands and Nova Scotia). Nevertheless, as the social anthropologist Malcolm Chapman has sardonically observed:

> Large groups of peoples – the Welsh, Irish, Scots and Bretons – are often called 'Celts' by others; and some of these 'Celts' are happy to use the term as a name for themselves. The Celts, after centuries of conceptual limbo, have been conjured once more into existence (Chapman 1992).

Conjuring the Celts, to use Chapman's phrase, has recently become a quite popular activity. Over the last 150 years, the Celts have been revived for romantic, political, commercial, religious and academic purposes. And at no time have things Celtic been more prevalent than at the beginning of the twenty-first century. At the same time, however, the academic community has embraced a stronger-than-usual scepticism regarding the Celts, in part because of the modern mania for things Celtic and Arthurian. The general public, complain the critics, are buying books which uncritically perpetuate old romantic myths about the Celts, and profit-seeking authors and publishers are allowing these myths to form current racial and political sentiments that are untrue and potentially dangerous.

Drawing upon recent trends in anthropology, archaeologists who study the European Iron Age have unleashed the most powerful criticism of the label Celt. They now question the association of Hallstatt and La Tène cultures with Celtic-speaking peoples and whether the specifically continental term *Keltoi* (or *Celtae*) should be used to describe the Iron Age inhabitants of Britain and Ireland (see James 1999; Collis 2003). Greek and Roman writers were inconsistent in their usage of the term, they say, and 'Celt' was never used to describe a person from the British Isles prior to the seventeenth century. The Greco-Roman construct of the barbarian other and the outmoded racial theories that pervade popular studies of the Celts impose uniformity on diversity. When Greek and Roman authors use labels such as Celts, Gauls and Britons, they ignore tribal or regional diversity to contrast for their audiences the exotic/uncivilised barbarians with the familiar/civilised Mediterranean peoples. This kind of stereotype was perpetuated by modern imperialists and is reflected in nineteenth-century racial theory. But since anthropology no longer believes in race theory nor in uniform and static 'cultures' (which had virtually defined Iron Age archaeology), such constructs as the Celts are no longer tenable.

Archaeologist Barry Cunliffe has suggested an alternative term – the Atlantic Zone – to explain the cultural similarities between long-term trading partners in Ireland, Wales, **Cornwall**, Brittany and Galicia (Cunliffe 2004). These lands in the early Middle Ages are thought to have produced a distinctive type of spirituality, reflected in their poetry, prayers and hagiography (see Oliver Davies 1999). Some medievalists, however, have attacked the notion of a '**Celtic Christianity**' or a uniform 'Celtic Church', stressing that the medieval Celtic Christians were both orthodox in their faith and similar to their English and Frankish neighbours in their manner of worship (see Hughes 1981; Wendy Davies 1992). Patrick Sims-Williams has pointed out our propensity to contrast the spiritual and natural Celt with the rational and materialistic Saxon (Sims-Williams 1986). Still, most have continued to use the term Celtic to describe – and lump together – the peoples and cultures of medieval Ireland, Scotland, Wales and Brittany. These lands are often referred to together as 'the medieval Celtic fringe', which assumes cultural similarities. While medieval writers never use the term Celt, many do perpetuate centuries-old stereotypes of barbarian Celts when describing the Irish, the Scots and the Welsh. In turn, some writers in medieval Ireland, Scotland and Wales – e.g. **Geoffrey of Monmouth**, Gerald of Wales, Robert and Edward Bruce – make claims to common origins, history and language (see Snyder 1996).

Despite this academically correct scepticism, Celt remains a convenient, recognisable and commercial label. It remains to be seen whether it will continue to be so or be replaced by a more accurate term or paradigm provided by scholars.

See also Art and Architecture; Britons; Gaels.

Further Reading

Chapman, Malcolm. 1992. *The Celts: The Construction of a Myth*. St. Martin's.

Collis, J. R. 2003. *The Celts: Origins, Myths and Inventions*. Tempus Publishing.

Cunliffe, Barry. 1997. *The Ancient Celts*. Oxford University Press.

———. 2004. *Facing the Ocean: The Atlantic and Its Peoples 8000 BC–AD 1500*. Oxford University Press.

Davies, Oliver (tr.). 1999. *Celtic Spirituality*. Paulist Press.

Davies, Wendy. 1992. 'The Myth of the Celtic Church'. Pp.12–21 in *The Early Church in Wales and the West*. Edited by Nancy Edwards and Alan Lane. Oxbow.

Haywood, John. 2001. *The Historical Atlas of the Celtic World*. Thames & Hudson.

Hughes, Kathleen Hughes. 1981. 'The Celtic Church—Is This a Valid Concept?' *Cambridge Medieval Celtic Studies* 1: 1–20.

James, Simon. 1993. *The World of the Celts*. Thames & Hudson.

———. 1999. *The Atlantic Celts: Ancient People or Modern Invention?* University of Wisconsin Press.

Koch, John (ed.). 1995. *The Celtic Heroic Age: Literary Sources for Ancient Celtic Europe and Early Ireland and Wales*. Celtic Studies Publications.

Kruta, Venceslas et al. (eds.). 1999. *The Celts*. Rizzoli.

Rankin, H. D. 1987. *Celts and the Classical World*. Croom Helm.

Russell, Paul. 1995. *An Introduction to the Celtic Languages*. Longman.

Sims-Williams, Patrick. 1986. 'The Visionary Celt'. *Cambridge Medieval Celtic Studies* 11: 71–96.

Snyder, Christopher A. 1996. 'Celtic Continuity in the Middle Ages'. *Medieval Perspectives* 11: 164–178.

Christopher A. Snyder

Ceolfrith (b. c. AD 642)

Ceolfrith (or Ceolfrid) was born c. AD 642 into a noble family of **Northumbria**. At eighteen, he entered monastic life at Gilling in modern Yorkshire, ruled by his brother Cynefrid. He, along with some other members of this community, was invited to transfer to the monastery at Ripon when St. **Wilfrid** refounded that community as a Benedictine Roman house. When Ceolfrith was twenty-seven in 669, St. Wilfrid ordained him a priest.

He travelled for a time in England, visiting and staying for some time at monasteries in East Anglia and Kent, where he served not only as a teacher but also as a miller and a baker. It is unknown when, or even if, Ceolfrith had met **Benedict Biscop** prior to Biscop's request for him at Monkwearmouth, but if so, it is probably during the trip through southern England when Biscop was serving as abbot of **St Augustine**'s and Ceolfrith was visiting the area. Biscop founded Monkwearmouth c. 674 and requested that Ceolfrith be sent to join him, the latter by this time having returned to Ripon. Ceolfrith was thirty-two then and became prior of the new foundation.

Ceolfrith assisted Biscop in acquiring Frankish workmen to complete the church. During this time, he found his position as prior, in part responsible for teaching the rule and setting an example in keeping it, a difficult one owing to the resistance of the monks under him. At some point, he resigned his position and returned to Ripon. Biscop persuaded him to return, and c. 679 when Monkwearmouth was completed, the two men went to Rome with the express purpose of acquiring books and other materials to enrich their foundation. On this trip, Ceolfrith experienced Roman Christianity first hand for the first time, met and brought back to **Northumbria** John the Chanter who taught the monks the Roman method of chant. When the pair returned, the king gave Biscop additional land to build a second foundation; this became **Jarrow**, and Ceolfrith was appointed its abbot, repairing there with a small group of monks in 681. Plague was ever present in this period in the north of England, and it killed all the monks except Ceolfrith at Jarrow in the following year and a small boy, whom most commentators assume to be **Bede**. But in spite of this, the new foundation was completed and the church was dedicated in 685.

With Biscop's death c. 689, Ceolfrith became abbot of both Monkwearmouth and Jarrow. He stepped down from that position in 716 to make a final pilgrimage to Rome. During this period, there is little that is datable. The two foundations continued to grow. Bede tells us that Ceolfrith doubled the size of the library, a rather impressive feat considering how well off Biscop had left the foundation's library with his multiple trips to Rome. It also appears that it is during the time of Ceolfrith's abbacy that the twin foundations became important scriptoria, bringing into being not just manuscripts that were sent to other foundations throughout England, but combining **Anglo-Saxon**, Celtic and Roman art in manuscript illumination and giving birth to the Northumbrian renaissance. It is also under Ceolfrith and with his blessing and encouragement that Bede was educated and came to prominence, the most important writer of the early period. It was Ceolfrith himself who ordered the creation of the three pandects of the Bible, of which only the *Codex Amiatinus* survives. It was this codex that Ceolfrith intended to deliver to Rome and the pope personally as thanks for Gregory's enterprise a little over a century earlier to convert the English nation. As fate would have it, Ceolfrith died in Langres, France, on 25 September 716 on his way to Rome.

See also Celtic Christianity; Monasticism.

Further Reading

Bede. 1965. *Lives of the Abbots of Wearmouth and Jarrow*. Translated by J. F. Webb. Penguin.
McClure, Judith. 1984. 'Bede and the Life of Ceolfrid'. *Peritia* 3: 71–84.
Wood, Ian. 1995. *The Most Holy Abbot Ceolfrid*. Jarrow Lecture.

Larry Swain

Ceramics and Glass

Prehistoric Pottery

Pottery first made its appearance in Britain in the **Neolithic** Period, in the fourth millennium BC. The earliest potteries were round-bottom pots, devoid of decoration and were produced by coiling. There are a number of distinct regional variations, such as Grimston-Lyles Hill, found in Ireland, Scotland and north and eastern England, which have simple, thickened or rolled rims and a generally corky appearance. In the south, **Windmill Hill** ware takes its name from a famous causewayed camp in Wiltshire where it is represented and has thickened rims and, sometimes, oval lugs to aid lifting. Hembury ware, found in the south-west, often have carinated (i.e. shouldered) profiles. They continued in use into the third millennium BC. Around 3000 BC, some decoration, most often incised or stabbed, was used on bowls found in the south of England. Later Neolithic pottery includes different types of pottery decorated with impressed decoration, most frequently produced by using twisted cords, fingertips or bird bones to create patterns. One regional variation is known as Peterborough ware. Flat bases were first employed in Grooved ware, which seems to have been a widespread tradition that appeared around 3000 and is found in Orkney, at **Skara Brae**, where decoration included designs of the type sometimes associated with Passage Grave art and high relief modelling. A variant of the tradition was employed at Durrington Walls in Wilts, an important henge monument.

In the later Neolithic Period, **Beaker** pottery was introduced to Britain by the early copper-workers. Beaker pottery is very distinctive, with thin walls and cord-impressed decoration. The subject of many different classificatory schemes over the years, the various groups are now divided into early (bell-shaped vessels with all-over cord decoration), which have been seen as of direct Continental derivation; middle (long- and short-necked beakers), which represent a local development in different parts of Britain and late, which show variations in style including the occasional use of handles and vessels with 'barbed wire' decoration.

Pottery of the earlier part of the **Bronze Age** continued earlier Neolithic traditions. Between c. 2000 and 1700 BC are found the so-called food vessels, which are flat-bottomed pots with simple decoration, sometimes over the whole vessel, sometimes only at the top. There are two main groups, bowl and vase food vessels. Early food vessels may have been used in a domestic context, but in the second millennium BC they were enlarged so that they could accommodate cremations. These are categorised as collared urns, food vessel urns and cordoned urns. Collared urns belong to the tradition of Neolithic pottery and have decorated, out-turned rims. Food vessel urns are enlarged food vessels, some with applied neck decoration. Some burials were also accompanied by smaller accessory vessels. These include perforated wall cups which have holes in the sides (formerly known as 'incense cups'), 'Aldbourne cups', which are small biconical vessels and 'grape cups', which have lumps of clay attached to the outside of the vessel.

In the Late Bronze Age, there were changes in pottery. In the south of England is found the Deverel-Rimbury tradition of bucket, barrel and globular urns. The bucket urns were inspired by beaten bronze buckets found on the Continent, with sharply angled shoulders and everted rims. They came into vogue in the early first millennium BC. Barrel urns, as the name suggests, are relatively plain barrel-shaped pots. Globular urns are the descendants of earlier Bronze Age or even Beaker pottery and have incised linear ornament. Outside the southern region, cinerary urns with cordoned decoration were made. A distinct late-Bronze Age tradition of potting is flat-rimmed ware, which, as the name suggests, has flat-topped rims, sometimes with a slight internal bevel. These are generally crude, undecorated pots of bucket shape and are found from Shetland southwards.

A considerable diversity of styles is apparent in **Iron Age** pottery. Until this time, all pottery was hand-made by coiling, but the use of a wheel began in this period. The earliest Iron Age pottery in Britain represents continuity from the Late Bronze Age in potting traditions. Continuing styles of Deverel-Rimbury origin are apparent in the south-east, for example at Eldon's Seat in Dorset. In the east of England, between c. 800 and 600 BC can be found pottery of the West Harling-Staple Howe tradition, which has jars and bowls with everted rims and shoulders, sometimes with fingertip decoration. A related regional variation is the Kimmeridge-Caburn, found along the south coast of England. Alongside these older traditions are found more sophisticated pots of Continental inspiration. In the eighth and seventh centuries BC in **Wessex** can be found the All Canning's Cross tradition, named after a site in Wiltshire. The forms include bucket-shaped pots, bead rim bowls and bulbous jars, decorated with stamps and incised zigzags. Some later versions employ a haematite (made with powdered iron ore) coating on the pots to imitate the appearance of metal. Some vessels in this period have painted decoration.

Between 600 and 300 BC (the Middle Iron Age), earlier potting traditions continued, but there were also some regional innovations. At Eastbourne, Sussex, some pots were made with pedestal feet and painted decoration, and in Wessex, the dominant tradition was that known as All Canning's Cross, which used haematite coating often on bowls with foot-ring bases and cordons. Wiped ware can be found in eastern England, in which the surface of the pot was wiped with a cloth or bunch of grass to produce striations. This type of pottery continued in many areas down to the third century BC, but in parts of the East Midlands, it seems to have continued until the arrival of the Romans.

In the later Middle Iron Age (c. 400/300–100 BC), pottery styles became more uniform, the dominant vessel being the 'saucepan pot', which had straight sides, rounded shoulders and beaded rim. Additionally, however, there were a number of distinctive regional traditions of decorative pottery. Among these can be singled out the south-western decorated wares of the south-west (formerly known as **Glastonbury** ware from its occurrence at a site in Somerset). The richly decorated necked bowls and jars were produced at various centres and widely traded, the source of the clay being Cornish. The Croft Ambrey-Breedon style of pots employed duck-shaped stamps in the decoration, while in Dorset – the **Maiden Castle** – Marnhull style of pottery sometimes had countersunk handles and decoration of grooved scrolls, arcs and wavy lines.

In the later Iron Age (c. 150 BC–AD 43), bead rim pots were dominant, but there were several regional traditions of richly decorated wares. Among these regional traditions is the Hunsbury-Draughton one, found in Northamptonshire with ornament of yin-yangs and running scrolls, possibly derived from metalwork. In Lincolnshire, the Sleaford-Dragonby style employed stamped circles with arcs and swags and employed patterns produced by a roulette (a wheel run over the surface of the pot).

A totally new tradition of wheel-made pottery made itself felt from the first century BC. This tradition, known as Swarling-**Aylesford** (after two cemeteries) or Belgic (after supposed incomers from the Continent who were seen to have introduced it), has distinctive vessel forms including tall pedestal urns, corrugated-sided urns, tazze (pedestalled bowls) and carinated cups. The vessels are often thin-walled, and burnishing (i.e. polishing) was sometimes employed. Combed decoration is also found.

During the later Iron Age, imported pottery came into southern Britain. These include from the second century BC wine amphorae from the Mediterranean and local wares from Brittany that arrived at the trading base of **Hengistbury Head**. In the south-east, a certain amount of Arretine pottery (red-gloss ware from the region of Arezzo in Italy) as well as Gallo-Belgic wares from Gaul was imported. These include terra nigra (a grey fabric ware with dark grey or black slip), terra rubra (orange-red ware with an orange-red slip probably intended to imitate arretine) and butt beakers, which were barrel-shaped rouletted vessels in a buff fabric. Some of these were imitated in Britain. A separate pottery tradition is apparent in the Iron Age of Atlantic Scotland, which starts in the Late Bronze Age and continues into the early medieval period.

Roman Pottery

The Roman conquest of Britain in AD 43 marked a sharp break in pottery styles, though some Swarling-Aylesford shapes continued in use through the first century AD. Pottery in Roman Britain can be divided into fine and coarse wares: the fine wares comprising almost entirely the large family of red-gloss wares known as samian or terra sigillata were imported from Gaul. Samian was imported in considerable quantities and can be found in both plain and decorated forms. The plain forms comprise various types of plates, cups and bowls, but rarer forms such as jars, inkwells and mortaria (for grinding food) are also found. Decorated forms mostly comprise bowls. The production may be said to have started with the Arretine ware imported before the conquest. This was imitated in southern Gaul (round La Graufesenque, near Lyons) from c. AD 20 and was imported to Britain until c. AD 110. South Gaulish in turn was copied by Central Gaulish potteries, which were the main suppliers of samian pottery to Britain from the late AD 70s to the end of the second century. Key factories were located round Lezoux. East Gaulish samian was produced in the region round Trier and Rheinzabern in Germany from the end of the first century, but only really came on its own in Britain in the early third century. Workshops frequently stamped their wares with the name of the factory owner, and this fact and the currency of known stamps used to build up the decoration on pots have meant that samian is quite closely datable. A small amount of samian was made around **Colchester** in the second century AD.

Glazed pottery made its appearance in Britain in the first century AD. Comparatively rare, this green-glazed fabric was imported by the army between c. AD 40 and 70. The army in Britain attempted to make some in the second century AD at Holt (Clwyd) and Little Chester (Derbys), but it was not common. Other early imports include mica-dusted ware, from the Rhineland and Gaul, imported in the early second century AD, and copied in East Anglia at the end of that century and into the early third.

A type of fine ware (though sometimes classed as 'coarse') produced in Britain was colour coated. This was used especially in the production of beakers, and the inspiration behind the British production was a series of beakers imported from the Rhineland with a metallic slip – Rhenish ware. These were made round Trier and Cologne form the late second century. Some have mottoes in white paint on a metallic dark slip, and rouletting was employed in the decoration. The main area of British copies was the lower Nene Valley (where the ware used to be termed 'Castor') and around Colchester. Much was produced around Water Newton in Cambridgeshire from the second to the fourth century. In addition to beakers, lidded boxes, mortaria and flagons were produced. A small series had relief decoration 'iced' on to the surface of the vessel ('en barbotine' decoration), and the ornament included animals and human figures. From the third century AD onwards, colour-coated wares were produced in the Oxford region. In addition to red colour-coated wares imitating samian, this area also produced white parchment ware with painted decoration. Stamps and rouletting were also applied. In the New Forest region of Hampshire, imitation samian was also produced from the third through the fourth century AD. Many of the wares were similar to those of the Oxford area, but a speciality was a type of metallic-surfaced beaker with indented sides.

Coarse wares make up the majority of pottery in use in Roman Britain. A particularly distinctive type is the black burnished, which, as the name suggests, has a polished exterior. There are two main groups; black-burnished ware category 1 (BB1) was gritty and handmade, with a surface that is often facetted with the burnishing. Typically, it was decorated with a trellis pattern. The forms found are almost entirely cooking pots, but from the late-second-century bowls are also found. It was made in Dorset, though a small amount was also made near Rossington Bridge in Yorkshire. Black burnished 2 (BB2), in contrast, was wheel-made and hard, with quartz in the fabric and a silky finish. The shades vary from black to grey. This seems to have been made first in the Thames estuary but was soon in production elsewhere. It was most common in the mid-second century AD but was rare after AD 250.

Among other distinctive coarse wares was the rusticated ware, on which the surface of the vessel was pinched up. This was popular between the conquest and c. AD 120, though some were produced again in the early third century. Roughcast wares were current in the late first to early second century and have a sprinkling of grit on the surface of the vessel. Among the specialist regional types, the ones that may be singled out are the Severn Valley ware, which was hard and orangey, and produced perhaps for the army in **Gloucester** and **Wroxeter** (Salop); Upchurch ware, produced in the North Kent Marshes; Huntcliff ware, which comprised handmade cooking pots with a lid seating and which was current from the mid-fourth century until the end of the Roman period in Yorkshire and on **Hadrian's Wall** and Crambeck ware, the production of which spans the fourth century and beyond and which is distinguished by grey cooking pots, flanged bowls, flaghons and mortaria, often with red-painted decoration.

An unusual fabric was the Derbyshire ware, which was fired to a high temperature and was orange-purple with a vitrified surface. It was used for cooking pots with hollow, everted rims and was a forerunner of the 'Midlands Purple' ware found in the same area in the later Middle Ages.

An enormous variety of pottery forms were produced in Romano-British kilns, ranging from large storage jars through cooking pots and 'pie dishes' and from beakers to cheese presses, candle holders and strainers. The most useful coarse forms for dating purposes are the different types of flagon and jug, and mortaria, the large bowls used in food preparation. Traditionally, it would appear these had to be cream-coloured, and where the underlying fabric was otherwise, they were given a creamy wash. The form of the rim changed frequently through time, and a number of them bear potters' names or marks. Until about AD 70, most mortaria were imported, but thereafter native products dominated the market, though there were a few imports, mostly from Germany. Among the British production centres were Colchester, St Albans and Hartshill/Mancetter near Nuneaton, the products of which dominated the market in the Midlands and north in the second century AD. A few mortaria were made in Scotland for the military market, and other kilns were located near **Cirencester**, Gloucester, **Caerleon** and **Lincoln**.

Early Medieval Pottery

In the fifth century AD, there was a limited amount of pottery production, though most of the main centres discontinued their output. Black-burnished ware seems to have been made in the neighbourhood of Poole Harbour, Dorset, possibly even into the sixth century. In **Cornwall**, pottery in a Romano-British tradition seems to have continued into the sixth century, and elsewhere in the province there was a limited amount of production at centres such as Lincoln into the fifth century.

Anglo-Saxon pottery represented a break with past traditions. The pots of the incomers were handmade and of the kind of thick, coarse fabric that had been in use in the pre-Roman Iron Age. For a number of years, archaeologists believed that Romano-Saxon pottery, which was Romano-British in fabric but germanic in shape and decoration, was produced by the Romans for the new Anglo-Saxon market, but it is now realised that this ware was purely Romano-British, albeit influenced by germanic taste. Some early Anglo-Saxon pots had pedestal bases and facetted shoulders or bosses on the angled shoulders instead of facets. They are found in the Thames Valley with some outliers. Similar pots are found around the river Elbe on the continent. During the fifth century, ornament consisting of arches or arched patterns were popular (*stehende bogen* urns) – these continued into the sixth century, when stamps, bosses orlinear ornament were also employed on them. After the middle of the fifth century, pots with pronounced bosses on the shoulders were in vogue, and these continued through the sixth century (they are known as *buckelurnen*). Most Anglo-Saxon pottery of the pagan period was plain, and it is best known from cemeteries mainly north of the Thames, where pots were used to contain cremation burials. The decorative schemes clearly held meanings for the Anglo-Saxons, as possibly did their shape and size, and pot stamps seem to have travelled quite long distances, perhaps having a heraldic value which was transmitted on marriage.

In south-east England, some wheel-made pottery was imported from France, mostly bottle-shaped vessels, a few of which were copied in England, where they were made on a slow wheel. Middle Saxon pottery generally continues some of the traditions of the pagan period. Some pottery, however, was now made on a slow wheel, notably **Ipswich** ware, named after a site in Suffolk, which may have begun in the seventh century and is associated with early urban expansion. In the north of England, there is some evidence that a fast wheel was used to produce Whitby-type ware, found in **Northumbrian** monasteries around the mid-ninth century. Of the imports, Tating ware, decorated with applied lozenges of tinfoil, seems to have been traded from Germany in this period.

Late Saxon pottery was mostly wheel-made, and a considerable industry flourished in the tenth and eleventh centuries, having probably originated in the late ninth century. These wheel-made pots are generally grouped as 'Saxo-Norman', as both forms and fabrics have some overlap with the **Norman Conquest**. They fall into three main fabric groups, Thetford-type ware, which is grey and gritty; St Neots-type ware, which is shell-gritted and Stamford-type ware, which is very fine, creamy coloured and lead glazed. These fabrics appear in a wide variety of forms, notably cooking pots, often with sagging bases; spouted pitchers and bowls are the most common, though less usual forms include lamps and lids. Rouletting was a decorative device that was employed sometimes.

Glazing seems to have rapidly spread in the ninth century from the East (where it was a feature of Islamic pottery) through Italy and France to England. It became particularly common in the tenth century onwards. A southern version of the more northerly Stamford Ware was Winchester ware, which was sometimes also decorated with applied strips. Among the products in Winchester ware were costrels (bottles) and strainers.

Many different types of imports are found in late-Saxon England. They include Badorf ware (large storage vessels or amphorae with rouletted applied strips, sometimes copied in Thetford ware), imported from Germany and Pingsdorf ware, also made in Germany, which had splashes of red paint and which was later produced in France and continued after the Norman Conquest.

In the Celtic West, very little pottery was produced except for the so-called souterrain ware, found mostly in northern Ireland and consisting of grass-marked bucket-shaped pots, similar (but unrelated) to the grass-marked ware in **Cornwall**, and pottery of ultimately Iron Age descent in the north-west of Scotland. Pottery was, however, imported from both Gaul and the Mediterranean. Red-slipped fine table wares from North Africa and storage amphorae from the east Mediterranean (the so-called A and B wares), which were imported probably through the agency of Byzantine merchants in the late fifth to the early sixth century and from the sixth- to the seventh-century mortaria (D ware) and a variety of cooking pots, jugs and bowls (E ware) from France, made their way to high-status sites of the **Brittonic Age** such as **Tintagel**, **South Cadbury**, **Dumbarton** and **Iona** ('**Tintagel ware**' q.v.).

Prehistoric Glass

Glass was probably first developed in Mesopotamia between 3000 and 2500 BC, where it was used for beads and inlays. By the late sixteenth century BC, it was being used for vessels in Egypt. The earliest glass found in Britain comprises imported beads, which first arrived in the second millennium BC, though there have been some suggestions that attempts were made to imitate them in Britain. Beads were imported throughout the Iron Age, and there is evidence that they were being produced at **Hengistbury Head** in Dorset, where lumps of imported glass for reworking have been found. Glass was used in the Iron Age in the production of enamels, and these are apparent on some of the earliest Iron Age products, such as the **Battersea Shield**. Vessel glass does not seem to have been imported until the Roman period, with the possible exception of a couple of pieces from pre-Conquest contexts at Sheepen, Colchester, Essex, and finds from Late Iron Age princely burials at Mount Bures, Essex, and Hurstbourne Tarrant, Hants.

Roman Glass

The Romans used glass quite extensively for everything, from enamels and beads through playing pieces, window glass, bracelets and vessels for the table. Most of the glass found in Britain was imported, particularly from the Rhineland and, in the early days following the Conquest, Italy, but glass was also manufactured in Britain. Although only partial remains of Romano-British glass-working sites have been discovered, it would appear that simple blown vessels were being produced along with window glass from the early second century AD. This glass was probably made using cullet – pieces of broken glass that were melted down and reworked. Some glass-workers were probably itinerant. Glass remained popular throughout the Roman period, and in the late first and second centuries AD, glass vessels were used for cremation burials.

Many different glass-working techniques are apparent in the finds from Roman Britain. They include blowing (both free blowing and mould blowing), casting (which also included polychrome-decorated items such as millefiori, marbles and stip and lace mosaic), painting and applying threads of glass to the surface of the vessel as in icing (snake-thread glass). Cut glass was quite popular in the fourth century AD, and some bowls have figured scenes.

Early Medieval Glass

Glass was both imported and worked by the pagan Anglo-Saxons. The products include a range of different types of vessels and beads. To this range, window glass can be added in the Christian period and is apparent in the Northumbrian monasteries of Monkwearmouth and **Jarrow** in the seventh to the eighth century and also at **Glastonbury** in Somerset. In the late ninth to tenth century, potash was used in the production of window glass at Winchester.

The imported glass in the pagan period was mostly products of the forest glass houses of Germany that continued in production from the end of the Roman period. A particular feature was the use of trailed and applied decoration, sometimes in a different colour. Claw beakers are tall drinking vessels with applied pieces of glass, which look a bit like lobster claws on the side. Other vessels include palm cups (round-bottomed for holding in the palm), drinking horns, bowls and beakers. Some palm cups were decorated with ribbing, produced by mould blowing.

Later, Anglo-Saxon glass vessels were found in fewer shapes, but often in stronger colours. Whether any vessels were produced in England is debated, though there was probably some production near Faversham in Kent. Beads, on the other hand, were both imported and locally made, usually out of recycled glass, though the only certain bead-making site is at **York**.

In the Celtic West, glass was similarly imported, though there is evidence for glass production as well as working at Dunmisk in County Tyrone, Ireland. The imported glass seems to have come from a different source from that of the pagan Anglo-Saxons, being imported from the region around Bordeaux. Particularly distinctive were fine, clear cone beakers with white-trailed decoration. There is some indication that there was an attempt to copy them in the monastic site of **Whithorn**, Dumfries and Galloway. When broken, the glass was reworked into beads and probably enamel. There is a limited amount of later glass, including some of Spanish origin from Tintagel, Cornwall, and some gold-glass tesserae used in mosaics in the Mediterranean, that were imported as scrap in the eighth century.

See also Art and Architecture; Roman Britain.

Further Reading

de la Bedoyère, Guy. 2000. *Pottery in Roman Britain*. Shire Books.

Gibson, A., and A. Woods. 1997. A *Prehistoric Pottery for the Archaeologist* (2nd edn.). Leicester University Press.

Gillam, J. 1971. *Types of Roman Coarse Pottery Vessels in Northern Britain*. Oriel.

Kennett, D. H. 1988. *Anglo-Saxon Pottery*. Shire Books.

Laing, Lloyd. 2003. *Pottery in Britain 4000 BC to AD 1900*. Greenlight.

Laingmaid, N. G. 1978. *Prehistoric Pottery*. Shire Books.

McCarthy, M., and C. Brooks. 1988. *Medieval Pottery in Britain, AD 900–1600*. Leicester University Press.

Price, J. (ed.). *Glass in Britain and Ireland, AD 350–1100*. British Museum Publications.

Tyers, P. 1996. *Roman Pottery in Britain*. Batsford.

Lloyd Laing

Cerdic (d.534)

According to the ***Anglo-Saxon Chronicle***, Cerdic was the founder of the **Wessex** (West Saxon) dynasty. He and his son Cynric, described by the chronicle as *aldormen*, are said to have come to Britain with five ships in the year AD 495. Landing on the Hampshire coast, they are attributed with victories over the **Welsh** (i.e. the **Britons**) in 508, 519, 527 and 530, during which time they gained possession of the Isle of Wight and established the West Saxon kingdom. The chronicle states that Cerdic died in 534, but that his son continued expanding the kingdom westwards.

There are problems with accepting this as historical evidence. The *Anglo-Saxon Chronicle* was written by Wessex scribes over a long period and appears in seven early manuscripts, but none dates to before the reign of **Alfred the Great** (871–899). Attributing only victories and no losses to Cerdic and Cynric may have been a conscious attempt to glorify the founders of Alfred's dynasty. The name Cerdic is also puzzling, for it appears to be a **Celtic** name, i.e. an **Anglo-Saxon** form of the British name *Caraticos* or **Caratacus** (cf. Ceredig, the traditional founder of British **Strathclyde**, and Ceretic, ruler of the British kingdom of **Elmet** in the seventh century). Some have conjectured that Cerdic was a Briton or had a British mother; others have argued that his regnal dates should be later, perhaps 538–554; many consider him an entirely legendary figure. **Bede** does not mention this Cerdic (he does mention a British Cerdic, probably referring to Ceretic of Elmet) and says that the West Saxons were first known as the **Gewisse**.

Further Reading

Crawford, O. G. S. 1952. 'Cerdic's Landing-Place'. *Antiquity* 26.104: 193–200.

Garmonsway, G. N. (ed. and tr.). 1994. *The Anglo-Saxon Chronicle*. Dent.

Johnstone, P. K. 1946. 'Cerdic and His Ancestors'. *Antiquity* 20.77: 31–37.

Yorke, Barbara. 1997. *Kings and Kingdoms of Early Anglo-Saxon England*. Routledge.

Christopher A. Snyder

Ceredigion

Ceredigion, from which Cardigan derives, was a traditional early medieval Welsh kingdom purportedly established by Ceretic, son of Cunedda, along the south-west Welsh coastline facing Ireland. Although its separate political existence ended in the ninth century, when it came under the control of rulers of adjacent kingdoms, it did contain one of the cultural centres of Wales at Llanbadarn Fawr. It eventually became part of the larger kingdom of **Deheubarth**.

The ninth-century ***Historia Brittonum*** reported the Welsh tradition that Cunedda, a leader from the region of Manaw **Gododdin** among the 'men of the North', had migrated south to Wales with his sons to evict the Irish and rule **Gwynedd**. Several Welsh kingdoms were named after his sons, including Ceredigion. While the mythic nature of the evidence has perplexed historians, it is clear that Ceredigion was one of the small Celtic kingdoms which emerged after the withdrawal of Roman forces from Britain early in the fifth century.

During the early Middle Ages, Wales was divided into numerous small kingdoms whose rulers strove to dominate and control their neighbours. For example, c. AD 730 King Seisyll ap Clydog of Ceredigion gained control over Ystrad Tywi, the kingdom south-east of Ceredigion, thereby creating a kingdom known as Seisyllwg. In 807, the major Welsh chronicle, *Brut y Tywysogyon*, tersely reports the death of Arthen, king of Ceredigion. The last known king of Ceredigion, Gwgon, drowned in 871, after which the kingdom came under the control of King **Rhodri Mawr** of **Gwynedd** and his sons. One of his sons, Cadell, probably ruled Ceredigion by 895 and also held **Dyfed** and Seisyllwg until his death in 909. Cadell's son, **Hywel Dda**, included Ceredigion among the territories which he ruled until his death in 950.

Thanks to its central geographic location, during the late tenth and eleventh centuries Ceredigion was fought over by rulers from the larger Welsh polities. Because of its long coastline, it was also subject to **Viking** attacks, including one on Llanbadarn Fawr in 998. This place was the site of a major 'clas' or religious community named in honour of the sixth-century Welsh holy man, Padarn. During the late eleventh century, this community was a major intellectual centre, thanks to the efforts of Sulien (1010–1091), who spent thirteen years being educated in Ireland and who twice served as bishop of **St David's**. Sulian's four sons, Rhygyfarch, Daniel, Ieuan and Arthen, continued his work. Ieuan wrote about the life of his father. Rhygyfarch wrote about the earliest known saint's life of **St. David** and c.1094 composed a poem lamenting the suffering endured by Ceredigion because of attacks by the **Normans**.

The first of these attacks occurred in 1074. In 1093, Roger de **Montgomery**, the earl of Shrewsbury, invaded Ceredigion and built Cardigan Castle at the mouth of the Teifi River. His son Arnulf proceeded south, captured the district of Penfro and erected Pembroke Castle there. The general Welsh uprising against Anglo-Norman inroads in 1096 temporarily regained Welsh control of Ceredigion. After the failure of the rebellion by the Montgomery family in 1102 and their exile from Britain, King Cadwgan ap Bleddyn of **Powys** gained Ceredigion for a few years.

See also Welsh People.

Further Reading

Davies, J. L., and D. P. Kirby (eds.). 1994. *Cardiganshire County History. Vol. I: From the Earliest Times to the Coming of the Normans.* University of Wales Press.

Davies, John. 1993. *A History of Wales.* Penguin.

Fred Suppe

Cernunnos

Cernunnos, 'the horned one', was an ancient deity depicted in art and inscriptions ranging from Romania to Ireland. Often considered a **Celtic** deity, his most well-known depiction is on the Gundestrup Cauldron, from southern Denmark, where he appears with antlers sitting cross-legged, wearing a torc and surrounded by animals. **Julius Caesar** equated Cernunnos with the Roman god Dis Pater. Stag figurines and antler amulets and headdresses found in **Iron Age** Britain may be related to him. Cernunnos has been interpreted by scholars as both the 'lord of beasts' (revered by hunters) and a fertility god. He is often depicted with serpents; a stone plaque from **Cirencester** shows him grasping two ram-horned snakes. There are depictions of monstrous individuals similar to Cernunnos in both medieval **Welsh** and Irish **literature**.

Further Reading

Bober, P. B. 1951. 'Cernunnos: Origin and Transformation of a Celtic Divinity'. *American Journal of Archaeology* 55.1: 13–51.

Green, Miranda. 1986. *The Gods of the Celts.* Alan Sutton.

MacKillop, James. 1998. *Oxford Dictionary of Celtic Mythology.* Oxford University Press.

Nussbaum, Alan J. 1986. *Head and Horn in Indo-European.* Walter de Gruyter.

Christopher A. Snyder

Chad (d.672)

St. Chad (Ceadda) was the first bishop of **Mercia** and Lindsey at Lichfield. He had three brothers, all of whom were active in the infant **Anglo-Saxon** church. His brothers are Cedd, Cenibal and Caelin. Cedd also became a bishop. Chad was a student of **St. Aidan** in **Northumbria** at **Lindisfarne** and spent some time of his early training in Ireland, where his closest associate was Egbert. In 664, King Oswiu of Northumbria chose **St. Wilfrid** as bishop of **York**, but Wilfrid delayed his return to France while travelling to Rome for consecration. In his place, Oswiu chose Chad and sent him to be consecrated by the archbishop of **Canterbury**, Deusdedit, rather than to Rome. Deusdedit died while Chad was travelling to Kent, and Chad was eventually consecrated by Wine, bishop of the West Saxons.

Chad was deposed by Theodore of Canterbury in 669 to restore Wilfrid. Chad retired then to Lastingham, where he was abbot, but was shortly thereafter installed by **Theodore** as bishop of Mercia and Lindsey. Here, he established monasteries, worked to fully evangelise the kingdom, built a cathedral on the site of the slaughter of Christians by the previously pagan Mercians and travelled his diocese on foot preaching and teaching laymen and monks alike. **Bede** tells us that Archbishop Theodore forced Chad into the saddle by physically putting him there to travel better. He died of plague on 2 March 672.

See also Celtic Christianity; Monasticism.

Further Reading

Bede. 1991. *The Ecclesiastical History of the English People*. Translated by Leo Shirley-Price. Penguin.

Larry Swain

Chester

The city of Chester, originally known as *Deva* from the river Dee on which it sits, has been an important site in north-west England since the arrival of the Romans in the first century AD. In AD 60, **Suetonius Paulinus** probably used Chester as a base for his attack on the Isle of Anglesey. The legionary fortress was under construction by AD 75 and the second legion was initially installed there. Covering an area of over 60 acres (24 hectares), the fortress was bigger than both **York** and **Caerleon**-on-Usk and contained a unique elliptical building near its centre, of a type unknown elsewhere in the Roman empire. Encircling the fortress was a substantial wall, and although refortified periodically, Roman masonry is still visible in several places. The amphitheatre was rediscovered in 1929 and Chester was also a thriving Roman port. The second legion left in AD 88 and was replaced by the twentieth legion. Between 120 and 210, the twentieth legion was busy building and manning the **Hadrian** and **Antoinine walls** and conducting campaigns in Scotland, leaving Chester thinly populated and parts of it became derelict. In the early third century, a period of reconstruction was undertaken and the archaeological finds from this period indicate a thriving fortress. Further reconstruction took place in the early fourth century, but by 350 the site was in decline and the final evidence of occupation are coin finds from the 390s.

Chester reappears in the historical record in 601 as the site of a synod of the British church and then again in 616 as the site of the important **Battle of Chester** between the forces of **Powys** and **Northumbria**. It next appears in 875 when the relics of St. Werburgh were brought there, and in 893, the ***Anglo-Saxon Chronicle*** reports that the Danes wintered at a deserted Roman site in the Wirral. The *Anglo-Saxon Chronicle* records the refortification of Chester in 907 by **Æthelflaed** and the walls were probably extended at this time to their present position, thereby doubling the size of the city. During her reign, Æthelflaed donated land near Chester to Ingimund, a Norse-Irish settler who subsequently tried to capture the city but failed. By the early tenth century, Chester also had a flourishing mint. King Edgar granted a charter to the church of St. Werburgh in 958, giving it various estates in the surrounding area and in 973 sailed up to Chester with a large fleet to receive homage from other kings who, as a sign of their submission, rowed him up the river Dee. Later accounts elaborate the number and identities of kings present, but it does seem to have been an event of some importance.

Chester was one of the last towns in England to fall to the **Normans** in 1070, and in 1071, Hugh of Avranches, nicknamed Hugh the Fat and nephew to William the Conqueror, was made the first earl of Chester. At this time, a castle was built overlooking the river on the site now occupied by the stone-built Chester Castle. The Anglo-Norman earls of Chester were some of the most powerful men in England, and by 1086, Hugh had expanded his frontier to include all of Flintshire and some of eastern Denbighshire in North Wales. Chester was often used as a staging post for the various campaigns against Wales until its final conquest in 1282. Chester became a cathedral city in 1075 when the bishop's seat of the diocese of Lichfield was moved to the church of St. John the Baptist; however, by 1095, it had moved to Coventry. The church of St. Werburgh was refounded in 1093 as a Benedictine Abbey by Hugh. The next earl was Hugh's son Richard, who was only seven years old, spent most of his life in France and was killed in the *White Ship* on his return in 1120. He was succeeded by Ranulf of Meschines, who was earl until his death in 1129, and then by his son **Ranulf II**, the most famous and ruthless of all the earls of Chester who played a major role during the anarchy of Stephen and helped capture the king at **Lincoln** in 1140. He died in 1153.

See also Romano-British Towns.

Further Reading

Husain, B. M. C. 1973. *Cheshire Under the Norman Earls 1066–1237*. Cheshire Community Council.

Mason, David. 2001. *Roman Chester: The City of Eagles*. Tempus.

———. 2007. *Chester AD 400–1066 from Roman Fortress to English Town*. Tempus.

Thornton, David E. 2001. 'Edgar and the Eight Kings, AD 973: Textus et Dramatis Personae'. *Early Medieval Europe* 10.1: 49–79.

Scott Lloyd

Chester, Battle of

The Battle of Chester in AD 616 is the earliest battle between the **Britons** and the **Northumbrians** that can be securely cited and dated. **Bede** (bk. II, ch. 2) is the earliest source of information and he tells us that **Æthelfrith**, the king of Northumbria '... collected a great army against the city of legions, which is called Legacaestir by the English and more correctly Caerlegion by the Britons, and made a great slaughter of that nation of heretics' (McClure and Collins 1994, 73). As the site is named in three different languages, the identification with Chester is not in doubt. Bede goes on to describe an assemblage of monks from the monastery of Bangor-is-y-Coed set apart in a safer place away from the main army and defended by the British ruler Brochmail. The monks were praying for the British forces, and Æthelfrith on being informed of their purpose stated, 'If they are praying to their God against us, then, even if they do not bear arms, they are fighting against us ...' (McClure and Collins 1994, 74). He ordered his first attack against the monks, who were easily slaughtered as Brochmail, and his men ran away, leaving the monks defenceless. Bede states that 1,200 monks were killed and only 50 escaped. He also relates how the victory for the English forces fulfilled the prophecy of **Augustine** that the Britons would suffer at the hands of their enemies for their failure to adopt the practices of the Roman Church. Although Bede is not specific about the exact date of the battle, the ***Irish Annals***, the ***Annales Cambriae*** and the ***Anglo-Saxon Chronicle*** place the battle variously between 605 and 616, with the latter date considered the most likely. The *Annales Cambriae* add that Selyf, son of Cynan, a ruler of **Powys**, also fell there. It is not known whether the Northumbrian victory was consolidated, as Chester is not mentioned again until the late ninth century.

The Roman site of Heronbridge, 1 mile (1.5 kilometres) south of Chester on the west bank of the river Dee, was first excavated in 1930, and a post-Roman cemetery containing approximately twenty skeletons was discovered. The skeletons were all male and displayed evidence of violent death in the form of blade-cuts to the skull and the lack of grave goods suggested a hurried burial. The battle cemetery was excavated again in 2004, and new skeletons were discovered and subjected to modern dating techniques. The skeletons dated from the period 530–660, making it highly likely that they belonged to the Battle of Chester. These recent finds make the Battle of Chester the best-attested battle from the Anglo-Saxon period, as nowhere else has a site been located so specifically and bodies dating from the correct period found.

See also Warfare and Weapons.

Further Reading

Chadwick, Nora K. 1963. 'The Battle of Chester: A Study of Sources'. Pp. 167–185 in *Celt and Saxon Studies in the Early British Border*. Edited by Kenneth Jackson et al. Cambridge University Press.

Mason, David. 2007. *Chester AD 400–1066 from Roman Fortress to English Town*. Tempus.

McClure, Judith, and Roger Collins. 1994. *Bede: The Ecclesiastical History of the English People*. Oxford University Press.

Scott Lloyd

Chichester

Chichester, Sussex, the Roman town of *Noviomagus*, was the regional capital of the *Regnenses*, a tribe ruled by the pro-Roman **Cogidubnus**. Mentioned in Ptolemy's *Geography*, the *Antonine Itinerary* and the *Ravenna Cosmography*, it was a military supply base in the opening years of the conquest. Around AD 47, when the Roman troops moved northwards, it became a town and was probably the centre of Cogidubnus's administration. In the second century, timber buildings were gradually replaced by stone ones and the settlement was enclosed by an earth rampart with stone gateways. In the third century, the earth defences were replaced in stone. Bastions to take catapults were added in the fourth century. At its greatest extent, it covered 99 acres (40 hectares).

Archaeological evidence for Roman Chichester includes indications that it possessed a large statue of Nero and a series of inscriptions, including a building inscription of AD 58. There is evidence to suggest that in the fifth century (after the Roman power had been relinquished in Britain), the **Britons** of Chichester continued to control a territory from which **Anglo-Saxon** settlers were excluded, though in due course it was absorbed into Anglo-Saxon territory. In the ninth century, Chichester was one of the **burhs** founded by **Alfred** the Great as part of his defence against the Danes, and it figures in the '**Burghal Hidage**', a document drawn up by Alfred's successor Edward the Elder, which lists the burhs and the number of men available, based on the extent of the town in terms of hides of land. The present name is an Anglo-Saxon one, the '-chester' element denoting a Roman site, with the 'Chich-' element probably being derived from a Saxon personal name. The Saxon town is first mentioned in the ***Anglo-Saxon Chronicle*** in an entry for AD 895. The cathedral is largely **Norman**, being consecrated in 1108, though it was extensively rebuilt.

See also Romano-British Towns.

Further Reading

Down, A. 1988. *Roman Chichester*. Phillimore.

Down, A., et al. 1978–1996. *Chichester Excavations*, vols. 1–6. Chichester District Council.

Woodward, S. (ed.). 1992. *Archaeology of Chichester and District: A Review of Fieldwork and Research*. Chichester District Council.

———. 1993. *Archaeology of Chichester and District: A Review of Fieldwork and Research*. Chichester District Council.

Jennifer Laing

Ciarán of Clonmacnois (c.512–c.544)

Ciarán (c. 512–c. 544) is traditionally regarded as one of the so-called Twelve Apostles of Ireland. According to legend, all twelve of them were trained in Clonard by St. Finnian, though the sources do not agree as to which saints are included in the twelve. Ciarán was responsible for the founding of the monastery of **Clonmacnois**, and the very great importance of this monastic foundation in the history of Ireland is reflected in the fame and reputation for holiness given to Ciarán.

Ciarán was reputed to have been born in **Connaught** between 510 and 520. One Irish and three Latin *Vitae* survive, and in the opinion of James Kenney, they would all seem to depend ultimately on an early text or collection of texts compiled at Clonmacnois (Kenney 1929). True to the genre of hagiography, they emphasise Ciarán's holiness by seeking to parallel events in his life with events in the life of Christ. Thus, they describe his father – to whom the name Beóit is given – as a carpenter, as well as a cartwright. His mother's name is given as Darerca, and the family is supposed to have fled from Antrim to escape persecution by the chieftain, though this could be another parallel with the infancy of Christ.

Ciarán is supposed to have travelled to Clonard at the age of fifteen, taking a cow with him to provide milk. According to legend, Finian regarded his pupil very highly and would have eventually resigned his abbacy in Ciarán's favour, but the latter refused. Ciarán went to the Aran Islands, where he made further monastic studies under Enda on Inís Mór and was ordained to the priesthood and then moved on again to Scattery Island in the mouth of the Shannon to visit the monastery founded by Senan. According to tradition, he founded other monasteries, one on Inis Aingin (Hare Island) in Lough Ree, where he stayed for three years. Leaving there with eight companions, he arrived on the banks of the Shannon, where he founded and erected the first buildings of what was eventually to become the great monastic complex of Clonmacnois.

Clonmacnois stood at an important cross roads; it was near the river Shannon, which was a major artery for travel and commerce, and close to one of the main roads of ancient Ireland. Thus, it was in one of the most strategically significant sites in the country. This was largely responsible for its great importance as a major monastic foundation for the next thousand years. Clonmacnois became a burial place for many of the kings of Ireland.

Ciarán died of plague very soon after founding the monastery, traditionally at the age of thirty-three, but whether this is historically accurate or another parallel with the life of Christ is not clear.

See also Celtic Christianity; Monasticism.

Further Reading

Kenney, James F. 1929. *The Sources for the Early History of Ireland: Ecclesiastical*. Columbia University Press.

Macalister, R. A. S. 1921. *The Latin and Irish Lives of Ciaran*. Society for Promoting Christian Knowledge.

Patricia Rumsey

Cirencester

Cirencester, a town in Gloucestershire on the river Churn at the point where it crossed with the Fosse Way, was a site first attested to by Ptolemy as the Roman town of *Corinium Dobunnorum*, with a history which continued into the medieval period. Associated with both the ***Cornovii*** and the ***Dobunni*** tribes and beginning as a fort in the mid-first century AD, the town continued to grow even after the military site was abandoned around AD 70. It showed considerable civic growth: public works included the construction of a forum, amphitheatre, basilica and substantial stone city walls, becoming the second largest town in Roman Britain by the early third century. Industries at Cirencester include a substantial centre for sculpture, tile and pottery manufacturing. One of the Roman city's best-known features is perhaps being the centre for the fourth-century Corinian school, whose floor mosaics of the fourth century included one of Orpheus, as well as others *in situ* at the nearby villas of Woodchester, Barton Farm and Chedworth. By the late Roman period, Corinium was the seat of the province of Britannia Prima, and it stands out as providing some of the earliest evidence for Christianity in Roman Britain: the Septimius Stone, which attests to Julian the Apostate's efforts to restore paganism in the 360s.

In the fifth or early sixth century, the amphitheatre in Cirencester had been further fortified, with the town continuing in occupation as a farming settlement of the **Britons**. It only finally fell to the Anglo-Saxons in the late sixth century after the battle of **Dyrham** in 576/577. This period saw a replacement of the earlier stone monuments by timber buildings, presumably due to a collapse in the stone industry, and in the ninth century, the ***Anglo-Saxon Chronicle*** records Danish occupation for the whole year of 878. Either in the late ninth century or in the early tenth century, a minster was established at Cirencester as a royal foundation, and after the **Norman Conquest**, the royal manor itself was granted to William Fitz-Osbern in the 1070s. Subsequently, the older church was demolished and the Augustinian Abbey was constructed. The abbey at Cirencester, which was completed and dedicated a century later by **Henry II**, along with the town's wool industry, allowed for the site to flourish in the Middle Ages, as it had in Roman times. Evidence also attests to a timber castle being constructed at Cirencester during King Stephen's reign in the 1140s, and by the thirteenth century, the town had a trading economy of international consequence.

See also Romano-British Towns.

Further Reading

Holbrook, Neil (ed.). 1998. *Cirencester: The Roman Town Defences, Public Buildings and Shops*. Cotswald Archaeological Trust.

McWhirr, Alan. 1981. *Roman Gloucestershire*. Alan Sutton.

Wacher, John. 1995. *The Towns of Roman Britain* (2nd rev. edn.). Batsford.

Wilkinson, D. J., and A. D. McWhirr (eds.). 1998. *Cirencester Anglo-Saxon Church and Medieval Abbey*. Cotswald Archaeological Trust.

Anne Sassin

Cist Burials

The custom of making interments in stone-lined boxes or cists is a practice that can be traced back to the **Bronze Age**. There are two main categories of such burials: short cists, which were of prehistoric date and long cists, which were predominantly of the early medieval period. In both types, slabs of stone are used to line the wall of a grave, normally with one or more slabs over the top and sometimes with an underlying slab or slabs.

In the later Roman period in Britain, extended, supine inhumation burial replaced cremation, and various types of burials are encountered. Burials in slab-lined graves are found in western Britain from the fourth century onwards, for example at Mary Major (**Exeter**, Devon), Brean Down or Lamyat Beacon (Somerset). Whether these burials were the inspiration for those to be found in the Celtic areas has been debated – a Continental origin has also been speculated – but in any event cist burials became very common in western and northern Britain and Ireland from the fifth century onwards. In Scotland, they are found in particular in the south-west and in the region round the Firth of Forth; they are very common in the **Isle of Man** and also occur in Wales and the south-west peninsula. The rite seems to have been taken to Ireland from Britain, perhaps as early as the fourth or fifth century. The skeletons are usually oriented east-west, with their arms at their sides, but occasionally may have their arms crossed at the pelvis. There is a group of slab-lined graves in Ireland dated to the fifth century with the hands crossed on the pubic area; they do not seem to have been wrapped in a winding sheet (which was the normal custom) and are found isolated, sometimes inserted in prehistoric burial mounds. Although normally only one body was laid in each grave, sometimes more than one body is found, and sometimes (in Ireland) additional skulls are also found. For the most part, long cist burials seem to belong to the fifth to seventh century, though later occurrences are known.

Related to cist graves are lintel graves, again of early medieval date. These have side slabs, but lack flooring stones, and are tapered, with slabs (lintels) laid across the burials. These are generally found later than other types of cist grave, starting in the seventh century and going on to a later period. Sometimes, the lintels are laid directly on the bodies, rather than on the side slabs.

Further Reading

Laing, Lloyd. 2006. *The Archaeology of Celtic Britain and Ireland, c. AD 400–1200.* Cambridge University Press.

O'Brien, Elizabeth. 1999. *Post-Roman Britain to Anglo-Saxon England: Burial Practices Reviewed.* British Archaeological Reports 289.

Thomas, Charles. 1971. *The Early Christian Archaeology of North Britain.* Oxford University Press.

Lloyd Laing

Cistercian Monasteries

One of the most successful reform movements in the long history of Christian **monasticism** was that led by the Cistercians in the twelfth century. The origins of the Cistercian order lie in the foundation of a reformed monastic house at Cîteaux near Dijon. In 1098, a group of monks from Molesme led by their abbot, Robert, settled there, intent on following a strict life of poverty in accordance with the rule of St. Benedict. From 1113, the ideas of the first Cistercians spread throughout Europe. The combination of founders who wished to establish houses following the way of life of the Cistercians (also known as White Monks) and recruits who wished to live it resulted in a wave of foundations. The first English Cistercian abbey was Waverley in Surrey (1128), established by William Giffard, bishop of Winchester, who drew the first monks from the monastery of L'Aumône in France. It was to L'Aumône also that Walter Fitz Richard de Clare went for a colony to begin a Cistercian monastery at Tintern, not many miles from his castle at Chepstow (1131). In the twenty years that followed, the 'white' monks spread rapidly all over Britain. In England, their most successful foundations were made on the moors and dales of the north, where abbeys such as Rievaulx (1132) and Fountains (1132) became dominant. Fountains abbey resulted from an acrimonious dispute about reform at the Benedictine abbey of St Mary's, York – ample testimony to the impact that the reforming ideals of the Cistercians had on the traditional monastic world.

A handful of English houses were founded from continental abbeys, in particular from St Bernard's abbey at Clairvaux, but most were the result of internal colonisation. Founders turned to English houses, notably Waverley, Rievaulx and Fountains, for monks to staff new houses, and their choice often reflected political and tenurial loyalties, for the Cistercians flourished amid the uncertainties and regional disorder experienced in the reign of King **Stephen** (r.1135–1154). It was to Rievaulx that the Scottish king **David I** turned in 1136 and again in 1142 for monks to establish first Melrose Abbey and then Dundrennan. These two houses became the mainstay of Cistercian expansion north of the border. When the Cistercian general chapter, the annual meeting of all abbots of the order, decided in 1152 to forbid further foundations, the main expansion in England was over.
In other parts of Britain and Ireland, it was a different story. In Wales, a turning point for the white monks was the political ascendancy of Rhys ap Gruffydd, who in 1165 took over the patronage of two existing Cistercian abbeys, Whitland and Strata Florida. Thereafter, the white monks secured the support of the Welsh princes of **Deheubarth**, **Powys** and **Gwynedd** and flourished under their patronage, although

their close association often made them objects of suspicion among English settlers in Wales and to the English crown. In Ireland, the premier foundation was Mellifont, founded from Clairvaux in 1142 by Donough O'Carroll, king of Oriel. Mellifont spawned a large number of daughter houses, starting with Bective in 1147 and ending with Hore in 1272, and spread into the third and fourth generations. Many Irish foundations were made by the Irish kings, but some were made by Anglo-Norman knights in the wake of the invasion of Ireland in 1169–1170. The foundation of thirty-three Cistercian houses in Ireland was a remarkable success, even by the standards of the order.

The success and impact of the Cistercians were remarkable. It was the first cohesive monastic order held together by administrative mechanisms as well as common observances. Thus, the abbot of a mother house was obliged to visit each of his daughter houses once a year to ensure uniformity in all manners. Once a year, all abbots took to the road to attend the general chapter at Cîteaux; originally intended as a means to uphold the bonds of charity that underpinned the order, the chapter became its legislative and disciplinary body. Cistercian monasteries were aware of being part of a monastic world that transcended political boundaries, even if the maintenance of links became strained under political pressures.

The Cistercians were characterised by their strict observances. Their desire for 'desert places' led them to remote sites, although critics such as Walter Map accused them of depopulating lands to create their own 'desert'. Their wish to develop an economic base that was not dependent on the work of others led them to reject manorial revenues and to create a distinctive pastoral economy based around granges, or outlying farms, staffed by *conversi* or lay brothers. The Cistercians became successful agricultural entrepreneurs, in particular in relation to sheep farming and the wool trade. Above all, the Cistercians are known for the austerity of their architecture, and the order is famed for the imposing style of the surviving remains of its buildings.

See also Celtic Christianity.

Further Reading

Burton, Janet. 1994. *Monastic and Religious Orders in Britain 1000–1300.* Cambridge University Press.

Kinder, Terryl. 2002. *Cistercian Europe: Architecture of Contemplation.* Eerdmans and Cistercian Publications.

Knowles, D. 1963. *The Monastic Order in England.* Cambridge University Press.

Stalley, R. 1987. *The Cistercian Monasteries of Ireland.* Yale University Press.

Janet Burton

Claudius (r. AD 51–54)

The Roman emperor Claudius (AD 51–54) was the son of Nero Claudius Drusus (brother of the Emperor Tiberius) and Antonia, the daughter of Mark Antony. As a child, he contracted infantile paralysis, which left him with a limp and a stammer. As a result, he was kept out of public life and devoted himself to antiquarian pursuits. In AD 41, his predecessor, the unpopular Caligula, was murdered by some of his own bodyguards (the Praetorian Guard). After much violence and confusion, Claudius was proclaimed and accepted as emperor since, despite his lack of experience in public life, he was a member of the Julio-Claudian dynasty. He carried out his new role competently. His achievements included the conquest of Britain in AD 43, which he celebrated in the new province, at **Colchester**. Having been married to Messalina (whose scandalous lifestyle led to her execution), in AD 49 Claudius married his niece, Agrippina, and adopted her son, Nero, as his heir. He died in AD 54, probably poisoned on the orders of his wife. He was succeeded by Nero, who became one of the most notorious emperors.

See also Roman Army; Roman Britain.

Further Reading

Levick, B. 2001. *Claudius* (rev. edn.). Routledge.

Scullard, H. H. 1992. *From the Gracchi to Nero, a History of Rome from 133 BC to AD 68* (5th edn.). Routledge.

Jennifer Laing

Clickhimin

The site of Clickhimin lies on a loch just outside Lerwick, Shetland. Originally on an island, it was approached from the mainland by a causeway. Occupation commenced in the Late **Bronze Age** with the construction of an oval house, which was long-lasting. Somewhat later, a ditch was dug across the peninsula on which it stood and a stone-walled fort was constructed, with wooden lean-to ranges round the inside. A two-storey blockhouse was next built around 100 BC, which had intramural chambers accessed from the first floor. These chambers, usually seen as guardrooms (as, for example, at the Ness of Burgi), may in this case have served as prison cells or for storage. The ground floor provided storage, and the first floor was residential. A stone external staircase provided access to the first floor.

The back of the blockhouse was furnished with an internal timber range butting against it. The entrance passageway of the blockhouse has a door-check halfway along it (a common feature of Atlantic **Iron Age** stone buildings), the passage extending to over 13 feet (4 metres). The blockhouse still stands to a height of over 10 feet (3 metres). Inside the fort were various structures. The stone fort was then extended, leaving the blockhouse free-standing. A flood in the second or first century BC created an island of the peninsula, and the ring wall was buttressed, and many of the timber buildings butted against it were demolished. The next stage in the development of the site was the construction of a developed round house (**broch**), which still survives to an impressive height. This somewhat unusually had several entrances and timber internal structures butted against the inner wall. It was associated with external buildings. It was replaced by a stone wheelhouse constructed inside it and other round houses on the outside. These continued in use into the seventh or eighth century. A pair of stone footprints, not dissimilar to that at **Dunadd**, may have been used in the early medieval period for inaugurations.

Further Reading

Hamilton, J. R. C. 1962. 'Brochs and Broch-Builders'. Pp. 72–88 in *The Northern Isles*. Edited by F. T. Wainwright. Nelson.

———. 1968. *Excavations at Clickhimin, Shetland*. Her Majesty's Stationery Office.

———. 1970. *The Brochs of Mousa & Clickhimin*. Her Majesty's Stationery Office.

Turner, V. 1998. *Ancient Shetland*. Batsford & Historic Scotland.

Lloyd Laing

Clonfert

Clonfert, in County Galway, is a church site dating back to the sixth century and the principal cult site of St. **Brendan** 'the Navigator' (feast day 16 May). The extant cathedral, dating from the twelfth century, is notable for its outstanding Romanesque portico.

According to the main collections of *Irish Annals*, Clonfert was founded by St. Brendan in the year 558, though this entry may not be contemporary. The AD 570 *obit* of Maenu 'bishop of Clonfert', five years prior to Brendan's own death in 575, if reliable, would indicate that the monastery was an episcopal seat more or less from the outset. Cuimmíne Fota (d. 662) was the most notable amongst subsequent bishops; he was probably the author of the paschal letter to **Ségéne** of **Iona** in c. AD 633 and one of the most significant of the Irish **penitentials**: *Paenitentiale Cummeani*. He later became the subject of a relic cult at Clonfert and a figure of legends.

The monastery of Clonfert was possibly the place of authorship of the ninth-century Latin tale ***Navigatio Sancti Brendani Abbatis***, as it is featured at the outset of the story under the Latin name *Saltus Virtutum*, a calque of *clúain fearta* ('meadow of miracles'). The *Navigatio*'s reference is confirmation that Brendan's cult centred upon Clonfert in the ninth century. The annals consistently acknowledge the residence of Brendan's *comarbai* at Clonfert, except for a brief period after 1068 when, according to the *Annals of Inisfallen*, Clonfert was abandoned and its leadership withdrew to **Munster** – most probably to Ardfert (County Kerry).

Nothing remains of early medieval Clonfert. The extant cathedral appears to have been built in the late twelfth century. Its most notable feature is the doorway in the West Front, built c. 1180. The doorway has distinctive sloping jambs and is topped by a pediment of human heads, carved in relief with further heads in blind arches underneath. Irish interlace and organic motifs decorate the six decorated orders of the arch. The Synod of Ráth Bressail (1111) made Clonfert one of the medieval dioceses of Ireland. In the twelfth century, a college of Augustinian Canons was founded at Clonfert, which became famous as a centre for education.

See also Celtic Christianity; Monasticism.

Further Reading

Higgins, J., and C. Cunniffe (eds.). 2007. *Navigatio: A Voyage of Research in Search of Clonfert*. Crowsrock Press.

O'Keefe, T. 1994. 'The Romanesque Portal at Clonfert and its Iconography'. Pp. 261–269 in *From the Isles of the North*. Edited by C. Bourke. HMSO.

Jonathan Wooding

Clonmacnois

Clonmacnois, County Offaly, is one of the most important early Christian monasteries in Ireland. Founded on the river Shannon by St. Ciaran around the mid-sixth century, it was already a major player in monastic affairs by the seventh century, claiming as its own many churches that some contemporaries felt were founded by St. **Patrick**. In 764, the monasteries at **Durrow** and Clonmacnois came to blows, Durrow being defeated. In 842, Clonmacnois was the victim of a **Viking** raid, and another followed in 845 when the churches (which were timber) were burned. Chronicles were kept at Clonmacnois from at least the eighth century; the *Annals of Tigernach* were compiled here, as well as a number of secular texts such as the *Book of the Dun Cow*, which contains the earliest version we have of stories of the **Ulster Cycle**. In the tenth century, Clonmacnois benefitted from the royal patronage of King Flann. There is an almost complete list of abbots down to the twelfth century. Clonmacnois continued to thrive into the twelfth century, but from the thirteenth century it went into decline. The English garrison at Athlone plundered it in 1552.

Clonmacnois has a number of major sculptures, notably the Cross of the Scriptures (erected around AD 909), the South Cross (probably mid-ninth century) and the fragmentary North Cross. The site also has the largest collection of cross-slabs in Ireland – over 600 – which range in date from the early eighth century to the twelfth century. There is also an early Ogam stone. The visible remains at Clonmacnois include the cathedral, built originally in 909, and a **round tower**, erected in the twelfth century. Since the 1980s, a very important series of excavations has been carried out at Clonmacnois, which has produced much information about early industrial activity including ironworking and the production of ornamental metalwork, and an underwater project has revealed the remains of a wooden bridge, dated by dendrochronology to 804.

See also Celtic Christianity; Monasticism.

Further Reading

King, H. (ed.). 2000. *Clonmacnois Papers, II.* Department of Environment, Heritage and Local Government, Dublin.

Manning, C. 1998. *Clonmacnois, Co Offaly* (2nd edn.). Deptartment of Environment, Heritage and Local Government, Dublin.

Lloyd Laing

Clontarf, Battle of

Battle of Clontarf was fought on Good Friday, 23 April 1014, just outside **Dublin**. The events of the battle are recorded in the Irish *Cogad Gáedel re Gallaib* as well as the Icelandic *Njal's Saga*. A general insurrection of the northern Irish kingdoms as well as Dublin and **Leinster** began in 1012. The Irish high king, **Brian Bóruma**, responded in 1013 by ravaging Leinster and attempting a siege of the Viking town of **Dublin**. The initial siege failed, but the high king mustered his forces the following spring for a renewed attempt.

Brian Boru faced the combined force of the Irish kingdom of Leinster and the Vikings of Dublin under Sitric Silkenbeard and externally recruited allies led by Sigurd the Stout, earl of Orkney. Máel Sechnaill, king of **Meath** and ally of Brian, withdrew from the field prior to the start of the battle, leaving Brian with only the men of **Munster** and southern Connacht. The intense fighting carried across the field of battle to the weirs of Clontarf. High tide floated the Viking fleet into the Bay of Dublin, stranding the Dublin–Leinster forces that had been driven from the field and were attempting to escape. A short-lived rally under Earl Sigurd prolonged the conflict. Fighting was hand-to-hand and desperately personal.

At the advanced age of seventy-two, Brian had remained near his tent giving tactical command to his son Murchad. A Viking warrior named Brodar, fleeing the field came upon King Brian, killing him. Casualties on both sides were heavy, probably numbering in the thousands. The names of twenty-six nobles are recorded as dead. The dead included the Irish high king Brian Bóruma, his son and heir Murchad, his grandson Tadc, as well as Máel Morda, king of Leinster and Sigurd, earl of Orkney. King Sitric of Dublin survived the battle.

History credits Brian with driving the Vikings from Ireland at the Battle of Clontarf. Current scholarship has discredited this assertion, although it continues in popular conception. The Vikings had been reduced to pawns in Irish politics long before Clontarf. Brian's forces failed to take Dublin and the survival of Sitric and the town long outlasted Brian. The most significant result of the battle was that Brian and his top field commander were killed and his forces suffered serious losses. The military power upon which he had risen to the high kingship was broken at

Clontarf. Brian's son Donnchad took command of the bloodied forces of the south and fought his way back to his centre at Kincora, facing resistance from previously subordinate kingdoms immediately. The position of Brian's descendants was significantly weakened, with Donnchad reduced to a regional power as he attempted to re-establish his authority.

See also Warfare and Weapons.

Further Reading

Ó Corráin, Donnchadh. 'Brian Boru and the Battle of Clontarf'. Pp. 31–40 in *Milestones in Irish History*. Edited by Liam De Paor. Mercier Press.

Ryan, John. 1938. 'The Battle of Clontarf'. *The Journal of the Royal Society of Antiquaries of Ireland* 68: 1–50.

David Beougher

Cluniac Monasteries

The Benedictine abbey of Cluny in Burgundy had a decisive impact on the development of monastic life. First, it elaborated the performance of the *Opus Dei*, the 'Work of God', that is the liturgy. The Rule of St. Benedict, the basis of monastic life in the medieval west, established the seven daily services which, along with the night office, formed the backbone of the monastic timetable around which were fitted periods of work and sacred reading. At Cluny, the number of services was increased by the addition of masses for the dead, and the liturgy was lengthened, enriched by music and performed in increasingly elaborate architectural settings. Critics of Cluny remarked that the emphasis on the liturgy squeezed out the two other activities laid down by Benedict, in particular, manual labour. Second, for the first time in the history of western **monasticism**, Cluny developed around itself a monastic congregation or family. Such was Cluny's fame that a number of existing Benedictine houses adopted its customs, though without compromising their independence and status as abbeys. In other instances, monastic houses were founded *de novo* as Cluniac houses: from their very inception, they were intended not only to follow Cluniac customs but also to be dependent on the mother house of Cluny. Although some new abbeys, especially ones with high status founders such as Reading Abbey in England and the abbey of May in Scotland, retained their autonomy, the majority of new houses were established as dependencies of Cluny or of major associated abbeys of the Burgundian house. Their dependent status was denoted by their designation as priories.

The first Cluniac foundation in England was Lewes Priory in Sussex (1077). The sources for the foundation were not free from difficulties, but it seems clear that William de Warenne, a Norman noble, was determined to found a religious house on the lands he had acquired as a result of the **Norman Conquest** of England. It was while he was staying at Cluny that he and his wife decided that the new house should be a Cluniac one. It was with some reluctance that Abbot Hugh of Cluny was persuaded to send monks overseas to make the foundation, having refused a similar request by **William I** of England. Lewes was the first and foremost Cluniac house in England and itself made foundations at Thetford and Castle Acre. The main springboard in English expansion, however, came from the French abbey of La Charité rather than Cluny or Lewes. Between 1079 and 1100, five significant Cluniac foundations were made from La Charité: Much Wenlock in Shropshire, where an Anglo-Saxon cult centre was revived, Bermondsey, Daventry, Pontefract and Northampton. With the exception of Alwin Child, the Anglo-Saxon founder of Bermondsey, all the founders were major Norman nobles, and Brian Golding has argued that Cluny had a particular appeal to the Norman newcomers in England, in that it allowed them to make foundations on English soil that had neither English nor Norman associations; they may have been more acceptable to the **Anglo-Saxons** because they did not have connections with the duchy.

The last twenty years of the eleventh century marked the high point of expansion. The congregation of Cluny in England and in Wales (where there was only one priory, that of St Clears) was never large. In Scotland, there were three houses, Paisley, Renfrew and Crossraguel, and in Ireland, there was only one, Athlone. The question that arises is how far the British houses were distinctive, or perceived to be different, from other houses, notably the Benedictine monks. In the late twelfth century, Gerald of Wales appears to have used the term *monachi nigri*, or black monks, to denote both Benedictine and Cluniac indiscriminately. Links between local houses and the mother house of Cluny are more likely to have been formal rather than close. Certainly, the mother house demanded the payment of the yearly tax in recognition of its status and maintained that the abbot of Cluny should appoint the prior of his dependencies. This led, on more than one occasion, to disputes, well documented in the thirteenth century, between the mother house and the local patron – for instance, the dispute between the abbot of Cluny and the earls of Warenne as patrons of Lewes – over the right of appointment of the prior. The argument of the abbot of Cluny was that the prior of Lewes was his deputy, or second in command, while Warenne claimed the traditional right of a monastic patron to oversee an election. There was, however, no formal machinery of control such as that found in the Cistercian order, and it was not until 1231 that Pope Gregory IX introduced into the Cluniac order visitation and a general chapter along Cistercian lines.

Further Reading

Burton, Janet. 2002. 'The Monastic World'. Pp.121–136 in *England and Europe in the Reign of Henry III*. Edited by B. K. U. Weiler and I. W. Rowlands. Ashgate.

Golding, Brian. 1980. 'The Coming of the Cluniacs'. *Anglo-Norman Studies* 3: 65–77.

Knowles, David. 1963. *The Monastic Order in England 940–1216* (2nd edn.). Cambridge University Press.

Wood, Susan. 1955. *English Monasteries and Their Patrons in the Thirteenth Century*. Oxford University Press.

Janet Burton

Cnut (r. 1016–1035)

Cnut, sometimes Cnut the Great, a son of the Danish king **Svein Forkbeard**, led an invasion of England and reigned as king there from 1016 to his death in 1035. During this period, he continued to extend his power in Scandinavia, receiving the throne of Denmark c. 1019 and seizing power over Norway in 1028. In addition, he repelled an invasion of Danish territory by Swedish forces, but it is doubtful if he ever held authority over that region.

Around 995–1000, Cnut was born, probably as the second son of King Svein Forkbeard of Denmark. His father led an invasion of England in 1013–1014, but died after only a few months in power, forcing Cnut to flee back to Denmark. There, his brother Harald had remained in control, and according to the principal narrative source for this period, the *Encomium Emmae Reginae*, Cnut lived under his brother's rule and prepared for a re-invasion of England. This was launched in 1015, and the English forces were fought to a standstill by 1016. However, there was no decisive victory and England was initially divided between Cnut and Edmund Ironside, the son of **Æthelred the Unready**. Edmund died shortly afterwards and Cnut seized complete control. Cnut married his predecessor's wife, Emma (also known by the English name Ælfgifu, in some sources), in 1017. However, he had already married (in some informal fashion) another English woman, known as Ælfgifu of Northampton, probably during his father's invasion in 1013–1014.

The stability of Cnut's early years in England relied on the combined authority of Englishmen who were too powerful to be removed and the military might of Cnut's own overly powerful Scandinavian allies, but after 1021 all of them had been executed or expelled. The royal followers selected to fill their places became Cnut's 'new men', an Anglo-Scandinavian social group who remained a significant force in English politics until the **Norman Conquest**.

Around 1019, Cnut's brother died, and Cnut sailed to Denmark to accept rule there. He began to consolidate his dynastic hold on this region (often using English administrative models and personnel for this task) and had to defend his interests there in battle in 1026 against a joint Swedish-Norwegian invasion. Immediately after this, Cnut travelled to Rome, where he played a significant role in the coronation of the new emperor, Conrad II. The grandeur of this visit and his negotiations with the emperor and the pope over such matters as tariffs for English merchants in Rome sealed his reputation as a formidable international statesman.

In 1028, Cnut led an invasion fleet into Norway. By a mixture of bribery and force, he inveigled himself into Norwegian politics and succeeded in causing the reigning king to flee. Under the regency of a Norwegian supporter and then a son by his first wife, Cnut held power there until 1034, when a rebellion of the Norwegian nobility caused his representatives to flee. Cnut's final years in England were remembered as peaceful and prosperous ones, and numerous records survive of his lavish patronage of religious houses and institutions. He died at Shaftesbury on 12 November 1035 and was buried in the Old Minster, Winchester.

See also Vikings; Warfare and Weapons.

Further Reading

Lawson, M. K. 1993. *Cnut: The Danes in England in the Early Eleventh Century*. Longman. (Reissued in

2004 with minor revisions under the title *Cnut: England's Viking King* [Tempus].)
Rumble, A. 1994. *The Reign of Cnut. King of England, Denmark and Norway*. Leicester University Press.

Timothy Bolton

Coel Hen

Coel Hen is the shadowy historical figure behind the nursery rhyme figure Old King Cole. Coel the Old (Welsh *Hen*) appears at the head of six of the thirty-three pedigrees of Welsh rulers found interpolated into the text of ***Historia Brittonum*** found in Harley manuscript 3859, a copy of a tenth-century version of the text made c.1100. In a number of these pedigrees, individuals can be identified who are known from other sources, including **Urien Rheged** and Dunod, son of Pabo, who seem to have lived in the decades around 600. From the appearance of such names among the descendants of Coel, it seems clear that, as a group, these families ruled in what is now northern England immediately prior to the **Anglo-Saxon** conquest. Whether they represent a single dynasty in which the kingship circulated between branches or several related dynasties ruling neighbouring kingdoms is open to speculation. Coel appears five generations before Urien and Dunod and thus, if truly historical, probably lived in the early to mid-fifth century.

The Welsh traditions tell us nothing of Coel's career beyond his place in the pedigrees, but this has not prevented modern scholars from speculating. Because his lifetime would seem to have coincided with the ending of Roman rule in Britain, and because most of the ruling families of what is now northern England claimed him as their ancestor, Coel Hen has been seen as the last holder of the office of *Dux Britanniae*, the Roman military command of the northern frontier. This interpretation is based upon the idea that the several *Coeling* kingdoms represent a fragmentation of a single unified territory. It is just as likely, however, that the dynasty expanded from a more local base and that different branches gradually took over neighbouring territories in much the same way as the dynasty descended from **Rhodri Mawr** gradually took control of most of Wales. Coel's name may be derived from the Roman name Caelius, although it is also a Welsh common noun meaning 'belief', 'trust' or 'omen'.

Later Welsh legend made Coel the maternal grandfather of Cunedda, the founder of the first dynasty of **Gwynedd**, through a daughter named Gwawl ('Wall'). His own wife was said to be the niece or granddaughter of Cynan, also known as Conan Meriadoc, the legendary leader of the migration of **Britons** to Brittany. **Geoffrey of Monmouth** borrowed Coel's name for two fictional kings of Roman Britain, one of whom gave his name, he claimed, to **Colchester**.

See also Welsh People.

Further Reading

Bartrum, P. C. 1966. *Early Welsh Genealogical Tracts*. University of Wales Press.
Bromwich, Rachel. 2006. *Trioedd Ynys Prydein: The Triads of the Island of Britain* (3rd edn.). University of Wales Press.

Alex Woolf

Cogidubnus

Cogidubnus (now more accurately called Togidubnus) was a British chieftain of the mid-first century AD who was pro-Roman and was allowed by Rome to control a territory in southern Britain. Almost nothing is known about him, apart from a reference in Tacitus's *Agricola* (14.1) to a Cogidumnus believed to be the same person:

> Certain states [in Britain] were handed over to king Cogidumnus, who has remained continuously loyal to our own times [i.e. the late first century] according to the old and well-established principle of Roman policy, which employs kings as agents of enslavement.

This reference is supported by an inscription found at **Chichester**, from a temple of Neptune and Minerva, which refers to 'Tiberius Claudius Cogidubnus, Great King of Britain'. Clearly, he thought it politic to take on the names of the current and previous emperors of Rome (if these were not bestowed on him by the Romans), and this must have happened before AD 54 when Claudius died and was succeeded by Nero.

One other clue about him is provided by coinage. An extremely rare silver unit bears the inscription CRAB, which has been read (not necessarily correctly) as *Cogidubnus Rex Atrebatum Britanniorum* ('Cogidubnus, king of the Atrebates of Britain'). The coins might suggest that Cogidubnus was the successor of

Verica of the ***Atrebates***. The area around Chichester seems to have been that of the tribe known as the ***Belgae***, presumably an offshoot of the tribe of the same name in Gaul, but after the conquest, the tribe changed its name to *Regnenses*, presumably after its king (*rex* in Latin). Cogidubnus must have ruled over at least the *Atrebates* and Regneses, if not other southern tribes. It has been suggested by its excavator that the Roman palace at Fishbourne, on Chichester harbour, was his palace. This is a possibility, though other owners for the palace have also been proposed.

See also Britons; Celts; Roman Britain.

Further Reading

Barrett, Anthony A. 1979. 'The Career of Tiberius Claudius Cogidubnus'. *Britannia* 10: 227–242.
Bogaers, J. E. 1979. 'King Cogidubnus of Chichester: Another Reading of RIB 91'. *Britannia* 10: 243–254.
Cunliffe, Barry. 1999. *Fishbourne Roman Palace*. Tempus.
Henig, Martin. 1998. 'Togidubnus and the Roman Liberation'. *British Archaeology* 37 (September).
Margary, I. D. 1971. 'The Fishbourne Story'. *Britannia* 2: 117–121.

Lloyd Laing

Coinage and Trade

Prehistoric Trade

Although it is probable that there was some trading going on in very early prehistory in Britain, it is not until the **Neolithic** Period that there is any real evidence for it. When considering prehistoric trade, it is important to realise that it was probably not a simple matter of barter, but was tied up with all sorts of social and even religious dimensions, most of which are difficult to discern. The earliest imports in Neolithic Britain appear to have been stone axes, the finest of which were made from jadeite imported from Switzerland or the Alps. They have been found as far afield as Scotland, **Wessex** and East Anglia, and one was found deposited under the Sweet Track, a roadway in Somerset. Clearly, such objects had ritual importance, and axes seem to have been tied up with religion through much of prehistory. In Neolithic Britain and Ireland, there is also evidence for the large-scale exploitation of suitable stone at axe factories, where roughouts were made and subsequently traded, to be finished off at their final destinations. Axes from the factory at Tievebulliagh in County Anmtrim were traded in Britain as well as Ireland, while products of the Great Langdale, **Cumbria**, and Graig Llwyd, Clwyd, factories were traded very widely in Britain. Flint was also exploited in mines, such as those at Grimes Graves, Norfolk or Cissbury in Sussex, and the products again were traded widely. Pottery too seems to have enjoyed a measure of trade – some pottery found at **Windmill Hill** in Wiltshire came from the south-west peninsula. At the end of the third millennium BC, stone axes were traded to Britain from the Baltic, from which source also came amber.

The development of metal technology at the end of the Neolithic Period by the **Beaker people** led to new requirements – metal ores. Copper knives from **Dorchester**, Dorset, and Roundway, Wiltshire, have been shown to be made of copper from central Europe, while a copper knife from Wiltshire was made of metal from Ireland. Jadeite axes were still imported; however, gold necklets known as *lunulae* were traded to the Continent.

In the Early **Bronze Age**, associated with the building of the final stage of **Stonehenge**, a rich culture flourished in Wessex. This society largely prospered though pastoralism, but an adjunct of the display of prestige was a trade network that stretched across to the Continent and north and west to Scotland and Ireland. The trade brought metalwork from central Europe, and the same area may have been the intermediary for the trade in Baltic amber and possibly also with the Mycenaean civilisation of Greece. Among the finds from Wessex are gold-bound amber discs that can be matched at Knossos in Crete, and bone mounts from a burial at Bush Barrow, Wilts, can be matched to one of the graves at Mycenae. Faience beads, made with glass frit, of types common in the east Mediterranean, including Egypt, have been found in Britain dating to this time.

About 1450 BC, metalworking in Britain seemed to parallel developments on the Continent, and there is evidence for a two-way trade – axes, twisted gold necklets and sheet metal were traded to the Continent, while composite tools and bar-twisted ornaments were imported from France. These European links continued through the later part of the Bronze Age. Sheet bronze metalworking technology spread from the east Mediterranean to north-west Europe, and there seems to have been a common trade network, with a route that stretched down the Atlantic coast, incorporating Iberia, Britain and France. Within this zone, there seems to have been a kind of currency – small bronze socketed axes, which were too soft for use but which turn up in large hoards. New types of sword and bronze cauldrons also form part of the extensive trade network of the Late Bronze Age.

The Early **Iron Age** saw a continuing pattern of external trade. In the seventh century BC, some bronze swords were imported from the Continent, and copied in Britain and Ireland, to be followed by a variety of other objects. These included iron objects, which were soon copied in Britain. A slight lull in overseas trade followed, from the sixth to fifth century BC, but trade picked up again thereafter. The overseas trade seems to have followed a pattern of trade routes linking Britain, Ireland and France, which had originated in all probability much earlier. By the first century BC, four routes (at least) were being followed. Travellers from Ireland went from **Wexford** past the Scillies to Brittany. Trade with the Mediterranean followed a route round the Gibraltar and up the Atlantic seaboard or by river via the Seine-Rhone, Loire-Rhone or Garonne-Aude. Other trade routes operated across the Channel. Classical writers refer to Tartessians (from Spain) and Carthaginians (from North Africa) trading with south-west Britain, and the likeliest export from this region was Cornish tin. Although a few may have been modern losses, there are a large number of Greek coin finds from Britain, especially from round the Isle of Wight (a likely embarkation point for the tin) and, perhaps slightly more surprisingly, from Kent. An important trading base was **Hengistbury Head** in Dorset, where Mediterranean wine amphorae, Breton pottery, figs and lumps of glass arrived, and from whence probably Kimmeridge shale, iron, salt, gold, copper, tin, lead and possibly grain were exported. Not all Iron Age trade was external, however, and there is evidence for a trade in pottery which took decorated vessels from **Cornwall** as far afield as Somerset. In the early first century AD, there was a vigorous trade between south-east England and Belgic Gaul, which saw Roman goods as well as Gallo-Roman pottery pouring into the country.

Iron Age Coinage

Coins were first used in Britain in the pre-Roman Iron Age, having been employed in the Greek world from the seventh century BC. The continental **Celts** seem to have begun by copying Greek coins struck by Philip II of Macedon and his son Alexander the Great in the fourth century BC, and such copies of gold staters of Philip of Macedon provided the models for the earliest coins found and struck in Britain. These had a debased version of the head of Apollo on the obverse and the remnants of a chariot (usually reduced to a horse and wheel) on the reverse.

The first Celtic coins to be used in Britain were imported gold issues struck in Belgic Gaul from the mid-second century BC – they are known as the Gallo-Belgic series – and probably reflect Britain's political ties with the Continent. The most influential of these coins was the Gallo-Belgic C, which, though comparatively rare as an import, inspired the first series of the British copies. Gallo-Belgic E, which followed it, was struck around 60–50 BC and was issued in considerable quantities; it has been surmised to facilitate war payments in the campaigns against **Julius Caesar** in Gaul.

From the end of the second century BC, a series of crudely designed cast potin (bronze with a high tin content) coins circulated in **Kent**, imitating the bronze coins of Massalia (Marseilles), with the head of Apollo on the obverse and a butting bull on the reverse. The earliest of these coins were the 'Thurrock' bronzes, named after a hoard found in Essex, which were succeeded by flatter, cruder issues, which continued until around the mid-first century BC.

The imported Gallo-Belgic gold coins gave rise in Britain to a series of uninscribed gold coins from around 70 BC. Usually these coins, and their successors, have been ascribed to tribes, but it is far from certain whether their issue and use were confined to the later tribal areas. After the campaigns of Julius Caesar in the south of the Thames, there arose a number of different coinages, including some bronze pieces struck round **Chichester**, Sussex. Inscribed coins make their appearance in this area, the earliest bearing the name of Commius–from Commius Attrebas, long believed to have been Caesar's opponent and sometimes ally. It is now thought that these coins belong to a later period and were struck by Commius's son, with the same dynastic name. From this time onwards, a variety of coins were issued bearing names, with some, such as Verica, being identified with historical parsonages.

In the years immediately preceding the Roman conquest under Claudius, coins were struck in south-east England that were very Roman in style and in some cases copied

Roman types – some may even have been made by craftsmen trained in Roman workshops. The most noteworthy series are those issued by Tasciovanus of the ***Catuvellauni/ Trinovantes*** in Herts and Essex and **Cunobelinus** of the *Trinovantes*.

Romano-British Trade

Trade greatly increased in the Romano-British period. One reason for the conquest was the perceived resources of Britain, and the exploitation of metal resources, which was under the control of the state, was put in hand within a few years of the Conquest. Mendip lead was transported from Southampton Water from at least as early as AD 49 (the date on some lead pigs). Subsequently, lead mines were established in Clwyd, Derbyshire and Yorkshire. Silver was obtained by cupellation from lead, and gold mines were exploited at Dolaucothi in South Wales.

The volume of imports that were part of a luxury trade was already considerable by the late first century AD. It included metalwork, art, pottery and glass. Lamps were imported from Gaul, Italy and Africa. Pottery included samian ware from Gaul, jars from the Eiffel-Rhine and slipped beakers from the Rhineland. A table leg from Paros in Greece found in **Colchester** suggests that furniture was imported. Metalware included fine silverware, represented in late Roman hoards such as those from **Mildenhall** and **Hoxne** in Suffolk. Textiles were imported from the Mediterranean; decorative glass was imported from Germany. On a more mundane level, hand-mills were imported from the Andernach region of Germany. Inscriptions suggest that perishable commodities were traded, such as salt (which was probably sent from Britain to Gaul), wine and fish sauce. Other exports from Britain included pottery and the famous *byrrus Britannicus*, a type of woollen duffel coat, which along with the *tapete Britannicum*, a type of woollen rug, is mentioned in Diocletian's 'Maximum Price Edict' in the early fourth century. The same edict lists British beer, priced at twice the Egyptian one. The wine trade enjoyed fluctuating fortunes: before AD 43, the source had been mainly Italy, but after the Conquest, much seems to have come from Spain. In the second century, this trade diminished, and German and French wine were imported instead.

Inscriptions mention the traders – a Salmanes from Syria is named in an inscription from the **Antonine Wall** in Scotland. Inscriptions also relate to traders from Gaul who operated in **York** and **Lincoln**. Internal trade was also considerable. Jet was traded from Yorkshire (Whitby), Kimmeridge shale from Dorset and oysters and other shellfish from Essex. Some pottery travelled often very long distances, such as the black-burnished ware of Dorset, which was traded to the northern frontier.

Romano-British Coinage

In the Roman period, coins poured into Britain, initially in army pay chests. The coins that circulated in Britain were mostly produced in mints on the Continent, initially (as was the case with most Roman coins of the period) in mints at Rome, but in the third and fourth centuries in mints at Trier (then Gaul, now Germany), Lyons and Arles. At a few periods, coins seem to have been struck in Britain. The earliest coins date from a period soon after the conquest, when imitations of the bronze asses of **Claudius** were copied due to a shortage of small change; some imitations were quite well done, others less so. These coins may have been semi-official. There might have been a mint in Britain at the time of Antoninus Pius, issuing coins with a reverse type of Britannia personified seated on a pile of rocks in an attitude of misery. These coins may have been issued by a travelling mint. In the third century, coins were struck at Colchester and London by the usurpers **Carausius** and Allectus; when control was restored by Constantius Chlorus, a mint was opened in **London** and coins were struck there by the Tetrarchy and by the House of Constantine. The London mint issued bronze coinage for insular use, and they also issued some gold coins from 312 to 314 and again from 383 to 388. It closed shortly after 388, however, and coins were thereafter sent to Britain from continental mints, usually from Gaul.

At various times during the Roman period, there were waves of counterfeiting. At the end of the second and the beginning of the third centuries, cast copies of *denarii* were produced. There was a considerable production of imitations of official *antoniniani* in the late third century, particularly of those issued by the Gallic Empire of Postumus, Victorinus, Tetricus I and II. These imitations are often termed as 'barbarous radiates' (the emperors wear a radiate crown). Although suggestions have been made that some may have been produced later, they appear to be largely contemporary with the coins they copied. A further wave of imitations was produced in the fourth century when the most common series copied was the 'Fel Temp Rep', inscribed centenionales of Constans and Constantius II, usually with a soldier spearing a fallen horseman as a type, though other coins were also copied, including issues of Magnentius. It used to be thought that these coins were struck after the departure of the Romans from Britain, but it is now known that, like the barbarous radiates, they were contemporary with the coins they copied.

Some Roman coins have types commemorating events in Britannia. Apart from the issues of Antoninus Pius mentioned above, coins were struck by Claudius commemorating the Roman conquest, and 'Britannia' types were issued by **Hadrian** around the time of his visit to the province and the building of **Hadrian's Wall**. Furthermore, commemorative coins were issued by Septimius Severus and his sons at the time of his campaigns in Scotland.

Coins continued to come into Britain on a fairly regular basis until the early fifth century. The last coins to be imported in significant numbers are issues of Honorius and Arcadius, minted in the first decade of the fifth century; there are also some examples of the coinage of **Constantine III** (407–411). That some coins continued to arrive in Britain later than 411 has been proven by the discovery of the Patching hoard from Sussex, deposited at the end of the fifth century and containing some Visigothic counterfeits. A distinctive feature of the Romano-British currency was the circulation of clipped Roman silver *siliquae* in the early fifth century.

Early Medieval Trade

There is abundant evidence for trade in high-status items in pagan Anglo-Saxon England, which coincided with the development of the élites in the sixth and, more particularly, the seventh centuries AD. Much of these items came by way of Kent. Amethyst beads may have been derived from the east Mediterranean or Spain, cowrie shells from the Red Sea, elephant ivory rings from the Mediterranean, amber beads from the Baltic, rock crystal possibly from Switzerland, garnets originally from India, bronze vessels from the east Mediterranean and Germany, gold (in the form of coins and pendants) from France and Denmark and Frankish **brooches** and pottery from France. Much of this trade seems to have been through close ties between Merovingian France and Kent. Many of these items are concentrated in Kent, the outliers being more thinly distributed, but there was also a measure of trade via the Humber. Gold coins, imported from the Frankish world, provided the raw material for Anglo-Saxon gold-working. Internal trade is more difficult to demonstrate, but certainly pottery seems to have been traded over quite considerable distances.

In the Christian period, the trade in exotic items dried up. But this period saw the growth of *emporia* (trading bases) on either side of the North Sea, such as Hamwic in Southampton, Fordwich and Ipswich in England, Dorestad and Quentovic in Frisia and, further north, Helgo in Sweden. The network of trade enjoyed by these emporia is well exemplified by the finds from Hamwic, which included some items from Frisia, glass from the Rhineland and probably the east, and pottery from the Meuse, Pas-de-Calais, Trier, Rouen and the Ardennes. The Niedermendig lava quarries continued exporting querns, and from the Canary Islands came the bone of a green turtle.

Late Saxon England saw a continuing urban expansion and developing trade. The trade developed both overseas and at home. Documentary sources such as **Ælfric**'s *Colloquy* allude to it, relating how merchants brought back 'purple robes and silk, precious gems and gold, rare garments and spices, wine and oil, ivory and brass, copper and tin, sulphur and glass and many suchlike things'. The other commodities mentioned in the documents were fish, blubberfish and slaves. Most of these commodities have left little or no trace in the archaeological record, but more mundane items include Near Eastern glass, schist whetstones from the Eiffel and pottery from the Rhineland and France.

An additional factor in the development of late-Saxon trade was the impact of the **Vikings**. Although they were responsible for important urban development in England and Ireland, the evidence for their overseas trade is fairly limited. Out of about 15,000 finds of the ninth century from Jorvik (**York**), only 500 were imported; one of these finds included a silk cap. Silk is also known from **Lincoln** and London. Walrus ivory, soapstone and schist (for making whetstones) were imported from Scandinavia.

Anglo-Saxon Coinage

The beginnings of Anglo-Saxon coinage coincide with developments in coinage on the Continent in the seventh century. The first coins to be struck in England were gold pieces, the counterparts of tremisses, which were probably known as 'shillings', but are now termed *thrymsas* in the numismatic literature. The earliest of these coins seem to have been struck around 630, in imitation of Frankish issues. An important hoard from Crondall, Hampshire, included one of these coins with the mint name of London. There may have been a limited output at York. In line with Frankish debasement, the first gold issues were rapidly followed by a pale gold phase assigned to the period 650–670; these coins often bore the names Pada or Varimundus, though a few seem to have borne the name of a king – Eadbald of Kent.

On the Continent, the Franks continued to debase their coins, producing silver pieces. Once again, this was paralleled in England, and the new silver units, conventionally called *sceattas* by numismatists (but probably more accurately termed 'pennies'), were issued in the 670s. Until the 720s, mints produced 'Primary Sceattas', which were made of good silver and had types displaying Roman influence. They were succeeded by more debased issues, the Secondary Sceattas, current between c. 720 and 755. The *sceatta* coinages display a great diversity of designs and were struck in a wide range of mints. The main areas in which these circulated was in a zone south of the Humber and east of Southampton – mints were located in Kent (Rochester and **Canterbury**), the Lower Thames and East Anglia (Ipswich) and in the emporium at Hamwic (Southampton) and York. In **Northumbria,** a few *sceattas* were issued in silver, usually in the name of kings or ecclesiastics. These were rapidly debased into copper alloy, and these *stycas* (as they are often erroneously called by numismatists) continued to be struck in the ninth century, at a time when they had been replaced by silver pennies further south. Alongside the English issues are to be found a series struck in Frisian mints but found equally on both sides of the Channel – these are sometimes termed 'porcupine' *sceattas* on account of the debased rendering of Romulus and Remus with the wolf, which looks more like a porcupine on the obverse. Most of the *sceattas* are uninscribed, but a few have names which seem to represent the moneyers rather than the issuing authority. A few in East Anglia have inscriptions in runes.

The next major landmark in the development of English coinage was the appearance of the silver penny. *Sceattas* were struck on small, dumpy flans made out of pellets of silver. The new pennies, like their continental counterparts, the deniers, were struck on flans cut from sheets of hammered silver. There were a few early issues of pennies copying the idea pioneered by Pippin III in 755. These pennies, issued by Kentish kings Heaberht and Ecgberht, were struck around 760. The Kentish (probably Canterbury) mint was annexed by **Offa** of **Mercia** when he assumed overlordship of Kent, and from the 760s, he issued a substantial coinage. Offa's coins were well made and designed, and following Roman precedent, he even issued some in the name of his wife, Cynethryth. Offa also issued a rare *dinar* for trade with moors in Iberia: the coins have inscriptions in Kufic script. From this point onwards, coins have the name of the king and usually also the moneyer who struck them.

As the ninth century progressed, there was increasing control over the design and issue of coins, and it would appear that in the 860s, Wessex and Mercia had an agreement which allowed coins of similar design to circulate throughout both areas. **Æthelstan** in the Grateley Decrees announced that all places of importance had to have mints and that there was to be one coinage in England (the king's). There were about thirty mints in operation, but his system did not work totally effectively.

In the late ninth century, there was a noteworthy output of coins in the Scandinavian-controlled areas of eastern England. The Danes of East Anglia struck coins in honour of St. Edmund. English pence and halfpence were copied in the Seven Boroughs, and in York, coins were issued in the name of a Cnut and a Siefred. Viking-age coin hoards often contain Kufic (Arab) *dirhems*; a huge number was present in the Cuerdale hoard (Lancs), which contained over 7,000 coins in total.

The next major development in Anglo-Saxon coinage was the coinage reform of 973, initiated by **Edgar**. The system ensured a proper control of the coinage: the coins had the name of the mint as well as that of the king and the moneyer. The types were standardised, but changed every six years (later every three), with a small cross type used as an emergency type when there was a shortage of coins. Only the current type could be used, so people had to change their money into coins of the current type when carrying out transactions. A device which was apparently deliberate was the progressive decline of the standard during the currency of each issue, which was then restored at the start of the new issue. This would have encouraged people to bring in old coins near the end of each issue, when a better exchange rate would have been offered. There were at first around fifty mints in operation, but this was increased by the time of Æthelred II to over seventy. The system, which was ahead of any other in Europe at the time, continued until 1125.

During the period of the Scandinavian rule in England, huge numbers of English coins reached Scandinavia, mostly in tribute, from the 990s to the 1040s. There are at least 50,000 Anglo-Saxon coins from the island of Gotland, and Scandinavian hoards could contain as many as 1,000 English coins. Although some Anglo-Saxon coins penetrated the Celtic areas, with the exception of some coins struck by Norse rulers in **Dublin**, coinage was absent in the Celtic-speaking areas. For a short period, the Anglo-Saxons had a mint at Rhuddlan, Clwyd, and a penny was issued in the name of **Rhodri Mawr** as a tribute by the Anglo-Saxon king Edgar at his mint in **Chester**.

Further Reading

Arnold, C. J. 1997. *An Archaeology of the Early Anglo-Saxon Kingdoms* (rev. edn.). Routledge.
Brooke, G. C. 1951. *English Coins*. Methuen.
Casey, John. 1980. *Roman Coinage in Britain*. Shire.
Cunliffe, Barry. 2005. *Iron Age Communities in Britain* (4th edn.). RKP.
Darvill, T. 1987. *Prehistoric Britain*. Batsford.
De Jersey, P. 1996. *Celtic Coinage in Britain*. Shire.
Dolley, M. (ed.). 1961. *Anglo-Saxon Coins*. Methuen.
Dolley, M. 1964. *Anglo-Saxon Pennies*. British Museum Press.
———. 1976. 'Anglo-Saxon Coins'. Pp. 349–372 in *The Archaeology of Anglo-Saxon England*. Edited by David Wilson. Methuen.
Hodges, Richard. 1989. *The Anglo-Saxon Achievement*. Duckworth.
Laing, Lloyd. 2006. *The Archaeology of Celtic Britain and Ireland, c. AD 400–1200*. Cambridge University Press.
North, J. J. 1974. *English Hammered Coinage, I, Early Anglo-Saxon to Henry III, c. 600–1272*. Spink.
Reece, Richard. 1987. *Coinage in Roman Britain*. Seaby.
Snyder, Christopher A. 1998. *An Age of Tyrants: Britain and the Britons, AD 400–600*. Sutton.
Van Arsdall, R. D. 1983. *Celtic Coinage of Britain*. Spink.

Lloyd Laing

Colchester

Colchester, **Essex**, was a major Roman town (*Camulodunum*) that began as a settlement in the Late **Iron Age**. The Roman (and pre-Roman) name means 'the strong place of Camulos', a **Celtic** war god. The Iron Age settlement lies at Gosbecks to the south-west of the present town and occupies an area between two rivers, the westward, undefended side being protected by a complex series of earthworks. This was the stronghold of the **Trinovantian** king, who was killed by **Cassivellaunus**, king of the neighbouring ***Catuvellauni***. The result was an appeal to Rome for help and the subsequent campaigns by **Julius Caesar** in 55 and 54 BC. By the early years of the first century AD, the site was the stronghold of the expansionist **Cunobelinus** and remained the regional capital until the time of Addedomarus, who is probably the person whose cremated remains were discovered in a richly furnished nearby barrow at Lexden.

Immediately after the invasion of AD 43 under Emperor **Claudius**, a legionary base was established at Colchester, the remains of which were excavated in 1965 and 1971–1975. In AD 49–50, this base was replaced by the town, named *Colonia Claudia Victricensis* (after Claudius), which housed army veterans who built public buildings, including a huge temple in honour of the emperor (the head of a life-size statue of him survives). An archway commemorated the Claudian conquest. The *colonia* was sacked in AD 61 by **Boudica**, queen of the ***Iceni*** tribe. Some evidence for her devastation has been found in excavations throughout the town, including a burnt couch in Lion Walk. The town was slowly rebuilt and defences were erected by AD 65. The main rebuilding took place around 120–130, and a new town wall was constructed around 150.

In the fifth century, Anglo-Saxon settlers moved into the old Roman town, and their ***grubenhäuser*** (distinctive buildings with sunken floors) have been found. A Roman lifestyle also continued; the baths were still in use (though not as baths). Sometime between 490 and 550, a winged building in Roman style was constructed within the baths and remained in use into the seventh century. Colchester had a late-**Saxon** church and the Saxon settlement was eventually occupied by the **Normans**, who built the castle.

See also Britons; Gaels; Roman Britain; Romano-British Towns.

Further Reading

Anonymous. 1980. *Roman Colchester*. Colchester Borough Council.

Crummy, Philip. 1997. *City of Victory*. Colchester Archaeological Trust.
Dunnett, R. 1975. *The Trinovantes*. Duckworth.
Hawkes, C. F. C., and M. R. Hull. 1947. *Camulodunum*. Society of Antiquaries Research Report.

Jennifer Laing

Columba, Saint (b. c.521)

Columba (Latin 'dove'), or Colmcille in Irish (Colum-cille = 'dove of the church'), is perhaps the most widely revered figure of the Age of the Saints in Britain and Ireland. Born c. 521 in the north of Ireland, Colmcille was a monk, a priest, a missionary and the founder and first abbot of **Iona**. Apart from these facts, we have few details of the life of this saint who was a figure of major importance in the development of Christianity in both Ireland and Scotland. What we know of him derives almost entirely from **Adomnán**'s *Vita Columbae*, which, although it is based on solid traditions within his monastery and earlier written accounts, was written almost a century after Colmcille's death and portrays him in idealised terms as the perfect disciple, specially chosen by God, and given 'prophetic revelations', the power 'to work miracles' and receive 'angelic visitations' (second preface). For Adomnán, Colmcille is a flesh and blood example of the ideal monk and Christian. Many common stories, such as that he had to flee Ireland after having made a pirate copy of a book, are much later inventions of folklore and hagiography.

Since the *Vita* is episodic, without a chronological frame (although Colmcille's death is at its end), much of our information comes from this statement: 'From his youth he devoted himself to growing in the Christian life, with God's help studying wisdom and keeping his body chaste ... [and] he spend thirty-four years as an island soldier of Christ' (second preface). We know that he studied with **Finnian of Clonard**, and then founded several monasteries in Ireland before setting out for Iona in 563, which became the centre for a large *familia* of monasteries in Ireland and Britain. Being in Iona made him a *peregrinator pro Christo*, 'a pilgrim for Christ', and allowed him to engage in missionary work among the **Picts**. He established many contacts both with other monasteries (e.g. **Bangor**) and with the rulers such as the Pictish king **Brude**. By the time of his death (traditionally, 9 June 597), Iona was an important monastic centre, forming the link between Ireland, Dalriada and **Northumbria**; this importance grew over the following two centuries.

Many aspects of insular monastic spirituality (e.g. the special place of islands) can be traced to the inspiration of Colmcille, and he may have inspired others (e.g. St. **Columbanus**) to combine the notion of monastic exile with that of missionary work. Traditionally, several Latin hymns (e.g. the *Altus prosator*) have been attributed to Colmcille, and his authorship cannot be excluded; Adomnán presents him as both a scholar and a scribe. Legend, reaching back almost to his lifetime (the *Amrae Coluimb Chille*), revered him as the patron of the poets.

The *Vita* has long been used as if it were a text apart from other *vitae*: they seemed contrived to present a model of edification, but that of Colmcille provided a precious glimpse into a 'Celtic' monastery in the pristine golden age. This impression, and it has been noted by generations of scholars going back to Bishop William Reeves in the later nineteenth century, is, however, no more than an incidental tribute to the artistry of Adomnán: he so absorbs us in his subject that we suspend our judgement and fail to notice that the structure, many incidents and, more significantly, the theology of holiness in the *Vita* are derived from Gregory the Great's *Dialogues* (and, in particular, *Dialogues* 2, dealing with St. Benedict). Just as the *Dialogues* made Benedict the ideal 'western monk', so also the *Vita* made Colmcille the ideal 'Celtic monk'.

See also Celtic Christianity; Monasticism.

Further Reading

Anderson, Alan Orr, and Marjorie Ogilvie Anderson (eds. and tr.). 1961. *Adomnan's Life of Columba*. Thomas Nelson and Sons Ltd.
Bieler, Ludwig. 1975. 'Hagiography and Romance in Medieval Ireland'. *Medievalia et Humanistica* 6: 13–24.
Bourke, Cormac (ed.). 1997. *Studies in the Cult of Saint Columba*. Four Courts Press.
Bruce, James. 2004. *Prophecy, Miracles, Angels, and Heavenly Light? The Eschatology, Pneumatology, and Missiology of Adomnán's Life of St Columba*. Paternoster.
Clancy, Thomas Owen, and Gilbert Márkus. 1995. *Iona: The Earliest Poetry of a Celtic Monastery*. Edinburgh University Press.
Herbert, Máire. 1988. *Iona, Kells and Derry: The History and Hagiography of the Monastic Familia of Columba*. Oxford University Press.

Sharpe, Richard (tr.). 1995. *Adomnán of Iona: Life of St Columba*. Penguin.

Anne Sassin

Columbanus, Saint (d.615)

Columbanus (d.23 November 615) was a monk in Ireland, who in his middle age left for the continent in search of a more perfect monastic life. He founded monasteries in the north-western region of the Alps, before moving to Bobbio in northern Italy where he died; he has left us a significant body of theological writing in Latin. He is the most famous of the medieval Irish *peregrini* on the continent; indeed, it is upon his exploits that the notion of 'the Irish re-converting Europe' is chiefly based. What we know of him comes from (1) a 'life' (*vita*) written by Jonas who entered his monastery at Bobbio soon after his death; (2) later lives of his companion St. Gall, which refer to him; and (3) what we can glean from his own writings.

Columbanus was born in **Leinster**, but we do not know when (the traditional date of c. 543 is without foundation). From Jonas, we learn that he studied with Sinell (*Vita* 1,3) and later with Comgall at **Bangor** (*Vita* 1,4). It is said that he became very learned in Latin and the scriptures. The quality of this education is borne out in his writings – he is the first Irish writer from whom a sizeable *corpus* is extant – which show him to have a fine Latin style and to be well acquainted with the main theological currents of his time. Around 590–591 (this date is the subject of controversy), he arrived in Gaul, and the Merovingian king Guntram gave him land in the Vosges, where he established several monasteries and convents, Luxeuil being the most famous. These houses quickly developed a reputation for the rigour of their monastic observance. This is reflected in his two works *Rules* for monastic living and a *Penitential* (attributed to Columbanus), which survive in a later form, but whose basic teaching goes back to Columbanus himself.

In 603, Columbanus came into conflict with the local bishops. They claimed that the problem was his Irish method of fixing the date of Easter, but clearly, this dispute also involved his recognition of their authority and his attacks on what he saw as their degenerate morals. Columbanus refused to appear before them at a council and appealed directly to Rome for support. His letter to the pope is interesting, as it reveals the perception of Europe, held by one born in the Ocean (*Vita* 1,2) (i.e. on an island in the ocean that surrounded the continents and, therefore, on the rim of the inhabited area), as a Christian cultural unit focused on Rome (*Letter* 1,1). Seven years later, Columbanus again fell foul of local authorities, this time King Theuderic. Theuderic, to secure the succession of his kingdom, had to recognise his illegitimate sons. This action was criticised by Columbanus, who refused to bless them. The king in response expelled Columbanus from his kingdom – an action undoubtedly welcomed by the local clergy.

Having left Luxeuil, Columbanus and a group of monks, including Gall, passed into Nuestria (southern Gaul) and the region of modern Switzerland. There is evidence to link him to Zürich, Bregenz and Chur. On this journey, he quarrelled with Gall, who then left him and became a hermit (later a monastery would be established at the site of this hermitage). Finally, around 612, he arrived at Bobbio in northern Italy and established a monastery, where he spent the remaining three years of his life. Bobbio flourished to become one of the great centres of learning of the early medieval period.

Columbanus's writings have been the subject of extensive debate. Of the thirty-four texts printed in the most used edition (Walker 1957), doubts have been cast on twenty-seven of them. There is agreement that eight of these are not genuine, and six are doubtful (or Columbanus plus accretions), and only recently has a consensus emerged that the thirteen *instructions* are his work (Stancliffe 1997). Thus, there are twenty works that can be used to establish his thought (O'Loughlin 2001).

See also Celtic Christianity; Literature.

Further Reading

Lapidge, Michael (ed.). 1997. *Columbanus: Studies in the Latin Writings*. Boydell & Brewer.

O'Loughlin, Thomas. 2001. 'Irish Preaching Before the End of the Ninth Century: Assessing the Extent of Our Evidence'. Pp.18–39 in *Irish Preaching 700–1700*. Edited by Alan J. Fletcher and Raymond Gillespie. Four Courts Press.

Stancliffe, Clare. 1997. 'The Thirteen Sermons Attributed to Columbanus and the Question of their Authorship'. Pp. 93–202 in *Columbanus: Studies in the Latin Writings*. Edited by Michael Lapidge. Boydell & Brewer.

Walker, G. S. M. (ed.). 1957. *Sancti Columbani Opera*. Dublin Institute for Advanced Studies.

Thomas O'Loughlin

Colum Cille, Saint

See Columba, Saint.

Connaught

Connaught, also spelled Connacht, was one of the five ancient kingdoms or provinces of Ireland. Once known as Cóiced Ol nEchmacht, Connaught includes the modern counties of Galway, Lentrim, Mayo, Roscommon and Sligo. According to the *Geography* of Ptolemy, a people known as the Nagnatae (or Fir Ol nEchmacht) inhabited this region in the early centuries AD, and it was not until the Connachta dynasty, descended from Conn Cétchathach (Conn of the Hundred Battles), in the early medieval period that the kingdom began to be known by its modern designation.

The area itself, situated west of the river Shannon and along the Atlantic seaboard to include the rocky Connemara plain, was overall unsuited for tillage but very capable of supporting livestock; thus, the high density of ringforts in the region is well accounted for. These include the most notable ones at Ardcloon and Letterkeen in County Mayo, the latter providing excellent evidence for the processing of grain through its querns, remains of a corn-drying kiln and possible threshing floor, as well as the crannog of Rathtinaun, Lough Gara in County Sligo, which though still unpublished is possibly of **Bronze Age** origins, making it highly important in the dating of this settlement type. Early ecclesiastical sites in Connaught are also extensive, though they are situated mostly along the chain of islands in the Atlantic, and they include Inishkea North, a site with a well-known early Christian crucifixion slab; Inishmurray, an island monastery with a massive enclosure and considerable number of carved cross-slabs and pillars; High Island, Croagh Patrick and Temple Macdara, all of which boast significant early stone oratories. A certain regionalism can possibly be detected in the ecclesiastical architecture of the region, as the rocky terrain made a move to stone church construction an obvious solution early on, and much later in the twelfth century, when the Transitional style of architecture had been introduced into the eastern half of the country by the **Normans**, the familiar Romanesque continued in Connaught for another three centuries after 1200.

Some of the more famous rulers associated with Connaught include Medb, the legendary queen from the **Ulster Cycle**, and Niall of the Nine Hostages, the late fourth to early fifth century king famous for his raids on Britain. However, for the most part, the sources before c. AD 800 are very few, though they increase considerably in the **Viking** Age, with numerous records of extensive devastation, and the annals are able to provide more solid evidence for the early medieval period. This is especially so over the struggles with the **Uí Néill** clan, including the battle of Cúl Dremne between the northern and southern factions in 561 in County Sligo. The powerful Uí Briúin (O'Brien) dynasty, which can be subdivided into at least three important family groups, was dominant from the eighth century onwards from their capital at Cruachain. They can be credited for bringing Connaught out of its earlier era of insignificance, having superseded the Uí Fiachrach dynasty of north Connaught in the seventh century and their best-known king, Guaire mac Colmáin or 'Guaire of the bounty', as well as the largest sub-kingdom, that of the Uí Maine, who occupied much of Roscommon and belonged to neither of the other families. In the tenth century, Conchobar mac Tadg began the reign of the O'Connor dynasty, whose ancestor Tairrdelbach mac Ruaidri Ua Conchobair (1119–1156), also known as Turlough O' Connor (one of the three main political families of Connaught along with the O'Rourkes and O'Flahertys), was commissioner of the Cross of Cong and the most powerful man in Ireland in the first half of the twelfth century. Turlough became one of the first high kings from the region in centuries, for unlike the other provinces, Connaught was not known for its over kingship, and his son Ruaidrí mac Tairrdelbach Ua Conchobair (Rory O'Connor) was also high king before his deposition in 1186, a period by which the Anglo-Norman administration had taken over.

See also Gaels; Kings and Kingship; Irish Language.

Further Reading

Byrne, J. F. 1973. *Irish Kings and High-Kings*. Batsford Press.

Edwards, Nancy. 1990. *The Archaeology of Early Medieval Ireland*. University of Pennsylvania Press.

Freeman, A. M. (ed.). 1944. *Annals of Connacht*. Dublin Institute for Advanced Studies.

Harbison, P. 1999. *The Golden Age of Irish Art*. Thames & Hudson.

Jennett, S. 1970. *Connacht: The Counties Galway, Mayo, Sligo, Leitrim and Roscommon in Ireland.* Faber Press.
Laing, Lloyd. 2006. *The Archaeology of Celtic Britain and Ireland, c. AD 400–1200.* Cambridge University Press.
Ó Cróinín, Daibhi. 1995. *Early Medieval Ireland 400–1200.* Longman Press.

Anne Sassin

Constantine I the Great (b. c. AD 270)

Constantine I (the Great) was the first Roman emperor to promote Christianity and was responsible for the founding of a new imperial capital in the East, Constantinople. Born c. AD 270, in the Danubian province of Moesia to the future emperor **Constantius I** and Helena (St. Helena, alleged finder of the True Cross), Constantine was proclaimed *Augustus* (emperor) by the army in the city of **York** following the death of his father in 306. Constantine spent some time consolidating the power of the Tetrarchy – the system of government that had been set up by Diocletian, whereby two *Augusti* ruled the two halves of the empire (East and West), with two *Caesares* as the '*Augusti*-in-waiting'. Constantine campaigned against the Franks and returned to Britain in 307. The Eastern Emperor Maximian came out of retirement, gave Constantine his support and allowed him to marry his daughter, Fausta. Constantine then campaigned in Germany, but found out that Maximian's son, Maxentius was claiming to be *Augustus*, with the support of his father. Constantine advanced on Marseilles, where Maximian surrendered. However, Maxentius remained a threat until he was defeated in 312 at the Battle of Milvian Bridge, when, according to his biographer, Bishop Eusebius, Constantine saw the Christogram (monogram of Christ) and decided to fight in the name of Christ.

One view is that converting to Christianity brought Constantine political gain. Though in 313, he began vigorously promoting Christianity (which had become legal with Galienus's Edict of Toleration issued in 311), it did not become the official religion of the empire until 395. In 324, Constantine defeated his one-time ally Licinius, emperor of the Eastern Empire and became master of the Roman world. His triumph was marked with the founding of a 'new Rome' on the ancient site of Byzantium, renamed after Emperor Constantinople. While the city was dedicated in 330, Constantine's base of operations was the Gallic city of Trier. He died in 337, with a legacy of reform, which included promoting the use of Germans in the military and Christians in his government.

See also Roman Army; Roman Britain.

Further Reading

Barnes, T. D. 1981. *Constantine and Eusebius.* Harvard University Press.
Bidwell, P. 2006. 'Constantius and Constantine at York'. Pp. 31–40 in *Constantine the Great.* Edited by E. Hartley et al. York.
Cameron, Averil. 2006. 'Constantius and Constantine: An Exercise in Publicity'. Pp.18–30 in *Constantine the Great.* Edited by E. Hartley et al. York.
Fox, Robin Lane. 1987. *Pagans and Christians.* Knopf.
Holloway, R. R. 2004. *Constantine and Rome.* Yale University Press.

Jennifer Laing

Constantine III

Constantine III, 'the Pretender', was an imperial usurper in the early fifth century AD, whose legacy went beyond the minor role he played in late-Roman politics. Our information about Constantine comes mostly from the works of imperial and church chroniclers, writings far removed from Britain – Olympiodorus (fragmentary), Sozomen, Orosius and Zosimus. The last of these men, giving the fullest account of Constantine's actions, wrote over a century later than the events described.

After the barbarians crossed the frozen Rhine in AD 406, the troops in Britain elected a series of *tyranni* (usurpers), hoping that they could be more effective than the legitimate emperor of the West, Honorius, in securing the safety of the western Roman provinces. The last of these usurpers, an obscure soldier with an auspicious name – Flavius Claudius Constantinus – thus became Constantine III and fulfilled the wishes of his British troops by taking them to Gaul to bring order back to that province. To further heighten comparisons with **Constantine** the Great, who had also been proclaimed emperor in Britain, he renamed his sons Constans and Julian, bestowing upon the eldest the title of Caesar.

After naming two of his own generals to the post of *magistri militum* in Gaul, Constantine crossed to Boulogne and stayed for a few days to put the local defences in order. Honorius's *magister militum* for the West – Stilicho – had Constantine's generals killed, but they were replaced by the Frank, Edobinchus and the Briton, Gerontius. Constantine garrisoned the Alpine passes to protect himself from an invasion from Italy and then sent Constans and Gerontius to Spain to suppress imperial loyalists. After some success there, Constans returned to his father, who began diplomatic negotiations with Honorius. Late in the year 409, things began to fall apart for Constantine. Gerontius, hearing that he was about to be replaced in Spain, proclaimed one of his own dependents as emperor and incited the barbarians in Gaul to revolt against Constantine. Constans, now elevated to Augustus and colleague of his father, was defeated and killed by the rebel Gerontious. Constantine attempted to invade Italy but was repulsed, perhaps by Alaric. Gerontius then laid siege to Constantine at Arelate but was replaced by a more powerful foe, Honorius's new *magister* Constantius, the future emperor Constantius III. A deserted and despairing Constantine laid down his power and took refuge in a church, where he was hurriedly ordained priest. The city gates were opened, and Constantine's troops turned the emperor and his son Julian over to Constantius. While being led captive back to Rome in 411, both prisoners were assassinated by the order of Honorius.

Zosimus claims that the barbarians took advantage of the careless government of Constantine III to harass Britain, and that around 410, the **Britons** had had enough and declared their independence from Rome. Constantine would resurface centuries later in the *History* of **Geoffrey of Monmouth** (c.1136), where he is made the father of Aurelius Ambrosius (i.e. **Ambrosius Aurelianus**) and Uther Pendragon, and thus the grandfather of King **Arthur**.

See also Roman Army; Roman Britain.

Further Reading

Birley, Anthony. 1980. *The People of Roman Britain.* University of California Press.

Demougeot, Emilienne. 1974. 'Constantin III, l'emperor d'Arles'. Pp. 83–125 in *Homage a André Dupont.* Federation Historique du Languedoc.

Paschoud, François (ed.). 1989. *Zosime: Histoire Nouvelle.* Les Belles Lettres.

Rodley, Ronald T. (tr.). 1982. *Zosimus: New History.* Australian Association for Byzantine Studies.

Snyder, Christopher A. 1998. *An Age of Tyrants: Britain and the Britons, AD 400–600.* Penn State Press.

Thompson, E. A. 1977. 'Britain, AD 406–410'. *Britannia* 8: 303–318.

Christopher A. Snyder

Constantius I (r. AD 305–306)

The Roman Emperor Constantius I 'Chlorus' (r. AD 305–306) was actively involved in the events in Britain. He came from Illyricum in northern Greece and rose through army ranks to become the governor of Dalmatia. He became praetorian prefect to Emperor Maximian and later married Maximian's daughter (or stepdaughter) Theodora, discarding Helena (later St. Helena), the mother of **Constantine** the Great. Constantius campaigned in Germany to end the breakaway 'empire' in Gaul and Britain, which had been established by **Carausius** in 286 and (following his assassination) continued by Allectus. Constantius besieged Boulogne and prevented the rebels getting out of the bay by building a mole. He crossed to Britain, defeated Allectus and marched on to **London**. A gold medallion from the Arras Treasure shows him being greeted by the city. The province of Britannia was then divided into four; two of the subdivisions – Flavia Caesariensis and Maxima Caesariensis – probably were named in his honour. The rest of his reign was regarded by Christian commentators as moral and pro-Christian. He returned to Britain in 305 or 306 to campaign against the **Picts**, this time accompanied by his son, Constantine. He was successful but died in the city of **York** on 25 July 306.

See also Roman Army; Roman Britain.

Further Reading

Bidwell, P. 2006. 'Constantius and Constantine at York'. Pp. 31–40 in *Constantine the Great.* Edited by E. Hartley et al. York.

Cameron, Averil. 2006. 'Constantius and Constantine: An Exercise in Publicity'. Pp.18–30 in *Constantine the Great.* Edited by E. Hartley et al. York.

Jennifer Laing

Coppergate Helmet

Found in a wood-lined shaft at the end of the excavations in Coppergate, **York**, associated with a spearhead, the Coppergate helmet is one of the four known helmets from **Anglo-Saxon** England, the others being those from

Sutton Hoo, Suffolk; Benty Grange, Derbyshire; and Wollaston, Northamptonshire (the 'Pioneer' helmet). Measuring 0.8 feet (24.6 centimetres) in height, it is made up of a cap made with a riveted iron frame, two curved cheek pieces and a neck protector of ring mail. There was no evidence of an inner cap. The curved eye openings have eyebrows in the form of animals, ending in a profile ferocious animal head. The nose guard has a pair of intertwined animals with hatched bodies and spiral hips. Between the eyebrows and facing down the nose guard is a snub-snouted animal head with incised eyes and comma-shaped ears. A band runs back over the crown with an inscription, which translates as 'In the name of the Lord Jesus, the Holy Spirit, God, and with all we pray. Amen. Oshere. Christ'. A cross strip carries two inscriptions which echo that given in full on the crest. On either side behind the eyebrows is an iron hinge for the cheek piece. It was deliberately buried, probably in the late eighth century.

These helmets evoke in their form and decoration both their Roman imperial origins and their Late **Iron Age** northern Europe artistic and cultural traditions. Like the other known helmets, it shares descent from the *spangenhelmen*, developed at the end of the Roman period and widely used in the Migration Period Europe. The animal decoration is echoed in some Anglo-Saxon sculpture of the period and also in Pictish metalwork and sculpture. The identity of the owner, presumably Oshere, is not known, but it is clear that the helmets were high-status items, only worn by those of the highest rank. It is possible that it was, like the Sutton Hoo helmet, a parade article, rather than one intended for use in battle.

See also Metalworking; Picts.

Further Reading

Tweddle, D. 1984. *The Coppergate Helmet.* York Archaeological Trust.

Webster, L., and J. Backhouse (eds.). 1990. *The Making of England, Anglo-Saxon Art and Culture, AD 600–900.* British Museum.

Lloyd Laing

Corbridge

Corbridge, the Roman site of *Corstopitum*, Northumberland, was a military fort that later developed into a town supplying **Hadrian's Wall**. The first Roman activity was at some distance from the now-visible remains and comprised a fort and bathhouse built c. AD 79 by the Roman general **Agricola** as a supply base for his northern campaign. It was demolished c. 87 when the first fort of turf and timber was built on the present site, probably to house the *Ala Petriana*, a cavalry regiment. This fort was burnt down but rebuilt around 104, to be in turn improved around 120 before being abandoned around 124 when Hadrian's Wall was built. It was taken back into commission during the advance into Scotland in the time of Antoninus Pius (138–161), before being finally abandoned soon after the mid-second century.

The Roman town of Corbridge flourished in the third and fourth centuries on the same site and lay on each side of the Stanegate (the east–west road which ran behind Hadrian's Wall). Among the surviving buildings are impressive granaries and a fountain, the edge of which has been worn down with the constant sharpening of knives. The finds from Corbridge include a rich array of sculptures, including the Corbridge lion and a suit of Roman armour.

See also Roman Britain; Romano-British Towns.

Further Reading

Bishop, M. C., and J. N. Dore. 1989. *Corbridge: Excavations of the Roman Fort and Town, 1947–1980.* Historic Buildings and Monuments Commission for England.

Jennifer Laing

Corieltauvi

The *Corieltauvi* were an indigenous Celtic tribe living in the **Iron Age** and **Roman Britain**, whose territory, according to the only surviving Roman account to shed light on their position, the *Geography* of Ptolemy, was north of the ***Iceni*** and east of the ***Cornovii***, with coins and pottery providing the best evidence of its extent, extending to modern Lincolnshire, Leicestershire and Nottinghamshire. Manuscripts of Ptolemy's texts convey both the name *Coritani* and the name *Coritavi*, with a graffited tile at Churchover contributing another proposed form (*Corieltauvi*). They were regarded as having been more pro-Roman and less significant than their neigbours, notably the ***Brigantes***, although this was because they were assumed to have had no coinage of their own. Since then, however, the coinage once ascribed to the *Brigantes* has been reassigned to them, and this implies some level of commercial activity, with wide trading connections. Evidence points to a number of Iron Age settlements with imported pottery (e.g. at North Ferriby) before the Roman advance.

Most of the early excavated settlements are in Lincolnshire (e.g. **Dragonby** or Ancaster) as well as in the Jewry Wall site at Leicester and Brayford Pool at Lincoln, though no place has produced remains that would seem similar to the ***oppida*** of southern Britain. The *Corieltauvi* do not figure in any Roman accounts before AD 70 (and very few for the entire period), and though this cannot be taken to mean that they did not create opposition, their territory quickly fell under imperial control. Besides the presence of forts at Longthorpe, Newton-on-Trent and East Bridgford (Margidunum) and military occupation at Little Chester and Chesterfield, there was a veteran colony at **Lincoln** from c. 90 and a significant Iron Age nucleus at Leicester (*Ratae Corieltauvorum*). The archaeological evidence does not indicate much difference between the two latter cities, though Lincoln may have been legally superior to the native *caput*, which probably received the transition of authority in the early second century. Though finds from levels beneath the Roman city of Leicester have made Iron Age settlement seem certain, the decision to make it the administrative capital of the *Corieltauvi* may very likely have come after Lincoln's foundation, with attention to the tribal land naturally coming second.

The late Roman period saw significant works in the private sphere (e.g. the Blackfriars mosaic), and minor settlements in the territory assist in providing a fuller picture of the countryside, to which the majority of the *Corieltauvi* seem to have been connected, though there is a rather sizeable gap in the knowledge and context of the villas (such as at Southwell), of which some seventy are known, a comparably small number for the size of the territory. There were also a number of small Iron Age **hillforts** with occupation that continued into the Roman period (e.g. Dorket Head and Fox Wood), and in addition to the shared tradition of **Romano-Celtic temples** (e.g. Colley Weston and Brigstock), the rural temple at Thistleton provided finds suggesting religious significance before the Roman conquest.

A rich agricultural territory with a wealth of minerals, ironworking seems to have been one of the chief industries of the *Corieltauvi*, with salt-production, stone-quarrying and pottery production as well, though by the later fourth and early fifth centuries manufacturing was beginning to go into a decline, having been preceded by an unsettled period of barbarian raiding, and at which point Germanic settlement dominated, leaving any continuity from the Romano-British families difficult to substantiate.

See also Britons; Celts.

Further Reading

Cunliffe, B. W. 2005. *Iron Age Communities of Britain* (4th edn.). RKP.

Todd, Malcolm. 1991. *The Coritani*. Alan Sutton.

Anne Sassin

Cork

Cork, a coastal town in south-west Ireland, was an important trading centre under the **Vikings** in the tenth century, and its name was derived from the Irish *corcach*, meaning 'marshy place'. Having one of the largest natural harbours in the world, the site's position on the river Lee was essential for its communications network, and the two islands in the middle of the river were the basis from which the medieval city later grew, linked together by timber bridges. Supposedly founded as a monastic establishment and centre of learning in the late sixth or early seventh century by Cork's patron saint Finbarr, who was later buried in Gill Abbey over which the present-day St Finabarre's Cathedral stands, there is not much solid evidence for Cork's early history, though the rather interesting 'Cork horns', representing **La Tène** decorated metalwork of the first or second century AD, are amongst the early finds of the area. After having undergone raiding and pillaging by the Vikings for the following few centuries, the community grew into a town, which seems to have been founded by the Scandinavians in the mid-ninth century. Unlike **Waterford** and **Dublin**, however, which have undergone extensive excavation, evidence for early Cork must rely almost entirely on the occasional documentary reference.

Gill Abbey in Cork, one of Cormac Mac Cárrthaigh's foundations, was probably a follower of the style begun at Cormac's

Chapel at Cashel, County Tipperary, which was completed in 1134, thus making Gill slightly later. The town itself seems to have controlled considerable hinterlands in the twelfth century, including the baronies of Kerrycurrihy and parts of Kinalea, and it was granted its official city charter around the year 1185. The excavations which were undertaken in the 1970s did not manage to shed light on the Hiberno-Norse occupation, but instead they focused on Skiddy's Castle on the city's north island and the Holy Trinity-Christchurch area on the south one; neither area yielded much occupation evidence before the thirteenth century. The excavated pottery from the Anglo-Norman settlement was analysed, with 80 percent of the report suggesting that it was imported, including half from Ham Green, attesting to the importance of trade with Bristol and half from kilns near Bordeaux. Bone pin beaters found in the excavation were also able to demonstrate the widespread nature of the textile industry at this time; with other finds were crucible fragments and slag from furnaces, worked wood and leather products. By the thirteenth century, the city had massive defences and was fully enclosed by a stone wall, of which some gates remain, and all of the excavated finds imply that Cork had become a city of some distinction with an integral role as a trading community.

See also Ceramics and Glass; Coinage and Trade; Gaels.

Further Reading

Barry, T. B. 1987. *The Archaeology of Medieval Ireland.* Methuen.

Edwards, Nancy. 1990. *The Archaeology of Early Medieval Ireland.* University of Pennsylvania Press.

Harbison, Peter. 1999. *The Golden Age of Irish Art.* Thames & Hudson.

Anne Sassin

Cornish

See Brythonic Language; Cornwall.

Cornish Rounds

'Cornish rounds' is a label commonly given to the ringforts of south-western Britain, the British equivalent of the Irish **rath**. Though examples can be found in Dorset, Devon, Somerset and even Brittany, there are nearly a thousand examples from **Cornwall** spanning later prehistory to the early Middle Ages. They are generally small, with a single entrance and modest defences (a single circular earthen mound and ditch) enclosing a few round huts or other small buildings. Two of the most well-known examples from the excavation are Grambla and Trethurgy. The majority date to the Roman period, where they appear to be defended farmsteads with high-status goods. Some received luxury items imported from Gaul and the Mediterranean in the **Brittonic Age**, and at Trethurgy, there is evidence of the Cornish tin trade.

Further Reading

Laing, Lloyd. 2006. *The Archaeology of Celtic Britain and Ireland c.* AD *400–1200.* Cambridge University Press.

Pearce, Susan. 2004. *South-Western Britain in the Early Middle Ages.* Leicester University Press.

Todd, Malcolm. 1987. *The South West to* AD *1000.* Longman.

Christopher A. Snyder

Cornovii

We know of two groups of people called *Cornovii* from Roman-era sources, one living near **Wroxeter** and another living near Caithness. The name was probably derived from British *corn-*, meaning 'horn', but it is unclear to what this might have referred in each case. Suggestions range from the meaning 'promontory dwellers' to 'worshippers of a horned deity'. In the absence of coinage and distinguishing archaeological remains, the *Cornovii* are difficult to distinguish from their neighbours. Their *civitas*-capital, apparently founded by the Romans, is named in several Roman sources as *Virconium*, Wroxeter, which was abandoned as a legionary base in the first century AD but rebuilt as a city in the first half of the second century AD. Wroxeter's post-Roman history is obscure, although it was apparently still occupied by the British (and Irish) by the end of the fifth century.

Relatively little is known about the *Cornovii* in Caithness. A third group of presumed Roman-era *Cornovii* can be discerned in **Cornwall**, although they are not attested until the Middle Ages. The Ravenna Cosmography (seventh or eighth century) lists in the south-west of Britain *Purocoronavis*, almost certainly an error for *Durocornovium*, 'fort of the *Cornovii*' (Rivet and Smith 350). In medieval sources, we hear of *Cornubia* as a sub-kingdom of **Dumnonia**. Charles Thomas has argued that the *Cornovii* lying behind the medieval Latinised form *Cornubia* (and the modern name for Cornwall in the Cornish language, *Kernow*) were immigrants from Armorica, traders of the *Veneti*, who in their new home gained the name *Cornovii* not as an ethnic signifier but as a description of their purported habit of dwelling on cliffs, along with other settlement, burial and pottery habits particular to them, which were arguably specific to Cornwall. The specificity of some of these archaeological features to Cornwall, in particular, burial habits, **Cornish rounds**, fogous and pottery, seems clear, although that of cliff forts is less so. The connections to Brittany or northern France illustrated by these remains are also clear. However, Thomas's theory as to the link between these archaeological connections to the name of the *Cornovii* via Venetic traders remains controversial.

See also Britons; Celts; Roman Britain.

Further Reading

Dark, Ken. 1994. *Civitas to Kingdom: British Political Continuity 300–800.* Leicester University Press.

Quinnell, Henrietta. 1986. 'Cornwall During the Iron Age and the Roman Period'. *Cornish Archaeology* 25: 111–134.

Rivet, A. L. F., and Colin Smith. 1979. *The Place-Names of Roman Britain.* BT Batsford.

Thomas, Charles. 1966. 'The Character and Origins of Roman Dumnonia'. In *Rural Settlement in Roman Britain: Papers Given at a CBA Conference Held at St Hugh's College,Oxford, January 1 to 3, 1965.* Edited by Charles Thomas. CBA Research Report No. 7. Council for British Archaeology.

Todd, Malcolm. 1987. *The South-West to AD 1000.* Longman.

Webster, Graham. 1975. *The Cornovii.* Duckworth.

Karen Jankulak

Cornwall

The county of Cornwall in the tip of the south-west peninsula of Britain was part of the British kingdom of **Dumnonia** until conquered by the English in the tenth century. Apart from what archaeology can tell us, the history of Cornwall is virtually unknown prior to the Middle Ages. The Cornish language, widely spoken up to the early modern period, disappeared as a spoken language in the eighteenth century. With its dramatic landscape stretching out into the Atlantic Ocean, Cornwall has proven to be an alluring mystery to historians and novelists alike.

Prehistoric Cornwall participated in the **Neolithic** revolution that began around 8000 BC and produced many types of Neolithic and **Bronze Age** stone monuments, including chambered tombs, tor enclosures, cairns, standing stones and stone circles. Because it has always been sparsely populated, many of these monuments have survived. There is the Blind Fiddler, a solitary standing stone; the Nine Maidens, a small stone circle on an isolated stretch of moorland; Lanyon Quoit, with its three upright stones supporting a massive stone table, originally covered by a mound; and Men-an-Tol, a large circular holed stone through which, according to folklore, children were passed for healing. Ancient Cornwall is known, above all, for its tin. Called 'the Brettanic metal' by the Greeks, Cornish tin was probably in great demand in Bronze Age Europe and was certainly so in the Roman world. By the **Iron Age**, the most distinctive settlement type was the univallate defended farmstead known as the **'Cornish round'**. The equivalent of the Irish **rath**, the rounds probably represented one extended family (up to about thirty people), with sufficient resources to control local agriculture and cattle and import high-status goods. While these rounds usually contained at least two or three timber round houses, in the Roman period some of the rounds contained cellular courtyard houses built of stone (e.g. Chysauster near Penwith). Often associated with these farmsteads were fogous, underground stone storage chambers, the Cornish equivalent to the Breton and Scottish **souterrains**. This pattern of enclosure of agricultural lands changed little from prehistory up to the eighteenth century.

Beginning in the Iron Age, Cornish princes controlled trade from promontory forts or 'cliff castles' (e.g. The Rumps) and resided in multivallate (and usually circular) **hillforts** (e.g. Castle Dore and Chûn Castle). Most spectacular of all these defended hilltop sites is **Tintagel**, which, like Castle Dore, has associations with the Arthurian legends. Originally interpreted as a monastic settlement, Tintagel now appears to have been a major emporium of the fifth and sixth centuries AD. Dated by the presence of **'Tintagel ware'** – hundreds of fine ceramics and vessels containing luxury items from the Mediterranean – Tintagel appears to have grown from a minor Roman settlement with the addition of several buildings, defences and a wharf. Because of its isolation and exposure to the elements, it has been suggested that Tintagel was seasonably occupied by a powerful lord who controlled the exchange of luxury goods. While the figures of King **Arthur** and King Mark are both associated with Tintagel in the **Brittonic Age**, it is probable that Tintagel was the seat of the British kings of Dumnonia.

The ***Dumnonii***, not the ***Cornovii***, was the ruling tribe in Cornwall from at least the late pre-Roman Iron Age. While the *Cornovii* appear to have been centred in Shropshire, the Ravenna Cosmography records a *Durocornavis*, 'fortress of the *Cornovii*', west of the river Tamar. The **Brittonic** element *corn-*, like the Latin *cornu*, means 'horn', and this may refer to the Cornish peninsula or one of its many promontories. If there was a *Cornovii* tribe in Cornwall, they must have been a subgroup of the *Dumnonii*, whose lands stretched from Somerset to Lizard's Point. Though they lacked **coinage** and large tribal centres, the *Dumnonii* were connected to an Atlantic trade network where they exchanged tin, lead and other products with western Gaul, Atlantic Spain and the Mediterranean lands. When the Roman *classis Britannica* ceased to operate in the Channel, the southern coast of Cornwall would have been susceptible to Germanic piracy. The north coast would likewise have been vulnerable to Irish sea raids, and the presence of **Ogam** inscriptions and Irish names in sixth-century western Cornwall could be evidence of Irish settlers, trade with Ireland or ecclesiastical contacts. British saints **Samson** and **Pol** are described as having travelled between Wales, Dumnonia and Brittany.

The ***Anglo-Saxon Chronicle*** describes the landing of several West Saxon lords on the southern coast of Britain and the gradual expansion of the kingdom of **Wessex** into the Dumnonian territory. While these victories attributed to the House of **Cerdic** over the *Westwalas* and *Cornwalas* (as the Saxons called these Britons) come from late and biased sources and cannot be taken as strictly historical, they do probably describe in general the process which was occurring in the south-west from the sixth to the tenth century. Of these, the battle of **Dyrham** (577) was probably the most significant, for it gave the Saxons access to the west coast and essentially separated the Britons of Dumnonia from those in Wales. The only Dumnonian king about whom we have much information is **Geraint** (*Gerontius rex*), who ruled from c. 670 to 710 and who corresponded with the English bishop **Aldhelm**. He appears as 'Geraint, son of Erbin', in medieval Welsh poetry and becomes one of Arthur's knights in later romances.

The growth of **Mercia** in the seventh century may have forced the kings of Wessex to look westward for territorial expansion. By the eighth century, Wessex kings were granting Devonshire lands to English churchmen, and the *Anglo-Saxon Chronicle* records that **Egbert** of Wessex 'harried Cornwall from east to west' in 814. In 838, a **Viking** host landed in Cornwall and joined the Britons in fighting against Egbert, but they were defeated at Hingston Down by Egbert, who then felt free to grant lands in Cornwall to the English clerics. The ***Annales Cambriae*** records the name of the last British king of Dumnonia, one 'Dungarth, king of *Cerniu*', who drowned in 875. By then, such British rulers were probably the vassals of the kings of Wessex, though Viking activity in the south-west may have delayed the complete conquest of Devon and Cornwall. This finally happened during the reign of **Æthelstan** (924–939), who compelled the Britons to leave **Exeter** (which he then fortified in stone) and fixed the left bank of the Tamar as the shire boundary. The conquering English kings expected the **Britons** to respect the new border and in return formally recognised the six 'hundreds' (the *kevran*, a district capable of raising 100 recruits for a warband) within Cornwall.

The distinctive character of the Cornish church is evident in hagiography like the *Lives* of Saints Samson, Pol and Petroc. Aldhelm and subsequent English bishops were often distressed with the Christians of Cornwall and paid visits to 'repress their errors'. In 1050, Cornwall was demoted to the status of archdeaconry within the new diocese of Exeter, and he would remain there until the creation of the see of Truro in 1877. The **Norman Conquest** led to the complete replacement of the existing ruling elite, with 80 percent of Cornish manors passing to Norman hands. A number of impressive motte and bailey castles were built by Anglo-Norman lords, including Launceston and Kilkhampton. A magnificent stone castle was begun in the 1140s by **Henry I**'s son Reginald, earl of Cornwall, and completed in the 1230s by Henry III's younger brother Richard, earl of Cornwall. After **Geoffrey of Monmouth** depicted the stone castle as the site of Arthur's conception and birth, it came to be known as King Arthur's Castle.

From the eleventh to the fourteenth century, Cornwall experienced a period of prosperity and population growth, with reorganisation of the countryside and the development of new hamlets, villages and towns. Cornish, the Brittonic language of Cornwall which Gerald of Wales stated was very similar to Breton in the twelfth century, was spoken widely in Devon until 950 and became a literary language in late medieval Cornwall, used especially for liturgical drama.

See also Celts; Roman Britain.

Further Reading

Conner, Patrick W. 1993. *Anglo-Saxon Exeter: A Tenth-Century Cultural History*. Boydell & Brewer.
Cornwall County Council. 2007. 'Cornwall's Archaeological Heritage: A Field Guide to Accessible Sites', http://www.historic-cornwall.org.uk/a2m/index.htm (cited 15 February 2008).
Filbee, Marjorie. 1996. *Celtic Cornwall*. Constable.
Olson, Lynette. 1989. *Early Monasteries in Cornwall*. Boydell & Brewer.
Orme, Nicholas. 2000. *The Saints of Cornwall*. Oxford University Press.
Pearce, Susan. 1978. *The Kingdom of Dumnonia*. Lodenek Press.
Rowe, Toni-Maree. 2005. *Cornwall in Prehistory*. Tempus.
Snyder, Christopher A. 2003. *The Britons*. Peoples of Europe Series. Blackwell.
Thomas, Charles. 1985. *Exploration of a Drowned Landscape*. Batsford.
———. 1997. *Celtic Britain*. Thames & Hudson.
Todd, Malcolm. 1987. *The South West to AD 1000*. Longman.
Yorke, Barbara. 1995. *Wessex in the Early Middle Ages*. Leicester University Press.

Christopher A. Snyder

Crannogs

The term *crannog* (from Irish *crann*, meaning a tree) is applied to circular or oval islands in lakes, with one or more houses, mostly dating from the **Iron Age** and early medieval periods. These islands can be either totally or partially human-made. They are found in Ireland and Scotland, with a couple of outliers in Wales.

The earliest crannogs are found in Scotland, where they are almost all of Early Iron Age date. Here, different types of constructional technique have been identified: those built on platforms sited on piles driven into the bed of the loch and those built up with alternate layers of brushwood and stones (packwerk). There are two main concentrations of Iron Age crannogs in Scotland, in Argyll and in Dumfries and Galloway, but there are also important crannogs in Perthshire. Crannogs with early Christian period occupation are rare and may have been due to the influence from Ireland. The classic sites of this period are Buiston (or Buston, Ayrshire) and Loch Glashan (Argyll). It appears that Scottish crannogs with early medieval occupation were in most cases reused sites, built originally at an earlier date.

In Ireland, there are at least 1,200 crannogs, nearly all of which are of the early medieval period. They are concentrated in the Midlands, west and north-west. They range in diameter from around 33 feet (10 metres) to 131 feet (40 metres) and are of the packwerk type of construction, with vertical piles anchoring the platforms. On the surface, there was usually a retaining palisade, within which were one or more buildings. In contrast to Scottish crannogs, there is little evidence for early construction: most date from the sixth to the thirteenth century. There are a few **Bronze Age** lakeside settlements, but the connection of these with the true crannogs is uncertain. A group of crannogs on Lough Gara have been dated by radiocarbon to around the end of the first millennium BC, and dendrochronology for the one at Coolure Demesne, Lough Derravarragh, suggests that the timbers employed were felled in AD 402–409.

It is usually assumed that crannogs were high-status residences, given the range of high-status artefacts recovered and the organisation necessary to construct them, but some claims have been made for lower-status crannogs, the outcome of teamwork by neighbouring families. Some crannogs, however, such as Lagore, County Meath, are known from documentary sources to have had royal residences, and others, such as Moynagh Lough, seem to have been the home and workplace of high-status smiths. The only crannog in Wales so far excavated is that at Llan-Gors, which was, like Lagore, a royal residence.

See also Irish Language; Scots.

Further Reading

Fredengren, C. 2002. *Crannogs: A study of People's Interaction with Lakes*. Wordwell.
Morrison, I. 1985. *Landscape with Lake Dwellings: The Crannogs of Scotland*. Edinburgh University Press.
O'Sullivan, Aidan. 1998. *The Archaeology of Lake Settlement in Ireland*. Royal Irish Academy.
———. 2000. *Crannogs: Lake Dwellings of Early Ireland*. Country House.

Lloyd Laing

Crickley Hill

Crickley Hill is one of the several prehistoric earthworks built on top or near the edge of the central Cotswold escarpment, high above the Severn Valley in Gloucestershire. The multiperiod site was excavated between 1969 and 1991. The first settlement on the site took place during the **Neolithic** Period around 4000 BC, when a small mound surrounded by pits was constructed on the highest part of the hill and at least three tiny beehive-shaped post-built huts were also built. In c. 3650 BC, a causewayed enclosure was built, and over the next century, it was extended and rebuilt several times and eventually replaced by a larger enclosure, with wooden palisades on top of the defences. Stone excavated from the ditches was used to form embankments on the outer sides, and hollows and ditches were consolidated by dry-stone walling. Fenced pathways led from two narrow entrances to the central enclosure, where substantial rectangular post-built buildings stood. Towards the end of the Neolithic occupation, a small stone shrine was erected at the western end of the hill, separated from the rest of the complex by fences and gates. This area was later covered by a long mound of rubble and earth and a small stone circle with a central slab for burning. Offerings appear to have been made at the long mound from the Neolithic to the Roman times, though the ritual involved remains unknown.

The Neolithic occupation came to an end when the site was violently attacked in c. 3450 BC. All the wooden structures were burnt, and clusters of arrowheads concentrated around the two main entrances and fanning out into the interior testify to the intensity of the fighting. The site appears to have been visited only sporadically during the **Bronze Age**: fragments of an all-over corded Beaker may indicate a disturbed burial, and an antler pick from the long mound has been dated to this period. During the **Iron Age**, the long mound was rebuilt and enclosed within a kerb of regularly placed slabs. A **hillfort** was built in the seventh or sixth century BC, with rubble from the ditch used to make the rampart, which was then topped by a timber palisade. Inside the hillfort were several rows of rectangular buildings. After these had been destroyed by fire, the fort was subsequently rebuilt with round houses and four-post granaries. These also burned down, and the fort was finally abandoned in the middle of the fifth century BC.

During the Roman period, a small farm was built to the north of the hillfort, and a little later, probably in the fifth century AD, two separate settlements were constructed, each of which contained small huts with stone footings and perhaps clay walling. The two settlements were burnt, then rebuilt and burnt again, and finally abandoned, perhaps in the sixth or seventh century. By the Middle Ages, Crickley Hill formed part of the pasture land of two adjacent parishes and was grazed. A small stone hut was built on the edge of the hill, perhaps to shelter the shepherd.

See also Art and Architecture.

Further Reading

Dixon, Philip. 1988. 'The Neolithic Settlement on Crickley Hill'. Pp. 75–87 in *Enclosures and Defences in the Neolithic of Western Europe*. Edited by C. Burgess, C. Mordant and M. Maddison. British Archaeological Reports 403.

———. 1994. *Crickley Hill. Volume 1: The Hillfort Defences*. Crickley Hill Trust and the Department of Archaeology, Nottingham University.

Sarah Milliken

Cross of Muiredach, Monasterboice

The church at Monasterboice, in County Louth, is one of the most important High Cross sites in Ireland, having two complete and at least two fragmentary crosses. The name suggests the traditional ascription of the site as the monastery of Buithe, about which very little is known with certainty.

The Cross of Muiredach is the best preserved and one of the most impressive of all the Irish High Crosses and probably dates from the second half of the ninth century. It gets its name from an inscription at the bottom of the west face, fitted in between the high-relief carving of two cats: OR DO MUIREDACH LASNDERNAD IN CHROS – 'A prayer for Muiredach, who caused this cross to be made'. This Muiredach is usually taken to be Muiredach mac Domhnaill, an abbot or *comarba* of the monastery who died in 923, but the name was a common one, borne by more than one abbot, so this is not certain.

As with all the High Crosses, the purposes of this Cross were several. The fact that there are at least four crosses remaining on this site suggests that they helped to establish the boundary of the *termon*, the sacred space of the monastic precinct, which provided sanctuary for those in need. Crosses also marked holy places connected with major monastic events and miracles believed to have been worked by the founding saints and others. They were certainly places where liturgical prayer was conducted, possibly following known customs in Jerusalem, where ceremonies were conducted before the True Cross in the Church of the Holy Sepulchre. A further parallel with Jerusalem can be seen in the shape of the capstone, which is that of a small house or shrine, taken to be a copy of the Temple of Jerusalem, as it was understood by the artist. There is a similar illustration in the ***Book of Kells***, where Christ is being tempted by the devil to throw himself down from the pinnacle of the Temple. The crosses may have also have served as teaching aids, to explain the mysteries of faith and the scriptures to the faithful.

Muiredach's cross is of sandstone and stands 18 feet (5. 5 metres) high. The head and shaft are carved from a single block of stone, with the capstone added on by means of a mortice and tenon. The figures are carved in deep relief and are well modelled and full of life, vigour and character. Because the details are particularly well preserved, it is comparatively easy to identify the scenes chosen. The scenes on the east and west faces should be read from the bottom up. They are (west face) the arrest of Christ, the incredulity of Thomas, the Mission of Peter and Paul, the Crucifixion and the Ascension. On the east face, they are Adam and Eve with Cain and Abel, David and Goliath, Moses striking the rock, the Adoration of the Magi, the Last Judgement (probably one of the richest depictions of this scene in contemporary Europe) and Christ in majesty. Thus, the whole epic of salvation was displayed both from events in the life of Christ and by using a sophisticated Old Testament typology.

See also Art and Architecture; Celts.

Further Reading

Harbison, Peter. 1992. *The High Crosses of Ireland: An Iconographical and Photographic Survey.* Dr. Rudolf Habelt GMBH.

Macalister, R. A. S. 1966. *Guide to Monasterboice.* Dundalgan Press.

Richardson, Hilary, and John Scarry. 1990. *An Introduction to Irish High Crosses.* Mercier Press.

Patricia Rumsey

Cú Chulainn

In the Ulster Cycle of tales, Cú Chulainn (*aka* Sétanta) figures as a young hero, admired and feared for his warrior skills, fighting fury, sense of honour and beauty. He epitomises the glorious and tragic sides of a warrior who lives fast and dies young. He single-handedly defends **Ulster** against its enemies and is unequalled as a fighter but is also forced to kill his only son and his beloved foster brother.

Most of the 'classical' tales involving Cú Chulainn are dated to the eighth and ninth centuries, but there are also somewhat older texts, including *Verba Scáthaige* ('The Words of Scáthach') and *Forfes Fer Fálchae* ('The Siege of the Men of Fálchae'). The latter belongs to a cycle involving the **Munster** character Cú Roí.

According to the earliest tale of his conception, *Compert Con Culainn*, Sétanta was born thrice. Dechtine, daughter of Conchobar mac Nessa, takes him with her from his supernatural parents at Brug na Bóinne. When the baby dies, it transforms itself into a small animal which Dechtine inadvertently swallows in a drink. In a dream, **Lug**, a Celtic deity, tells Dechtine that he is the father and that the boy will be called Sétanta. The Ulstermen think she is pregnant from Conchobar and she is betrothed to the human Súaltaim mac Róich. Ashamed, Dechtine procures an abortion, but when she gets pregnant again from her husband she gives birth to Sétanta. The triple conception signifies his extraordinary personality.

In the *macgnímrada* ('boyhood deeds'), one of the finest sections of *Táin Bó Cúailnge* ('The Cattle-raid of Cooley'), Sétanta goes alone to the playing field of **Emain Macha** when he is five years old. There, 150 boys attack him. Overcoming all resistance, the boy is taken in by Conchobar, who has the legal obligation to protect him. Later, when Sétanta arrives late at a feast of Culann the smith and kills Culann's ferocious watchdog, he takes the guarding of the territory upon himself, hence earning the name Cú Chulainn ('Hound of Culann'). At the age of seven, Cú Chulainn takes up arms, drives with his charioteer Láeg to the midlands and decapitates three fearsome warriors. Still in his fighting rage, he returns to Emain Macha, where only the sight of naked women makes him hide his face, after which he is cooled down by being thrown into three vats of cold water successively.

Further adventures take place in Alba (Scotland) where the father of his lover Emer entices him to train with the female warrior

Scáthach ('Shadowy'). He does so, overcoming many difficulties, and also fathers a son of Aífe, whom he leaves with her. In another story, Cú Chulainn kills his strong young son to uphold the honour of the Ulstermen. After winning Emer, Cú Chulainn defends Ulster against the forces of queen Medb of Connacht, her husband Ailill and their allies, including a number of exiled Ulster heroes. The Ulstermen are disabled by a curse which renders them powerless, but since Cú Chulainn's father is a foreigner, he is not affected. By tricks, duels and martial feats, he keeps the invaders at bay, as related in the *Táin*. The war forces Cú Chulainn to kill a number of his foster brothers, but he receives aid from one of his foster fathers, the exiled Fergus mac Róich. During the fighting, Cú Chulainn displays his fighting rage, in which he closes one eye, his hair stands on end, his limbs turn inside out and his internal organs are visible – a gruesome spectacle. In the *Táin*, Cú Chulainn is seventeen years old. In other tales, his age is usually not given, but according to the annals he was twenty-seven when he was killed in AD 2 by his enemies. According to literature, he was doomed after he had violated his *gessa* ('taboos').

Cú Chulainn appears to have a mythological background, and as the son of Lug, he is sometimes regarded as a Celtic demigod. His behaviour is often discussed in the context of the warrior band (*comitatus*), the Old Norse *berserkirs* and the Greek hero Achilles.

See also Gaels; Irish Language; Literature.

Further Reading

Enright, Michael. 2002. 'Fires of Knowledge: A Theory of Warband Education in Medieval Ireland and Homeric Greece'. Pp. 342–367 in *Irland und Europa im früheren Mittelalter: Texte und Überlieferung.* Edited by Próinséas Ní Chatháin and Michael Richter. Four Courts Press.

Jaski, Bart. 1999. 'Cú Chulainn, *Gormac* and *Dalta* of the Ulstermen'. *Cambrian Medieval Celtic Studies* 37: 1–31.

McCone, Kim. 1990. *Pagan Past and Christian Present in Early Irish Literature.* An Sagart.

Bart Jaski

Cumbria

Cumbria is a district in north-western England, just below the Scottish border, which was long the home of a **Brittonic** population before its conquest and conversion to an English county. Stretching from Lancaster in the south to **Carlisle** in the north, it includes an area of glaciated mountains and glacial lake known collectively as the Lake District. The modern county of Cumbria was formed from the older counties of Cumberland, Westmorland and parts of North Lancashire and North Yorkshire.

In Neolithic times, the mountains of the Lake District were a major source of stone axes, and stone circles were erected at Castlerigg, Long Meg and elsewhere. Later, Cumbria was mined for copper, iron ore, graphite and green slate. In the **Iron Age**, Cumbria was under the control of the tribal confederation known as the ***Brigantes***, though the area around Carlisle belonged specifically to a smaller, dependent tribe called the ***Carvetii***. Native settlement types dating back to the **Bronze Age**, such as round huts and enclosures, continued to dominate in the Iron Age and early Roman period. The Romans planted several forts in Cumbria but no villas and no towns apart from Carlisle, which served as the capital of the *civitas Carvetiorum*. Stone and lead mining continued, and the fort of *Glannoventa* (Ravenglass) may have served as a base for the naval fleet patrolling the Irish Sea. Continuity of occupation from Roman to medieval times can be seen best in Carlisle, which may have served as the bishopric for the *civitas*.

Although the details are unclear, the **Britons** survived the withdrawal of Roman troops by eventually defending towns and reoccupying hillforts, forming kingdoms in the north-west such as Elmet, Craven and **Rheged**. Cumbria probably formed part of Rheged, a large and powerful kingdom in the north of Britain in the late fifth and sixth centuries. Known to us almost solely through medieval Welsh poetry, Rheged was ruled by **Urien Rheged** and his son **Owain ap Urien** in the late sixth century. At its height, Rheged may have extended from Galloway in south-west Scotland to Lancashire, but it suffered in the seventh century from the expansion of the English kingdoms of **Northumbria** and **Mercia** as well as the British kingdom of **Strathclyde**. Because British place names dominate particularly in northern Cumbria, it is unlikely that there was much influx of English peasantry in this period of transition from Rheged to Northumbrian rule.

Viking raids devastated the north-western coast of Britain in the ninth century, and a weakened Strathclyde was overwhelmed by the new Scottish kingdom united by **Kenneth MacAlpin**. Scottish kings in the tenth century seem to have created a new entity – Cumberland – and chose kings from among the surviving British aristocracy to rule Cumbria under Scottish suzerainty. These new kings of Cumberland revived hostility towards the English, allowing Hiberno-Norse settlement in the region. These settlers introduced such Scandinavian place-name elements as thwaite ('clearing'), fell ('mountain with grazing'), gill ('ravine') and force ('waterfall'). A coalition of **Scots**, northern Britons and Hiberno-Norse was crushed by **Æthelstan** at the battle of **Brunanburh** in 937, and in 945, **Edmund** defeated the Cumbrian king Dunmail map Owain and blinded two of his sons in an attempt to end the dynasty. Edmund granted Cumberland to Malcolm I of Scotland, and the death of Owen the Bald c.1018 signalled the end of the British royalty in the north.

Norman rule of Cumbria begins with **William II**'s conquest of Carlisle in 1092. Richard Sharpe has discussed the administrative structures that were put in place by the Normans (see Sharpe 2006). By 1101, Ranulf Meschin had control of both Carlisle and Appleby, with wide but undefined powers under the king. He surrendered his role in 1121–1122, and from then until 1133, Cumberland and Westmorland were run by minor local officials answerable to the Exchequer. The creation of a bishopric for this area in 1133 went along with the establishment of normal shire institutions in Cumberland, including a sheriff who remained in office under Scottish rule. This happened officially in 1136, when King **Stephen** granted **David I** Carlisle, but by then Scottish forces were already established in the area. **Henry II**, who had been knighted by David in 1149, reneged upon an agreement with the Scots in 1157 and made Malcolm IV resign Northumberland, Cumberland and Westmorland to him in return for the earldom of Huntingdon.

See also Roman Army; Roman Britain.

Further Reading

Higham, N. J. 1986. *The Northern Counties to AD 1000.* Longman.
Higham, N. J., and Barri Jones. 1991. *The Carvetii.* Sutton.
McCarthy, Mike. 2002. 'Rheged: An Early Historic Kingdom Near the Solway'. *Proceedings of the Society of Antiquaries of Scotland* 132: 357–381.
Phythian-Adams, Charles. 1996. *Land of the Cumbrians: A Study of British Provincial Origins AD 400–1120.* Ashgate.
Sharpe, Richard. 2006. *Norman Rule in Cumbria 1092–1136.* The Cumberland & Westmorland Antiquarian & Archaeological Society.
Winchester, A. J. L. 1987. *Landscape and Society in Medieval Cumbria.* John Donald.

Christopher A. Snyder

Cumbric

See Brythonic Language; Cumbria.

Cummian

Cummian (also spelled 'Cummin' or 'Cumian') the Fada, meaning 'the tall', was an Irish Benedictine bishop and writer of theology from the first half of the seventh century, who is best known for the Paschal letter which he wrote, though he collected and owned several other manuscripts and commentaries, displaying his high level of knowledge. Born c. AD 590, Cummian was a son of Fiachna, king of West **Munster**, and after receiving his monastic instruction at **Durrow**, his early career was spent as a monk and later as abbot at **Clonfert**, before he became abbot and founder of Kilcummin monastery in Killala Bay, County Mayo.

A stout defender of Roman liturgical practice, Cummian argued especially in favour of the Roman Church's calculation of the date of Easter, particularly against the Celtic abbot of **Iona**. A decree that asked the Irish to take their problems to Rome if all else were to fail was amongst the many sections of his famous Paschal, which was composed of five folios and contained sections from the Vulgate and commentaries including those of Jerome, Augustine and Gregory the Great, and it was also notable for the ecclesiastical history which it provided and synodal decrees from both Nicea and Arles. Amongst the many manuscripts in Cummian's collection was a possible letter from **Pelagius**, and he may have also been the author of a penitential, a commentary on Mark and a hymn on the apostles. In keeping with the Irish monks' love of travel, Cummian seems to have moved his work to the monastery of Bobbio in Italy near the end of his life, and upon his death on 12 November 662, he was buried back in Ireland in the cemetery of Kilcummin.

See also Celtic Christianity; Literature; Monasticism.

Further Reading
The Benedictine Monks of St Augustine's Abbey, Ramsgate. 1989. *The Book of Saints: A Dictionary of Servants of Gods Canonized by the Catholic Church* (6th edn.). Morehouse Publication.
O'Loughlin, T. 2000. *Celtic Theology*. Continuum.
Walsh, M., and D. Ó Cróinín (eds.). 1988. *Cummian's Letter De Controversia Paschali*. Pontifical Institute of Medieval Studies.

Anne Sassin

Cunobelinus

Cunobelin, Latinised as Cunobelinus, was one of the most powerful and influential British kings in the years just prior to the Roman conquest of Britain in AD 43. Although he is briefly mentioned by Suetonius and Cassius Dio, most information about him has been pieced together through his copious coinage. He appears to have come to power c. AD 9 and ruled over both the *Catuvellauni* and the *Trinovantes*. His coins name him as Tascio F(ilius), 'Son of Tasciovanus', though this may simply mean a close relative. His coins were issued at **Colchester** (the new Catuvellaunian capital) and also at **St Albans**, where Tasciovanus had been based.

Cunobelinus acquired the Roman-style title *Rex* (Suetonius calls him *Rex Britanniarum*, 'King of the **Britons**'), and his extremely Roman-style coins were probably produced by engravers trained in Roman workshops. To judge by the distribution of his coins, he was influential over a large area of south-east England and encouraged trade with his Roman neighbours, importing olive oil and fish sauces (from Spain), wine, Roman metal vessels, glass and Gallo-Belgic pottery (produced on the Continent and imitated at Colchester).

The family of Cunobelinus had varying territorial interests and opinions of Rome. A brother named Epaticcus (d. c. AD 35) seized control of the ***Atrebates*** during Cunobelinus's lifetime and minted coins at **Silchester**. He was succeeded there by one of Cunobelinus's sons, **Caratacus**, who, with his brother Togodumnus, led the British resistance against the Roman invasion of AD 43. Another son, Adminius, controlled Kent but was banished by Cunobelinus, and sought help from the Roman Emperor Caligula. Cunobelinus died around AD 40 but appears in Geoffrey of Monmouth's *History of the Kings of Britain* (c.1136) as 'Cymbeline' and then (via Holinshed) in Shakespeare's 1610 play of that name.

See also Celts.

Further Reading
Allen, D. 1944. 'The Belgic Dynasties of Britain and Their Coins'. *Archaeologia* 110: 1–46.
Cunliffe, Barry. 2005. *Iron Age Communities of Britain* (4th edn.). RKP.
Snyder, Christopher A. 2003. *The Britons*. Peoples of Europe Series. Blackwell.
Stevens, C. E. 1951. 'Britain Between the Invasions (54 BC–AD 43): A Study in Ancient Diplomacy'. Pp. 332–344 in *Aspects of Archaeology in Britain and Beyond*. Edited by W. F. Grimes. Edwards.
Todd, Malcolm. 1999. *Roman Britain* (3rd edn.). Blackwell.

Jennifer Laing

Cunomorus

Cunomorus is the Latin name of a sixth-century British ruler known to readers of the romances of **Tristan** and Isolde as King Mark of **Cornwall**. Cornwall was then part of a larger British kingdom called **Dumnonia**. Gildas (writing in the early sixth century) gives us the name of the king of Dumnonia in his day as *Constantinus*. This Constantine appears in later Welsh genealogies as Custennin, son of Cynfawr. *Cynfawr* is Welsh, but the earlier Latinised British form would be *Cunomorus*, which means 'Hound of the Sea'. The earliest evidence for him is the inscription on the so-called Tristan stone, found near Castle Dore in Fowey. It reads DRUSTANUS HIC IACIT CUNOMORI FILIUS, 'Here lies Drustanus son of Cunomorus'. *Drustan* is the Cornish (or perhaps Pictish) original of Tristan, and Wrmonoc in the *Life of St. Pol de Leon* mentions a 'King Mark (*Marcus*) who is called by another name Cunomorus'. This evidence has led many to conclude that Cynfawr/Cunomorus was the sixth-century lord of Castle Dore, the King Mark of the Tristan legends and the March ap Meirchion, who is **Arthur**'s nemesis in the Welsh Triads. However, there are two earlier references to a Cunomorus in Brittany: Gregory of Tours describes him as a Breton count, and in the *Life of St. Samson*, he is a minor Breton lord of Carhaix, who rebels against Judhael, king of Domnonée (see Pearce 1978, 141). Either the Dumnonian Cunomorus held authority in both Britain and Brittany or the genealogists are confusing two different rulers.

See also Britons; Celts; Literature.

Further Reading

Pearce, Susan. 1978. *The Kingdom of Dumnonia*. Lodenek Press.
Snyder, Christopher A. 2003. *The Britons*. Peoples of Europe Series. Blackwell.

Christopher A. Snyder

Currach

The *currach*, or coracle, is a traditional western European craft made by the stretching of hides or waterproofed cloth over a woven wood frame. It played a particular role in early medieval Britain and Ireland as a craft for **penitential** and monastic use, both because it was an inexpensive craft appropriate to Atlantic navigation and because the hide of its covering was a metaphor for the soul travelling in a mortal vessel. Strabo, Avienus and Sidonius attest to the use of hide-covered craft by peoples on the Atlantic seaboard in antiquity. Some of these references have vaguely supernatural overtones, arising from the classical conception of the ocean as a place of peril and mortality (Wooding 2001). The Christian imagery of the hide boat can also signify mortality, encounter and trial.

It is debatable whether the *currach* was as ubiquitous in early Ireland as has sometimes been assumed. The *currach* was one of the many types used in the past, and its prominence in the early twentieth century – through which it came to be a symbol of '**Gaelic**' culture – was not necessarily typical of even nineteenth-century use. Terminology is also problematical. Latin *curuca* is used by **Adomnán** (*Vita Columbae*, II. 45) to describe what are apparently small craft, but larger craft clearly made of hide are described by the term *nauis* (II. 42) and its diminutive *nauicula*. The latter term may relate to the Irish word *naomhóg* (a diminutive of Irish *noe*, cognate of *nauis*), used interchangeably for *currach* in modern Irish.

In early Irish law, the 'one hide' craft was used for voyages of penance and is found in that context in **Muirchú**'s *Vita Patricii* in the story of Maccuill. The *currach* was a favoured symbolic and actual craft for religious exile (***peregrinatio***). Boats of three hides are used in the tales *Immram curaig Maíle Dúin* ('The Voyage of Máel Dúin's *currach*') and the *Immram curaig Ua Corra* ('The Voyage of the *currach* of the Uí Chorra'); three Irishmen who arrived at the court of King Alfred in 891, according to the ***Anglo-Saxon Chronicle***, did so in a boat of 'two and a half hides'. The ***Navigatio Sancti Brendani*** is probably the most famous text to depict an ocean voyage in a *currach*. The author of an Irish commentary on Mark in the seventh century describes the stilling of the tempest (Mark 4:38) in terms of a journey in a *currach*: the wood of the frame being the cross of Christ supporting the mortal flesh of the hide. Episodes in *Vita Columbae* and *Immram curaig Ua Corra* in which infernal beasts attempt to pierce the hide of the ship are used to remind readers that God protects us even in the frailty of our flesh.

See also Literature.

Further Reading

Hornell, J. 1938. *British Coracles and Irish Curraghs*. Sheed and Ward.
Wooding, J. M. (ed.). 2000. *The Otherworld Voyage in Early Irish Literature*. Four Courts Press.
Wooding, J. M. 2001. 'St Brendan's Boat: Dead Hides and the Living Sea in Columban and Related Hagiography'. Pp. 77–92 in *Studies in Irish Hagiography: Saints and Scholars*. Edited by John Carey, Máire Herbert and Padraig Ó Riain. Four Courts Press.

Jonathan Wooding

Cuthbert, Saint

St. Cuthbert was an inspirational English monastic figure who served as the bishop of Lindisfarne in the late seventh century. There are few bishops of the period whose lives are so well documented and yet about whom so little is actually known. Cuthbert's life was treated no fewer than four times in the first fifty years after his death: at his translation in 698, an anonymous monk at **Lindisfarne** composed a life, a few years later **Bede** composed a poetic life, followed some years later a prose life also written by Bede and finally an extensive treatment again by Bede in the *Historia Ecclesiastica*.

Born c. 635, probably to noble parents in **Northumbria**, Cuthbert led a normal life until 651. Sometime during that year, he saw a vision and entered the monastery at Melrose under the direction of Boisil. Later, c. 660, Abbot Eata took Cuthbert with him to the newly founded monastery at Ripon, but they soon returned to Melrose when St. **Wilfrid** was given the monastery. Cuthbert's mentor, Boisil, died of plague, possibly in 664, and Cuthbert succeeded him as prior. Here, his reputation increased due in large part to his constant pastoral visits to the surrounding countryside to preach and teach. One result of this was not only the series of miracles recorded by his biographers, but also that the king's sister, Aebbe, requested that Cuthbert come to her monastery and address those who dwelt there.

When the Council of Whitby was held in 664 and King Oswiu decided in favour of the Roman dating of Easter, Cuthbert was among those who accepted this decision. Sometime in the decade after Whitby, he was moved to the monastery at Lindisfarne at the invitation of its new abbot, Eata. While prior there, he met resistance to the strict adherence to the rule Cuthbert advocated. He responded by becoming a hermit, first on what was to become St Cuthbert's island, and later he removed further from Lindisfarne to Farne Island. He became very well known as a hermit, so his advice was sought by the king's family and he was often visited by various political and religious figures of the time.

In 685, Cuthbert was reluctantly made bishop. He was to go to Hexham, but he refused the bishop's office unless Eata would trade with him and he became bishop of Lindisfarne instead. While a bishop, Cuthbert preserved his strict adherence to the hermit's way of life as best he was able to while engaging in an active pastoral career visiting not only the monasteries but the villages in his see to preach and teach. While teaching in the villages, he developed a reputation as a healer and miracle worker. He naturally enjoyed the connections with the royal family of Northumbria.

Sensing his imminent death, in early 687, Cuthbert resigned his bishopric and retired again to Farne Island and died there on March 20. According to Bede, he advised the community at Lindisfarne to bury him on the island, so that the pilgrims visiting his tomb would not disturb the community. The community, however, buried him in their chapel on the south side of the altar dedicated to St. Peter. He was reinterred in 698 when his body was found incorrupt in a wooden casket and elevated above the altar.

Cuthbert is presented in his lives as a man who was unyielding in passion, particularly when it came to the rule and the eremitic life, and yet had a deep pastoral concern. His habit of preaching and teaching in the countryside was only one example of this and a habit that was not shared by all his contemporaries. Other examples are the lessons he gave to monks who came to visit him on Farne Island and his kind treatment of the young monk who came to spy upon him at prayer. Furthermore, Cuthbert was kind to his horse, whom he fed first from a miraculous provision of food. Cuthbert, at least as Bede presents him, is a saint who is already aware of his greatness.

Bede presents him as a complex figure. Cuthbert eschews worldly position and power and takes up a hermit's life. But Cuthbert is also a man of position and world power: he travels on horseback with a large retinue, he has regular concourse with the king's family, and the magnificent pectoral cross, gospel book and tapestry found in his coffin speak of a man of wealth and position. In spite of these two poles, the hermit and the man of worldly position and power, there is also the pastoral Cuthbert and the Cuthbert who wields spiritual power over nature and performs miracles. The Cuthbert presented to us is a multifaceted individual, even if a complete picture cannot be now drawn of him.

See also Celtic Christianity; Monasticism.

Further Reading

Bonner, G., D. W. Rollaston and C. Stancliffe (eds.). 1989. *St. Cuthbert, His Cult and His Community to AD 1200.* Boydell Press.

Colgrave, Bertram (ed.). 1940. *Two Lives of St. Cuthbert.* Cambridge University Press.

Johnson-South, Ted, and D. S. Brewer (eds.). 2002. *Historia de sancto Cuthberto: A History of Saint Cuthbert and a Record of His Patrimony.* Anglo-Saxon Texts 3. D. S. Brewer.

Stevens, Clifford. 1991. 'St Cuthbert: The Lindisfarne Years'. *Cistercian Studies* 26.1: 25–39.

Thacker, Alan. 2002. 'The Making of a Local Saint'. Pp. 45–73 in *Local Saints and Local Churches in the Early Medieval West.* Edited by Alan Thacker and Richard Sharpe. Oxford University Press.

Larry Swain

Cymry

Cymry (also *cumbri)* is the name by which the **Welsh** have referred to themselves since as early as the seventh century AD. Derived from the Latin *combrogi*, meaning 'fellow countrymen', the sense of nationality which it portrayed was both cultural and linguistic. The first reference to *cymry* can be found in a praise poem to Cadwallon, possibly dating from c. 633. The vernacular term appears to have derived ultimately from the Latin *cives* (meaning 'citizens'), which distinguished

Roman citizens in Britain from barbarian neighbours like the **Picts** and the **Scots**. In the fifth century, it came to denote Christian **Britons**, even those living beyond **Hadrian's Wall**, who were then opposing the expansion of new barbarian settlers, the *Saxones* or *allmyn* (i.e. the **Anglo-Saxons**). Latin *cives* evolved from there into the early British *combrogi* and then into the Old Welsh *cymry*, which was used in addition to the earlier vernacular term *Brython/Brythoniaid* (itself derived from the Latin *Britto/Brittones*) that encompassed all the other **Brythonic** speakers (as opposed to the **Goidelic** branches of Celtic) of south-western and northern Britain as well as Armorica. It appears in the tenth-century ***Armes Prydein*** ('The Great Prophecy of Britain') as *Kymry*, who are called upon to ally with other Britons and the Dublin Danes to overthrow the English king **Æthelstan**. By the time of the 1197 entry in the *Brut y Tywysogyon*, *cymry* had come to replace the term 'Briton' as the label preferred by Welsh writers.

Though **Geoffrey of Monmouth** in the twelfth century claimed that *cymry* derived from Camber, the son of **Brutus**, this is not a favoured origin, and it has been suggested that this need for a sense of identity stemmed from the Britons struggle for survival in early post-Roman centuries. Considering that the British of southern Scotland also associated themselves with this term, it may indeed support a derivation from a 'Cumric' distinctiveness in the **Brittonic Age**. Later, Bishop Bernard of St David's would write that law was the one distinguishing factor between the Welsh and other Britons. The survival of *cymry* can be seen in place names in England (e.g. the many *cumber-* places, as in Cumberland and Cumberton), where perhaps the English newcomers were identifying settlements of surviving Britons in their midst. The Welsh needing to differentiate themselves from the Romans, the English and the Norman French certainly outlasted the Middle Ages. Despite the eventual Normanisation of Wales, with its introduction of feudalistic and ecclesiastical overlords in Wales, the *Cymry* were able to retain their language and, more importantly, their sense of identity, occasionally managing to overcome princely disputes to join forces against their English foes in the High Middle Ages.

Further Reading

Dark, K. R. 1994. *Civitas to Kingdom*. Leicester University Press.

Snyder, Christopher A. 1998. *An Age of Tyrants: Britain and the Britons, AD 400–600*. Sutton Publishing.

———. 2003. *The Britons*. Peoples of Europe Series. Blackwell.

Anne Sassin

Cynewulf

Cynewulf is one of only two English poets whose name is preserved from the period before the **Norman Conquest**, the other being **Cædmon**, but Cynewulf is in fact unique in passing his name down to us, unlike Cædmon, whose name descends to us from **Bede**'s account of the miraculous revelation of his poetic gift. Four **Old English** poems preserve in their final lines coded, runic characters which may be interpreted to spell 'Cynewulf', leading scholars to assume for a long time that all four poems are indeed the work of a single poet of that name who encoded brief autobiographical comments into his compositions, signing them as described. The four poems are those known as 'Elene', 'Juliana', 'Fates of the Apostles' and 'The Ascension' or 'Christ II', which happens to be the second of three poems in the ***Exeter Book*** on the revelation of Christ.

'Elene' and 'Juliana' are both saints' lives, the first describing the life of St. Helen, the mother of Emperor **Constantine,** who established Christianity in the Roman Empire. Helen is credited with having gone to Jerusalem and located the true cross and returned it to Rome. 'Elene' is found in an English manuscript known as *The Vercelli Book*, because it seems to have been located in Vercelli, Italy, throughout its documented history. 'Juliana' is, like 'Christ II', found in the *Exeter Book*, and like 'Elene', it is a hagiographical work. She was one of the martyrs of the Diocletian persecution of Christians at the beginning of the fourth century. The narrative centres around her conversion of a devil sent to torture her while she was being held captive. 'The Fates of the Apostles', also in the *Vercelli Book*, traces the martyrdoms of Christ's apostles as they spread the church through Europe and Asia Minor, and even India. 'The Ascension' is homiletic in its style and therefore exhibits a less coherent narrative, but it focuses on interpreting the events surrounding Christ's ascension.

Scholars date the period during which Cynewulf flourished between the late eighth and the late tenth centuries, the former dating is based on a debate about the probable period during which the poet might have spelled the second syllable of his name **e** and not the expected **i**, and the latter is based on the dating of the manuscripts in which his work appears. For a number of years, scholars accepted that the poems could be dated to the ninth century because if a series of near-rhymes in 'Elene' were corrected to perfect rhymes, they would uniformly represent a ninth-century dialect. Near-rhyme, however, is sufficiently common in Old English poetry that one cannot argue that any such pairing requires correcting to exact rhyme. Moreover, I have argued that Cynewulf's source in 'The Fates of the Apostles', depends upon Usuard's martyrology, a document which is narrowly datable to 875 and which is unlikely to have been available in England until after the middle of the tenth century (Conner 1993). This would make Cynewulf a contemporary, more or less, with the manuscripts in which his poems appear. It would be inappropriate, however, to conclude that the issue of dating Cynewulf's poetry is a closed one.

Technical issues aside, Cynewulf is an excellent Old English poet. Although his work embraces the orthodox subject matter of his time, he sets significant rhetorical challenges for himself, such as the re-creation of the cross that appeared to Constantine at the beginning of 'Elene', and invokes them with great mastery. Moreover, he creates two strong heroic women whom he, nevertheless, differentiates with great care, in a way that is rare for a single author's *oeuvre* in the early Middle Ages. Cynewulf's style has been carefully analysed over the years, most recently by Andy Orchard, who sees him actively combining in new and imaginative ways the vernacular oral and literate Latin traditions he inherited.

See also Literature.

Further Reading

Bjork, Robert E. (ed.). 2001. *The Cynewulf Reader*. Routledge.

Conner, Patrick W. 1993. *Anglo-Saxon Exeter: A Tenth-Century Cultural History*. Boydell & Brewer.

Greenfield, Stanley B., and Daniel C. Calder. 1986. *A New Critical History of Old English Literature* (rev. edn.). New York University Press.

Patrick W. Conner

D

Dál Riata

See Dalriada.

Dalriada

Dalriada, or as it is more often now termed Dál Riata, is the name given to an area of northern Ireland (roughly County Antrim) and a kingdom which was its offshoot in western Scotland (mainly modern Argyll). The homeland of the settlers was traditionally centred on Dunseverick, and they were known as Scotti – **Scots** – in Roman sources, which documented them as having taken part in raids on **Roman Britain**. The name of Dál Riata means 'the portion of Riata' and is seen to be a reference to the mythical king Riata or Reuda, who according to **Bede** was the founder of the kingdom in Scotland. Bede suggested that Reuda came to Scotland and 'won lands from the **Picts**', adding that 'they are still called Dalreudini after this leader' (*HE*, 1). Another foundation legend suggests that Reuda was Cairpre of Riata, who settled in Scotland some ten generations before Fergus mac Eric, i.e. in the second or third century AD.

There is some evidence for contact between the Irish Dál Riata and Scotland before the traditional date of colonisation, and possibly there were marriage alliances. The supposed colonisation took place in the later fifth century, when traditionally Fergus mac Eric migrated with his brothers to establish the new territory. An entry in the *Annals of Tigernach* for AD 500 states that 'Feargus mor mac Erc with the nation of Dál Riata took part of Britain and died there', but modern scholarship suggests that this is taken from a tenth-century entry in the *Chronicle of Clonmacnois* and some scholars have argued that the migration story is a myth intended to serve the aims of tenth-century Scottish kings. This does not, however, explain how an Irish kingdom was established in western Scotland, and the lack of archaeological evidence for the settlement is perhaps to be explained by the lack of information we have about the archaeology of both Antrim and Argyll in the fifth century; at the very least, there must have been an aristocratic takeover to establish Irish overlordship, which may have been occasioned by pressure from the leading Irish dynasty, the **Uí Néill**, at the time.

Another source, the *Senchus fer nAlban* ('The Tradition of the Men of Scotland', composed in the eighth century but surviving in a tenth-century manuscript), provides a potted history of the kingdom from Fergus down to the seventh century. According to the *Senchus*, Dál Riata was divided between the sons of Fergus mac Erc, the family (or Cenél) of Loarn occupying northern Argyll, the family of Angus (the Cenél Oengusa) occupying Islay and the family of Gabran (the Cenél nGabrain) in Kintyre and Knapdale. The same source provides a useful list of the manpower available on land and sea in the kingdom.

The early history of Dál Riata is one of family feuding between the lines of Loarn and Gabran. The history is fragmented, and the first king to figure who was active outside his own territory was Gabran, who campaigned at the end of the sixth century against the **Britons** adjacent to the Forth, and possibly in Pictland. The next major figure was **Aedán mac Gabráin**, a dynamic leader active round the Forth and in Pictland, who had an expedition to the Orkneys in 581. He sent aid to the Britons against the **Angles** at **Degsastan** in 603, in which the Anglo-Saxons were victorious. By the mid-seventh century, Dál Riata was broken up under the control of four families, each with its own king, but with a high king over all. Under Ferchar 'the Tall', Dál Riata was reunited at the end of the seventh century, but during most of the eighth and the ninth centuries the Picts were the dominant people in northern Scotland. Some Scottish kings seem to have ruled in Pictland, however, and in 843/844, **Kenneth MacAlpin** of Dál Riata, under somewhat obscure circumstances, came to rule Picts and Scots in a united kingdom, subsequently known as Alba.

The language spoken in Dál Riata was initially 'common Gaelic', spoken in both Ireland and now Scotland. Out of this common Gaelic evolved Scottish Gaelic, which probably through the agency of clerics from **Iona** had spread to neighbouring Pictland before the union of Picts and Scots in the ninth century, and the dissemination of Scottish Gaelic was furthered by Irish-Norse activity in the tenth century. A few inscriptions in the ogham script are known, including one from **Dunadd**, a Dalriadic centre in the Crinan Moss of Argyll.

The archaeology of Dál Riata is inadequately understood, though the centre of Dunadd has been extensively excavated, and important excavations have also been carried out at Dunollie, another fort just outside modern Oban. Much information has also come from a long series of excavations at the monastic site of Iona, off Mull. Apart from the main sites mentioned, there are a series of **duns** that were occupied in the period, and the same is also the case with a **crannog** at Loch Glashan.

See also Celts; Gaels; Kings and Kingship.

Further Reading

Anderson, M. 1973. *Kings and Kingship in Early Scotland*. Edinburgh University Press.
Bannerman, J. 1974. *Studies in the History of Dalriada*. Edinburgh University Press.
Foster, S. 1996. *Picts, Gaels and Scots*. Batsford.
Laing, Lloyd, and Jennifer Laing. 2001. *The Picts and the Scots* (2nd edn.). Alan Sutton.
Smyth, Alfred P. 1984. *Warlords and Holy Men, Scotland AD 80–1000*. Edward Arnold.

Lloyd Laing

Damnonii

The *Damnonii*, sometimes referred to as the ***Dumnonii***, were one of the indigenous **Brythonic** tribes of **Iron Age** and **Roman Britain**, whose territory lay in western central Scotland, in the area around **Strathclyde**, including modern Ayrshire, Dumbartonshire, Lanarkshire and Renfrewshire. Similar to their neighbours, the ***Votadini***, the *Damnonii* formed a buffer state between the **Caledonians** and Britannia, and according to Ptolemy's *Geography*, 'towns' (i.e. settlements) which lay in their territory included Colanica, Coria, Victoria and Vindogara, the last associated with Ayr in Strathclyde. Although no *civitas* capital has been identified, the Damnonian stronghold may have been at **Dumbarton** Rock, upon which sat Dumbarton Castle, the capital of the early medieval kingdom of Alt Clut, which flourished as a major industrial centre and citadel from the sixth to the ninth century AD. From here, it seems that they conducted trade with the Romans, attesting to their friendly relations and probably *foederati* status, though unfortunately the region has not provided much evidence for Roman occupation, apart from the fort at Castledykes.

The Iron Age remains in the territory are varied and include **hillforts**, particularly in the Clyde valley and in Ayrshire, and **crannogs**. Other tribes in Britain share the *Dumnonii* name, including those which occupied Devon and **Cornwall**, as well as the Irish Damnonians. Though the territory of the *Damnonii* does not seem to have been immediately affected by the Roman withdrawal from Britain and barbarian raids of the fifth century, it eventually contributed to the formation of the kingdom of Strathclyde in the tenth century.

See also Celts; Picts; Scots.

Further Reading

Breeze, David. 1981. *The Northern Frontiers of Roman Britain*. Batsford.

Cunliffe, B. W. 1991. *Iron Age Communities in Britain* (3rd edn.). RKP.

Harding, D. W. 2004. *The Iron Age in Northern Britain: Celts and Romans, Natives and Invaders*. Edinburgh University Press.

Anne Sassin

Danebury

Danebury, Hampshire, is one of the few Early **Iron Age hillforts** to have been extensively excavated (by Sir Barry Cunliffe). Its construction began in the sixth century BC with the building of an earth rampart with timber facing, furnished with two gates joined by a roadway. Internally, circular houses and storage buildings were built immediately behind the rampart. Considerable numbers of storage pits were discovered, as well as a building in the centre, which was interpreted as a shrine.

Danebury was attacked and refortified in the fifth century BC. One of the original gates was blocked and the remaining gate was given highly elaborate defensive works. The rampart was heightened with material from a quarry ditch. Between this ditch and the rampart were storage buildings and working areas. The main road remained in use and houses were rebuilt over two or three centuries. Buildings were confined to zones, and rows of four- and six-post buildings were constantly replaced. Danebury continued in use until around 100 BC, and the ramparts seem to have been refortified in the fifth or sixth century AD.

See also Britons; Celts.

Further Reading

Sir Barry Cunliffe, B. W. 1991–1996. *Danebury: An Iron Age Hillfort in Hampshire*, 6 vols. Council for British Archaeology.

———. 1993. *The English Heritage Book of Danebury* (rev. edn.). Batsford.

———. 2003. *Danebury Hillfort*. Tempus.

Jennifer Laing

Danelaw

Danelaw was the name of the north-eastern area of England where, according to treaty, the Danes settled in the 870s following their defeat by King **Alfred** of **Wessex**.Until the mid-tenth century, the Danelaw included, at various times, Northumbria, parts of Mercia and East Anglia. Its southern border was Watling Street, running from London to Chester. The area became known as the Danelaw in the early eleventh century because it was believed that all the inhabitants of the region lived under Danish law. The Danelaw was the result of decades of battles between the Danish forces and the House of Wessex under Alfred, his elder brothers, **Æthelberht**, **Æthelbald** and **Æthelred** I, and their father, Æthelwulf. It was reunited with southern England under Edgar in the 960s.

On 15 April 871, King Æthelred died, probably of a wound inflicted in battle with the **Vikings**. Because his children were minors, Æthelred's brother, Alfred, was elected king without contest. Alfred continued to fight the Viking invaders, with minimal success and frequent failure, until a surprise invasion caught him totally unprepared and robbed him of his kingdom. After losing a battle to the Danish forces in 875, Alfred sought to purchase peace from the Vikings, as many other rulers in England and France had before.

Because the Danes were not Christian and were therefore not committed to Christian oaths, Alfred attempted to attain peace by requiring **Guthram** to swear an oath on a pagan relic in addition to exchanging hostages. The Vikings , however, not adhering to this oath either, murdered their Anglo-Saxon hostages, continued to harass the countryside, and drove Alfred out of Wessex with a small band of retainers. Legend holds that Alfred, while hiding in the fens of Somerset, infiltrated the Viking camp and learned of their battle plans. After assuring his men of an easy victory, Alfred led the Wessex forces to a decisive victory at the battle of **Edington** in May 878. Using a fleet of messengers to quickly and stealthily call up the *fyrd*, Alfred and his troops chased the surprised Vikings back into their stronghold of Chippenham and laid seige. After several days, the Danes submitted to their hunger, thirst and fear, surrendering to Alfred and agreeing to his terms.

But Alfred learned from his past mistake in negotiating with the Danes. If the pagans could not be trusted to adhere to their word, they must convert to Christianity. Alfred became the godfather of Guthram and arranged a truce that split the English isle neatly in two. The Danes controlled the north-eastern section of the country, above Watling Street (the Danelaw), and Alfred controlled the south-west (the Anglalaw). Each territory was so named because the people there lived under the differing rules, English written and customary law in Alfred's territory and Danish customary law in the Danelaw. The remainder of Alfred's reign was free from major Danish incursions, although the ***Anglo-Saxon Chronicles*** tell repeatedly of Alfred's successes in various battles, suggesting that the kingdom was never fully at peace. The relative peace that followed the formation of the Danelaw granted Alfred the ability to begin a program of national reform from the reorganisation of military institutions, to monetary reforms, urban planning and the revitalisation of England's literary glory.

Although Guthram converted to Christianity in the peace agreement struck by Alfred, there is no absolute surety that the entire Scandinavian population contained by the Danelaw also converted. Scholars have argued that the majority of the Danish population converted at the same time, and it is true that the spread of Christianity throughout groups often occurred alongside or quickly following the conversion of the group leader. Several Anglo-Saxon authors (such as **Asser** and the anonymous author of the *Anglo-Saxon Chronicle*), however, continued to refer to the Scandinavians as pagans even after the conversion of Guthram and the creation of the Danelaw. Christian iconography existed in Scandinavian coins, prominent individuals were often buried near churches, and stone sculptures appeared in and around churches, indicating perhaps a widespread recognition of the Christian faith. And yet, authors mentioned prominent Scandinavian settlers who had converted as well as those who had remained pagan. It appears, from the juxtaposition of Christian and pagan elements, as well as the listed converts and holdouts, that the total conversion of the Danish settlers was a longer process than originally believed. One factor that most likely contributed to the increased Christianisation of the Danish settlers was their eventual integration with the indigenous Anglo-Saxon population living within their borders. The Danes did not utterly replace the English who had lived north of Watling Street when Alfred negotiated the Danelaw; while it is entirely possible that they dispossessed some indigenous landholders, in many cases the Danish settlers may have bought land or married into English families that possessed land. The continued association between the pagan or nominally Christian Danes and the solidly Christian English may have spread Christianity gradually to the new settlers.

Linguistically, the settlement of the Danes brought some changes to the English language, much of which is only recorded later in Wessex documents. In some cases, Old Norse terms merged with Anglo-Saxon words. Our modern word 'dream' combines the **Old English** word *drēam* ('joy') with the Old Norse *draumr* ('vision in sleep'). Additionally, certain sound combinations re-entered our phonological system. Because the Anglo-Saxon sound combination [sk], written sc, shifted to [š], many of our words with [sk] come from the Danes: the Old English word *scyrte*, for example, became our modern word shirt, while the Danish cognate *skyrta* became our modern skirt. In addition to the replacement of existing Old English words, a small number of Scandinavian terms also crept into the Anglo-Saxon lexicon to label objects or concepts previously unnamed: for example, certain legal terms specific to Danish administration or nautical terms for the ships the Vikings used to raid.

Further Reading

Abels, Richard Philip. 1998. *Alfred the Great: War, Kingship, and Culture in Anglo-Saxon England*. Longman.

Algeo, John, and Thomas Pyles. 2005. *The Origins and Development of the English Language* (5th edn.). Thomson Wadsworth.

Baugh, Albert C., and Thomas Cable. 2002. *The History of the English Language* (5th edn.). Prentice Hall.

Hadley, D. M. 2000. *The Northern Danelaw: Its Social Structure, c.800–1100*. Leicester University Press.

———. 2006. *The Vikings in England: Settlement, Society and Culture*. Mancheter University Press.

Hadley, D. M. and Julian D. Richards. 2000. *Cultures in Contact: Scandinavian Settlement in England in the Ninth and Tenth centuries*. Brepols.

Hart, Cyril R. 1992. *The Danelaw*. Hambledon Press.

Richards, Julian C. 2001. *Blood of the Vikings*. Hodder & Stoughton.

Britt Rothauser

Danes

See Vikings.

David I (r. 1124–1153)

David I, king of **Scots** from 1124 to 1153, played an instrumental role in shaping the medieval Scottish kingdom and has gone down in history as one of the most important of the medieval Scottish kings.

The youngest son of **Malcolm III** and Margaret (later St. Margaret), David was probably born in the early 1080s. In the unstable political environment that followed the death of his mother and father in 1093, he was sent to the English court, where he grew up; his sister, Matilda, married **Henry I** in 1100, which gave David and his brother **Alexander I** elevated status. As a protégé of Henry I, David acquired lands, wealth and prominence in England. In 1114, he married a wealthy widow, Maud de Senlis, which brought him the earldoms of Huntingdon and Northampton. At about the same time, he was given lands and jurisdiction in southern Scotland. One English writer remarked that David's upbringing at the court of the English king 'rubbed off all tarnish of Scottish barbarity' (Anderson 1908, 157), a reminder that residence at the court of Henry I allowed David the opportunity to assimilate contemporary Anglo-French culture. As an example of this, David was knighted by Henry and came to be regarded as a paragon of contemporary knighthood. David's familiarity with the English kingship, government and culture was to have particular significance when he became king of Scots.

David, already middle-aged, succeeded to the kingship of the Scots on the death of his brother, Alexander, without legitimate heirs in 1124. He seems to have faced some resistance early in his reign from rival contenders for the kingship (one of whom was possibly an illegitimate son of Alexander), but by the mid-1130s the situation had stabilised. Relations with England remained good while Henry I was alive, but David involved himself in the struggles that followed Henry's death. Despite a Scottish defeat at the battle of the Standard near Northallerton in 1138, David took control of a substantial portion of northern England between the Ribble and the Tees, which was not relinquished until the reign of Malcolm IV (1153–1165).

David's long reign saw the transformation of Scottish society, but innovations were carefully balanced by respect for traditional institutions and members of the native ruling elite. The minting of coins and the development of urban centres signalled economic transformation, while government and administration were enhanced by the development of sheriffdoms on an English model. Military and social aspects of society were altered by the introduction of knights and knights' fees, and David also brought Anglo-Norman colonists to Scotland from south of the border; some of these families, such as the **Bruces**, fitzAlans (later Stewarts) and Morvilles played important roles in subsequent Scottish history. David was also a patron of the reformed Continental religious orders, and following the trends begun by his brother Alexander and his mother, he founded or endowed a number of religious houses; David also reformed the Scottish episcopate and founded several new bishoprics.

When David died on 24 May 1153, he was already something of a legend among contemporaries, most of whom praised him highly as an ideal and pious ruler. Modern historians have regarded him as one of the greatest of the medieval Scottish kings, whose reign was instrumental in medieval Scottish state building.

See also Plantagenets.

Further Reading

Anderson, A. O. (ed. and tr.). 1908, repr. 1991. *Scottish Annals from English Chroniclers AD 500 to 1286.* Paul Watkins.

———. 1922, repr. 1992. *Early Sources of Scottish History AD 500 to 1286.* Oliver and Boyd. Paul Watkins.

Barrow, G. W. S. 1984, repr. 1992. 'David I of Scotland: The Balance of New and Old'. Pp. 45–66 in *Scotland and Its Neighbours in the Middle Ages.* Hambledon.

Duncan, A. A. M. 1975. *Scotland: The Making of the Kingdom.* Oliver and Boyd.

———. 2002. *The Kingship of the Scots 842–1292.* Edinburgh University Press.

R. Andrew McDonald

David, Saint (d. 589)

St. David, or Dewi Sant as he is known in **Welsh**, was a church official in the sixth century AD who later became the patron saint of Wales. Although there is no certainty about the dates of his lifetime, 589 seems to have been the year of his death, with a range from 462 to 530 put forward for his birth, though c. 487–500 is a better approximation. Unlike many of the key figures who lived in the Age of Saints, an extensive amount has been written on David and the events in his life, even if they are unfortunately sometimes in contradiction. The *Life of Saint David* written by Rhygyfarch (Ricemarch) of Llanbadarn in 1090–1095 is the earliest work of the lives of the Welsh saints; however, earlier sources include the mention of David in an Irish martyrology in c. 800 and in a list of saints from Ireland of around the same period. The *Life of Paul of Léon*, written in 884, also describes David, in this instance, as an *aquaticus* (waterman), a reference to his push for drinking only cold water, one of the many indications of his asceticism. Early in the tenth century, he figured in a poem, the '**Armes Prydein Vawr**'. Gerald of Wales (c. 1200) and the anchorite of Llanddewibrefi (c. 1346) also gave accounts of him.

In spite of the incredible nature of some of the material, a select number of events described may be plausible, though David's early life is certainly the most unclear. According to legend, the saint was the result of a violation to his mother Non, the daughter of the lord of Caer Goch in Pembrokeshire, and was born on a cliff top during a storm, supposedly very near the location of **St David**'s today. Rhygyfarch cites David as being son of *sanctus rex ceredigionis,* who has been interpreted as Sandde, king of **Ceredigion**, although as he seems to have been the brother of the king Urai, he was more likely a prince. This still made David of the house of Ceredigion, however, and his education has been associated with Windci-Lantquendi, often identified as Whitland, under the instruction of the St. Paulinus, though he was also said to have studied under **St. Illtud** at Llantwit Major.

Due to his evangelical lifestyle, several monastic establishments in southern Wales have been attributed to David, and though many of them are probably later fabrications, a few of the legitimate foundations may include Betws, Llanarthne and Llangyfelach. The saint was also associated with some work at **Bath** and **Glastonbury**, where according to **William of Malmesbury** he supposedly had an extension added to the abbey. But it was the foundation of Mynyw in the Ross Vale, the port of Menevia, which would become the church for which he is most famous. According to legend, following this foundation there was an attempt to seduce him by the wife of a hostile Irish chieftain, one of the many contacts which either David or his disciples had with Ireland, including one Aidan who left Wales to establish the monastery at Ferns. According to the sources, David was well known for his emphasis on hard work and vegetarianism (perhaps explaining the use of a leek for his symbol), which made him one of the most respected Christian leaders in Wales, and this allowed him to preside over two important synods in his lifetime, both of which were concerned with wiping out the spread of **Pelagianism**. The first synod was that at Llanddewibrefi in Cardiganshire, held perhaps in 545, although as with all the events in David's life this is uncertain, when he performed one of his best-known miracles of raising a hill at his own feet so that the crowd could hear him better. This was followed by the Synod of Lucus Victoriae, possibly in 569, and along with his disciples Teilo and Padarn (both of whom would become saints), he also travelled to Jerusalem to be consecrated as bishop, supposedly journeying to Rome, **Cornwall** and Brittany in his lifetime as well.

Though it has been suggested that David was an archbishop, there is no evidence that the Welsh Church at the time recognised such a post, and it seems unlikely that he received any status higher than his bishopric, despite the increasing evidence of his fame from the tenth century onwards speaking of his pre-eminence and the devotion amongst his successors of his memory. By the year 1200, there were more than sixty churches dedicated to the saint, and with the Welsh Church having lost some of its independence to the **Norman** administration by that time, revival in his work and history served an important role in trying to assert more authority. Rhygyfarch cites 1 March 589 as being the date of David's death, a day that would become the Welsh national holiday, and he was buried in what is today St David's Cathedral in Pembrokeshire, invoking centuries of pilgrimage thereafter, with his formal canonisation secured in 1119 by the Bishop Bernard.

See also Celtic Christianity; Monasticism.

Further Reading

Davies, John. 1993. *A History of Wales*. Penguin Books.
Dumville, D. N. 2001. *Saint David of Wales*. Kathleen Hughes Memorial Lectures on Mediaeval Welsh History. Hughes Hall and Department of Anglo-Saxon, Norse and Celtic.
Harris, S. M. 1940. *Saint David in the Liturgy*. University of Wales Press.
Rhigyfarch. 1967. *Rhigyfarch's Life of St David: The Basic Mid Twelfth Century Latin Text with Introduction, Critical Apparatus and Translation by J.W. James*. University of Wales Press.
Walker, D. 1990. *Medieval Wales*. Cambridge University Press.

Anne Sassin

Deceangli

The *Deceangli* were one of the indigenous tribes of **Iron Age** and Roman Wales, whose territory seems to have encompassed the modern county of Clwyd, possibly extending further west, although this is not certain. According to the records of **Tacitus**, these **Britons** were the target of the first campaigns of Ostorius Scapula (c. AD 47–52), and though the dearth of military forts in the territory has been taken to imply a compliant attitude of the indigenous population, excavation has brought to light the strong possibility of forts at Ruthin, Rhuddlan and Ffrith, whose existence would only be natural considering the proximity of the legionary fortress at **Chester**. Although they were not designated to be a hostile tribe like the ***Ordovices***, the *Deceangli* also never attained *civitas* status, and they remained initially under military supervision, despite the probability of eventual administrative duties being granted to the tribal leaders. Lacking an urban focus other than the civilian settlement at Chester, the territory of the *Deceangli* has also had little evidence of villas, and there is an overall fairly close correlation between pre- and post-Roman settlement, with a variety of dwelling types, especially farmstead enclosures and **hillforts** (e.g. Dinorben), the latter type often yielding evidence of a late Roman presence.

Evidence of the rural landscape has suggested that parts of the territory may have been subordinate to the ***Cornovii*** to the east, with cultural links closer to the central Marches than to the other areas of Wales, and its rich copper and lead deposits would have made the region prime for industrial exploitation, with an imperial hand in lead–silver extraction and processing specifically attested to as early as the first century at Ffrith. Evidence for subsistence is rather more slight, although both cereal processing and beef and mutton consumption are apparent through excavation, and both pottery and tile kilns have been identified at the military site of Holt. Little is known of the British kingdom that immediately replaced that of the *Deceangli*, though they are said to have left their name at the sixth-century stronghold of **Deganwy**, and while this section fell under the power of the early medieval kingdom of **Gwynedd**, the remainder of the old tribal territory was encompassed by the realm of **Powys**.

See also Welsh People.

Further Reading

Arnold, C. J., and J. L. Davies. 2000. *Roman and Early Medieval Wales*. Sutton.
Cunliffe, B. W. 2005. *Iron Age Communities of Britain* (4th edn.). RKP.
Laing, Lloyd. 2006. *The Archaeology of Celtic Britain and Ireland, c. AD 400–1200*. Cambridge University Press.
Todd, Malcolm. 1999. *Roman Britain* (3rd edn.). Blackwell.

Anne Sassin

Deer Park Farms

This platform **rath** or ringfort in County Antrium, northern Ireland, was excavated by Chris Lynn in the 1980s and is notable for the remarkable conservation of organic remains. It was a multi-phase settlement, occupied between the sixth century and at least the eighth century AD. Originally a simple univalate enclosure, it was slowly raised in height through refurbishment and introduction of stone and earth to deal with problems of on-site waterlogging. At around AD 700, there were five houses within the enclosure, built with basket-woven wickerwork walls, constructed almost entirely with hazel and double-lined to provide a forerunner of 'cavity wall insulation'. These houses had diameters of 13–23 feet (4–7 metres). The walls originally had stood at 8 feet (2. 5 metres) in height (or more) and were remarkably well preserved. The data of felling of the timbers for a doorway were provided by dendrochronology to AD 648.

Among the interior details was a bed frame, partly bonded with the wall, and what has been interpreted as a frame for the processing of linen. The bed frame was made with slit oak, into which wooden panels were fitted, and the bed itself has a 'mattress' of brushwood. These houses were replaced by a succession of some thirty houses, which were, however, poorly preserved. The site was an enclosed farmstead, as with most Irish raths, with an economy based on dairying and some arable farming. The small finds included a range of ironwork, glass beads and copper-alloy objects, as well as wooden objects such as troughs, bowls, a shoe last and textiles (woollen tabby weaves). Finer items included a stud with gold-wire grill, dated to the eighth century. Among the other organic finds were a leather plate for tablet weaving, woad pads, puffballs and fish fins.

See also Art and Architecture.

Further Reading
Lynn, C. J. 1989. 'Deer Park Farms'. *Current Archaeology* 113: 193–198.
———. 1994. 'Houses in Rural Ireland, AD 500–1000'. *Ulster Journal of Archaeology* 57: 81–94.

Lloyd Laing

Degannwy

Degannwy is a fortified hilltop in the cantref of Rhos in **Gwynedd**, lying between the modern towns of Conwy and Llandudno. In the post-Roman centuries, the summit of the hill, comprising about one-third of a hectare, was enclosed by a dry stonewall. Archaeological evidence, including imported pottery, appears to show a continuity of occupation on the site from the Roman period. It has been suggested that the site's importance may have been tied to the copper mines on the nearby Great Orme's Head or to the control of the mouth of the river Conwy or both. By the later middle ages, the site was associated with the sixth-century ruler **Maelgwn Gwynedd**, **Gildas**'s Maglocunus, and there is no particular reason to doubt this connection. He was said to have died of the plague at the nearby church of Llanrhos while staying at Degannwy.

Degannwy is mentioned in two ninth-century entries in the ***Annales Cambriae***, where it is described as *arx Decantorum*, 'the citadel of the Decanti'. In the first entry, under the year 811, we are told that it was burned down following a lightning strike, an incident which may have inspired the hagiographical account of the destruction of the fortress of Benlli in ***Historia Brittonum***, written a few years later. In 822, we are told that that *arx Decantorum* was destroyed by the **Saxons** (of **Mercia**) and that the country of **Powys** was taken into their power. This has led some commentators to suggest that Degannwy lay in Powys rather than Gwynedd. From the eleventh century, at least, the area between the Conwy and Clwyd rivers, known as Perfeddwlad – the 'Middle Country' – was a debatable land. It seems more likely, however, that in this earlier period Rhos was intimately connected with Gwynedd and the annalistic entries for 816 and 817 make it clear that the Mercians were as interested in attacking Gwynedd as Powys.

We do not hear of Degannwy again until 1080 when the **Norman** adventurer Robert of Rhuddlan erected a castle there. In the course of the twelfth century, the kings of Gwynedd regained the castle, and by the early thirteenth century, it had become one of the principal castles of Llywelyn ab Iorwerth (1199–1240), the first prince of Wales. The castle was later extended by Henry III of England.

See also Hillforts; Roman Britain; Welsh People.

Further Reading
Alcock, Leslie. 1967. 'Excavations at Degannwy Castle, Caernarvonshire, 1961–6'. *Archaeological Journal* 124: 190–201.
Arnold, Christopher J., and Jeffrey L. Davies. 2000. *Roman and Early Medieval Wales*. Sutton.
Lane, Alan. 1988. 'Degannwy Castle'. Pp. 50–53 in *Early Medieval Settlements in Wales, AD 400–1100*. Edited by Nancy Edwards and Alan Lane. University of Wales Press.

Alex Woolf

Degsastan, Battle of

The Battle of Degsastan, an early conflict in the history of Anglo-Scot relations, was fought in AD 603 and resulted in **Æthelfrith** of **Northumbria** defeating **Áedán mac Gabráin** of the **Dál Riata Scots**. Under Áedán, who became king of Dál Riata in 574, the Scots had become very formidable, with objectives of settlement extending beyond Dál Riata, to take in the Forth and Scottish lowlands and even expeditions to the Orkneys. Upon the advance of **Bernicia** in the late sixth and early seventh centuries, however, a kingdom which also saw dramatic enlargement due to its King Æthelfrith, Áedán and several Irishmen who were commissioned by his ally Máel Umai mac Báetáin of **Ulster**, brother of the high king, attacked the English in 603. Despite the possibility of additional aid from the **Britons** of **Strathclyde**, Æthelfrith's brother Theodbald was killed and overall the Bernicians suffered heavy losses. Yet the end result was that Áedán was driven from the field and the Scottish resistance crushed almost entirely, notwithstanding having had the larger army.

The location of Degsastan has long been debated, and though one possibility is that it is located somewhere in the Tweed basin, it has generally been identified with Dawston in Liddesdale. However, as the **Old English** form is thought to be more likely 'Daystone', this theory may not be correct, and Ian Smith has implicated Addinston in Berwickshire as the battle spot, leaving its precise location unidentified. As the more important aspect of

Degsastan was the outcome, due to both his victory there and the overall conquest of territory, Æthelfrith was remembered even as soon as the eighth century as a king who was 'very powerful and most eager for glory' (Higham 1993, 99). The Battle of Degsastan assisted the **Angles** of Bernicia in their colonisation of the north, even beyond the Forth. Thereafter, the Britons in Strathclyde became the only real rivals of Bernicia for possession of the Scottish lowlands, with the Dálriatan threat eliminated, and although the prediction was to be short-lived, Degsastan, according to **Bede**, ended the threat of the kings of the Scots against the English.

See also Warfare and Weapons.

Further Reading

Cramp, Rosemary. 1995. *Whithorn and the Northumbrian Expansion Westwards*. Friends of the Whithorn Trust.

Higham, N. J. 1993. *The Kingdom of Northumbria AD 350–1100*. Alan Sutton.

Morris, John. 1973. *The Age of Arthur*. Weidenfeld and Nicolson.

Smyth, A. P. 1984. *Warlords and Holy Men*. Edward Arnold.

Anne Sassin

Deheubarth

Deheubarth, together with **Gwynedd** and **Powys**, was one of the three major kingdoms of medieval Wales. Created early in the tenth century by the combination of **Dyfed**, **Ceredigion** and Ystrad Tywi, it dominated the south-west corner of Wales (the name Deheubarth means 'the southern part'). Its two greatest rulers were **Hywel Dda**, during the first half of the tenth century, and 'The Lord Rhys', during the latter half of the twelfth century.

In 904, Llywarch ap Hyfaidd, king of Dyfed, died. His brother and heir, Rhydderch, died the next year and two sons of King **Rhodri the Great** of Gywnedd, Anarawd and Cadell, invaded the region to take advantage of the power vacuum. Cadell became king of Dyfed and Ystrad Tywi and the new polity came to be called Deheubarth. After Cadell's death in 910, his son Hywel (later known as Hywel Dda, 'the Good') became king of Deheubarth, eventually controlling Gwynedd and Powys too during the final years before his death in 950. Hywel cemented his claim to Deheubarth by marrying Elen, the daughter of Llywarch ap Hyfaidd. He enjoyed good relations with the English king Æthelstan after submitting to him in 927 and was a frequent visitor to his court. According to later **Welsh** tradition, Hywel commissioned a group of legal scholars to compile a collection of traditional Welsh laws. After Hywel's death, his son Owain and the latter's sons Einion and Maredudd ruled Deheubarth until Maredudd died in 999.

For most of the eleventh century, several rival royal families, including the line of Hywel Dda, contended for Deheubarth. Between 1056 and 1063, **Gruffudd ap Llywelyn** controlled the kingdom, along with the rest of Wales. Finally in 1079, Owain ap Hywel Dda's great-great-grandson, **Rhys ap Tewdwr**, gained control over Deheubarth. Rhys decisively defeated rivals at the battle of Mynydd Carn in 1081 and maintained control until his death at the hands of Bernard de Neufmarché in 1093. Rhys was the last ruler in medieval Wales to use the title 'king'. The next member of this royal dynasty, Gruffudd ap Rhys (d.1137), was an exile or marginal figure for most of his career, but he did maintain the family's claim to the territory. The most accomplished of Gruffudd's four sons, 'The Lord Rhys', ruled Deheubarth from 1155 to 1197. After initially fighting against the aggressive English king **Henry II**, Rhys negotiated a diplomatic accommodation, whereby the English ruler recognised Rhys's authority as lord over southern Wales in return for Rhys's agreement to maintain peace there. He is also famous for holding the first recorded eisteddfod (Welsh competitive poetry and music festival) at his court in 1176. His court was based at Dinefwr Castle, which was regarded in Welsh tradition as the centre of Deheubarth, just as Aberffraw and Mathrafal fulfilled that function for Gwynedd and Powys, respectively.

See also Kings and Kingship.

Further Reading

Davies, John. 1993. *A History of Wales*. Allen Lane, Penguin.

Maund, Kari. 2000. *The Welsh Kings: The Medieval Rulers of Wales*. Tempus.

Turvey, Roger. 1997. *The Lord Rhys Prince of Deheubarth*. Gomer.

Fred Suppe

Déisi

The *Déisi* were a group of people who originated in Ireland, and according to legend, they left their home in **Munster** and settled in the area of the ***Demetae*** in western Britain either in the third or in the fourth century AD. Also known as the *Dési*, derived from *déis* meaning 'subject' or 'vassal', the name itself seems to have applied to several groups in Ireland of no relation but of the same class designation; thus, they probably did not exist as a distinct tribal group until a later interpolation. The supposed sept which originated in **Tara** in County Meath and settled in Munster as tributaries to the Eóganachta are the best known, however, namely for the late-eighth- or early-ninth-century legend, the 'Expulsion of the Déisi', which tells of their being driven out from counties Waterford and Tipperary. The **Féni**, a powerful expansionist group from the middle of Ireland, may have been the catalyst for the initial migration, which was led by Eochaid Allmhuir mac Art Corb, and by the late third or fourth century, it seems that Irish colonists known as the *Déisi* occupied the old tribal territory of the *Demetae* in south-west Wales. It is not known exactly what the relationship with the *Demetae* was, but the contribution to **Welsh** literature and the long-lasting nature of the dynasty (corresponding for twelve generations with later Welsh genealogies) suggests that it was not a simple invasion, possibly even leading to the later regional name **Dyfed**. The *Annals of the Four Masters* record this invasion as taking place in the year AD 265, though a more recent study has suggested that they were just one of the groups of Irish raiders and settlers in western Britain from the fourth century onwards, which included the ***Attacotti*** and Uí Liatháin.

One problem with the *Expulsion* is that its chronology can be distorted, and later, twelfth-century manuscripts such as the Harleian MS 3859 either parallel the Irish version of genealogy or diverge and provide British pedigrees, perhaps in deliberate attempt to stifle Irish origins post-eighth century. The real aim for writing the legend may have been to legitimise the *Déisi* of Munster (*Déisi Muman*) by providing them with an ancestry at Tara, and the group described as actually migrating, a branch of the Dál Fiachach Suidge who later headed the *Déisi Muman*, attest to the small size of the relocation rather than the entire tribal movement once assumed. Another possible translation of *Déisi* as *Aithechthúatha* or 'rent-paying tribes' suggests that, like the Uí Liatháin, who also migrated from Munster to south-west Wales (as well as possibly Cornwall), the *Déisi* may have been established as *foederati*, barbarians employed by the Romans as federates in the buffer zones. Munster's role in raiding can be attested to in the Irish distribution of Roman finds of the fourth and early fifth centuries, and as the raiding *Attacotti* tribe had come to terms with the Roman authorities by c. 395, this has further supported the growing consent that the *Déisi*'s settlement was, at this time, the only dominant power in Dyfed until at least the tenth century.

See also Celts.

Further Reading

Ó Cathasigh, T. 1984. 'The Déisi and Dyfed'. *Éigse* 20: 1–33.

Powell, T. G. E. 1980. *The Celts*. Thames & Hudson.

Rance, Philip. 2001. 'Attacotti, Déisi and Magnus Maximus: The Case for Irish Federates in Late Roman Britain'. *Britannia* 32: 243–270.

Thomas, Charles. 1972. 'The Irish Settlements in Post-Roman Western Britain: A Survey of the Evidence'. *The Journal of the Royal Institution of Cornwall* VI. 4: 251–274.

Anne Sassin

Deira

Deira was the more southerly of the two **Anglo-Saxon** kingdoms that were to be combined in the late seventh century to become **Northumbria**. Its original core area largely corresponds with the East Riding of Yorkshire and it seems in some sense to have been a successor state to the Romano-British *civitas* of the *Parisi*. Its name, in Old English, *Deru*, derives from the British name for the river Derwent. Small numbers of Anglo-Saxon inhumation burials from as early as the late fifth century are scattered quite widely across Yorkshire, but in the early sixth century a concentration of large cremation cemeteries, very similar to those found in East Anglia, appear in the region of Newbald and Sancton, on the south-western edge of the Wolds. This region appears to be the core of the historical kingdom. *Historia Brittonum* seems to suggest that the first king of Deira was Soemel, son of Saefugel, who appears in the pedigrees six places above Eadwine (617–632) and might, thus, have lived in the mid-fifth century. The pedigree is somewhat suspect, however, in that Soemel and the five men above him all have alliterating names beginning with 's', whereas those below him, until one gets to **Ælle**, Eadwine's father, alliterate on 'w', suggesting that two or more pedigrees may have been spliced.

Ælle is the earliest king of whom anything is recorded, and he may have been succeeded by his brother **Ælfric**. In 604, however, the kingdom was conquered by the northern kingdom of **Bernicia**. **Æthelfrith**, the Bernician king, seems to have consolidated his power by marrying Ælle's daughter Acha. Her brother Eadwine returned from exile in 617 and, after killing Æthelfrith, not only regained control of Deira but also conquered **Bernicia** and attained some degree of hegemony over much of Britain. He was instrumental in introducing Christianity to the region. Following his death at the hands of the British king Cadwallon, Deira and Bernicia went their separate ways for a year with Osric, Ælfric's son, ruling the southern kingdom. After his death, **Oswald** (634–642), son of Æthelfrith and Acha, reunited the two kingdoms. On Oswald's death, Oswine, son of Osric, assumed the Deiran kingship (c. 642–651) but, under threat from Oswald's brother **Oswiu**, now king of Bernicia (642–671), was abandoned and murdered by his retainers. Oswald's son Æthelwald then took the kingship of Deira (c. 651–656), but he also fell foul of his uncle after allying himself to Penda of Mercia. After this, Deira was ruled in succession by the three sons of Oswiu, Alhfrith (c. 656–664), Ecgfrith (c. 664–671) and Ælfwine (c. 671–679). During this period, Deira was reduced to the status of a sub-kingdom of Bernicia, but the fact that Ecgfrith and Ælfwine were the sons of Eadwine's daughter Eanflæd seems to have facilitated integration. After Ælfwine's death in battle with the Mercians in 679, Ecgfrith, who had earlier been promoted to the Bernician kingship, seems to have affected the complete union of the two kingdoms. In cultural terms, Deira had been, and remained, much closer to its southern neighbours than Bernicia was ever to be.

See also Kings and Kingship.

Further Reading

Kirby, David P. 1992. *The Earliest English Kings*. Routledge.

Yorke, Barbara. 1991. *Kings and Kingdoms of Early Anglo-Saxon England*. Seaby.

Alex Woolf

Demetae

The *Demetae* were one of the indigenous **Celtic** tribes of **Iron Age** and Roman Wales. Their territory encompassed the fertile Tywi and Teifi valleys of the south-west and extended into the Cambrian mountains, which became roughly the early Christian kingdom of **Dyfed** and the recent counties of Pembrokeshire and Carmarthenshire.

It has been assumed that the slight archaeological evidence for settlement indicated that this client tribe was hostile to the neighbouring ***Silures*** to the east and thus did not require military occupation by the Roman invaders other than the garrison at **Carmarthen**. Though there does seem to be a rather peaceful picture of hamlet and village occupation, a fort existed at Llandeilo, and the Roman road running west from the auxiliary fort at Carmarthen presumably led to an, as of yet, undiscovered fort or forts in Pembrokeshire. However, by Hadrian's reign, the territory was considered pacified, and the *Demetae* were only one of two tribes, along with the *Silures*, to have satisfied Roman requirements sufficiently to be granted *civitas* status in the early second century AD. Presumably, this represented a pro-Roman sentiment amongst the native aristocracy, and a *caput* was established at Carmarthen (*Moridunum*), suggesting that the tribal élite were wealthy enough to create an urban focus.

Carmarthen's situation in the fertile lowlands provided an agricultural surplus, and a level of production and exchange was achieved early on, especially in metalworking (both iron and bronze), though there seems to have been less prosperous retail properties and higher-status housing than that at the other *caput* at **Caerwent**, indicating Carmarthen's more peripheral location. Although there seems to have been a period of some neglect and even abandonment of buildings in the late second century, defences appear to have been remodelled at Carmarthen in the late third century, and the *caput* was able to maintain its status as a major town until the end of the Roman period.

Much of the more hospitable regions of the rural Demetian territory were densely settled with a diversity of site types, many of which were a continuation of pre-Roman patterns. These include small ringfort-like enclosures like the 'Cornish rounds' (e.g. Walesland Rath, whose community of circular huts appears to date from the first century BC), promontory forts (e.g. Coygan Camp, which remained in use into sub-Roman times), a few villas in the southern part of the territory and other defended enclosures (e.g. Gateholm), many of which show signs of early Roman abandonment and later reoccupation in the third or fourth century. Overall, a long-lived pattern of uninterrupted indigenous development seems to be suggested, with settled pastoralism as well as cereal cultivation, while other industries include supposed exploitation of the gold mines of Dolaucothi (*Luentinum*) and pottery production (based on the kilns at Carmarthen), though the scarcity of artefacts and excavation in many instances makes assessment often difficult. The end of the Demetae's history is uncertain, for by the end of the Roman period it seems that Irish colonists known as ***Déisi*** occupied their territory, though there is not much solid information about their cultural interaction, and the sub-Roman period saw the *civitas* succeeded by the early medieval kingdom of Dyfed.

See also Britons; Roman Britain; Roman Roads; Welsh People.

Further Reading

Arnold, C. J., and J. L. Davies. 2000. *Roman and Early Medieval Wales*. Sutton.

Cunliffe, B. W. 2005. *Iron Age Communities of Britain* (4th edn.). RKP.

Lloyd Laing

Derry

Derry, or Londonderry, is a city in the north-west of Ireland, wrapped around a lazy curve of the river Foyle, just below its mouth into Lough Foyle. Legend suggests that **St. Colum Cille** (Columba) founded Derry in AD 535, though more contemporary documents suggest otherwise. The *Annals of Ulster*, for example, put the founding of 'Daire Cholmcille' at c. 545 but names no founder. In the early 1600s, the site became the seat of the new-walled plantation city of Londonderry, the core of the modern city of the same name.

The monastic site is linked by legend to St. Colum Cille of the Cenél Conaill, a branch of the northern **Uí Néill**. Their seat of power at that time was the nearby **hillfort** Grainan of Aileach. The settlement was built on a hillock on the west bank of a bend of the Foyle. It was surrounded by both the river and the bogland. Legend has it that the place was named Daire for the plentiful oak trees on the land. The monastery was not particularly wealthy, and the kings at Aileach provided excellent protection from raiders such as the **Vikings**. Therefore, unlike many other similar places in Ireland, Derry never really developed a thriving medieval trading settlement.

Derry did gradually develop a township, especially after it passed to the Cenél Eóghain under Domnall Mac Lochlainn. Domnall brought his challenge for the high kingship to Derry, where he defeated a fleet of Muircertach O'Brien's in 1100. O'Brien later sacked and destroyed the Grainan of Aileach. Like many places in Ireland, Derry underwent repeated attacks, pillages and violence during the **Norman** invasion of Ireland. For example, John de Courcy captured it and then used it as his base to plunder most of the Inishowen area.

Derry's situation made it an important site for the English as they worked to quell the Irish throughout the later medieval times. The township was devastated by the English response to the rebellion of Sir Cahir O'Doherty in 1608, but already the future plans for Londonderry were being developed by King James I's treasurer, Robert Cecil Lord Salisbury. The city that was built by The Honourable The Irish Society was the first planned city in Ireland, completely walled with four gates and fortified by canon on the same hillock as the monastery. It was this city that James II laid siege to in 1688–1689, leading to the first major Jacobite defeat in Ireland, and ultimately to James's routing at the Battle of the Boyne in 1690.

Since then, the city has expanded to straddle both sides of the Foyle, whilst becoming a font of political division throughout Ulster. During the Troubles, it was plagued with sectarian violence and tragedies such as Bloody Sunday, 30 January 1972. It has more recently begun to craft a new identity for itself as one of the ten best cities of its kind to live in the United Kingdom.

See also Gaels; Monasticism.

Further Reading

Gébler, Carlo. 2005. *The Siege of Derry: A History*. Little, Brown.

Lacy, Brian. 1990. *Siege City: The Story of Derry and Londonderry*. Blackstaff Press.

John J. Doherty

Derrynaflan Hoard

The Derrynaflan hoard is one of the most significant finds of **Celtic** ornamental metalwork made in Ireland. It was found in 1980 by a metal detector, on the site of a monastery, where it had been buried for safe keeping. The hoard was covered by a large copper-alloy bowl or basin and comprised a number of pieces of liturgical plate of different dates but deposited in the late ninth or early tenth century.

The earliest and finest item is the paten (a plate used in mass to hold the host), which is the only early medieval example from Britain or Ireland and which is one of few from early medieval Europe. This comprises a silver plate, 1 foot (38.6 centimetres) in diameter, with a flattened rim, turned on a lathe, attached to a double-walled hoop of copper alloy, to which decorative elements had been affixed. The rim displays twelve mounts, with two flanking panels of filigree wire work. In the centre of each frame is a decorative stud, inlaid with enamel. Twelve smaller studs where the panels adjoin cover locking pins. There are twelve die-stamped gold foils with traditional Celtic ornament and around the rim is trichinopoly work (knitted silver wire). The filigree panels display complex symbolism, and the subjects include animals, real and imaginary, and men. Tiny letters, 0.04 inch (1 millimetre) high, were engraved to aid in the assembly, and the style of these helps to date the paten to the (probably late) eighth century.

The paten had been used with a stand, which may be of a later period, and has die-stamped silver foils. The chalice is closely similar in style to the artistically superior **Ardagh Chalice** but belongs to a later period than the latter one. It stands 0.6 feet (19.2 centimetres) high and comprises a bowl and base with a collar, with two lifting handles which spring from escutcheons. It displays eighty-four filigree panels and fifty-seven amber studs. It also has cast interlace and animal patterns. It probably dates from the ninth century. The chalice and paten are both inspired by Byzantine prototypes. Along with these items was found a strainer-ladle, probably of eighth-century date, but not matching the paten. Used to strain liturgical wine, it is ornamented with silver foils, decorated studs and millefiori-inlaid plaques.

See also Art and Architecture.

Further Reading

Ryan, M. 1983. *The Derrynaflan Hoard I, a Preliminary Account*. National Museum of Ireland.

Youngs, S. (ed.). *The Work of Angels: Masterpieces of Celtic Metalwork, 6th–9th Centuries* AD. British Museum.

Lloyd Laing

Dicuil

Dicuil was an Irish monk, teaching in Frankish lands, probably in the palace school, in the early ninth century, from whom three works survive. All knowledge about him comes from internal evidence in these writings. He was at least twenty-five years old in 795 and was teaching on the continent by 814 when he dedicated a work to the emperor, Louis; in 825, he published three works: *De mensura orbis terrae* and two works on grammar, *De prima syllaba* and *De quaestionibus decim artis grammaticae*, which are lost. It is not known when he died. In addition, it is known that he was a monk and his teacher was named Suibne, whom some scholars have identified with a contemporary abbot of **Iona** and hence have explained Dicuil's going to the continent as a flight from **Viking** attacks on Iona at the end of the eighth century. However, we cannot know if the 'Suibne' mentioned by Dicuil and the abbot of Iona are identical because 'Suibne' was a common name. Moreover, while Dicuil did know about the Faeroes and the northern latitudes – awareness appropriate to someone who had lived on Iona – such an argument could be deployed for a number of places that he mentions in his geographical book.

Dicuil's output exhibits several of the basic educational concerns of Carolingian scholarship. He was interested in Latin grammar: he wrote on the origins of language, on grammatical problems, and left us some verses written on a copy of Priscian. This is the work of every schoolmaster of the time. Then there is his work on astronomy in five books written between 814 and 818. This is often referred to as if it were two separate works: (1) the *Liber de astronomia* (bks. 1–4), which is a *computus* (for calculating the date of Easter – or, more precisely, explaining how that date is arrived at) and (2) the *Liber censuum* (bk. 5), which deals with other measurements and weights. What combines these works, and links them with his work on grammar, is their dependence on, and development of, numerical skills for all the various tasks his students might need, whether they became scholars, pastors or tax clerks. Dicuil's major work is the *De mensura orbis terrae*, which continues the mathematical theme but applies it to the size of the earth and its geography. This is a theme he takes over from Isidore and **Bede**, and although he cited about thirty authorities, many of them Greek, he actually wrote his book by relying upon Pliny, Solinus, Priscian and Isidore – and so we can see the book as belonging to the tradition of textbook compilations. It is, however, our most explicit glimpse into how the Carolingians saw the world.

See also Literature; Monasticism.

Further Reading

Bergmann, Werner. 1993. 'Dicuils "De Mensura Orbis Terrie" '. Pp. 524–537 in *Science in Western and Eastern Civilization in Carolingian Times*. Edited by P. L. Butzer and D. Lohrmann. Birkhäuser Verlag.

Tierney, James J. 1967. *Dicuili Liber De Mensura Orbis Terrae*. Dublin Institute for Advanced Studies.

Thomas O'Loughlin

Dinas Emrys

This small hierarchically organised fort in **Gwynedd**, North Wales, was excavated by H. N. Savory between 1954 and 1956. It figures prominently in **Welsh** legend; from the ninth century, it was associated with **Ambrosius Aurelianus** and also later with **Vortigern** and **Merlin**. It figures in the story of Llud and Llefelys in the *Mabinogion*.

There are indications of some use of the site in the earlier Roman period (late first/early second century AD), without identifiable structures. There was more extensive activity on the site in the late third/fourth century, associated with pottery and glassware. A series of post holes along the line of the inner rampart probably relate to Roman-period occupation. In the post-Roman period, two ramparts were constructed to utilise the defences of the hill, on top of late Roman material. Post-Roman imported Mediterranean pottery (B ware amphora) and glass, and sherds of a Chi-Rho marked North African A ware plate, were found and dated to the late fifth and early sixth centuries (**'Tintagel ware'** q.v.). Savory believed a cistern was built to water sheep and cattle within the ramparts in the early medieval period, but radiocarbon dating suggested that this feature was late medieval (AD 1265–1410). The final phase of occupation was in the later medieval period, when a castle was built in the twelfth century.

See also Ceramics and Glass.

Further Reading

Edwards, Nancy, and Alan Lane (eds.). 1988. *Early Medieval Settlements in Wales AD 400–1100*. University of Wales Press.

Laing, Lloyd, and Jennifer Laing. 1990. *Celtic Britain and Ireland, AD 200–800: The Myth of the Dark Ages*. St Martin's.

Savory, H. N. 1960. 'Excavations at Dinas Emrys, Beddgelert, Caernarvonshire, 1954–56'. *Arch Cambrensis* 109: 13–77.

Lloyd Laing

Dinas Powys

The hilltop settlement of Dinas Powys, Glamorgan, South Wales, is one of the most significant settlements of early medieval date to be excavated in the principality. It was investigated by Leslie Alcock in 1954–1958, who believed there was an Early **Iron Age** occupation, then a period of abandonment before re-occupation in the later fifth or sixth century AD. There was an amount of Roman material from the site, which the excavator argued had been brought there in the post-Roman period, but there is no real reason for accepting the arguments and Roman-period activity seems probable.

In the early medieval period, earthworks were constructed to defend the settlement. There are five banks at Dinas Powys, of which Bank 2, of dump construction, was considered to be early medieval; the others, the excavator believed, were of **Norman** date, on account of twelfth-century pottery from the top of Bank 1, which was stone revetted. Current opinion favours the view that all the banks are early medieval. It was inferred that early medieval structures included a hall with bowed-out sides and a smaller structure set at right angles to it. These structures formed a courtyard, containing a number of hearths which were used for various activities including metalworking. No structural remains of these buildings were found, and their existence was inferred from eaves-drips.

Middens on the site produced a range of imported pottery of Mediterranean and Continental European origin (A, B, D and E wares) and Continental glass (**'Tintagel ware'** q.v.). Ornamental metalworking was carried out on the site, as attested by sherds of crucibles (with gold and bronze residues) and a lead model of Irish type for making penannular brooches. Ironworking was also undertaken, and other evidence pointed to wood and leatherworking and possibly the production of bone combs and pins. Other finds included a millefiori rod and a mount from an **Anglo-Saxon** bucket. The site has been interpreted as a defended farmstead of the **Brittonic Age** and possible secondary distribution point for imported foodstuffs, ceramics and glass.

See also Hillforts; Roman Britain; Welsh People.

Further Reading

Alcock, Leslie. 1963. *Dinas Powys, an Iron Age, Dark Age and Medieval Settlement in Glamorgan.* University of Wales Press.

———. 1987. *Economy, Society and Warfare Among the Britons and Saxons.* University of Wales Press.

Edwards, Nancy, and Alan Lane (eds.). 1988. *Early Medieval Settlements in Wales, AD 400–1000.* University of Wales Press.

Graham-Campbell, J. 1991. 'Dinas Powys Metalwork and the Dating of Enameled Zoomorphic Penannular Brooches'. *Bulletin Board of Celtic Studies* 38: 220–233.

Laing, Lloyd, and Jennifer Laing. 1990. *Celtic Britain and Ireland AD 200–800: The Myth of the Dark Ages.* Irish Academic Press.

Snyder, Christopher A. 1998. *An Age of Tyrants: Britain and the Britons, AD 400–600.* Sutton.

Lloyd Laing

Dobunni

The *Dobunni* were one of the indigenous tribes who lived in **Iron Age** and **Roman Britain**, and their tribal territory, based on coin distribution, seems to have centred in Gloucestershire, extending into north Somerset, north and west Wiltshire, west Oxfordshire and most of Worcestershire. They were one of the few tribes that are known to have issued coinage (the earliest uninscribed gold coinage, known as British R) before the arrival of the Romans, with a large number found in Essex and Lincolnshire, possibly implying contact with the ***Trinovantes*** and ***Corieltauvi***. Three centres in Dobunnic territory appear prominent from such evidence: Bagendon, Camerton and **Bath**. Sometime in the Late Iron Age, it seems that the region was split between two ruling households, Bodvoc (Boduocos) and Corio, who remained in control of the northern and southern *Dobunni*, respectively, and this division can be seen both in coinage and in the native pottery distribution of the first century BC. Pottery north of the Bristol Avon (a 'saucepan pot' tradition, suggesting close contact with the south) was exported widely to the Cotswolds and **Welsh** border. There was a completely different style in north Somerset (a 'Glastonbury ware'), which suggests contact with **Cornwall** and the ***Durotriges***. Acculturation begins to be apparent in the first century AD, as Atrebatic and Catuvellaunian wheel-turned pottery types replaced the indigenous traditions at several sites, and coinage suggests alliances with both tribes. The areas closest to the ***Catuvellauni*** began to develop earthworks similar to south-eastern ***oppida***, e.g. Minchinhampton and Bagendon, the latter the predecessor of the town of **Cirencester**. Evidence of **metalworking**, coin-minting and Gallo-Belgic pottery at Cirencester suggests that it was an important settlement by the first century AD, in the centre of a large road network, and it would become the *caput* of the *civitas* (*Corinium Dobunnorum*) and one of the largest towns in Roman Britain.

It seems that **hillforts** continued for some time and were actively defended in the more remote areas (e.g. Bredon Hill and Worlebury), although refortification is not overly apparent after the later first century AD, and a few smaller settlements also suggest continuation from the Iron Age into the Roman period (e.g. Langford Down and Butcombe), with numerous rich villas around the *caput* itself. Burial evidence is slight, though one point of interest is the survival of inhumation at the cemetery at both Barnwood and Birdlip in Gloucestershire, possibly representing a strong indigenous maintenance of a pre-Belgic tradition, and by the later Roman period, there were many rural shrines (e.g. **Lydney**) and Romano-British villas (e.g. Chedworth). Overall, it is clear that the *Dobunni* practiced mixed farming in fertile valleys and engaged in industries, which, in addition to their own mint and potteries, included iron extraction and the production of salt, brick and tile. Although it is difficult to say what became of the tribal inhabitants, by the **Brittonic Age** (fifth and sixth centuries AD) the Romano-British population in the area clashed with the **Saxon** invaders, though their success in holding them off was short-lived (as in the battle of **Dyrham**).

See also Britons; Celts; Ceramics and Glass; Coinage and Trade.

Further Reading

Cunliffe, B. W. 2005. *Iron Age Communities of Britain* (4th edn.). RKP.

Todd, Malcolm. 1999. *Roman Britain* (3rd edn.). Blackwell.

Van Arsdell, R. D. 1994. *The Coinage of the Dobunni.* Oxford University Committee for Archaeology.

Anne Sassin

Domesday Book

The *Domesday Book* is arguably the most famous public record produced during the Middle Ages. Compiled from records gathered for a survey of property ordered by King **William I** at his Christmas court in 1085, the *Domesday Book*'s two volumes preserve some of the earliest evidences of landholding for approximately 15,000 places throughout 35 English counties south of the river Tees. The earliest recorded use of the *Domesday Book*'s ominous name appears in a twelfth-century administrative manual, *The Dialogue of the Exchequer*, whose author declared that the records entered in it 'like those of the Last Judgment, are unalterable' (Johnson 1950, 64).

The survey on which the *Domesday Book*'s records were based was completed with remarkable speed and efficiency. Teams of royal commissioners were appointed to enquire what lands and rights were held by the king in each county and establish their level of taxation, as well as to determine what lands and privileges were held by the various other individuals and institutions throughout the kingdom. Each group of commissioners travelled throughout one of seven regional circuits conducting inquests, probably in conjunction with meetings of the various shire courts. At these inquests, local officials presented reports to the commissioners, who then recorded their information. The entire survey was completed by 1 August 1086, when the records of the inquests were presented to the king at **Salisbury**. Two of what appear to be original circuit returns are preserved: the volume known as *Little Domesday*, which records information from the counties of Essex, Sussex and Norfolk, and the *Exon Domesday*, which records information regarding the south-western counties. Several other local 'satellite' records related to the inquests survive, including the *Inquisitio Eliensis*, which appears to have been compiled for the abbot of Ely, and the *Inquisitio Comitatus Catabrigiensis*, which appears to be based upon a commissioner's report on Cambridgeshire.

The information recorded in the *Domesday Book* is organised both geographically and tenurially: in other words, estates were listed in each shire according to the honour of the landholder (first the king, followed by ecclesiastical lords and then followed by lay lords); also, each landholder's estates were listed according to the administrative district (hundred and vill) in which they were located. In addition, notices of over 3,200 land disputes are recorded in the *Domesday Book*.

The data collected by the commissioners from the thirty-two counties not included in *Little Domesday* were eventually recorded in a massive single-volume compilation referred to as *Great Domesday*. Unlike *Little Domesday*, which was recorded by several scribes, the records entered on the 382 folios of *Great Domesday* appear to have been compiled and edited by a single scribe. Exactly why, when and under what circumstances *Great Domesday* was compiled is a matter of controversy. Two long-established views argue that *Great Domesday* was an official record of the 1086 inquests compiled shortly after the survey was completed to either aid in the collection of taxes (*geld*) or record feudal relationships and dues under the new **Norman** regime. Recently, David Roffe has called into question the proposition that *Great Domesday* was an intended product of the Domesday inquests, arguing instead that it was compiled independently from the 1086 inquests sometime after the accession of King **William Rufus** for largely political purposes.

Whether it was created as a royal administrative aid or a political instrument, the *Domesday Book*'s significance was transformed in the popular imagination during the Middle Ages to become both a tangible symbol of royal governance and a record of traditional rights. Because the book records a comparison of each holding's value from two temporal perspectives, *Tempore Regis Edwardi* (TRE), 'in the time of King Edward' (i.e. January 1066), and *Tempore Regis Williami* (TRW), 'in the time of King William' (i.e. 1086), modern scholars consult the *Domesday Book* to explore the social and economic impact of the first twenty years of Norman rule over England. It is also an important source of information for place and personal names, administrative and legal developments, military service, taxation and land use in eleventh-century England.

Further Reading

Fleming, Robin. 1998. *Domesday Book and the Law: Society and Legal Custom in Early Medieval England*. Cambridge University Press.

Holt, J. C. (ed.). 1987. *Domesday Studies*. Boydell & Brewer.

Johnson, C. (ed.). 1950. *Dialogus de scaccario: The Course of the Exchequer and the Constitutio domus regis*. Nelson's Medieval Classics. Oxford University Press.

Roffe, D. 2000. *Domesday: The Inquest and the Book.* Oxford University Press.
Williams, A., et al. (eds.). 2002. *The Digital Domesday Book.* Alecto.

Jonathan Herold

Donald III Bán (b. c.1037)

Donald III Bán was also known as Donald Bán ('Fair-haired') or Domnall mac Máel Choluim. Donald's intermittent kingship of the **Scots** (1093–1094 and 1094–1097) represented a backlash against the foreign influence introduced during Malcolm III's reign and a final surge of Gaelic/Scandinavian control.

Little is known of Donald's early life, except that, according to John of Fordun, he was born c.1037 and fled to the Western Isles in exile around 1042. He emerged in the chronicles in 1093, after the death of his brother Malcolm III, an aged man prepared to claim the title King of Scots forcibly. The native Scot aristocracy supported his claim and indeed chose him in a final exercise of tanistry. After Donald III's final defeat, the laws of primogeniture prevailed. To please the nobles, Donald 'drove out all the English who were with King Malcolm before' (Anderson 1908, 117–118). The surviving sons of Malcolm and Margaret were most likely included in this expulsion.

Challenges to his title dominate our knowledge of his time as king. His first rivals were Duncan II, son of Malcolm, and his first wife Ingebjorg, who challenged Donald less than one year after he took power. Duncan, a supporter of the English king **William II**, entered Scotland in late 1093 or early 1094 with a French and English army and enjoyed success. Duncan's claim to the title King of Scots was short-lived, however (Berchán implies less than two months), as Donald and his Scot supporters led a successful revolt against Duncan. It is worth noting that Malcolm's son Edmund supported his uncle in this revolt; Edmund was the only son of Malcolm and Margaret who did no homage to the English king. Some scholars claim that after the death of Duncan II, Donald and Edmund ruled Scotland jointly, while others speculate that Edmund was the designated successor as Donald had no legitimate heir. This ambiguous relationship continued until the two were defeated by Edmund's brother Edgar in 1097.

Edgar entered Scotland in 1097 with the aid of the king of England. As vassal of the English king **William II**, Edgar began calling himself king of Scotland in 1095 but was 'set up as king' by William in 1097. Donald Bán succumbed to this final challenge most unfortunately. According to the *Chronicles of the Kings of Scotland*, he was captured by Edgar, Malcolm's son, and died in Rescobie (Anderson 1922, vol. 2, 90). Some sources claim that Donald was blinded at the urging of Edgar's brother David (later **David I**). He spent the remainder of his days as a prisoner and died in either 1097 or 1099. The sources do not agree on this point. There is speculation that he was kept prisoner for the remainder of his natural life, but this decision was revoked and his murder ordered. He was buried at **Dunkeld**, though later king lists claim that his bones were exhumed and taken to **Iona**. One of Donald's legacies was his daughter Bethoc, who was the ancestress of the Comyn claimants to the Scottish kingship.

See also Kings and Kingship.

Further Reading

Anderson, A. O. (ed. and tr.). 1908, repr. 1991. *Scottish Annals from English Chroniclers AD 500 to 1286.* Paul Watkins.
———. 1922, repr. 1992. *Early Sources of Scottish History AD 500 to 1286.* Paul Watkins.
Barrow, G. W. S. 1981. *Kingship and Unity: Scotland 1000–1306.* University of Toronto Press.
Duncan, A. A. M. 1975. *Scotland: The Making of a Kingdom.* Oliver and Boyd.
———. 2002. *The Kingship of the Scots 842–1292.* Edinburgh University Press.
Hudson, Benjamin T. 1996. *Prophecy of Berchán: Irish and Scottish High-Kings of the Early Middle Ages.* Greenwood Press.

Trudy Tattersall

Dorchester

The Roman town of Dorchester (*Durnovaria*), situated in modern Dorset, was the *civitas* capital of the tribe of the ***Durotriges***. It seems to have partly superseded the **hillfort** of **Maiden Castle**, which lies about 2 miles (3 kilometres) to the south of the present town (although it is clear that the hillfort saw post-conquest occupation). The origins of Dorchester itself are the source of some dispute, although recent interpretations favour a military origin for the town, suggesting that a Roman military establishment dating to the conquest period was replaced by a civilian settlement around AD 65.

Excavations during the early 1980s showed that the street grid and a number of buildings were laid out sometime prior to AD 70 on an area that had previously been open pasture. A series of shafts found during these excavations contained votive offerings and have been interpreted as ritual deposits relating to the foundation of the town. The earliest buildings on the site appear to have been modest timber structures, which were later replaced by buildings with stone foundations. Little is known of the layout of the town, although the position of a forum is postulated on the basis of some walls and a gravelled area close to Cornhill.

The best known of Dorchester's public buildings is the amphitheatre. This is situated at Maumbury Rings, about 2,625 feet (800 metres) to the south of the Roman town. Its unusual circular form is caused by the fact that it was built on a **henge** monument of **Neolithic** date. This seems to have been adapted in the first century AD, when the interior of the monument was excavated to a depth of 9 feet (3 metres) to create an oval arena (190 feet × 157 feet [58 metres × 48 metres]), with the excavated material piled onto the surrounding bank to increase the height of the seating.

Dorchester's public baths are situated in the south-east of the town and were partially excavated in 1977, when a substantial series of heated rooms and a possible *palaestra* were revealed. The excavators suggested that the first phase of the baths was erected around AD 75–100. The baths were supplied with water by the town's aqueduct, which is one of the best-understood water-supply systems of **Roman Britain**. Recent work has shown that the water was transported to the town in a covered wooden channel some 6 miles (9 kilometres) in length, with the source probably near **Frampton**, where a small stream was dammed to create a headwater.

The earliest domestic housing was built in timber, although we know much more about the later housing, in particular that in the area of Colliton Park, where a number of dwellings of varying scale were excavated. The largest of these included an impressive series of mosaics. Numerous other mosaics have been discovered in the town and in villas in its hinterland. It has been postulated that a mosaic workshop was active in the region in the fourth century, although little of its work has been found within the town itself.

A number of cemeteries have been found on the outskirts of the town, of which the most extensively investigated is the late Roman cemetery at Poundbury. This contained predominantly inhumation burials with few grave goods, and it is probable that many of those interred were Christian.

See also Romano-British Towns.

Further Reading

Putnam, Bill. 2007. *Roman Dorset*. Tempus.

Wacher, John. 1975. *The Towns of Roman Britain*. Batsford.

Woodward, Peter, Susan Davies and Alan Graham. 1993. *Excavations at the Old Methodist Chapel and Greyhound Yard, Dorchester 1981–1984*. Dorset Natural History and Archaeological Society.

Woodward, Peter, and Ann Woodward. 2004. 'Dedicating the Town: Urban Foundation Deposits in Roman Britain'. *World Archaeology* 36.1: 68–86.

William Bowden

Dorchester-on-Thames

Dorchester-on-Thames, a small town on the river Thames in Oxfordshire, is an important site for discussing the origins of **Anglo-Saxon** England and later became an important English bishopric in an area disputed between **Wessex** and **Mercia**. Though a minor Roman town was established at Dorchester, finds from Dyke Hills to the south-west of the town give us important clues about the first Anglo-Saxon settlers in Britain. In 1874, workmen discovered a military belt set and, nearby, a female skeleton, with both a cruciform brooch and a disc brooch. The belt set is typical of officers' dress in mid-fifth century Gaul, while the **brooches** are a style popular in northern Germany (Welch 1992). It is possible that this cemetery belonged to one of the first groups of Saxons settled by the Britons c. 449 to protect their towns and villas.

Dorchester-on-Thames served as a bishopric, first of **Wessex** from c. 635 to c. 666 and later of **Mercia** from c. 869 to c. 1072. The first bishop of Dorchester was Birinus, a missionary sent to England by Pope Honorius (625–638). Birinus focused his efforts in Wessex, receiving the city as a grant from Cynegils, king of Wessex (611–643), and **Oswald**, king of **Northumbria** (634–642). Birinus baptised Cynegils at Dorchester-on-Thames in 635, establishing a close relationship between the see and the royal family of Wessex. Both Cynegils's son and grandson were also baptised at Dorchester-on-Thames in 636 and 639, respectively. In 660, Cenwahl, king of Wessex (643–645; 648–672), decided to establish another bishopric at Winchester, probably due to Mercian aggression, as Dorchester-on-Thames lay close to Mercian territory. Agilbert, a Frank who had been serving as bishop of Dorchester-on-Thames for ten years, moved to Northumbria and was present for the **Synod of Whitby** in 664. It is not fully clear if the Dorchester-on-Thames see was vacant or occupied between 660 and 666. Cenwahl may have appointed a successor to Agilbert, who served for less than a year, and it is also possible that Wine, who had been appointed as bishop of the newly created see in Winchester, was briefly transferred to Dorchester-on-Thames before being transferred to **London** in 666. Following the military victories of the Mercian king Wulfhere (657–674) in 661, Dorchester-on-Thames was incorporated into Mercian territory and placed under the authority of the bishops of Leicester. During the Danish invasions of the ninth century, the bishops of Leicester fled to Dorchester-on-Thames, using the city as their new seat, with a brief vacancy between c. 896 and c. 909. The bishopric was transferred to **Lincoln** in 1072, following the **Norman Conquest**.

See also Celtic Christianity.

Further Reading

James, Edward. 2001. *Britain in the First Millennium.* Arnold.

Welch, Martin. 1992. *Discovering Anglo-Saxon England.* Penn State Press.

Yorke, Barbara. 1995. *Wessex in the Early Middle Ages.* Leicester University Press.

Deanna Forsman

Dover

The town of Dover is strategically placed at the shortest crossing point of the Channel where the close proximity of the Continent has ensured Dover's standing as a highly important port since at least the Roman period. The river Dour has been central to Dover's very existence, providing both a sheltered haven for shipping and a constant supply of fresh water in the past. The original estuary has long since disappeared as a result of infilling with silt and shingle, and much of modern Dover is built across the infill site of the ancient haven.

The earliest evidence for human occupation of the region is lower and middle **Palaeolithic** handaxes found on the plateau surface adjacent to the valley. Within the valley, fragmentary evidence for **Neolithic** activity occurs, but it is only in the **Bronze Age** that there is significant evidence for prehistoric occupation. A 3,500-year-old boat discovered during roadworks in the town centre represents a particularly significant find, which suggests the use of the river-mouth by sea-going vessels at this early date (Clark 2004).

The Roman period saw the development of a major harbour and the only two known Roman lighthouses in Britain that were associated with a unique second-century Roman naval fort (Classis Britannica fort). This fort was succeeded during the late Roman period by the Saxon Shore fort together with various other buildings and harbour installations (Philp 1981, 1989). The principal area of Roman occupation was situated on the south-west side of the valley and this has remained the primary settlement focus up to the present day. Archaeological evidence attests Anglo-Saxon settlement by the start of the sixth century AD within the walls of the late Roman fort here (Philp 2003) and the settlement seems to have grown in importance during the later Saxon period, for by the mid-tenth-century Dover possessed a mint (Tatton-Brown 1984). According to the ***Domesday Book***, the Anglo-Saxon phase came to an abrupt end when the town was burnt, with a major fire destroying much of the settlement.

Following the **Norman Conquest** in 1066 and the construction of an earthwork castle on the eastern heights, urban development continued on the western side of the valley. By the late twelfth century, a new suburb had been established on the eastern side of the Dour at the foot of Castle Hill. In 1295, Dover was subjected to a massive French attack, and although the French were driven off, it seems probably the town sustained considerable damage during the raid. Subsequently, the town was walled for protection, but today the precise line of the town wall remains uncertain in many places.

See also Romano-British Towns.

Further Reading

Clark, P. 2004. *Dover Bronze Age Boat.* English Heritage.

Philp, B. J. 1981. *The Excavation of the Roman forts of the Classic Britannica at Dover, 1970–1977.* Kent Archaeological Rescue Unit Monograph Series 3.

———. 1989. *The Roman House with Bacchic Murals at Dover.* Kent Archaeological Rescue Unit Monograph Series 5.

———. 2003. *The Discovery and Excavation of Anglo-Saxon Dover.* Kent Archaeological Rescue Unit Monograph Series.

Tatton-Brown, T. 1984. 'The Towns of Kent'. Pp.1–36 in *Anglo-Saxon Towns in Southern England*. Edited by J. Haslam. Wiley.

Martin Bates

Dragonby

The prehistoric and Roman settlement of Dragonby near Scunthorpe, Lincolnshire, is of particular importance for its occupation in the Early **Iron Age**. There was some activity on the site in the **Mesolithic**, **Neolithic** and **Bronze Age** and again in the **Anglo-Saxon** and later Medieval periods, but most of the excavated remains belonged to the Iron Age and **Romano-British** eras. Excavations began in earnest in 1963, with the main campaign being carried out under Jeffrey May between 1964 and 1973.

The Iron Age activity on the site probably began in the second century BC or earlier. It was characterised by ditched enclosures, perhaps used to define property boundaries, associated with an irregular pattern of streets and wooden round houses. At its greatest extent, it probably covered about 20 acres (8 hectares). It may have served as a clan centre for a subgroup within the tribe of the ***Corieltauvi,*** which depended on agriculture and stock rearing but also engaged in craft activities and trade. Spelt and barley were the main crops, supplemented by Celtic beans, hazelnuts, sloes, crab apples and other berries. The evidence for textile manufacture was supported by the occurrence of woad in a pit of the mid-first century AD. The Iron Age settlement was directly succeeded by a Romano-British one, in which the earlier buildings were succeeded by rectangular, aisled structures on stone foundations. This settlement continued until the end of the fourth and possibly into the fifth century AD.

Dragonby is particularly noteworthy for its pottery sequence, the analysis of which was a major feature of the published report. The pottery is characterised by gradual and small-scale changes. Some Gallo-Belgic imported pottery, as well as ceramic types usually associated with the '**Swarling-Aylesford**' tradition of the south-east, was among the finds. Among individual finds, mention may be made of a parcel-gilt silver 'Birdlip' brooch of the first century AD and a Roman bronze figurine of Mars in native style.

See also Ceramics and Glass.

Further Reading

May, J. 1996. *Dragonby: Report on Excavations at an Iron Age and Romano-British Settlement in North Lincolnshire*, 2 vols. Oxbow.

Lloyd Laing

'Dream of the Rood'

The 'Dream of the Rood' is one of the earliest and finest examples of **Anglo-Saxon** religious literature. It belongs to the genre of dream poetry and a portion of it is carved in four columns of runic lettering on the Ruthwell Cross, which dates to c. AD 750. The complete poem was not discovered until 1822 in the tenth-century *Vercelli Book* in northern Italy. The poem may represent the liturgical celebration of the finding of fragments of the True Cross in Rome during the pontificate of Pope Sergius I (687–701).

In the poem, the unknown writer describes how in a dream he recognised the 'rood' or Cross of Christ, adorned with gold and precious jewels, which covered over the ancient wounds inflicted during the crucifixion when the Cross and Christ suffered together. In an interesting and original example of inculturation, Christ is described in the heroic terms familiar to Anglo-Saxon society as an eager young warrior who faces death bravely and fearlessly:

> Then the young hero (who was God almighty)
> Got ready, resolute and strong in heart.
> He climbed onto the lofty gallows-tree,
> Bold in the sight of many watching men,
> When he intended to redeem mankind.
> (Hamer 1970, 163)

Once the instrument of Christ's suffering and death, the Cross is now the splendid and glorious emblem of humankind's salvation, and the poet is bidden to make his dream known to encourage sinners with the hope of redemption:

> Now, my dear warrior, I order you
> That you reveal this vision to mankind,
> Declare in words this is the tree of glory
> On which Almighty God once suffered torments
> For mankind's many sins, and for the deeds
> Of Adam long ago. (Hamer 1970, 167–169)

While very much within the early tradition which saw the Cross as the sign of Christ's glorious triumph over suffering and death, 'The Dream of the Rood' is original both as poetry and as theology: Ó Carragáin describes it as 'the first major English contribution to the Western theological tradition' (1999, 61). This originality involved the rethinking of the crucifixion to present the event from the point of view of the Cross. The poem dramatises the dilemma faced by the Cross at having to bear the Lord to his death and parallels this dilemma with that of Mary at the Annunciation. No other piece of medieval poetic literature expresses the realisation that the Incarnation and the Passion both involved an encounter between the Lord and a fearful creature or that the Cross brought to completion the work which Mary had begun by her willing, though apprehensive, consent to Christ's conception. This may be connected to the fact that in early medieval England and Ireland it was believed that the first Good Friday fell on 25 March, the feast of the Annunciation. The *Martyrology of Tallaght* has the following entry for that date: 'Dominus noster Iesus Christus crucifixus est et conceptus et mundus factus est' (Best and Lawlor 1931, 27).

See also Literature.

Further Reading

Best, Richard Irvine, and Hugh Jackson Lawlor (eds. and tr.). 1931. *The Martyrology of Tallaght*. Henry Bradshaw Society.

Hamer, Richard. 1970. *A Choice of Anglo-Saxon Verse*. Faber and Faber.

Ó Carragáin, Éamonn. 1982. 'Crucifixion as Annunciation: The Relation of *The Dream of the Rood* to the Liturgy Reconsidered'. *English Studies* 63: 487–505.

———. 1987–1988. 'The Ruthwell Crucifixion Poem in its Iconographic and Liturgical Contexts'. *Peritia* 6–7: 1–71.

———. 1999. 'Rome, Ruthwell, Vercelli: "The Dream of the Rood" and the Italian Connection'. Pp. 59–105 in *Vercelli Tra Oriente Ed Occidente Tra Tarda Antichitá e Medioevo*. Edited by Vittoria Dolcetti Corazza. Edizioni dell'Orso.

Patricia Rumsey

Druids

The druids were the priestly class in **Celtic** society, not only in Britain and Ireland but also in Gaul, and although their study has been steeped in mythology and lore, contemporary evidence suggests that they were involved in politics, sacrificial ritual and prophecy, as well as controlling the divine world, for which they were both feared and revered. Described as philosophers and as men who were learned in religious affairs by Diodorus Siculus, they also served as teachers, orators, royal advisors and, in rare instances, rulers themselves. Pliny has stated that their name derived from the Greek for 'oak'. While *dru-* is the Indo-European word for oak, the link between druids and oak trees may have been made by ancient Celts or Romans because of the role of oak groves in druidic ceremonies. Some scholars now believe the word druid means 'wisdom'. Though Pliny believed the druids and their religion to have originated in Gaul and from there to have been taken to Britain, **Caesar** made comments to the opposite effect.

The most famous account of the druids in Britain was **Tacitus**'s reference to their 'barbarous superstitions' (especially human sacrifice) and description of the attack in AD 61 on the sacred groves of Mona (Anglesey), where the druids may have been driven after the Roman invasion of Wales. The attack on Anglesey was led by the Roman governor **Suetonius Paulinus**, who saw the druids as a source of native insurrection. While Paulinus's massacre of the priests and priestesses on Anglesey may have put an end to the druidic order in Britain, fourth- and early-fifth-century writings from Gaul make it clear that some Gallic families proudly remembered druidic ancestors. After the collapse of the western Roman empire in the fifth century, however, literary references to the druids in both Gaul and Britain come to an end. Ireland, never conquered by Rome, continued to produce druids throughout the early Middle Ages. Early references can be found in the seventh-century *Lives* of St. **Brigid**, who was supposedly the foster child of a druid, and St. **Patrick**, whose coming was predicted by the druids Lochru and Lucat Mael. This period of overlap between traditional pagan practices and Christianity was also preserved in vernacular mythic texts, which, though written down in Christian times, may contain genuine accounts of pre-Christian beliefs and practices. Represented as either receptive or hostile towards the new faith, druids were sometimes presented as prophets of Christianity, as in the *Aided Conchobar*, where the druid tells his king that an earthquake had been caused by the crucifixion of Christ. Other references include *The Siege of Druim Damhghaire,* which linked druids to birds (i.e. the druid Mog Ruith who wore a speckled bird-dress); a 'bird-man' described in the eleventh-century *Story of Da Derga's Hostel*; the shape-shifting druid Cathbadh attached to the court of Conchobar in the *Ulster Cycle*; and the druidess Bodhmall in the *Fenian Cycle*. Irish saints also battle 'wizards' among the **Picts** of Scotland, and there is a rare reference to druids in Wales in the twelfth century *Life of Saint Beuno*.

Early Irish **literature** attested to four great seasonal festivals marking important points in the farming calendar and the passing of the seasons, the two most important being **Beltaine**, the May festival linked with druids by the ninth century writer Cormac, and **Samhain**, the beginning of winter at which time druids were required to control forces flowing from the open Otherworld portal. In some Irish texts, the learned class was divided into druids, bards and ***filid*** (seer poets), of which the druids were the most politically influential, but by the seventh century many of their functions had been taken over by the *filid* when the old pagan system had begun to lose hold. Presumably, the *filid* at that time took over prophesying, divination and teaching, as well as sharing the role of advisor to the king, while druids retained their powers of magic, arbitration and war craft. Thus in literature, they are portrayed as wielding immense power and influence, with Caesar claiming that they trained for twenty years. They had very close relationships to kings, as their ability to predict the future meant that they were dependant on for guidance, though early eighth-century Irish canons declared that a just king was not to heed their superstition.

As there are no inscriptions or images which can be identified with certainty as druidical, literary evidence is the only source which directly mentions them by name. Attempts to use archaeological material must thus be approached with caution. Often inferences are based on the suggestion of ritual practice and sacrifice or veneration of natural elements, such as tree groves, lakes and springs. References made by Pliny to a druidic talisman (*anguinum*), an egg-like object allegedly made from the spittle and secretions of angry snakes which was used as an amulet to gain victory in law courts, has been connected to the serpentine egg amulet of possible Roman date from Bu Sands, Orkney, as well as two others from Cairnhill, Aberdeenshire, in what may have been a ritual deposit. Headdresses, possibly worn by the druid class, are numerous from the period, examples including the red deer antlers associated with fourth-century material near the Roman bath-suite at Hooks Cross, Hertfordshire, and bronze ritual head-dresses and diadems from Romano-Celtic temples at Hockwold-cum-Wilton, Norfolk, and Cavenham, Suffolk. The early Romano-British wooden wheel-shaped Wavendon Totem from Buckinghamshire, found in a waterlogged pit, has been interpreted as a solar symbol.

Over 300 military and high-status objects which were cast into the water at Flag Fen, Cambridgeshire (a site with activity from 1200 to 200 BC), have been seen as suggesting possible druidic associations. Cauldrons such as that found at Llyn Fawr, Wales (c. 600 BC), may also have been votive offerings, as were later first-century AD ritual deposits in lochs at Blackburn Mill, Berkwickshire, and Carlingwark, Kirkkudbright.

Ritual murder, commonly attested to in sources, may be confirmed by the famous **Lindow Man** bog body of the first century AD from Cheshire, with evidence for others at such Iron Age **hillforts** as **South Cadbury**, Somerset, and **Danebury**, Hampshire. Witch-craft and ritual behaviour may be apparent at the fourth-century Romano-British cemetery at Lankhills, Winchester, which contained burials of several old women who had been decapitated with their heads placed by their legs. This was a similar pattern to that which was found at Kimmeridge, Dorset, where the late-third-century burials were also decapitated, with their lower jaws removed and placed at their feet, each accompanied by a spindle-whorl. As this was a symbol of fate and destiny, and the removal of their jaws might imply the possible desire to prevent the women from speech, they have been interpreted as possible witches or druidesses, though whether correct cannot be said.

Healing shrines of the Roman period, such as at Nettleton Shrub, Wiltshire, and **Lydney**, Gloucestershire, have been identified as possibly druidic, as has the site at Lowbury Hill in Oxfordshire, which is regarded as the location of a probable first-century AD temple, with a sacred enclosure formed by trees. Having been entwined with superstition for over a millennium, as well as being the object of revival since the eighteenth century, it is thus very difficult to distinguish fact from legend in the study of druids, despite the immense impact they had on Britain's Celtic past.

See also Roman Britain.

Further Reading

Chadwick, Nora. 1997. *The Druids* (rev. 2nd edn.). University of Wales Press.
Freeman, Philip. 2006. *The Philosopher and the Druids.* Simon and Schuster.
Green, Miranda, J. 1997. *Exploring the World of the Druids.* Thames & Hudson.
Kendrick, T. D. 1927. *The Druids: A Study in Keltic Prehistory.* Methuen Press.
Piggott, Stuart. 1975. *The Druids.* Thames & Hudson.
Ross, Anne. 1999. *Druids.* Tempus.
Snyder, Christopher A. 2003. *The Britons.* Peoples of Europe Series. Blackwell.

Anne Sassin

Dublin

Dublin (*Dyflinn*) was the principal town and port of **Viking** Age Ireland and developed in the Middle Ages and Modern periods to become the nation's capital city. Originally, its location on a ridge on the south bank of the river Liffey, just where it opened up into the estuary, overlooked an important pre-**Viking** fording point across the river Liffey (at a place known in the sixth century AD as *Áth Cliath*, 'ford of the hurdles'). Early medieval **ringforts** and churches are known from the vicinity, and historical records also attest to the existence of probable early churches, burial places and monastic sites. Probably, there was a native Irish, early Christian settlement here at *Áth Cliath* and also nearby at *Linn duib* ('Black pool', situated to the south of the confluence of the river Poddle and the river Liffey).

The early medieval ***Annals of Ulster*** state that in the year AD 841, there was a 'naval camp at *Duiblinn* (*Longport oc Duiblinn*) from which the Laigin and the **Uí Néill** were plundered ...'. The longphort was probably a defended enclosure on the riverbank that was variously used as a raiding base, a semi-permanent settlement and, perhaps, a trading base. The precise location of this longphort is not known, but it has been suggested that it was located further upstream on the river Liffey near Islandbridge-Kilmainham (e.g. where a range of ninth-century Viking burials were found in the nineteenth century and the 1930s that imply at least the use of native Irish cemeteries). It has also been suggested that the longphort was somewhere north of the present location of Dublin castle. Recent archaeological excavations in Temple Bar and at Golden Lane in Dublin city have uncovered burials of probable Viking raiders, probably dating to the same period as – or perhaps even before – the historically attested longphort.

In AD 902, according to the *Annals of Ulster*, the Norse longphort at Áth Cliath was reputedly sacked by the Irish **kings** of Brega and Leinster, and its inhabitants 'abandoned a good number of their ships, and escaped half dead after they had been wounded and broken'. It is thought that the site's Norse inhabitants, or at least the political elite of the settlement, were expelled at this time, whence they went to northern England and the Isle of Man. In AD 917, Norse settlers returned and re-established the town of Dublin proper at *Duiblinn*, overlooking the river Liffey and protected from the south-east by Poddle. By the reign of *Amlaíb Cuarán* (**Olaf Cuarán,** 945–980), Dublin had become a permanent settlement and the annalists refer to a stronghold (Irish *dún*) there in the tenth century AD. This was an ideal location for a fortified base for Norse kings responsible for raids into the Irish countryside, and it was also ideally located as a trading settlement with access to the river for ships and boats. Although initially located at the eastern end of a natural promontory between the rivers, the town gradually expanded westwards along High Street, so that by the late tenth century and eleventh century it was a large thriving urban settlement, with streets and houses inhabited by a large, ethnically mixed (i.e. part Irish, part Norse, with undoubtedly others from the Atlantic seaways) population of traders, craftsmen and slaves. After around 980, Dublin was drawn closely into the Irish political system, and from 1052, the overlord of Dublin was usually an Irish high king.

The Norse town of *Dyflinn* was enclosed within a series of large earthen banks, topped with post-and-wattle fences. There is good archaeological evidence for houses, streets and plot boundaries, particularly at Fishamble Street and Temple Bar West. At Fishamble Street, twelve tenement plots have been traced more or less constantly across time, with the occupation of at least 150 different houses over a period of c.150 years. These houses were probably owned by individuals, but the evidence suggests that the town was laid out according to the instructions of a central regulating authority. Norse Dublin's houses were entered from the street; each had vegetable plots, gardens and midden spaces out in the back. Other structures included pigpens, workshops and storehouses. Other features associated with Norse practices and beliefs included the Thingmót – a place of public assembly to the east of the town – and the Norse burials placed in **barrows** (Norse *haugr*) to the east of the town on the edge of the Liffey marshes, particularly along the southern bank. By c.1050, the town had doubled in size to encompass an area of about 30 acres (12 hectares), with an estimated population of c. 4,500 people. In the eleventh century, the town was enclosed within stonewalls, and the Christianised population had a stone-built cathedral at Holy Trinity (known today as Christ Church), as well as several other parish churches within and outside its walls and at least three monasteries in the vicinity.

The town was a major centre for craft production, with such raw materials as wood, leather, bone, antler, amber and metals used for domestic equipment and high-status goods. In terms of economy, it is likely that the townspeople were largely self-sufficient, raising pigs and goats, while beef cattle, cereals, other agricultural produce and various raw materials were brought in from the surrounding countryside, where there were probably both Norse and native Irish rural populations (within a district later known as *Dyflinaskiri*) involved in the provisioning of the town with food and other materials. There is also evidence that the people of Norse Dublin consumed a lot of fish and shellfish – perhaps more than the native Irish. Archaeological evidence suggests that fishing was clearly important, as lead line-weights, wooden net-floats and stone sinkers found in excavations indicate fishing using lines and nets from both the shoreline and off-shore in boats. Archaeozoological studies of deposits from Dublin, and also from the Norse towns of **Waterford** and **Cork**, confirm this focus on marine species, with bones from hake, cod, ling, plaice and herring all known from these towns. It is also likely that the **Vikings** were involved in hunting marine mammals, such as porpoise, whales and seals. Indeed, an iron harpoon head found at Fishamble Street was probably used for this purpose. Wildfowl such as teal, duck and mallard were also trapped in the estuarine marshlands.

By the tenth and eleventh centuries AD, Dublin was one of the most important trading ports in Atlantic Europe, with its own ships being the key to trade and commerce with the Baltic, Mediterranean and Russia. Between AD 920 and 1170, Dublin had trading links with **York**, Scandinavia, **Anglo-Saxon** England and other parts of Ireland. Gold and silver ingots and a large number of imported coins indicate the importance of trade with England, particularly the Chester area, and with the north-west of France. The presence of walrus ivory (available only in the Arctic circle), soapstone vessels and amber indicates that trade was maintained with Scandinavia, while the discovery of silks shows that Dublin was part of a trading network which stretched as far as the Silk Road to China. Silver coins from Samarkand, Taskent, and Baghdad, Iraq, have all been found in Dublin. Almost certainly, the town's major exports were wool, hides and slaves (as slavery was to be the source of Bristol's and Liverpool's wealth in the post-medieval period). There is also good archaeological and historical evidence for the development of the late medieval town of Dublin after the Anglo-**Norman** colonisation of 1169.

See also Brian Boru; Celts; Gaels; Houses; Coinage and Trade; Warfare and Weapons.

Further Reading

Bradley, J. (ed.). 1984. *Viking Dublin Exposed: The Wood Quay Saga*. The O'Brien Press.

Clarke, H. B. 2002. *Dublin. Part I to 1610. Irish Historic Towns Atlas, No. 11*. Royal Irish Academy.

Geraghty, S. 1996. *Viking Dublin: Botanical Evidence from Fishamble Street*. Royal Irish Academy.

Holm, P. 1986. 'The Slave Trade of Dublin, Ninth to Twelfth Centuries'. *Peritia* 5: 317–345.

Ó Floinn, Ragnaill. 1998. 'The Archaeology of the Early Viking Age in Ireland'. Pp.131–165 in *Ireland and Scandinavia in the Early Viking Age*. Edited by H. B. Clarke, M. Ní Mhaonaigh and R. Ó Floinn. Four Courts Press.

O'Brien, E. 1998. 'A Reconsideration of the Location and Context of Viking Burials at Kilmainham/ Islandbridge, Dublin'. Pp.35–44 in *Dublin and Beyond the Pale: Studies in Honour of Patrick Healy*. Edited by C. Manning. Wordwell.

Valante, M. 2000. 'Dublin's Economic Relations with Hinterland and Periphery in the Later Viking Age'. Pp.69–83 in *Medieval Dublin I*. Edited by S. Duffy. Four Courts Press.

Wallace, P. F. 1987. 'The Economy and Commerce of Viking Age Dublin'. Pp.200–245 in *Untersuchungen zu Handel und Verkehr der vor- und frühgeschichtlichen Zeit in Mittel- und Nordeuropa*.

———. 1988. 'Archaeology and the Emergence of Dublin as the Principal Town of Ireland'. Pp.123–160 in *Settlement and Society in Medieval Ireland*. Edited by J. Bradley. Kilkenny.

———. 1992a. 'The Archaeological Identity of the Hiberno-Norse Town'. *Journal of the Royal Society of Antiquaries of Ireland* 122: 35–65.

———. 1992b. *The Viking-Age Buildings of Dublin*, 2 vols. Royal Irish Academy.

———. 2001. 'Ireland's Viking Towns'. Pp.37–50 in *The Vikings in Ireland*. Edited by A. Larsen. Roskilde.

———. 2005. 'The Archaeology of Ireland's Viking Age Towns'. Pp. 814–840 in *A New History of Ireland: I Prehistoric and Early Ireland*. Edited by D. Ó Cróinín. Oxford University Press.

Aidan O'Sullivan

Dumbarton

Dumbarton (*Dun Breatainn* in **Scots** Gaelic) was the government seat for the early medieval kingdom of **Strathclyde**, centred on Dumbarton Castle, which was in turn built upon the basalt core of an extinct volcano, Dumbarton Rock, a natural high point on the north shore of the Firth of Clyde, overlooking the area where the river Leven flows into the estuary. The builders of Dumbarton Castle found an ideal site for fortifications, but they were not the first to do so; the castle was constructed upon the remains of earlier fortifications, and there is archaeological evidence to suggest that the site was occupied at least as early as the Roman era, if not earlier. *Dun Breatainn* means 'fortress of the **Britons**', while the Britons themselves called it *Alt Clut*, the 'Rock on the Clyde'. It appears in **Bede**'s *History* as *Alcluith*, and **Adomnán** states that **Rhydderch ap Tudwal**, known in Welsh sources as Rhydderch Hael ('Roderick the Generous'), was 'King of Dumbarton' in the late sixth century.

Through much of the early medieval period, the Britons of Strathclyde were at war with the Scots of **Dalriada** to the west and south-west as the Scots established their presence in western Scotland. The **Angles** of **Northumbria** to their east and south also became a chronic foe until their power faded in the eighth century, but **Viking** incursions from Ireland in the ninth century devastated Strathclyde just as they did much of the western region of what later became Scotland. Viking assaults that began in 866, and again in 870–871, were rugged blows for the kingdom. The 870–871 campaign was disastrous. King Arthgal and many of his people barricaded themselves within Dumbarton Castle to escape the marauding Norsemen under King Olafr of Dublin, trusting that the castle's defences would keep them safe. However, the summer of 870 was an unfortunate time for those in the castle; as the Vikings besieged the castle, a severe drought besieged the Britons as well. While the garrison held out for four months, they were forced to give up when the well that supplied the castle dried up. The castle was destroyed, but the Britons eventually rebuilt it in the early tenth century. However, the kingdom declined in strength as compared with its Scottish and **Anglo-Saxon** neighbours, and in the early eleventh century, it merged with the growing Scot kingdom.

Nevertheless, because of its strategic position, Dumbarton Castle remained in nearly continuous use through the medieval period and an important component of the Scot kingdom. King Alexander II (1214–1249) made Dumbarton a royal burgh in 1222, and the burgh was used by him, and his successor, Alexander III, as a base from which the Scots expanded their control over the western coastal areas and Western Isles. The castle also provided shelter for David II, son of Robert the Bruce, and his queen, Joan, in 1333, following the Scots defeat at Halidon Hill. Perhaps more famous are William Wallace's associations with Dumbarton; Blind Harry describes Wallace's dramatic escape from the burgh at one point as English forces closed in. Later, when Sir John Menteith captured Wallace in 1305, he kept Wallace prisoner in the fortress there before turning him over to the English. Finally, infant Mary, Queen of Scots, was moved there for her safety after her father's disastrous defeat at the Battle of Pinkie in 1548.

See also Kings and Kingship; Warfare and Weapons.

Further Reading

Hudson, Benjamin T. 1994. *Kings of Celtic Scotland*. Greenwood Press.
McDiarmid, Matthew P. (ed.). 1969. *Blind Harry's Wallace*, vol. II. Scottish Text Society. William Blackwood and Sons.
Snyder, Christopher A. 2003. *The Britons*. Peoples of Europe Series. Blackwell Press.

Darlene Hall

Dumnonia

Dumnonia was a post-Roman British kingdom in the south-west which had its origins in the Roman period or the pre-Roman **Iron Age** and which survived until its gradual incorporation into the English kingdom of **Wessex**.

The earliest mention of the post-Roman kingdom of Dumnonia (as *Damnonia,* reproducing a common scribal error) comes c. 540 in the *De Excidio Britanniae* of **Gildas**. Although it has been speculated that Gildas might have been speaking of a kingdom taking its name not from the south-western ***Dumnonii*** but rather from a people of the same name living in southern Scotland, several factors strongly argue against this. The names *Dumnonia* and *Dumnonii* are conspicuously absent from Scotland during the post-Roman period; moreover, the name of the ruler of Dumnonia cited by Gildas, Constantine, is a well-established dynastic name in the south-west. Finally, it seems likely that Gildas's own area of interest in this section was confined to Wales and southern Britain.

We know of one other named ruler of Dumnonia, **Geraint**. These rulers, Constantine and Gerontius (Geraint), have late Roman names. The continuity of the Romano-British regional name Dumnonia nonetheless implies continuity of a Romano-British ruling elite. Other possible rulers in the region include Marcus, also known as Cunomorus, and Drustanus, who feature in the **Arthurian** stories. The admittedly sparse and fragmentary medieval **Welsh** genealogical material gives us the closest thing we have to a king list, albeit legendary, of Dumnonia. In one text, Geraint figures several times as the grandson of *Custennyn Gorneu* (Constantine of Cornwall?); in another text, Geraint's lineage includes *Kynvawr* (Cunomorus?) (Bartrum 1966, 25, 58). The list could easily be a list of rulers of the south-west rather than strictly familial relationships, and it is worth noting that while Constantine and Geraint are relatively secure in their historicity, the others named are far less so. Archaeological evidence such as imported ceramics ('**Tintagel ware**') has identified **Tintagel** as a high-status site, and others have been identified on the basis of place names that include the element *llys* ('court') and from folkloric traditions, many of which are associated with King Arthur.

It seems likely that within the post-Roman kingdom of Dumonia, there also existed a sub-kingdom of *Cornubia*. Both *Cornubia* and *Domnonia* are mentioned in an eighth-century poem attributed to Aldhelm, the former described as 'nasty', the latter as 'devoid of any flowering vegetation or grasses in any abundance' (Lapidge and Rosier 1985, 177). Immigration of **Brythonic** speakers from the south-west to what became medieval Brittany resulted in early Breton kingdoms bearing the names Dumnonée (in the north and north-west) and Cornouaille (in the south-west). The possibility that some Dumnonian rulers' sway extended to both sides of the Channel cannot be discounted. The matter is obscured even more by the identical names used for these regions in both countries.

All but the west of the kingdom was lost to **Anglo-Saxon** conquest by the eighth century. The absorption of Cornwall into the kingdom of Wessex was more gradual, **Cornwall** apparently having its own king as late as 875, in which year the ***Annales Cambriae*** record that Dungarth, *rex Cerniu*, was drowned (Dumville 2002, 12). Cornwall retained its British (Celtic) language (which survived into the eighteenth century), a native pottery sequence and, possibly, pre-Roman territorial divisions. Even by the time of the **Domesday Book** (1086), the **Norman** clerics could still discern in the county distinctive institutions and practices.

See also Britons; Celts; Roman Britain.

Further Reading

Bartrum, P. C. 1966. *Early Welsh Genealogical Tracts.* University of Wales Press.

Dark, Ken. 1994. *Civitas to Kingdom: British Political Continuity 300–800.* Leicester University Press.

Dumville, David (ed. and tr.). 2002. *Annales Cambriae, AD 682–954: Texts A-C in Parallel.* Department of Anglo-Saxon, Norse and Celtic, University of Cambridge.

Lapidge, M., and J. L. Rosier (tr.). 1985. *Aldhelm: The Poetic Works.* D. S. Brewer.

Pearce, Susan. 1978. *The Kingdom of Dumnonia.* Lodenek Press.

Preston-Jones, Ann, and Peter Rose. 1986. 'Medieval Cornwall'. *Cornish Archaeology* 25: 135–186.

Snyder, Christopher A. 2003. *The Britons.* Peoples of Europe Series. Blackwell.

Todd, Malcolm. 1987. *The South-West to AD 1000.* Longman.

Winterbottom, Michael (ed. and tr.). 1978. *Gildas: The Ruin of Britain and Other Documents.* Phillimore.

Karen Jankulak

Dumnonii

Roman-era sources speak of two peoples called the *Dumnonii*, one in the south-west of what is now England, which later became the post-Roman kingdom of **Dumnonia**, and another in what is now Scotland, which disappeared, apparently superseded or replaced by the post-Roman kingdom of **Strathclyde**.

There is no consensus on the derivation of the **Celtic** name *Dumnonii*, which has been interpreted either as 'people of the land' or as 'people of the god *Dumnōnos'. According to several Roman-era sources, the *Dumnonii* lived in the south-west of England, taking in most of modern **Cornwall** and Devon (the latter takes its name from Dumnonia), part of Somerset (west of the river Parrett) and perhaps part of Dorset (around the estuary of the Axe at Seaton), extending west as far as the Lizard peninsula, which is called *Dumnonium Promontorium* by Ptolemy (Rivet and Smith 1979, 342–344). The area was relatively underpopulated, and its material culture relatively poor. During the Romano-British period, as Malcolm Todd has noted, the south-west was 'one of the least Romanised regions of **Roman Britain**' (1987, 216). There is also very little evidence of Roman military activity, suggesting that Romanisation, such as it was, came relatively peacefully. *Isca Dumnoniorum* (**Exeter**), the *civitas*-capital, was a notably moderate Roman town, with few or no indications of wealth and with a remarkable absence of villas, both in the vicinity of the *civitas* and farther afield.

The northern *Dumnonii* are far less well attested. They are often referred to by modern historians as *Damnonii,* but this is arguably derived from the same scribal error that produced this form in the sources relating to the south-western *Dumnonii.*

See also Scots.

Further Reading

Dark, Ken. 1994. *Civitas to Kingdom: British Political Continuity 300–800.* Leicester University Press.

Pearce, Susan. 1978. *The Kingdom of Dumnonia.* Lodenek Press.

Rivet, A. L. F., and Colin Smith. 1979. *The Place-Names of Roman Britain.* BT Batsford.

Thomas, Charles. 1966. 'The Character and Origins of Roman Dumnonia'. Pp. 74–98 in *Rural Settlement in Roman Britain: Papers Given at a CBA Conference Held at St Hugh's College, Oxford, January 1 to 3, 1965.* Edited by Charles Thomas. CBA Research Report No. 7. Council for British Archaeology.

Todd, Malcolm. 1987. *The South-West to AD 1000.* Longman.

Karen Jankulak

Dún Aonghusa

Dún Aonghusa (or Dún Óengussa, 'fortress of Angus') is a stone fortress located in Kilmurvy on Inishmore in the Aran Islands in Galway Bay on the western coast of Ireland. It is located on the edge of a 330-foot (100-metre) cliff and consists of four semicircular limestone walls ending at the cliff face. The initial **hillfort** at Dún Aonghusa dates from the Late **Bronze Age**, and several artefacts including swords, spearheads and pottery from

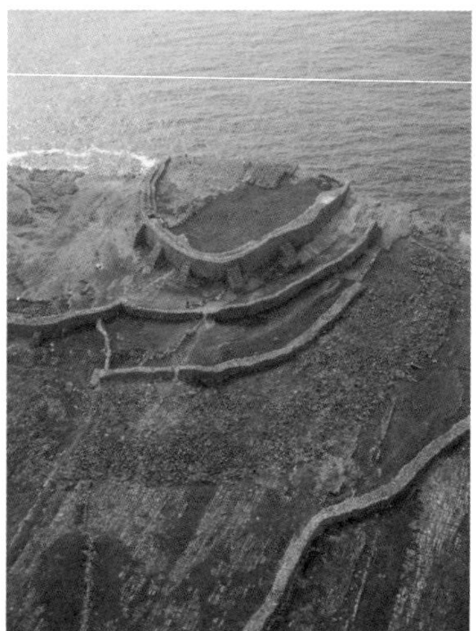

11. Ruins of Dun Aengus on the Aran Islands, Ireland, Late Bronze Age to early medieval.

that era have been discovered through excavations. The site continued to be occupied during the **Iron Age**. However, the majority of the extant remains at Dún Aonghusa are the product of early medieval construction.

According to Irish mythology, Dún Aonghusa was apparently named after Óengus mac Úmóir, a king of the legendary people known as the ***Fir Bolg***. However, the stories concerning Óengus mac Úmóir are part of a rather confused set of tales, incorporating various mythological traditions. The medieval Irish poems *Loch Aindind* and *Carn Conall* ('Cairn of Conall') recount the exploits of the family of the mythological figure Úmór, whose name means 'big-eared'. Úmór seems to function as an ancestral deity of the *Fir Bolg*, a population that invaded Ireland in popular tradition. The *Fir Bolg* were also called the Builg, a name related to that of the Continental and British tribe known as the ***Belgae***. *Loch Aindind* states that Úmór and his followers travelled from Greece to **Tara** in Ireland. Interestingly, *Carn Conall* mentions that they were from the land of the *Cruithne*, a term that can refer either to the **Picts** of Scotland or to a population of **Ulster** in Ireland. Therefore, they would have been of some type of **Celtic** origin before their stay in Greece. After their arrival in Ireland, Cairbre Nia Fer, the king of Laigin ('people of Leinster') who had earlier seized control of Tara, taxed the family of Úmór, which angered them. And under their king, the Laigin had defeated the family of Úmór. As a result of this, the forces of Laigin apparently drove away the family of Úmór to the Aran

Islands in the western part of **Connacht**, and Óengus settled at Dún Aonghusa.

It has been suggested that this account of Úmór and his family was later reworked and transformed into the tale of *Cath Maige Tuired* ('Battle of Mag Tuired [Moytura]') from the ***Lebor Gabála*** (*Book of Invasions*). In *Cath Maige Tuired*, it is the ***Tuatha Dé Danann***, rather than the Laigin, who defeated the *Fir Bolg*. After the battle, the *Fir Bolg* escaped to the Scottish islands instead of to the west of Connacht. This latter discrepancy may have resulted from a confusion of the Aran Islands of Ireland with Arran Island, which is located off the south-western coast of Scotland.

Further Reading

Gwynn, Edward. 1991a. *The Metrical Dindshenchas, Part III*. Dublin Institute for Advanced Studies.

———. 1991b. *The Metrical Dindshenchas, Part IV*. Dublin Institute for Advanced Studies.

Jones, Carleton. 2004. *The Burren and the Aran Islands: Exploring the Archaeology*. Collin Press.

O'Rahilly, Thomas F. 1984. *Early Irish History and Mythology*. Dublin Institute for Advanced Studies.

Joseph Calise

Dunadd

This rocky outcrop once isolated by the Crinan Moss was a major citadel (Irish *Dún Add* = 'Fortress of Add') occupied by the **Scots** of **Dál Riata** and is usually assumed to have been their capital, though this cannot be proven. It was first excavated in 1905 by David Christison, who recovered a considerable body of material and provided an account of the defences, though no sequence of occupation was given. Excavations on a more limited scale were carried out by Hewat Craw in 1929, but little further progress was made in interpretation. This was in great part rectified by excavations during 1980–1981 by Alan Lane and Ewan Campbell, which, though limited, recovered much evidence about the development of the site.

It would appear that Dunadd was first occupied in the **Iron Age**, when a stonewalled fort or dun was probably constructed. The main defences, however, belong to the early medieval period, when an oval summit fort was built in the fourth or fifth century AD, to which were added outer enclosures, the construction of which was effected by the seventh century. This plan, however, was further modified with the construction of the outer enclosure wall, and this phase was dated to sometime between the eighth and tenth centuries AD. The site was possibly occupied down to the twelfth century.

The defences were of stone, sections of walling joining up natural outcrop. Within the enclosures, there was at least one stone-built structure, apparently rectilinear. Among the main features of the 1980–1981 excavations was the investigation of the debris from a workshop producing ornamental metalwork in the seventh century – there were more than 900 mould fragments as well as other evidence for the production of brooches and pins and buckles employing gold, silver and copper alloys. This metalworking debris shed important light on the development of **Celtic** ornamental metalworking in the period and also for contact with the **Anglo-Saxon** world. Other finds include imported Continental pottery and glass and inscribed stones.

Dunadd has been identified as the capital of the Cenél nGabráin dynasty; however, historical evidence reveals that it was certainly controlled by Cenél Loairn dynasty during the eighth century. The medieval Irish *Annals of Ulster* record that Dunadd and Dundurn were besieged in 683. Unfortunately, the record does not give any details regarding the circumstances surrounding the siege, including the names of the antagonists. According to *Annals of Ulster*, the Pictish king **Óengus** mac Forgusso/Fergusa (r. 729–761) attacked Dál Riata in 736, seized Dunadd and captured the Scots leaders Dúngal mac Selbaig (king of Dál Riata in 723–726 and 733–736) and his brother Feradach mac Selbaig, who were from Cenél Loairn. It has been suggested that both Dúngal and Feradach were killed after their capture and that this event began a period of Pictish control over Dál Riata; however, this is uncertain.

On top of the summit enclosure at Dunadd, there is a rock carved with the figure of a boar and two footprints. In addition, there is a poorly preserved **Ogam** inscription consisting of two lines, also present on this rock. The condition of the inscription makes it nearly impossible to decipher its meaning and context. The boar carving has been dated between the sixth and eighth centuries, and it has been suggested that the boar was left by the invading Pictish army, which captured Dunadd in 736. However, the style of the boar does not resemble other known Pictish boar symbols. In addition, it seems unlikely that the Scots would have allowed such a triumphal memento to have remained intact after the

Picts had withdrawn. Therefore, it seems improbable that the boar carving commemorates this invasion. It has some other significance; it has also been suggested that all the carvings on this rock surface relate to ceremonies and rituals involving the inauguration of Scots kings of Dál Riata upon this site.

See also Hillforts; Kings and Kingship.

Further Reading

Alcock, Leslie. 1981. 'Early Historic Fortifications in Scotland'. Pp.158–179 in *Hill-Fort Studies: Essays for A.H.A. Hogg*. Edited by Graeme Guilbert. Leicester University Press.

———. 2003. *Kings & Warriors, Craftsmen & Priests*. Society of Antiquaries of Scotland.

Craw, I. H. 1929–1930. 'Excavations at Dunadd and OTHER sites in the Poltalloch estates, Argyll'. *Proceedings of the Society Antiquaries of Scotland* 64: 111–147.

Lane, Alan. 1984. 'Some Pictish Problems at Dunadd'. Pp.43–62 in *Pictish Studies*. Edited by J. G. P. Friell and W. G. Watson. British Archaeological Reports British Series 125.

Lane, Alan, and Ewan Campbell. 2000. *Dunadd: An Early Dalriadic Capital*. Oxbow.

Lloyd Laing and J. M. P. Calise

Duncan I (c.1015–1040)

Duncan I, properly Donnchad mac Crínáin, was the son of Bethoc, daughter of King Malcolm II, and Crinan, the comarb of Dunkeld. His direct male line ruled in Scotland from 1058 to 1286, and his descendants include the reigning monarch of the United Kingdom. He has achieved literary immortality due to Shakespeare's drama *Macbeth*. Some of the first precise dates in Scottish history are attached to his reign, thanks to the interest of an Irish chronicler named Marianus Scotus, whose amanuensis gathered the information while travelling across Scotland during the reign of his son **Malcolm Canmore**.

Duncan began his reign on 30 November 1034, five days after the death of his grandfather Malcolm II. The *Prophecy of Berchán* describes him as young, which is corroborated by the *Annals of Tigernach*. His early reign was uneventful, although a folktale preserved by Andrew Wyntoun claims that a casual liaison between Duncan and the daughter of the miller of Forteviot produced the future king Malcolm III 'Canmore'. The events leading to his downfall and death began c.1039. A Northumbrian noble named Ealdred, son of Uchtred, raided the **Britons**, apparently the men of **Strathclyde**, who John of Worcester claims had been ruled by Duncan prior to his elevation to the kingship. Duncan retaliated the following year with a raid on Durham. Using cavalry and infantry, the attack was an utter failure for the Scots, who retreated with heavy losses. Assisting Duncan was **Macbeth**, described by Marianus Scotus as his *dux*, who was probably his cousin. Despite the military fiasco, Duncan decided to travel throughout his realm, collecting taxes. Outside Elgin, he was challenged to battle by Macbeth on the *nativitas* of Mary, which was celebrated on August 16 by the Scots, at *Bothngouane*, possibly Pitgaveny. Duncan was slain after a reign of five years and nine months.

Duncan's family was still powerful after his death. His sons Malcolm and Domnall 'Ban' remained in the kingdom for several years before fleeing: Malcolm to England and Domnall to the Hebrides. Malcolm's sojourn in England could reflect ties to the Northumbrian aristocracy. The Scottish king lists claim that Duncan's wife was named Suithen and that she was a kinswoman of Earl Siward of Northumbria, while Duncan's brother Maldred had married into the native Northumbrian aristocracy. In support of his grandsons, Duncan's father Crinan attempted a *coup d'etat* in 1045, but it failed and Crinan died.

The restoration of Duncan's family to the kingship in the person of Malcolm III oversaw the refurbishing of his memory. The poem known as 'Duan Albanach' describes Duncan as pure and wise, while a verse added to the *Prophecy of Berchán* claimed that he was elderly. In the thirteenth century, his descendant King Alexander II endowed a mass chaplaincy near Elgin in memory of King Duncan. The final restoration came with the evolution of the Macbeth legend. In the fourteenth-century story of John of Fordun, Duncan is a gentle, old man, who is too mild to rule his kingdom and too trusting of his lieutenant. In the final retelling of his legend, Shakespeare's drama presents Duncan as the innocent victim of his murderer's vaulting ambition.

See also Kings and Kingship; Scots.

Further Reading

Anderson, A. O. (ed.). 1990. *Early Sources of Scottish History AD 500–1286*. Stroud.

Hudson, Benjamin. 1990. 'From Senchus to Histore: Traditions of King Duncan I'. *Studies in Scottish Literature* 25: 100–120.

———. 1994. *Kings of Celtic Scotland*. Greenwood.
———. 1996. *Prophecy of Berchán*. Greenwood.
Kappelli, W. 1976. *The Norman Conquest of the North*. University of North Carolina Press.

Benjamin Hudson

Duncan II (c. 1066–1094)

King Duncan II of **Scots**, correctly Donnchad mac Máel Choluim, was the son of **Malcolm III 'Canmore'** and his first wife Ingibjorg of the Orkneys. Duncan first appears in historical records in 1087 as a hostage at the English court who was freed by King **William II** upon his succession. He was also given arms, according to the chronicler John of Worcester, which apparently means that he was knighted. The beginning of his captivity is unknown, but Duncan may have been among the Scots hostages given to King **William I** in August 1072 at Abernethy. Duncan continued to reside at the English court, where he learned of the death of his father in an ambush at Alnwick on 13 November 1093. The ***Anglo-Saxon Chronicle*** claims that upon learning of the succession of his uncle Domnall 'Ban', Duncan gave oaths of fealty to William in return for troops to attempt a seizure of the kingship. The expedition was memorable, probably because of its speedy execution, and Duncan was king before the end of the year. Ailred of Rievaulx, in his *Relatio de bello standardo*, mentions it as an example of Anglo-Scots cooperation.

The exact length of Duncan's brief reign is uncertain, although contemporary records agree that he was slain in 1094. Duncan is probably the king intended in the contemporary *Prophecy of Berchán*, who would reign for a month and four nights, apparently an example of poetic license. One Scottish king list (E) claims that he reigned less than a year only, while others allot six months to his rule. As was customary among his family, he was a patron of the community of **St. Cuthbert** at Durham. A charter survives in which he grants lands in Lothian to the community. His reliance on foreign supporters was a source of unhappiness to his subjects and Duncan barely escaped from an ambush that killed many of his foreign troops. The rebels were reconciled with the king on the condition that his mercenaries would be dismissed.

The king was unwise to make such an agreement. Without his supporters, Duncan was unable to withstand the plots made for his murder. He was killed by his own subjects; the usual date given for this event is 12 November 1094. The *Anglo-Saxon Chronicle* and the Irish *Annals of Inisfallen* claim that sole responsibility of the killing rested with his uncle Domnall, while **William of Malmesbury** and the *Annals of Ulster* claim that his half-brother Edmund, the son of Malcolm's second wife Margaret, was also involved, and the later Scots historical materials such as the king lists and the *Chronicle of Melrose* attribute his death to a mormaer of the Mearns named Máel Petair mac Máel Choluim; the place of his death is traditionally placed at Mondynes, near Fordun. Taken together, this probably means that Domnall and Edmund agreed on the murder, but the deed was carried out by Máel Petair.

Duncan was married to Æthelthryth or Octreda, the daughter of Gospatric I, earl of Dunbar. Their son was known as William Fitz Duncan, and he was an important commander for his uncle King **David I**.

See also Kings and Kingship.

Further Reading

Anderson, A. O. (ed. and tr.). 1908. *Scottish Annals from English Chroniclers AD 500 to 1286*. Paul Watkins.
——— (ed.). 1990. *Early Sources of Scottish History AD 500 to 1286*, 2 vols. Stamford.
Duncan, A. A. M. 1999. 'Yes, the Oldest Scottish Charter'. *Scottish Historical Review* 78: 1–38.
Hudson, Benjamin. 1996. *Prophecy of Berchán*. Greenwood.
Kapelle, William. 1979. *The Norman Conquest of the North*. University of North Carolina Press.
Ritchie, R. L. G. 1954. *The Normans in Scotland*. Edinburgh University Press.

Benjamin Hudson

Dundurn

Dundurn (Irish *Dún Duirn*) is a fortress at the east end of Loch Earn in Perthshire in Scotland. It is placed on a pyramid-shaped knoll known as St Fillan's Hill above the foot of Loch Earn, a location that would have been within the traditional boundaries of Pictland. However, it is uncertain as to what group actually possessed the fortress. It has been suggested that it may have been a stronghold of the **Picts**, **Scots** or **Strathclyde Britons**, considering that it is situated in an area which bordered on the territory of these three populations. It is even possible that Dundurn may have changed hands among these three groups at various times. Also, Dundurn was in an important strategic location between **Dunadd** and Dunollie (which were important to the Scots) and Forteviot and **Scone** (which were important to the Picts), which would have made it a perfect target for siege. The medieval Irish *Annals of Ulster* record that Dundurn and Dunadd were besieged in 683. Unfortunately, the record does not give any details regarding the circumstances surrounding the siege, including the names of those laying siege to Dundurn or the names of those being besieged.

Archaeological excavations have been carried out at Dundurn during 1976–1977. Evidence acquired from these excavations suggests that Dundurn was occupied between the sixth and ninth centuries. It also appears that the site was first fortified during the seventh century and had several stages of construction. Dundurn initially consisted of a citadel with a wooden-stockaded terrace rampart of hazel wattling and oak beams with a dry-stone wall. The rampart was located below the citadel. This early fortress was completely burned down but was refortified soon after with dry-stone walls. The refortification may have been prompted by the siege of 683, but this cannot be proven with any historical certainty. Interestingly, most of the stone used for the fortifications were brought from the bottom of the hill rather than quarried from rock on the site. Excavations at Dundurn have also revealed a wide variety of artefacts and remains, including imported pottery, domesticated animal bones (cattle, sheep and pig), crucibles and moulds (for metalworking), decorated glass and metal objects, and a **Saxon**- or **Viking**-style knife. However, the nature of the finds makes it difficult to discern whether the fortress belonged to the Picts, Scots or Strathclyde Britons. On the top of the hill upon which the fortress of Dundurn was built, there is also a carved rock boss known as St Fillan's Chair. It has been suggested that this may have been a throne for the inauguration of kings of Strathearn; however, this proposition is uncertain.

Further Reading

Alcock, Leslie. 1981. 'Early Historic Fortifications in Scotland'. Pp.150–180 in *Hill-Fort Studies: Essays for A. H. A. Hogg*. Edited by Graeme Guilbert. Leicester University Press.

———. 2003. *Kings & Warriors, Craftsmen & Priests*. Society of Antiquaries of Scotland.

Alcock, Leslie, Elizabeth Alcock, and S. T. Driscoll. 1989. 'Reconnaissance Excavations 3: Excavations at Dundurn'. *Proceedings of the Society of Antiquaries of Scotland* 19: 189–226.

Anderson, M. O. 1980. *Kings and Kingship in Early Scotland* (2nd edn.). Edward Arnold.

Foster, Sally. 1998. 'Before Alba: Pictish and Dál Riata Power Centres'. Pp.1–31 in *Scottish Power Centres*. Edited by Sally Foster, Allan Macinnes and Ranald Macinnes. Cruithne Press.

Joseph Calise

Dunkeld

Dunkeld (Irish *Dún Callan* or *Dún Caillenn*) is a location in Tayside between Pitlochry and Perth in central Scotland. During the early medieval period, Dunkeld became an important ecclesiastical centre. A monastery and church were established there as a replacement for **Iona**, which was subject to frequent **Viking** attacks. It has been suggested that Dunkeld was originally a monastery started by the religious reform movement known as the *Céli Dé* ('clients of God'). In medieval Scottish regal lists, the foundation of Dunkeld is attributed to Causantín mac Fergusa (Constantin filius Uurguist), king of Fortriu and, probably, king of **Scots** (c. 811–820). This event may have been associated with the visit of Diarmait, abbot of Iona, to Scotland in 818 with the relics of St. **Columba** (d. 597), who had founded the monastic community of Iona in 563 and was its first abbot. Later relics of St. Columba were transferred from Iona to Dunkeld in 849 by Cináed mac Alpín (**Kenneth MacAlpin**), king of **Dál Riata** (c. 840–858) and king of **Picts** (c. 842–858 or 848/849–858). Most importantly, these relics which were taken to Dunkeld included the symbol of St. Columba's (and his successor's) authority, the *Scrín Choluim Chille* ('Shrine of Columba'). This act marked Dunkeld as the main Columban church and monastery in Scotland, thus reducing the importance of Iona. There is some evidence that Dunkeld was the source of a medieval chronicle composed between 849 and 903, which was the basis for some historical entries later incorporated into a Scottish regal list known as the *Chronicle of Picts*. However, this is uncertain.

During the ninth century, Dunkeld appears to have been attached to the episcopal see of Fortriu since the 865 obit of Tuathal mac Forgusso, abbot of Dunkeld, also names him as bishop of Fortriu. However, this link must have been temporary, as subsequent abbots of Dunkeld were not labelled as bishops. Dunkeld itself became the object of Viking attacks in the ninth century. The monastic community there later became important not only in religious matters but also, more significantly, in secular ones. Abbots of Dunkeld even became involved in disputes over the throne during the tenth and eleventh centuries. In fact, two abbots were actually killed in battles between Scots during that time. Abbot Dúnchad was slain in 965 during a civil war, which erupted between Dub mac Máel Choluim and Cuilén mac Iduilb over the throne. In 1045, the abbot Crínán and 180 warriors were killed in battle under uncertain circumstances. This incident may have been part of a rebellion against the Scottish king Mac Bethad mac Findláech (d.1057), who is the **Macbeth** made infamous by Shakespeare.

See also Celtic Christianity; Monasticism.

Further Reading

Anderson, M. O. 1980. *Kings and Kingship in Early Scotland* (2nd edn.). Columbia University Press.

Broun, Dauvit, and Thomas Owen Clancy (eds.). 1999. *Spes Scotorum: Hope of Scots*. T & T Clark.

Clancy, Thomas Owen. 1996. 'Iona, Scotland, and the Céli Dé'. Pp.111–114, 120, 122, 124–125 in *Scotland in Dark Age Europe*. Edited by Barbara Crawford. St. John's House Papers No. 6. Scottish Cultural Press.

Hudson, Benjamin T. 1994. *Kings of Celtic Scotland*. Greenwood Press.

Joseph Calise

Dunnichen, Battle of

The Battle of Dunnichen (middle Irish *Dún Nechtain*, 'fortress of Nechton/Nechtan'), also known by its English title, the Battle of Nechtansmere (Old English *Nechtanesmere*, 'Nechtan's mere'), was fought on 20 May 685 near Strathmore in Forfarshire (Angus) in Scotland, which would have been in Pictish territory. In this battle, the **Picts** under Bruide mac Bile (Bridei son of Bili), king of Fortriu (671/672–692/693), defeated the **Anglo-Saxon** Northumbrians under Ecgfrith, son of **Oswiu**, king of **Northumbria** (670/671–685), who was killed in the battle. The Battle of Dunnichen was the culmination of Northumbrian attempts to subjugate the Picts and place them under Northumbrian rule, a move that particularly began during the reign of Ecgfrith's father, Oswiu, son of **Æthelfrith** (642–670 or 643–671).

It is possible that Northumbria tried to control the Picts through the installation of puppet kings, since one Pictish king, Talorcán mac Anfrait (Talorgen son of Eanfrith) (653–657), may have been a son of Oswiu's brother Eanfrith. However, the Picts revolted against Northumbria around the time of Oswiu's death. Although initially defeated by the Northumbrians under the sub-king Beornhæth, the Picts were able to defeat Ecgfrith at Dunnichen when he attempted to invade Pictish territory. As a result of this Pictish victory, the Picts prevented Northumbria from further incursions into Pictland and re-conquered land previously taken by the Northumbrians. The battle also helped to end the Northumbrian bishopric of Abercorn (now in West Lothian, Scotland), which had been established under Trumwine for those Picts who had been conquered by Northumbria.

The most thorough medieval accounts of the Battle of Dunnichen occur in **Bede**'s *Historia Ecclesiae Gentis Anglorum* ('Ecclesiastical History of the English People') (bk.IV, ch.26, where the battle is unnamed), various texts of the ***Irish Annals*** (where it is called *Dún Nechtain*) and the ***Historia Brittonum*** (ch.57, where it is called *Lin Garan*). Various manuscripts of the ***Anglo-Saxon Chronicle*** also mention the battle but usually only mention the death of Ecgfrith, without naming either the battle or his opponents. Similarly, the anonymous *Vita Sancti Cuthberti* (*Life of St. Cuthbert*), Bede's *Vita Sancti Cuthberti* (*Life of St. Cuthbert*) and *Life of* ***Wilfrid*** all record that Ecgfrith was killed by the Picts, without naming the battle or giving the specifics.

In 1805, a Pictish stone was found on Dunnichen Hill (now in the Meffan Institute in Forfar). This stone has three Pictish symbols carved on it. It has been suggested that the elaborately carved Pictish red sandstone cross-slab (known as **Aberlemno** 2) in the Aberlemno kirkyard in Forfarshire (3.25–4 miles [5–6 kilometres] north of Dunnichen) depicts the battle of Dunnichen on its reverse side. The reverse of this stone has two Pictish symbols and depicts a scene of mounted and unmounted warriors engaged in combat. Some of the warriors wear helmets, while others do not. Those wearing helmets have been identified as Northumbrians, and those without helmets have been identified as Picts. However, the equation of this scene with the battle of Dunnichen is uncertain and speculative.

See also Warfare and Weapons.

Further Reading
Anderson, M. O. 1980. *Kings and Kingship in Early Scotland* (2nd edn.). Columbia University Press.
Cruickshank, Graeme. 1999. *Battle of Dunnichen*. The Pinkfoot Press.
Fraser, James E. 2002. *Battle of Dunnichen 685*. Tempus Publishing Ltd.
Mack, Alistair. 1997. *Field Guide to the Pictish Symbol Stones*. The Pinkfoot Press.
Stenton, Frank. 1998. *Anglo-Saxon England* (3rd edn.). Oxford University Press.

Joseph Calise

Duns

Duns (the name means 'fort' in Gaelic) is the term given to a distinct group of small stonewalled forts found in Scotland. They are distributed in Argyll and the Inner Hebrides, with an outlying group in Perthshire, and a few are found south of the Forth–Clyde line, where they are believed to have been constructed in the Roman period by refugees from further north. Generally speaking, the stonewalls enclose an area no more than about 4,036 square feet (375 square metres) and have a single entrance, sometimes with door checks and with small guard-chambers at the entrance. Very small duns (with a diameter of less than 49 feet [15 metres]) may have been roofed – these have been termed 'dun houses'; these dun houses are in a majority in Argyll. They seem to have been the homesteads of individual families.

It is the dating of the duns that is problematical. Only one in Argyll, Rahoy, has been proved to be of **Iron Age** date, though examples in Perthshire seem to have belonged to this period. The majority of the western Scottish duns that have been excavated have produced finds of early medieval date, though these may not represent primary occupation. Good examples in this category are Kildonan, Ardifuir and Dùn Fhinn (all Argyll). A group of duns show features of rectilinear planning, perhaps influenced by Roman architecture. Some duns, arguably of post-Roman date, have outer enclosures. These are particularly characteristic of the Isle of Mull.

Stone forts, also known as cashels, are also known from Ireland, where they have been typically dated to the early medieval period. The cultural and chronological relationships between Scottish duns and Irish cashels, particularly down the maritime provinces of the Atlantic façade, remain a subject of debate.

See also Art and Architecture; Scots.

Further Reading
Alcock, Leslie. 2003. *Kings and Warriors, Craftmen and Priests*. Society of Antiquaries of Scotland.
Harding, D. W. 2004. *The Iron Age in Northern Britain: Celts and Romans, Natives and Invaders*. Routledge.
Henderson, Jon C. (ed.). 2000. *The Prehistory and Early History of Atlantic Europe*. Archaeopress.

Lloyd Laing

Dunstan, Saint

St. Dunstan was a Benedictine monk and the archbishop of **Canterbury** (960–988). He is noted as the principal architect of the Benedictine Reform movement of the English Church, in both its episcopal and its monastic manifestations, during the tenth century. Dunstan's primary objectives were to enforce clerical celibacy, convert the Cathedral chapterhouses into monastic communities, restore stringent adherence to the Benedictine order in English monasteries and install monks as bishops throughout the episcopal network of England. Traditionally, the authorship of the *Regularis Concordia* and a key stage in the development of the *Ordo* of Coronation were attributed to him; however, recent scholarship has challenged this.

Dunstan's life spanned the reigns of nine **Anglo-Saxon** kings: from Edward the Elder (899–924) to **Æthelred the Unready** (978–1016).

His first biographer, known to us by the initial 'B' appended to his work, tells us that Dunstan was born to Heorstan and Cynethryth at Baltonsborough near **Glastonbury**. Modern scholars have dated the birth to around 909. In his youth, he was placed into the care of the community at Glastonbury to receive an education. Expelled, he relocated to Winchester, where Ælfheah, bishop of Winchester (934–951), convinced him to take monastic vows. Dunstan then returned to Glastonbury to the household of **Æthelflæd**, matron and niece of King **Æthelstan**, where he acted as her confessor and spiritual guide.

Dunstan's relationship with the royal court alternated between fair and falling foul of the King's will and was, for the greater part, dictated by the crown's position on reform of the clergy. In 934 or 935, he was expelled from the court of Æthelstan (924–939) and then again in 939 from that of Edmund (939–946) – who, however, recalled Dunstan the next day after a harrowing escape from death while hunting in Cheddar Gorge. The following year, Edmund appointed Dunstan as abbot of Glastonbury, and it was from this point on that Dunstan took steps to implement his reform agenda. It was also at this time that he took an interest in the education of **Edgar**, infant son of Edmund and Aelfgifu, during the boy's fosterage to Æthelstan, half-king of **Mercia**. The relationship forged between Edgar and Dunstan during these years would prove exceedingly beneficial to Dunstan.

Dunstan's presence at court continued under Edmund's successor, Eadred (946–955), and his efforts to reform the church were greatly enhanced by the support of the dowager queen, Eadgifu, wife of Edward the Elder.

Upon his enthronement in 955, however, Eadwig dispossessed his grandmother Eadgifu and exiled Dunstan. B script explains the expulsion as a consequence of Dunstan's intervention in Eadwig's affairs on the night of the king's coronation. Dunstan had entered the king's chamber to remove him from the company of a woman, Ælfgifu, later his wife. Eadwig was so incensed that he drove Dunstan from court. That the expulsion was motivated by Eadwig's desire to establish his control over a court dominated by factions supporting his grandmother and Dunstan is indicated in the nature and number of the charters issued in his first year as king. Dunstan, for his part, removed to the monastery of Blandin, outside Ghent in Flanders, where he reportedly came within the scope of the continental Benedictine reform movement emanating from Fleury, the 'fount of the cult of Benedict', in Lotharingia (Dales 1988, 75). It was here as well that Dunstan modified his script, adopting Caroline forms prevalent on the continent in place of the insular miniscule script he had learned at Glastonbury. Scholars have dubbed this modified hand, Dunstan B script.

In 957, Eadwig's younger brother Edgar, by now approximately fourteen years of age, was selected to rule over a combined Mercia and **Northumbria** as separate kingdom. The reign of Edgar marks the apogee of Dunstan's career. Edgar immediately recalled his mentor from exile and soon appointed him as bishop of Worcester. Following Eadwig's death in 959, Edgar was crowned King of England, and Dunstan rose to be bishop of **London** and archbishop of Canterbury.

At a time when lay overlords treated monastic foundations within their domains as extensions of their estates to be disposed of at their discretion, the charters advanced by Dunstan and his fellow reformers while active in the court of Edgar served to reformulate the terms by which a monastery held its lands; in doing so, real property rights were transferred into the hands of powerful churchmen such as Dunstan and the monasteries. The result was the marginalisation of local magnates from church affairs. As the reform gathered momentum, the Easter Synod at Winchester 964 called for the foundation of monasteries throughout England, codified the terms of monastic landholding and sanctioned the expulsion of the secular clergy from the offices of the church. During the reign of Edgar, twenty-two monasteries were founded.

Dunstan also provided the inspiration for the *Regularis Concordia*, a version of the Rule of St. Benedict, written by Æthelwald, intended to standardise Benedictine practices among the monasteries and mandated compulsory clerical celibacy. It was promulgated at the council of Winchester c. 970.

After the death of Edgar in 975, the succession was contested; Dunstan supported the elder son, Edward, while Æthelwald supported Æthelred. Edward the Martyr (975–978) was not much older than ten when he succeeded the throne. Being a regency government, the crown was not strong enough to preserve all the advances made during Edgar's tenure, and Edward's short reign was plagued by the seizure of church lands by force. Dunstan retreated from court during the reign of Æthelred the Unready (978–1016) and died 19 May 988, aged nearly eighty.

The historiographical footprint of Dunstan has changed over time. When he died, his sanctity was immediately recognised, but few efforts were made to promote his cult. The initial manifestation of this cult appeared upon the continent, and the first Lives were composed in continental houses; B wrote between 994 and 1004 and Adelard, writing in 1011, was a monk of Blandin in Flanders. The first English Life, appropriately composed at Canterbury, was written over sixty years after Dunstan died.

After the **Norman Conquest** of 1066, the Norman Archbishop Lanfranc (1070) questioned the veracity of some Anglo-Saxon cults and removed Dunstan from the Calendar of the Saints. Nonetheless, modest recognition continued in the post-conquest era with Osbern, writing c. 1070–1093, Eadmer c. 1100 and **William of Malmesbury**, writing at the behest of Glastonbury, in 1125 during the conflict between Glastonbury and Canterbury.

There was a revival of interest in Dunstan under Henry VIII. As that monarch defied the Pope in his effort to secure a divorce from his wife, the king's supporters found in Dunstan's refusal to conform to the demands of a pope a useful precedent. Dunstan's usefulness to the English crown was short-lived, however. After 1530, his memory was modified to support the Protestant position against the papacy. Protestant reformers argued in defence of royal supremacy over the church; the example of Dunstan served as a warning to the dangers of an over-mighty church (Parish 2001, 57). The reworking of Dunstan's memory at the hands of Protestant writers tarnished his memory until his image was rescued by Bishop Stubbs in 1874.

See also Celtic Christianity; Monasticism.

Further Reading

Conn, Marie. 1996. 'Rites of King-Making in Tenth-Century England'. Pp.111–127 in *The Propagation of Power in the Medieval West: Selected Proceedings of the International Conference*, Groningen 20–23 November 1996. Edited by Martin Grosman, Arjo Vanderjagt and Jan Veenstra. Egbert Forsten.

Dales, Douglas. 1988. *Dunstan: Saint and Statesman*. Lutterworth Press.

Parish, Helen. 2001. ' "Impudent and Abominable Fictions": Rewriting Saints' Lives in the English Reformation'. *Sixteenth Century Journal* 32.1: 45–65.

Ramsey, Nigel, Margaret Sparks and Tim Tatton-Brown. 1988. *St. Dunstan: His Life, Times and Cult*. Boydell Press.

Whitelock, Dorothy. 1981. *History, Law and Literature in 10th–11th Century England*. Variorum Press.

Sue Schulze

Durham

The site of Durham has been occupied at least since the **Neolithic Period**, as indicated by archaeological evidence including burial finds. Its medieval history begins when the see of Durham was founded out of the relocated see of **Lindisfarne**. Its primary function was to house the body of the revered St. **Cuthbert**, which had been held for 200 years in Lindisfarne as a relic. After transferring his body into a new wooden coffin, which still survives, the monks fled with it from Lindisfarne to protect it from Danish raids. They wandered over considerable territory, stopping at

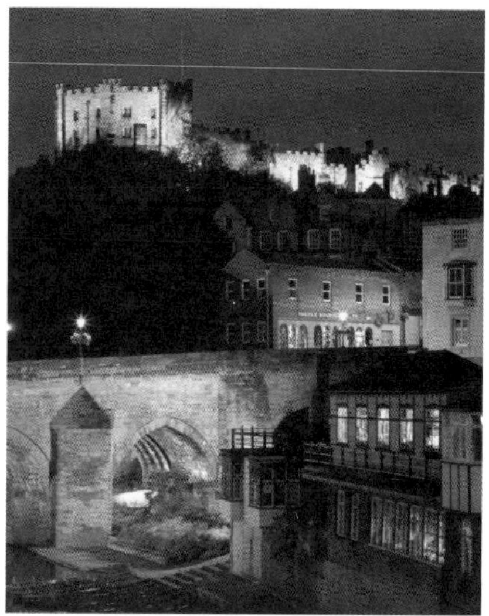

12. Durham Castle and Elvet Bridge, United Kingdom.

nearby Chester-le-Street for a century before carrying it on ultimately to Durham, which has remained the home of Cuthbert and his foundation for a thousand years. This foundation began with the 'White Church', a wooden structure built around 998 on a bend in the river Wear by Aldhun of Lindisfarne. Aldhun was related through his daughter to Uchted, the earl of Northumberland and protector of Durham. The White Church sufficed for three years, while a second structure, also known as the White Church, was built beside it. This church soon became a pilgrimage site and even King **Cnut** visited (and granted many privileges and much land to the foundation, aiding in its growth). In 1022, Durham acquired the body of the Venerable **Bede**, among the greatest of **Anglo-Saxon** churchmen and the father of English history.

During the **Norman Conquest**, the monks fled Durham, again taking the beloved Cuthbert with them, sheltering in Lindisfarne briefly before returning to Durham. The Anglo-Saxon bishop Æthelwin was replaced by Walcher of Lorraine, a **Norman**. His successor, William of St-Calais, oversaw the construction of the grand new cathedral, beginning c.1093. This massive and imposing structure declared not only the importance of their relics but also the power of the bishop and his Norman backers. Following the Conquest, the bishops became prince bishops, with military as well as ecclesiastical authority, and the neighbouring castle was the administrative centre for northern England for much of the Middle Ages. This military function was echoed in the west towers' balustrades, which mimic crenellations with open tracery.

Built in only forty years, the present structure has been hailed as the greatest of the Romanesque churches of Europe. However, its design embodies a transformation in Anglo-Norman architecture. Durham bears consistent rib vaulting, pointed arches and nascent (concealed) flying buttresses, the three defining features of Gothic architecture. In typical Norman fashion, the nave is very long, with an emphasis on linearity rather than height. Its massive, incised columns, alternating with compound piers, are highly distinctive. The body of Bede is housed in the Galilee Chapel, added by Bishop Hugh of Le Puiset c.1175–1180. The original rounded apse was replaced in the thirteenth century by a second transept containing nine altars. The see was dissolved in 1539.

See also Art and Architecture; Monasticism; Vikings.

Further Reading

Coldstream, N., and P. Draper (eds.). 1980. *Medieval Art and Architecture at Durham Cathedral.* British Archeological Association Conference Transaction.

Jackson, Michael (ed.). 1993. *Engineering a Cathedral.* Thomas Telford.

Shipley, Debra. 1992. *Durham Cathedral.* Tauris Parke Books.

Asa Mittman

Durotriges

The *Durotriges* were one of the indigenous tribes of the **Iron Age** and **Roman Britain**. More of a close-knit confederacy of smaller units than an actual tribe, the Durotriges's territory was centred on Dorset but extended to cover the southern portions of modern Wiltshire and Somerset as well. Overall, it was a very marked territory and dissimilar to that of neighbouring ***Atrebates***. Lacking ***oppida***, Durotrigian urbanisation seems to have been focused on the older Iron Age **hillforts**, with expansion and rebuilding taking place around the time of the Roman invasion, as at **Maiden Castle**, **Hod Hill**, Hambledon Hill and **South Cadbury**, all of which suggest being heavily active prior to AD 43 and hostile to the Roman invaders (e.g. Maiden Castle). Former garrisons for the Romans became towns and possible *caputs* of the *Durotriges* after c.70, as at **Dorchester** (*Durnovaria*) and Ilchester (*Lindinis*). The marginal sitting and overseas dependence of **Hengistbury Head**, an important trading centre with evidence for an advanced metal industry and possible mint, could be considered the equivalent of a south-eastern *oppidum* and may argue against centralisation in the Duotrigian region. Though a certain cultural isolation can be detected in the coinage, with a silver currency adopted before **Julius Caesar**'s invasion and retained until the later first century AD, it was also the result of trading contacts with Armorica. This can also be seen in the large quantities of imported black burnished pottery from the same period, and though there seems to be little regional variation or change from previous periods as far as locally produced ware, the assumption has been that the overall assemblage represents considerable commercialisation, possibly with an influx of potters from France.

Unlike Atrebatic areas, Durotrigian culture seems to have differed from the 'Belgic' culture of the south-east, especially with the continued use of inhumation, as can be seen at Maiden Castle, as well as the two rich burials within the territory (a male warrior at Whitcombe near Dorchester and, possibly, a female at West Bay near Bridport). Although it seems that the *Durotriges* developed on their own with little eastern influence, trading still took place, though they seem to have suffered a decline in their earlier cross-Channel trade with Brittany after Caesar's invasion, turning thereafter to trade with the ***Catuvellauni***. Rural farm settlements have been extensively excavated (e.g. on Cranbourne Chase), which seem to fall within traditions going back to the second millennium BC, and an equal continuation of hillfort occupation has suggested the possibility of suffering from internal tribal struggles longer than some of their neighbours. Durotrigian shale products such as armlets were found in other areas, including that of the *Catuvellauni*, and salt extraction along the Dorset coast was also an enterprise. There is evidence of the Romans exploring stone quarries in the area, as well as the potteries which continued into the late Roman period. Though little is known of the *Durotriges* after the departure of the Roman administration in the early fifth century, there is some archaeological evidence for continuing occupation in the area by the **Britons** (e.g. at Ilchester) before it fell to the West **Saxons**.

See also Celts.

Further Reading
Cunliffe, B. W. 1978. *Hengistbury Head*. Elek.
———. 2005. *Iron Age Communities of Britain* (4th edn.). RKP.
Sharples, N. 1991. *English Heritage Book of Maiden Castle*. Batsford.

Anne Sassin

Durrow

Durrow, one of St. **Columba**'s monastic foundations in County Offaly in the kingdom of **Meath**, was one of the most important ecclesiastical establishments in early medieval Ireland. Located on the important east-west land route, the *Slighe Mhór*, which is marked today by a line of oak trees, Durrow's name seems to have been derived from *Daru*, meaning 'plain of the oaks'. The specific date for Durrow's establishment by Columba is not certain, which is often given as between AD 553 and 556, though as late a date as 586 has been conjectured, and while **Bede** attests to Durrow's foundation as taking place before Columba's departure to **Iona** in 563, **Adomnán** tells of the saint having to send an angel from Iona to save a Durrow monk who had fallen during the construction of the church there.

Little is known of the early church of the monastery, though it is presumed to have been of timber construction, and the attack of a stone church at Durrow is recorded in the Annals for 1020, implying that by this period it had definitely replaced the earlier structure of Columba's. Of the monuments themselves which survive from the site, the earliest are five likely seventh-century sandstone slabs bearing Latin crosses with circular centres and geometric designs, and a small cross-head of tenth- to twelfth-century date, which once hung on the church gable, is now housed in the National Museum. However, it is the high cross at Durrow of mid-ninth century date which is probably the most famous standing monument, and while the inscription on the west face does not bear a readily identifiable name, that on the north side cites the king Máel Sechnaill, who died c. 862 and was the father of Flann, though whether it was commissioned by him or commemorating his achievements is uncertain. Being iconographically close to the Cross of the Scriptures at **Clonmacnois**, the cross's decoration includes trunco-pyramidal arm-ends, perhaps copied from metal boss design, a scene of John the Baptist on its narrow side, a panel of the Raised Christ, the Sacrifice of Isaac on the east face shaft and Passion scenes on the west. However, it is the capstone, shaped like a church with a shingled roof and finials, which most usefully serves as one of the only artistic representations of what early wooden churches may have looked like.

A fragment of what is known as the Crozier of Durrow is also housed in Dublin's Museum, but the most famous portable object associated with the monastery, the ***Book of Durrow***, one of the earliest illuminated manuscripts which dictated the layout, organisation and design of later ones, may not have even been produced there. With arguments for its origin including Iona and **Northumbria**, as well as a date range throughout the seventh century, it is known from an inscription on the now-lost cover that its origin was in Ireland at the time of the High King Flann Sinna (who lived from 879 to 916). It has been claimed that its arrival post-700 would have been more difficult to justify, and the retreat of an Irish party from the **Synod of Whitby** in 664 has been seen as one very probable opportunity for it to appear at Durrow, attesting to the pre-eminent position which the monastery held.

This richness in artefacts also implicates the semi-urban status that Durrow, along with other monasteries, would have had, with an estimated population in the ninth century between 1,500 and 2,000 people, and though excavations have not uncovered them, presumably there would have been workshops and streets as at Clonmacnois. Battles between monasteries are attested to in the Annals, including records by 764 of war with Clonmacnois, and its attractiveness as a target to both **Vikings** and Irishmen is apparent, especially in the eleventh and twelfth centuries, having been attacked by **Meath** in 1059, burned along with its books in 1095, and burned again twice in one month in 1155. Though Columba's church seems to have existed at least up until the **Norman** invasion, the Augustinian Priory of St. Mary was also established at Durrow in the twelfth century, founded by Murchadh O'Maeleachlainn under the direction of St. Malachy, and after the Anglo-Norman arrival of **Henry II**, Meath was granted to Hugh de Lacy, who had a motte built at Durrow in the 1180s.

See also Celtic Christianity; Monasticism.

Further Reading
Byrne, M. 1987. *Tullamore Catholic Parish: A Historical Survey*. Offaly Heritage Books.

Edwards, Nancy. 1990. *The Archaeology of Early Medieval Ireland.* University of Pennsylvania Press.
Harbison, P. 1999. *The Golden Age of Irish Art.* Thames & Hudson.

Anne Sassin

Dyfed

Dyfed was the traditional **Welsh** kingdom located in the extreme south-west corner of Wales. It consisted of six cantrefs: Pebidiog, Cemaes, Emlyn, Rhos, Penfro and Gwarthaf and included the site of **St David's** cathedral church. It provides the setting for two of the tales in the ***Mabinogi*** ('Pwyll, prince of Dyfed' and 'Manawyddan, son of Llŷr'). During the early tenth century, Dyfed was joined with Ceredigion and Ystrad Tywi to form **Deheubarth**.

During pre-Roman times, a Celtic tribe called the ***Demetae*** lived in this region, and 'Dyfed' derives from that tribal name. (In Welsh, an 'm' can mutate into the 'v' sound represented in Welsh by 'f'.) In post-Roman times, there is evidence, including twenty stones with **ogam** inscriptions, for a strong Irish presence in the region. One of these stones bears the name Voteporix in both Latin and Irish ogam versions, and **Gildas** describes him as *tyrannus* of the *Demetae*.

The first royal dynasty of Dyfed traced its connections to the Irish ***Déisi*** tribe. Late in the eighth century, Seisyll ap Clydog took territory from Maredudd, the king of Dyfed. After Maredudd's death in 796 or 797, the reduced territory of Dyfed was called Rheinwg, after the name of his son Rhain. Rhain died in 808 and left a son Tryffin, who died in 814. Rhain's brother Owain had a daughter, Tangwystl, who married Hyfaidd ap Bleddri, who controlled Dyfed between 870 and 892. This marriage illustrates the pattern of a previously lower-status family marrying into one of the older royal dynasties and then supplanting it – a frequent occurrence during this period of Welsh history. Hyfaidd was one of several Welsh rulers who allied themselves to King **Alfred** the Great for protection against the aggressive king **Rhodri Mawr** of **Gwynedd**. After Hyfaidd died in 892, his son Llywarch held Dyfed, although enduring an attack by Rhodri Mawr's son Anarawd in 894. The marriage of Llywarch's daughter Elen to Anarawd's nephew, Hywel ap Cadell, and the beheading of Llywarch ap Hyfaidd's brother Rhodri in 904 indicate the end of the old royal line. The political turmoil of this period may have been one factor in the decision of **Asser**, a scholar at St David's, to travel to **Wessex** to serve King Alfred as an adviser.

When the Normans attacked south-west Wales in 1093, Arnulf de Montgomery took Penfro and built his strong castle of Pembroke there. Although the **Montgomery family** lost its English and Welsh lands after its failed rebellion in 1102, the area remained under English domination. In 1105, King **Henry I** established a colony of Flemish settlers in the cantrefs of Rhos and Daugleddau. They brought with them expertise in raising sheep, and their Flemish language persisted in the region until the mid-fourteenth century.

See also Kings and Kingship.

Further Reading

Davies, J. L., and D. P. Kirby (eds.). 1994. *Cardiganshire County History. Volume I: From the Earliest Times to the Coming of the Normans.* University of Wales Press.
Davies, John. 1993. *A History of Wales.* Allen Lane, Penguin.
Davies, Wendy. 1982. *Wales in the Early Middle Ages.* Leicester University Press.

Frederick Suppe

Dyrham, Battle of

The Battle of Dyrham in 577 was fought between the **Britons** and the **Saxons** in south-west Britain. The battle is recorded in the ***Anglo-Saxon Chronicle***, which claims that the West Saxon king Ceawlin (560–593) and his son Cuthwine defeated three otherwise unknown British kings, Conmail, Condidan and Farinmail, and as a result gained control of the British cities of **Gloucester**, **Cirencester** and **Bath**.

In older scholarship, the Saxon victory at the Battle of Dyrham was emphasised as a significant turning point in the expansion of the Anglo-Saxon kingdoms, both in opening the Severn Valley to Saxon colonisation and in isolating the British kingdoms in Wales and **Dumnonia**. More recent scholarship has downplayed the significance of Dyrham for several reasons, ranging from the historical accuracy of the *Anglo-Saxon Chronicle* – a ninth-century source – for sixth-century battles to limited archaeological evidence for sixth-century Saxon settlement as far west as Gloucestershire. Although it is clear that a powerful West Saxon state was emerging in the late sixth and early seventh centuries, its centre was in the upper Thames, and many of its cultural features represent a blending of Germanic and British practices.

See also Warfare and Weapons.

Further Reading

Snyder, Christopher A. 2003. *The Britons*. Peoples of Europe Series. Blackwell.
Stenton, F. M. 1971. *Anglo-Saxon England*. Oxford University Press.
Yorke, Barbara. 1995. *Wessex in the Early Middle Ages*. Leicester University Press.

Deanna Forsman

E

East Anglia

See Angles.

Edgar, King of England (r.957/959–975)

Edgar (*Eadgar*) was the king of England from 957/959 to 975 and is primarily remembered for his patronage of the monastic reform movement of the late tenth century. Edgar was born c. 943 and was the second son of King Edmund (d. 26 May 946). After Edmund's death, the kingship passed to his brother Eadred, until his death on 23 November 955. Eadred died with no male heir, and so Edmund's two sons, Eadwig and Edgar, held the closest claims to the throne. Eadwig initially received the full kingship. However, in the second half of 957, in unknown circumstances, Mercian noblemen withdrew their support from Eadwig and chose Edgar as king. The country was apparently peacefully divided between the two brothers. On 1 October 959, Eadwig died and Edgar was chosen as king of the entire kingdom.

Edgar appears to have built up his position through alliances, and after his brother's death, he invited Dunstan (later St. **Dunstan**) to return from exile and appointed him to the see of **Canterbury** in 960 and appointed Oswald to **Worcester** by 961. Additionally, he restored to power some of the figures denigrated by his brother, and c. 961, he took a new wife, Wulfthryth, who was well connected to a powerful West Saxon family. Edgar proved to be a solid and steady ruler, continuing **Æthelstan**'s reforms of the English coinage, enforcing the regulation of weights and measures, and significantly contributing to legislation.

However, the aspect of his reign that has received the most attention is his support for the monastic reform movement. An account in **Old English** traces the origin of Edgar's support of the monasteries to a religious vow made in his youth. However, there is little evidence of any reforming zeal before the appointment of Æthelwold to the see of Winchester in 963, and perhaps instead we should see its beginnings in that act. The widespread foundation of monasteries by Æthelwold, Dunstan and Oswald, with royal support, grew in strength from this date, and led to the emergence of a network of reformed monastic houses across England.

All this lead up to the zenith of Edgar's authority on 11 May 973, when he was re-consecrated as king at **Bath**. The date of this coronation, some fourteen years after he began to wield authority over England, has caused some puzzlement. It appears most probable that this was a second coronation with imperial overtones; it is implied by the fact that immediately after this event, he travelled to **Chester** and received the submission of a number of sub-kings of Britain.

Edgar died on 8 July 975 and was buried in **Glastonbury**. His marriages had resulted in a number of heirs, and a violent dynastic struggle for the throne ensued between his two surviving sons, Edward and **Æthelred** (later 'the Unready').

See also Kings and Kingship; Monasticism.

Further Reading

Barlow, F. 1979. *The English Church 1000–1066* (2nd edn.). Longman.
Parsons, D. 1975. *Tenth-Century Studies: Essays in Commemoration of the Millennium of the Council of Winchester and Regularis Concordia*. Phillimore.
Robinson, J. A. 1923. *The Times of Saint Dunstan*. Oxford University Press.

Timothy Bolton

Edgar Ætheling

Edgar *Ætheling* (an Anglo-Saxon term for 'prince') was the great-grandson of **Æthelred the Unready**, grandson of Edmund Ironside, son of Edward the Exile and cousin of **Edward**

the Confessor. Notably, Edgar was passed over as heir to Edward in favour of **Harold Godwinsson** in 1066. However, upon Harold's death at the Battle of **Hastings**, Edgar was the chosen heir by the surviving English nobles. Although he found support among the English, who at the time were well noted for their dislike of **Normans** in general, Edgar was not able to resist William's conquest of England. After a brief period of exile in Scotland, Edgar submitted to William's rule and became an active commander in the service of both **William I** and his son, **William Rufus**.

Born during his father's exile from the court of King **Cnut**, Edgar was brought up in the court of King Salomon of Hungary. Some confusion and quite a bit of romance surround the family's exile, seen in the *Leges Edwardi Confessoris*, Geffrei Gaimar's *L'Estorie des Engleis* and John of Worcester's *Chronicon*. In 1057, Edward the Exile returned to England, but died before meeting with Edward the Confessor. Barring a child born to the allegedly unconsummated marriage of Edward and Edith, Edgar Ætheling was then the closest relation to the king and a viable choice as heir. But in 1066, Edgar was most likely only fourteen years old, and probably not a wise choice of ruler in a country torn by internal strife and threatened with external invasion. Additionally, Edgar had no strong allies in England to oppose Harold's claim. The family's extended exile on the western edge of Christendom had done nothing to bolster the support of friends.

After the death of Harold II at the Battle of Hastings, England was again left without a clear English heir to the throne. Although William continued to conquer all the English territories that had not yet submitted to his rule, a faction in **York**, led by Archbishop Ealdred, nominated Edgar as their king. For the next six years, Edgar continued to harass William with Scottish, Northumbrian and, perhaps, Danish allies. However, an offer from Philip of France of the castle of Montreuil and urging from **Malcolm Canmore** of Scotland prompted Edgar to make peace with William. Edgar held minor significance under the Norman kings until he and William Rufus raised a joint army in 1097 to put Edgar's nephew, Edgar, on the Scottish throne.

For the final chapter of Edgar's career, he travelled to the Holy Land, although the impetus for this journey is ambiguous. Oderic Vitalis noted in his *Ecclesiastical History* that Edgar was in charge of the English fleet that left in 1096 for the Crusade; however, Edgar's activities in Scotland cast some doubt on this claim. **William of Malmesbury**, in a more plausible story, recorded Edgar's pilgrimage to Palestine in 1102. On his return from the Holy Lands, Edgar joined a brief campaign against **Henry I** and was captured at the battle of Tinchebrai. Released, probably because he posed little political threat, Edgar retired, unmarried, to his estates and faded into obscurity, dying perhaps in his seventies, sometime after 1125.

See also Kings and Kingship; Warfare and Weapons.

Further Reading

Hooper, Nicholas. 1985. 'Edgar the Ætheling: Anglo-Saxon Prince, Rebel and Crusader'. *Anglo-Saxon England* 14: 197–214.

Stenton, F. M. 1971. *Anglo-Saxon England*. Clarendon Press.

Britt Rothauser

Eddington, Battle of

The Battle of Eddington in 878 was fought between **Alfred**, the king of Wessex (871–899), and **Guthram**, the king of the Danes. Beginning in the late eighth century, England experienced sporadic Danish raiding – the most notorious incident being the sack of **Lindisfarne** in 793. In the mid-ninth century, raiding became regular, and in 865 a large Danish army, known as the 'Great Army' invaded. Four years later, in 871, the 'Great Army' was joined by another large contingent of Danes, known as the 'Summer Army'. By 877, these Danish armies had conquered **Northumbria**, East Anglia and most of **Mercia**. Invasion of **Wessex** began in the winter of 878, and the Danes successfully occupied the portion of Wessex near Chippenham. Alfred rallied his forces and managed to defeat the Danish army at the battle of Eddington, in the vicinity of Wiltshire. As a result of his defeat at this battle, Guthram agreed to receive baptism and withdrew to East Anglia, where he reigned as king for ten years (880–890).

Eddington is seen as a turning point in the history of the ninth-century Danish invasions. Prior to this battle, the Danish had successfully conquered most of the Anglo-Saxon kingdoms. After Eddington, Alfred was able to reconquer **London** and establish Watling Street (a Roman road that ran north from London to **Chester**) as the boundary between the territory of the Danes (known as the **Danelaw**) and that of the English. Although a third large Danish army attacked Alfred's territory between 893 and 896, a new English navy and the extensive defensive system of ***burhs*** that Alfred had constructed enabled him to deal with them quite easily. According to the entry in the ***Anglo-Saxon Chronicle*** for 896, after Alfred's victory at Eddington, the English faced a greater threat from the mortality of men and cattle than from the invading Danish armies.

See also Kings and Kingship; Vikings; Warfare and Weapons.

Further Reading

Campbell, James. 1991. *The Anglo-Saxons*. Penguin.
James, Edward. 2001. *Britain in the First Millennium*. Arnold.

Deanna Forsman

Eddius Stephanus (fl.669–720)

Eddius Stephanus (fl. 669–720) was the author of the *Life of Wilfrid*. He was a native of **Kent**, invited to **Northumbria** by **Wilfrid** c. 669 to serve as a singing master in his churches. He was a strong partisan of Wilfrid, accompanying him to Rome in 702. Eddius Stephanus ended his career as a monk in Wilfrid's foundation at Ripon.

Eddius Stephanus wrote the *Life of Wilfrid* within no more than ten years of Wilfrid's death, and the traditional date of composition is between 709 and 720. It is likely that Stephanus composed this work in response to the popularity created by the *Anonymous Life of Cuthbert*, written between 698 and 705. He has been criticised for his glorification of Wilfrid, his excoriation of anyone who crossed the saint and his alteration of facts to achieve his aim. Stephanus's trustworthiness as a witness to Wilfrid's life has also been called into question, particularly in his portrayal of the years Wilfrid spent in Lyon. Although Stephanus's version of these events conflicts with sources from the continent, the tension is due more to exaggeration and Stephanus's desire to enhance Wilfrid's sanctity rather than lack of accurate information. When Stephanus's account is compared with **Bede**'s description of Wilfrid in the *Ecclesiastical History*, there is a high degree of reliability between the two sources.

Stephanus's Latin demonstrates a high level of learning, although it is not quite as good as Bede's. His narrative style is clear and readable with few obscure passages, although he does have a fair share of grammatical errors. The *Life of Wilfrid* survives in two independent manuscripts, dating from the eleventh and twelfth centuries. Along with Bede, Stephanus provides important information about the **Synod of Whitby** in 664, which launched Wilfrid – for better or worse – into Northumbrian politics.

See also Celtic Christianity; Literature.

Further Reading

Colgrave, Bertram (ed. and tr.). 1985. *The Life of Bishop Wilfrid by Eddius Stephanus*. Cambridge University Press.
Fouracre, Paul, and Richard A. Gerberding. 1996. *Late Merovingian France: History and Hagiography 640–720*. Manchester University Press.
Goffart, Walter. 1988. *The Narrators of Barbarian History (AD 550–800): Jordanes, Gregory of Tours, Bede and Paul the Deacon*. Princeton University Press.

Deanna Forsman

Edmund, Saint

St. Edmund was the king of **East Anglia** who was killed by the **Viking** army in AD 870 and came to be venerated as a saint in the church. Most of the details of his life and death come from the account by Abbo of Fleury, who wrote the first life of the saint in the later tenth century, and from the entry for the year 870 in the ***Anglo-Saxon Chronicle***. These sources relate that **Ivar the Boneless** and his brother **Halfdan** led a Danish army into East Anglia in 865 to conquer land on which to settle. Though the *Anglo-Saxon Chronicle* indicates that King Edmund of East Anglia at first made peace with the Great Army, and even supplied the Danes with horses, the invaders' demands quickly outpaced the King's generosity. Edmund refused to give in to Viking demands and was killed in 870.

Abbo recounted the tale of Edmund's martyrdom in his *Life of Saint Edmund*, written initially in Latin but also translated into Anglo-Saxon and accompanied with a preface by Aelfric of Eynsham. In it he recounts that he heard the tale from St. **Dunstan**, who had heard it from Edmund's own sword bearer at the court of King **Æthelstan** (r. 924–939), while Dunstan was a young man. This could be chronologically possible, but just barely. According to the *Life's* account of the martyrdom, Edmund refused to fight against the **Danes**, to save the lives of his people, and equally refused to submit to non-Christians. The Danes thus tied Edmund to a tree, shot him with many arrows and beheaded him, hiding his head in thick brambles. After the Danes left, people found the body and went searching for the head, which cried 'Here, here, here!' miraculously, so that they could find it. The head had been guarded by a wolf, which kept it from being attacked by other animals. Once the head and body were reunited, they became one, leaving no scars except for a thin red line where the head had been severed from the body. Subsequently, miracles followed at the tomb. While Abbo notes Edmund's refusal to fight the Danes, the *Anglo-Saxon Chronicle* states that he brought an army against them and was killed in the fighting.

Edmund's cult was founded by 895, at which point the first of a series of St. Edmund coinage was issued. More than likely, the community of Bury St. Edmunds had formed around Beadoriceworth, where the king's body was interred, by this point. Through the tenth and eleventh centuries, Edmund's cult enjoyed royal patronage and devotion by the kings of **Wessex** and then England. In addition to being a royal saint, Edmund became the patron of the monastery of Bury St. Edmunds. His body was ceremoniously translated to the new abbey church in 1095, and in 1098, Baldwin, the abbot of Bury, commissioned *De miraculis sancti Edmundi*, a work that forwarded the abbey's political claims.

See also Celtic Christianity; Kings and Kingship.

Further Reading

Rudyard, Susan. 1988. *The Royal Saints of Anglo-Saxon England: A Study of West Saxon and East Anglian Cults*. Cambridge University Press.

Sawyer, P. H. 1978. *From Roman Britain to Norman England*. St. Martin's Press.

Nicole Lopez-Jantzen

Edward the Confessor (c.1005 1066)

Edward the Confessor (c.1005–1066) was an **Anglo-Saxon** king who ruled England between 1042 and 1066 and was canonised by Pope Alexander III in 1161. Edward died childless, and thus after his death, there was a struggle over who would exercise legitimate kingship. This struggle culminated in the **Norman Conquest** in 1066, an event that has dominated the interpretation of Edward's reign since his earliest biographers and hagiographers in the later eleventh and twelfth centuries. Scholars have long sought to answer the question of whether or not Edward promised the kingdom to **William** of Normandy ('the Conqueror') in 1051 or 1052.

The eldest son of King **Æthelred** the Unready and Emma of Normandy, Edward was born c.1005, when he is first mentioned in the charters, at Islip in Oxfordshire. Edward spent most of his early years in Normandy, where he fled with his family in 1013. When the Danish king **Cnut** conquered England after Æthelred's death, Emma of Normandy returned to England from Normandy to marry him and had a second son, **Harthacnut**. Upon Cnut's death in 1035, his son by his first wife, **Harold Harefoot**, seized the throne, although the rest of his sons also made claims to it. Edward and his brother Alfred returned to England briefly in 1036 to support their claims, but Edward quickly returned to Normandy after Alfred's murder. By 1037, Harold had gained the throne but was succeeded by Harthacnut on his death in 1040. Edward returned once again from Normandy when he was associated with Harthacnut in kingship in 1041 and then succeeded his half-brother upon his death in 1042. On 3 April 1043, he was crowned at Winchester, and later that year, accompanied by the three most important earls of the kingdom, **Godwin** of Wessex, Leofric of **Mercia** and Siward of **Northumbria**, he seized the wealth and land of his mother Emma.

Although the male line of the Danish royal family in England ended with Harthacnut, two Danes still laid claim to the throne. The first, Harold, who was related to Cnut through marriage, was killed in 1043, while the other, Swein, the son of Cnut's sister Esthrith, was locked in a struggle with **Magnus**, king of Norway, over Denmark. Edward recognised that if Swein secured his position in Denmark, he would soon turn to England and thus kept a fleet ready at Sandwich. By 1047, Magnus had defeated Swein and soon after died, but his successor Harald Hardrada made peace with England, ending the threat of the northern invasion. Soon after, Edward first reduced and then disbanded his fleet, abolishing the annual tax that had been levied for its maintenance in 1051.

Soon after the northern threat had abated, there was a major internal conflict in the realm. Edward had been closely allied with

Godwin of Wessex early in his reign, cementing his familial ties in 1045 by marrying Godwin's daughter Edith. However, in 1049, Edward rejected Godwin's candidate for archbishop of **Canterbury**, instead appointing the **Norman** Robert of Jumièges. Problems between the king and the earl reached a breaking point in 1051 over a riot in Dover. After Edward ordered Godwin to punish the townspeople of **Dover** for an attack on his kinsman, Eustace of Boulogne, Godwin refused. Godwin and his sons began to prepare an army and were joined by Godwin's other son Swegn, who had previously been outlawed. Godwin and his family fled the kingdom, but after they returned with an army in 1052 Edward reinstated them and dismissed his Norman advisors. Although Godwin died in 1053, his sons advanced through the 1050s and 1060s. When Edward died on 5 January 1066, Harold Godwinsson, Godwin's son, was crowned the next day.

The major source for historical information about Edward's reign is the ***Anglo-Saxon Chronicle***. Nevertheless, there are three important sources for the growth of Edward's cult. The first, the *Vita AEdwardi Regis*, was written around the time of Edward's death by a monk associated with Edith to glorify the family of Earl Godwin. The first true saint's life, the *Vita Beati Regis Eadwardi*, was written by Osbert of Clare, elected prior of Westminster in 1136. When Henry I came to the throne in 1154, he could lay claim to descent from both the **Saxon** and the Norman royal lines and thus promoted the cult of his royal predecessor and kinsman to lend authority to his reign. Pope Alexander III canonised Edward on 7 February 1161. Following the canonisation, Ailred of Rievaulx rewrote Edward's *Life*, in time for the translocation of his body to a new tomb in Westminster Abbey, a ceremony over which Thomas Becket, Archbishop of **Canterbury**, presided. Ailred's *Life* is the archetype for all subsequent versions of St. Edmund's *Life*.

See also Kings and Kingship.

Further Reading

Barlow, Frank. 1970. *Edward the Confessor*. University of California Press.

Blair, Peter. 2003. *An Introduction to Anglo-Saxon England* (3rd edn.). Cambridge University Press.

Stafford, Pauline. 1989. *Unification and Conquest: A Political and Social History of England in the Tenth and Eleventh Centuries*. Edward Arnold.

Stenton, F. M. 1971. *Anglo-Saxon England* (3rd edn.). Clarendon Press.

Nicole Lopez-Jantzen

Egbert I of Kent (r.664–673)

Egbert I was the king of **Kent** from 664 to 673. He was the son of Eorcenbert, king of Kent (640–664), and Seaxburh, the daughter of Anna, king of East Anglia (d. 654). His sister Eormenhild married Wulhere, king of Mercia (657–674), and another sister, Eorcengota (d. 660), was a nun in the Frankish monastery of Faremoutiers-en-Brie.

Egbert succeeded his father as king after Eorcenbert died of the plague. One of his first acts was to work together with **Oswiu**, king of **Northumbria** (641–670), to select the next archbishop of **Canterbury**. Together, the two appointed the priest Wigheard, whom they sent to Rome for consecration. Wigheard died soon after his arrival in Rome, and the Greek **Theodore** of Tarsus was consecrated and sent to England in his stead. On his journey from Rome to Canterbury, Theodore was delayed in the Frankish kingdoms until Egbert obtained his release by sending an official across the Channel to conduct Theodore to Canterbury. The incident with Theodore demonstrates Egbert's strong connections with the Merovingian palace. Under Egbert's rule, Kent exercised control over a portion of the kingdom of the East Saxons, as demonstrated by his donation of a sizeable portion of land for the foundation of the monastery of Chertsey in Surrey c. 666. According to the eighth-century *Legend of St. Mildrith*, Egbert had his cousins Æthelbert and Æthelred (sons of Eorcenbert's brother Eormenred) murdered at his succession. In reparation for this crime, Egbert founded the double monastery of Minster-in-Thanet under the authority of his cousin Æbbe, daughter of Eormenred and sister of Æthelbert and Æthelred. Minster-in-Thanet functioned as an important proprietary monastery for the royal family of Kent through the late eighth century.

See also Kings and Kingship; Monasticism.

Further Reading

Stenton, F. M. 1971. *Anglo-Saxon England*. Oxford University Press.

Yorke, Barbara. 1990. *Kings and Kingdoms of Early Anglo-Saxon England*. Routledge.

Deanna Forsman

Egbert II of Kent (c.765–c.780)

Egbert II (c. 765–c. 780) is one of several eighth-century kings of **Kent** who is attested only through charter evidence. He served as co-ruler with Heabert (c. 764–c. 765), both of whom are attested in the same charter as kings of Kent. Egbert's rule corresponds with the territorial expansion of **Mercia**, and it is clear that he initially ruled under the authority of **Offa**, king of Mercia (757–796). The ***Anglo-Saxon Chronicle*** records a battle at Otford, fought between the Mercians and Kent in 776, but it does not record the victors. Charter evidence indicates that Egbert and his successor Ealmund (c. 784) ruled independently of Mercia between 776 and 784, so it is likely that Kent won the battle at Otford, probably under Egbert's leadership. Egbert maintained a close relationship with the bishops of Kent. Jænbert, archbishop of **Canterbury** (765–792), was related to one of Egbert's ministers, and several of Egbert's surviving charters grant land to the bishops of Rochester. It is likely that Offa's request to reduce the authority of the archbishop of Canterbury and establish a new archbishopric in Lichfield was related to resistance of the church in Kent to his rule.

See also Kings and Kingship; Monasticism.

Further Reading

Sawyer, P. H. 1968. *Anglo-Saxon Charters: An Annotated List and Bibliography*. Royal Historical Society. http://www.trin.cam.ac.uk/chartwww/eSawyer. 99/eSawyer2.html.

Stenton, F. M. 1971. *Anglo-Saxon England*. Oxford University Press.

Yorke, Barbara. 1990. *Kings and Kingdoms of Early Anglo-Saxon England*. Routledge.

Deanna Forsman

Egbert of Wessex (r.802–839)

Egbert was the king of **Wessex** from 802 to 839 and *Bretwalda* was king from 829 to 839. Egbert was the son of Ealmund, who may have served as king of **Kent** (c. 784). Egbert traced his ancestry back to **Ine**, king of Wessex (688–726). Egbert's predecessor Beorhtric (786–802) and **Offa**, king of **Mercia** (757–796), drove Egbert into exile, and he spent at least three years in Francia, probably at the Carolingian court. Although the later tradition that Egbert married the sister of a Frankish king is probably not true, it is clear that Egbert's descendants maintained close ties with the Franks as Egbert's son **Æthelwulf** (839–858) married Judith, the daughter of Charles the Bald (840–877). Upon the death of Beorhtric in 802, Egbert succeeded the throne of Wessex, possibly returning from exile with Frankish support.

In 815, Egbert consolidated his control in Devon and fought several victorious battles in **Cornwall**. Ten years later in 825, he fought a major battle against the Mercian king Beornwulf (823–825). Beornwulf was defeated, and Egbert was involved in the subsequent **East Anglian** revolt against Mercia, in which Beornwulf was killed. At this point, Egbert expanded West Saxon influence into Kent, sending his son Æthelwulf to expel Baldred (c. 825), who had been ruling Kent under the authority of Mercia, and receiving the submission of Kent, Surrey, Essex and Sussex. These territories were never again independent, serving as sub-kingdoms under the authority of the heir to the throne of Wessex throughout the ninth century.

In 829, Egbert invaded Mercia again, this time defeating and expelling the Mercian king Wiglaf (827–840). He continued on to the borders of **Northumbria**, harassing the kingdom and receiving submission and tribute from Eanred, king of Northumbria (c. 808–c. 840). Egbert ruled Mercia for about a year before Wiglaf was able to reclaim his throne. In spite of West Saxon expansion, Wiglaf had enough influence to summon a council of all South English bishops in 836, something Egbert never did. In 838, Egbert defeated a combined invasion force of West Welsh (i.e. Cornish) and Danes at Hingston Down. The same year, he granted land to the churches of **Canterbury** and Winchester, seeking the friendship of the church for himself and his heirs. Upon his death, Egbert was succeeded by his son Æthelwulf, and the throne of Wessex remained among Egbert's direct descendants, creating dynastic stability on the eve of accelerated Danish invasions. Egbert was buried in Winchester.

See also Kings and Kingship; Saxons.

Further Reading

Campbell, James. 1991. *The Anglo-Saxons*. Penguin.

Yorke, Barbara. 1995. *Wessex in the Early Middle Ages*. Leicester University Press.

Deanna Forsman

Eleanor of Aquitaine (1122–1204)

Eleanor of Aquitaine, wife of two kings and mother of two more, was one of the most powerful and influential women in medieval Europe. Born around 1122, Aliénor (her

13. Tomb of Eleanor of Aquitaine, Queen (Louis VII) of France, Queen (Henry II Plantagenet) of England. A thirteenth-century polychrome stone at Fontevrault Abbey, Maine-et Loire, France.

Occitan name, from the Latin *alia Aenor*, 'the other Aenor', Aenor being her mother's name) was the eldest child of William X, duke of Aquitaine, and became his heir after the death of her younger brother, William Aigret, at age four. The duke accordingly let her receive an excellent education, preparing her to act as the undisputed ruler of one of the wealthiest territories bordering the kingdom of France. Her home, the court of Poitiers, was one of the most cultured centres of western Europe in the early twelfth century. Furthermore, Eleanor was the granddaughter of William IX, the first and most famous *trobador* (troubadour) who virtually invented the notion of 'courtly love'. As the duchess of Aquitaine, she wielded considerable political power in her own right, even if her two successive husbands and her sons tried in various ways to encroach on it.

Eleanor received the oaths of her father's vassals when she was fourteen. In 1137, she married the heir of Louis VI 'the Fat', king of France, a few weeks after her father's death. The future Louis VII so became the duke of Aquitaine, but the marriage contract stipulated that Aquitaine will only become part of France (and not a sovereign Duchy anymore) in the next generation. It is unclear whether William X, who died as a pilgrim on his way to St James of Compostela, ever wanted this matrimonial alliance with France, or whether he entrusted his daughter to his liege lord the king of France while waiting to a suitable husband for her. Louis VI died a few months after the marriage, and Eleanor became Queen of France at Christmas 1137.

Despite Louis VII's early enthusiasm for his bride, the new queen was not very popular at the royal court, in the Merovingian capital Paris, which was then colder and less open to courtly ideas than the relaxed southern culture to which she was used. The Queen Mother, as well as Abbot Suger, the king's counsellor, considered her a bad influence, especially since she reminded the French of another queen from Provence, the rather infamous Constance d'Arles. Her entourage of *trobadors*, singing their love for their queen, displeased the more sedate Parisian courtiers.

Eleanor's attempts to 'interfere' in matters of the state do not help, nor did the fact that her first child, after several stillbirths, was a daughter, Marie, later countess of Champagne and the patroness of the Arthurian poet Chrétien of Troyes. Burdened by guilt for burning a church and meddling in the church's matrimonial policy on behalf of Eleanor's sister, Petronilla, Louis VII answered the call of Pope Eugenius III to crusade. Since a crusade is considered a pilgrimage, Eleanor accompanied her husband, with a huge retinue that would cause problems on the way and be a liability when they would be in the East. The queen's affectionate relationship with her uncle, Raymond of Antioch, as well as her unlucky interventions in military decisions, brought about serious disagreements with Louis VII.

Eleanor wished for a divorce. However, on their way back after the failure of the crusade, Pope Eugenius managed to arrange a reconciliation, which resulted in the birth of another daughter, Alix, in 1151. Faced with the opposition of his barons to his wife, and fearing that she would not be able to give him a son and heir, Louis VII eventually resolved to dissolve the marriage: this was done in early 1152, on the grounds of consanguinity. A few weeks later, Eleanor, once again one of the most powerful heiresses in Europe, married Henry Plantagenet, the future Henry II, whom she had met the year before and whom she probably secretly informed of her 'availability'.

Henry was eleven years younger than Eleanor, and they were more closely related than she was to Louis. Also, since Henry became duke of Aquitaine through his marriage to Eleanor, it meant he became the vassal of the king of France for a territory bigger than half of the French kingdom. Between 1153 and 1166, Eleanor gave birth to five sons and three daughters. All of her children except for the youngest, John 'Lackland', would die before her, and her sons would fight constantly among themselves and against their father.

Henry II was a less accommodating husband than Louis VII; he used his wife as a pawn in extending his empire on a large and composite territory, either delegating her to rule in his stead in her duchy or having her represent him in England when he was campaigning elsewhere. Eleanor acted as a patroness of arts and protector of numerous writers but was limited to a cultural and aesthetic role. Eleanor resented her being allowed very little real power, disagreed with her husband on important matters of policy (especially regarding Thomas Becket) and was insulted by the king's flaunting his affairs and illegitimate children. After the birth of her last child, Eleanor returned to Poitiers, where she ruled in the name of her husband, but in effect on her own.

Henry II's autocratic tendencies succeeded in alienating his sons, especially Henry 'the Young King', officially associated to the crown but left with very little power. The 'Younger Henry' revolted against his father in 1173–1174, attracted to his side his two younger brothers, Richard and Geoffrey, as well as his mother, and sought an alliance with the king of France. Although Henry II eventually was reconciled with his rebellious son (until the next time, in 1183, when the Young King would die ignominiously of dysentery while campaigning against his father), he did not forgive his wife. Eleanor spent the next fourteen years as a prisoner in England, although after the Younger Henry's death her captivity was somewhat softened. It is said that Henry II wanted to provoke her into seeking an annulment of their marriage: if Eleanor became the abbess of Fontevrault, of which she was a patroness, her lands and properties would go back to her husband – and to the Plantagenet empire.

When Richard 'the Lion-Hearted' became king in 1189 after his father's death, Eleanor was freed and played an important part during her son's reign: she acted as regent when he was absent during the Third Crusade, she brought him the bride she had chosen for him, Bérengère de Navarre and she was instrumental in gathering the huge ransom asked for the captive king. Although she had energetically fought her last son John's attempts to usurp the power while Richard was still alive, she immediately gave him her support when he became king in 1199 after his brother's untimely death. She still engaged in a few diplomatic missions, but the internecine conflicts that divided her family, as well as the war between John Lackland and Philip 'August', Louis VII of France's son, contributed to dispirit even her exceptional personality. She retired to Fontevrault in 1200 and died there in 1204.

See also Kings and Kingship; Literature.

Further Reading

Duby, Georges. 1997. *Women of the Twelfth Century, Volume 1: Eleanor of Aquitaine and Six Others.* University of Chicago Press.

Meade, Marion. 2002. *Eleanor of Aquitaine (Women in History).* Weidenfeld & Nicholson.

Wheeler, Bonnie, and John Carmi Parsons (eds.). 2002. *Eleanor of Aquitaine: Lord and Lady.* Palgrave Macmillan.

Weir, Alison. 2001. *Eleanor of Aquitaine: A Life.* Ballantine Books.

Anne Berthelot

Elfoddw (d.809)

Elfoddw (d. 809) was an important reformer in the pre-conquest church of Wales, most notable for changing the way the British church calculated Easter to conform with Rome. The ***Annales Cambriae*** under the entry for the year 768 states that 'Easter was altered among the **Britons**, the reform being the work of that man of God Elfoddw' (Morris 1980, 47). According to **Bede**, the British way of celebrating Easter was one of the main points of contention between the British church and St. **Augustine** sent from Rome in 603 and this was the final change the British church made to confirm to Roman practice. It has been suggested (Evans 1986, 77) that the term *servus dei* (Servant of God), used to describe Elfoddw in the B text of the *Annales Cambriae*, may reflect a connection with the Irish term ***Céli dé*** (Servant of God). According to Gerald of Wales, the *Céli dé* (sometimes referred to as Culdee) community was still present at Penmon on Anglesey in the late twelfth century.

The *Annales Cambriae* also notes Elfoddw's death in 809 and, in doing so, refers to him as the Archbishop of **Gwynedd**. The episcopal organisation of Wales during this period is little understood and the only other archbishop named in pre-Norman Wales is Nobis, the archbishop of **St David's** c. 900, according to **Asser** in his *Life of Alfred the Great.*

Later medieval Welsh sources associate Elfoddw with Abergele on the North Wales coast, which is also mentioned later in the *Annales Cambriae* under the year 856, suggesting a site of some importance. The twelfth-century **Welsh** poet Einion ap (son of) Gwalchmai (fl. 1170–1220) associates Elfoddw with Abergele and a holy well dedicated to Elfoddw was recorded in 1697, although it is no longer present, where pins were offered and people would flock to every Easter morning. Medieval Welsh tradition adds that Elfoddw was the son of Tudclyd of Caer Gybi (Holyhead on the Isle of Anglesey), but the authenticity of this cannot be substantiated. Despite the obvious importance of Elfoddw in the history of the church in Wales, no ecclesiastical sites were ever dedicated to him.

The fame of Elfoddw as a man of learning is also evident in the preface to the eleventh-century Nennian recension of the ***Historia Brittonum***: 'Ninnius, pupil of Elvodug' (Morris 1980, 9). This preface is not found in the earliest recension of the *Historia Brittonum*, but as the text was written in Gwynedd c. 830 and **Nennius** is known from other sources to date from this period, some sort of association may be possible.

See also Celtic Christianity.

Further Reading

Baring-Gould, S., and John Fisher. 1908. *The Lives of the British Saints,* vol. II. The Honourable Society of the Cymmrodorion.

Evans, J. W. 1986. 'The Early Church in Denbighshire'. *Transactions of the Denbighshire Historical Society* 35: 61–82.

Morris, John. 1980. *Nennius British History and the Welsh Annals.* Phillimore.

Thorpe, Lewis. 1978. *Gerald of Wales, the Journey Through Wales/the Description of Wales.*Penguin.

Scott Lloyd

Elmet

Elmet was a minor British kingdom which emerged in north-western Britain in the years following Britain's independence from Rome c. AD 410. Elmet is attested in early written sources, but the exact territory which it covered is not easy to discern. From place name evidence, it appears that Elmet once covered much of west and south Yorkshire. A series of linear earthworks (dykes) to the south and north-east may have been constructed by the **Britons** to separate themselves from the **Anglo-Saxon** kingdoms of **Mercia** and **Deira**. North-west of Elmet was the tiny British kingdom of Craven, about which almost nothing is known. Bede claims that Leeds lay within 'the forest of Elmet', and poetic sources mention two early kings of Elmet, Cwallawc and Madog. According to the ***Annales Cambriae*** and the ***Historia Brittonum***, the last British king of Elmet was one Ceredig, who was defeated by Edwin of Deira and expelled from Elmet c. 617. The English takeover of Elmet may have been inevitable due to the expansion of Deira, and Mercia and Deira may have split Elmetian territory between them for *Elmetsœte* is given only 600 hides in the **Burghal Hidage** (late seventh century).

See also Kings and Kingship.

Further Reading

Eagles, Bruce. 1980. 'Anglo-Saxons in Lindsey and the East Riding of Yorkshire in the Fifth Century'. Pp. 285–287 in *Anglo-Saxon Cemeteries 1979.* Edited by Philip Rahtz et al. British Archaeological Reports No. 82.

Snyder, Christopher A. 2003. *The Britons.* Peoples of Europe Series. Blackwell.

Taylor, C. M. 1992. 'Elmet: Boundaries and Celtic Survival in the Post-Roman Period'. *Medieval History* 2: 111–129.

Wood, P. N. 1996. 'On the Little British Kingdom of Craven'. *Northern History* 32: 1–20.

Christopher A. Snyder

Ely

Ely is home of one of England's monastic cathedrals, along with **Canterbury**, **Durham**, Norwich, Rochester, Winchester and **Worcester**. These foundations were unique in the Middle Ages, with a single figure serving as abbot of the monastery and bishop of the see.

Bede notes that Ely (originally *Elge*) is named so for the quantity of eels in the region. Once an island in the now-drained fens, Ely was a quiet and remote location, well suited to monastic retreat from the world. Considerable documentation survives for the founding and history of Ely Cathedral. The church was founded by St. Æthelthryth (also known as Etheldreda or Audrey), who has been claimed as the most popular female saint in England, especially in the Middle Ages. She was a seventh-century princess who was married to Prince Tondbert. He died shortly after their marriage, and she then married King Egfrid of **Northumbria** with whom, Bede tells us, she lived chastely for twelve years. She then persuaded him to allow her to become a nun. She journeyed to the Isle of Ely, then an island in the fens, which she owned from the dowry of her first marriage. St. **Wilfrid**, Archbishop of **York**, established her as an abbess around 672 and she ran a monastic community at Ely for seven years before dying of the plague. Her sister Seaxburh succeeded her.

The present cathedral structure was begun in the mid-1080s under the auspices of Abbot Simeon, with the new Norman cathedral built by his brother Walkelin as his model. The foundation possessed the bodies of four famed saints, Æthelthryth, Seaxburh, Wihtburh and Eormenhild, and was designed with pilgrimage clearly in mind. The shrine of Æthelthryth, located behind the main altar, is splendid, embellished with silver and crystal. The cathedral is one of the largest and finest Anglo-Norman structures and is characteristic of their style of architecture. The body of the church is very long, but low and narrow. The exterior creates a dramatic silhouette and the interior presents an impressive processional space, with a nave stretching for thirteen bays and an additional four bays in the choir. Unlike many of the Norman cathedrals, Ely bears a timber vault, added in 1858 during extensive repairs and bearing an extensive and lyrical series of Victorian paintings begun by Henry Le Strange and finished by Gambier Parry.

The most notable feature of the cathedral is its octagonal crossing tower, added between 1322 and 1328 and credited to Sacrist Alan of Walsingham, the mason John and the royal carpenter William Hurley. The octagon replaced a tower that collapsed in 1322 and may have been inspired by the octagonal cap on the west tower. The structure is a blend of a powerful timber vault lodged in the stone fabric. From below, the fan vaulting supporting it makes the tower seem to float gently above the viewer.

See also Art and Architecture.

Further Reading

Meadows, Peter, and Nigel Ramsay (eds.). 2003. *A History of Ely Cathedral*. Boydell Press.

Zarnecki, George. 1958. *The Early Sculpture of Ely Cathedral*. Alec Tiranti.

Asa Mittman

Emain Macha

Emain Macha, now **Navan Fort** in County Armagh, is one of a group of sites in Ireland traditionally regarded as the provincial capitals of the 'Five Provinces', the others including **Tara** (capital of **Meath**), Knockaulin (Dun Ailinne, capital of **Leinster**) and Cruachan (capital of **Connaught**). Emain in the **Ulster Cycle** was represented as the stronghold of the Red Branch warriors under Conchobar mac Nessa, whose champion was **Cú Chulainn**. The existing remains are prehistoric (in keeping with those on the other sites that have been investigated). Emain consists of a circular enclosing rampart, 787 feet (240 metres) in diameter, comprising a bank surviving up to 49 feet (15 metres) wide and 13 feet (4 metres) high, with an internal ditch up to 13 feet (4 metres) deep. Excavations have shown that the construction of this rampart took place around 90 BC. Inside the enclosure is located a ring barrow and a substantial mound.

Excavations have shown a long period of activity, stretching from the **Neolithic** through to the **Iron Age**, the large mound being put up in 95 BC, on the site of a complex timber building. This was 120 feet (37 metres) in diameter and was composed of five concentric circles, each of about 275 posts. In the centre was a tall post. The whole building was roofed, then ritually set alight, before the mound was built.

Further Reading

Raftery, Barry. 1994. *Pagan Celtic Ireland*. Thames & Hudson.

Waterman, D. M. 1997. *Excavations at Navan Fort, 1961–71*. HMSO.

Lloyd Laing

Emma of Normandy (c.984–1042)

Emma was the daughter of Richard I of Normandy, the wife of two English kings, **Æthelred the Unready** and Cnut, and the mother to **Edward the Confessor**. Born to Richard I and the Danish-born Gunnor, little is known about Emma's life before her marriage to Æthelred in 1002, and she is most prominent in the sources as an English queen.

Emma's marriage to Æthelred was one of a series of events orchestrated by her brother, Richard II, to help establish his rule, a peacemaking marriage in the face of **Viking** attacks in the Channel. With Æthelred she had three children: Edward by 1005, Alfred by 1013 and her daughter Godgifu c.1007. In 1013, after the

Danish king Svein conquered England, Emma and her children fled to Normandy, followed by Æthelred. Upon Svein's death in 1014, Æthelred returned to England to reclaim the throne, along with Emma, while Svein's son **Cnut** was proclaimed king by the Danish army. Upon Æthelred's death in 1016, his son and Emma's stepson Edmund became the English claimant to the throne. When Edmund died later in 1016, however, the English nobles swore oaths of loyalty to Cnut and confirmed the peace in 1017. Emma's marriage to Cnut occurred in 1017, in the context of peacemaking between Cnut and the conquered English.

Although Emma's life in this period, 1016–1035, was not chronicled, she appears in several witness lists and was an important patron. She also had two children with Cnut, **Harthacnut** and Gunnhild. After Cnut's death on 12 November 1035, Harold, his son by his first wife Aelfgifu, seized the throne. In 1036, while Emma remained at Winchester and Harthacnut advanced his claims to the kingdom from Denmark, she sent greetings to her sons, asking for one of them to come to England to advance a claim. Both Alfred and Edward came separately, but *en route* Alfred was captured, blinded and died. When she was forced into exile in 1037, Emma went to Flanders, where she continued trying to get support for her goals of putting a son on the throne and thus her continuation as queen mother.

After Harold's death in 1040, Harthacnut became king of England and, in 1041, invited Edward back, to share rule of the kingdom. On 8 June 1042, Harthacnut died, leaving Edward the sole king. During this period, Emma commissioned the *Encomium Emmae Reginae*, a political work written by a Flemish monk in 1041 and 1042, which set out to explain Emma's actions in a positive light and depict her as a queen above all else. Soon after, in 1043, Edward deprived her of her treasures and land, giving her back just enough to live off of in Winchester and ordering her to stay there, thereby retiring her from political life. Although Emma was partially restored in 1044, returning to court in that year, she no longer exercised power. On 6 March 1052, she died at Winchester and was buried in the church of St Swithun, next to Cnut.

See also Kings and Kingship; Normans.

Further Reading

Stafford, Pauline. 1997. *Queen Emma and Queen Edith: Queenship and Women's Power in Eleventh Century England.* Blackwell Publishers.

Strachan, Isabella. 2004. *Emma the Twice-Crowned Queen: England in the Viking Age.* Peter Owen Publishers.

Nicole Lopez-Jantzen

Éoganachta

From the early medieval period until the late tenth century, princes from the Éoganachta dynasties held the southern Irish kingship of **Cashel**. A number of their kings extended their influence beyond the borders of their province of **Munster** and even challenged the **Uí Néill** kings of **Tara**. Brief periods of powerful rulers could not counter their gradual division and decline, so that they fell prey to the ambitions of the Uí Néill and were later eclipsed by the Dál Cais of Thomond.

The six main branches of the Éoganachta were spread out over the whole of Munster: Éoganacht Chaisil in the east; Éoganacht Áine, Éoganacht Airthir Chliach and Éoganacht Glendamnach in the centre; Éoganacht Raithlind in the south; and Éoganacht Locha Léin in the west. They all counted Éogan Már (*alias* Mug Nuadat, 'Slave of Núadu'), son of Ailill Ólumm, as their eponymous ancestor. The Uí Liatháin and Uí Fhidgeinte were also descendants of Éogan Már, but not of Conall Corc, who according to legend founded Cashel (from Latin *castellum*), the new seat of the kings of Munster. Conall Corc is the subject of a number of dynastic legends, which usually slander the forefathers of the Éoganachta Locha Léin and others.

Cathal mac Finguine (721–742) is the first king of Cashel, of whom it is recorded that he was militarily active in **Leinster** and the midlands. In 737, he and Áed Allán, king of Tara, promulgated the Law of Patrick over the whole of Ireland. After his death, the rulers of Munster were of lesser stature; some of them held the abbacy of the community of Ailbe at Emly. This changed when Feidlimid mac Crimthainn (820–847) took the kingship. During the worst period of **Viking** incursions, he continued his dynasty's struggle with the kings of Tara. His actions against a number of midland monasteries may be related to his membership of the reform-minded monastic movement of the ***Céli Dé*** ('Clients of God').

In the year 854, the king of Tara, Máel Sechnaill, took hostages of the king of Cashel for the first time. His son Flann Sinna was equally successful. The last resurgence of the Éoganachta took place during the reign of the bishop of Cashel, Cormac mac Cuilennáin (903–908). This learned man, probably the compiler of the Psalter of Cashel as well as the alleged author of Cormac's Glossary and many poems, met his end in a battle in Leinster against Flann Sinna and his allies. The already disunited Éoganachta never recuperated, and this paved the way for the emergence of the Dál Cais. In 963, Mathgamain of the Dál Cais took the kingship of Cashel, while his brother and successor **Brian Bóru** used the kingship for his eventual acquisition of the kingship of Ireland. Finally, only the Mac Carthaigh (McCarthy) family of Éoganacht Chaisil remained a dominating force in southern Munster until and after the coming of the Anglo-**Normans**.

See also Kings and Kingship.

Further Reading

Byrne, F. J. 2000. *Irish Kings and High-Kings*. Four Courts Press.

Sproule, David. 1985. 'Politics and Pure Narrative in the Stories About Corc of Cashel'. *Ériu* 36: 11–28.

Bart Jaski

Eorls

An *eorl* (also known as earl) was a high magnate in late-Anglo-Saxon England. Beginning with the reign of **Cnut** (1016–1035), England was divided into four territories (**Northumbria**, East Anglia, **Mercia** and **Wessex**), each under the authority of an eorl. The **Old English** *eorl* is related linguistically to the Old Norse *jarl*, and it seems to come into use in the **Danelaw**, those parts of England under Scandinavian control in the ninth and tenth centuries. By the eleventh century, the eorls were the greatest magnates in England, and the king would consult them in matters of state. On the eve of the **Norman Conquest** in 1066, the four eorls were the power of the land, creating a system in which the king of England had more status than actual power and was largely dependent upon the eorls for his maintenance.

During the tenth century, the term *eorl* increasingly replaced the Old English *ealdorman*. Traditionally, an ealdorman was in charge of a shire, and there would be several ealdormen in each Anglo-Saxon kingdom. During the reign of **Æthelstan** (924–939), provincial organisation of the English kingdom was changed, and certain ealdormen were given authority over multiple shires, and we see the establishment of ealdormen ruling in Mercia, East Anglia and Northumbria with vice-regal authority, although other large areas, such as Wessex, were still divided between two and three ealdormen. Although the development of eorls represents a consolidation of power among fewer men, it is clear that men in control of smaller territories within England continued to play a vital role in late-Anglo-Saxon politics.

Further Reading

Campbell, James. 1991. *The Anglo-Saxons*. Penguin

Stenton, F. M. 1971. *Anglo-Saxon England*. Oxford University Press.

Deanna Forsman

Eric Bloodaxe (r. c.947–948 and c.952–954)

The last Scandinavian king of **York** was Eric, called Bloodaxe by later saga writers, who also connected him with a king who ruled briefly in Norway. The historical Eric reigned from York twice, c. 947–948 and again c. 952–954. Contemporary evidence is sparse, but several sagas discuss him in some detail; this makes separating fact from fiction very difficult with this king.

According to later Icelandic sources, Eric Bloodaxe was the oldest son and presumed heir of Harald Finehair, the king who united south-western Norway under his rule. One of Harald's younger sons was Hakon, who lived in the royal household of the kings of **Wessex** as a fosterling. The lateness of the sources is a real problem here – *Egils Saga* and *Heimskringla* both assert that **Æthelstan** supported Hakon over Erik when Harald died, helping Hakon take control of western Norway. But according to the ***Anglo-Saxon Chronicle***, Æthelstan died in 939, several years before Harald Finehair's death. (One problem is that most scholars give the range for the death of Harald as between 930 and 940, so it is possible, in this scenario, that Æthelstan did aid Hakon's succession.) These sources further assert that Eric left Norway peacefully and quietly, without fighting his brother, and headed off to York.

The historical facts surrounding King Eric while he was in York can be very difficult to ascertain. As early as 945, and certainly by 947, a king named Eric had seized control of York and **Northumbria**, the last part of the **Danelaw** still unconquered by the **Anglo-Saxon** kings. He was certainly not a descendant of **Ivar** of Dublin, and no contemporary source tells us that he was a member of any Norwegian royal family. By 948 or 949, he was driven from the throne, supposedly by the people of York themselves at the behest of the Anglo-Saxon king Eadred, son of Edward the Elder, who was furious that the people of Northumbria had 'taken Eric for their king'. This was the same year that **Olaf Cuarán** came from Dublin and claimed the kingdom of York. In 952, the *Anglo-Saxon Chronicle* states that the people of York once again accepted Eric as their king, having driven out Olaf this time. Eric died in 954 at Stainmore in Northumbria, after he was driven from York for the last time, and Eadred added Northumbria to his Anglo-Saxon kingdom. The sagas add to history here, assuring us that Eric Bloodaxe was a pagan and that Odin and great **Viking** heroes of the past welcomed him into Valahlla upon his death.

One of the most concrete pieces of evidence, we have for the historical king Eric is the coinage he issued at York. There were two types, likely corresponding to his two reigns. The earlier was modelled directly on Anglo-Saxon pennies, probably made by moneyers who also worked for either **Edmund** (Æthelstan's half-brother and first heir, who died in 946) or Eadred. The later type is modelled on earlier Viking coins from Northumbria, with the inscription 'Eric Rex' and a sword. The use of the earlier style may have been an attempt by Eric to demonstrate a more independent, more Scandinavian, Northumbrian kingdom.

See also Kings and Kingship.

Further Reading

Bately, Janet M. 1986. *Anglo-Saxon chronicle 3 MS A*. Boydell and Brewer.

Downham, Clare. 2004. 'Eric Bloodaxe – Axed? The Mystery of the Last Scandinavian King of York'. *Mediaeval Scandinavia* 14: 51–77.

SigurDur, Nordal. 1933. *Egils Saga Skalla-grímssonar*. HiD íslenzka fornritafélag.

Mary Valante

Essex

See Saxons.

Exeter

Exeter, the capital city of Devon and home to the magnificent Exeter Cathedral, has an occupational history going back to at least the late pre-Roman **Iron Age**. Exeter was a major settlement of the ***Dumnonii*** tribe, and when the Romans took the area in AD 50, they recognised its importance in the south-west by making it first a camp for the Second Augustan legion and then a *civitas*-capital, *Isca Dumnoniorum*. Walls were constructed around the city towards the end of the second century, and the Romans recognised Exeter's importance as a crossing-place of the river Exe. The city might have played an important role in the trade between Britain and the Mediterranean throughout the Roman period and beyond, for its port at Topsham was the first Roman port reached by ships rounding the Iberian Peninsula.

A story in the seventh-century *Life of St. John the Almsgiver* suggests that tin from **Cornwall** may have passed through Exeter on its way to the Mediterranean. There are a few signs that urban life continued into the fifth century after the withdrawal of the Roman army from Britain. An early Christian cemetery (and possible monastery) has been excavated, which was succeeded by a **Saxon** church and graveyard. Though the **Anglo-Saxon** saint Boniface grew up and may have been trained in the area, Exeter continued to be associated with the **Britons** until the ninth century. In 876, the Danes briefly occupied the city but were defeated by **Alfred** the Great, who rewarded his biographer **Asser** with Exeter and all its parishes. According to **William of Malmesbury**, Alfred's grandson **Æthelstan** (r. 924–939) attacked the Britons and compelled them to withdraw from Exeter. Having cleansed the city of its defilement by wiping out that filthy race, he fortified it with towers and surrounded it with a wall of square-hewn stone (*Gesta Regum Anglorum* 2.134).

Æthelstan held a council at Exeter in 928, and in 1050, the diocese of Exeter was created. The so-called ***Exeter Book***, a manuscript kept in the library at Exeter Cathedral since the second half of the eleventh century, contains the largest and most varied selection of poetry in **Old English** in all surviving Anglo-Saxon manuscripts, including 'The Wanderer', 'The Ruin' and nearly 100 riddles. Leofric, the first bishop of Exeter, claimed that he had brought the manuscript into Exeter's library after his installation by **Edward the Confessor**. The old Saxon minster of St Mary and Peter's became the new cathedral.

Soon after his victory at **Hastings**, **William the Conqueror** came to Exeter and assumed control of the city. The Rougemont castle was built around this period on the highest point of the city's walls. The **Normans** built their Cathedral of St Peter on the site of the English cathedral starting in 1114. The Norman North Tower was dedicated in 1133 and rebuilt after King Stephen's siege in 1136. The cathedral underwent major rebuilding over the years, particularly in 1360, and stands as a magnificent example of Decorated Gothic style. Despite the rebuilding, its twin Norman towers still remain and can be seen from all over the city.

See also Roman Britain.

Further Reading

Allan, J., et al. 1984. 'Saxon Exeter'. Pp. 385–414 in *Anglo-Saxon Towns in Southern England*. Edited by J. Haslam. Phillimore.

Bidwell, Paul T. 1980. *Roman Exeter: Fortress and Town*. Exeter Museums Service.

Conner, Patrick W. 1993. *Anglo-Saxon Exeter: A Tenth-Century Cultural History*. Boydell & Brewer.

Snyder, Christopher A. 1996. *Sub-Roman Britain (AD 400–600): A Gazetteer of Sites*. British Archaeological Reports British Series 247.

———. 2003. *The Britons*. Peoples of Europe Series. Blackwell.

Christopher A. Snyder

Exeter Book

The *Exeter Book* is the usual name for a manuscript kept in the Dean and Chapter Library at **Exeter** Cathedral since the second half of the eleventh century, if not before, where its shelfmark is D & C Library, MS 3501. MS 3501 is a large manuscript of 262 pages, and it contains the largest and most varied selection of poetry in **Old English** in all surviving Anglo-Saxon manuscripts. The most important of these include 'Christ I' (or 'The Advent Lyrics'), 'Christ II' (or 'The Ascension'), 'Christ III' (or 'The Last Judgement'), two poems on the life of St. **Guthlac**, 'The Phoenix', 'Juliana', all of the Old English elegies extant, including **'The Wanderer'** and 'The Seafarer', 'Widsith', 'Deor', 'The Wife's Lament', 'The Ruin' and a collection of nearly 100 riddles.

Critical and scholarly commentaries on many of the poems in the *Exeter Book* abound, but less attention has been paid to locating a thematic centre for the book's contents. The question is important, because the collection is both diverse and unified. The riddles, for example, are all gathered into the last portion of the manuscript; the main body of shorter, elegiac poems occupy the mid-portion of the manuscript; 'Christ' and 'Guthlac', both longer poems with defined sub-units, occupy the first part of the manuscript. As late as AD 1072, when Bishop Leofric at Exeter described the book as 'A large English book with everything written out in the manner of poetry' in a list of books he had 'brought into' Exeter's library, the manuscript had become a single collection. Nevertheless, the reading of any poem in it is likely to profit from looking at the other poems adjacent to it and in trying to understand by what logic editors have isolated and identified the poems in the manuscript.

Because any contemporary grasp of this manuscript is at least partly based on the work of editors who have hewn the texts scholars use from the rough stone of the manuscript where no item is titled, and many items display unclear indications of their beginnings and endings, the editorial history of this manuscript is important. John Josias Conybeare is generally credited with announcing the manuscript's existence to antiquarians and the interested public in a series of short articles in the journal *Archaeologia* in 1814 and, later in 1826, in *Illustrations of Anglo-Saxon Poesie*. In 1831, the British Museum commissioned a facsimile transcription of the manuscript to be kept with its own Anglo-Saxon manuscript collection. The first edition of the entire codex was made by Benjamin Thorpe and published in 1842. A photographic facsimile of the manuscript (*The Exeter Book of Old English Poetry*) was published in 1933, edited by R. W. Chambers with the aid of Max Förster and Robin Flower. These scholars undertook the first systematic historical account of the manuscript, and their essays on it remain valuable. Two important editions depended upon this facsimile: William S. Mackie edited the manuscript for the Early English Text Society in 1934, and George Phillip Krapp and Elliot Van Kirk Dobbie edited it for The Anglo-Saxon Poetic Records in 1936. In 2006, Bernard J. Muir published a much-anticipated electronic facsimile of the manuscript with an accompanying edition and a full apparatus.

See also Literature.

Further Reading
Conner, Patrick W. 1993. *Anglo-Saxon Exeter: A Tenth-Century Cultural History*. Boydell & Brewer.
Muir, Bernard J. 2006. *The Electronic Exeter Anthology of Old English Poetry*. Exeter University Press. [CD ROM].

Patrick W. Conner

F

Féni

In the medieval Irish sources, Féni has three related meanings: the class of freemen, a conglomeration of free peoples and a population group. The first meaning is especially current in legal texts, but its employment is not consistent. The dynastic or ethnic identity of the Féni was already subject to various interpretations in the early medieval period.

The literal meaning of Féni is usually given as 'those belonging to the woods'. It is connected to Old Irish *fid* ('wood, forest') and also to the *fían* ('band of hunters, troop of warriors'). In legal sources, Féni can often be translated as 'freemen' (noblemen and commoners), but sometimes it denotes the commoners only. Expressions such as *bélrae Féni* ('language of the Féni') and *breth Féni* ('judgement of the Féni') primarily refer to native freemen law, excluding the laws of the clergy (canon law) and poets, who had their own jurisdictions. Yet poets were supposed to be versed in *Fénechas* ('Féni-lore'), which is mainly expressed in ancient alliterative poetry and legal maxims. As a genre, it has an oral background. The common formula *la Féniu* ('according to the Féni'), which is usually translated as 'in Irish law', often occurs in legal enumerations and the question-and-answer style used in instructive literature. Its use is typical for the *Senchas Már* legal school of the midlands, which was perhaps centred in Slane in Brega. The tract *Trecheng Breth Féni* ('The Triads of the Judgements of the Féni') assigns the *Fénechas* of Ireland to Cloyne and the *bélrae Féni* of Ireland to **Cork**, but the judgement of Ireland to Slane. Slane was a foundation strongly attached to the community of **Patrick**, who figures prominently in the *Senchas Már* ('Great [Legal] Tradition'), an extensive compilation of early Irish law-tracts.

Some Old Irish law-tracts in the *Senchas Már* regard the Féni as a population group which had legal dealings with the **Ulaid** of **Ulster** in the time of the Ulster Cycle of tales and in one reference in the time of Congal Cáech (d. 637). Some modern scholars take the Féni to be an historical alliance between the Connachta (including the **Uí Néill**) and the **Éoganachta** of **Munster**. It has been suggested that because of this alliance the kings of Ulster and **Leinster** never promulgated ecclesiastical laws (*cánai*) in the period between 697 and 825 independently, and even that the alliance of the Féni created the standard Old **Irish language** (Charles-Edwards 2000, 160, 579–580, 583–584). However, the first interpretation and the theories based on it are not without problems, regarding other references to the Féni and those associated to them. The uncertainties reflect the difficulties medieval Irish scholars had in defining the Féni. Only their fictitious eponymous ancestor, Fénius Farsaid ('the Pharisee', a Jewish legal expert), is well established in ***Lebor Gabála*** and other texts.

See also Literature.

Further Reading
Charles-Edwards, Thomas M. 2000. *Early Christian Ireland*. Oxford University Press.
Hamp, Eric P. 1992. 'Goídil, Féni, Gwynedd'. *Proceedings of the Harvard Celtic Colloquium* 12: 43–50.
O'Brien, David. 1932. 'The Féni'. *Ériu* 11: 182–183.

Bart Jaski

Feudalism

'Feudalism' is neither a medieval term nor does it not have a single, agreed-upon definition. In recent decades, some historians have even questioned the historical and heuristic value of the term. Lordship, dependent tenures and manors were real institutions in the eleventh through fourteenth century, even if the words used to connote them also bore other meanings and differed from region to region. Feudalism, on the other hand, is a historical construct that one must define before using. Like all historical constructs feudalism, however defined, describes an 'ideal type' rather than any particular historical society. This article will begin with descriptions of the traditional models of feudalism, emphasising the one favoured by Anglophone historians, and then explain the current historiographical controversies this term has generated.

Definitions of Feudalism

The earliest and in some ways most enduring definition of 'feudalism' is the legal framework for the possession and descent of 'fiefs', that is, estates held as dependent tenures either from the crown or from some other lord. The term 'feudal' was invented by Renaissance Italian jurists to describe what they took to be the common customary law of property. Giacomo Alvarotto's (1385–1453) treatise *De feudis* ('Concerning Fiefs') posited that despite regional differences the regulations governing the descent of aristocratic land tenure were derived from common legal principles, a customary shared 'feudal law'. Alvarotto and his contemporaries drew upon twelfth- and thirteenth-century compilations of land law and customals dealing with the descent of fiefs, most notably the Italian *Libri Feudorum* (mid- to late twelfth century), the German *Sachsenspiegel* of Eike von Repgow (1220s), the thirteenth-century Norman *Summa de legibus*, Philippe de Beaumanoir's *Coutumes de Beauvaisis* (1280/1283), and the English legal treatises (mistakenly) attributed to Glanvill (late twelfth century) and Bracton (second quarter of the thirteenth century). The English Common Law of real property as expounded in the eighteenth century by the great English jurist William Blackstone (1723–1780) in his *Commentaries on the Laws of England* (1765–1769) finds its roots in *Glanvill* and *Bracton* and derives much of its technical vocabulary from 'feudal' law. The conception of feudalism as the law of fiefs was subsequently extended to cover the aggregate of institutions connected with the support and service of knights and with the descent of their tenures ('fiefs').

Traditionally, British and American historians have used feudalism as a shorthand to describe a political, military and social system that bound together the warrior aristocracy of western Europe between c.1000 and c.1300. This 'system', it is asserted, only gradually took shape and differed in detail from region to region. Its key institutions were lordship, vassalage and the fief. Lordship and vassalage represent the two sides of a personal bond of mutual loyalty and military service between nobles of different rank that found its roots in the Germanic war-band. The superior in this relationship was termed a lord, and the subordinate, who pledged loyalty and military service to his lord, was his 'vassal'. A 'fief' (Latin *feudum*) was a grant of land tenure or of revenues held by a vassal from a lord, whose property, in theory, the tenements remained, in return for specified services, which were usually a combination of military and social duties (e.g. attendance at the lord's court, hospitality to the lord and his men) and miscellaneous payments ('feudal incidents') that reflected the lord's continued rights over the property. The most important of the services required from a fief-holder was knight service. When summoned to war by his lord, the holder of a fief was obliged to send to the lord's host or retinue the quota of knights owed from his fief. These knights were then to render to the lord military service for a period of time fixed by custom, which amounted to forty days in thirteenth-century France and England. British and American historians have traditionally regarded knight service as the *raison d'etre* of 'feudalism'. 'Feudalism', as defined in this fashion, can be thought of as a military recruitment system in which land tenure was exchanged for the service of heavily armed warriors on horseback.

In the Anglo-American paradigm, feudalism is associated with the fragmentation of central authority, as political power and jurisdiction in the tenth and eleventh centuries devolved into the hands of 'private' individuals, that is, of nobles who held franchises, immunities or banal rights. In theory, the king stood at the apex of a feudal network of personal loyalty and land tenure, since he was the lord of lords and the ultimate source of all rights over land. Before the late twelfth century, however, feudal kings were often merely the first among equals, and their claims to authority often masked their limited actual power.

Among the leading theorists of this approach are the Belgian historian Francois-Louis Ganshof (1895–1980), the English historians John Horace Round (1854–1928) and Sir Frank Merry Stenton (1880–1967), and the American historians Carl Stephenson (1886–1954) and Joseph Strayer (1904–1987). Ganshof's definition of feudalism may be offered as prototypical of this school: 'a body of institutions creating and regulating the obligations of obedience and service – mainly military service – on the part of a free man (the vassal) towards another free man (the lord), and the obligations of protection and maintenance on the part of the lord with regard to his vassal. The obligation of maintenance had usually as on its effects the grant by the lord to his vassal of a unit of real property [actually the grant of tenure] known as a fief' (Ganshof 1944, xvi).

An alternative definition of feudalism favoured by Marxist historians focuses on the economic and juridical privileges enjoyed by a landowning aristocracy over a subordinate peasantry. This economic definition of feudalism derives from the eighteenth-century Enlightenment. French Enlightenment *philosophes*, notably Montesquieu in his *The Spirit of the Laws* (1748), understood the 'feudal law' to be a system of exploitation of peasants viewed against the backdrop of the parcelling out of national sovereignty to private individuals. For them, *féodalité* denoted the aggregate of seigneurial privileges and prerogatives, which could be justified neither by reason or justice. When the National Constituent Assembly abolished the 'feudal regime' in August 1789, this is what they meant. Across the channel, Adam Smith coined the phrase 'feudal system' in the *Wealth of Nations* (1776) to describe a form of production governed not by market forces but by coercion and force. For Smith, the 'feudal system' was the economic exploitation of peasants by their lords, which led to an economy and society marked by poverty, brutality, exploitation, and wide gaps between the rich and the poor. This economic definition of feudalism found its way into the writings of Karl Marx (1818–1883), who saw feudalism as a particular mode of production standing between the slave economy of the ancient world and modern capitalism.

French historians have tended to combine the two definitions through the linked phrase *Féodalité et Seigneurie*, the 'Feudal and Seigneurial Systems'. For historians such as Marc Bloch (1886–1944), Georges Duby (1919–1996) and their followers, feudalism is a general term that embraces the key aspects of the prevailing medieval social, political and economic arrangements. German historians have also tended to use the term feudalism (*Lehnswesen*) broadly, emphasising the twin elements of landed lordship over peasants (*Grundherrschaft*) and political decentralisation. Like the French historians of feudalism, German scholars emphasise the emergence of a regime of serfdom in place of the slave and free peasant rural economy of the Carolingian era. German historians such as Otto Hintze (1861–1940), Heinrich Mitteis (1889–1952) and the Austrian Otto Brunner (1898–1992) have presented feudalism as an 'ideal' stage in state formation not limited to the medieval West.

Vassalage and the Fief

'Vassalage' was the protective relationship set up by one free man (the lord) over another (his 'man'). Like feudalism, vassalage is a modern construct. In the eleventh and twelfth centuries the words most widely used to describe honourable dependents were *miles* (soldier), *fidelis* (faithful man) and *homo* ('man'). The term 'vassal', derived from a **Celtic** word (*gwassawl*) meaning a servant or young boy, was rarely used after the ninth century, except in *chansons de geste*, where it most often connoted a warrior. The ceremony through which an individual became the vassal of a lord included the vassal's sacred oath of loyalty and an act of ritual submission ('homage'). The origins of the lord-man relationship may be found in the conditions of seventh and eighth centuries western Europe that made such a private pledge of mutual protection and support necessary. The breakdown of central authority in the west (due to the abandonment of the Roman cities for the countryside; the breakdown of central administrative institutions, including the army and bureaucracy; decay of roads, communications, etc.) led to dangerous times. Lordship became the dominant societal bond – or at least the dominant vertical bond (kinship and friendship remained powerful ties) – in the tenth century because of the **Viking** invasions that shattered the remaining vestiges of central authority of the Carolingian kings of West Francia (soon to be France).

The antecedents of medieval vassalage were complex and various. Among them, one can number the Roman patron/client relationship; Roman 'friendship' agreements, *convenientiae*, used to end legal disputes or to forge alliances among the powerful; the *bucellarii*, Roman soldiers detached to serve as the personal bodyguards of private landowners in the late Roman Empire; and the Germanic war-band, termed the *comitatus* by the Roman historian Tacitus, c. AD 100. From the patron/client relationship and the *convenientiae* came the notion of contract and mutual obligations that were religiously and morally binding (*fides* – fealty/faith). The Germanic war-band and the institution of the *bucellarii* contributed to vassalage the idea of military service in exchange for maintenance (support through gifts of food, clothing, shelter and weapons), oaths, the ceremony of homage and, perhaps most importantly, the erosion of the boundaries between 'state' and 'household'. One should not, however, draw too fine distinctions among the four sources, as they historically and conceptually overlap. By the sixth century, Roman *bucellarii* and Germanic war-bands had merged into the Merovingian *obsequia*, the entourages of Frankish kings and nobles, but even before that the military followings of Roman and German magnates probably shared much in common.

Just as lords had many vassals, vassals could have several lords. 'Liege lordship' was the mechanism developed for determining the table of priorities of loyalty. The liege lord was a vassal's primary lord, to whom he owed loyalty and service above all others. In the second half of the twelfth century, **Henry II** of England (1154–1189) and then King Philip Augustus of France (1179–1223), in imitation of Henry, developed an ideal of royal liege lordship in which the king was defined as the primary lord of every free man who held land in the realm, regardless of who that man's immediate personal lord might be.

Fief (*feudum*) is the word from which feudalism derives. The word most often used to denote dependent tenures in Merovingian and Carolingian Francia was *beneficium*, while in **Anglo-Saxon** England such holdings were termed *lænland*. Neither word, however, implied a specific type of service. Both could range from the large endowments of royal vassals in return for loyalty and military obligation to quite modest precarial tenures whose tenants rendered their lords menial services. In the tenth and eleventh centuries, the Latin term *feodum* (also *feudum*, *fevum*, and in French, *fief*) began to be used interchangeably with *beneficium*. In this period, however, fief still lacked a precise definition: it could be used either to describe dependent tenure held by a man from his lord, as it is used now by historians, or it could denote simply property. In thirteenth-century charters from England, France, Germany, Spain and Italy, the term was used to describe a dependent tenure held from a lord by a vassal in return for a specified amount of knight service and occasional financial payments. These payments are sometimes termed 'feudal incidents', because earlier historians saw them as 'incidental' to the fundamental obligation of military service. (But see below on the problem of regarding military service as the essence of the lord/vassal relationship.)

Giving fiefs was beneficial to both lord and vassal. Land meant that the vassal could marry and raise a family. Possession of landed estates was equivalent to manhood. The grant of fiefs was also beneficial to the lord, since the lord's 'honour' (complex of lands) usually consisted of widely scattered holdings that were difficult to exploit or control anyway. Interestingly, there is a series of charters from twelfth-century Montpellier analysed by historian Frederic Cheyette that suggests that the same land could be granted *in alodio*, that is, as property, repeatedly by the same donor to the heirs of the original recipient and then granted back to the donor as a *feudum*. As Cheyette observes, this:

> practice raises far more questions than that: it suggests that an analysis of the rights one or another individual might hold in the property is here simply beside the point. What seems to be important for the participants is the entire ritual of donation, return grant, and oath of fidelity, a ritual that served to implant a personal relationship, what the document from Pignan refers to as 'love', into the landscape. The particular words that the scribe scratched on parchment were of less importance than the action and the words that were uttered. (Cheyette 1996, 1004)

The confusion over the definition of property created a problem for the lord: how was he to maintain his legal ownership of the property in face of its *de facto* ownership by the vassal? The tension between the vassal's desire to transform the fief into hereditary property and the lord's desire to retain the fief as his property resulted in a compromise, the so-called feudal incidents mentioned earlier. The fief, thus, became hereditary tenure; the eldest son of a deceased vassal would inherit, but first he had to do homage and swear fidelity to the lord and pay a 'relief' for the land (a monetary recognition of the lord's continuing proprietary rights over the property). King Henry II of England's use of the concept of royal liege lordship to enhance his rights and power as king transformed these incidents into important sources of royal income and patronage. Baronial discontent with royal claims to arbitrarily assessed 'reliefs' and other feudal payments under Henry's son King John led to the *Magna Carta* in 1215.

The second problem faced by the lord was the difficulty of exacting as much service as he wished from his feudal tenants. Services over the tenth and eleventh centuries tended to become fixed as customary obligations. Thus, throughout northern France in the twelfth and thirteenth centuries, military service for fiefs was limited for offensive campaigns to forty days for a knight. In England before 1066 landowners were required to supply and send one soldier to the king's army (***fyrd***) for every five 'hides' of land – i.e. from every estate rated for taxation as possessing 600 acres of arable – for a period of sixty days. This limitation on military service highlights an irony about 'feudalism': there seems to have been no period in which feudal obligation was the chief form of military recruitment. Military historians of Anglo-Norman England not only emphasise the central role played by the military households of the king and his barons in warfare but recognise that voluntary and stipendiary military service existed side by side with feudal obligation from at least the eleventh century on. In pre-conquest England and Normandy, many nobles would have answered a king's summons to war with a retinue appropriate to their rank and dignity, even if it exceeded the number of **thegns** or knights owed from their lands. By the twelfth century, English and French kings and barons were already commuting military service for cash payments (scutages), with which they could purchase the service of mercenaries.

This brings us back to the idea of the fief as a social institution. Knight-service in war was far less common than (1) castle-guard, the obligation of a vassal to serve in a castle garrison of the lord; (2) suit in court, that is, the vassal's obligation to attend the lord's court, to give him counsel and to help him judge disputes; (3) accompanying the lord when he travelled or attended the court of his lord – meant to increase the social status of the lord or (4) hospitality to the lord or to his servants. Most feudal incidents, indeed, reflected the social relationship between the lord and his vassal and the mixed proprietary rights each had over the fief. To go by the legal treatises attributed (perhaps mistakenly) to Glanvill (late 1180s) and Bracton (second quarter of the thirteenth century), the most important rights that a lord in late-twelfth-century England could claim over vassals who held land from him were relief, wardship and marriage, aids and escheat. Wardship and marriage referred to a lord's right to control descent of fief by choosing husbands of female heirs and guardians of minors, preferably in consultation with the heirs' closest male adult kinsmen. An 'aid' was economic help given by the vassal to his lord. Fief-holders in twelfth-century England were expected to help defray the lord's expenses incurred through knighting his eldest son, the marriage of his eldest daughter or for ransoming his person. Escheat was the reversion of the fief to the lord in default of an heir.

Debate Over the Origins of Feudalism in England

The debate over English feudalism has largely revolved around the question of whether **William the Conqueror** introduced the conjoined institutions of vassalage, fief and knight service from Normandy in 1066, or whether the origin of these institutions is to be sought in **Edward the Confessor**'s England. Those who wish to portray the **Norman** conquerors as the architects of the feudal system have minimised the resemblance of the royal army of pre-conquest England to the Anglo-Norman host, Anglo-Saxon commendation to Norman vassalage and Anglo-Saxon land tenure to that found in *Domesday Book* (1087). Others have argued with vehemence that the Anglo-Saxons developed dependent military tenures at least a century before **Hastings**. The argument extends back to the seventeenth century when the antiquary Sir Henry Spelman first recognised the applicability of the feudal terminology formulated by early modern French legal writers to describe the laws governing the descent of fief to the situation of medieval England. The modern debate, however, began in 1891 with the publication of an essay by John Horace Round on the introduction of knight service into England. Taking exception to Edward A. Freeman's argument for continuity in English tenurial and political history, Round represented the conquest as a dividing line between a pre-feudal and feudal England. According to Round, William the Conqueror revolutionised the military organisation of England by imposing upon the fiefs he distributed to his followers precisely defined quotas of knight service. Round, who had previously argued that 1066 marked a tenurial revolution, posited that the Norman Conquest marked a dramatic and absolute break with English traditions of military service, which he saw as arising from a public duty incumbent upon all free men.

The most prominent advocate of Round's thesis was Sir Frank Stenton, who rejected Round's animus against the Anglo-Saxons, but who embraced his view that 1066 marked the beginnings of English feudalism. Not everyone, however, was persuaded. Round's distinguished contemporary, the legal historian Frederic Maitland (1850–1906), remarked, tongue firmly in cheek, 'Now if an examiner were to ask who introduced the feudal system into England? One very good answer, if properly explained, would be Henry Spelman.... If my examiner went on with the question and asked me, when did the feudal system attain its most perfect development? I should answer, about the middle of the last century' (Maitland 1908, 142). Whereas Maitland argued for tenurial continuity, others discovered evidence of 'feudal' institutions in pre-conquest England. In the 1960s, Eric John revived the arguments of the late-nineteenth-century historian H. Munro Chadwick for Anglo-Saxon royal armies made up of noble warriors who were personally commended to the ealdormen under whom they fought. C. Warren Hollister both argued for elements of continuity between the military organisations of Anglo-Saxon and Anglo-Norman England and, more radically, demonstrated that 'feudal' military service never constituted the main source of warriors for the Norman kings. John Gillingham followed Hollister by critically re-examining the evidence for William's sudden imposition of knight quotas, and David Bates demonstrated that Normandy before 1066 was not as 'feudal' as Round had supposed. The author of this article demonstrated that, in 1066, English armies were organised according to the principle of lordship and raised, in part, through the obligation of those who held their lands freely, 'with sake and soke', to render military service to the crown, the extent of which was determined by a rough approximation of the value of their lands (Abels 1998). Since around 1990, the debate has died down, in large part because of increasing doubts of the validity of the feudal paradigm itself. The consensus at present is that both England and Normandy possessed rudimentary elements of a 'feudal system' – dependent tenures, lordship and dependent military tenures – before 1066, but they coexisted with other forms of tenure and military obligation, and English feudalism as exemplified in the works of Glanvill and Bracton was the result of an evolutionary process that had much to do with the unsettled conditions that followed the Norman Conquest.

Marc Bloch's First and Second Feudal Ages

In 1939, Marc Bloch, one of the fathers of the '*Annales* school' and arguably the most prominent modern medievalist after Henri Pirenne (1862–1935), published the first volume of *Feudal Society*, a study of feudalism as a system of social relations. (The second volume appeared in the following year while Bloch was in hiding from the Nazis.) Bloch, appreciating the difficulty of trying to define feudalism, opted instead to describe the characteristics of a 'feudal society':

A subject peasantry; widespread use of the service tenement (i.e. the fief) instead of a salary, which was out of the question; the supremacy of a class of specialised warriors; ties of obedience and protection which bind man to man and, within the warrior class, assume the distinctive form called vassalage; fragmentation of authority – leading inevitably to disorder; and, in the midst of all this, the survival of other forms of association, family and State, of which the latter, during the second feudal age, was to acquire renewed strength (2: 446).

Bloch identified two distinct feudal ages. The First Feudal Age, lasting from the collapse of the Carolingian Empire to the mid-eleventh century, was characterised by the breakdown of the central authority of the state, in part as a consequence of the Viking raids. Authority during this period devolved upon the localities. Motte-and-bailey castles, man-made hills with wooden towers on top of them and enclosures created by ditches and palisades at their base, sprang up all over the western half of the Carolingian Empire. The castellans who controlled these castles were essentially politically autonomous, despite the efforts of counts and dukes to rein them in and the exalted theocratic claims made by kings and their ecclesiastical supporters. The economy was primitively agrarian, the little trade that there was largely long-distance luxury trade, in which the west exchanged slaves and raw materials for the luxuries of the east.

Bloch's Second Feudal Age, which began around 1050 and continued until around 1250, was the product of a European economic take-off. Agricultural revolution (three field rotation, heavy plough, horse harness, windmills) and the expansion of commerce led to the growth of towns and the rebirth of a cash economy. These economic changes helped kings and the great princes of Europe consolidate power, as feudal monarchies arose that were to be the basis of the modern European nation states. These economic changes also led to a transformation of feudal relations and the definition of nobility. The knightly class became a hereditary nobility by the year 1100. The influx of wealth led to an increasing emphasis upon expenditure and conspicuous consumption as a reflection of nobility. Since this was also an age of rampant inflation, the aristocracy found itself continually pressed for money, which led, in many instances, to attempts to increase the economic exploitation of manorial resources through the use of professional bureaucratic staff in noble households and on manors. By the thirteenth century, aristocrats in England, France, Germany and Italy tended to be literate, at least in the vernacular, and all great landowners had professional administrators to look after their affairs. (Here is where the universities became especially important in the secular history of medieval Europe.) The aristocracy, faced by the emergence of the merchant class, began to define itself as a special order with the help of the church. This led to chivalry and to the rituals of knighthood (e.g. the dubbing ceremony, courtly love). Though still defining itself as a warrior class, the military value of knights in the Second Feudal Age declined due to the rigid customary limitations on service. Already by the middle of the twelfth century, English and French kings were relying on mercenaries, many of whom were poor or landless knights. The aristocracy, however, continued to display its martial prowess in games (tournaments) as well as in war. Feudal incidents began to displace military service as the most important render owed by a feudal tenant to his lord.

The Feudal Revolution Debate

Marc Bloch was vague about precisely when his 'First Feudal Age' began. Georges Duby, arguably the most influential French medieval historian of the second half of the twentieth century, remedied this. In *La société aux XIe et XIIe siècles dans la région mâconnaise* (1953), Duby proposed that France underwent a 'feudal transformation' around the year 1000. His study of the charters of the abbeys of Cluny and St Vincent of Mâcon persuaded him that between the years 980 and 1030 the Mâconnais experienced a breakdown in public law and order coincident with the emergence of a 'new and harsh regime of lordship' based on castles and knights. Lords, according to Duby, imposed new obligations on the peasants, both those of servile and free descent, who became a new class – the serfs. Public law and order gave way to violence, custom and violent custom. J. F. Lemarignier (1957) chronicled the devolution of power in the late Carolingian period, as kingdoms fractured into principalities, counties and, by the end of the tenth century, into castellanies. The Capetian idea of kingship was weakened and finally, by the 1020s, swamped in the 'seignurial tide and lost its public character'. Pierre Bonnassie found the same process in the Spanish March, discovering that in the 1020s 'an old public order based on Visigothic law preserving peasant property and slavery was smashed by castle-generated violence', which produced a revolutionary change in the social order (Bisson 1994, 7). Duby further linked this new form of domination to the development and popularisation in the 1020s of the paradigm of the Three Orders – the heaven-sanctioned obligation of the many who work to serve those who fight and those who pray. A summary of this view was offered by J-P Poly and Eric Bournazel, *The Feudal Transformation, 900–1200* (French 1980, trans 1991). This feudal transformation (mutation) or revolution described a cluster of changes: (1) collapse of public justice, (2) new regimes of arbitrary lordship over recently subjected and often intimidated peasants, (3) the multiplication of knights and castles and (4) a new ideology of the Three Orders. Thus, while fiefs and vassals could be found in the eighth and ninth centuries, feudalism arose only around the year 1000. The most extreme statement of this view is by Guy Bois (1989) who saw the persistence of the antique order characterised by private property and slave labour – lasting until around the year 1000 when it was swept away.

The reaction against the 'Feudal Transformation' thesis was not slow in coming. Dominique Barthélemy's research on the Vendomais proved to him that the feudal transition was a phantom. He contended that changes to terminology had been misinterpreted as actual social and political changes. The new paradigm also drew fire from the 'hyper-Romanists', who saw the persistence of Roman order into the twelfth century and who challenged the validity of the public versus private paradigm itself. The question of whether there was a 'Feudal Transformation' around the year 1000 was vigorously debated in the journal *Past and Present.* In 1994, T. N. Bisson (vol. 142) initiated this debate with a defence of Duby's thesis, but with important modifications, followed by criticisms by Barthélemy and White (1996, vol. 152) and by T. Reuter and Chris Wickham (1997, vol. 155). Bisson emphasises the transformation of violence from the 'political' (maintenance of public order through public officials and courts) to the non-political and the non-constructive (the use of violence by castellans and others to increase or maintain their power, without any sense of creating political institutions or structures). Bisson's restatement takes into account that the shift from slavery/free peasants to serfs was gradual and that serfdom coexisted with both in the tenth and in the twelfth centuries. He also acknowledges that the revolution was not complete by 1200 and was, in fact, a continuing process. Bisson makes the interesting point that even in the twelfth century the 'officers and agents' of counts, dukes and kings did not enforce law and order or implement the orders and regulations of their lords, but ruled with arbitrary force under their lords.

This debate is far from over. Richard Barton's findings for the county of Maine have echoed Barthélemy's for the Vendomais. Recently, David Bates, a specialist in early Norman history, has considered whether England experienced something akin to Bisson's 'Feudal Revolution' of the year 1000. Unsurprisingly, given his area of specialisation, Bates focuses on the impact of the Norman Conquest and in doing so touches on many of the same issues raised by the insular debate over the introduction of feudalism into England. Bates argues that, despite the 'massive tenurial change, violence and castle-building' associated with the Norman Conquest, 'when the whole is set in a broad context, continuity and evolution are the predominant characteristics' (2000, 633) of English society, economy and politics not only over the course of the eleventh century but also between c. 850 and c. 1200. 'The main messages from England for French historiography', he concludes, 'are that feudalism, castle-building and cultural violence can co-exist with power which for the sake of convenience we can call public' (2000, 646). Bates also finds that the evidence for Normandy 'points to a paradigm which acknowledges evolutionary change'.

The evidence does suggest a breakdown in public order maintained through public officials and courts in late-tenth- and eleventh-century France and Italy, and although the transformation from the free/slave peasant dichotomy to general servility (serfdom) was gradual and hardly unidirectional, the trend from 950 to 1150 was towards the domination of peasant villages by lords claiming proprietary and juridical rights over these lands and the authority to command the labour of their inhabitants. Such 'banal' lordships, moreover, derived their power from the possession of castles and the service of knights. England and Germany, however, cannot easily be accommodated under the 'feudal transformation paradigm, and White, Janet Nelson and Barthélemy are right in maintaining that the Carolingian world of the ninth and tenth centuries was also marked by the use of extra-judicial violence as a tool for resolution of disputes among the elites. One also must acknowledge that the idea of public (i.e. royal) authority continued throughout this period in the person of counts and dukes, whatsoever their actual powers and their *de facto* relationship with the kings whom they nominally served.

Criticism of the Construct of 'Feudalism'

The variety of definitions of feudalism employed by scholars led the American historian Elizabeth Brown to question the utility of the term for the study of the Middle Ages. In an article in the *American Historical Review* 79 (1974) entitled, 'The Tyranny of a Construct: Feudalism and Historians of Medieval Europe', she contended that it would be best to discard entirely the term feudalism because it is fundamentally misleading. 'As far as pedagogy is concerned', Brown declared, 'students should certainly be spared an approach that inevitably gives an unwarranted impression of unity and systematisation.... To advocate teaching what is acknowledged to be deceptive and what must later be untaught reflects an unsettling attitude of condescension toward younger students' (1974, 1078). Brown's criticism is far-reaching. She regards not only feudalism but all isms – 'abstract analytic constructs formulated and defined as a shorthand means of designating the characteristics that the observers consider essential to various time periods, modes of organisation, movements, and doctrines' – as artificialities that distort through simplification and which are fraught with the unstated assumptions of those who coined these terms. As Brown concludes, 'The tyrant feudalism must be declared once and for all deposed and its influence over students of the Middle Ages finally ended. Perhaps in its downfall it will carry with it those other obdurate isms – manorial, scholastic, and human – that have dominated for far too long the investigation of medieval life and thought' (1974, 1088).

Brown's criticisms have been developed further by Susan Reynolds in an influential monograph, *Fiefs and Vassals* (1994). Reynolds surveyed the documentary evidence for dependent military tenures in England, France, Germany and Italy, and concluded that even terms such as fief, benefice and vassal lacked any technical meaning until the late twelfth century when they were given legal definition by the Italian lawyers who produced the *Liber Feodorum*. In essence, Reynolds argued that in the early Middle Ages custom rather than law ruled, and that this custom was both highly localised and mutable. There is no evidence, to her mind, for precise 'feudal' institutions or obligations in the tenth or eleventh century. If anything, dependent tenures were less important than inheritable family lands and horizontal bonds of association were more important than the vertical bonds (lordship) that historians have traditionally emphasised. Reynolds argues for the persistence of public power and the centrality of community in the eleventh century. The feudalism of history textbooks owes far more to the *Libri Feudorum* of late-twelfth-century professional Italian lawyers than to the institutions and practices of earlier centuries. Reynolds' book pays far more attention to *fiefs* than to *vassals*, but her work has inspired others to challenge received wisdom about the latter.

Paul Hyams's essay, 'Homage and Feudalism: a Judicious Separation', makes an important contribution to the debate by demonstrating that another of the favourite terms of medieval historians, 'homage', had a broader meaning than traditionally believed. Hyams, a self-pronounced sceptic of the utility of feudalism as an analytical model, demonstrates in a carefully argued paper that the ritual of 'intermixed hands' was not specific to 'the creation of honourable lordship', as is usually believed, but was used for various purposes to make manifest 'an act of submission, the conveyance of self into some state of dependence' (Hyams 2003, 49).

I am more ambivalent. The pendulum has threatened to swing too far in the other direction, away from vertical ties and power relations towards horizontal bonds, consensus making and community. Both types of social bonds appear in the sources for the tenth and eleventh centuries, not only in France, Italy and Germany, but in pre-conquest England as well. If defined narrowly, as in Ganshof's definition, feudalism remains a useful shorthand term to describe vertical social and political relations among the aristocracies of England and France from the mid-eleventh through the thirteenth century (and of Germany in the thirteenth century). Susan Reynolds is right in noting that vassalage and fiefs were not the only – and perhaps not even the most prevalent – political and material ties among the European nobility of the tenth and eleventh centuries. Nonetheless, lords, retainers and dependent tenures did exist in France, Italy and England during those centuries and were to become ubiquitous by the early thirteenth century. This development probably had less to do with professional Italian lawyers systematising feudal law than with the realisation by rulers that they could enhance their authority by defining themselves as royal liege lords of all free men and as the fount of all landholding in their realms. It is telling that the most 'feudalised' societies of the twelfth century were Norman England, Norman Sicily and the Crusader principalities, all polities established through conquest. William the Conqueror's distribution of lands to his followers was on the basis of fiefs. *Domesday Book* describes the lands of England's tenants-in-chief in 1087 as held *de rege* ('from the king), and Henry II's *Cartae Baronum* of 1166 enumerates the military obligations attached to them fifty years later. Whether Normandy (or Anglo-Saxon England) was 'feudal' or not in 1066, it is indisputable that William structured the Norman settlement of his newly acquired kingdom upon the principle of dependent military tenures. One must, however, always be aware that an ideal construct only approximates reality; the danger is mistaking the construct for reality, and either interpreting source evidence through the construct or judging the actual social, political and tenurial relationships in a particular society, whether medieval European or not, against this ideal. The question 'Was this society feudal?' is less important than understanding the institutions and relationships of that society in their historical context.

Further Reading

Abels, Richard. 1988. *Lordship and Military Obligation in Anglo-Saxon England.* University of California.

Barthélemy, Dominique, and Stephen D. White. 1996. 'Debate: The Feudal Revolution'. *Past and Present* 152: 196–223.

Bates, David. 2000. 'England and the "Feudal Revolution" '. *Il Feudalesimo Nell'Alto Medioevo. Settimane Di Studio Del Centro Italiano Di Studi Sull'Alto Medioevo* 47: 611–645.

Bisson, Thomas. N. 1994. 'The Feudal Revolution'. *Past and Present* 142: 6–42.

Bloch, Marc.1939 (French edn.), 1964 (English tr.). *Feudal Society.* Translated by L. A. Manyon. University of Chicago Press.

Bois, Guy. 1989. *The Transformation of the Year One Thousand.* Fayard.

Brown, Elizabeth A. R. 1974. 'The Tyranny of a Construct: Feudalism and Historians of Medieval Europe'. *American Historical Review* 79: 1063–1088.

Cheyette, Frederic L. (ed.). 1975. *Lordship and Community in Medieval Europe: Selected Readings.* Robert E. Krieger.

———. 1996. Review of Susan Reynolds, *Fiefs and Vassals. Speculum* 71: 998–1006.

Ganshof, F. L. 1944 (original French edn.), 1964 (rev. English tr.). *Feudalism.* Translated by P. Grierson. Harper-Torch.

Gillingham, John. 1982. 'The Introduction of Knight Service into England'. *Anglo-Norman Studies* 4: 53–64.

Herlihy, David (ed.). 1970. *The History of Feudalism.* Humanities Press.

Hollister, C. Warren. 1965. *Military Organization of Norman England.* Oxford University Press.

Hyams, Paul. 2003. 'Homage and Feudalism: A Judicious Separation'. Pp.13–49 in *Die Gegenwart des Feudalismus.* Edited by Natalie Fryde. Marx-Planck-Institut fur Geschichte.

Lemarignier, Jean-François. 1957. 'Political and Monastic Structures in France at the End of the Tenth and the Beginning of the Eleventh Century'. In *Lordship and Community in Medieval Europe.* Edited and translated by Frederic Cheyette. Holt, Rinehart, and Winston, 1968.

Maitland, Frederic William. 1908. *The Constitutional History of England.* Edited by Hal Fisher. Cambridge University Press.

Milsom, S. F. C. 1976. *The Legal Framework of English Feudalism.* Cambridge University Press.

Poly, Jean-Pierre, and Eric Bournazel. 1980 (French edn.), 1991 (English tr.). *The Feudal Transformation, 900–1200.* Translated by Catherine Higgit. Holmes & Meier.

Reuter, Timothy, and Chris Wickham. 1997. 'Debate: The Feudal Revolution'. *Past and Present* 155: 177–225.

Reynolds, Susan. 1994. *Fiefs and Vassals: The Medieval Evidence Reinterpreted.* Oxford University Press.

Round, J. H. 1895. *Feudal England.* Swan Sonnenschein & Co. (Includes the essay, 'The Introduction of Knight Service into England'. *English Historical Review* 6, 1891: 417–443, 625–645.)

Stephenson, Carl. 1942 *Mediaeval Feudalism.* Cornell University Press.

Stenton, Frank M. 1932. *The First Century of English Feudalism 1066–1166.* Oxford University Press.

Richard Abels

Filid

Fili (plural *filid*) is the Old Irish word for poet. They were not mere verse-makers, but high-status professionals who performed many different functions within their society. The term *fili* originally seems to have referred to men who were poets, judges and storytellers. Some law texts suggest that the profession of a judge (*brithem*) started out as a specialist within the *filid*, though not all texts agree. The *Senchas Már* does hint that poets were lawmakers, 'true laws of the poets ... and the advice of judges'.

It is clear from legal sources that all *filid* were born into poetic families and were fully trained. They belonged to the noble, or *nemed*, class. In fact, they were the only professionals (as opposed to lords and kings) who were members of that class. There were seven grades of professional poets, the highest of which was the *ollam*. Poets, like clergy, kept their status when they left their own *túath*, which meant they could travel more easily that most members of their society.

The duties and powers of the poet were many. First and foremost they were to praise and to satirise, so their job was associated with maintaining (or destroying) the public honour of important people. They were also thought to have magical powers, including the ability to curse and to prophesy. The *firt filed* was the poet's curse, or sometimes 'miracle'. In the ***Annals of Ulster*** for 1024, a powerful *fili* was murdered and he cursed his killers so that they all became putrid within an hour of his death. The *Annals of* ***Connacht*** under the year 1414 record another incidence of the poet's curse.

Prophecy was another poetic skill. Bretha Nemed and the Triads both agree that a poet's status derived in part from 'knowledge which illuminates' (Bincy 1978, 1533), or prophecy. One famous example appears in the *Táin* when queen Medb of Connacht meets the poetess Fedelm. To each of Medb's inquiries about the fate of her army, Fedelm answers 'I see it crimson, I see it red', foreshadowing Connacht's defeat.

The poets had other, more prosaic duties as well. They were storytellers, historians, genealogists and were knowledgeable about place names. Poets were commissioned and paid for their work and the members of the highest grades were trained to produce the most complicated poems. They could therefore demand the highest fees for their work. One tenth-century Hiberno-Scandinavian king of **Dublin** apparently commissioned just such a praise poem for himself:

> Olaf of Dublin the hundred-strong,
> who gained the kingship of Howth;
> I bore off from him as a price of my song
> a horse of the horses of Achill.
> (Gwynn 1903, 53)

There were women poets as well (*banilid*), and though they were rare they were hardly unknown. Fedelm was a literary example, but another is named in the *Annals of Inisfallen* in the year 934. Fergus Kelly has suggested that perhaps a poet with no sons might train a daughter. With full *nemed* status on their own, they would have had legal right usually denied to women.

See also Irish Language; Literature.

Further Reading

Bincy, D. A. (ed.). 1978. *Corpus Iuris Hibernici*, 6 vols. Dublin Institute for Advanced Studies.

Breatnach, Liam. 1987. *Uraicecht Na Ríar: The Poetic Grades in Early Irish Law*. Dublin Institute for Advanced Studies.

Fergus, Kelly. 1988. *A Guide to Early Irish Law*. Dublin Institute for Advanced Studies.

Gwynn, Edward (ed. and tr.). 1903. *Metrical Dindsenchus I*.

Mary Valante

Fir Bolg

The *Fir Bolg* (*Men of Bags*) are the legendary people who invaded Ireland (Ériu) in pre-Christian times. They were first mentioned in the well-known ninth-century ***Historia Brittonum*** ('The History of the Britons'), attributed to the Welsh monk **Nennius**. Nennius mentions *Builc*, as a person, without the prefix *Fir* (Men) (ch.14). They are described as *Fir Bolg* in more detail in the eleventh-century pseudo-historical ***Lebor Gabála Érenn*** (*The Book of Invasions* or *Book of the Taking*).

Irish history is presented in four cycles: the Ulster cycle, the Mythological cycle, the Historical cycle and the Fenian cycle. The *Lebor Gabála*, written in Middle Irish, forms the major part of the so-called Mythological cycle and describes how the island was subjected to a succession of invasions. The first 'taking' of Ireland took place before the flood by Cessair, granddaughter of Noach. The next 'taking' was undertaken by Partholón, a Scythian who arrived hundreds of years later. Then came the invasion of the Nemedians, named after their leader, Nemed. After the *Fir Bolg*, who were the fourth wave, the ***Tuatha Dé Danann*** ruled the island until they were succeeded by the last invaders of Ireland, the Milesians (after Mil).

When the *Fir Bolg* arrived in Ireland, they divided into three tribes, or nations: the *Fir Domnann*, the *Fir Bolg* and the *Gaileoin*. The *Lebor Gabála* gives an explanation of their names: 'Fir Domnann, from Inber Domnann, the name of the creek where they landed. *Fir Bolg*, then, from the bags in which they used to carry the earth are they named. The Gaileoin, from the javelins are they named' (Macalister and Stewart 1941, section 6, 17).

Five sons of the *Fir Bolg* (Slainge, Gann, Sengannd, Genannd and Rudraige) then divided Ireland into five *cóicid*, or fifths: the modern-day provinces **Ulster**, **Leinster**, **Munster**, **Connaught** and **Meath**. They held Ireland for thirty-seven years until the arrival of the *Tuatha Dé Danann*, who wanted to live peacefully with the *Fir Bolg*. But the *Fir Bolg* did not wish their companionship and decided to drive them back into the sea where they came from. The result was written down in the famous eleventh-century tale *Cath Maige Tuired* ('The [first and second] Battle of Moytura'). The *Tuatha Dé Danann*, however, being near halfgods, were gifted with magical powers and were too powerful for the *Fir Bolg*. The Men of Bags lost the battle and were forced to live on the outskirts of Ireland.

See also Gaels; Kings and Kingship.

Further Reading

Carey, John. 1993. *A New Introduction to Lebor Gabála Érenn, the Book of the Taking of Ireland*. Irish Texts Society.

Gray, Elizabeth A. 1982. *Cath Maige Tuired: The Second Battle of Mag Tuired*, vol. 52. Irish Texts Society.

Macalister, Robert, and A. Stewart. 1941. *Lebor Gabála Érenn: The Book of the Taking of Ireland*, Part 4. Irish Texts Society.

Morris, John (ed. and tr.). 1980. *Nennius: British History and The Welsh Annals*. Phillimore.

Nicki Bullinga

Fishbourne

Fishbourne, **Sussex**, is the site of a Roman military base at the time of the Claudian invasion of AD 43 and a later palace that was excavated by Sir Barry Cunliffe from 1960 to 1967, and intermittently since. The earliest occupation was represented by a pre-Roman ditch containing imported Roman Arretine pottery, imported pottery from Gaul, local wares and the probable mount from a Roman sword scabbard. This occupation may have been associated with a native phase of activity in the early first century AD, strongly encouraged by the Romans. The first Roman constructional activity on the site was a series of timber buildings that were probably a supply base for the campaigns of the commander Vespasian (later, emperor) in the south-west in AD 44. These buildings were demolished in the late 40s or early 50s, and a substantial timber dwelling with painted wall plaster was erected. The secondary building was probably for servants. This secondary building in turn was replaced around the 60s or early 70s by a stone structure of imposing design, the 'proto-palace', which had a colonnaded garden, a suite of domestic rooms, baths and servants' quarters. It was notable for having painted wall plaster (which included a scene of a harbour, not unlike one from Stabiae in Italy), stucco work and paved floors employing *opus sectile*, a type of mosaic.

Splendid though this building was, it was replaced by one that was even grander. This consisted of a series of four ranges round a formal garden, which extended to 4 ha – a complex that was more extensive than any found at the time outside Italy. The domestic wing was on the south (mostly under the present road). On the west was the 'official' wing at which guests were received, with an imposing apse audience chamber. The east wing had an elaborate entrance chamber and accommodation for official visitors. The whole complex was built and decorated by immigrant craftsmen, in the most up-to-date style. It has been suggested that this palace was the residence of **Cogidubnus**, a Roman client king, though it has also been suggested that it might have been a palace of the Roman provincial governor.

Around the end of the first century, two new bath suites were built, perhaps indicating that the palace was split up and new mosaics were laid in the north wing, of which the most notable dates from the mid-second century and depicts a cupid riding a dolphin surrounded by sea panthers and sea horses. The palace flourished into the late third century, when it was destroyed by fire – the lead from the roof melted over the mosaic floors. It was robbed for building materials, and the site used for a series of late-Roman burials.

See also Roman Britain; Romano-British Towns.

Further Reading

Cunliffe, B. W. 1971. *Excavations at Fishbourne*, 2 vols. Society of Antiquaries Research Report.

———. 1971. *Fishbourne: A Roman Palace and Its Garden*. Thames & Hudson.

Manley, J., and D. Rudkin. 2003. 'Fishbourne Before the Conquest Royal Capital of a Client-Kingdom?' *Current Archaeology* 187: 290–298.

Jennifer Laing

Frampton

Frampton, Dorset, is the site of a Roman villa investigated in 1796–1797 by Samuel Lysons, who uncovered an outstanding series of Roman mosaics. Apart from the meticulous engravings executed by Lysons at the time and published in his *Reliquiae Britannico Romanae* (1813–1817), no documentation survives relating to the villa's mosaics, but his drawings show that they contained an array of scenes from Classical mythology and, in the case of one famous example, a Chi Rho (the first two letters of the word 'Christ') in a border. A couplet about Neptune points to the level of education of villa owners in fourth-century Britain.

Dorset is notable for its Roman mosaics, which occasionally use Christian subject matter. The most famous is that from Hinton St Mary, in which the central roundel shows a head in front of a Chi Rho (which strongly suggests that the head represents that of Christ). The rest of the composition (which includes Bellerophon and the Chimaera) is pagan in subject matter, but can be interpreted in Christian terms.

See also Romano-British Towns.

Further Reading

Cosh, S. R., and D. S. Neal. 2006. *Roman Mosaics of Britain, 2, South-West Britain*. Illuminata Barham.

Neal, D. S. 1981. *Roman Mosaics in Britain: An Introduction to their Schemes and a Catalogue of Paintings*. Britannia Monographs 1.

Jennifer Laing

Franks Casket

The confusingly named Franks Casket, also known as the Auzon Casket, is a rectangular whalebone box, measuring 9 inches (23 centimetres) long, 7 inches (19 centimetres) wide and 5 inches (13 centimetres) high, that was purchased by Sir Augustus Franks in Paris in 1860 and donated by him to the British Museum in 1867 with four of its five panels intact (the right-hand panel, which had become separated from the casket, is now housed in the Bargello Museum in Florence.) The casket has been identified on the basis of its orthography and iconography as a product of the Northumbrian 'Renaissance' of the early eighth century. Late antique models, such as the early-fifth-century Brescia Casket, have clearly influenced the design, construction and iconography of the Franks Casket. The purpose of the Casket is uncertain. Because of its inclusion of pagan scenes, commentators have been reluctant to see it as a reliquary, despite it having been modelled upon late antique reliquaries, and the most frequent suggestion is that it was meant to be a jewel box for a great layman.

Each of the Casket's five panels is decorated with carvings in relief accompanied by runic inscriptions. The iconography mixes scenes from Roman, Biblical and Germanic history and legend in a manner suggestive of an illustrated world-chronicle such as the eighth-century *Scaliger Barbarus*. The front panel depicts the stories of Weland the Smith and the Adoration of the Magi. On the back panel, we find Titus's capture of Jerusalem in AD 70, helpfully confirmed by an inscription. On the left side, Romulus and Remus are shown suckled by a pair of wolves (left-hand end). On the right side is a mysterious tableau derived from Germanic pagan religion with an equally cryptic inscription. On the lid, we see warriors attacking a fortified enclosure defended by a single archer; above the archer's head appears the name 'Ægili' in runes. Each of these pictures is surrounded by **Anglo-Saxon** inscriptions written in runes, some of which are as obscure as the images they complement. Whatever else we make of the iconography, the one thing that stands out most clearly is that the designer saw nothing incongruous about mixing together images from the Bible, Roman history and Germanic legend.

The front panel has elicited, perhaps, the most general comment because of its clear juxtaposition of Germanic and Biblical stories. On its right-hand side we see the three Magi, dressed as Roman soldiers, bringing their gifts to the infant Christ seated on Mary's lap

14. Franks Casket relief, whalebone front plate, Northumbria, early eighth century, British Museum, London.

in a manger represented by the artist as an elaborate arched structure, reminiscent of the Jerusalem Temple of the back panel. Oddly, the Magi are preceded by a bird. So that we make no mistake about the meaning of this tableau, the artist had '*mægi*' inscribed over the first two figures. On the left-hand side of the panel, we find what is for most of us a less familiar scene. Here a man, right leg bent, stands in a forge, tongs in his left hand and a cup in his right hand. At the man's feet lies a headless body, and in the tongs we see the head, held over an anvil. The smith is offering the cup to a robed woman, who reaches for it. Another woman stands immediately to her right, clutching a traveller's pouch. Next to her a man is strangling birds. These are episodes from the story of Weland the Smith.

That Weland was a well-known character in early and middle **Saxon** England is evidenced by the casual references to him in the early Anglo-Saxon poem 'Deor' and in King **Alfred**'s translation of Boethius's *Consolation of Philosophy*. Weland's story as told in later Scandinavian sources, the poem 'Volundarkviða' in the Elder Edda and mid-thirteenth-century Ðiðrekssaga, is consistent with what we see on the Franks Casket (Souers 1943). In its broad outlines it tells how King NiDhad captured the heroic smith, lamed him by severing his knee joints and imprisoned him in a forge on an island, where he put him to work making wondrous things. Weland, as any proper hero would, plotted and achieved his revenge. He prepared for his escape by having his brother Egil strangle birds and collect their feathers. From these Weland fashioned wings upon which he could fly away. But before escape came vengeance. When the king's two sons visited his smithy to view his treasure, Weland killed them both. He made cups out of their skulls as a gift for their father, and gems out of their eyes for their mother. When NiDhad's daughter Beadohild subsequently came to Weland with a broken ring for repair, he gave her a cup of drugged beer (in the Casket, the cup is made from the skull of her murdered brother) and then raped and impregnated her. Satisfied, he flew away boasting of his revenge.

The pairing of the stories, on its face, seems incongruous. What has Weland's revenge to do with the Adoration of the Magi? Some scholars, inspired by the reference in 'Deor' to Beadohild's sorrows, have ingeniously sought a link in the birth of Beadohild's son, the hero Widia, seeing in him a sort of Germanic prefiguration of Christ. This reading, however, is unpersuasive. The Casket's imagery clearly focuses on Weland's revenge and not on the birth of the hero. Others have interpreted the panel more straightforwardly, as a dramatic representation of the fundamental opposition between bloody paganism and the mercy of Christianity. There is no hint, however, that the designer intended his audience to condemn Weland and the revenge he took. The scenes in the front panel are more plausibly interpreted as complementary rather than adversarial. The images, on this reading, represent two aspects of reciprocity: vendetta and gift-giving. The design of the casket as a whole is coherent and best understood as a self-conscious fusion and synthesis of native Anglian, Roman and Christian traditions. This sense of syncretism is reinforced by the designer's clever manipulation of the inscriptions, which mixes together Anglo-Saxon and Latin words and runic and Roman letters.

See also Art and Architecture; Literature; Northumbria.

Further Reading

Becker, Alfred. 1973. *Franks Casket. Zu den Bildern und Inschriften des Runenkästchens von Auzon*, vol. 5. Regensburger Arbeiten zur Anglistik und Amerikanistik.

———. 2007. 'Franks Casket', http://www.franks-casket.de/english/index.html (cited 17 March 2008).

Davidson, H. R. Ellis. 1969. 'The Smith and the Goddess' *Frühmittelalterliche Studien* 3: 216–226, 217.

Napier, A. S. 1901. 'The Franks Casket'. Pp. 362–381 in *An English Miscellany Presented to Dr. Furnivall in Honour of His Seventy-Fifth Birthday*. Clarendon Press.

Souers, Philip W. 1943. 'The Wayland Scene on the Franks Casket'. *Speculum* 18: 104–111.

Webster, Leslie. 1982. 'Stylistic Aspects of the Franks Casket'. Pp. 20–31 in *The Vikings*. Edited by R. T. Farrell. British Archaeological Reports.

———. 1999. 'The Iconographic Programme of the Franks Casket'. Pp. 227–255 in *Northumbria's Golden Age*. Edited by Jane Hawkes and Susan Mills. Sutton.

Richard Abels

Fursa, Saint (d.649)

St. Fursa (Fursu, Fursey) was one of a number of Irish monastic exiles (***peregrini***) who were active in northern Gaul in the early seventh century. Though his life was spent at monasteries, which he founded in East Anglia and at Lagny, near Paris, his cult flourished posthumously at Péronne, in Picardy, which as 'Peronne of the Irish' (*Perrona Scotorum*) became one of the major centres of Irish spirituality on the continent. His feast day is 16 January.

The early Irish martyrologies and saints' genealogies place Fursa's origins among the Conailli Muirthemne of County Louth. His *Life* emphasises the nobility of his birth, as does **Bede**'s. Later traditions place Fursa's origins in Connacht, linking his lineage to that of another, even more famous, Irish visionary traveller, **St. Brendan**. Such augmentation of a genealogy is characteristic of medieval Irish historiography and need not be accorded much credence.

In the early 630s, after some years preaching widely on the basis of his claimed visions, Fursa abandoned evangelism in Ireland and travelled to East Anglia, then under the rule of King Sigebert (631–634). Here, later joined by his brothers Fóillán and Ultán, he established the monastery of *Cnobheresburh* in a fortress (possibly **Burgh Castle**, near Yarmouth), under the patronage of King Anna (635–654). He left East Anglia after some years and travelled to Gaul, where, under the patronage of Erchinoald, the *maior palatii* of Neustria, he built a monastery at Lagny, near Paris. He died in 649, while away from his monastery, and his body was taken to a new monastery at Péronne. After four years, his incorrupt body was exhumed and placed in a shrine created by Eligius of Noyen. In time, Fursa's shrine at Péronne came to be a focal point of Irish monks and a centre for the dissemination of Irish saints' cults on the Continent.

The *Life of Fursa*, possibly written around the time of the elevation of Fursa's remains, is one of the most important texts for the development of the idea of post-mortem purgation. Around two-thirds of the *Life* is made up of two mystical journeys, one an 'out-of-body' experience, the other a 'near-death' experience in which the saint is carried to a place outside of Paradise in which he witnesses the cleansing of sinners by a purgatorial fire, each one according to the desserts of his works. This process is reminiscent of the Irish **penitential** traditions of 'tariffed penance'; its extension to a post-mortem context stands near the beginning of a long tradition of such visions in western literature leading to Dante's *Purgatorio*. The *Life* was also paraphrased by Bede and by **Ælfric**. The originality and power of its vision of salvation provides rare insights into the appeal of the teaching of the *peregrini* in Frankish Gaul.

The circumstances of Fursa's family are unusually well documented and reveal the variety of ways in which the Irish *peregrini*, with their compelling interpretations of theology, became influential in Frankish society. In seventh-century Gaul, the tensions between the Merovingian dynasty and rival aristocratic families were expressed both in political machinations and in claims of special sanctity for members of the nobility. Fursa and his brothers were of significance both for their claimed knowledge of the afterlife and for their access to a variety of networks of patronage in Gaul and in Ireland. Fóillán and Ultán ultimately followed their brother to Gaul. Some sources claim that Fóillán then took up residence at Péronne, only to be expelled, travelling into Austrasia and going on to found a monastery at Fosses-la-Ville. Here Fóillán and Ultán enjoyed the patronage of Itta, a member of the Pippinid family (later to become the Carolingian dynasty), and of her daughter, St. Geretrud of Nivelles. Fóillán was murdered on 31 October 655 and his body was miraculously discovered on St. Fursa's day (16 January) the following year, in the course of a coup which sent the future King Dagobert II into exile in Ireland.

See also Celtic Christianity; Monasticism.

Further Reading

Dunn, M. 2002. *The Birth of Monasticism*. Edinburgh University Press.

Moreira, I. 2000. *Dreams, Visions and Spiritual Authority in Merovingian Gaul*. Cornell University Press.

Groves, Nicholas (tr.). 'First Life of St Fursey', University of Wales Lampeter Celtic Christianity e-Library, http://www.lamp.ac.uk/celtic/VitaSFursey.htm (cited 17 March 2008).

Fouracre, P., and R. Gerberding. 1996. *History and Hagiography in Late Merovingian France*. Manchester University Press.

Jonathan Wooding

Fyrd

Fyrd is the term used in law-codes and the ***Anglo-Saxon Chronicle*** to denote a royal army or military expedition. **Anglo-Saxon** kings, with the notable exception of **Alfred** the Great, did not maintain standing armies. *Fyrds* were levies summoned in times of need. Throughout the Anglo-Saxon period, *fyrds* retained the characteristics of royal war-bands since they composed of the king's own retainers, whom he had summoned personally, and their followers. A *fyrd* could be local or national. Local royal armies were led by ealdormen/earls; national *fyrds* were usually commanded personally by the king and were composed of the forces of multiple shires.

Fyrds were organised territorially, by shire and hundred, and led by royal officials, ealdormen/earls, bishops, sheriffs and the king's thegns. The rank and file was probably composed mainly of sokemen and 'free men', small landowners who held a place in society between the nobility and the dependent peasantry. From the late eighth century on, liability to serve in *fyrds* rested upon the dual foundation of lordship and land tenure. By 1066, all those who held 'bookland' (land held by charter which gave the possessor exemption from royal burdens other than military service, fortification repair and bridge work) were obliged to send soldiers on royal expeditions on the basis of the assessed value of their estates, expressed in 'hides'. According to a royal customal in the Berkshire folios of ***Domesday Book***, one soldier was to be sent on expedition from every five hides of land (i.e. 600 acres); he was to serve at the land-holder's expense for sixty days. Although this custom could not have been followed throughout England, since the tax liability in some shires was expressed in carucates rather than hides, it is likely that a similar principle was in general use in 1066.

See also Kings and Kingship.

Further Reading

Abels, Richard. 1988. *Lordship and Military Obligation in Anglo-Saxon England*. University of California Press.

Halsall, Guy. 2003. *Warfare and Society in the Barbarian West, 450–900*. Routledge.

Hollister, Warren. 1962. *Anglo-Saxon Military Institutions*. Clarendon Press.

Hooper, Nicholas. 1979. 'Anglo-Saxon Warfare on the Eve of the Conquest: A Brief Survey'. *Anglo-Norman Studies* 1: 84–93.

Keynes, Simon, and Michael Lapidge (tr.). 1983. *Alfred the Great: Asser's Life of King Alfred and Other Contemporary Sources*. Penguin.

Swanton, Michael (ed. and tr.). 2000. *The Anglo-Saxon Chronicles* (rev. edn.). Phoenix.

Richard Abels

G

Gaelic

See Irish Language.

Gaels

In denoting the Irish of Ireland and those who colonised parts of Britain, medieval Irish authors most often use the Latin term *Scotti* (**Scots**) or the originally **Welsh** term *Goídil* (Gaels). The native term **Féni** has a restricted use, and *Hibernenses* derives from a geographical term and refers to the inhabitants of Ireland only.

In historical terms, *Scotti* and *Goídil* are synonyms. In the seventh-century British poem '**Y Gododdin**', the phrase *Gŵyðel a Phryden* linguistically reflects 'Gaels and British', but is best translated as '*Scotti* and *Picti*', the combination also employed by late Latin writers such as **Patrick** and **Gildas**. There is no linguistic relationship between *Scotti* and *Goídil*, but both terms originally referred to the same group of peoples. It is generally accepted that *Goídil* and *Goídelc* derive from the British pre-forms **Wēdeli* and **Wēdelica*; in the latter, the suffix *-ca* is of Latin origin. In archaic Welsh, these words developed into **Guoidil* and **Guoidelec*, and in the seventh century these words were borrowed into **Irish** as *Goídil* and *Goídelc*. These words gave rise to the modern terms Gaels and Gaelic (Modern Irish *Gaeilge*, Scottish Gaelic *Gàidhlig*).

The borrowing of 'Gael(s)' in Irish is shown in the genealogies of the supposedly British dynasty of Dal nAraidi in **Ulster**, which contain the personal name Góedel, who lived at c. 650. In 776, one Góedel of Clonard died. The term *Goídil* occurs in two early **Leinster** poems, which perhaps date from the late seventh century. The *Irish Annals* first employ the term in 772. In the Irish-origin legend, the Góedil derive their name from Góedel Glas. He was the son of Scotta, daughter of the Pharaoh of Egypt, and Nél, son of Fénius Farsaid. After him the Irish language was called *Goídelc*. According to one version, Moses blessed Góedel before the former crossed the Red Sea. In due course, the term *Goídil* came to be the standard word to refer to the native inhabitants of Ireland and those who had colonised parts of Scotland and the **Isle of Man**, and who spoke a common language, Gaelic.

This development happened notwithstanding the negative connotations attached to **Guoidil.* It is commonly related to Middle Welsh *gwyδ* and Old Irish *fíad,* 'wild, feral, uncultivated', as well as to Old Irish *fid* and Old English *widu, wudu,* 'tree, wood'. Hence, **Guoidil* means literally 'Forest People', and negatively 'Wild People, Savages'. It is the negative sense that has continued in Middle and Modern Welsh and probably reflects the reputation of the Irish plunderers among the Romans and British in the fourth and fifth centuries. Hence, it appears that the Irish (both in Ireland and outside) took over an originally negative term for themselves, just like the Welsh did when they took over the **Anglo-Saxon** word *wealas,* 'foreigners; speakers of a different language; slaves; serfs' (singular *wealh*), for themselves.

That the Irish adopted the foreign words *Scotti* and *Goídil* and their derivatives *Scotice* and *Goídelc* for the Irish people and language suggests that they had no previous concept of being one people with an identical language and culture. It was outsiders who familiarised them with these notions, where previously only a geographical 'identity' had existed. The raids and colonies of the Irish on the British coast in the fourth and fifth centuries expanded the Irish linguistic and cultural horizons across the Irish Sea. The Irish were instrumental in spreading Christianity in Britain in the sixth and seventh centuries. Such activities not only set them apart from other peoples, it also created a sense of commonness, which stimulated the adoption of (foreign) markers of a common identity. In due course, the Gaels were geographically divided between the Irish and the Scots, and 'Gaels' became an ethno-linguistic term, mainly denoting speakers of a Gaelic language (Irish, Scots Gaelic, Manx).

See also Celts.

Further Reading

Hamp, Eric P. 1992. 'Goídil, Féni, Gŵynedd'. *Proceedings of the Harvard Celtic Colloquium* 12: 43–50.

Koch, John T. 2000. 'On the Origins of the Old Irish Terms *Goídil* and *Goídelc*'. Pp. 3–16 in *Origins and Revivals: Proceedings of the First Australian Conference of Celtic Studies.* Edited by Geraint Evans, Bernhard Martin and Jonathan M. Wooding. University of Sydney.

———. 2003. 'Celts, Britons, and Gaels – Names, Peoples, and Identities'. *Transactions of the Honourable Society of Cymmrodorion* 9: 41–56.

Bart Jaski

Gallarus Oratory

The Gallarus Oratory, in the Dingle Peninsula of County Kerry, is a drystone-built corbelled structure, somewhat reminiscent of an upturned boat. Built on a 1:1.5 length–breadth ratio, it has a single entrance in one of the short sides and small window on the other. Next to it, an unexcavated platform of stones marks the site of an earlier oratory; associated with it is a cross-slab, possibly of the seventh century.

Its importance lies in the fact that it was for long seen as one of the earliest ecclesiastical buildings in Ireland still standing, and various dates from the sixth century onwards were assigned to it; Petrie in the nineteenth century even suggested that it belonged to the fifth century. H. G. Leask, among others, saw it as a stone version of a timber structure, the corbelled design echoing the cruck construction of a timber predecessor. This interpretation, however, has been subsequently questioned, and arguments were put forward for suggesting that it could belong to as late as the twelfth century. Those in favour of a late date have pointed to its use of squared stones and a round-headed window, and its general similarity to the features of the known twelfth-century church at Kilmalkeddar. It also has an upwards-swinging door, which is only paralleled in the church at **Glendalough** known as St Kevin's Kitchen, which is dated to the twelfth century.

See also Celtic Christianity.

Further Reading

Harbison, P. 1970. 'How Old Is Gallarus Oratory?' *Medieval Archaeology* 14: 34–59.

Leask, H. G. 1955. *Early Irish Churches and Monastic Buildings, I: The Early Period and the Romanesque.* Dundalk.

Lloyd Laing

Geoffrey, Count of Anjou

Geoffrey, count of Anjou, known as le Bel ('The Fair') or **Plantagenet**, after the sprig of broom (*planta genesta*) that he wore when hunting, was the father of King **Henry II** of England and the founder of the Plantagenet or Angevin dynasty.

Geoffrey was born in 1113, the eldest son of Fulk, count of Anjou, and Eremburge of La Flèche. In 1127, Geoffrey married **Matilda**, a decade his senior, daughter and designated successor of King **Henry I** of England. The following year his father left to take the crown of Jerusalem and resigned the county of Anjou into his hands. Geoffrey's early years as count were occupied with establishing his authority over rebellious vassals. In 1135, he came into conflict with his father-in-law in an attempt to gain the castles promised in his wife's dowry. Shortly after, King Henry died suddenly, and the throne was seized by **Stephen** of Blois.

When Stephen was crowned king, Geoffrey and Matilda moved quickly to gain a foothold in Normandy, but an ambitious campaign in 1136 was derailed by an outbreak of illness among the troops and injury to Geoffrey himself. In 1139, Matilda invaded England, and for a time in 1141, she looked poised to oust Stephen. The king was captured and imprisoned and Matilda took the title *Domina Anglorum* (Lady of the English), but her imperious behaviour lost her party support and by the end of the year Stephen was free and Angevin hopes for the crown had faded for the time being. Had Matilda pressed the advantage, it is possible that Geoffrey would have crossed to England and had himself crowned, but instead he continued to concentrate on the conquest of Normandy. By 1141, he controlled most of the duchy south and west of the Seine and in 1143 he crossed the Seine to complete the conquest. In 1144, when Rouen fell, he was invested as duke of Normandy and was recognised as such by King Louis VII of France, whom he accompanied on the Second Crusade (1147–1149).

Geoffrey's relations with his wife were stormy, with much of their marriage spent apart, and at times of crisis such as in late 1141 Geoffrey refused to answer Matilda's pleas for aid. Nonetheless, it was fruitful in terms of both children and political gain. A son, Henry, was born to Matilda in 1133, and two more sons, Geoffrey and William, were born in the following years. When Matilda returned to France in 1148 after failing to take the crown, her eldest son became the focus of Angevin ambition. In 1150, Geoffrey ceded the duchy to Henry, who would go on to take the throne of England in 1154. Geoffrey died suddenly on 7 September 1151 and was buried in Le Mans. He is described as handsome, energetic, skilled in warfare, possessed of an unusual interest in learning and was also cold and cunning. By consolidating his power in Anjou, conquering Normandy and ceding his title, Geoffrey left a powerful legacy to his son and the Plantagenet dynasty.

See also Kings and Kingship; Normans.

Further Reading

Gillingham, John. 1984. *The Angevin Empire*. Edward Arnold.

Hallam, Elizabeth (ed.). 1986. *The Plantagenet Chronicles*. Weidenfeld & Nicolson.

Michael Staunton

Geoffrey of Monmouth (d. 1155)

Geoffrey of Monmouth, although relatively obscure as a person, is the author of one of the most popular texts of the Middle Ages, *Historia Regum Britanniae* ('The History of the Kings of Britain'), which presented for the first time a coherent and detailed (if far from accurate) story of the history of Britain from its foundation to the decisive establishment of the Anglo-Saxons as rulers of England. In terms of Arthurian literature, Geoffrey's *Historia* provided a pivotal transition from a character, the British warrior **Arthur**, known only from fragmentary and even sometimes contradictory references, to a more fully rounded character of story and romance that forms the basis of the modern well-known King Arthur.

Our most significant sources of information about Geoffrey's life, apart from his own literary works, are six charters in favour of religious foundations in the Oxford area, which he signed as a witness from c. 1129 to 1151. In four of these charters he signs himself 'Geoffrey Arthur' (*Galfridus Arturus*), to which he added, in two, the description *magister,* 'teacher'; in the last two he signed as 'bishop [elect] of St Asaph'. His contemporaries also referred to him as 'Geoffrey Arthur'. The *Historia Regum Britanniae* had been completed by 1139, and parts of it were circulating by 1136. Sometime later, probably between 1148 and 1151, Geoffrey wrote the *Vita Merlini* (*Life of* ***Merlin***) in Latin verse. In each work Geoffrey described himself as 'Geoffrey of Monmouth' (*Galfridus Monemutensis*). We know that Geoffrey was ordained at Westminster in February 1152 and consecrated bishop later in the same month. Later that year, as 'Geoffrey bishop of St Asaph', he witnessed the Treaty of Westminster between **Stephen** and Empress **Matilda,** which ended the civil war between them. According to the Welsh chronicle *Brut y Tywysogion*, Geoffrey died in 1155.

Geoffrey's life and work raise several fascinating but ultimately unanswerable questions. Indications of his own cultural identity are endlessly suggestive. He has been claimed as a Breton, on the basis of several propositions: his *Historia* celebrates the Bretons as the remnants of the heroic past of the British; Monmouth, suggested by the epithet used by him in his writings to have been his place of origin, was under the control of Breton barons from the time of **William I**; the epithet 'Arthur', which has often been taken as a patronymic, was notably more popular among Bretons than anyone else (including the **Welsh**). The last of these propositions, the most seemingly conclusive identifier of Geoffrey's identity, has been discredited, with 'Arthur' now mostly viewed as a nickname, and the question of Breton ancestry is now regarded as unanswerable and ultimately irrelevant. A further related question concerns the extent and directness of Geoffrey's contact with the Brythonic material which undoubtedly provided much of the material which appeared in Geoffrey's writings, albeit for the most part considerably reworked. Scholars do not believe Geoffrey's claims that in producing the *Historia* as well as the *Prophetiae Merlini* ('Prophecies of Merlin'), a section of the *Historia* probably originally separate, he was merely 'translating' from existing books in the 'British language'. There are no such originals extant, and it is probable that there never were, although there is general agreement that the ninth-century ***Historia Brittonum*** provided Geoffrey with much of his overall structure and themes (structures and themes also central to medieval vernacular Welsh pseudo-historical material) and is therefore the closest thing to the 'very ancient book' Geoffrey claimed to have received from Walter, archdeacon of Oxford. Geoffrey was clearly familiar with both the detail and the overall thrust of medieval **Brythonic** tradition as we know it from surviving texts, in Latin as well as in Welsh, from Wales and to a lesser extent Brittany. But there is little visible evidence in Geoffrey's writings of a profound knowledge of Welsh or Breton, aside from some suggestive puns and place name etymologies.

Geoffrey is clearly a writer of active, and inventive, intelligence. It is difficult to differentiate between traditional material (inasmuch as we can identify it) 'misunderstood' by Geoffrey and that material 'adapted' by Geoffrey. Recently it has been argued that Geoffrey was perhaps instrumental in creating what scholars have for some time thought of as already existing medieval Welsh tradition such as the 'Myrddin' legend in its northern 'madman of the woods' aspect (Padel 2006). Part of the difficulty, of course, comes with the fact that the writing down of our existing medieval Welsh literature happened during or after the circulation of Geoffrey's immensely influential *Historia,* which had a lasting impact through its original Latin version, through Latin variants and through translations into the vernacular, including Welsh, which then in some cases visibly altered some of the Welsh material which Geoffrey had clearly used as a source in the first place.

Geoffrey's motives in writing *Historia Regum Britanniae* are not immediately obvious. Though he was writing at a time of impending civil war, and though he addresses several patrons in various dedications, there is no single political target to which it is obviously directed. The work champions notions of unity and good governance in general, but it does so in the service of providing a glorious and above all civilised past for the British, surely a politically ambiguous concept during the twelfth century. In writing his *Historia*, Geoffrey 'provided', as John Gillingham has argued (1990, 118), 'a powerful rejoinder ... [to] the "twelfth-century Renaissance" perception of the Celtic peoples in general, and the Welsh in particular, as barbarians', as exemplified in the writings of those such as **William of Malmesbury**. The objections of contemporary writers and historians to his work, partly on the entirely reasonable grounds that, in the words of William of Newburgh, Geoffrey had 'by means of the Latin language cloaked the fables about Arthur in the respectable name of history' (as quoted in Padel 2006, 76), did nothing to stem the remarkable popularity and influence of Geoffrey's history. In particular Arthur, very much Geoffrey's creation whatever later writers would make of him, was pressed into service in a number of political and literary roles.

See also Literature.

Further Reading
Clarke, Basil (ed. and tr.). 1973. *Life of Merlin*. University of Wales Press.
Crawford, T. D. 1982. 'On the Linguistic Competence of Geoffrey of Monmouth'. *Medium Ævum* 51: 152–162.
Crick, Julia 1999. 'The British Past and the Welsh Future: Gerald of Wales, Geoffrey of Monmouth and Arthur of Britain'. *Celtica* 23: 60–75.
Curley, Michael J. 1994. *Geoffrey of Monmouth*. Twayne Publishers.
Dalton, Paul. 2005. 'The Topical Concerns of Geoffrey of Monmouth's *Historia Regum Britanniae:* History, Identity, Prophecy, Peacemaking, and English Identity in the Twelfth Century'. *Journal of British Studies* 44: 688–712.
Gillingham, John. 1990. 'The Context and Purpose of the *History of the Kings of Britain*'. *Anglo-Norman Studies* 13: 99–118.
Padel, O. J. 2006. 'Geoffrey of Monmouth and the Development of the Merlin Legend'. *Cambrian Medieval Celtic Studies* 51: 37–65.
Roberts, B. 1976. 'Geoffrey of Monmouth and Welsh Historical Tradition'. *Nottingham Mediaeval Studies* 20: 29–40.
Thorpe, Lewis (tr.). 1966. *Geoffrey of Monmouth: The History of the Kings of Britain*. Penguin.

Karen Jankulak

Geraint

More than one king of the south-western early medieval British kingdom known as **Dumnonia** may have borne the name Geraint. The best attested is that addressed as *Geruntius rex* in a letter from Aldhelm, then abbot of Malmesbury, datable to sometime after 672. This letter clearly addresses the sole ruler of a relatively stable kingdom, and one that was entirely different from English kingdoms in its ecclesiastical habits (Lapidge and Herren 1979, 155). Sherborne abbey claimed to have been granted land in **Cornwall** from Geraint, at least according to a fourteenth-century copy of a perhaps eleventh-century list of benefactors; if authentic, this grant could be interpreted as a sign of conciliation between Aldhelm (later first bishop of Sherborne) and Geraint (O'Donovan 1988, 81). At any rate, according to the ***Anglo-Saxon Chronicle*** in 710 the West **Saxon** king **Ine** fought against a 'Geraint, king of the Britons' (*Wealas*); if this was not the same Geraint, then he was probably a member of the same family (Whitelock et al. 1961, 26). Apart from these two pieces of evidences, all instances of the name Geraint show up in relatively legendary contexts.

Depending on how its date is assessed, and there continues to be considerable debate on this subject, the earliest mention of a Geraint may come in the Welsh-language poem **'Y Gododdin'**, although with no identifying context apart from the phrase 'before/against? the men of the south' (*rac deheu*) (Koch 1997, 124). Another **Welsh** poem, dated between the ninth and eleventh centuries, discusses a battle involving a Geraint whose men were 'of the region Dyfnaint [i.e Devon]' (*o godir Dyfneint*, stanza 17) (Rowland 1990, 459, 505). This poem seems to belong not to the genre of praise poems addressed to living (or recently dead) historical rulers, but to a narrative, storytelling genre concerning semi-legendary figures. This is not to say that the Geraint of the poem might not have been based on a historical figure, but only that it would be unwise to take the poem as evidence of his historicity. The fact that **Arthur** or his men appear alongside, or against Geraint in the poem further obscures assessment of its sense of historicity and chronology. The location of the battle in question, *Llongborth*, cannot be determined. In the more recent of the two surviving versions of the poem, Geraint is provided with a partial lineage: he is Geraint fab Erbin, Geraint son of Erbin (the patronymic also appears in the title, although not in the body of the older version). This patronymic allows us to identify this Geraint, at least in medieval Welsh tradition, with others of the same name. Geraint son of Erbin is mentioned in passing in the medieval Welsh Arthurian tale *Culhwch ac Olwen,* in the catalogue poem *Englynion y Clyweit,* in one of the Welsh triads and in the *Life of St. Cuby*, although there as the father rather than the son of Erbin. Geraint is also identified as a son of Erbin in the medieval Welsh genealogical material, which links him to other purported rulers of Dumnonia.

Geraint's name and patronymic were substituted for the character Eric when Chrétien de Troyes's romance *Eric et Enide* (itself probably of Breton origin) was transformed into the later medieval Welsh romance *Geraint vab Erbin*. This gave Geraint, in subsequent Welsh tradition, a wife named Enid. A local Cornish saint named Gerent is attested from the tenth century.

See also Kings and Kingship; Literature.

Further Reading
Bartrum, Peter C. 1996. *Early Welsh Genealogical Tracts*. University of Wales Press.
Grimmer, Martin. 2001. 'Saxon Bishop and Celtic King: Interactions Between Aldhelm of Wessex and

Geraint of Dumnonia'. *The Heroic Age* 4, http://www.mun.ca/mst/heroicage/issues/4/Grimmer.html (cited 17 March 2008).
Koch, John (ed.). 1997. *The Gododdin of Aneirin. Text and Context from Dark-Age North Britain.* University of Wales Press.
Lapidge, Michael, and Michael Herren (tr.). 1979. *Aldlhelm: The Prose Works.* D.S. Brewer.
O'Donovan, M. A. (ed.). 1988. *Charters of Sherborne.* Oxford University Press.
Rowland, Jenny. 1990. *Early Welsh Saga Poetry: A Study and Edition of the Englynion.* Boydell & Brewer.
Whitelock, Dorothy with David C. Douglas and Susie I. Tucker. 1961. *The Anglo-Saxon Chronicle: A New Translation.* Eyre & Spottiswoode.

Karen Jankulak

Germanus of Auxerre, Saint

St. Germanus of Auxerre was at the centre of the ecclesiastical politics of both Britain and Gaul in the fifth century AD. Only sketchy details of Germanus's early life are presented in the surviving texts. The most important source is the *Life of Saint Germanus* written by Constantius of Lyon c. 480. Germanus was born at Autissiodorum (Auxerre) to a prominent but not noble Gallo-Roman family. He was well educated in the Gallic schools before studying law in Rome. He practiced law as an advocate and made a successful marriage. His secular career prospered, and according to Constantius, he became a *dux* (general) with command over several provinces. This may have been a major military office in north-western Gaul, the *dux tractus Armoricani et Nervicani.* Such a military command, rather than a civilian governorship, would have been an unusual step for someone on Germanus's career ladder. Some scholars believe that Constantius used the term *dux* in error, but there are in fact other allusions to Germanus's military experience elsewhere in Constantius's *Life of St. Germanus.*

In 418, while still in secular office, Germanus was unexpectedly chosen as the successor of St. Amator, bishop of Auxerre. Thus began an eventful career as bishop that lasted thirty years (c. 415–446). The crucial question for historians is the overall reliability of Constantius's work and how much stock to place in the literal meanings of his words. Constantius wrote a hagiography, not a history. His purpose was to glorify St. Germanus and to edify his readers, not to transmit accurate biographical details. But did Constantius record aspects of a real episcopal career or invent wholesale a blueprint for the future lives of bishops? Did Constantius recount the life of an historical individual or simply compose an allegorical icon whose didactic purpose was to guide his readers on the journey to salvation? Saints' *Lives* were works of spiritual propaganda, and it is this quality that makes it so difficult to penetrate beyond genre to recover details suitable for constructing a historical narrative.

Constantius was a younger contemporary of Germanus, but composed the *Vita* more than thirty years after Germanus's death. Despite a lack of explicit dates, the story of Germanus's career as presented in the *Vita* is internally consistent. Portions of the narrative, particularly for events in Gaul and Italy, are rich in place names, personal names and offices. Many of the details concerning Germanus's actions are both highly personal and unconventional in the context of hagiographic genre. Constantine evidently made serious efforts to discover the recoverable details of Germanus's career. It is these details that counterbalance historical distrust of the *Vita* and link the individual experiences of St. Germanus to the wider currents of fifth-century history.

In 429, Bishop Germanus, accompanied by Bishop Lupus of Troyes, journeyed to Britain to combat the **Pelagian** heresy. While there, he not only battled heretics but also led the **Britons** to the 'Alleluia' victory over a combined invading force of **Picts** and **Saxons**. His actions in Britain illustrated not only the need for an educated clergy to counter heresy, but also the growing conflation of secular and spiritual skills and powers in an age of declining imperial authority. Germanus may have returned to Britain in the 440s to deal with a revived Pelagian threat. The bare outline of his activity in Britain recorded by Constantius is almost the last glimpse through Gallo-Roman eyes of Britannia becoming sub-Roman Britain.

In Gaul, Germanus's actions illustrate the growing historical importance of bishops as leaders and representatives of their communities in contact with both the imperial authorities and the barbarians. In the mid-430s, Germanus travelled to Arles and successfully obtained tax relief for his people. In the 440s, he mediated between the rebelling population of Armorica and Alanic federates sent by the imperial authorities to crush the uprising. By his own hand, Germanus stayed the action of Goar, the Alan king. In these and other actions, he discharged the increasingly important role of bishop as patron, mediator and buffer. After the incident with Goar, Germanus travelled to the imperial court at Ravenna to prevent further reprisals against the Armoricans. He died there, probably in 445 or 446.

Constantius's *Life of Saint Germanus* provides rare and vivid evidence for aspects of crisis and continuity in fifth-century Gaul. His work is a window into the historical transformations of Late Antiquity.

See also Brittonic Age.

Further Reading

Borius, René (ed.). 1965. *Constance de Lyon: Vie de saint Germain d'Auxerre*. Les Editions du Cerf.

Constantius de Lyon. 1954. 'Vita Sancti Germani'. Pp. 284–320 in *The Western Fathers*. Edited and translated by F. R. Hoare. Sheed & Ward.

Drinkwater, John, and Hugh Elton (eds.). 1992. *Fifth-Century Gaul: Crisis of Identity*? Cambridge University Press.

Jones, Michael E. 1986. 'The Historicity of the Alleluja Victory'. *Albion* 18: 363–373.

Levison, Wilhelm. 1904. 'Bischof Germanus von Auxerre und die Quellen zu zeiner Geschichte'. *Neues Archiv der Gesellschaft für ältere deutsche Geschichtskunde* 29: 95–175.

——— (ed.). 1920. 'Vita Sancti Germani in Monumenta Germaniae Historica'. *Scriptores rerum Merovingicarum* 7: 224–283.

Mathisen, Ralph. 1981. 'The Last Year of Saint Germanus of Auxerre'. *Analecta Bollandiana* 99: 151–159.

Thompson, E. A. 1984. *Saint Germanus of Auxerre and the End of Roman Britain*. Boydell & Brewer.

Michael E. Jones

Gesta Stephani

The *Gesta Stephani* is an anonymous account of the troubled reign of King **Stephen** (1135–1154). Detailed, vivid and providing much unique information, it is one of the best sources for the events in question.

The *Gesta Stephani* is in two parts, the first book covering the years 1135–1141 and the second, briefer, book covering the period 1141–1154. It begins with the death of King **Henry I** and a eulogy of Stephen, describing how the count of Blois appeared as the fitting candidate to restore peace. He is characterised as 'peculiarly eminent for many conspicuous virtues': rich but unassuming, brave, judicious and patient (ch. 2). Energetic in calming the kingdom and establishing peace, he was good-natured and agreeable to all, and often forgot his exalted rank, seeing himself as the equal or inferior to his courtiers (ch. 12). England settled into peace and established freedom for the church (ch. 13). The author acknowledges, however, that the peace-loving king was easily inclined to grant the requests of petitioners, and sometimes led astray by bad advice, and he criticises the king's arrest of the bishops in 1139, while blaming it on his counsellors (ch. 34). The author's loyalty to Stephen's cause does not falter with his capture in 1141: God, he writes, cast him down, as he had other kings, so that his elevation might be loftier and more surprising (ch. 55). His rivals, **Matilda** and Robert of Gloucester, are harshly treated, with Matilda dismissed as the 'countess of Anjou'. However, when Matilda's son Henry **Plantagent** (later **Henry II**) enters the scene, he is repeatedly cast as the 'rightful heir to the kingdom', and the work concludes with his succeeding Stephen to the honour and the applause of all (ch. 120).

On the basis of circumstantial evidence, various ecclesiastics have been identified as the author, including Robert of Lewes, bishop of **Bath** 1136–1166, but there is no consensus as to the likely candidate. The work is marked by detailed topographical descriptions, accounts of sieges and battles, and information on local politics, much of which centres on the area around Bristol and Bath. Though concerned with secular politics, the author shows a good deal of interest in ecclesiastical affairs and discusses the king's changing fortunes in terms of biblical history. Early in the reign, the redness of the sky is compared to Old Testament portents of doom; the king's subjects are like the people of Israel, softened by luxury and hence afflicted by defeats (39–40). Stephen himself is implicitly compared to the flawed but penitent King David.

The *Gesta Stephani* covers some similar ground to **William of Malmesbury** and **Henry of Huntingdon,** but is independent of these writers. The work was printed in 1619 from a manuscript, now lost, in the episcopal library at Laon. In the 1950s, another copy was discovered in a fourteenth-century manuscript at the Municipal Library at Valenciennes. This copy contained additional material which brought the narrative up to 1154, though gaps in the narrative remain.

See also Kings and Kingship.

Further Reading

Gransden, Antonia. 1974. *Historical Writing in England c. 550–c. 1307*. Routledge.

King, Edmund. 2006. 'The Gesta Stephani'. Pp.195–206 in *Writing Medieval Biography, 750–1250: Essays in Honour of Professor Frank Barlow*. Edited by D. Bates, J. Crick and S. Hamilton. Boydell and Brewer.

Potter, K. R., and R. H. C. Davis (eds.). 1976. *Gesta Stephani* (2nd rev. edn.). Oxford Medieval Texts. Clarendon Press.

Michael Staunton

Gewisse

See Saxons; Wessex.

Gildas (c.485–c.570)

Gildas was a British cleric and writer active around the year AD 500. He is the author of one substantial work, *De Excidio Britanniae* ('Concerning the Ruin of Britain'), an extended sermon on the political and ecclesiastical ills of Britain in the fifth and sixth centuries. The *De Excidio* is our chief source of evidence for both **Ambrosius Aurelianus** and the Battle of **Badon Hill**, which Gildas says was fought in the year of his own birth. Two other writings have been attributed to him: *Fragmenta*, 'Fragments' of letters concerning ecclesiastical organisation and *De Poenitentia* ('On Penance'), probably the earliest of the monastic **penitential** to be produced in the British Isles. **Columbanus** described Gildas to Pope Gregory the Great as an expert on monastic discipline, while **Bede** (who draws heavily on Gildas) and subsequent medieval writers saw him as Gildas Sapiens, the respected historian of the **Britons**. Another tradition depicts him as the founder of the monastery of St. Gildas de Rhuys in Brittany, and two late *Vitae* were produced in the eleventh and twelfth centuries. The most famous is the *Life of Gildas* written by Caradoc of Llancarfan, which states that Gildas was the son of a king of **Strathclyde** and a student of St. **Illtud** at Llantwit Major.

The oldest extant manuscript of the *De Excidio Britanniae* dates to the tenth century and is now in the British Library, though it was badly damaged by fire in 1731. Theodor Mommsen produced the first modern critical edition in the nineteenth century, and the standard English translation is that of Michael Winterbottom. The *De Excidio* has been the focus of much recent scholarship, which has removed old prejudices about Gildas's rustic style and cultural isolation. He is now viewed as the recipient of a classical education (which included grammar, rhetoric and legal studies) who was well read and who wrote in the style of fifth-century Christian rhetoricians like Sidonius and Ennodius. The *De Excidio* shows particularly a 'biblical style' of writing, especially influenced by Jeremiah's prophetic warnings and Stephen the Martyr's speeches in Acts, and the work is also an example of the type of 'providential history' produced by early medieval writers like Bede. According to Columbanus, Gildas communicated with a British scholar named *Uinniau* or 'Finnio' (possibly Finnian of Clonard), who may have established in Ireland Gildas's reputation for monastic discipline. Two later chronicles disagree over Gildas's death date, the ***Annales Cambriae*** recording the year as 570 while the *Annals of Tigernach* dating it to 569. His feast day is 29 January.

Many people have attempted to use Gildas' writings to write the history of Britain in the fifth and sixth centuries and, in particular, to write the history of King **Arthur**. However, it should be noted that not only does Gildas never mention Arthur (he and Guinevere do appear in Caradoc's *Life of Gildas*), but that Gildas does not ever purport to be writing a history or chronicle of his own day. The *De Excidio* is, rather, in the form of an epistle (like the *Fragmenta*) and seldom mentions specific names, places and events. The exception is for his own time, which he says is noted by the tyranny of five British kings: Constantine of **Dumnonia**, Aurelius Caninus, Vortipor of the ***Demetae*** and Maglocunus. The last is almost certainly **Maelgwn**, king of **Gwynedd**. Attempts to date Gildas more securely by using Badon, Maelgwn and the annals have not been convincing.

See also Brittonic Age; Literature.

Further Reading

Higham, N. J. 1994. *The English Conquest: Gildas and Britain in the Fifth Century*. Manchester University Press.

Lapidge, Michael, and David Dumville (eds.). 1984. *Gildas: New Approaches*. Boydell.

Snyder, Christopher A. 1998. *An Age of Tyrants: Britain and the Britons, AD 400–600*. Penn State Press.

———. 2003. *The Britons*. The Peoples of Europe Series. Blackwell.

Winterbottom, Michael (ed. and tr.). 1978. *Gildas: The Ruin of Britain and Other Works*. Phillimore.

Christopher A. Snyder

Glastonbury

Glastonbury is a small town in Somerset, England, with a long history and a vast accumulation of legend. It is cradled in a cluster of hills overlooking level country. During the last pre-Christian centuries, and early in the Christian era, the hill-cluster was almost surrounded by water and could be reached by vessels navigating the river Brue from the Bristol Channel. The highest of the hills is the Tor, a whaleback formation rising a little over five hundred feet above sea level, with terracing (variously explained) around the sides, and a medieval tower on top.

Glastonbury's nucleus, and its original *raison-d'être* as a town, is its Benedictine Abbey. This was the successor of British and **Saxon** monasteries on the same site. There was perhaps an affiliated community on the Tor. The origins can be traced back to the sixth century AD and may have been earlier. According to legend, they were much earlier. Traces of Roman buildings have been found in the neighbourhood. A chalybeate spring below the Tor, now enclosed in a garden and known as Chalice Well, is apparently mentioned in the Grail romance *Perlesvaus*.

Prehistoric Glastonbury is glimpsed through archaeology. **La Tène** objects are associated with a small Celtic population inhabiting 'lake-villages' in the adjacent waters. Nothing shows their relationship, if any, with the almost insular hill-cluster, though there is some evidence for its having had religious significance. The abbey's medieval chronicles make the first Christian settlement contemporary with at least one of the lake-villages. Here, the newcomers are led by Joseph of Arimathea, the wealthy convert who laid the body of Christ in the tomb. Reputedly, he came to Britain with several companions in AD 63 and formed a small community on the future site of the abbey.

15. Glastonbury Abbey, Glastonbury, Somerset, United Kingdom.

This tradition portrays Christian Glastonbury as beginning during the apostolic era. While it cannot be accepted as serious history, it is on record during the Middle Ages (unlike a modern fancy that Jesus himself was here with Joseph, on a previous visit). The Joseph theme is involved in some way with romances of the Grail, which introduce him as its first custodian and have him bring the sacred vessel to Britain, though the relation between the different stories is uncertain.

The Glastonbury Joseph legend, and others that made the place extremely ancient, arose from the fact that the first Christian building on the site really was so old that eventually no one knew who had put it there. By the time **William of Malmesbury** tried to write the abbey's history (c.1130), it was called simply 'the Old Church'. It was a wattle-built structure, with reinforcements of lead. Because of its age and anonymity, stories gathered around it and continued to grow, some as monastic propaganda, some with elements of reality.

The place name 'Glastonbury' is puzzling. A Celtic root *Glasto*, meaning 'woad', may have designated this as a place where woad grew (i.e. 'the woad place). The modern English form derives from Old English *Glastingburi/Glæstingeberia*, 'the fortress of the people living at Glaston'. The name *Glastonia* is also recorded early. A **Welsh** name, *Ynys-witrin*, 'the Isle of Glass', may have resulted from a misunderstanding of the first syllable, but this etymology is open to question. Wherever the 'glass' notion came from, it opened up possibilities for the evocation of magic and mystery, preparing the way for Glastonbury's acquisition of a more resonant name, **Avalon**.

'Avalon' means 'apple-place' and is attached to an otherworldly island where, according to legend, the wounded **Arthur** was taken after his last battle. About 1130, the Welsh hagiographer Caradoc of Llancarfan gave an account of Arthur visiting Glastonbury, which connected him with it before his passing, and in 1191 the monks took a momentous further step by announcing that they had exhumed his bones in their own graveyard. It followed that the Isle of Avalon, his last destination, was no Celtic fairyland. It was simply Glastonbury, or rather the quasi-insular hill-cluster in which the abbey and the town lay.

Arthur's grave is usually, though not unanimously, dismissed as a hoax, contrived to enhance the abbey's prestige and attract money that was needed for rebuilding after a fire. Whatever its real nature, the discovery was accepted as genuine during the Middle Ages, and 'Avalon survived as an alternative name for Glastonbury. It survives to this day, with a romantic aura still clinging to it.

Glastonbury Abbey became the greatest and richest in England, or an equal-first with Westminster. It maintained an important school and a famous library, and owned the land for miles around. The monks and their tenants carried out reclamation work in the waterlogged levels, embanked the river to prevent flooding, and held back the Bristol Channel with sea walls. Popular superstition came to venerate a tree on one of the hills, the Holy Thorn, an unusual hawthorn that blossomed at Christmas. It became part of the Joseph story, having sprung from his staff when he drove it into the ground. Descendants still exist, correctly blooming round about Christmas. They resemble trees found in Palestine and Syria. Some pilgrim or crusader may have brought back the original parent.

Thanks to the abbey's antiquity and the Arthurian halo, it flourished as a sort of national shrine till its dissolution by Henry VIII in 1539. The last abbot, Richard Whiting, was executed with two companions on trumped-up charges. The buildings passed into private ownership, were used as a quarry for building materials and survive today only as fragmentary though deeply impressive ruins.

The last survivor of the community, Austin Ringwode, is said to have prophesied that Glastonbury would rise again. The fact that it did, after centuries of silence, is unavoidably part of the story. Unlike other defunct abbeys, Glastonbury came back to life, though not as the prophet would have imagined. In 1908, the Church of England acquired the site, and subsequent decades saw a series of developments inspired by its rebirth. A revival of pilgrimage and excavations shedding light on the early history were doubtless foreseeable. Not foreseeable was a Glastonbury Festival of music and drama, organised by the composer Rutland Boughton and publicised by Bernard Shaw and other eminent supporters. The later twentieth century brought a new festival, perhaps best described as pop-mystical, which has become a recurrent event and internationally famous. It was launched on a farm some distance from the town, but it was always the Glastonbury Festival and so, unequivocally, it remains.

Meanwhile, a medley of fantasies and 'New Age' activities made Glastonbury unique. It harboured enthusiasts who claimed to see signs of the zodiac in the surrounding country. Others announced that the true deity of the place was not God but 'the Goddess' and founded a temple for her. There were many more fantasies. Happenings like these showed a continuing fascination at work, taking numerous forms and manifestly far more than an afterglow. The causes are a legitimate object of inquiry. They have even been detected in the configuration of the landscape.

See also Brittonic Age; Britons; Literature; Monasticism.

Further Reading

Ashe, Geoffrey. 1984. *Avalonian Quest*. Fontana.
——— (ed.). 1968. *The Quest for Arthur's Britain*. Pall Mall.
Benham, Patrick. 2006. *The Avalonians* (2nd edn.). Gothic Image Publications.
Carley, James P. 1988. *Glastonbury Abbey*. Boydell & Brewer.
Scott, John. 1981. *The Early History of Glastonbury*. Boydell & Brewer.

Geoffrey Ashe

Glendalough

Glendalough, the 'valley of the two lakes' (*Glenn dá Locha*), is situated approximately eight miles north of Rathdrum in County Wicklow, Ireland. The original monastery was founded by St. **Kevin** (Coemgen) and was one of the most important Irish monastic houses in the early Middle Ages. Because of the sanctity of its founder, it soon became a famous pilgrimage destination; seven visits to Glendalough were reckoned to be the equivalent to one pilgrimage to Rome. This fame persisted right through the centuries (in his *Félire* written c. 800, Óengus the **Culdee** described Glendalough as 'the sanctuary of the Western world') and even today Glendalough is one of Ireland's main tourist attractions.

Although today Glendalough appears to be isolated and off the beaten track, it was originally at a junction of important roadways and so was a well-chosen site for communications in all directions. It eventually became a large and prosperous monastery, but as land suitable for farming in the valley is limited by the surrounding hills and the lakes, it is unlikely that the monks could have been entirely self-sufficient.

Pilgrims approached the monastic complex in Glendalough by means of 'Coemgen's Road'. This roadway was developed from trackways going back to Neolithic times and the enormous effort the builders put into its construction in order to provide a solid road-bed all year round suggests how importantly they viewed the journey to the monastery and the relics of the saint.

There is a whole complex of monastic buildings in the area, dating from the eleventh and twelfth centuries, but standing on the site of earlier buildings. The gateway, which originally marked the entrance to the monastic sanctuary, is the only surviving example in Ireland. The round tower, which is one of the finest in Ireland and stands just over 98 feet (30 metres) high, dates from the late tenth or early eleventh century. The cathedral is the largest of Glendalough's churches. It was dedicated to Sts. Peter and Paul and the oldest parts of the building also date from the late tenth or early eleventh century. St Kevin's Cross now stands in the cemetery; it was carved from a single block of granite and stands about 10 feet (3 metres) high. It is unusual among High Crosses because the ring remains solid and is not perforated. St Kevin's Church is a unique building, which combines a small round tower, nearly 16 feet (5 metres) high, with the church. The original building probably goes back to the late tenth century. St Mary's Church stands outside the main monastic enclosure and may have been built originally for nuns (as at **Clonmacnois**). Reefert Church is the site of royal burials, as Glendalough was the cemetery of the kings of **Leinster**: Óengus the Culdee called it 'the cemetery of the west of the world' (Stokes 1905). St Saviour's Church dates from probably the twelfth or thirteenth century and is connected with St. Laurence O'Toole, who was abbot of Glendalough and archbishop of **Dublin** in the twelfth century. There are also various sites in the valley traditionally associated with St. Kevin and popular with pilgrims through the ages: Kevin's Cell, Kevin's Bed and Kevin's Well.

See also Art and Architecture; Celtic Christianity; Gaels; Monasticism.

Further Reading

Hughes, Kathleen, and Ann Hamlin. 1977. *The Modern Traveller to the Early Irish Church*. SPCK.

MacShamhráin, A. S. 1989. 'Prosopographia Glindelachensis: The Monastic Church of Glendalough and Its Community, 6th to 13th Centuries'. *Journal of the Royal Society of Antiquaries of Ireland* 119: 79–97.

Plummer, Charles (ed. and tr.). 1922. 'Life of Coemgen (II)'. Pp.127–150 in *Lives of Irish Saints*. Clarendon Press.

Stokes, Whitley (ed. and tr.). 1905. *The Martyrology of Oengus the Culdee (Félire Óengusso Céli Dé)*. Harrison and Sons.

Patricia Rumsey

Gloucester

Gloucester, a town near the **Welsh** border on the river Severn, began as a Roman fortress and town and continued as a thriving trading centre throughout the Middle Ages. The early history of the site includes the fort at Kingsholm, which was founded in AD 49, as well as a subsequent legionary fortress which was established further south a decade later. Though there was a re-stationing of legions after this point, by the end of the first century a veteran colony was established at Gloucester. Known as *Glevum*, and founded as a town in the AD 90s, material evidence for the Roman occupation includes remains of the settlement's walls, pottery, tile and brick kilns, and a putative temple; though inscriptions seem to be overall lacking, the remains also include a couple of notable altars.

After the Roman withdrawal, **Britons** continued to occupy the forum area, replacing stone buildings with timber, and there is some evidence of both local and imported pottery. The Christian population included one prominent member buried in a timber mausoleum beneath the later Saxon chapel of St. Mary de Lode. Following the Battle of **Dyrham** in 577/578, the West Saxons took control of the region. In 681, the Abbey of St. Peter was founded under Osric (his sister Kyneburga became its first abbess), assisting in the town's revival and considerable growth. The abbey was replaced in the late eleventh century by the cathedral founded by Abbot Serlo and consecrated in 1100. Considerable Gothic additions, as well as the shrine of Edward II, were made in the thirteenth century. The abbey's foundation, which attracted pilgrims on account of its shrine containing the remains of St. **Oswald**, assisted in the town's increased industrial and market activity, becoming a burgh in the late ninth century, with a mint by the tenth century.

In 1085, Gloucester became the site where the ***Domesday Book*** was ordered to be compiled under **William I**. By the late eleventh century, a timber castle was constructed, replaced by one of stone in the twelfth, as its precarious position near the border with Wales made a strong garrison a necessity. Its location in the Cotswalds also served to contribute to Gloucester's thriving wool market, with its position along the Severn providing both fishing and trading industries. Robert, first earl of Gloucester, was the illegitimate son of **Henry I,** who played a major role in the war between Stephen I and Matilda. He aided the future king **Henry II** and was a patron of **Geoffrey of Monmouth**, who depicted Gloucester as a town of great import and antiquity among the Britons.

See also Roman Britain; Romano-British Towns.

Further Reading

Baker, N. 2004. *Urban Growth and the Medieval Church: Gloucester and Worcester*. Ashgate.

Heighway, Carolyn. 1987. *Anglo-Saxon Gloucestershire*. Sutton.

Hurst, H. R. 1986. *Gloucester: The Roman and Later Defences*. Gloucester Archaeological Publications.

Anne Sassin

Godfrey Haraldsson

Godfrey and Magnus were two brothers, sons of a man named Harald and leaders of a fleet of Danish **Vikings**. They started out as raiders in Wales, Ireland and Scotland. **Welsh** Chronicles name them first, placing Magnus at Anglesey in northern Wales in 971. The ***Annales Cambriae*** tell us that Godfrey son of Harald collected a Danegeld from Anglesey the next year. Unfortunately, no contemporary sources say where their initial bases were or where the men came from originally. There was no single power in the region when the sons of Harald arrived, but descendants of Godfrey of **Dublin** were active there. But the Hiberno-Scandinavian family disappears from the sources just as the Haraldssons rise to power, which is surely not a coincidence. Magnus attacked **Limerick** in 974, and the two brothers continued to harass Wales. Over the next several years, they allied themselves with and fought against various Welsh princes. In 982, Godfrey raided **St David's** and other sites in Dyfed.

By 984, the Haraldssons were powerful enough to attract the attention of **Brian Boru**, king of **Munster** at this time and, later, king of Ireland. He had captured the Hiberno-Scandinavian town of Waterford, and it was there, according to the *Annals of Inisfallen*, the men met. They agreed to attack Brian's rivals in Leinster, the Haraldssons by sea and Brian's troops by land. The Haraldsson family and the descendants of Brian, the Ua Briain, remained allies for nearly two centuries.

The Haraldssons had other Irish allies as well. According to the *Banshenchas*, a daughter of Harald son of Godfrey (possibly a mistake for Godfrey son of Harald) married a king from Ossory, and her son became king a few years after his father's death. Her name is a Christian one, so she must have converted at some stage, possibly in order to secure the marriage. Whether or not her father ever converted is unknown.

Magnus disappears from the historical records after the meeting with Brian Boru in 984, though his death is not mentioned in any contemporary source. In 987, Godfrey attacked the Isle of Man alone, and over the next few years he continued to attack Anglesey and to demand tribute from its rulers. By 989, Godfrey Haraldsson controlled Anglesey, Man and some of the Hebrides. When he was killed in the kingdom of the **Dál Riata** in Scotland, the ***Annals of Ulster*** call him 'king of the islands of the Foreigners'.

Godfrey's descendants continued to rule and to be active in the Irish Sea. Godfrey's son Ragnall, like his father called 'king of the Isles', died in Ireland in 1005. Another son, Lagmann, seems to have inherited the title and was active in Normandy. Olaf son of Lagmann was killed at the Battle of Clontarf fighting on Dublin's side, possibly on behalf of *jarl* Signurd of Orkney. Godfrey's grandson Echmarcach was a king in Galloway in Scotland, and Echmarcach's grandson Olaf died fighting in the same region (though his obit does not call him a king).

See also Gaels; Kings; Kingship and Scots.

Further Reading

Hudson, Benjamin T. 2005. *Viking Pirates and Christian Princes: Dynasty, Religion, and Empire in the North Atlantic*. Oxford University Press.

Dumville, David N. (ed. and tr.). 2002. *Annales Cambriae, AD 682–954: Texts A-C in Parallel*. Cambridge ASNAC.

Mac Airt, Seán (ed. and tr.). 1951. *The Annals of Inisfallen*. Dublin Institute for Advanced Studies.
Mac Airt, Seán, and Gearóid Mac Niocaill (eds. and tr.). 1983. *The Annals of Ulster: To AD 1131*. Dublin Institute for Advanced Studies.

Mary Valante

Gododdin

Gododdin, a northern British kingdom of the **Brittonic Age**, was the successor of the **Iron Age** tribe the ***Votadini***, whose territory covered the Borders region of north-east England and south-east Scotland. Extending west to the kingdom of **Strathclyde**, south to the kingdom of Bryneich (**Northumbria**), and possibly north to Stirling, the latter which was the centre of the sub-kingdom Manau (Manaw), the kingdom was focused especially on the Lothians. Its name is possibly derived from the **Brythonic** word for the *Votadini*, the *Guotodin*. By AD 470 the Votadinian lands seem to have come under the control of Gododdin, following the death of the legendary **Coel Hen** ('Ole King Cole'), who may have ruled as an over-king over the former northern provinces. Cunedda, legendary founder of the kingdom of **Gwynedd**, is also believed to have been a Manau Gododdin warlord, who migrated south-west with his fellow Votadinians.

Gododdin is perhaps best known through the poem 'Y Gododdin', attributed to the bard Aneirin in the late sixth century. This poem gives an account of the feast given by Mynyddog, king of Gododdin, to his warriors on the eve of the Battle of **Catraeth**. Aneirin depicts this British raid on the Angles as a devastating defeat for Mynyddog and the **Britons**. Catraeth has since been identified by most scholars as Catterick, Yorkshire, though there has been some debate over both the date of the poem and the identification of this Gododdin leader (see Koch 1997).

Gododdin does not seem to offer substantial evidence for occupation via archaeology, although there are sites which suggest settlement in the period, including **hillforts** of which many were Iron Age in origin and later reoccupied, such as Crock Cleugh and Ruberslaw in Roxburghshire; Hownam Law in the Borders; and the Dod, Tweed basin, whose rectangular buildings, including an apse-ended one interpreted as a possible church, suggest an important post-Roman site. Some of the best evidences for timber halls in the period also come from the region, including Doon Hill, **Yeavering** and Dunbar. Being so close to Pictland and possibly seeing some occupation by the **Picts** for a time, Pictish evidence can also be found, such as symbol stones from Edinburgh and Borthwick, as well as place names in the Lothians (e.g. Pitcox and Pittendreich). Evidence of Christianity in the region besides putative churches such as **Traprain Law** and the Dod is present, though the religion was possibly not that wide-ranging at first, with both long-cist cemeteries (e.g. Parkburn) and memorial stones (e.g. at Peeble and Yarrow) having been found.

The hillfort of Traprain Law in East Lothian served as a major centre for the *Votadini* from the first century onwards, from which the famous Traprain Law hoard came. Discovered in 1919, this hoard was thought to have been a Roman payment to the tribe and consisted of over one hundred pieces, including bowls, cups and coins (some with Christian iconography), which were likely deposited in the early fifth century when the fort saw its final refortification. Although it has been suggested that Traprain Law served as the early capital of Gododdin before it was replaced by Din Eidyn and saw some Pictish occupation, it is possible that the cultural interaction detected in artefacts (e.g. Pictish silver chains) may have been through simple trade, rather than occupation. Edinburgh, or Din Eidyn as it is cited in 'Y Gododdin', seems to have become the kingdom's stronghold since at least the sixth century, and excavations from the midden at Castle Rock have been interpreted as evidence of occupation both during and after the Roman period. This was based on finds (e.g. double-sided composite comb) of early medieval date, and though the site has been assumed as a thriving nuclear fort and royal residence of the period, the oldest remaining part of the present castle and site is the twelfth-century St Margaret's Chapel. After the Anglian advance into **Bernicia** in the sixth century, the **Angles** had continued to press north, killing the Gododdin men at Catraeth and, according to the ***Annals of Ulster***, Din Eidyn may have fallen to them in 638, soon after which Gododdin came under the rule of Bernicia, becoming part of the kingdom of **Northumbria** and falling under English control.

See also Warfare and Weapons.

Further Reading

Davies, Wendy. 1992. *Wales in the Early Middle Ages*. Leicester University Press.

Driscoll, S. T., and P. A. Yeoman. 1997. *Excavations Within Edinburgh Castle in 1988–1991.* Society of the Antiquaries of Scotland, Monograph 12.
Koch, John T. 1997. *The Gododdin of Aneirin: Text and Context from Dark Age Northern Britain.* Cardiff.
Morris, John. 1995. *The Age of Arthur: A History of the British Isles from 350 to 650.* Phoenix Press.
Snyder, Christopher A. 1998. *An Age of Tyrants: Britain and the Britons, AD 400–600.* Sutton.
———. 2003. *The Britons.* Peoples of Europe Series. Blackwell.

Anne Sassin

Godwin

Godwin, earl of **Wessex,** was the most powerful earl in the English court in 1051 and was the father of the future king **Harold II**. He possessed a vast earldom stretching from **Kent** to **Cornwall** along the south coast of England. His father was named Wulfnoth, a thegn who held an estate in Compton, Sussex, which passed to Godwin according to the will of Æthelred II's son Æthelstan the Ætheling (1012–1015). Both Stenton and Barlow identified Godwin's father with Wulfnoth Cild, a Sussex thegn who, according to the ***Anglo-Saxon Chronicle***, ravaged the south coast of England with a fleet of twenty ships in 1009 after being accused (possibly of treason) by Eadric Streona's brother, Earl Brihtric.

Godwin was also the father-in-law of King **Edward the Confessor**. Rumoured to have been responsible for the blinding and subsequent death of Edward's brother, Alfred the Ætheling, Godwin's power prompted his disobedience to the Crown through his refusal to punish his **Dover** subjects for an altercation with some of the king's French relatives. Feeling threatened by his own actions, Godwin raised an army against the king. This army, combined with those Godwin's sons, Swein and Harold, took Edward by surprise, forcing the king to swell his own ranks with the aid of three powerful earls, Leofric, Siward and Ralf. The disastrous consequences of in-fighting between all of the most powerful earls of the country were realised and the armies never met. Rather than opening the borders to invasion, each side gave hostages as collateral to ensure that Godwin and his sons appeared in London to answer the charges brought against them by the king.

As the court date neared, Godwin's followers recognised his weakened position and the superior numbers of Edward's army, some of whom came from Godwin's own territories. Disheartened, Godwin's remaining loyal retainers dispersed. Godwin, along with his sons Swein and Harold and their immediate families, was sent into exile. Queen Edith also suffered from her father's disobedience and was dismissed into retirement at Wherwell Abbey.

In 1052, Godwin, learning from his earlier error of using indigenous Englishmen to fight the English king, hired a band of mercenary sailors to attack England. The people of England, in their growing resentment of the **Normans**, were more disposed to welcome Godwin and offered their support to his campaign (especially Kent, Surrey, **Sussex** and Hastings.) He stealthily entered England to gain assurances and then retreated to exile in Flanders. The seafaring force of **Edward the** Confessor grew tired of the delays in action, abandoned their post and left the south coast of England undefended. Godwin used this to his advantage and began harrying the coastal inhabitants of the Isle of Wight, Portland and further west. There, he joined forces with his son, Harold, and began winning the support of the coastal communities, eventually extending as far as **London**. Realising the danger in the situation, Edward sued for peace. Godwin was restored to the 'full friendship' of the Crown, returned to his earldom and was restored of all his and his family's confiscated possessions. All the Normans that had recently come to England, excepting a few chosen by the king and believed loyal to England, were sent into exile, along with the archbishop of **Canterbury** and the bishop of **Dorchester**. The property of the archbishop and bishop was divided between Godwin, Harold and the queen, who returned from retirement.

Godwin died on 15 April 1053, leaving a powerful family legacy to his son, Harold Godwinsson, that continued until the family's ultimate overthrow at the hands of **William the Conqueror**.

Further Reading

Barlow, Frank. 2002. *The Godwins: The Rise and Fall of a Noble Dynasty.* Longman.
John, Eric. 1991. 'The End of Anglo-Saxon England'. Pp.214–239 in *The Anglo-Saxons.* Edited by James Campbell. Penguin Books.
Mason, Emma. 2003. *The House of Godwine: The History of Dynasty.* Hambledon Press.
Stenton, F. M. 1971. *Anglo-Saxon England.* Clarendon Press.

Walker, Ian. 1997. *Harold: The Last Anglo-Saxon King.* Sutton.

Britt Rothauser

Goidelic

See Irish Language.

Grubenhäuser

The *grubenhaus* ('pit-house') is a type of sunken-floor building found in both England and on the continent. Their main period of construction lies between the fifth and the late seventh centuries, but later examples of buildings with sunken features occur in the late-**Saxon** period at sites such as **London**, Thetford, **York** and **Chester**. These show differing features and can be found down to the twelfth century, but they differ from their early **Anglo-Saxon** predecessors.

The majority of *grubenhäuser* are identified from the sunken element, which tends to be sub-rectangular, measuring about 129 square feet (12 square metres) in area and up to 1.6 feet (0.5 metres) in depth. This lay beneath a timber superstructure, which is often represented by a pair of post holes opposite one another on the short sides of the pit, for uprights to take a ridge-pole, though there can be more post-holes (up to six) and also post-holes at the corners. Classic examples include some from **Mucking, Essex**; **Dorchester on Thames**, Oxfordshire; and **West Stow**, Suffolk.

Since *grubenhäuser* were first identified at Sutton Courtenay, Berks, in the 1920s, there has been considerable debate about their use. Frequently they have been seen as buildings with low roofs into which you step down to the floor level. This interpretation was believed to have been supported by the fill of the sunken element, which included pottery and bones. It can now be seen, however, that the contents were largely deposited after the abandonment of the building, and that these structures had suspended floors, the area underneath being useful for storage, particularly of perishable food. On account of the weaving equipment found in several buildings, it has been suggested that they were mostly weaving sheds, but this also cannot be supported as a universal explanation, though some may have been used for this purpose.

See also Art and Architecture; Houses.

Further Reading

Rahtz, P. A. 1976. 'Buildings and Rural Settlement'. Pp. 49–98 in *The Archaeology of Anglo-Saxon England.* Edited by David M. Wilson. Methuen.

Tipper, J. 2004. *The Grubenhaus in Anglo-Saxon England.* Landscape Research Centre.

Lloyd Laing

Gruffudd ap Cynan (d. 1137)

During the last third of his life Gruffudd ap Cynan (d. 1137) was king of **Gwynedd** and brought peace and prosperity to this land. He is particularly remarkable as being the subject of one of the earliest medieval biographies, the **Welsh**-language *Historia Gruffed vab Kenan*. Gruffudd claimed descent from **Rhodri Mawr**, king of Gwynedd between 844 and 878. Gruffudd was born in **Dublin** in 1054 and was the son of Cynan ab Iago and Ragnhildr, the daughter of Olaf Sihtricson, the Scandinavian king of Dublin.

Gruffudd's grandfather, Iago, had been king of Gwynedd before **Gruffudd ap Llywelyn** defeated him in 1039 and exiled Iago's son Cynan to Ireland. Gruffudd made several efforts to regain political control of Gwynedd for his family line before finally succeeding. In 1075, he sailed with supporters from Dublin to the island of Anglesey off the north-west corner of Wales to fight against Trahaearn ap Caradog from Arwystli and Cynwrig ap Rhiwallon from Powys. He was initially successful, killing Cynwrig in battle and defeating Trahaearn. However, a resurgence of support for Trahaearn then forced Gruffudd to flee to **Wexford** in Ireland. He tried again in 1081, this time in alliance with **Rhys ap Tewdwr**, and defeated and killed Trahaearn at the decisive battle of Mynydd Carn. However, shortly after taking control of Gwynedd, Gruffudd was captured by the Anglo-Norman Robert of Rhuddlan and spent at least the next twelve years as a prisoner of Robert's overlord, Earl Hugh of Chester before escaping.

Circumstances near the end of the eleventh century allowed Gruffudd to finally attain his goal. The Anglo-Norman earls of Chester and Shrewsbury invaded north-western Wales and forced Gruffudd and his ally Cadwgan ap Bleddyn to retreat to Anglesey and then to Ireland. However, a surprise attack near Anglesey by King Magnus Bareleg of Norway killed Earl Hugh of Shrewsbury, creating a power vacuum, which benefited Gruffudd. By 1099, he had control of Gwynedd and he ruled it successfully until his death in 1137. The minority of the young earl of Chester between 1101 and 1114 and the generally good relations with the English king **Henry I** favoured Gruffudd's rule. The English king apparently granted him Llŷn, Eifinionydd, Ardudwy and Arllechwedd, all districts adjacent to his core holdings of Anglesey and the coastal district opposite it. Henry I twice led campaigns against Gruffudd in 1114 and 1121, but the latter wisely submitted to the English king and agreed to pay tribute.

Gruffudd's wife was Angharad, the daughter of Owain ab Edwin, ruler over Dyffryn Clwyd in north-eastern Wales. Their children included three sons: Cadwallon, Owain Gwynedd and Cadwaladr. While he was alive Gruffudd granted his sons territories peripheral to his core holdings. Towards the end of his life he was blind. Gruffudd died in 1137 at the age of eighty-two, and he was buried in the cathedral at **Bangor**. His chief poet, Meilyr Brydydd, celebrated his accomplishments in a formal elegy. A Latin version of his biography was probably composed in the mid-twelfth century during the reign of his son Owain Gwynedd, both to celebrate Gruffudd's accomplishments and to buttress Owain's rule. During the thirteenth century this Latin work was used as the basis for the *Historia Gruffud vab Kenan*. Thanks to Gruffudd's persistent efforts, his dynasty supplied the rulers of Gwynedd until the English king Edward I conquered Wales in 1283 and suppressed the native Welsh ruling families.

See also Kings and Kingship.

Further Reading

Evans, D. Simon. 1990. *A Medieval Prince of Wales: The Life of Gruffudd ap Cynan*. Llanerch Enterprises.

Maund, Kari. (ed.). 1996. *Gruffudd ap Cynan: A Collaborative Biography*. Boydell Press.

Pryce, Huw. 2004. 'Gruffudd ap Cynan'. Pp.133–135 in *Oxford Dictionary of National Biography*, vol. XXIV. Oxford University Press.

Frederick Suppe

Gruffudd ap Llywelyn (d. 1063)

Gruffudd ap Llywelyn was ruler over the **Welsh** kingdoms of **Gwynedd** and **Powys** and managed to gain power over all of Wales for eight years before his death in 1063 – something achieved by no other medieval Welsh ruler. He was son of Llywelyn ap Seisyllt, who had been king of Gwynedd between 1018 and 1023, and was grandson of Maredudd ab Owain, the king of **Deheubarth** between 986 and 999. In 1039, Gruffudd seized power in Gwynedd from Iago ab Idwal and drove the latter's son Cynan into exile in Ireland. From this time Gruffudd also ruled Powys. The next year he defeated the men of **Mercia** at the battle of Rhyd y Groes ('ford of the cross') on the river Severn – the first of many efforts to extend his power into the Anglo-Welsh borderlands.

For the next fifteen years, Gruffudd strove to gain control of Deheubarth, fighting first against Hywel ab Edwin and then after 1044 against Gruffudd ap Rhydderch. During this period, he experienced mixed success. In 1042, he was briefly captured by Scandinavian raiders. In 1046, he allied for about a year with the English earl, Swein Godwineson, while campaigning in southern Wales. The next year he experienced a major setback when the men of Ystrad Tywy, the south-west Welsh district next to **Dyfed**, killed 140 men of his bodyguard or *teulu*. Finally, in 1055 he killed Gruffudd ap Rhydderch, who then ruled both Deheubarth and Morgannwg. From this point on Gruffudd held sway over all of Wales.

In 1055, Aelfgar, son of Earl Leofric of Mercia, was forced into Irish exile by the political competition among the rival English families of earls. Aelfgar returned from Ireland with a fleet recruited from the Scandinavians of Dublin and allied himself with Gruffudd. The two allies successfully attacked the March border town and castle of Hereford and killed the earl of Hereford, Ralph of Mantes. Earl **Harold Godwinsson** of **Wessex** reacted by refortifying Hereford and installing there his warlike cleric, Leofgar, as the new bishop of Hereford. However, when Leofgar led an army against Gruffudd in 1056, the English forces were utterly defeated. According to the twelfth century collector of stories, Walter Map, this situation was resolved by a peace negotiation between Gruffudd and the English king, **Edward the Confessor**, which occurred at Awst on the river Severn. At some time during this period, Gruffudd gained control over a number of manors along the northern **Marches,** which had previously been English, most notably Bishopstree near Mold.

Earl Aelfgar died in 1062. Deprived of this alliance, Gruffudd was more vulnerable. That year Earl Harold attacked Gruffudd at his court in Rhuddlan, but he temporarily escaped. However, Harold and his brother, Earl Tostig, then blockaded and besieged Gruffudd at his retreat in the mountains of north-west Wales. Gruffudd was finally betrayed by some of his associates, who beheaded him and gave his head to Earl Harold. The earl then presented Gruffudd's head and the figurehead of his ship to King Edward.

Gruffudd had married Ealdgyth, the daughter of his ally Aelfgar, and by her had a daughter named Nest, who later married the eleventh-century Marcher baron Osbern fitz Richard. However, Gruffudd left no sons to carry on his political dynasty, so his territorial sway over Wales disintegrated. Gwynedd and Powys were given to his half-brothers, Bleddyn ap Cynfyn and Rhiwallon ap Cynfyn. Deheubarth became the focus for intense political competition until **Rhys ap Tewdwr** gained control of it in 1081. Gruffudd's widow, Ealdgyth, married her husband's nemesis, Earl Harold. Although Gruffudd's political line ended with him, memories of his exploits were still current on the Marches a century after his death, with stories about him preserved by Walter Map.

See also Kings and Kingship; Warfare and Weapons.

Further Reading

Maund, Kari. 2000. *The Welsh Kings: The Medieval Rulers of Wales*. Tempus.

Walker, David. 2004. 'Gruffudd ap Llywelyn'. Pp.136–137 in *Oxford Dictionary of National Biography*, vol. XXIV. Oxford University Press.

Frederick Suppe

Gruffudd ap Rhys (d.1137)

Gruffudd ap Rhys (d.1137) was the son of **Rhys ap Tewdwr**, who established the final royal dynasty of **Deheubarth** before his death in battle in 1093. For most of his adult life Gruffudd strove vainly against both the English and **Welsh** rivals to regain his father's position and territories. However, after his death his youngest son, 'the Lord Rhys', reached a political understanding with the English king **Henry II** and became the greatest ruler of Deheubarth.

After Gruffudd's father, Rhys ap Tewdwr, was killed in 1093, the family's political position reached a nadir. Rhys's daughter Nest, reputed to be the most beautiful woman in Wales, married Gerald of Windsor, an Anglo-Norman who was steward of Pembroke Castle, which had been built in the south-west corner of Deheubarth by Arnulf de Montgomery. Rhys's son Gruffudd fled to Ireland, where he spent the next decade in exile. He returned to south-west Wales in 1113, staying intermittently with kinsmen or with Gerald of Windsor. In 1115, he was accused of fomenting rebellion against the English king **Henry I** and therefore fled, together with his brother Hywel, for refuge with King **Gruffudd ap Cynan** in **Gwynedd**. Henry's agents persuaded Gruffudd ap Cynan to hand over his guest to the English, but the latter escaped, first finding sanctuary in the church at Aberdaron on the Llŷn peninsula and then fleeing south to Ystrad Tywi. Once there, Gruffudd ap Rhys rallied many young Welsh warriors who were disaffected with Welsh leaders in alliance with the Anglo-Norman invaders to join him in attacking the Anglo-Norman hold on Deheubarth. His forces burned Narberth Castle, attacked Llandovery and forced William of **London** to abandon his castle at Ogmore. However, his attack on the motte-and-bailey castle at Aberystwyth failed and his followers then dispersed.

The next dozen years of his career are obscure, but by 1127 he held only a small remnant of Deheubarth, the commote of Caeo in Cantref Mawr given to him by King Henry I, though still maintaining a claim to the whole of Deheubarth. That same year he fled briefly to Ireland because of an accusation against him by his Anglo-Norman neighbours. After Henry I died in 1135, English political weakness encouraged a major uprising by many Welsh leaders. Gruffudd ap Rhys was allied with Gruffudd ap Cynan and his sons in participating in this rebellion. Gruffudd ap Rhys had married Gwenllian, daughter of the king of Gwynedd, and she led Welsh troops against Cydweli (Kidwelly) Castle, where she was killed in battle. Shortly thereafter, however, Gruffudd ap Rhys and two of Gruffudd ap Cynan's sons won a major victory at the Battle of Crug Mawr, near Cardigan, defeating Stephen, the constable of Cardigan Castle, and a force of Anglo-Normans and Flemings. During 1137, the last year of his life, Gruffudd ap Rhys led a campaign into the commote of Rhos in south-west **Dyfed**. Thus, although he spent most of his adult life in exile or as a marginal political figure, he did lay the groundwork for his four surviving sons to restore the family's control over Deheubarth. The greatest and most successful of these sons, usually known as 'the

Lord Rhys' because of his political alliance with King Henry II, ruled Deheubarth from 1155 to 1197.

See also Kings and Kingship; Warfare and Weapons.

Further Reading

Babcock, Robert. 1993. 'Imbeciles and Normans: The *Ynfydion* of Gruffudd ap Rhys Reconsidered'. *The Haskins Society Journal* IV: 1–9.
Maund, K. L. 1991. *Ireland, Wales, and England in the Eleventh Century*. The Boydell Press.
Tout, T. F., revised by Huw Pryce. 2004. 'Gruffudd ap Rhys (d.1137)'. Pp.139–140 in *Oxford Dictionary of National Biography,* vol. XXIV. Oxford University Press.

Frederick Suppe

Guthlac, Saint

See Æthelbald.

Guthram

Guthram was a **Viking** leader associated with the 'Great Heathen Army' that attacked **Anglo-Saxon** England, beginning in 866. He is associated with the end of the depredations of the Great Army, but very little is actually known about him.

In 878, Guthram's army attacked **Wessex** and its king, **Alfred** the Great, was forced to flee with his men into the far south-west. Alfred and his men, bolstered by troops from the now-defeated kingdom of **Mercia**, fought back and defeated the Danish army decisively at Edington. Alfred made peace with Guthram in the Treaty of Wedmore. Both sides agreed to a division of territory, 'Up the Thames, and then up the Lea, and along the Lea to its source, and then in a straight line to Bedford, then up the Ouse to the Wattling Street' (Attenborough 1922, 98–101). The Danes held all lands north and east of the division (the area became known as the **Danelaw**), and Alfred and the House of Wessex ruled all lands to the south. As part of the agreement, Guthram and thirty of his most prominent followers agreed to be baptised as Christians; Alfred himself sponsored Guthram.

Guthram remained in East Anglia and his forces settled down and started to farm. In 880, most of what was left of Guthram's fighting forces followed him to Carolingian Frankia. About half the force returned in 885, the rest remaining behind to raid. Guthram ignored the treaty with Alfred and attacked the Anglo-Saxon kingdom. Guthram's forces were defeated, and in 886 he and Alfred renewed the treaty. Guthram behaved himself this time and died in 890, without having attacked Alfred's lands again. No descendant of Guthram is named in future sources, so his lasting influence would appear to be limited. But Guthram set the stage for the future – the Danelaw lasted, in whole or in part, until 954 when Alfred's descendant Eadred defeated the Scandinavian King Eric of **York**. The example of Christianising the pagan enemy as a means to peace was also followed successfully by future kings from Wessex. Finally, along the borders of the Danelaw Alfred and his descendants built a series of fortifications called ***burhs*** that helped keep Wessex safe and helped push the boundary between Anglo-Saxon England and the Danelaw ever northwards.

See also Kings and Kingship; Warfare and Weapons.

Further Reading

Attenborough, F. L. 1922. *The Laws of the Earliest English Kings*. Cambridge University Press.
Bately, Janet M. 1986. *Anglo-Saxon Chronicle*. 3 MS A. Boydell and Brewer.
Graham-Campell, James. 1989. *Cultural Atlas of the Viking World*. Facts on File.
Jones, Gwyn. 1968. *A History of the Vikings*. Oxford University Press.

Mary Valante

Gwynedd

Gwynedd, along with **Powys** and **Deheubarth**, was one of the three major medieval **Welsh** kingdoms. Based on the mountains of Snowdonia and the island of Anglesey in north-west Wales, Gwynedd was established soon after the Roman withdrawal from Britain in the early fifth century. Its foundation is attributed to the shadowy Cunedda, who is said to have migrated to northern Wales with his sons from Manaw Gododdin in southern Scotland. Gwynedd was the strongest of the three major Welsh kingdoms and experienced a number of strong rulers, including two in the thirteenth century who came close to creating a unified Wales based upon Gwynedd.

The first known king of Gwynedd was **Maelgwn Gwynedd**, the great-grandson of

Cunedda according to later Welsh genealogies, who died in 547 of the plague. His dynasty ruled Gwynedd until the death of Hywel ap Rhodri in 825. Then **Merfyn Frych** ('the freckled') ap Gwriad, a man of obscure origins despite later genealogical claims, gained power and ruled until his death in 844. Merfyn's son, **Rhodri**, was later known as Mawr ('the Great'), for he also gained control of Powys in 855 and of Ceredigion and Ystrad Tywi in 872 – thus ruling most of Wales during the final five years of his life. Rhodri fended off the first **Viking** attack on his realm in 855 and died in 877 while fighting another battle against them. **Gruffudd ap Llywelyn** (d.1063) seized power in Gwynedd and Powys in 1039 and eventually ruled all of Wales during the final eight years of his life. After several decades of political competition, **Gruffudd ap Cynan** finally managed to achieve a long period of control over Gwynedd from 1099 to 1137. His son, Owain Gwynedd, solidified the family's hold over the kingdom, first by taking advantage of the period of English weakness during King **Stephen**'s reign (1135–1154) and then by submitting to the aggressive King **Henry II** after the latter's 1157 campaign into northern Wales.

After Owain's death in 1170, rival factions contended for Gwynedd, but Llywelyn ap Iorwerth gained control in 1199 and maintained it until his death in 1240. His court was at Aberffraw on the island of Anglesey and he negotiated with King John of England, being mentioned by name in article 58 of the Magna Carta. During his reign, he developed a cadre of officials and governmental institutions imitating those of England and France. His grandson, Llywelyn ap Gruffudd, ruled Gwynedd from 1255 until his defeat and death while fighting the English King Edward I in 1282. The treaty of Montgomery in 1267 had recognised Llywelyn as prince of Wales and he came very close to using the strong Gwynedd developed by his grandfather as the base for a unified Wales. The long elegy composed by the Welsh poet Gruffudd ab yr Ynad Coch to lament Llywelyn's death, with multiple lines beginning with the word 'head', recognised that he had been beheaded and that his defeat deprived Wales of its national leader. After his three Welsh wars, Edward I had complete control of Wales and the ancient kingdoms, including Gwynedd, were extinguished.

See also Kings and Kingship; Warfare and Weapons.

Further Reading

Davies, John. 1993. *A History of Wales*. Penguin Press.
Davies, Wendy. 1982. *Wales in the Early Middle Ages*. Leicester University Press.
Maund, Kari. 2000. *The Welsh Kings: The Medieval Rulers of Wales*. Tempus.
Thornton, David. 2003. *Kings, Chronologies, and Genealogies. Studies in the Political History of Early Medieval Ireland and Wales*. Prosopographica et Genealogica. The Unit for Prosopographical Research, Linacre College, Oxford University.

Frederick Suppe

Timeline

Lower Palaeolithic Period (800,000 BC)

c.500,000 BC

The earliest documented human occupation, individuals known as *Homo heidelbergensis*, at Boxgrove.

The earliest stone tools, such as Acheulian hand-axes and cleavers, appear.

Middle Palaeolithic Period (250,000 BC)

c.245,000 BC

Neanderthals and Mousterian tools first appear.

Upper Palaeolithic Period (40,000 BC)

c.25,000 BC

Modern humans (*Homo sapiens*) and composite tools first appear.

Mesolithic Period (10,000 BC)

10,000 BC

The end of the last Ice Age. Britain and Ireland are separate islands for the first time.

The first modern humans appear in Ireland.

Early Neolithic Period (4000 BC)

4000 BC

The first pottery appears in Britain, known as the Grimston-Lyles Hill tradition.

Causewayed camps appear in Britain (Windmill Hill Culture).

Middle Neolithic Period (3400 BC)

3400 BC

Decorated bowls first appear. Large hilltop enclosures first appear (e.g. Hambeldon Hill and Maiden Castle).

The construction of Newgrange.

c.3200–2400 BC

Construction of the stone monuments at Avebury.

Late Neolithic Period (3000 BC)

c.2950 BC

The first building activity at Stonehenge.

c.2700 BC

Beaker culture reaches Britain.

Early Bronze Age (2600 BC)

c.2500 BC

Copper working is introduced from the Continent.

c.2400 BC

The circle of trilithons and the circle of sarsens are erected at Stonehenge; beginning of the Wessex Culture.

2268–2251 BC

Timbers felled by a metal axe at Corlea, County Longford.

c.2000 BC

Move from inhumation to cremation. Bronze metallurgy begins in Britain.

Middle Bronze Age

1600 BC

Bronze dagger evolves into rapiers and spearheads.

Late Bronze Age

1200 BC

Introduction of Hallstatt culture to Britain.

Appearance of the first true hillforts in Britain.

Early Iron Age (700 BC)

c.650 BC

British smiths begin forging iron.

Middle Iron Age

Third century BC

La Tène style iron swords are produced in Britain.

Second century BC

Iron 'currency bars' appear.

Late Pre-Roman Iron Age

55 and 54 BC

Julius Caesar's expeditions to Britain.

50 BC

Commius flees to Britain, becomes leader of the *Atrebates*.

AD 7

Catuvellauni conquer the *Trinovantes*, and their king Cunobelinus issues coins in his name.

40/43

Death of Cunobelinus; his sons, Caratacus and Togodumnus, conquer the *Atrebates*.

Roman Period (AD 43–410)

43

Roman emperor Claudius orders the invasion of Britain, led by Aulus Pluatius.

51

Caratacus defeated in battle, betrayed by Cartimandua and sent to Rome.

60/61

Revolt of Boudica.

83

Agricola defeats Caledonians at the Battle of Mons Graupius.

122

Hadrian visits Britain and work begins on Hadrian's Wall.

140–143

Antonine conquests in Scotland, culminating in the construction of the Antonine Wall.

197/213

Britain divided into two provinces.

208–211

Campaigns of Septimius Severus in Britain.

259/260–274

Britain part of the Gallic Empire.

287

Carausius seizes Britain.

296

Britain recaptured by Constantius I.

306

Constantine I proclaimed emperor at York.

Early Christian Period

314

British bishops at the Council of Arles.

367–369

The 'barbarian conspiracy' in Britain, subsequent recovery by Count Theodosius.

383–388

Britain under the rule of Magnus Maximus.

Brittonic Age (AD 400–600)

c.402

Stilicho withdraws troops from Britain.

406–407

Marcus, Gratian and Constantine III proclaimed in Britain.

409–411

Saxons raid Britain, Britons declare their independence from Rome, and Constantine III is assassinated.

429 and c.445

St. Germanus of Auxerre visits Britain to combat Pelagianism.

431

Palladius is sent by Pope Celestine as the first bishop 'of the Irish who believe in Christ', succeeded sometime afterwards by St. Patrick.

c.449

Rebellion of Saxon mercenaries in Britain.

469

British army under Riothamus is betrayed and defeated by the Visigoths at Bourg-de-Déols.

c.485

Britons defeat the Saxons at the Battle of Badon Hill.

c.490

Ancestors of the Uí Néill conquer central Ireland.

c.529

Gildas writes *De Excidio Britanniae.*

540s

Plague in Britain and Ireland.

c.547

Death of Maelgwn, king of Gwynedd.

Accession of Ida, first king of Bernicia.

554–584

Reign of Brude mac Maelchon in Pictland.

563

St. Columba comes to Britain and founds a monastic community on Iona.

570

Death of Gildas, according to the *Annales Cambriae.*

c.572

The Battle of Catraeth.

572–579

Reign of Theodoric, king of Bernicia, enemy of Urien of Rheged.

c.574–606

Reign of Áedán mac Gabráin, king of Dál Riata.

577

The Battle of Dyrham in which, according to the *Anglo-Saxon Chronicle*, the British towns of Gloucester, Cirencester and Bath fall to the Saxons.

591

St. Columbanus, a monk from Bangor (County Down), begins founding monasteries among the Franks.

592–616

Reign of Æthelfrith, king of Bernicia and Deira.

597

Death of St. Columba on Iona and arrival of St. Augustine in Kent.

Medieval Anglo-Saxon Period (AD 600–1000)

c.600

St. Kentigern (Mungo) founds the first church in Glasgow.

601

Death of St. David, according to the *Annales Cambriae.*

603

The Battle of Degsastan, in which Áedán mac Gabráin is defeated by Æthelfrith.

c.615

The Battle of Chester, in which Æthelfrith defeats the Britons and slays 1,200 monks from Bangor.

616

The death of Æthelberht of Kent; Æthelfrith is defeated and killed by Rædwald, king of the East Angels.

616–633

Reign of Edwin, king of Northumbria.

617

Edwin defeats the last British king of Elmet and annexes his kingdom.

c.625

The deaths of Rædwald and Cadfan, king of Gwynedd.

627

The Easter baptism of Edwin of Northumbria by bishop Paulinus.

c.632

Cummian writes his letter on the Easter Controversy to Ségéne, abbot of Iona.

633

Cadwallon of Gwynedd and Penda of Mercia kill Edwin at the Battle of Hatfield Chase.

634

Cadwallon is defeated and killed by Oswald of Bernicia at the Battle of Heavenfield.

635

The foundation of the monastic community at Lindisfarne by St. Aidan.

637

Domnall mac Áeda defeats and kills Congal Cáech, king of Tara, at the Battle of Mag Rath.

c.640

The siege of Edinburgh and fall of the kingdom of the Gododdin.

642

The deaths of Oswald, Cynegils of Wessex and Domnall Brecc of Dál Riata.

650

Agilbert, a Frank, becomes bishop of the West Saxons.

651

The deaths of Oswine of Deira and St. Aidan.

655

Penda is defeated and killed by Oswiu, king of Northumbria.

660–680

The Anglian conquest of Cumbria.

664

The Synod of Whitby.

669

The arrival of Theodore, 'archbishop of the island of Britain', at Canterbury; Wilfrid installed as bishop of York.

670–c.710

The death of Oswiu of Northumbria. The reign of Geraint, king of Dumnonia.

674

The foundation of Monkwearmouth by Benedict Biscop.

c.675

Cogitosus writes his *Life of Brigit.*

679

Æthelred of Mercia defeats Ecgfrith of Northumbria at the Battle of the Trent; the Synod of Hatfield is summoned by Theodore.

680

The death of Hild, abbess of Whitby.

682

Foundation of Jarrow by Benedict Biscop, beginning of the abbacy of Ceolfrith.

The death of Cadwaladr, king of Gwynedd.

685

Bridei son of Derilei, king of Fortriu, defeats and kills Ecgfrith at the nettle of Nechtanesmere.

686

The first visit of Adomnán, abbot of Iona, to Northumbria; Cædwalla, king of the West Saxons, conquers the Isle of Wight.

687

St. Cuthbert dies at Lindisfarne.

c.688–694

Promulgation of the laws of Ine, king of the West Saxons.

689/690

The deaths of Benedict Biscop and Archbishop Theodore.

c.695

Muirchú writes his *Life of St. Patrick.*

697

The Synod of Birr and promulgation of the Law of the Innocents by Adomnán.

704

The deaths of Adomnán and Aldfrith, king of Northumbria.

709

The death of Wilfrid.

715

The death of Cellach Cualann, the last Uí Máil king of Leinster.

716

The monks of Iona adopt the Roman Easter; the deaths of Ceolfrith and Osred of Northumbria.

725

The death of Wihtred, king of Kent, and control of his kingdom by Æthelbald, king of Mercia.

c.730

Whithorn becomes a Northumbrian see.

731

Bede completes his *Ecclesiastical History*.

735

The death of Bede; recognition of the archbishopric of York.

750–752

Tewdwr ap Bili, king of the Strathclyde Britons, becomes overlord of the Picts.

757

Æthelbald of Mercia dies, and his successor is killed by Offa.

768

Elfoddw convinces the Britons of Wales to adopt the Roman Easter.

770

Donnchad mac Domnaill of the Uí Néill brings an army into Leinster and enforces his overlordship.

c.784

Construction of Offa's Dyke.

793

The sack of Lindisfarne by Vikings.

794

Æthelberht, king of East Anglia, is executed by Offa.

796

The deaths of Offa and his son Ecgfrith; Coenwulf succeeds to the throne of Mercia.

802–839

The reign of Egbert, king of Wessex.

806

Vikings attack Iona and kill sixty-eight monks.

c.807

Cellach, abbot of Iona, founds the monastery at Kells.

809

The death of Elfoddw, archbishop of Gwynedd.

821

The death of Coenwulf of Mercia.

822

Degannwy falls to the Mercians, giving them temporary control of Powys.

825

Egbert, king of the West Saxons, takes control of Sussex, Kent and Essex. Abbot Blathmac is martyred on Iona.

826

The death of Hywel, king of Gwynedd, and the succession of Merfyn Frych.

c.830

Composition of the *Historia Brittonum*.

838

The Battle of Hingston Down, in which Egbert of Wessex defeats the Britons of Dumnonia and their Viking allies.

839–858

The reign of Æthelwulf, king of Wessex.

841

Vikings establish a base in Dublin.

843

Kenneth MacAlpin unites the Scottish and Pictish thrones.

844

The death of Merfyn, king of Gwynedd, and beginning of the reign of his son, Rhodri Mawr.

856

Rhodri the Great, king of Gwynedd, slays the Viking leader Horm.

866

The city of York falls to the Danes.

870–871

Olaf the White and Ivarr sack Dumbarton.

871–899

The reign of Alfred the Great.

876

Constantine I, king of Scotland, falls in battle against the Vikings.

878

Alfred defeats Guthram at the Battle of Eddington.

c.885

Asser leaves the monastery of St David's and enters the service of Alfred the Great.

892

Asser completes his *Life of King Alfred.*

899–924

The reign of Edward 'the Elder'.

900

Scots annex Strathclyde; migration of the Strathclyde British aristocracy to North Wales.

903

Vikings from Dublin invade Anglesey and kill Merfyn ap Rhodri.

925–941

Reign of Æthelstan.

927

Morgan, king of Gwent and Glywsying, and Hywel Dda, king of Deheubarth, submit to Æthelstan at Hereford.

c.935–950

Composition of the 'Armes Prydein Vawr'.

937

The Battle of Brunanburh, in which Æthelstan defeats an alliance of Scots, Dublin Danes and Strathclyde Britons.

939–946

Reign of Edmund, brother of Æthelstan.

945

Edmund ravages Cumbria and Strathclyde and grants conquered British territory to Malcolm, king of the Scots.

950

The death of Hywel Dda.

959–960

Edgar succeeds as king of England and makes Dunstan archbishop of Canterbury.

973

Edgar receives the submission of Kenneth II of Scotland, Malcolm, king of Strathclyde and Cumbria, and Iago and Hywel of Gwynedd.

975–978

Reign of Edward (later St. Edward), son of Edgar.

978

Beginning of the reign of Æthelred 'the Unready'.

Anglo-Norman Period (AD 1000–1200)

1000

Composition of the poem, 'The Battle of Maldon'.

1002

Máel Sechnaill submits to Brian Bóruma, who becomes high-king of Ireland.

1012

The Leinstermen and the Ostmen of Dublin revolt against Brian Bóruma.

1013

King Sweyn of Denmark and his son Cnut conquer England; Æthelred flees to Normandy.

1014

Good Friday — The Battle of Clontarf, in which Leinster and its Viking allies are defeated, but Brian Bóruma is slain.

1016

23 Apr — Death of Æthelred, succession of his son Edmund 'Ironside'.

30 Nov — Death of Edmund, Cnut chosen king of England.

1018

The Battle of Carham, in which Malcolm II of Scotland and Owen the Bald of Strathclyde defeat the English of Bernicia; Llywelyn ap Seisyll slays Aeddan ap Blegywryd.

1022

Death of Máel Sechnaill, high-king of Ireland.

1023

Archbishop Wulfstan II of York writes his *Homilies*.

1035

12 Nov Death of Cnut, followed by a succession dispute.

1036

Sitric Silkenbeard is banished from Dublin.

1037

Harold I 'Harefoot' proclaimed king of England.

1040

17 Mar Death of Harold I 'Harefoot'.

June Succession of Harthacnut.

16 Aug MacBeth kills Duncan and becomes king of Scots.

1042

8 June Death of Harthacnut.

1043

3 Apr Edward 'the Confessor' crowned at Winchester.

c. 1050

The four branches of the *Mabinogi* are composed; Cornwall is demoted to the status of archdeaconry within the new diocese of Exeter.

1051

Harold Godwinsson flees to Ireland after his father rebels against King Edward.

1052–1070

Reign of Diarmait, 'king of the Isles'.

1056–1063

Gruffudd ap Llwelyn establishes himself in Morgannwg and becomes ruler of all Wales.

1057

MacBeth is killed at Lumphanan.

1058–1093

Reign of Malcolm III 'Canmore'.

1061–1070

Murchad, son of Diarmait, reigns as king of Dublin and the Isle of Man.

1063

Harold Godwinsson, earl of Wessex, invades Wales; the assassination of Gruffudd ap Llywelyn.

1065

28 Dec Dedication of Westminster Abbey.

1066

Death of Edward the Confessor; the crowning of Harold II; Harold II defeats Harald Hardrada at the Battle of Stamford Bridge; Norman invasion of England; William the Conqueror defeats Harold Godwinsson at the Battle of Hastings.

1070

29 Aug Lanfranc consecrated archbishop of Canterbury.

1086

Completion of the *Domesday Book*; the death of Toirdhealbhach Ua Briain, king of Munster and Dublin, grandson of Brian Bóruma.

1087

9 Sep The death of William I.

26 Sep Coronation of William II 'Rufus' at Westminster.

1093

25 Sep Anselm consecrated archbishop of Canterbury.

13 Nov Death of Malcolm III of Scotland.

16 Nov The death of Malcom III's wife Margaret.

1100

2 Aug The death of William II.

5 Aug Coronation of Henry I.

1101

The reforming Synod of Cashel.

1103

Norse king Magnus Barelegs is killed while raiding in Ulster.

1106

28 Sep Henry I conquers Normandy and captures Robert Curthose.

1107

Death of Edgar and succession of Alexander I as king of Scotland.

1114

Muirchartach Ua Briain of Munster falls from power; Henry's daughter Matilda marries Emperor Henry V.

1119

Succession by Tairrdelbach mac Ruaidri Ua Conchobair of Connacht.

1120

25 Nov The wreck of the White Ship.

1124

David I, youngest son of Malcolm III and Margaret, becomes king of Scotland.

1125

William of Malmesbury finishes his *Gesta Regum Anglorum*.

1128

15 June Matilda, now widowed empress, marries Geoffrey of Anjou.

David I founds Holyrood House in Edinburgh.

1132

Foundation of the Cistercian abbey of Rievaulx, Yorkshire.

1133

5 Mar Matilda gives birth to Henry II, the future king.

1135

1 Dec The death of Henry I.

22 Dec Coronation of Stephen of Blois.

c. 1136–1139

Geoffrey of Monmouth completes his *History of the Kings of Britain*, incorporating an earlier work, *The Prophecies of Merlin*.

1137

Death of Gruffudd ap Cynan, king of Gwynedd, who is succeeded by Owain Gwynedd.

1138

Defeat of the Scots at the Battle of the Standard.

1139

30 Sep Empress Matilda and Robert of Gloucester invade England.

1141

2 Feb The Battle of Lincoln and capture of Stephen of Blois.

14 Sep Defeat of Matilda's forces and capture of Robert of Gloucester

1142

First Cistercian abbey in Ireland founded at Mellifont, Louth.

1146

Birth of Gerald of Wales.

1152

18 May Marriage of Henry Plantagenet (Henry I) and Eleanor of Aquitaine.

1153

6 Nov The Treaty of Winchester acknowledging Henry as Stephen of Blois's heir.

Malcolm IV succeeds David I as king of Scotland.

1154

25 Oct Death of Stephen of Blois at Canterbury.

19 Dec Coronation of Henry II at Westminster.

1155

Henry II appoints Thomas Becket Chancellor of the Realm; the English pope Adrian IV issues *Laudabiliter*.

1156

Death of Tairrdelbach mac Ruaidri Ua Conchobair and succession of his son Ruaidrí (Rory O' Connor).

1159

John of Salisbury completes his *Polycraticus*.

1162

3 June Thomas Becket consecrated archbishop of Canterbury.

1164

Death of Somerled, 'king of the Hebrides and Kintyre'.

1166

Issuance of the Assize of Clarendon.

1 Aug Diarmait Mac Murrough is ejected from Leinster and flees to England.

1167

Aug Diarmait Mac Murrough returns to Ireland with a band of Flemish mercenaries from Pembrokeshire but is defeated by Ruaidrí.

1169

1 May A large band of Anglo-Norman mercenaries, led by Robert fitz Stephen, lands in County Wexford.

1170

23 Aug Richard Fitz Gilbert de Clare ('Strongbow') takes Waterford and marries Diarmait's daughter, Aoife.

29 Dec The murder of Thomas Becket in Canterbury Cathedral.

1171

17 Oct Henry II invades Ireland and accepts the submission of Irish kings.

1172

Meath falls into the hands of the English baron Hugh de Lacy.

1173

21 Feb Canonisation of St. Thomas of Canterbury.

13 July Capture of William, king of Scots, at Alnwick.

1176

The Lord Rhys hosts the first *eisteddfod* at Cardigan.

1183

11 June The death of Henry the Young King.

1189

6 July Death of Henry II at Chinon.

3 Sep Coronation of Richard I at Westminster.

1190

Massacre of the Jews of York; Richard leaves on the Third Crusade.

c. 1190

Glastonbury monks excavate the grave of Arthur and Guinevere; Layamon publishes his *Brut*.

1199

6 Apr Death of Richard I at Chalus.

27 May Coronation of John at Westminster.

Sources

Barrell, A. D. M. 2000. *Medieval Scotland*. Cambridge University Press.

Bartlett, Robert. 2000. *England Under the Norman and Angevin Kings 1075–1225*. Oxford University Press.

Charles-Edwards, Thomas. 2003. *After Rome: A Short History of the British Isles*. Oxford University Press.

Duffy, Seán. 1997. *Ireland in the Middle Ages*. St. Martin's Press.

Palmer, Alan, and Veronica Palmer. 1992. *The Chronology of British History*. Century.

Snyder, Christopher A. 1998. *An Age of Tyrants: Britain and the Britons, AD 400–600*. Pennsylvania State University Press.

———. 2003. *The Britons*. Peoples of Europe Series. Blackwell.

Royal Genealogies

Rulers of Early Britain and Ireland

Kings of the *Catuvellauni*

Cassivellaunus
Tasciovanus
Cunobelinus
Epaticcus
Adminius
Togodumnus
Caratacus (or Caratacos)

Kings of the *Cantiaci*

Dubnovellaunus
Vosenios
Eppilus
Cunobelinus probably annexes the *Cantiaci*
Adminius possibly appointed to rule the *Cantiaci*

Kings of the *Atrebates*

Commius (or Commios)
Tincommius
Eppillus
Verica (or Berikos)
Tiberius Claudius Cogidubnus

Rulers of the *Iceni*

Can[...]
Anted[ios], Aesu[...], and Saenu[...]
Prasutagus (made client king of Rome c. AD 47, d. c. 60)
Boudica (60/61)

Rulers of the *Brigantes*

Cartimandua and Venutius of the *Carvetii*
Cartimandua and Vellocatus

Roman Governors of Britain

Aulus Plautius (AD 43–47)
Publius Ostorius Scapula (47–52)
Aulus Didius Gallus (52–57)
Quintus Veranius (57–58)
Gaius Suetonius Paullinus (c. 58–61)
Publius Petronius Turpilianus (61/62–63)
Marcus Vettius Bolanus (63–69)
Quintus Petillius Cerealis (71–73/74)
Sextus Julius Frontinus (73/74–77/78)
Gnaeus Julius Agricola (77/78–83/84)
Sallustius Lucullus (83–96)
Publius Metilius Nepos (by 98)
Titus Avidius Quietus (97/98–100/101)
Lucius Neratius Marcellus (100/101–103 or later)
Marcus Appius (or Atilius) Bradua (c.115–118)
Quintus Pompeius Falco (118–122)
Aulus Platorius Nepos (122–124 or later)
Sextus Julius Severus (c.130/131–132/133)
Publius Mummius Sisenna (132/133–135 or later)
Quintus Lollius Urbicus (138/139–c.143)
Cornelius Priscianus (c.143–145)
Gnaeus Papirus Aelianus (146)
Gnaeus Julius Verus (158)
? (c.158–161)
Marcus Statius Priscus (161/162)
Sextus Calpurnius Agricola (162/163–c.166)
Quintus Antistius Adventus (c.169–?)
Caerellius Priscus (?–c.180)
Marcus Antius Crescens Calpurianus (acting governor c.182–184)
Ulpius Marcellus (184/185)
Publius Helvius Pertinax (185–c.187)
Decimus Clodius Albinus (191/192, proclaimed emperor 193, d.197)
Virius Lupus (197–c.202)
Gaius Valerius Pudens (202/203–c.205)
Lucius Alfenus Senecio (205/207)
Gaius Junius Faustinus Postumianus (c.208–213)
Ulpius Marcellus (c.211/212)
Gaius Julius Marcus (by 213)
Britain divided into two provinces, each with a governor (197–213)
Pollienus Auspex, Rufinus, Marcus Martiannius Pulcher (Britannia Superior, 197/c.250)
Marcus Antonius Gordianus (Britannia Inferior, by 216)
Modius Julius (Britannia Inferior, by 219)
Tiberius Claudius Paulinus (Britannia Inferior, 220)
Marius Valerianus (Britannia Inferior, 221–222)
Calvisius Rufus, Valerius Crescens Fulvianus (Britannia Inferior, 222/235)
Claudius Xenophon (Britannia Inferior, 223)
Maximus (Britannia Inferior, by 225)
Claudius Appellinus (Britannia Inferior, c.235)
(T)uccianus (Britannia Inferior, by 237)
Maecilius Fuscus, Egnatius Lucilianus (Britannia Inferior, 238/244)
Nonius Phillipus (Britannia Inferior, by 242)
Aemilianus (Britannia Inferior, after c.244)
Titus Desticius Juba (Britannia Superior, 253/255)
Octavius Sabinus (Britannia Inferior, 263/268)
Lucius Septimius (Britannia Superior, after 274)
Britain becomes a diocese consisting of four (later five) provinces (after 296)
Aurelius Arpagius (Britannia Inferior or Britannia Secunda, 296/305)
Hierocles Perpetuus (province unknown, late third/early fourth century)
Lucius Papius Pacatianus (vicarius of the diocese, by 319)
Flavius Sanctus (province unknown, c. 350)
Martinus (vicarius, 353/354)
Alypius (vicarius, 357/358–360)
Civilis (vicarius, 367)
Chrysanthus, Victorinus (vicarii, c. 395/406)

Kings of Gwynedd, Deheubarth and Morgannwg

Gwynedd

Maelgwn (Maglocunus) (d. c. AD 547)
Cadfan (late sixth century)

Cadwallon (d. 635)
Cadwaladr (d. 682)
Caradog (d. 798)
Gwriad (late eighth/early ninth century)
Merfyn Frych (c. 825–844)
Rhodri Mawr (844–877)
Gwynedd ruled by Rhodri's surviving sons, Cadell (d. 910) and Anarawd (d. 916), and split into northern and southern halves.

South Gwynedd and Deheubarth

Hywel ap Cadell (Hywel Dda) (910–c. 950), who became the first king of Deheubarth in 920.
The sons of Idwal defeated the sons of Hywel and left them only with Deheubarth:
Owain ap Hywel Dda (c. 950–988)
Maredudd ap Owain (d. 999) temporarily reunited in Gwynedd in 986
Rhydderch ab Iestyn (d. 1033), king of Morgannwg, seizes control of Deheubarth
Rhys ap Tewdwr, king of Deheubarth (d. 1093)
Gruffudd ap Rhys, king of Deheubarth (1093–1137)
Rhys ap Gruffydd (Lord Rhys), king of Deheubarth (1155–1197)

North Gwynedd

Idwal Foel ap Anarawd (d. 942)
The north is ruled by the sons of Idwal: Idwal (d. 980), Meurig, Iago, Rhodri (d. 968) and Ieuf (d. 988)
Llywelyn ap Seisyll (1010–1023) displaced the sons of Meurig ap Idwal in 1010
Iago ap Idwal ap Meurig (c. 1023–1039) regained control after the death of Llywelyn
Gruffudd ap Llywelyn (1039–1064) killed Iago and drove out the king of Deheubarth, becoming king of all Wales.
Gruffudd ap Cynan (d. 1137)
Owain Gwynedd (1137–1170)
Cynan ap Owain (c. 1170–1175)
Dafydd ap Owain (1175–1194) and Rhodri ap Owain (d. 1195)
Llewelyn ap Iorweth (c. 1194–1240)

Kings of Powys

Bleddyn ap Cynfyn (d. 1075)
Cadwgan ap Bleddwyn (1075–1111)
Owain ap Cadwgan (1111–1116)
Maredudd ap Bleddyn (1116–1132)
Madog ap Maredudd (1132–1160)
Gruffydd Maelor ap Madog (1160–1191)
Owain Cyfeiliog ap Gruffydd (1191–1197)
Gwenwynwyn ap Owain (1197–1216)

Kings of Dumnonia and Cornwall

List of kings in Jesus College, Oxford, MS 20	**List of kings in Bonedd y Saint, the 'Lineage of the Saints'**
Eudaf Hen	
Cynan	
Gadeon	
Gwrwawr	
Tudwawl	
Kynwawr (Cynfawr)	Custennyn Gorneu
Erbin	Erbin
Gereint	Gereint
Cado	Selyf
Peredur	Kyby
Theudu (daughter ?)	
Judhael	

Probably composed in the twelfth century without regnal dates.

Kings of Rheged

Urien Rheged (late sixth century AD)
Owain ap Urien (early seventh century)
Rhun (early seventh century)
Royth (seventh century)
Riemmelth, great-granddaughter of Urien, is married to the Northumbrian king Oswiu (c. 635)

Kings of Strathclyde and Cumberland

Ceredig, first recorded king of Strathclyde (fifth century)
Cynwyd ap Ceredig
Dyfnwal Hen ap Cynwyd
Clynog ap Dyfnwal
Tudwal ap Clynog (sixth century AD)
Rhydderch Hael ap Tudwal (d. c. 614)
Nwython (d. c. 620)
Beli ap Nwython
Ywain ap Beli (fl. 642)
Gurad ap Ywain (d. 658)
Elfin ap Ywain (d. 693)
Dyfnwal ap Ywain (d. 694)
Beli ap Elfin (d. 722)
Tewdwr ap Beli (d. 752)
Rhodri ap Beli (d. 754)
Dyfnwal ap Tewdwr (d. 760)
Ywain ap Dyfnwal
Rhydderch ap Ywain
Dyfnwal ap Rhydderch
Arthgal ap Dyfnwal (d. 872)
Rhun ap Arthgal (d. 873)
Eochaid map Rhun (d. 889)
Strathclyde is annexed by Donald II, king of Scots (c. 889); Scottish monarchs choose subsequent 'kings of the Cumbrians'
Dyfnwal ap Rhun, king of Cumberland
Ywain ap Dyfnwal, king of Cumberland (fl. 935)
Edmund, king of England, blinds two of Dyfnwal's sons and grants Cumbria to Malcolm I, king of Scotland (c. 945)
Rhydderch ap Dyfnwal, king of Cumberland (fl. 971)
Dyfnwal ap Ywain (or Dunmail map Owain), king of Cumberland (d. 975)
Malcolm ap Dyfnwal, king of Cumberland (d. 997)
Ywain ap Dyfnwal (Owen the Bald), king of Cumberland (d. 1018)
Duncan, king of Scots (d. 1040), assumes the kingship of Cumberland and Strathclyde

Pictish Kings

Brude mac Maelchon (d. 584)
Brude mac Bile (c. 671–693)
Brude mac Derile (d. 706)
Nechtan (706–732)

Óengus mac Fergus (732–761)
Óengus II (d. 834)
Brude mac Feredach (d. 843)
Kenneth I MacAlpin unites the Scottish and Pictish thrones (843)

Kings of the Dalriada Scots

Áedán Mac Gabráin (c. 574–606)

Kings of Alba (Scotland)

Kenneth I MacAlpin (843–858)
Donald I (858–862)
Constantine I (862–877)
Áed (877–878)
Eochaid and Giric (878–889)
Donald II (889–900)
Constantine II (900–943)
Malcolm I (943–954)
Indulf (954–962)
Dub (962–71)
Kenneth II (971–995)
Constantine III (995–997)
Kenneth III (997–1005)
Malcolm II (1005–1034)
Duncan I (1034–1040)
Macbeth (1040–1057)
Lulach (1057–1058)
Malcolm III Canmore (1058–1093)
Donald III Bàn (1093, dep. May 1094)
Duncan II (1094)
Donald III Bàn (restored 12 Nov 1094, dep. 1097)
Edgar (1097–1107)
Alexander I (1107–1124)
David I (1124–1153)
Malcolm IV the Maiden (1153–1165)
William the Lion (1165–1214)

Kings of East Anglia

Rædwald (?–625)
Erpwald (625–630/631)
Sigebert (c. 630–640)
Ethelhere (654–655)
Ethelwald (655–663/664)
Aldwulf (663/664–713)
Elfwald (713–749)
Kingdom is divided (749)
(St.) Edmund (855–869)
Guthram (869–c. 880)
Edward, king of Wessex, conquers East Anglia (917)

Kings of Kent

Hengist (legendary founder of the dynasty)
Oisc (late fifth/early sixth century)
Eormenric (512–60)
Æthelbert I (560–616)
Eadbald (616–640)
Eorconbert (640–664)
Egbert I (664–673)
Lothere (July 673–685)
Edric (685–c. 692)
Swefhard and Oswin (c. 690–692)
Witred (c. 692–725)
Æthelbert II, Edbert and others (725–765)
Egbert II (765–c. 780)
Ealmund (784–796)
Edbert (796–798)
Cuthred of Mercia (c. 780–796)
Baldred (807–c. 825)
Egbert, king of Wessex, unites Kent with Wessex (c. 825)

Kings of Bernicia

Ida (547–559)
Glappa (559–560)
Adda (560–568)
Ethelric (568–572)
Theodric (572–579)
Frithuwald (579–585)
Hussa (585–592/593)
Æthelfrith, first king of all Northumbria (592/593–616)
Edwin, king of all Northumbria (616-632)
Eanfrith (632–633)
Oswald, king of all Northumbria (634–642)
Oswiu (642–670), king of all Northumbria (655–670)
Bernicia was part of Northumbria (670–867)
Egbert I (867–873)
Ricsig (873–876)
Egbert II (876–878)
Eadwulf (878–913)
Aldred (913–927)
Æthelstan, king of all England (927–939)

Kings of Deira

Ælle (560–592/593)
Edwin (592/593–633)
Deira was part of Northumbria (592/593–633)
Osric (633)
Deira was part of Northumbria (634–642)
Oswine (644–651)
Ethelwald (651–655)
Deira was part of Northumbria (655–867)
Deira became part of the Danelaw (867)

Kings of Northumbria

Æthelfrith (592/593–616)
Edwin (616–633)
Oswald (634–642)
Oswiu (642–670)
Ecgfrith (670–685)
Aldfrith (685–705)
Eadwulf (705–705/706)
Osred I (705/706–716)
Cenred (716–718)
Osric (718–729)
Ceolwulf (729–737)
Edbert (737–758)
Oswulf (758–759)
Ethelwald Moll (758/759–765)
Alred (765–774)
Ethelred I (774–778/779 and 790–796)
Elfwald I (778/779–788)
Osred II (788–790)
Osbald (796)
Eardwulf (796–806/808)
Elfwald II (806/808)
Eanred (808/810–840)

Ethelred II (840–844 and 844–848)
Radwulf (844)
Osbert (848–867)
Northumbria becomes part of the Danelaw (867)

Kings of Mercia

Penda (c. 632–Nov 655)
Mercia under the rule of Northumbria (655–58)
Wulfhere (658–674)
Æthelred (674–704)
Cenred (704–709)
Ceolred (709–716)
Æthelbald (716–757)
Offa (757–796)
Egfrith (796)
Coenwulf (796–821)
Ceolwulf I (821–823)
Beornwulf (823–825)
Ludeca (825–827)
Wiglaf (827–840)
Betwulf (840–852)
Burgred (852–873)
Ceolwulf II (873–879)
Æthelred II (879–911)
Æthelflaed (911–918)
Elfwyn (918–919)
Mercia united with Wessex (919)

Kings of Wessex

Cerdic (c. 519–534)
Cynric (534–560)
Ceawlin (560–591)
Ceol (591–597)
Ceolwulf (597–611)
Cynegils (611–642)
Cenwell (642–672)
Queen Seaxbur, wife of Cenwel (672–674)
Escwin (674–676)
Centwine (676–685)
Cadwalla (685–688)
Ine (688–726)
Ethelhard (726–740)
Cuthred (740–756)
Sigeburt (756–757)
Cynewulf (757–786)
Britric (786–802)
Egbert (802–839, king of all Anglo-Saxon kingdoms 829–830)
Æthelwulf (839–855)
Æthelbald (855–860)
Æthelbert (860–865)
Æthelred (865–871)
Alfred the Great (Apr 871–899)
Edward the Elder (Oct 899–924)
Elfward (July 924–925)
Æthelstan, king of all England (4 Sep 925–939)

Cenél nÉogain Kings of Tara

Muirchertach mac Ercae (d. 536)
Forggus (d. 566)
Domnall (d. 566)
Eochaid (d. 572)
Báetán (d. 572)
Colmán Rímid (d. 604)
Áed Allán/Uaridnach (d. 612)
Suibne Mend(d. 628)
Fergal (d. 722)
Áed Allán (d. 743)
Náill Frossach (d. 778)
Áed Oirdnide (d. 819)
Náill Caille (d. 846)
Áed Findlíath (d. 879)

Kings of the Danelaw

Danish Vikings from York create the Danelaw (867)
Aelle (867–875/876)
Halfdan I (875/876–877)
Guthfrith I (883–895)
Sigfrid and Cnut (895–899/900)
Æthelwald, prince of Wessex (899/900–902)
Halfdan II and Eowils (902–910)
Ragnald I (911–921)
Sihtric (921–927)
Guthfrith II (927)
Æthelstan, king of all England (927–939)
Olaf I Guthfrithsson (939–941)
Olaf II Sihtricsson (941–943)
Ragnald II Guthfrithsson (943–944)
Edmund, king of all England (944–946)
Eadred, king of all England (946–947 and 954–955)
Eric 'Bloodaxe' (947–948 and 952–954)
Olaf II Sihtricsson (949/950–952)

Kings of England

Æthelstan (925–941)
Edmund I (Oct 939–946)
Eadred (May 946–955)
Eadwig (Nov 955–959)
Edgar I (Oct 959–975)
Edward the Martyr (July 975–18 Mar 978)
Æthelred the Unready (Mar 978–1013 and 1014–1016)
Svein Forkbeard, king of Denmark, acknowledged as king of England (Sep 1013–Feb 1014)
Edmund II Ironside (Apr–Nov 1016)
Cnut (Nov 1016–12 Nov 1035)
Harold I 'Harefoot' (1035/1037–1040)
Harthacnut (June 1040–1042)
Edward the Confessor (3 Apr 1043–1066)
Harold II Godwinsson (23 Jan–14 Oct 1066)
William I (25 Dec 1066–1087)
William II Rufus (26 Sep 1087–1100)
Henry I (5 Aug 1100–1135)
Stephen of Blois (22 Dec 1135–1154)
Henry II (19 Dec 1154–1189)
Richard I (3 Sep 1189–1199)
John (27 May 1199–1216)

Sources

Charles-Edwards, Thomas. 2000. *Early Christian Ireland*. Cambridge University Press.
———. 2003. *After Rome: The Short Oxford History of the British Isles*. Oxford University Press.
Palmer, Alan, and Veronica Palmer. 1992. *The Chronology of British History*. Century.
Salway, Peter. 1993. *The Oxford Illustrated History of Roman Britain*. Oxford University Press.
Snyder, Christopher A. 2003. *The Britons*. Peoples of Europe Series. Blackwell.

List of Illustrations

Volume I

Volume II

List of Maps

Volume I

Volume II

Select Bibliography

Internet Resources

Anglo-Saxon Charters (Trinity College, Cambridge) http://www.trin.cam.ac.uk/sdk13/chartwww/chartho me.html

Arthuriana: The Journal of Arthurian Studies, http://faculty.smu.edu/arthuriana/

Bede's World: The Museum of Early Medieval Northumbria at Jarrow, http://www.bedesworld.co.uk/

CELT: Corpus of Electronic Texts, http://www.ucc.ie/celt/

The Celtic Coin Index, http://web.arch.ox.ac.uk/coins/ccindex.htm

The Celtic Inscribed Stones Project (CISP), http://www.ucl.ac.uk/archaeology/cisp/database/

Creighton, John. 'Understanding the British Iron Age: An Agenda for Action', http://www.rdg.ac.uk/~lascretn/IAAgenda.htm

The Heroic Age: A Journal of Early Medieval Northwestern Europe, http://www.heroicage.org/

Peritia: Journal of the Medieval Academy of Ireland, http://www.ucc.ie/peritia/index.html

The Pictish Arts Society, http://www.pictart.org/

Russell, Paul, and Alex Mullen. *Celtic Personal Names of Roman Britain (CPNRB)*. Department of Anglo-Saxon, Norse, and Celtic, University of Cambridge, http://www.asnc.cam.ac.uk/personalnames/

Snyder, Christopher A. 1997. 'A Gazetteer of Sub-Roman Britain (AD 400–600): The British Sites'. *Internet Archaeology* 3, http://intarch.ac.uk/journal/issue3/snyder_index.html

Stone Pages (the archaeology of megalithic Europe) http://www.stonepages.com/

The Sutton Hoo Society, http://www.suttonhoo.org/

Vindolanda Tablets Online, http://vindolanda.csad.ox.ac.uk/

Bibliographies and Other Reference Works

Bartrum, Peter C. 1993. *A Welsh Classical Dictionary*. The National Library of Wales.

Farmer, D. H. (ed.). 2003. *The Oxford Dictionary of Saints*. Oxford University Press.

Hinton, D. A. 1974. *A Catalogue of the Anglo-Saxon Ornamental Metalwork 700–1100 in the Department of Antiquities, Ashmolean Museum*.

Koch, John (ed.). 2006. *Celtic Culture: A Historical Encyclopedia*, 5 vols. ABC-Clio.

Koch, John. 2007. *An Atlas for Celtic Studies: Archaeology and Names in Ancient Europe and Early Medieval Ireland, Britain and Brittany*. Oxbow.

Laing, Lloyd. 1993. *A Catalogue of Celtic Ornamental Metalwork in the British Isles, c. AD 400–1200*. British Archaeological Reports No. 225.

Lapidge, Michael, et al. (eds.). 1999. *The Blackwell Encyclopedia of Anglo-Saxon England*. Blackwell Publishing.

Lapidge, Michael, and Richard Sharpe. 1985. *A Bibliography of Celtic-Latin Literature 400–1200*. Royal Irish Academy.

Sawyer, P. H. 1968. *Anglo-Saxon Charters*. Royal Historical Society, http://www.trin.cam.ac.uk/chartwww/eSawyer. 99/eSawyer2.html

Sims-Williams, Patrick. 2006. *Ancient Place-names in Europe and Asia Minor*. Blackwell.

Primary Sources (individual printed works and collections)

Anderson, A. O. (ed. and tr.). 1922. *Early Sources of Scottish History AD 500 to 1286*. Oliver and Boyd.

Bartrum, P. C. 1966. *Early Welsh Genealogical Tracts*. University of Wales Press.

Bede. 1994. *The Ecclesiastical History of the English People*. Translated by Bertram Colgrave. Oxford University Press.

Bieler, Ludwig (ed.). 1963. *The Irish Penitentials, Scriptores Latini Hiberniae*, vol. 5. Dublin Institute for Advanced Studies.

Birch, W. de Gray. 1885–1999. *Cartularium Saxonicum: A Collection of Charters Relating to Anglo-Saxon History*, 4 vols. Whiting & Co.

Bjork, Robert E. (ed.). 2001. *The Cynewulf Reader*. Routledge.

Borius, Rene (ed. and tr.). 1965. *Constance de Lyon: Vie de Saint Germain d'Auxerre*. Éditions du Cerf.

Bromwich, Rachel (ed. and tr.). 1978. *Trioedd Ynys Prydein: The Welsh Triads*. University of Wales Press.

Bromwich, Rachel, and D. Simon Evans (eds.). 1992. *Culhwch and Olwen: An Edition and Study of the Oldest Arthurian Tale*. Medieval Academy of America.

Caesar. 1996. *The Gallic War*. Translated by Carolyn Hammond. Oxford University Press.

Colgrave, Bertram (ed.). 1940. *Two Lives of St. Cuthbert*. Cambridge University Press.

Collingwood, R. G., and R. P. Wright. 1995. *The Roman Inscriptions of Britain, Volumes I and II*. Alan Sutton.

Davies, Brian, and Gillian Evans (tr.). 1998. *Anselm of Canterbury: The Major Works*. Oxford University Press.

Davies, Oliver, and Thomas O'Loughlin. 1999. *Celtic Spirituality*. Paulist Press.

Davies, Wendy (ed.). 1979. *The Llandaff Charters*. National Library of Wales.

Doble, G. H. 1971. *Lives of the Welsh Saints*. Edited by D. Simon Evans. University of Wales Press.

Dumville, David N. 2002. *Annales Cambriae, AD 682–954: Texts A–C in Parallel*. Department of Anglo-Saxon, Norse and Celtic, University of Cambridge.

Evans, D. Simon. 1990. *A Medieval Prince of Wales: The Life of Gruffudd ap Cynan*. Llanerch.

Evelyn White, Hugh G. (tr.). 1919. *Ausonius*, Loeb edn., 2 vols. Harvard University Press.

Farmer, D. H. (ed.). 1998. *The Age of Bede*. Penguin.

Finberg, H. P. R. 1963. *The Early Charters of Devon and Cornwall*. Leicester University Press.

Flobert, Pierre (ed. and tr.). 1997. *La Vie Ancienne de Saint Samson de Dol*. CNRS.

Ford, Patrick K. (ed. and tr.). 1974. *The Poetry of Llywarch Hen*. University of California Press.

Garmonsway, G. N. (ed. and tr.). 1994. *The Anglo-Saxon Chronicle*. J.M. Dent.
Gildas. 1978. *'The Ruin of Britain' and Other Works*. Edited and translated by Michael Winterbottom. Phillimore.
Gregory of Tours. 1974. *The History of the Franks*. Translated by Lewis Thorpe. Penguin.
Haddan, Arthur West, and William Stubbs (eds.). 1964. *Councils and Ecclesiastical Documents Relating to Great Britain and Ireland*, 3 vols. Clarendon Press.
Ireland, Stanley. 1996. *Roman Britain: A Sourcebook* (2nd edn.). Routledge.
Jarman, A. O. H. 1990. *Aneirin: Y Gododdin: Britain's Oldest Heroic Poem*. Gomer Press.
Jones, Gwyn, and Thomas Jones (tr.). 1961. *The Mabinogion*. J.M. Dent.
Jones, Thomas (tr.). 1952. *Brut y Tywysogyon, or 'The Chronicle of the Princes'*. Peniarth MS 20 Version. University of Wales Press.
———. 1955. *Brut y Tywysogyon, or 'The Chronicle of the Princes'*. Red Book of Hergest Version. University of Wales Press.
Kenney, James F. 1966. *The Sources for the Early History of Ireland: Ecclesiastical*. Four Courts Press.
Keynes, Simon D., and Michael Lapidge (eds.). 1984. *Alfred the Great: Asser's Life of King Alfred & Other Contemporary Sources*. Penguin.
Koch, John T. (ed.). 1995. *The Celtic Heroic Age: Literary Sources* (2nd edn.). Celtic Studies Publications.
Lapidge, Michael, and James Rosier (eds. and tr.). 1985. *Aldhelm: The Poetic Works*. Brewer.
Lapidge, Michael, and Michael Herren (eds. and tr.). 1979. *Aldhelm: The Prose Works*. Brewer.
Mommsen, Theodor et al. (eds.). 1826–. *Monumenta Germaniae Historica*. Anton Hieserman.
Morris, John (ed. and tr.). 1980. *Nennius: British History and the Welsh Annals*. The Phillimore Press.
Nash-Williams, V. E. 1950. *The Early Christian Monuments of Wales*. University of Wales Press.
Orosius. 1936. *Seven Books of History Against the Pagans*. Translated by I. W. Raymond. Columbia University Press.
Parry, Thomas (ed.), and Rachel Bromwich (tr.). 1982. *Dafydd ap Gwilym: A Selection of Poems*. Gomer Press.
Patrick, Saint. 1978. *His Writings and Muirchu's 'Life'*. Edited and translated by A. B. E. Hood. Phillimore.
Platnauer, Maurice (ed. and tr.). 1922. *Claudian*, Loeb edn., 2 vols. Harvard University Press.
Potter, K. R. (ed. and tr.). 1976. *Gesta Stephani*. Clarendon Press.
Ridley, Ronald T. (tr.). 1982. *Zosimus: New History*. Australian Association for Byzantine Studies.
Rowland, Jenny.1990. *Early Welsh Saga Poetry: A Study and Edition of the Englynion*. D. S. Brewer.
Royal Commission on the Ancient and Historical Monuments of Scotland. 1999. *Pictish Symbol Stones: An Illustrated Gazetteer*. RCAHMS.
Sharpe, Richard (tr.). 1995. *Adomnán of Iona: Life of St Columba*. Penguin.
Sozomen. 1855. *The Ecclesiastical History*. Translated by Edward Walford. Henry G. Bohn.
Strabo. 1917–1933. *Geography*. Translated by Horace Leonard Jones and John Robert Sitlington Sterrett. W. Heinemann.
Swanton, Michael (ed. and tr.). 2000. *The Anglo-Saxon Chronicles* (rev. edn.). Phoenix.
Tacitus. 1991. *Agricola*. Translated by Herbert W. Benario. University of Oklahoma Press.
Wade-Evans, A. W. 1944. *Vitae Sanctorum Britanniae et Genealogiae*. University of Wales Press.
Williams, Ifor (ed.), and Rachel Bromwich (tr.). 1972. *Armes Prydein ('The Great Prophecy of Britain') from the Book of Taliesin*. Dublin Institute for Advanced Studies.
Winterbottom, M., and R. M. Thomson (eds.). 2002. *William of Malmesbury: Saints' Lives (Lives of SS. Wulfstan, Dunstan, Patrick, Benignus and Indract)*. Oxford Medieval Texts. Clarendon Press.
Wright, Neil (ed.). 1984. *The 'Historia Regum Britannae' of Geoffrey of Monmouth I: The Bern MS*. D.S. Brewer.

Prehistory

Barton, Nick. 2005. *Ice Age Britain*. Batsford.
Bradley, Richard. 1984. *The Social Foundations of Prehistoric Britain*. Longman.
———. 2007. *The Prehistory of Britain and Ireland*. Cambridge University Press.
Burgess, C. 2001. *The Age of Stonehenge* (rev. edn.). Phoenix.
Burl, A. 1979. *Prehistoric Avebury*. Yale University Press.
———. 2000. *The Stone Circles of Britain, Ireland and Brittany*. Yale University Press.
Clarke, D. 1970. *Beaker Pottery of Great Britain and Ireland*. Cambridge University Press.
Clarke, D. V., T. G. Cowie and A. Foxton (eds.). 1985. *Symbols of Power at the Time of Stonehenge*. HMSO.
Cleal, R. M. J., K. E. Walker and R. Motague. 1995. *Stonehenge in Its Landscape*. English Heritage.
Conneller, Chantal, and Graeme Warren. 2006. *Mesolithic Britain and Ireland: New Approaches*. Tempus Publishing Ltd.
Cooney, Gabriel. 2000. *Landscapes of Neolithic Ireland*. Routledge.
Cunliffe, Barry. 2001. *Facing the Ocean: The Atlantic and Its Peoples, 8000 BC–AD 1500*. Oxford University Press.
Cunliffe, Barry (ed.). 1998. *Prehistoric Europe: An Illustrated History*. Oxford University Press.
Daniel, G. 1950. *The Prehistoric Chamber Tombs of England and Wales*. Cambridge University Press.
Darvill, T. 1987. *Prehistoric Britain*. Batsford.
Garrod, D. A. E. 1926. *The Upper Palaeolithic Age in Britain*. Clarendon Press.
Gibson, A., and A. Woods. 1997. *Prehistoric Pottery for the Archaeologist* (2nd edn.). Leicester University Press.
Harding, A. F. 1987. *Henge Monuments and Related Sites of Great Britain*. British Archaeological Reports British Series 175.
Harding, J. 2003. *Henge Monuments of the British Isles*. Tempus.
Harrison, R. J. 1980. *The Beaker Folk: Copper Age Archaeology in Western Europe*. Thames & Hudson.
Henderson, Jon C. (ed.). 2000. *The Prehistory and Early History of Atlantic Europe*. Archaeopress.
Malone, Caroline. 1989. *Avebury*. Batsford/English Heritage.
———. 2001. *Neolithic Britain and Ireland*. Tempus Publishing Ltd.

Pearson, M. P. 1993. *Bronze Age Britain*. B.T. Batsford.
———. 2005. *The Bronze Age* (2nd rev. edn.). Batsford.
Piggott, Stuart. 1954. *Neolithic Cultures of the British Isles*. Cambridge University Press.
———. 1982. *Scotland Before History*. Edinburgh University Press.
Powell, T. G. E. 1966. *Prehistoric Art*. Thames & Hudson.
Rowe, Toni-Maree. 2005. *Cornwall in Prehistory*. Tempus.
Sandars, N. K. 1965. *Prehistoric Art in Europe*. Penguin.
Smith, Christopher A. 1992. *Late Stone Age Hunters of the British Isles*. Routledge.
Stout, Geraldine. 2002. *Newgrange and the Bend of the Boyne*. Cork University Press.
Stringer, Chris. 2006. *Homo Britannicus: The Incredible Story of Human Life in Britain*. Allen Lane.
Wainwright, G. 1989. *The Henge Monuments, Ceremony and Society in Prehistoric Britain*. Thames & Hudson.

The Iron Age

Chadwick, Nora. 1966. *The Druids*. University of Wales Press.
———. 1998. *The Celts*. Penguin.
Champion, T. C., and J. R. Collis (eds.). 1996. *The Iron Age in Britain and Ireland: Recent Trends*. University of Sheffield.
Collis, John R. 1984. *Oppida: Earliest Towns North of the Alps*. University of Sheffield.
———. 1996. 'The Origin and Spread of the Celts'. *Studia Celtica* 30: 17–34.
———. 1997. *The European Iron Age* (2nd edn.). Routledge.
———. 2003. *The Celts: Origins, Myths and Inventions*. Tempus Publishing.
Collis, John R. (ed.). 1977. *The Iron Age in Britain—A Review*. University of Sheffield.
Cunliffe, Barry. 1974, repr. 1991. *Iron Age Communities in Britain*. Routledge.
———. 1995. *English Heritage Book of Iron Age Britain*. B.T. Batsford.
———. 1997. *The Ancient Celts*. Oxford University Press.
———. 2003. *The Extraordinary Voyage of Pytheas the Greek*. Penguin.
Forde-Johnson, J. 1976. *Hillforts of the Iron Age in England and Wales*. Liverpool University Press.
Green, Miranda J. 1986. *The Gods of the Celts*. Alan Sutton.
———. 1997. *Exploring the World of the Druids*. Thames & Hudson.
Harding, D. W. 1974. *The Iron Age in Lowland Britain*. Routledge.
———. 2004. *The Iron Age in North Britain: Celts and Romans, Natives and Invaders*. Edinburgh University Press.
Hill, J. D. 1996. 'Weaving the Strands of a New Iron Age'. *British Archaeology* 17 September.
James, Simon. 1993. *The World of the Celts*. Thames & Hudson.
———. 1998. 'Celts, Politics and Motivation in Archaeology'. *Antiquity* 72.275: 200–209.
———. 1999. *The Atlantic Celts: Ancient People or Modern Invention?* University of Wisconsin Press.
James, Simon, and Valery Rigby. 1997. *Britain and the Celtic Iron Age*. British Museum Press.
Jope, E. M. 2000. *Early Celtic Art in the British Isles*. Clarendon Press.
Kruta, Venceslas et al. (eds.). 1991. *The Celts*. Thames & Hudson.
Megaw, Ruth, and Vincent Megaw. 1989. *Celtic Art: From Its Beginnings to the Book of Kells*. Thames & Hudson.
———. 1996. 'Ancient Celts and Modern Ethnicity'. *Antiquity* 70.267: 175–181.
Piggott, Stuart. 1968, repr. 1985. *The Druids*. Thames & Hudson.
Powell, T. G. E. 1980. *The Celts*. Thames & Hudson.
Raftery, Barry. 1994. *Pagan Celtic Britain*. Thames & Hudson.
Rankin, H. D. 1987. *Celts and the Classical World*. Areopagitica Press.
Ross, Anne. 1967, repr. 1992. *Pagan Celtic Britain*. Constable.
Stead, I. M. 1996. *Celtic Art*. British Museum Press.
Turner, R. C., and R. G. Scaife (eds.). 1995. *Bog Bodies: New Discoveries and New Perspectives*. British Museum Press.
Van Arsdale, R. D. 1983. *Celtic Coinage of Britain*. Spink.
Wait, G. 1985. *Religion and Ritual in Iron Age Britain*. British Archaeological Reports British Series No. 149.

Roman Britain

Allason-Jones, Lindsay. 1989. *Women in Roman Britain*. British Museum Press.
Birley, Anthony. 1980. *The People of Roman Britain*. University of California Press.
Birley, Robin. 1990. *The Roman Documents from Vindolanda*. Roman Army Museum Publications.
Blagg, T. F. C., and A. C. King (eds.). 1984. *Military and Civilian in Roman Britain*. BAR British Series 136.
Braund, David. 1996. *Ruling Roman Britain: Kings, Queens, Governors, and Emperors from Julius Caesar to Agricola*. Routledge.
Breeze, D. J., and B. Dobson. 2000. *Hadrian's Wall* (4th edn.). Penguin.
Burnham, B. C., and H. B. Johnson (eds.). 1979. *Invasion and Response: The Case of Roman Britain*. BAR British Series 73.
Casey, P. J. 1994. *Carausius and Allectus: The British Usurpers*. Yale University Press.
Clayton, Peter (ed.). 1980. *A Companion to Roman Britain*. Phaidon.
Creighton, John. 2006. *Britannia: The Creation of a Roman Province*. Routledge.
De la Bédoyère, Guy. 1999. *The Golden Age of Roman Britain*. Stroud.
———. 2006. *Roman Britain*. Thames & Hudson.
Esmonde Cleary, A. S. 1989. *The Ending of Roman Britain*. Batsford.
Faulkner, Neil. 2000. *The Decline and Fall of Roman Britain*. Stroud.
Frere, S. S. 1987. *Britannia: A History of Roman Britain* (3rd edn.). Routledge.
Hall, Jenny, and Ralph Merrifield. 1986. *Roman London*. HMSO.
Hanson, W. S. 1987. *Agricola and the Conquest of the North*. Edinburgh University Press.
Henig, Martin. 1984. *Religion in Roman Britain*. St. Martin's.

———. 1995. *The Art of Roman Britain*. Batsford.
Hingley, Richard. 1989. *Rural Settlement in Roman Britain*. Seaby.
Holder, P. A. 1982. *The Roman Army in Britain*. St. Martin's.
Johns, Catherine. 1996. *The Jewellery of Roman Britain: Celtic and Classical Traditions*. University of Michigan Press.
Johnson, Stephen. 1976. *The Roman Forts of the Saxon Shore*. Elek.
———. 1980. *Later Roman Britain*. Scribner.
Jones, Barri, and David Mattingly. 1990. *An Atlas of Roman Britain*. Blackwell.
Jones, Michael E. 1996. *The End of Roman Britain*. Cornell University Press.
Laing, Jennifer. 1997. *Art and Society in Roman Britain*. Alan Sutton.
Manley, J. 2002. *AD 43: The Roman Invasion of Britain*. Tempus.
Mattingley, David. 2006. *An Imperial Possession: Britain in the Roman Empire*. Penguin Books.
Maxwell, G. 1989. *The Romans in Scotland*. Edinburgh University Press.
Miles, David (ed.). 1982. *The Romano-British Countryside*, 2 vols. BAR British Series 103.
Millett, Martin. 1990. *The Romanization of Britain*. Cambridge University Press.
———. 1995. *Roman Britain*. English Heritage/Batsford.
Neal, D. S. 1981. *Roman Mosaics in Britain: An Introduction to Their Schemes and a Catalogue of Paintings*. Britannia Monographs 1.
Reece, Richard M. 1980, 'Town and Country: The End of Roman Britain'. *World Archaeology* 12: 77–92.
———. 1987. *Coinage in Roman Britain*. Seaby.
Rivet, A. L. F., and Colin Smith. 1979. *The Place-Names of Roman Britain*. Princeton University Press.
Salway, Peter. 1967. *The Frontier People of Roman Britain* (2nd edn.). Cambridge University Press.
———. 1981. *Roman Britain*. Oxford University Press.
———. 1993. *The Oxford Illustrated History of Roman Britain*. Oxford University Press.
Todd, Malcolm. 1999. *Roman Britain* (3rd edn.). Blackwell.
Tyers, P. 1996. *Roman Pottery in Britain*. Batsford.
Wacher, J. S. 1978. *Roman Britain*. Dent.
———. 1979. *The Coming of Rome*. Routledge.
———. 1995. *The Towns of Roman Britain* (2nd edn.). Batsford.
Watts, Dorothy. 1998. *Religion in Late Roman Britain: Forces of Change*. Cambridge University Press.
Webster, Graham. 1978. *Boudica: The British Revolt Against Rome*. Batsford.
———. 1981. *Rome Against Caratacus: The Roman Campaigns in Britain, AD 48–58*. Batsford.
———. 1986. *The British Celts and Their Gods Under Rome*. Batsford.
———. 1993. *The Roman Invasion of Britain* (rev. edn.). Barnes & Noble.

The Brittonic Age

Alcock, Leslie. 1971. *Arthur's Britain*. Penguin.
———. 1987. *Economy, Society, and Warfare Among the Britons and Saxons*. University of Wales Press.
Ashe, Geoffrey (ed.). 1968. *The Quest for Arthur's Britain*. Pall Mall.
Bammesberger, A., and A. Wollman (eds.). 1990. *Britain 400–600: Language and History*. Pp.149–178. Winter.
Bartholemew, Philip. 1982. 'Fifth-Century Facts'. *Britannia* 13: 261–270.
Campbell, Ewan. 2007. *Continental and Mediterranean Imports to Atlantic Britain and Ireland AD 400–800*. Council for British Archaeology.
Charles-Edwards, Thomas. 1991. 'The Arthur of History'. Pp.15–32 in *The Arthur of the Welsh*. Edited by Rachel Bromwich et al. University of Wales Press.
Dark, K. R. 1993. *Civitas to Kingdom: British Political Continuity, 300–800*. Leicester University Press.
———. 2000. *Britain and the End of the Roman Empire*. Tempus.
Dark, K. R. (ed.). 1996. *External Contacts and the Economy of Late Roman and Post-Roman Britain*. Boydell and Brewer.
Dumville, David N. 1977. 'Sub-Roman Britain: History and Legend'. *History* 62: 173–192.
———. 1995. 'The Idea of Government in Sub-Roman Britain'. Pp.177–216 in *After Empire: Towards and Ethnology of Europe's Barbarians*. Edited by Giorgio Ausenda. Woodbridge.
Evans, Jeremy. 1990. 'From the End of Roman Britain to the Celtic West'. *Oxford Journal of Archaeology* 9: 91–103.
Higham, Nicholas. 1992. *Rome, Britain and the Anglo-Saxons*. Seaby.
———. 1994. *The English Conquest: Gildas and Britain in the Fifth Century*. Manchester University Press.
———. 2003. *King Arthur: Myth-Making and History*. Routledge.
Lapidge, Michael, and David N. Dumville (eds.). 1984. *Gildas: New Approaches*. Boydell and Brewer.
Snyder, Christopher A. 1996. *Sub-Roman Britain (AD 400–600): A Gazetteer of Sites*. BAR British Series 247.
———. 1998. *An Age of Tyrants: Britain and the Britons, AD 400–600*. Penn State University Press.
Thomas, Charles. 1981a. *Christianity in Roman Britain to AD 500*. University of California Press.
———. 1981b. *A Provisional List of Imported Pottery in Post-Roman Western Britain and Ireland*. Institute of Cornish Studies.
———. 1993. *Tintagel: Arthur and Archaeology*. Batsford/British Heritage.
———. 1994. *And Shall These Mute Stones Speak? Post-Roman Inscriptions in Western Britain*. University of Wales Press.
Thompson, E. A. 1977. 'Britain, AD 406–410'. *Britannia* 8: 303–318.
———. 1983. 'Fifth-Century Facts?' *Britannia* 14: 272–274.
———. 1984. *St. Germanus of Auxerre and the End of Roman Britain*. Boydell and Brewer.
Wood, Ian. 1987. 'The Fall of the Western Empire and the End of Roman Britain'. *Britannia* 18: 251–262.

Anglo-Saxon England

Abels, Richard. 1988. *Lordship and Military Obligation in Anglo-Saxon England*. University of California.
———. 1998. *Alfred the Great: War, Culture and Kingship in Anglo-Saxon England*. Longman.
Arnold, C. J. 1997. *An Archaeology of the Early Anglo-Saxon Kingdoms* (2nd edn.). Routledge.

Backhouse, J. et al. 1984. *The Golden Age of Anglo-Saxon Art.* British Museum Press.
Barlow, Frank. 2002. *The Godwins: The Rise and Fall of a Noble Dynasty.* Longman.
Bartholemew, Philip. 1984. 'Fourth-Century Saxons'. *Britannia* 15: 169–185.
Bassett, Steven (ed.). 1989. *The Origins of Anglo-Saxon Kingdoms.* Leicester University Press.
Biddle, Martin. 1976. 'Towns'. Pp. 99–150 in *The Archaeology of Anglo-Saxon England.* Edited by David M. Wilson. Methuen.
Blair, John. 2005. *The Church in Anglo-Saxon Society.* Oxford University Press.
Bruce-Mitford, R. 1979. *The Sutton Hoo Ship Burial.* British Museum Publications.
Campbell, James (ed.). 1982. *The Anglo-Saxons.* Cornell University Press.
Carver, Martin. 1998. *Sutton Hoo: Burial Ground of Kings?* University of Pennsylvania Press.
———. 2005. *Sutton Hoo: A Seventh Century Princely Burial Ground and Its Context.* British Museum Press.
Conner, Patrick W. 1993. *Anglo-Saxon Exeter: A Tenth-Century Cultural History.* Boydell and Brewer.
Donoghue, D. 2004. *Old English Literature: A Short Introduction.* Blackwell.
Dumville, D. N. 1992. *Wessex and England from Alfred to Edgar.* Boydell.
Evison, Vera I. (ed.). 1981. *Angles, Saxons, and Jutes: Essays Presented to J.N.L. Myres.* Clarendon.
Fernie, E. 1983. *The Architecture of the Anglo-Saxons.* Batsford.
Foot, Sarah. 2006. *Monastic Life in Anglo-Saxon England c. 600–900.* Cambridge University Press.
Greenfield, Stanley B., and Daniel C. Calder. 1986. *A New Critical History of Old English Literature* (rev. edn.). New York University Press.
Härke, Heinrich. 1997. 'Early Anglo-Saxon Social Structure'. Pp. 125–170 in *The Anglo-Saxons from the Migration Period to the Eighth Century: An Ethnographic Perspective.* Edited by John Hines. Boydell.
Hawkes, Jane. 1999. *Northumbria's Golden Age.* Sutton.
Hawkes, Sonia Chadwick (ed.). 1989. *Weapons and Warfare in Anglo-Saxon England.* Oxbow.
Higham, N. J. 1986. *The Northern Counties to AD 1000.* Longman.
———. 1993. *The Kingdom of Northumbria AD 350–1100.* Alan Sutton.
Hill, D. 1981. *An Atlas of Anglo-Saxon England.* University of Toronto Press.
Hines, John. 1990. 'Philology, Archaeology and the *Adventus Saxonum vel Anglorum*'. Pp. 17–36 in *Britain 400–600: Language and History.* Edited by Alfred Bammesberger and Alfred Wollmann. C. Winter.
———. 1994. 'The Becoming of the English: Identity, Material Culture and Language in Early Anglo-Saxon England'. *Anglo-Saxon Studies in Archaeology and History* 7: 49–59.
Hodges, Richard. 1989. *The Anglo-Saxon Achievement.* Cornell University Press.
Hooke, Della. 1998. *The Landscape of Anglo-Saxon England.* Leicester University Press.
Howe, Nicholas. 2001. *Migration and Mythmaking in Anglo-Saxon England.* University of Notre Dame Press.
Hunter Blair, Peter. 2003. *An Introduction to Anglo-Saxon England.* Cambridge University Press.
James, Edward. 2001. *Britain in the First Millennium.* Oxford University Press.
Kirby, D. P. 1968. *The Making of Early England.* Schocken Books.
———. 2000. *The Earliest English Kings* (rev. edn.). Routledge.
Leahy, K. 2003. *Anglo-Saxon Crafts.* Tempus.
Lucy, S. 2000. *The Anglo-Saxon Way of Death.* Sutton Publishing.
Mayr-Harting, Henry. 1972. *The Coming of Christianity to Anglo-Saxon England.* Batsford.
O'Brien, Elizabeth. 1999. *Post-Roman Britain to Anglo-Saxon England: Burial Practices Reviewed.* BAR British Series 289.
Orchard, Andy. 2005. *A Critical Companion to Beowulf.* D. S. Brewer.
Pollington, Stephen. 2001. *The English Warrior from Earliest Times till 1066.* Anglo-Saxon Books.
Pratt, David. 2007. *The Political Thought of King Alfred the Great.* Cambridge University Press.
Richards, Julian D. 1995. 'An Archaeology of Anglo-Saxon England'. Pp. 51–74 in *After Empire: Towards and Ethnology of Europe's Barbarians.* Edited by Giorgio Ausenda. Boydell and Brewer.
Rollason, David. 2003. *Northumbria, 500–1100: Creation and Destruction of a Kingdom.* Cambridge University Press.
Rudyard, Susan. 1988. *The Royal Saints of Anglo-Saxon England: A Study of West Saxon and East Anglian Cults.* Cambridge University Press.
Russo, Daniel G. 1998. *Town Origins and Development in Early England, c. 400–950 AD.* Greenwood.
Smyth, Alfred P. 1996. *King Alfred the Great.* Oxford University Press.
Stafford, Pauline. 1989. *Unification and Conquest. A Political and Social History of England in the Tenth and Eleventh Centuries.* Edward Arnold.
Stenton, F. M. 1971. *Anglo-Saxon England.* Clarendon Press.
Taylor, H. M., and J. Taylor. 1965–1968. *Anglo-Saxon Architecture,* 3 vols. Cambridge University Press.
Underwood, Richard. 2000. *Anglo-Saxon Weapons and Warfare.* Tempus Publishing.
Webster, L., and J. Backhouse. 1991. *The Making of England.* British Museum.
Welch, Martin G. 1992. *Discovering Anglo-Saxon England.* Penn State Press.
Whitelock, Dorothy. 1952. *The Beginnings of English Society.* Penguin.
Williams, Ann. 1999. *Kingship and Government in Pre-Conquest England c. 500–1066.* Palgrave Macmillan.
Wilson, D. M. 1984. *Anglo-Saxon Art.* Thames & Hudson.
Yorke, Barbara. 1992. *Kings and Kingdoms of Early Anglo-Saxon England.* Routledge.
———. 1995. *Wessex in the Early Middle Ages.* Leicester University Press.
———. 2006. *The Conversion of Britain: Religion, Politics and Society in Britain, c. 600–800.* Pearson.

The Medieval Celtic Fringe

Alcock, Leslie. 2003. *Kings and Warriors, Craftsmen and Priests in Northern Britain AD 550–850.* Society of Antiquaries of Scotland, Monograph Series.

Anderson, Marjorie O. 1973. *Kings and Kingship in Early Scotland*. Scottish Academic Press.

Armit, I. 1997. *Celtic Scotland*. Batsford.

Arnold, Christopher J., and Jeffrey L. Davies. 2000. *Roman and Early Medieval Wales*. Tempus.

Bannerman, John. 1974. *Studies in the History of Dalriada*. Scottish Academic Press.

Barrell, A. D. M. 2000. *Medieval Scotland*. Cambridge University Press.

Barrow, G. W. S. 1981. *Kingship and Unity: Scotland 1000–1306*. University of Toronto Press.

Barry, T. B. 1987. *The Archaeology of Medieval Ireland*. Methuen.

Bhreathnach, E. (ed.). 2005. *The Kingship and Landscape of Tara*. Four Courts Press.

Bitel, Lisa M. 1993. *Isle of the Saints: Monastic Settlement and Christian Community in Early Ireland*. Cornell University Press.

———. 1996. *Land of Women: Tales of Sex and Gender from Early Ireland*. Cornell University Press.

Blair, John, and Richard Sharpe (eds.). 1992. *Pastoral Care Before the Parish*. Leicester University Press.

Bradley, Ian. 1999. *Celtic Christianity: Making Myths and Chasing Dreams*. Edinburgh University Press.

Bromwich, Rachel et al. (eds.). 1991. *The Arthur of the Welsh: The Arthurian Legend on Medieval Welsh Literature*. University of Wales Press.

Brown, Shirley Ann, and Michael W. Herren. 2002. *Christ in Celtic Christianity: Britain and Ireland from the Fifth to the Tenth Century*. The Boydell Press.

Byrne, J. F. 1973. *Irish Kings and High-Kings*. Batsford Press.

Carney, James. 1973. *The Problem of St Patrick*. University of Wales Press.

Carr, A. D. 1995. *Medieval Wales*. St. Martins.

Charles-Edwards, Thomas. 1995. 'Language and Society Among the Insular Celts, AD 400–1000'. Pp.706–710 in *The Celtic World*. Edited by Miranda J. Green. Routledge.

———. 2000. *Early Christian Ireland*. Cambridge University Press.

Charles-Edwards, T. M. et al. (eds.). 2000. *The Welsh King and His Court*. University of Wales Press.

Clancy, Thomas Owen, and Gilbert Márkus. 1998. *Iona: The Earliest Poetry of a Celtic Monastery*. Edinburgh University Press.

Conneely, Daniel. 1993. *St Patrick's Letters: A Study of Their Theological Dimension*. An Sagart.

Davies, John. 1993. *A History of Wales*. Penguin.

Davies, Oliver. 1996. *Celtic Christianity in Early Medieval Wales*. University of Wales Press.

Davies, Oliver, and Thomas O'Loughlin. 1999. *Celtic Spirituality*. Paulist Press.

Davies, Wendy. 1982. *Wales in the Early Middle Ages*. Leicester University Press.

———. 1990. *Patterns of Power in Early Wales*. Oxford University Press.

———. 1992. 'The Myth of the Celtic Church'. Pp.12–21 in *The Early Church in Wales and the West*. Edited by Edwards and Lane. Oxbow.

De Paor, Liam. 1993. *Saint Patrick's World*. University of Notre Dame Press.

Dumville, David N. et al. 1993. *Saint Patrick, AD 493–1993*. Boydell and Brewer.

Duncan, A. A. M. 1975. *Scotland: The Making of a Kingdom*. Oliver and Boyd.

———. 2002. *The Kingship of the Scots 842–1292*. Edinburgh University Press.

Edwards, Nancy. 1990. *The Archaeology of Early Medieval Ireland*. University of Pennsylvania Press.

Edwards, Nancy, and Alan Lane (eds.). 1988. *Early Medieval Settlements in Wales AD 400–1100*. University of Wales Press.

———. 1992. *The Early Church in Wales and the West*. Oxbow Monograph No. 16.

Elliott-Binns, L. E. 1955. *Medieval Cornwall*. Methuen.

Etchingham, Colmán. 1999, repr. 2000. *Church Organisation in Ireland AD 650 to 1000*. Laigin Publications.

Filbee, Marjorie. 1996. *Celtic Cornwall*. Constable.

Foster, S. 1996. *Picts, Gaels and Scots*. Batsford.

Hanson, R. P. C. 1968. *St. Patrick: His Origins and Career*. Oxford University Press.

Harbison, P. 1992. *The High Crosses of Ireland*, 3 vols. Royal Irish Academy.

———. 1999. *The Golden Age of Irish Art*. Thames & Hudson.

Henderson, George. 1987. *From Durrow to Kells: The Insular Gospel Books 650–800*. Thames & Hudson.

Henderson, Isabel, and George Henderson. 2004. *The Art of the Picts*. Thames & Hudson.

Henken, Elissa R. 1987. *The Traditions of the Welsh Saints*. D.S. Brewer.

———. 1991. *The Welsh Saints: A Study in Patterned Lives*. D.S. Brewer.

Herbert, Máire. 1988. *Iona, Kells, and Derry: The History and Hagiography of the Monastic Familia of Columba*. Oxford University Press.

Hill, Peter. 1997. *Whithorn and St Ninian: The Excavation of a Monastic Town*. Sutton.

Howlett, David R. 1995. *The Celtic Latin Tradition of Biblical Style*. Four Courts Press.

Hudson, Benjamin T. 1994. *Kings of Celtic Scotland*. Greenwood Press.

Hughes, Kathleen. 1966. *The Church in Early Irish Society*. Methuen.

———. 1972. *Early Christian Ireland: Introduction to the Sources*. Sources of History Limited.

———. 1980. *Celtic Britain in the Early Middle Ages*. Boydell.

———. 1981. 'The Celtic Church—Is This a Valid Concept?' *CMCS* 1: 1–20.

Jackson, Kenneth. 1994. *Language and History in Early Britain*. Four Courts Press.

Jaski, Bart. 2000. *Early Irish Kingship and Succession*. Four Courts Press.

Kelly, Fergus. 1988. *A Guide to Early Irish Law*. Dublin Institute for Advanced Studies.

Koch, John T. 1997. *The Gododdin of Aneirin: Text and Context from Dark-Age North Britain*. University of Wales Press.

Laing, Lloyd. 1975. *Settlement Types in Post-Roman Scotland*. BAR British Series 13.

———. 2006. *The Archaeology of Celtic Britain and Ireland c. AD 400–1200*. Cambridge University Press.

Laing, Lloyd, and Jennifer Laing. 2001. *The Picts and the Scots* (2nd edn.). Alan Sutton.

Leask, H. G. 1955. *Early Irish Churches and Monastic Buildings, I, The Early Period and the Romanesque*. Dundalk.

MacQueen, John. 1990. *St Nynia*. Polygan.

Maund, Kari. 2000. *The Welsh Kings*. Tempus.

McCone, Kim. 1990. *Pagan Past and Christian Present in Early Irish Literature*. An Sagart.
McDonald, R. Andrew. 1997. *The Kingdom of the Isles: Scotland's Western Seaboard c.1100–c.1336*. Tuckwell.
———. 2003. *Outlaws of Medieval Scotland: Challenges to the Canmore Kings, 1058–1266*. Tuckwell.
McManus, Damian. 1991. *A Guide to Ogam*. An Sagart.
Meehan, B. 1994. *The Book of Kells*. Thames & Hudson.
Morrison, I. 1985. *Landscape with Lake Dwellings: The Crannogs of Scotland*. Edinburgh University Press.
Mytum, H. 1992. *The Origins of Early Christian Ireland*. Routledge.
Ó Corrain, Donnchadh. 1972. *Ireland Before the Normans*. Gill and Macmillan.
Ó Cróinín, Dáibhí. 1995. *Early Medieval Ireland, 400–1200*. Longman.
———. 2003. *Early Irish History and Chronology*. Four Courts Press.
O'Donoghue, Noel Dermot. 1987. *Aristocracy of Soul: Patrick of Ireland*. M. Glazier.
Okasha, Elisabeth. 1993. *Corpus of Early Christian Inscribed Stones of Southwestern Britain*. Leicester University Press.
Olson, Lynette. 1989. *Early Monasteries in Cornwall*. Boydell and Brewer.
O'Loughlin, Thomas. 1999. *Saint Patrick: The Man and His Works*. Triangle.
———. 2000. *Celtic Theology: Humanity, World and God in Early Irish Writings*. Continuum.
———. 2005. *Discovering Saint Patrick*. Paulist Press.
O'Rahilly, T. F. 1957. *The Two Patricks*. Dublin Institute for Advanced Studies.
O'Rahilly, Thomas R. 1971. *Early Irish History and Mythology*. Dublin Institute for Advanced Studies.
Orme, Nicholas. 2000. *The Saints of Cornwall*. Oxford University Press.
O'Sullivan, Aidan. 1998. *The Archaeology of Lake Settlement in Ireland*. Royal Irish Academy.
———. 2000. *Crannogs: Lake Dwellings of Early Ireland*. Country House.
Padel, O. J. 2000. *Arthur in Medieval Welsh Literature*. University of Wales Press.
Patterson, Nerys Thomas. 1994. *Cattle-Lords and Clansmen: The Social Structure of Early Ireland*. University of Notre Dame Press.
Pearce, Susan. 1978. *The Kingdom of Dumnonia*. Lodenek.
———. 2004. *South-Western Britain in the Early Middle Ages*. Leicester University Press.
Phythian-Adams, Charles. 1996. *Land of the Cumbrians: A Study of British Provincial Origins AD 400–1120*. Ashgate.
Pryce, Huw. 1993. *Native Law and the Church in Medieval Wales*. Oxford University Press.
Richardson, Hilary, and John Scarry. 1990. *An Introduction to Irish High Crosses*. Mercier Press.
Ritchie, Anna. 1999. *Picts*. Historic Scotland.
Ross, Anne. 1992. *Pagan Celtic Britain* (rev. edn.). Constable.
Rowland, Jenny. 1990. *Early Welsh Saga Poetry: A Study and Edition of the Englynion*. Boydell and Brewer.
Russell, Paul. 1995. *An Introduction to the Celtic Languages*. Longman.
Sharpe, Richard. 1991. *Medieval Irish Saints' Lives: An Introduction to Vitae Sanctorum Hiberniae*. Clarendon Press.
Smyth, Alfred P. 1984. *Warlords and Holy Men: Scotland AD 80–1000*. Arnold.
Snyder, Christopher A. 1996. 'Celtic Continuity in the Middle Ages'. *Medieval Perspectives* 11: 164–178.
———. 2000. *Exploring the World of King Arthur*. Thames & Hudson.
———. 2003. *The Britons*. Peoples of Europe Series. Blackwell.
Thomas, Charles. 1994. *And Shall These Mute Stones Speak? Post-Roman Inscriptions in Western Britain*. University of Wales Press.
———. 1997. *Celtic Britain*. Thames & Hudson.
———. 1998. *Christian Celts: Messages and Images*. Tempus.
Thompson, E. A. 1999. *Who Was St. Patrick?* (2nd edn.). Boydell.
Todd, Malcolm. 1987. *The South West to AD 1000*. Longman.
Tolstoy, Nikolai. 1985. *The Quest for Merlin*. Little Brown.
Walker, David. 1990. *Medieval Wales*. Cambridge University Press.
Williams, Ifor. 1970. *Lectures on Early Welsh Poetry*. Dublin Institute for Advanced Studies.
———. 1980. *The Beginnings of Welsh Poetry*. Edited by Rachel Bromwich. University of Wales Press.
Winchester, A. J. L. 1987. *Landscape and Society in Medieval Cumbria*. John Donald.
Wooding, Jonathan. 1996. *Communication and Commerce Along the Western Sealanes, AD 400–800*. BAR International Series 654.
Wooding, Jonathan M. (ed.). 2000. *The Otherworld Voyage in Early Irish Literature*. Four Courts Press.
Woolf, Alex. 1998. 'Pictish Matriliny Reconsidered'. *Innes Review* 49: 147–167.
Yeoman, Peter. 1995. *Medieval Scotland: An Archaeological Perspective*. B.T. Batsford Ltd.
Youngs, S. (ed.). *The Work of Angels: Masterpieces of Celtic Metalwork 6th-9th Centuries AD*. British Museum.

The Vikings

Barrett, James (ed.). 2003. *Contact, Continuity, and Collapse: The Norse Colonization of the North Atlantic*. Brepols.
Clarke, H., and B. Ambrosiani (eds.). 1991. *Towns in the Viking Age*. Leicester University Press.
Crawford, Barbara 1987. *Scandinavian Scotland*. Leicester University Press.
Fell, Christine, et al. (eds.). 1983. *The Viking Age in the Isle of Man*. Viking Society for Northern Research.
Forte, Angelo, Richard Oram and Frederik Pedersen (eds.). 2005. *Viking Empires*. Cambridge University Press.
Graham-Campbell, James. 1989. *Cultural Atlas of the Viking World*. Facts on File.
Hadley, D. M. 2000. *The Northern Danelaw: Its Social Structure, c.800–1100*. Leicester University Press.
Hall, R. A. 1978. *Viking Age York and the North*. Council for British Archaeology.
———. 2004. *Aspects of Anglo-Scandinavian York*. Council for British Archaeology.
Hudson, Benjamin T. 2005. *Viking Pirates and Christian Princes: Dynasty, Religion, and Empire in the North Atlantic*. Oxford University Press.

Jones, Gwyn. 1968. *A History of the Vikings*. Oxford University Press.

Kinvig, R. H. 1975. *The Isle of Man: A Social, Cultural, and Political History* (3rd edn.). Liverpool University Press.

Richards, Julian C. 2001. *Blood of the Vikings*. Hodder & Stoughton.

Smyth, Alfred P. 1977. *Scandinavian Kings in the British Isles: 850–880*. Oxford University Press.

Wilson, David M. 1974. *The Viking Age in the Isle of Man: The Archaeological Evidence*. Odense University Press.

Wainwright, F. T. 1975. *Scandinavian England*. Phillimore.

The Anglo-Norman Period

Amt, Emilie M. 1993. *The Accession of Henry II in England: Royal Government Restored, 1149–1159*. Boydell.

Aurell, Martin. 2007. *The Plantagenet Empire: 1154–1224*. Longman.

Barber, Richard. 1996. *The Devil's Crown: A History of Henry II and His Sons*. Combined Books.

Barlow, Frank. 1999. *The Feudal Kingdom of England: 1042–1216* (8th edn.). Addison Wesley Longman.

Barrow, G. W. S. 1981. *The Anglo-Norman Era in Scottish History*. Oxford University Press.

Bartlett, Robert. 1982. *Gerald of Wales 1146–1223*. Oxford University Press.

———. 2000. *England Under the Norman and Angevin Kings 1075–1225*. Oxford University Press.

Bradbury, Jim. 1996. *Stephen and Matilda: The Civil War of 1139–53*. Sutton Publishing.

———. 1998. *The Battle of Hastings*. Sutton Publishing.

Brown, Shirley Ann. 1988. *The Bayeux Tapestry: History and Bibliography*. Boydell Press.

Burton, Janet. 1994. *Monastic and Religious Orders in Britain 1000–1300*. Cambridge University Press.

Chibnall, Marjorie. 1986. *Anglo-Norman England, 1066–1166*. Basil Blackwell.

Crouch, David. 2000. *The Reign of King Stephen, 1135–1154*. Longman.

———. 2003. *William Marshal: Knighthood, War and Chivalry 1147–1219* (2nd edn.). Longman.

Davies, R. R. 1979. *Historical Perception: Celts and Saxons*. University of Wales Press.

———. 1991. *The Age of Conquest: Wales 1063–1415*. Oxford University Press.

———. 1996. *The Matter of Britain and the Matter of England*. Oxford University Press.

Davies, R. R., et al. (eds.). 1984. *Welsh Society and Nationhood*. University of Wales Press.

Duby, Georges. 1987. *William Marshal: The Flower of Chivalry*. Pantheon.

Fernie, Eric. 2000. *The Architecture of Norman England*. Oxford University Press.

Fleming, Robin. 1998. *Domesday Book and the Law: Society and Legal Custom in Early Medieval England*. Cambridge University Press.

Gillingham, John. 1984. *The Angevin Empire*. Edward Arnold.

———. 1990. 'The Context and Purpose of Geoffrey of Monmouth's *History of the Kings of Britain*'. *Anglo-Norman Studies* 13: 99–118.

Gransden, Antonia. 1974. *Historical Writing in England c. 550–c. 1307*. Routledge.

Green, Judith. 2006. *Henry I: King of England and Duke of Normandy*. Cambridge University Press.

Griffiths, Ralph. 1994. *Conquerors and Conquered in Medieval Wales*. St. Martin's.

Hallam, Elizabeth (ed.). 1986. *The Plantagenet Chronicles*. Weidenfeld and Nicolson.

Harper-Bill, Christopher, and Nicholas Vincent (eds.). 2007. *Henry II: New Interpretations*. Boydell.

Hollister, C. Warren. 1965. *Military Organization of Norman England*. Oxford University Press.

———. 2001. *Henry I*. Yale University Press.

Hosler, John D. 2007. *Henry II: A Medieval Soldier at War, 1147–1189*. Brill.

Kappelli, W. 1976. *The Norman Conquest of the North*. University of North Carolina Press.

Knowles, David. 1963. *The Monastic Order in England 940–1216* (2nd edn.). Cambridge University Press.

Le Patourel, John. 1984. *Feudal Empires: Norman and Plantagenet*. Hambledon Continuum.

Legge, M. D. 1963. *Anglo-Norman Literature and Its Background*. Oxford University Press.

Loyn, Henry R. 1982. *The Norman Conquest* (3rd edn.). Hutchinson.

Morillo, Steve (ed.). 1996. *The Battle of Hastings, Sources and Interpretations*. Boydell and Brewer.

Nelson, Lynn. 1966. *The Normans in South Wales, 1070–1171*. University of Texas Press.

Orphen, Goddard Henry. 1968. *Ireland Under the Normans: 1169–1216*. Clarendon Press.

Partner, Nancy. 1977. *Serious Entertainments: The Writing of History in Twelfth-Century England*. University of Chicago Press.

Reeves, A. C. 1983. *The Marcher Lords*. Christopher Davies.

Reynolds, Susan. 1994. *Fiefs and Vassals: The Medieval Evidence Reinterpreted*. Oxford University Press.

Ritchie, R. L. G. 1954. *The Normans in Scotland*. Edinburgh University Press.

Roffe, D. 2000. *Domesday: The Inquest and the Book*. Oxford University Press.

Southern, Sir Richard. 1990. *St Anselm: A Portrait in a Landscape*. Cambridge University Press.

Stenton, Frank M. 1932. *The First Century of English Feudalism 1066–1166*. Oxford University Press.

Strickland, Matthew (ed.). 1992. *Anglo-Norman Warfare: Studies in Late Anglo-Saxon and Anglo-Norman Military Organisation and Warfare*. Boydell and Brewer.

Suppe, Frederick C. 1994. *Military Institutions on the Welsh Marches: Shropshire, AD 1066–1300*. Boydell and Brewer.

Thompson, R. M. 2003. *William of Malmesbury*. Boydell Press.

Walker, David. 1995. *The Normans in Britain*. Blackwell.

Warren, Wilfrid L. 2000. *Henry II*. Yale University Press.

Weir, Alison. 2001. *Eleanor of Aquitaine: A Life*. Ballantine Books.

Wheeler, Bonnie, and John Carmi Parsons (eds.). 2002. *Eleanor of Aquitaine: Lord and Lady*. Palgrave MacMillan.

Wilks, Michael (ed.). 1985. *The World of John of Salisbury*. Blackwell.

About the Editor and Contributors

Editor

Christopher A. Snyder is Professor of European History and Director of the Honours Programme at Marymount University in Arlington, Virginia. He also serves as Director of the National Celtic Heritage Center. Dr Snyder earned his PhD in medieval history at Emory University. He is the author of six books, including *The Britons* (Blackwell, 2003) and *The World of King Arthur* (Thames & Hudson, 2000). He lectures frequently at the Smithsonian Institution and has appeared on the History Channel, The Learning Channel and BBC Television and Radio.

List of Contributors

Richard Abels
Department of History
US Naval Academy
Annapolis, Maryland

Geoffrey Ashe
Independent Scholar
Glastonbury, Somerset, United Kingdom

Martin Bates
Department of Archaeology and Anthropology
University of Wales, Lampeter
Ceredigion, Wales

Deborah L. Bauer
Seminole Community College
Casselberry, Florida

David Beougher
Department of Military Science and Leadership
Eastern Michigan University
Ypsilanti, Michigan

Anne Berthelot
French and Medieval Studies
Modern and Classical Languages Department
University of Connecticut
Storrs, Connecticut

Timothy Bolton
Specialist in Western Medieval Manuscripts
Sothebys
London, United Kingdom

William Bowden
Department of Archaeology
University of Nottingham
Nottingham, United Kingdom

Nicki Bullinga
University Library
Utrecht University
Utrecht, the Netherlands

Barry Burnham
Department of Archaeology and Anthropology
University of Wales, Lampeter
Ceredigion, Wales

Thomas S. Burns
Department of History
Emory University
Atlanta, Georgia

Janet Burton
Department of History
University of Wales, Lampeter
Ceredigion, Wales

Joseph Calise
Department of History
Quinnipiac University
Hamden, Connecticut

Jane Cartwright
Department of Welsh
University of Wales, Lampeter
Ceredigion, Wales

Martin Carver
Department of Archaeology
University of York
York, United Kingdom

Ros Coard
Department of Archaeology and Anthropology
University of Wales, Lampeter
Ceredigion, Wales

John Collis
Department of Archaeology
University of Sheffield
Sheffield, United Kingdom

Patrick Conner
Department of English
West Virginia University
Morgantown, West Virginia

Marios Costambeys
School of History
University of Liverpool
Liverpool, United Kingdom

John Doherty
e-Learning Centre
Northern Arizona University
Flagstaff, Arizona

Penny Dransart
Department of Archaeology and Anthropology
University of Wales, Lampeter
Ceredigion, Wales

Peter J. Field
Department of English
Bangor University
Bangor, Gwynedd, Wales

Deanna Forsman
Department of History
North Hennepin Community College
Brooklyn Park, Minnesota

Philip Freeman
Department of Classics
Luther College
Decorah, Iowa

Mary Frances Giandrea
Department of History
American University
Washington, DC

Peter Goodrich
Department of English
Northern Michigan University
Marquette, Michigan

Darlene Hall
Department of Art and Sciences
Lake Erie College
Painesville, Ohio

Gregory Hays
Centre of Medieval Studies
Graduate Student
University of York
United Kingdom

Jonathan Herold
Centre for Medieval Arts
University of Toronto
Toronto, Ontario, Canada

Benjamin Hudson
Department of History and Religious Studies
Penn State University
State College
Pennsylvania

Karen Jankulak
Department of History
University of Wales, Lampeter
Ceredigion, Wales

Bart Jaski
Faculty of Arts
Department of Celtic
Utrecht, the Netherlands

Michael Jones
Department of History
Bates College
Lewiston, Maine

Joel A. Konrad
Department of History
McMaster University
Hamilton, Ontario, Canada

Jennifer Laing
Harlaxton College
University of Evansville
Grantham, United Kingdom

Lloyd Laing
Department of Archaeology
University of Nottingham
Nottingham, United Kingdom

Rhett Leverett
Department of History and Politics
Marymount University
Arlington, Virginia

Scott Lloyd
Department of History and Welsh History
Aberyswyth University
Ceredigion, Wales

Nicole Lopez-Jantzen
Department of History
Fordham University
Bronx, New York

Thomas O'Loughlin
Department of Theology and Religious Studies
University of Wales, Lampeter
Ceredigion, Wales

Andrew McDonald
Department of History
Brock University
St. Catherine's, Ontario, Canada

David W. Marshall
Department of English
California State University of San Bernardino
San Bernardino, California

Sarah Milliken
Institute of Archaeology
University of Oxford
Oxford, United Kingdom

Asa Mittman
Department of Art and Art History
California State University
Chico, California

Aidan O'Sullivan
University College
Dublin, Ireland

Britt Rothauser
Medieval Studies Programme
University of Connecticut
Storrs, Connecticut

Patricia Rumsey
c/o Sister Francisca
Arkley, Barnet, Hertfordshire, United Kingdom

Anne Sassin
Department of Archaeology
University of Nottingham
Nottingham, United Kingdom

Susan Schulze
Department of Art and History
George Maron University
Fairfax, Virginia

Thomas Shippey
Department of English
Saint Louis University
Saint Louis, Missouri

Charles R. Smith
Department of History and Politics
Marymount University
Arlington, Virginia

Christopher A. Snyder
Department of History and Politics
Marymount University
Arlington, Virginia

Michael Staunton
School of History and Archives
University College
Dublin, Ireland

Frederick Suppe
Department of History
Ball State University
Munice, Indiana

Larry Swain
University of Illinois at Chicago
Chicago, Illinois

Trudy Tattersall
Department of History
Brock University
St. Catherine's, Ontario, Canada

Owen Thomas
Department of Welsh
University of Wales, Lampeter
Ceredigion, Wales

Kisha Tracy
Medieval Studies
University of Connecticut
Storrs, Connecticut

Mary Valante
Department of History
Appalachian State University
Boone, North Carolina

James Williams
Graduate Student
Department of History
Purdue University
West Lafayette, Indiana

Jonathan Wooding
Department of Theology and Religious Studies
University of Wales, Lampeter
Ceredigion, Wales

Alex Woolf
Department of Scottish History
University of St. Andrews
Fife, United Kingdom